Facaros and

CENT

ITALY

'In Italy's long, narrow peninsula,
dense with cities and great monuments,
autostrade and pizzerias, sultry sunglassed
signorinas and Vespa-wrangling dudes,
Abruzzo and Molise come as
breath of fresh air.'

CADOGANguides

Contents

Introducing

The Guide

About the authors

Dana Facaros and **Michael Pauls** have written over 30 books for Cadogan Guides, including all the Italy series. For three years they lived in a tiny Umbrian hilltop village, where they suffered massive overdoses of food, art and wine, and enjoyed every minute of it. They have since lived all over Europe, but have recently moved to a farmhouse surrounded by vineyards in the Lot Valley.

About the updater

Mary-Ann Gallagher has written and updated more than a dozen titles for Cadogan Guides, and writes regularly for other travel publishers and magazines.

Acknowledgements

Huge thanks to Lawrence and everyone at City Guesthouse, Paul and Lara, Clothilde and Daisy. Thanks to the hardworking editors at Cadogan – Dom, Linda, Christine – and especially to Dana and Michael for letting me be their DB.

Cadogan Guides
Highlands House, 165 The Broadway,
London, SW19 1NE
info.cadogan@virgin.net
www.cadoganguides.com

The Globe Pequot Press
246 Goose Lane, PO Box 480, Guilford,
Connecticut 06437–0480

Cover and photo essay design by Kicca Tommasi
Book design by Andrew Barker
Photograpy: Kicca Tommasi
Maps © Cadogan Guides,
drawn by Map Creation Ltd
Managing Editor: Christine Stroyan
Editor: Dominique Shead
Art direction: Sarah Rianhard-Gardner
Indexing: Isobel McLean
Proofreading: Daphne Trotter
Production: Navigator Guides Ltd

Printed in Spain by Mateu Cromo
A catalogue record for this book is available
from the British Library
ISBN 1-86011-112-2

Please help us to keep this guide up to date. We have done our best to ensure that the information in this guide is correct at the time of going to press, but places and facilities are constantly changing, and standards and prices in hotels and restaurants fluctuate. We would be delighted to receive any comments concerning existing entries or omissions. Authors of the best letters will receive a copy of the Cadogan Guide of their choice.

Central Italy
a photo essay

by Kicca Tommasi

01

WSS
MARI

Pere

MONTES PACEM POPVLO ET

MONUMENTUM
BENEDICTUS·XIV·PONT·

Lago di Scanno, Abruzzo

Forum, Rome

Temple of Vespasian, Rome

Colosseum, Rome

Civita Retenga, Abruzzo

Gran Sasso, Abruzzo

Scanno, Abruzzo

frescoes, San Pellegrino, Bominaco, Abruzzo

Ponza, Lazio

San Clemente a Casáuria, Abruzzo

Viterbo, Palazzo Papale, Lazio

Roman wall, Hadrian's Villa

Sperlonga, Lazio

cathedral, Gaeta, Lazio

Villa Farnese, Caprarola, Lazio

Trastevere, Rome

Campo di Fiorio market, Rome

nightlife, Rome

About the photographer

Kicca Tommasi left sunny Rome for London to pursue photography and design. She spends much of her time travelling, trying to forget the long English winters. Her pictures are regularly published in travel guides and magazines.

Introduction

02

This guide to central Italy is probably one of the remaining Italian guides left for these authors to write. The truth is, after many years and a dozen or so books, we're running out of territory to cover. Which is a pity; we do get just a little sentimental about Italy, and we wish there were more of it. If anyone could stretch the peninsula out a bit for us, and throw in a few more cathedrals, some good frescoes and one or two rare varieties of tasty shellfish, we would be grateful. We suspect that many readers, veterans of a few trips to Italy, feel the same way. After tramping over the hill towns of Tuscany and Umbria, watching a sunset from the Amalfi coast and learning to navigate the canals of Venice, most people are ready to come back for more. For these people, we may just be able to stretch the peninsula out a bit. We have some new delights to offer, a part of Italy that is fresh and green, full of surprising interest and gratifyingly lacking in tour buses. It is hiding right in the middle of the country where everyone should know all about it; you could see a lot of it from the top of the Vatican dome.

Such a paradoxical state of affairs requires some explaining. A century or two ago, you wouldn't likely be wandering around Lazio or the Abruzzi (Abruzzo). On the coasts, your reception committee would have been made up of malaria mosquitos; in the mountains, it would be desperate bandits. Such intrepid travellers who did venture far beyond the gates of Rome testified that the food was awful, accommodation nearly non-existent, and the poverty of the people heart-rending. For centuries, these regions had suffered two of the most extravagant brands of misgovernment Europe ever invented, Lazio as part of the Papal States, and the Abruzzi under the Kingdom of Naples.

But Italy is fertile soil for more than just vines and olives, and given half a chance a good region grows back. Whatever the vicissitudes of history, the Italians, like gardeners, always come out after the drought or the storm and work hard and long until they get their landscapes and their historic towns back to just the way they want them.

The heart of Italy is beating quite soundly just now. You can travel comfortably anywhere, the cooking is wonderful, and there will be attractions to catch your fancy whatever you like or wherever you go. As you might expect, this region carries a nice balance of influences from the north and south of Italy, but beyond that there are few generalizations to be made, few tidy phrases that sum up the region as a whole. A difficult history, and a map full of mountains, have made these central Italian places particular and introspective. Every range, every valley and sometimes every town is a world in itself – these days, they even seem to have all developed their own particular shapes of pasta. All of these little worlds are worthy of a close look. If you have the time for them, you'll begin to see how the little differences that make for richness and depth in a civilization also bring those qualities to the traveller's experience of it.

Chapter Divisions

The Best of Central Italy

Rome, everybody knows; as for the rest of the territory, here are some of the highlights:

Around Rome: Many of Lazio's attractions are easily seen as day-trips from Rome – Tívoli, Ostia and a garland of lovely hill towns in the Castelli Romani. Northern Lazio was the homeland of the enigmatic Etruscans of antiquity; it contains no fewer than 28 excavated Etruscan sites, including the spectacular tombs of Tarquínia and Cervéteri.

Northern Lazio also offers the fine old city of Viterbo, seat of the papacy through much of the Middle Ages, and a string of idyllic lakes: Bracciano, Vico and Bolsena, set in sweet landscapes of jumbled hills. To show what the great Roman families got up to in the Renaissance, there are lavish villas and gardens at Caprarola and Bagnaia, and the 'Monster Park' at Bomarzo.

In **Southern Lazio** you'll see new land and new towns: the reclaimed Pontine Marshes, with Mussolini-founded towns such as Latina and Sabaudia. The coast was the playground of the ancient Roman élite, who leave us ruins everywhere. Towards the south you'll find a delicious slice of Tyrrhenian shore, including the old walled port of Gaeta, the resorts of Sperlonga and Terracina, the Pontine Islands, and the wetlands wilderness of the Monte Circeo national park. Inland, the mountains are embellished with a string of quietly lovely hill towns. Anagni and Subiaco hold rare treasures of medieval art. Others, like Alatri and Ferentino, with their impressive Cyclopean walls, are among the oldest towns in Europe. At the end is Montecassino, once the greatest monastery in Christendom.

Abruzzo and Molise: Across the Apennines, you'll find roads even less travelled than those of Lazio – though since the opening of the tunnel through the Gran Sasso it has been possible to drive by *autostrada* from Rome to the northern Abruzzo in an hour and a half. Nobody's ever heard of Atri, Penne or Loreto Aprutino, but these north Abruzzo art towns will make you glad you went out of your way. The coast, lined with beaches and postwar lidos, may not, though at the southern end you'll find a truly secret corner of Italy around the attractive resorts of Vasto and Térmoli. There is a remarkable concentration of medieval monastic churches and art in the hills south-east of Pescara, the Abruzzo's modest, modern metropolis. L'Áquila, the region's other big city, is an attraction in itself and also the gateway to the scenic and natural wonders of the central Apennines. A third of the Abruzzo's territory is protected in four national or regional parks – all paradises for hiking and climbing, and boasting great downhill and cross-country skiing in central Italy.

Historical Outline

03

The city of Rome, the north of Lazio, southern Lazio and the Abruzzo have such different histories that we have treated them individually within each chapter. To tie all the stories together, here is an outline of the main events.

BC

c. 1,000,000 Oldest known Europeans inhabit the Molise
c. 5000 Neolithic culture and technology comes to Italy
c. 2000–1000 Arrival of new peoples

Celto-Ligurians begin to occupy the north, while various 'Italic' peoples move into the peninsula, and other groups from the Balkans find a home along the Adriatic coast.

c. 900 Arrival of the Etruscans in Italy

This talented nation, migrating from the eastern Mediterranean (see p.186), gives Italy its first advanced culture, building a federation of strong cities, developing mining and agriculture, and importing Hellenic culture wholesale into Italy. Also at this time the Italic peoples begin to take the form in which they were recorded by the first written histories: the most important are the Latins and Volsci of southern Lazio (see p.231), and the Samnites of the southern Apennines. From the 8th to the 5th centuries, the culture of the Piceni flourishes in the Marches and northern Abruzzo.

753 Legendary date of Rome's founding

Uncomfortably fitted between the Etruscans of the north and the Greeks of Campania, the new Latin city on its strategic site grows and prospers just the same. In the 6th century, the Tarquinii, a dynasty of Etruscan kings, make Rome a proper city, draining the Forum and building the Temple of Jupiter on the Capitol.

c. 750 Greek colonization of southern Italy begins
510 Establishment of the Roman Republic
499 Victory of Rome over Latins and Etruscans at Lake Regillus
494 Tribunate established at Rome to defend plebeian interests
491 Treason of Coriolanus in Rome–Volsci wars
474 Naval defeat of the Etruscans by Greeks at Cumae
450 Rome's basic law, the Twelve Tables, is codified
423 Samnites take Capua, expand to the coast
407 Rome captures Tarquínia
396 Rome captures Veii
390 Rome sacked by Gauls
351 Final annexation of southern Etruria by Romans

The expansion of this powerful nation of the southern Apennines meant the greatest obstacle to Rome's own ambitions in Italy, resulting in a series of wars that resulted in a final Roman victory. Rome was also busy against the Volsci of southern Lazio, who were finally defeated in 304. Rome's conquest of its neighbours generally meant decay and impoverishment, and a decline of their cities that was especially sharp in the lands of the Latins and Etruscans, while vast lands were confiscated and redistributed to the Roman élite.

343 First Roman–Samnite War; Rome annexes Campania
338 Rome absorbs Latin cities
326 Second Roman–Samnite War
312 Appian Way begun by censor Appius Claudius
268 Rome annexes the lands of the Piceni
264–238 First Punic War
218–201 Second Punic War
151–146 Third Punic War; destruction of Carthage
133–121 Agrarian reforms; murders of Tiberius and Caius Gracchus
115–102 Last Celtic raids on Italy
100 Julius Caesar born, 12 July
92–89 Social War

Italy had been conquered, but its spirit was yet unbroken. When Rome refused to extend citizenship to the other peoples of the peninsula, they combined (except for the Latins) for one last massive revolt, called the Social War. They pooled their forces, and planned a new capital at Corfinium, renamed Italia, but Rome's offer of citizenship to all Italians brought over most of the rebels, and the Roman armies mopped up the rest. Italy was now truly unified, but the Republic's constitutional inadequacies, the bitter fight between the privileged and everyone else, and the ability of military commanders to meddle in politics meant that Italy still faced another 60 years of civil war, beginning in 82 with a grisly reign of terror during the dictatorship of the victorious General Sulla.

50 Caesar crosses the Rubicon and seizes Rome
44 Caesar done in by friends
43–32 *Second Triumvirate: Octavian, Mark Antony and Lepidus*
31 Battle of Actium leaves Octavian sole ruler of Rome
27 Octavian proclaimed Princeps, as Augustus Caesar
27 BC–AD 14 *Augustus*

The Roman Republic was dead, but Augustus, not a Roman but a provincial Italian (from Velletri), gave the new Empire a foundation firm and fair enough to ensure two centuries of peace and prosperity. Rome turned from a 'city of brick to one of marble', as Augustus boasted, while much of Lazio filled up with the grand villas of the emperors and the Roman élite.

AD

14–37 *Tiberius*
19 Death of Virgil
41–54 *Claudius*
54–68 *Nero*

54 Draining of Lake Fucino
64 Great fire in Rome
67 Martyrdom of Peter and Paul in Rome
69–79 *Vespasian*
81–96 *Domitian*
81 Colosseum completed
98–117 *Trajan*
106 Founding of Civitavécchia
117–138 *Hadrian*
118 Hadrian builds his Villa at Tívoli
138–161 *Antoninus Pius*
161–180 *Marcus Aurelius*
193–211 *Septimius Severus*
250–270 Military disasters in Germany and the Middle East

Rome didn't fall all at once. The military disasters and chronic economic crisis of the 3rd century, and the gradual abandonment of Rome by the emperors, made this an especially hard period for central Italy.

270–275 *Aurelian*
271 Aurelian builds the walls of Rome
284–305 *Diocletian*
305 Diocletian's reforms turn the Empire into a bureaucratized despotism
306–337 *Constantine*
312 Constantine wins Battle of the Milvian Bridge with the Christian cross on his banners
326 First basilica of St Peter built
330 Pagan temples closed by order of Constantine
336 Final division of the Empire into eastern and western halves
379–95 *Theodosius*
410 Alaric the Goth sacks Rome
476 Western Empire ends; last Emperor, Romulus Augustulus, pensioned off to Naples; Italy becomes a Gothic Kingdom
493–514 *Theodoric*
c. **500** St Benedict comes to Subiaco
529 St Benedict founds Montecassino
539–53 Greek–Gothic Wars
553 Byzantines abolish Roman Senate, found Exarchate of Ravenna
567–8 Invasion of the Lombards

Eastern Emperor Justinian's decision to reconquer Italy did more damage to the already stricken peninsula than any of the barbarian invasions. After Greeks and Goths had exhausted each other, the way was clear for the truly barbarous Lombards. Under King Alboin they overran most of Italy. Their Kingdom of Italy at Pavia in the north lasted until the coming of the Franks; after that, Lombard successor states, the duchies of Spoleto and Benevento, still controlled parts of central Italy.

590–604 *Pope Gregory the Great*
c. 590 Lombards convert to Christianity
728 'Donation of Liutprand' marks the beginning of the Papal States
750s Campaigns of Frankish King Pepin the Short increase papal power
778 Charlemagne defeats the last Lombard kings; Frankish troops occupy much of central Italy
795–816 *Pope Leo III*
800 Charlemagne crowned Holy Roman Emperor

The 9th century, beginning with so much promise with the rebirth of the Empire under Charlemagne, turned out instead to be a sad time of decay, impoverishment and Saracen raids. The Muslims destroyed coastal towns including Formia and Vulci, sacked St Peter's, and occupied Farfa and Minturno as bases.

c. 880–96 Theodora Senatrix and her daughter Marozia rule Rome
936–73 *Emperor Otto the Great*
962 Otto the Great occupies north Italy; is crowned at Rome the same year
987–98 *Crescenzio rules Rome*
1073–80 *Pope Gregory VII (Hildebrand)*
1075–1122 Investiture conflict between popes and emperors
1084 Robert Guiscard's Normans sack Rome while supposedly allied to the Pope
1097 First Crusade begins
1112–54 *King Roger II of Sicily*
c. 1130 Arrival of the Cistercians in southern Lazio
1140 Normans occupy Pescara

With the conquest of most of Abruzzo by the Normans of Sicily, this region's fate joins that of the south; Abruzzo would be part of the Norman Kingdom and its successor, the Kingdom of Naples, for the next 700 years.

1145 Revolution of Arnold of Brescia in Rome

In Rome, the Republic is temporarily re-established, as Pope Eugenius III becomes the first of many popes to take refuge in Viterbo. With the continuing anarchy in Rome, the popes would be spending considerable time in Viterbo, and other towns such as Anagni, for the next century and a half.

1152–90 *Emperor Frederick I (Barbarossa)*
1170 Viterbo destroys its neighbour Férento
1197 Romans destroy Tusculum
1198–1216 *Pope Innocent III*
1212–46 *Frederick II Emperor and King of Sicily*

The 13th and 14th centuries, a great time for culture and commerce in all of Italy, were also a period of continuous factional strife. Whatever the local reasons, foes tended to take sides in the greater Italian struggle between supporters of the popes, the Guelphs, and partisans of the emperors, the Ghibellines.

1223 St Francis of Assisi comes to Greccio and makes the first Christmas crib
1226 Death of St Francis
1240 Emperor Frederick founds L'Áquila
1243 Frederick besieges Viterbo
1251 Charles of Anjou invades Italy at behest of the pope
1266 Charles defeats the last Hohenstaufens
1278 Papal States chartered in deal with Emperor Rudolf
1294–1303 *Pope Boniface VIII*
1300 First Roman jubilee
1303 The 'Slap of Anagni': humiliation of Pope Boniface VIII
1309 French pope Clement V moves papacy to Avignon
1314 Dante completes the *Divina Commedia*
1347 Cola di Rienzo establishes Roman Republic once again
1348–9 Black Death wipes out one-third of the Italians
1354 Rienzo returns to Rome, is murdered by a mob
1354 Building of the Rocca at Viterbo

While the popes are in France, Cardinal Albornoz initiates his largely successful campaigns to shore up papal power, seizing control of recalcitrant towns and building castles to guard them, as at Viterbo.

1377 Papacy moves back to Rome once and for all
1382 Destruction of Ninfa
1435–58 *Alfonso the Magnanimous of Naples*
1447–55 *Pope Nicholas IV*
1492–1503 *Pope Alexander VI (Borgia)*
1494 Wars of Italy begin with French invasion of Charles VIII
1500–1503 Wars of Cesare Borgia in central Italy
1503–13 *Pope Julius II*
1519–56 *Emperor Charles V*
1523–34 *Pope Clement VII*
1527 Sack of Rome by Imperial troops
1530s–60s Turkish pirate raids on the Tyrrhenian and Adriatic coasts
1534–50 *Pope Paul III*

The accession to the papal throne of Alessandro Farnese marks the height of papal graft and nepotism, as much of central Italy (and other parts) fall under Farnese control. Rome and Lazio, which played only a small role in the beginnings of the Renaissance, now become the stage for scores of new palaces, gardens and churches by the greatest architects and artists of the day, sponsored by the Farnese and the other great noble families.

1540 Inquisition unleashed on Italy
1559 Treaty of Câteau-Cambresis confirms Spanish control of Italy
1626 St Peter's in Rome consecrated

1642 Death of Galileo
1798 Napoleon abducts pope, declares Rome a republic
1808 French capture Rome for the second time, and exile pope
1814 Overthrow of French rule
1848 Revolutions across Italy; pope chased from Rome
1849 Restoration of papal rule by a French army
1849–78 *Vittorio Emanuele II*
1859–61 Piedmont, with French help, annexes most of northern Italy; Garibaldi's 'Thousand' conquer Sicily and Naples
1870 Italian troops enter Rome; unification completed and Rome becomes capital
1900–1945 *Vittorio Emanuele III*
1915 Italy enters First World War
1918 Victory in the Veneto
1919 Fiume seized by Gabriele D'Annunzio; Italian claims generally ignored at Versailles
1922 Mussolini's March on Rome
1923 Creation of the Abruzzo National Park
1925–6 Conversion of Italy to a Fascist dictatorship
1926–35 Reclaiming of the Pontine Marshes; founding of Latina
1927 Founding of modern Pescara
1940 Italy enters Second World War
1943 Allies land in Sicily; Mussolini deposed, later rescued by Germans to found puppet government in the north. Provisional government in south surrenders in September.

After the Germans built their Gustav Line from Cassino to the southern Abruzzo, central Italy suffered more than any other region from the fighting in the Italian campaign. Great battles took place at the River Sangro (1943) and Montecassino (1944). While the Germans declared Rome an 'open city' sparing it from Allied bombing, many other cities and towns were virtually destroyed, including Viterbo, Formia, Civitavécchia, Ortona, Pescara, Cassino and Avezzano. Italian determination and skill got these cities rebuilt afterwards, and most of their monuments repaired; they've done so well, in fact, that today it is difficult to see just how big a job it really was.

1944 Anzio landings, liberation of Rome; Vittorio Emanuele III abdicates
1946 National referendum makes Italy a Republic
1956 Italy becomes charter member of the Common Market
1950s–60s Continuing 'economic miracle' integrates Italy more closely into western Europe.
1960 Olympic Games in Rome
1990s Decade of political upheavals

The 'Tangentopoli' scandals lead to fall of Christian Democrat and Socialist parties, while Communists reform as PDS and rightists converge under Silvio Berlusconi's Forza Italia. Emergence of a new left-wing city government in Rome under Francesco Rutelli.

2000 Jubilee year

Italy's monuments and museums are spruced up, Rome's infrastucture is given a major overhaul, and thousands of new hotels are prepared for the arrival of 30 million pilgrims. Francesco Storace, from the extreme right Alleanza Nazionale party, is elected President of the Lazio regional council.

2001 Walter Veltroni of the left-wing Democratici di Sinistra (DS) party is elected mayor of Rome when Rutelli leaves to run (unsuccessfully) for prime minister.

Art and Architecture

04

The Etruscans

Although Rome and Latium stood on the fringes of the Etruscan world, the young city could hardly help being overwhelmed by the presence of a superior culture almost on its doorstep. Along with much of its religion, customs and engineering talent, early Rome owed its first art to the enemies from the north. Not that there was ever much of it. For the first five centuries of the city's history, the high point came under the rule of the Etruscan kings – the Tarquins' monumental building programmes, including the first temple of the Capitoline Jupiter, in its time the biggest in Italy. Reconstructions show this lost building as a typical Etruscan work, deriving its form from the Greek temple but with a much more ornate decoration on the frieze and pediment, and perhaps statues along the roofline. Other Etruscan temples, with projecting pediments steeper than the Greek, and an emphasis on the exposed ends of beams and rafters, must have seemed an odd cross between a classical temple and an oriental pagoda.

Thanks to the Villa Giulia National Museum, with finds from all over Etruria, and the wonderful tombs in nearby Cervéteri, Rome can show you much of the best of Etruscan art. Enigmatic, often fantastical and always intensely vital, Etruria's artistic magpies were able to steal from every style and technique that came out of Greece – from the Archaic, through the Classical and Hellenistic eclecticism – and turn it into something uniquely their own. In their remarkable portrait sculpture (usually, like their architectural decoration, in terracotta), they often excelled even the Greeks. For this, for their love of fresco painting, and for their distinctive 'grotesque' decoration, embodying the Etruscan fancy for the excessive and outlandish, every period of later Roman art is in their debt.

The Romans Learn Building and Just Can't Stop

The greatest builders of antiquity, no less – though even in late imperial times, when it was a question of aesthetics, they would usually hire a Greek. In architecture, ancient Roman practicality found its greatest expression. They did not invent the arch, or concrete, or the aqueduct; they learned how to build roads and bridges from the Etruscans. Nevertheless, they perfected all these serviceable things to build works never dreamed of before, combining beauty and utility for their most significant contribution to Western culture. Speaking strictly of design, the outstanding fact of Roman building was its conservatism. Under the Republic, Rome adopted Greek architecture wholesale, with a predilection for the more delicate Corinthian order (and a progressive weeding out of Etruscan styles). When the money started rolling in, the Romans began to build in marble; the 2nd century BC Temple of Portunus, still standing by the Tiber, was one of the first examples. But for 400 years, until the height of the Empire, very little changed.

As Rome became the capital of the Mediterranean world, its rulers introduced new building types to embellish it: the series of **imperial fora**, variations on the Greek *agora*, the first of which was begun by Julius Caesar; **public baths**, a custom imported from Campania; **colonnaded streets**, as in Syria and Asia Minor; and **theatres**. Unlike

Greek theatres, these were enclosed (though not covered), with a semicircular orchestra and columned stage buildings. Theatre buildings were illegal in Republican Rome; Pompey and Caesar got around the law by adding temples, quadrangles and meeting halls, and claiming the whole as a religious sanctuary. Rome's own contribution was the *basilica*, a large rectangular hall supported on columns, impossibly noisy as a courtroom but still the perfect stage for Romans in their togas to act out their boisterous public life.

In a city of over a million and a half people, some advances in planning and design could be expected. The Forum of Trajan (AD 107–12, by **Apollodorus of Damascus**) makes the work of many modern planners look primitive. Besides providing noble buildings and open space in the crowded city centre, the Forum skilfully combines divergent land uses – temples, libraries, government and a big market – to create the first and finest of large-scale civic centres.

Concrete may not seem a very romantic subject, but in the hands of imperial builders it changed both the theory and practice of architecture. Volcanic sand from the Bay of Naples, used with rubble as a filler, allowed the Romans to cover vast spaces cheaply. Roman concrete lasts almost for ever; it's better than anything in use now. First in the palaces (such as Nero's Golden House), and later in the Pantheon, with its giant concrete dome (AD 128), and in the huge public baths (those of Caracalla and Diocletian were the largest and most elaborate), an increasingly sophisticated use of arches and vaults made the old Greek architecture of columns and lintels obsolete. Concrete seating made the Colosseum and the vast theatres possible, and allowed *insulae* – Roman apartment blocks – to climb six storeys and occasionally more.

Near the Empire's end, the tendency towards gigantism becomes an enduring symptom of Roman decadence; the clumsy forms of late monsters like Diocletian's Baths (298–306) and the Basilica of Maxentius (306–10) show a technology far outstripping art, while the nascent Christian Church was failing in its attempts to find an original architectural inspiration for its worship. When Constantine, the last of the big builders, financed Christian foundations around Rome, they all took the form of the basilica – an interesting comment on the early Roman church, that it would choose not a contemplative temple for its gatherings, but a form that to any Roman mind signified temporal authority.

Roman Sculpture, Painting and Mosaics

In the beginning, Romans couldn't have cared less for such stuff. Even after the conquests of the 2nd century BC followed by the methodical looting of the cultured East, it was a long time before Rome would be producing anything of its own. As in architecture, the other arts were dependent for centuries on the Greeks, either by importing artists or copying classical works. Portrait sculpture, inherited from the Etruscans, is the notable exception, with a tradition of almost photographic, warts-and-all busts and funeral reliefs extending well into the imperial centuries. Augustus, who did so much else to decorate Rome, first exploited the possibilities of sculpture as a propaganda tool; the relief scenes of his reign on the Ara Pacis (13 BC) exemplify the clarity and classical restraint Romans preferred. Neither state policy nor private tastes encouraged experimentation, and Rome's sculptors continued to churn out endless copies of celebrated Greek works, even with the originals on display in the emperor's gardens and temples.

As in architecture, sculptors began to consider new departures only in the confident, self-assured age of the Flavian and Antonine emperors. Some scholars have called the new style in reliefs 'impressionism', with a greater emphasis on effects of light and shadow, at times creating the illusion of depth, and more dynamic, 'unposed' compositions (as on the Arch of Titus or Trajan's Column). More than any other art, sculpture provides a compelling psychological record of Rome's history. In the 3rd century, as that confidence was undergoing its first crisis at the hands of German and Persian invaders, sculpture veers slowly but irreversibly towards the introverted and strange. Already under the late Antonines the tendency is apparent, with the grim, realistic battle scenes on Marcus Aurelius' column, or the troubled portraits of that emperor himself. Later portraits become even more unsettling, with rigid features and staring eyes, concerned more with psychological depth than outward appearances. Third-century reliefs can be either vigorous and queerly contorted, tending towards the abstract, or awkward and stiff, as in the large number of imperial propaganda reliefs (Arch of Constantine), where emperors on campaign or distributing gifts appear in static arrangements of figures, hardly more than symbols, a trend that presages the hieratic church art of Byzantium and medieval Italy.

In any case, during the 3rd and 4th centuries there was little public art at all. In its brief revival under Constantine, we see how far the process of decay had gone. No work better evokes the Rome of the psychotic, totalitarian late empire than the weird, immense head of Constantine in the Capitoline Museum. Gigantism, as in architecture, survived the final disappearance of individuality and genuinely civic art, while the imperial portraits freeze into eerie icons.

Painting and mosaic work were never exposed to the same storm and stress as sculpture. Though both were present from at least the 1st century BC, Romans considered them little more than decoration, and only rarely entrusted to them any serious subjects. Both are a legacy from the Greeks, and both found their way to Rome by way of talented, half-Greek Campania to the south. Painting, in the days of Caesar and Augustus, usually meant wall frescoes in the homes of the wealthy, with large scenes of gardens (as in the reconstructed room in the National Museum at Diocletian's Baths) or architectural fantasies in the form of window views, making small Roman rooms look brighter and bigger. Mythological scenes were also popular (the careers of Hercules and Dionysus remained favourite subjects for centuries), and there are mentions of 'battle paintings', an early sort of propaganda brought home by victorious generals ready to go into politics; none of these survive. Like the Etruscans, though less ambitiously, Romans liked to paint the walls of their tombs; you can see some in the excavations under St Peter's.

No important advances ever occurred in Roman painting. Skill and grace gradually deteriorated over the centuries; few of the paintings in the Christian catacombs, for example, are anything more than primitive. Mosaics, another import, had their greatest centre at Antioch, in Hellenized Syria, and only became a significant medium at Rome in the 2nd century AD, as painting was declining. Rome is full of simple black and white floor mosaics, but occasionally a virtuoso would turn out a marvellous small scene for a wealthy patron (like the cats and bunnies at Diocletian's Baths, or the debris of a banquet in the Vatican's Gregoriano Profano museum); the *tesserae* used could be as small as 1/32 inch. Sparkling mosaics of tinted glass chips were also used in fountains and the bottoms of pools, though none of this survives. If Rome too had been buried under volcanic lava, at whatever period, it is unlikely that much would be found to surpass the 2nd- and 1st-century BC paintings and mosaics discovered at Pompeii.

Early Christian and Medieval Art

Almost from the beginning, Rome's Christians sought to express their faith in art. The cartoon scrawls in the catacombs are no indication of the sophistication they often reached. On dozens of carved sarcophagi and statues, dating from the 3rd century on (many in the Vatican Museums), the figure of Christ is represented as the 'Good Shepherd', a beardless youth with a lamb slung over his shoulder. Occasionally he wears a proper Roman toga. Familiar New Testament scenes are common, along with figures of the early martyrs. The 4th-century building programme financed by Constantine filled Rome with imposing Christian basilicas, though little of the original work remains. The Lateran Baptistry, begun in the 320s, is the oldest in Christendom; its octagonal shape was copied for baptistries all over Italy for over a thousand years. Sculpture and architecture may have been in decline, but 4th-century mosaic artists were still able to create graceful syntheses of antique art and Christian symbolism, as in Santa Pudenziana church, or the imperial family mausoleum in Via Nomentana, now Santa Costanza.

Through the 5th and early 6th centuries, Christian art – now the only art permitted – changed little in style but broadened its subject matter, including scenes from the Old Testament (as in the Santa Maria Maggiore mosaics) and the Passion of Christ (the Crucifixion on the wooden doors of Santa Sabina may be the oldest one in existence). The new symbolism included the representation of Christ as the Lamb (as in SS. Cosma e Damiano), the animal symbols of the four Evangelists, and the four rivers, representing both the 'four rivers of Paradise' and the four Gospels. There was little money, and few artists, to continue after the destructive Greek–Gothic Wars, but the elegant chancel of San Lorenzo, really the original church, begun in 579, shows how the Romans could build even in the worst of times. More monuments from the advent of the Dark Ages are the mosaics of Sant'Agnese (638). The profound, unearthly gaze of the beautiful St Agnes, and the rich gold background, introduce the Byzantine influence into Roman art. Ravenna, not Rome, was now the artistic centre of Italy, and through it came the formal, mystical art ('hieratic', the Italians call it) of Byzantium. Greek dominance increased in the next three centuries, with an influx of artists fleeing Antioch and Alexandria after the Arab conquests, and from Constantinople itself during the persecutions of the iconoclast emperors.

An impressive revival of Roman building came in the late 8th century, with peace, relative prosperity and the enlightened reigns of popes like Hadrian, Leo III and Paschal I. New churches went up – Santa Maria in Cosmedin, Santa Prassede, Santa Maria in Domnica – all decorated with mosaics by Greek artists. The return of hard times after the collapse of the Carolingian Empire put an end to this little Renaissance, and very little was done in Rome until the 1100s.

When the real revival of art and architecture came to Italy after 1000, Rome was usually too caught up in the continuous fighting of its noble houses to play much of a role. The new Romanesque architecture and sculpture found its greatest triumphs in the far north of Italy, in Lombardy, and in the far south, in Puglia. The towns of central Italy outside Rome shared in the church-building boom of the emerging medieval world, but their productions usually mirror forms already established elsewhere. Notable exceptions include the remarkable churches of Tuscánia, and the Benedictine monasteries founded from Montecassino, and decorated by the school of artists developed there in the mid-11th century under Abbot Desiderius, who later went on to the papacy as Victor III. Desiderius imported large numbers of Byzantine painters, sculptors and architects, and had them train Italian monks in their arts. Although thanks to recurrent wars and earthquakes almost nothing remains of their labours at Montecassino itself, Benedictines created some of the finest frescoes of the period, at Anagni, Subiaco and Bominaco. The oldest of these are strongly Byzantine, though succeeding generations show the increasing influence of the highly stylized Romanesque art of France. Benedictine sculptors carved scores of excellent church portals, pulpits, 'paschal candlesticks' and choir screens; the Abruzzo is full of them, particularly around the Pescara valley where a large number of monasteries were founded or refounded from Montecassino.

When Rome began building again, it was largely with native artists, and stylistically there was almost a clean break with the past. The **Cosmati**, originally a single family of artisans, but eventually a name for a whole school, ground up fragments of coloured glass and precious stone from Rome's ruins and turned them into intricate pavements, altars, paschal candlesticks, pulpits and other decoration, geometrically patterned in styles derived from southern Italy, and ultimately from the Muslim world. Their work can be seen in countless churches around Lazio, notably at Civitá Castellana, Anagni, Subiaco and Ferentino.

Some of the Cosmati school eventually became accomplished sculptors, architects and mosaicists, such as **Pietro Vassalletto**, who built the cloisters at the Lateran and St Paul's (late 12th century) and **Iacopo Torriti** (mosaic of the Coronation of the Virgin at Santa Maria Maggiore; late 13th century). One of the Cosmati artists, Pietro Oderisi, even made it to London, to design Henry III's tomb in Westminster Abbey.

Perhaps the greatest Roman artist of the Middle Ages was **Pietro Cavallini** (*c.* 1250–1330), whose new freedom in composition and brilliant talent for expressive portraiture make him a genuine precursor of the Renaissance, equally at home in mosaics (Santa Maria in Trastevere) and fresco painting (Santa Cecilia). Further nudges towards the Renaissance came from outsiders, often Tuscans, such as the sculptor and architect **Arnolfo di Cambio**; though more famous for Florence's Cathedral and

Palazzo della Signoria, he also left considerable work in Rome (in San Clemente, San Paolo, St Peter's). Giotto also visited Rome, though almost none of his work at St Peter's survives. Outside influences even went so far as to give Rome a Florentine Gothic church (Santa Maria sopra Minerva, 1280), the one exception to Rome's haughty, almost neurotic avoidance of what at the time was Europe's International Style. Gothic architecture flourished in southern Lazio thanks to the Cistercian Order, which came down from France *c.* 1130 to reclaim vacant lands around the Pontine Marshes, and left a string of lovely abbey churches at Fossanova, Casamari and Ferentino in Lazio, and Lanciano in Abruzzo.

In 1308 came the 'Babylonian Captivity', and with no popes to order the work, and no money from tithes or pilgrims to pay for it, Rome's very promising career as a leader in Italian art came to an abrupt end.

The Renaissance in Rome

Rome had nothing to do with the beginnings of the Renaissance – its first century belonged to Tuscany and to Venice – but with yet another revival of the papacy the city was to have the last word. Almost every Tuscan Renaissance master is represented by something in Rome (minor works of Donatello at St Peter's and the Aracoeli, Botticelli, Ghirlandaio and Perugino in the Sistine Chapel, Masolino at San Clemente, Pinturicchio in the Vatican, Aracoeli, and Santa Maria del Popolo, Melozzo da Forlì in the Vatican and Santa Croce, among others); they came, however, as cultural missionaries to a city that had been a backwater since 1308. Pius II, the most artistically inclined of the early Renaissance popes, preferred to expend most of his patronage on his native Tuscany. Paul II (1464–71) commissioned many works, including Rome's first proper Renaissance palace, the Palazzo Venezia. Alexander VI (1492–1503), one of the most intelligent of all papal patrons, ordered the Pinturicchio frescoes in his Vatican apartments. Provincial centres in central Italy produced two important artists in this period, both of whom left only a few works: **Lorenzo da Viterbo**, who left some fine painting in Santa Maria della Verità in his native city, and **Andrea di Litio** of the Abruzzo, whose remarkable frescoes can be seen in the cathedral of Atri.

Rome's high Renaissance begins with Julius II (1503–13). **Michelangelo Buonarroti** (1475–1564) had already arrived, to amaze the world of art with his *Pietà* in St Peter's (1499), but the true inauguration of Rome's greatest artistic period was the arrival of **Donato Bramante** (1444–1514), an architect who had already made a name for himself in Milan. In Rome, where the example of the ancients impressed him deeply, he immediately left off the busy, somewhat eccentric style of his youth and began creating a refined classicism that seemed to exemplify the aspirations of the Renaissance more completely than anything that had gone before. This new marriage of the Renaissance and ancient Rome can best be seen at Bramante's Tempietto at San Pietro in Montorio (1503), or at his cloister for Santa Maria della Pace (1504). The round Tempietto, the first modern building to depend entirely on the proportions of the classical orders (the Doric, in this case), was the most sophisticated attempt at creating a perfect 'temple', fusing the highest conceptions of faith and art, an ideal taken from the architectural fantasies of early Renaissance paintings (for example, in Perugino's *Donation of the Keys* in the Sistine Chapel).

For painting and sculpture, the High Renaissance meant a greater emphasis on emotion, dynamic movement and virtuosity. Following in Bramante's footsteps was **Raphael**, Raffaello Sanzio of Urbino (1483–1520), who arrived from Florence in 1508. Learning the grand manner from antique sculpture and the ancient approach to decoration from the paintings in Nero's recently unearthed Golden House, he applied these lessons in the frescoes of the Vatican Stanze (begun 1509), one of the definitive achievements of the age. A versatile artist, Raphael excelled at portraiture, painted mythological frescoes (as in the Villa Farnesina), and was at times capable of almost visionary religious work (the *Liberation of St Peter* in the Vatican Stanze). He was the most influential painter of his time, with an easy virtuosity and sunny personality that patrons found irresistible – though he would have been mortified to know that his weakness for sweet Madonnas, clouds, putti, and floating holy celebrities was introducing a kitsch element that would plague European sensibilities for the next three centuries.

Michelangelo, unwashed and overworked as ever, spent much of his time sulking over the successes of these two men, whom he claimed stole all their ideas from him. Pope Julius kept him busy enough, with the gargantuan project for his papal tomb that was to bother the artist for much of his life, finally scaled down to a small ensemble, including the famous *Moses*, at San Pietro in Vincoli. Michelangelo tried to flee his terrible patron in 1506, but Julius snatched him back and put him up on the ceiling of the Sistine Chapel two years later. The artist responded to the unusual commission (ceilings are not exactly the best place for great art, though this one started a fad that would last for centuries) with the most profound and imaginative synthesis of art and faith Renaissance Rome would know.

After Julius came the Medici pope, Leo X, open-handed to artists, though greatly overrated as a patron – thanks largely to Voltaire, who wrote of the 'Age of Leo X' as an unsurpassed golden age of culture. Raphael and Michelangelo kept at their work (at least until 1520, when the former died and the latter returned to Florence). Poetry and humanist scholarship were still fostered at the papal court, but through his reign and that of the other Medici, Clement VII, nothing in art appeared that was as revolutionary as the works done under Julius.

The End of the Renaissance

The Sack of Rome in 1527 brought a rude interruption to artistic endeavours of all kinds. Many of the most promising artists left Rome for ever, including **Rosso Fiorentino** and **Giulio Romano** (one of the rare native Romans, a man who had worked for years as assistant to Raphael). Recovery was swift, though the creative intensity of the years before 1527 was never recaptured. Among the artists who returned to Rome, there was of course Michelangelo, who began the *Last Judgment* in the Sistine Chapel in 1536. Its sombre tones, not to mention its subject matter, illustrate more clearly than any other work the change in mood that had come over Roman art.

In his later years, Michelangelo produced little sculpture or painting. Pope Paul III, one of the more serious patrons to occupy the papal throne, appointed him architect of St Peter's in 1547 – when he was 72. Other late works include the civic centre on the Campidoglio (1547) and Santa Maria degli Angeli (1563). His antagonist, taking up Bramante's old job, was **Antonio da Sangallo the Younger**, most accomplished of a family of Tuscan architects. A more accomplished, though less flamboyant architect than Michelangelo, Sangallo continued the High Renaissance tradition, giving Rome some of its finest buildings (Farnese Palace, 1546), while also building some of the most elegant fortresses ever (the Rocca at Civita Castellana).

Tuscan Mannerism, the often eccentric, avant-garde tendency that rebelled against the Olympian high art of the Renaissance, found a place in Rome only for its less shocking exponents: painters such as **Francesco Salviati**, **Perin del Vaga** and **Baldassare Peruzzi** of Siena (1510–63), who besides his paintings contributed original architectural creations like the Villa Farnesina and Palazzo Massimo alle Colonne on Corso Vittorio Emanuele (1536).

Two other distinctive architects of this period created fanciful buildings with a touch of Mannerist restlessness – at least in their secular commissions: **Giacomo da Vignola** and **Pirro Ligorio**. At a time when the great papal families such as the Farnese were rolling in loot, these architects were on hand to indulge them with some of the most spectacular palaces, villas and gardens ever built. Vignola in particular gave them two of the Renaissance's last masterpieces: Rome's Villa Giulia (1550), and the Villa Farnese at Caprarola (1559); he also did the original design for the Villa Lante at Bagnaia near Viterbo; Ligorio's contributions include the Casino of Pius IV in the Vatican Gardens (1558) and the Villa d'Este at Tívoli (1550). Their works, some of the most delightful and challenging buildings of the Roman *cinquecento*, found no one to follow their example in the tough years that followed. The inspiration of the Renaissance was gradually becoming exhausted, just as political conditions were constraining artists to be very, very careful.

The Art of the Counter-Reformation

The decades of the rampant Counter-Reformation and the advent of the Inquisition put a chill on the Italian imagination that would never really be dispelled. In 1563, the final documents of the Council of Trent decreed the new order for art; it was to be conformist and naturalistic, a propaganda tool entirely in the service of the new totalitarian Church, with a touch of Spanish discipline and emotionalism to remind everyone where the real power lay. Largely under the direction of the Jesuits, a costly building programme was undertaken, with large, extravagant churches meant to overawe the faithful and provide an opulent background for the pageantry and bombastic sermons of the new Catholicism: the Gesù Church (1568), Santa Maria in Vallicella (1575), and Sant'Andrea della Valle (1591), all on Corso Vittorio Emanuele, remain the chief works of the transitional order which past centuries called the 'Jesuit Style'.

The leading architect of the age, **Giacomo della Porta** (Sant'Andrea, façade of the Gesù, Palazzo della Sapienza), earns a place as the last of the Renaissance tradition, with a coolly classical style immune to the artistic decay and political stresses of the time. By the end of the 1500s, painting and sculpture were in a bad way, with technically proficient but terminally boring artists like the **Cavaliere d'Arpino** (frescoes in St Peter's dome) holding sway among Roman patrons. **Taddeo Zuccaro** (frescoes at Caprarola, Bracciano and Farfa) and his brother **Federico** rank among the more serious men who thought Mannerism would last for ever, and sought to steer it towards a stiff, respectable academicism.

Rome itself was ordained to become the urban symbol of the Church resurgent, the most modern, most beautiful city in the world. Under the papacy of Sixtus V (1585–90), **Domenico Fontana** and other architects commenced an epochal planning scheme, uniting the sprawling medieval city with a network of long, straight avenues sighted on obelisks in the major piazzas. Fontana's attempts at architecture, such as the drab Lateran Palace (1586), were less fortunate, but other architects were pointing the way towards the dawning Baroque. **Carlo Maderno**'s façade for Santa Susanna (1603) was one of the first symptoms, though the more conventional façade he designed for St Peter's ten years later has been universally condemned ever since as one of the missed opportunities of Roman art.

Times were right for a change. The militant, intolerant atmosphere of the early Counter-Reformation could never last too long among the worldly aristocrats of Rome, no matter how much mischief they were causing to the rest of Europe, and hedonism and artistic innovation resurfaced under a very thin veneer of piety and propriety. Many of the first challenges came from the painters: first **Annibale Carracci**, who reintroduced mythological subjects, taboo in the early Counter-Reformation terror, along with an intense, dynamic style of presenting them that harks back to Michelangelo's Sistine ceiling (Palazzo Farnese gallery, begun 1597); his greatest follower, a figure whose dramatic altarpieces and ceilings contributed much to the birth of the Baroque, was **Guercino** (Casino Ludovisi frescoes, 1621, and the sensuous Venus in the Accademia di San Luca).

Carracci's artistic rival, **Michelangelo Merisi da Caravaggio**, worked in Rome at roughly the same time (1590–1603) before leaving town over the little matter of a homicide. Rome's first certified bohemian (whom modern Italy suavely co-opted by putting his face on a L100,000 note) might have been the last person to pick a fight with at the tavern, but he was all business at painting. His impeccable draftsmanship, combined with a revolutionary, *tenebroso* use of light and shadow and a new, naturalistic manner of portraying biblical subjects (San Luigi dei Francesi, S. Maria del Popolo), made him many followers, and inspired many others to find their own approach to breaking out of the High Renaissance straitjacket.

To Roman opinion, however, the dry, academic painting of the expiring Renaissance was a pinnacle of artistic achievement. And to many later critics, especially in the 1700s, **Guido Reni** (in Rome about 1604–14) and **Domenichino** (1613–31) ranked with Raphael and Michelangelo as the greatest of all time; today the former's brilliantly coloured but often lifeless art, and the latter's vapid classicism, hardly ever get a second glance from visitors to Rome's museums.

The Age of Baroque

No one is really sure where the word 'Baroque' originated. One possibility, according to Luigi Barzini in *The Italians*, is the irregular, oversized pearls still called *perle barocche* in Italy. Barzini goes on to explain how 'the term came to be used metaphorically to describe anything pointlessly complicated, otiose, capricious and eccentric...' Such is the reputation Baroque has acquired in our time. The opprobrium is deserved. Italy was subjected to reactionary priests and despotic tyrants, and art was reduced to mere decoration, forbidden to entertain any thoughts that might be politically dangerous or subversive to Church dogma. But in this captive art there was still talent and will enough for new advances to be made, particularly in architecture.

Plenty of churches, fountains and palaces were still going up in Rome, and there was every opportunity for experimentation. A second landmark, after Maderno's Santa Susanna, was the fountain of the Acqua Paola, built by Flaminio Ponzio in 1610. However, the real breakthrough came in the 1630s, with three great masters who between them inaugurated the Roman High Baroque and determined the course of European architecture for the next century: first **Pietro da Cortona**, with his intricate, flowing façade and dome for SS. Luca e Martina; then **Francesco Borromini**, with his earliest and most memorable works, San Carlo alle Quattro Fontane (1646) and Sant'Ivo (1642), and finally **Gianlorenzo Bernini**, who began the famous colonnades in front of St Peter's in 1656, and the church of Sant'Andrea al Quirinale two years later.

These three men came to architecture from diverse backgrounds, between them exposing something of the range of talents and ambitions of the Baroque movement. Cortona, from the town of Cortona and steeped in the tradition of Florentine Mannerism, began as a painter and designer, already famed for his ceiling frescoes in the Palazzo Barberini (1633–9). Borromini, a profound architect and the son of an architect, came from Lombardy, and brought to Rome the centuries-old tradition of Lombard building skills. The exotic geometry behind his two great churches, mentioned above, was a medieval throwback, repudiating the classical Vitruvian architecture of the Renaissance, but he used it to create amazingly sophisticated forms and spaces. Few architects were able to match this tortured soul's grasp of the art, or the sincere piety that informed it – Borromini himself, in his later career, created nothing as interesting as those first two churches – but everyone who followed did his best to conjure up even more striking and unusual combinations of shapes.

Among the first to catch the fever was Bernini. Neapolitan by birth, with some experience as a playwright and stage designer, Bernini always thought of himself as a sculptor first, and in fact his best-known and most original works are decorations, occupying the vague ground between sculpture and architecture: the St Peter's colonnades, the essential statement of Baroque flourish and grandiosity, and the Fountain of the Four Rivers in Piazza Navona (1651). As architect of St Peter's from 1629 on, and the most popular artist in Rome for decades thereafter, Bernini had an opportunity to transform the face of the city afforded to no other man before or since; his churches, palaces and fountains can be seen all over Rome, and in the Castelli Romani at Ariccia.

Other distinctive contributions to the High Baroque came from **Martino Longhi** (SS. Vincenzo ed Anastasio, 1646) and **Carlo Rainaldi** (Santa Maria in Campitelli, 1663–7).

In sculpture, the Baroque meant a new emphasis on cascading drapery and exaggerated poses, typecasting emotion or saintliness or virtue in a way Renaissance artists would have found slightly trashy. Here Bernini led the way, with such works as his early *David* in the Galleria Borghese (1623), the florid papal tombs, equestrian statue of Constantine, and bronze baldachin, all at St Peter's, and the incredible *Ecstasy of St Teresa* in Santa Maria della Vittoria (1652). His careful, eloquent portrait sculptures seem hardly to come from the same hand – for apparently the less this self-assured and somewhat arrogant artist was able to follow his fancy, the better. Bernini proved a hard act to follow; the only other Roman Baroque sculptors worthy of mention are the more sober **Alessandro Algardi**, and **Francesco Duquesnoy**, from Brussels, whose modest works, scattered around Rome's museums, often recall something of the freshness and lack of affectation of the early Renaissance.

Painting was on a definite downward spiral, though one usually had to look up to see it. Decorative ceiling frescoes, such as those of Pietro da Cortona, were all the rage, though few artists could bring anything like Cortona's talent to the job, **Andrea Sacchi**'s *Divina Sapienza* fresco (1633) in the Palazzo Barberini being a notable exception. After this, preciosity and tricky illusionism rapidly gained the upper hand, most flagrantly in GB Gaulli's ceiling for the Gesù Church (1679) and the Jesuit Andrea Pozzo's *trompe l'œil* spectacular in Sant'Ignazio (1694). Serious painting was breathing its last, but while you are in Rome's galleries keep a look out for the works of Pier Francesco Mola (1612–68) and two of the more endearing genre painters: scenes of Roman life and ruins by Michelangelo Cerquozzi (1620–60), and the landscapes of Salvator Rosa (1615–73).

The Last of Roman Art

From Rome, the art of the High Baroque reached out to all Europe – just as the last traces of inspiration were dying out in the city itself. The death of Pope Alexander VII (1667) is often mentioned as a convenient turning point, after whom there was less money, and less intelligent patronage. But as the Baroque trudged slowly off to its grave, bad paintings and sculptures were still being cranked out by the hundreds. Ironically, at the time when Rome's artistic powers were reaching their lowest ebb, the popes chose to restore dozens of churches after the degraded tastes of the age, destroying much of Rome's early Christian and medieval artistic patrimony in the process.

At the tail end of the Baroque, Rome's most popular architect was **Carlo Fontana** (San Marcello in Corso, 1683, the cathedral at Montefiascone, plenty of undistinguished palaces, and unrealized plans for extending Piazza San Pietro, even worse than the one finally built by Mussolini). After him, though, Roman architecture bounced back for a brief flurry of surprisingly creative work, beginning with **Francesco de Sanctis**' Spanish Steps of 1726, and **Filippo Raguzzini**'s lovely, arch-Rococo San Gallicano hospital in Trastevere (1724). Raguzzini also designed the intimate, stage-set ensemble in Piazza Sant'Ignazio (1728). Another accomplished architect to embellish

Rome in the 18th century was **Ferdinando Fuga**, who designed the Palazzo della Consultà (1737) and rebuilt S. Maria Maggiore (1743). Some things had not changed; all these works continued the Baroque love of the grand gesture – and a hint of stage decoration, nowhere more so than in **Nicola Salvi**'s endearing and utterly Roman Trevi Fountain of 1762.

By this time, a more introspective Rome was looking backwards. Meaningful sculpture and painting were gone for ever, and antiquarianism became a major concern of the few remaining Roman artists, most notably in the endless engravings of **GB Piranesi** (1720–78) and in the sketches, drawings, measurements and monologues of the hordes of Grand Tourists from the north. Another symbol of the age was the founding of the Vatican Museums in 1769. By the century's end, what passed for artistic life in Rome was entirely in the hands of foreigners, such as the German Johann Winckelmann, who became the pope's Superintendent of Antiquities in 1763, the Swiss painter Angelica Kauffmann, the French sculptor Jean-Antoine Houdon, the Icelandic sculptor Thorvaldsen. In the train of Napoleon came two Gallicized Italians, the architect **Valadier**, who gave Piazza del Popolo its present form, and the neoclassical sculptor **Antonio Canova**.

In the 19th century art in Rome continued to lose ground. The fathers of the new Italy, after 1870, knew in their hearts that liberation and Italian unity would unleash a wave of long-suppressed creativity, and they spent tremendous sums to help it along. They were mistaken. The sepulchral, artless monuments and ministries they imposed on Rome helped ruin the fabric of the city, while providing an enduring reminder of the sterility of the Risorgimento and the corrupt regimes that followed it. The modest revivals of Italian painting – the Italian Impressionists, the Tuscan *Macchiaioli* and the 20th-century Futurists – can all be seen in Rome's Galleria d'Arte Moderna, but few of the artists involved in these movements had anything to do with Rome itself. One exception to this dismal picture is the Roman artist **Giulio Aristide Sartorio** (1860–1932), influenced equally by Michelangelo and contemporary poster art; his masterpiece is the series of frescoes in the parliament chamber at Palazzo Montecitorio. Another exception is the delightful, eccentric neighbourhood of Art Nouveau fantasy houses and flats around Via Dora, just off Piazza Buenos Aires.

Mussolini too wanted his revolution to have its artistic expression. The sort of painting and sculpture his government preferred is best not examined too closely, but his architecture, mashing up Art Deco simplicity with a historical pomposity fit for a Duce, now and then reached beyond the level of the ridiculous (the ticket hall of Termini Station and municipal buildings on Via Petroselli in Rome, the post office at Ostia Lido, and especially the planning and public buildings of the new towns in the reclaimed Pontine Marshes, Latina and Sabaudia).

Rome today is moribund as an art centre, and even architecture has not recovered from the post-Risorgimento, post-Mussolini hangover. There are no first-rate contemporary buildings in Rome or anywhere else in central Italy. Not few – none. Efforts at planning the city's postwar growth, with satellite towns and housing schemes, resulted in confusion and concrete madness, and the hideous apartment and office blocks of the suburbs (a particularly vile nest of them can be seen along the road to the airport, around Via Magliana, where Fellini shot one of his last films, *Fred and Ginger*). Until recently it seemed impossible that Rome could ever again produce inspired architecture. However, Paolo Portoghesi's mosque, a playful postmodern extravaganza out near the Villa Ada, together with plans for a glass case by Richard Meier to go around the Ara Pacis in Rome, could be a sign that the tide is about to turn.

Topics

05

The King of the Wood

> *In this sacred grove there grew a certain tree round which at any time of the day, and probably far into the night, a grim figure might be seen to prowl. In his hand he carried a drawn sword, and he kept peering warily about him as if at every instant he expected to be set upon by an enemy. He was a priest and a murderer; and the man for whom he looked was sooner or later to murder him and hold the priesthood in his stead. Such was the rule of the sanctuary.*
>
> Sir James Frazer, *The Golden Bough*

Sir James Frazer was the son of a pharmacist from Glasgow who got a law degree because his strait-laced parents wanted him to, and instead of practising law then went off to become a classics fellow at Cambridge. In 1871 he happened to read about the singular customs of the sacred grove at Lake Nemi, 'Diana's Mirror' in the Alban Hills, where her priest, an escaped slave known as the 'King of the Wood', ruled over the grove and its famous temple, until another would come to take his place. The challenge, for the intruder, took the form of chopping the mistletoe from an oak in Diana's grove; an invitation to a fight that could only be to the death.

Frazer wondered *why*, but not in the innocent way that a less scholarly soul might wonder. Possessing some extreme strain of Scottish doggedness, he devoted the next twenty years of his life to finding out, and finally gave the world his answer in the thirteen volumes of *The Golden Bough* (1890), the foundation of modern anthropology.

If the cult of Diana goes back to the remotest antiquity, it did not necessarily do so in Italy. As ancient writers attested, it was one of many Latin religious imports from the East. According to legends, Diana's worship was brought to Italy by the hero Orestes from the Crimea, along with an image of the goddess hidden in a bundle of sticks. The Crimea, or the Chersonese, as it was known in classical times, was famous for outlandish religious practices, which usually involved blood, knives and horses. But the Latins, by way of the Greeks, would also have known other local variants of this most peculiar and dangerous of all goddesses – from Asia Minor, for example, where as the Ephesian Artemis she was worshipped in the form of an icon sprouting hundreds of breasts; her priests castrated themselves in her honour.

Diana's shrine at Nemi may have been the partial superimposition of foreign practices on a cult that already existed among the Latins. For Diana was not alone in her grove. As a classic ancient triple-goddess, she shared it with the crone Hecate and the mysterious nymph Egeria, who may have been the original goddess of the sanctuary. She was the lover of Rome's legendary second king, Numa Pompilius, and taught him the laws and religious rituals that the Romans were to follow for centuries; it is entirely possible that Rome's earliest kings were more sacred rulers than political leaders and, if he did not have to face death at the hands of a usurper, sacrifices of others may have been made in his place – Roman legends and the archaeological records are full of dark hints of human sacrifice, something the Romans suppressed all memory of in more civilized times.

As Rome gained ascendency over the other Latin cities, the Romans took care to bring their gods and sacred places a little closer to home. A spring near the Appian Way was said to be the real home of Egeria, while Diana herself received a new sanctuary in a temple within the city walls. But perhaps Diana preferred to remain around her beautiful lake, for her worship, along with the strange custom of the grove, survived for centuries more. They were still at it in the enlightened reign of Hadrian, and how long after that no one knows. By this time, everything connected with Diana's cult had become associated with the lower classes; Diana's Roman temple was built on the Aventine hill, the working man's district, and classical writers report that the grove at Nemi was constantly full of beggars, many of them from Rome's large population of impoverished Jews.

Even so, some of the more louche emperors took a special interest in Nemi, notably Caligula, who built luxurious pleasure barges on the lake, the famous ships that were later raised and displayed in the nearby Museum of Roman Ships. It is said that when Caligula tired of one King of the Wood he purposely set a slave to kill him. Archaeologists entertain the grisly thought that in these later days the murder of the King had been brought out from the woods, and provided a bloody imperial entertainment in the theatre attached to the temple complex.

It was not the sensationalism of this ancient rite, however, that set Frazer off on his twenty years of intellectual exploration. The main question was, why must the King die? Frazer tracked down innumerable ill-fated sacred Kings in cultures around the world, from ancient Sweden to the Zulu to the 'King of Calicut' on the Malabar coast to the Dinka and Shilluk tribes of the upper Nile. And he made the connection to the myriad gods of the Mediterranean and beyond who died too: Adonis, Attis, Osiris were the most famous, not to mention Jesus Christ, but ancient Greeks also showed visitors the 'tombs' of Dionysos and even Zeus, local relics of the days before gods became immortal.

Another question: why mistletoe? Ancient authorities linked the mistletoe to the golden bough plucked by Aeneas before his descent into the underworld; it was sacred to the Celtic Druids, and it formed the weapon that killed the Scandinavian god Balder. That led Frazer into a consideration of sacred trees around the world, which filled a volume or two of his great work. One thing led to another: taboos, the 'external soul' (as the mistletoe, engendered by thunder, was the 'soul' of the oak), the 'corn spirit', and magical charms and rituals for the good of the crops, the cycle of the year, and its turning-points at the summer and winter solstices. The sacred king, this universal figure who hides at the magical roots of all religion, was in fact the spirit of the year, and he dies with it for the 'good of the crops', dies so that the eternal recurrence of death and rebirth in nature might be induced to continue.

This mighty theme, and the fascinating trip through the world's antiquities and curiosities that illustrates it, made *The Golden Bough* one of the most popular and influential books of the last century; cast in Frazer's flowing, silvery prose it is also a masterpiece of literature. The single-volume summation has been in print for over a century. In its wake, people began to look at the epics and myths of the past in a new way, and find the thread of Frazer's idea running through everything from the Arthurian cycle to the story of Gilgamesh; it had a profound effect on many of the greatest 20th-century poets too, notably Eliot and Yeats.

Lake Nemi and the grove are still there, still beautiful and a bit uncanny, somehow magically preserved from the modern world and the noise of motor traffic (plenty of oaks, no mistletoe, but patches of pale, pretty violets everywhere; voices of women screaming far away, a crumpled pack of 'Diana' cigarettes by the roadside). Something still lives here. As we watch the dawn of a new millennium, obsessed with technics and parroting the fashionable rationalism of the day, desperately trying to convince ourselves it's true, an old ghost waits quietly to tell us something different about our world and ourselves, something deep and strange, something that won't go away.

Montecassino, 1944

After the invasion of Sicily, people all over Italy felt the sudden menace of the troops and the bombs that would undoubtedly be coming their way. But Mars, whose actions are notoriously unpredictable, decreed this time that central Italy would suffer the worst. The Allied landings at Salerno, followed by the uprising of the people of Naples, occasioned a quick German withdrawal to the hastily built fortifications of the Gustav Line, which stretched from the River Sangro in the Abruzzo to southern Lazio. There it was anchored on the heights of Montecassino, a mountain that was crowned by the most famous monastery in Christendom.

When the Allies reached Montecassino, they could not count on simply getting around it. The landings at the Ánzio beachhead were in a precarious state, and the Allies had to hit the Gustav Line hard to take pressure off the beleaguered troops further north. On 15 February 1944 the Americans sent B-17 Flying Fortresses to drop 287 tons of bombs on the monastery. There were no Germans in it. The Nazis, surprisingly, were often more scrupulous than the Allies about endangering Italian art centres, and Italians still blame the tragedy of Montecassino on the American commander, General Mark Clark.

Clark deserves better, facing a crucial objective in this most bloody and confusing front of the war. Lacking a clear message from the Germans, he naturally expected that the monastery was fortified. On 18 March the Allies dropped 2,500 tons more explosive, and by this time they were close enough to have 900 cannon blasting at the site – still with no foes inside. After the monastery had been reduced to a shambles, an élite brigade of German paratroops took up positions inside the ruins, and they were able to hold up the Allies for another month and a half. For a rest between attacks, they would go down to the crypt of Montecassino's church, the only part of the complex not destroyed, still covered with the gorgeous gold mosaics made by German monks only thirty years before.

The polyglot Allied forces, including New Zealanders, Poles, Indians, Moroccans, Canadians, Algerians and Free French, as well as British and American divisions, made unsuccessful attacks between January and May. On both sides, the fighting was some of the fiercest in the war; very few prisoners were taken. One Gurkha battalion got bogged down on the slopes after a doomed attack in February and refused to retreat; the command had to cut off their supplies to get them back down. Much of the worst fighting took place on the plain below, in the town of Cassino. The Allied bombers and artillery did such a good job of reducing it to rubble that the New Zealanders' tanks couldn't get down the streets, delaying the capture of the city centre for weeks.

It was the desperate men of the Polish 2nd Corps under General Anders, some of them escaped veterans of the resistance, who were charged with taking the monastery; over two weeks, they launched one impossible attack after another on the Germans' impregnable position, losing over a thousand men. They might have lost a thousand more before they got in, but the Moroccan units, experts in mountain fighting, had achieved considerable success in flanking Montecassino from the south, and just as the Poles were ready to break through, the Germans started to withdraw.

The Nazis, along with Mussolini's newly founded Italian Social Republic in the north, had used the defence of Montecassino as a major propaganda symbol. On 18 May, it was photos of the red and white flag of Poland over the ruins of the monastery that grabbed the world's front pages. The war moved on to the liberation of Rome, but when the spring of 1944 blossomed scarcely a single tree on the slopes of Montecassino was left standing. Just below the monastery, on the spot where much of the bloodiest fighting took place, there is a monument; the Polish inscription on it reads:

Passer-by, tell Poland that we died faithfully in her service; for our freedom and yours, we Polish soldiers gave our souls to God, our bodies to the soil of Italy and our hearts to Poland.

The Worst Pope

It would be no easy job to decide which popes made the greatest contributions to religion and culture. The best of them, no doubt, are written up in heaven in St Peter's book; just for fun we have tried to find the worst for ours. This too has its difficulties; out of the myriads of scoundrels, drunkards, thieves, children, idiots, poison artists, political tools, gluttons and perverts who have decorated St Peter's throne over two millennia, we have found some prime candidates, based on a bare minimum of scholarship and a good dose of spleen. We cannot agree with the obvious choice: **Alexander VI**, the notorious Borgia pope. Though a reasonably effective looter of Church money, a sex-crazed hedonist and possibly a closet pagan, his greatest sins seem to have been, first, not spreading the grease widely enough, and second, not being an Italian. The constant vilification he received from his contemporaries convinces us he wasn't such a bad fellow after all, and didn't poison nearly as many people as he is given credit for.

Sifting through the evidence, here are some of the top contenders for the prize: **Benedict IX** (1033–46), heir of Marozia, the third pope in succession to come from the family of the Counts of Tusculum. Elected at the age of ten, this 'Nero of the papacy' took to rapine and homicide at an early age. Twice he was deposed, and once put the papacy up for auction in order to marry an unwilling sweetheart. **Boniface VIII** (1294–1303), the most arrogant and unlovable of popes, who wrecked the powerful medieval papacy with his impostures. He got his job by tricking his predecessor, the saintly but not too clever hermit Celestine V, into abdicating. During a council at the Castel Nuovo in Naples, Boniface whispered through a hidden tube into the pope's cell, pretending to be the voice of God commanding him to quit. **John XII** (955–63). Another of the house of Tusculum, and another teenager, best known for the harem he maintained at the Vatican. **Leo X**, the Medici pope (1513–22). 'Let us enjoy the papacy, since God has given it to us,' said Leo. In fact it wasn't God, but Leo's father, Lorenzo de' Medici, whose money purchased the office. Enjoy it he did – and almost bankrupted it, while his attempts to make up the deficit by selling indulgences and bishoprics were an immediate cause of the Reformation. **Stephen VII** (896–7), an agent of the Dukes of Spoleto, who was so rotten that he exhumed the corpse of his predecessor, Pope Formosus, and put it on trial.

No one could dispute the credentials of **Paul IV** (1555–9), one nasty piece of work. Giovanni Carafa was the real father of the Inquisition, and his reign of terror in his native Naples caused a revolution there. As pope, he presided over the height of the Counter-Reformation, burning more books and more Christians than any other, all the while milking the Church to enrich his family. Paul's hobby was persecuting Jews, and one of the proudest acts of his reign was the creation of the Roman Ghetto. Recent revelations have added a new contender to the list, one with outstanding credentials: **Pius XII**, happy collaborator with the Fascists who also did more than anyone to make possible the Nazi takeover of Germany, by ordering the deputies of the Catholic Centre party to abstain during the crucial vote in 1933 that made Hitler chancellor.

But there is a sentimental favourite. Not as vicious as many, and living in a quiet and decorous age, he nevertheless could claim the award for his pure grasping, grubby mediocrity – **Innocent X** (1644–55). Felix I didn't have a very happy papacy, and Urban VI was really a country boy from Campania, but it is this Innocent who can claim the honour of the most misnamed pope. A tremendous grafter, Innocent devoted his undistinguished papacy entirely to the enrichment of his vile family, the Pamphili. A fair judge of art, he oversaw the development of Piazza Navona (meant to increase property values around his new family palace) and installed all the metal fig leaves and dresses on the Vatican's nude statues.

Innocent met a memorable end – dragging out his last hours while his relatives looted everything around him, even his clothes. Finally there was nothing left but the brass candlestick on his night table – until a servant came back and stole that too. No one could be found to pay for a funeral, and for a while the body lay in a tool shed in the Vatican crypt, in a plain coffin so small that the pope's feet stuck out the end. Francis Marion Crawford, who tells the tale (in *Ave Roma Immortalis*), remarks that eventually the corpse was taken to Sant'Agnese in Piazza Navona, where, 'in the changing course of human and domestic events, it ultimately got an expensive monument in the worst possible taste'.

The Pope who Quit

'The Faith,' as the Romans say, 'is made here and believed elsewhere.' And among the elsewheres, few places have such a sincere natural piety as earnest, hard-working Abruzzo, just across the mountains from the eternal cynicism and intrigues of papal Rome. Almost every village seems to have its special sanctuary or pilgrimage site. In the Dark Ages, its emptier spaces filled up with Benedictine monasteries. Travelling around the valley of the Pescara or the Maiella Mountains, you'll soon notice that the only attractions around are medieval Benedictine churches; imagine what it must have been like 900 years ago, when the monks made up most of the population, living amidst the beautiful scenery like the early fathers in the desert.

Pietro Angelieri, later known as Pietro da Morrone, was a man who liked to be alone. Born in Isérnia in 1215, he started off as a hermit, then became a Benedictine, but soon left the order to return to ascetic solitude in the mountains north of Sulmona. There he proved so good at his trade that he began to attract attention, and followers, who were eventually formalized as the Celestine Order. By the time he was nearing eighty, the Church was in a bad way: corrupt and worldly, and controlled by a greedy, self-serving bureaucracy in the Roman Curia. Politics got into everything, and even the sincere reformers were divided into factions. In 1294, the cardinals had spent two quarrelsome years unable to agree on a pope. Their patience finally ran out; at about the same time, someone had the unique idea of elevating a genuine holy man to the papal throne, someone who might be able to put the Church back on track by direct inspiration from God, or at least by honesty and common sense. The venerable hermit of Monte Morrone, much to his surprise, received a message that he had just been elected pope.

Morrone was indeed a holy man but rather naïve, and as Celestine V he proved all too susceptible to anyone who got his ear. That, as it turned out, was usually the King of Naples, and the cardinals who had hoped to use him as their instrument were disappointed. It soon became evident to the powers in the Church that the new pope wasn't quite turning out the way they had hoped. Celestine himself worried that this high office was proving dangerous for the salvation of his soul – though the evidence suggests that the Curia did everything it could to impede his papacy and manoeuvre him into quitting the job. Whatever the circumstances, he did resign, after only five months – the only pope ever to do so voluntarily. Benedict Caetani, the arch-schemer of the Curia who helped to engineer Celestine's departure, took his place as Boniface VIII. And just to make sure that no one would question the change in power, he locked Celestine up in the castle of Fumone in Lazio and held him there until he died in 1296.

Once Boniface was gone, his successors began the process of Celestine's canonization, perhaps as a kind of posthumous compensation, and he rests as St Peter Celestine in the beautiful church he founded in L'Áquila, Santa Maria di Collemaggio. A privilege Celestine V granted this church during his brief office – practically the only thing he did, in fact – is a Holy Door, like that of St Peter's in Rome, which is opened annually on 28 August for the faithful to pass through and receive a papal indulgence. Celestine gained an additional, somewhat embarrassing claim to fame in 1988 when his saintly remains were stolen and held for ransom, only to be returned without further ado when it became clear to the 'kidnappers' that nobody was going to pay them anything near what they wanted. The Abruzzans couldn't imagine any locals doing such a thing; they suggested the perpetrators must have been some hoods from Rome.

Cyclopean Walls

Wherever you go in southern Lazio, the oldest outstanding feature of a hill town will usually be the ancient, pre-Roman walls, built of stones so large it seems only giants could have put them in place. These walls are the trademark of the region, works as impressive in their way as anything around the Mediterranean. Any architect of antiquity would tell you that big stones are better for a defensive wall than small ones – attackers would be less able to pry them loose to weaken the wall. But the Latins and the other Italic peoples of central Italy took it to extremes. If you've ever built a stone wall in your garden, and mastered the art of finding and shaping the stones to fit tight, you'll appreciate the skill on display here.

Some of these stones, irregular but perfectly fitted, weigh as much as six tons (they are often called 'polygonal' walls, since they are made of many-sided stones set in place as the builders found them, not squared off; only the outer faces were chiselled smooth, to make climbing impossible). In the oldest walls, there are smaller stones fitted into cracks, but by the 5th century BC the builders had their art down so well that the outward face of the wall was constructed of nothing but the biggest stones, fitting so closely together they look as if they had been cut to fit. They've been in place for two and a half millennia, and nothing will shift them for a few millennia to come.

The style of building isn't entirely unique to Lazio. Similar walls can be seen in various places in southern Italy, at Erice in Sicily, in Sardinia and even among the Etruscans, at Volterra in Tuscany. The walls of southern Lazio, and their corbel-arch gates, bear an uncanny resemblance to those of Mycenaean Greece, as at Mycenae and Tiryns, but these precede the Italian models by a thousand years, making it difficult to claim any cultural connection. Ancient writers such as Pausanias, the compiler of Greek antiquities and the author of history's first guidebook, referred to the Mycenaean works as 'Cyclopean' walls, built of stones so large they might have been lifted by the gigantic Cyclops of Homeric legend. Oddly enough, Rome itself did not build Cyclopean walls; the city's first, the so-called Servian Wall, parts of which can still be seen near Termini Station and elsewhere, were built of easily worked volcanic tufa, in the neat ashlar masonry called *opera quadrata*.

But what does it say about the ancient Latins, Hernici, Volsci and Samnites, that such walls should be their only monuments? None of these peoples distinguished themselves in art or culture; nearly everything they had came from the Etruscans or the Greeks. So did their alphabets, and in these early years even the Romans had nothing to say in them that has survived beyond a few short inscriptions. Their deeds did not attract any attention from the historians of classical Greece until Rome started building an empire for itself in the 3rd century. Just as modern historians still wonder how Rome grew so strong, so fast, in the all-important 5th and 4th centuries BC they cannot really explain how the Italic peoples managed such colossal works while leaving behind so little else. Not noted for trade and commerce, and not blessed with the rich mines that financed Etruscan civilization, how did they generate the economic surplus necessary to build? The military necessity was clear; central Italy was a cockpit of competing ambitions, but each city had little to defend with such tremendous walls but its freedom.

These peoples of central Italy have never been favourites of modern archaeologists. Italy's Greek and Etruscan cities were largely abandoned later on; their clear sites are easier to excavate, and promise more in the way of precious art and inscriptions. Consequently, surprisingly little is yet known about the Latins and their neighbours. When Greece was at the height of its classical age, Italy was what today might be called an 'emerging nation'. And it was emerging with dramatic speed and force, growing in wealth and strength as it assimilated culture from the East. Above all, these Cyclopean walls are an expression of discipline and raw power, the same power that Italy, after its unification by Rome, would draw on to build the biggest empire the Western world has ever known.

Passing the Time of Day in Ancient Rome

Recreating some of the atmosphere of the old days is not hard: a score of books have been written on the subject, of which one of the best is *Daily Life in Ancient Rome* by Jerome Carcopino. Roman poets such as Horace, Martial and especially Juvenal also have plenty to say about it. Life in Rome at the height of Empire was an imperial pain: ridiculously high rents, high taxes, street crime, noise around the clock and neighbours from Baetica or Rhaetia with peculiar habits – but naturally everyone in the Empire dreamed of some day moving there. The most significant difference between the way they lived then and our times was the sharp contrast between the quality of life in public versus private places. The average Roman citizen, usually unemployed or underemployed, could loll about magnificent baths and forums all day; only with reluctance did he drag himself home to his nasty, cramped fourth-floor flat at night.

Public Rome

The Roman *forum*, developed from the Greek *agora*, took the form of an open space surrounded by temples, basilicas and colonnades. In the centre, the original Roman Forum and the Fora of Augustus and Trajan made up a single vast complex, the public stage of Roman life. A typical Roman citizen would be there in the morning, to meet friends, transact business, watch the cosmopolitan crowd go by, or indulge in the favourite pastime of watching court proceedings in the basilica. Often they would have their own actions running; the Romans were easily the most litigious nation in all history. Surrounding the *fora* would be the market-places, some of them imposing buildings like the Market of Trajan (in its time not unlike today's covered market in Istanbul).

For all their skill at plumbing, the Romans never managed to bring running water into their flats. The baths, therefore, were a daily spot on any respectable Roman's agenda. He could have stayed all day, for these great establishments were a stage for public life, and cheap and accessible even to the poorest man. Every neighbourhood had some and, counting the ones built by the emperors, they covered almost 10 per cent of Rome. The biggest ones, with bathing halls bigger than St Peter's, also included parks, museums, libraries, lunch counters and, of course, *palaestrae* – athletic grounds for the Romans' favourite games. No civilization, perhaps, ever conceived a more useful way for its citizens to spend their leisure time. There were other places to pursue the classical *dolce vita* – the emperors' extensive gardens (usually open to the public), the temples, which in an irreligious age were really glorified art museums, and the taverns – one on every block, usually with upstairs and gambling in the back room. Romans were terrible gamblers; even the virtuous Augustus would regularly present his children, slaves and dinner guests with bags of *sestertii* to wager against him. Finally there were the races and games in the Colosseum or the Circus Maximus, all of them extraordinarily brutal and bloody, which occupied an average of around 90–100 days a year. These were free, though you needed a ticket just to remind you of the imperial largesse that made it all possible. You also needed a toga, unless you were in the plebeian cheap seats, for these were among this informal city's few dress-up occasions.

Private Rome

Over 90 per cent of Romans lived in flats, in pretty but generally poorly built *insulae* up to 10 storeys in height. From the outside they looked much the same as some of the older Roman apartment blocks today, only with more imaginative façades of brick, stucco and patterned timbers. Many had balconies, and every part of these balconies and windows that received any sun would be full of climbing vines and flowers. Unfortunately most of the streets were less than 12ft across. Rich and poor Romans lived mixed together in every *regio*: the very rich in walled houses (like those at Pompeii), set perhaps next to a four-storey block with wine and oil shops, taverns and ironmongers on the ground floor, middle-class bureaucrats and clients of the rich on the first (with perhaps three or four slaves), and the very poor above them. These had the furthest to climb, and were doomed in case of fire or collapse. Both were constant worries. Crassus, who ruled Rome in the first Triumvirate with Caesar and Pompey, got his start as a weasling building contractor, following the fire squads.

People who lived in flats did not use them much for entertaining, or even for cooking. They had paid water-carriers, but no heating except braziers, no glass windows and little furniture. The shops that filled the ground floors of most buildings always spilled out into the narrow streets, joining the market barrows and the grammar school classes, which rented space under shop awnings or in porticoes – learning to live with distractions was a part of any Roman's education. Traffic problems were probably Rome's biggest headache after the 2nd century BC; Julius Caesar decreed an end to chariots and carriages (the rich had to get by with slave-borne litters) and banished wagons during daylight hours.

Food and Drink

06

In Italy, the three Ms (the Madonna, Mamma and *Mangiare*) are still a force to be reckoned with, and in a country where millions of otherwise sane people spend much of their waking hours worrying about their digestion, standards both at home and in the restaurants are understandably high. Everybody is a gourmet, or at least thinks he or she is, and food is not only something to eat but a subject approaching the heights of philosophy. Although ready-made pasta, tinned minestrone and frozen pizza in the *supermercato* tempt the virtue of the Italian cook, few give in (although many a working mother wishes she could at times).

For the visitor this national culinary obsession comes as an extra bonus to the senses – along with Italy's remarkable sights, music, and the warm sun on your back, you can enjoy some of the best tastes and smells the world can offer, prepared daily in Italy's kitchens and fermented in its countless wine cellars. Eating *all'italiana* is not only delicious and wholesome, but now undeniably trendy. Foreigners flock here to learn the secrets of Italian cuisine and the even more elusive secret of how the Italians can live surrounded by such a plethora of delights and still fit into their sleek Armani trousers.

Restaurant Generalities

Breakfast (*colazione*) in Italy is no lingering affair, but an early morning wake-up shot to the brain: a *cappuccino* (*espresso* with hot foamy milk, often sprinkled with chocolate – incidentally, first thing in the morning is the only time of day at which any self-respecting Italian will touch the stuff), a *caffè latte* (white coffee) or a *caffè lungo* (a generous portion of *espresso*), accompanied by a croissant-type roll, called a *cornetto* or *brioche*, or a fancy pastry. This repast can be consumed in any bar and repeated during the morning as often as necessary. Breakfast in most Italian hotels seldom represents great value.

Lunch (*pranzo*), generally served around 1pm, is the most important meal of the day for the Italians, with a minimum of a first course (*primo piatto* – any kind of pasta dish, broth or soup, or rice dish or pizza), a second course (*secondo piatto* – a meat dish, accompanied by a *contorno* or side dish – a vegetable, salad, or potatoes usually), followed by fruit or dessert and coffee. You can, however, begin with a platter of *antipasti* – the appetizers Italians do so brilliantly, ranging from warm seafood delicacies, to raw ham (*prosciutto crudo*), salami in a hundred varieties, lovely vegetables, savoury toasts, olives, pâté and many many more. There are restaurants that specialize in *antipasti*, and they usually don't take it amiss if you decide to forget the pasta and meat and just nibble on these scrumptious hors-d'œuvres (though in the end it may well cost more than a full meal). Most Italians accompany their meal with wine and mineral water – *acqua minerale*, with or without bubbles (*con* or *senza gas*), which supposedly aids digestion – concluding their meals with a *digestivo* liqueur.

Cena, the **evening meal**, is usually eaten around 8pm – earlier in the north and later in the south. This is much the same as *pranzo* although lighter, without the pasta;

a pizza and beer, eggs or a fish dish. In restaurants, however, they offer all the courses whatever the time of day, so if you have only a sandwich for lunch you can have a full meal in the evening.

In Italy the various terms for types of **restaurants** – *ristorante, trattoria* or *osteria* – have been confused. A *trattoria* or *osteria* can be just as elaborate as a restaurant, though rarely is a *ristorante* as informal as a traditional *trattoria*. Unfortunately the old habit of posting menus and prices in the windows has fallen from fashion, so it's often difficult to judge variety or prices. Invariably the least expensive eating place is the *vino e cucina*, a simple establishment serving simple cuisine at simple everyday prices. It is essential to remember that the fancier the fittings, the fancier the **bill**, though neither of these points has anything at all to do with the quality of the food. If you're uncertain, do as you would at home – look for lots of locals.

People who haven't visited Italy for years and have fond memories of eating full meals for under a pound will be amazed at how much **prices** have risen; though in some respects eating out in Italy is still a bargain, especially when you figure out how much all that wine would have cost you at home. In many places you'll often find restaurants offering a *menu turistico* – full, set meals of usually meagre inspiration for a reasonable set price. More imaginative chefs often offer a *menu degustazione* – a set-price gourmet meal that allows you to taste their daily specialities and seasonal dishes. Both of these are cheaper than if you had ordered the same food *à la carte*.

As the pace of modern urban life militates against traditional lengthy home-cooked repasts with the family, followed by a siesta, alternatives to sit-down meals have mushroomed. Many office workers now behave much as their counterparts elsewhere in Europe and consume a rapid snack at lunchtime, returning home after a busy day to throw together some pasta and salad in the evenings.

The original Italian fast food alternative is known as the 'hot table' (*tavola calda*), a buffet serving hot and cold foods, where you can choose a simple prepared dish or a whole meal, depending on your appetite. The food in these can occasionally be truly impressive, though nowadays they are becoming harder to find among the growing number of international and made-in-Italy fast food franchises. However, bars often double as *paninotecas* (these make sandwiches to order), and if everywhere else is closed, you can always try the railway station bars – these will at least have sandwiches and drinks. Some of the station bars also prepare *cestini di viaggio*, full-course meals in a basket to help you survive long train trips.

Common snacks you'll encounter include *panini* of prosciutto, cheese and tomatoes, or other meats; *tramezzini*, little sandwiches on plain, square white bread that are always much better than they look; pizza, of course; or, in Lazio, the native snack called *supplì* (rice croquettes filled with ham and mozzarella, rolled in breadcrumbs and fried). Little shops that sell pizza by the slice (*al taglio*) are common in city centres; some, called *gastronomie*, offer other take-out delicacies as well. At any delicatessen (*pizzicheria*), or grocer's (*alimentari*) or market (*mercato*) you can buy the materials for countryside picnics; some places in smaller towns will make the sandwiches for you.

Food

What may come as a surprise is the tremendous regional diversity at the table; often next to nothing on the menu looks familiar, or is disguised by a local or dialect name. Expect further mystification, as many Italian chefs have embraced the concept of *nouvelle cuisine*, or rather *nuova cucina*, and are constantly inventing dishes with even more names. If your waiter fails to elucidate, the menu decoder in this chapter may help.

Specialities of Rome and Lazio

In spite of the presence of cosmopolitan Rome, the traditional cuisine of Lazio is Italian soul food, or *cucina povera*: beans, chickpeas, greens, game, tripe, salt cod (*baccalà*), and kid and lamb. The idea of an *antipasto* (outside Rome) is fairly recent in the region's restaurants. In late spring and summer there are artichokes (*carciofi*), especially young ones served *alla giudea* ('Jewish style,' fried in olive oil until brown and crisp) or *alla romana* (stewed in oil, with mint and garlic). Marinated lake fish is a favourite by the lakes. In southern Lazio, in particular, you can start with a salad featuring *mozzarella di bufala*, the real McCoy made from buffalo milk, much better than cow's milk imitations. Two very traditional dishes are *panzanelle* (stale bread softened in water, mixed with fresh herbs, cucumber and tomotoes, vinegar and olive oil), and 'cooked water' – *acqua cotta* – perhaps the ultimate *cucina povera* dish: boiled wild herbs and mushrooms, and streaky bacon, boiled together in water and poured over stale bread, with olive oil, and whatever else anyone was lucky enough to have on hand.

Pasta is as ever a favourite first course: all over Lazio you'll find freshly made *fettuccini* (ribbons of egg pasta, served with porcini mushrooms, tomato sauce, ragu or *al burro* – with a double dose of butter, cream and Parmesan cheese), *pappardelle* (very fat noodles) with hare, boar or mushroom sauce, spaghetti *alla carbonara*, or spaghetti (or hollow *bucatini*, or fat *lombrichelle*) *all'amatriciana*, with a rich sauce of bacon, tomatoes, chilli pepper and onions, topped with grated pecorino (a hard, tangy sheep's milk cheese). *Maccheroni alla ciociara* is covered with ham, bacon and sausage. *Gnocchi alla romana* are semolina dumplings served with butter and cheese. *Stracciatella*, a chicken or beef broth with a beaten egg, grated cheese and semolina, is another popular *primo* around Rome, while the mountain villages are all proud of their pasta with beans, beans with wild fennel, chestnut and chickpea soup, and lentil dishes. By the lakes try *sbroscia*, a delicious soup made from freshwater fish, while in the Maremma region they make an unusual soup with lamb (*giubba e calzoni*).

For *secondo*, the seaside resorts naturally wait to beguile you with **seafood** (Ánzio with its busy fishing fleet has the best collection of fish restaurants outside Rome; look for the tasty scampi like *mezzancole*, a speciality of this coast, while lobster-lovers can usually find *aragosta* on the menu on Ponza) and the lakes offer freshwater fish and eels in interesting guises – at least once try *corregone*, whitefish from the lakes of northern Lazio, prepared in a wide variety of ways: other favourite lake fish are *tinca* (tench), *luccio* (pike) and *persico* (perch). A big eel is a *capitoni*, caught only from September to December. But fish (except for *baccalà*) figures little in traditional Lazio cuisine compared to **lamb**, often grilled chops of *abbacchio* (milk-fed lamb) or just its head (*testarelle di abbacchio*, sprinkled with rosemary and roasted) or lamb stew (*brodettato*) or insides (*coratella* – the intestines, lungs and heart, usually cut in small bits and fried). In Viterbo province the *pièce de résistance* is *pignattaccia*, beef and pork and offal, with onions, potatoes, celery and other vegetables, baked in an earthenware casserole. Mountain villages pride themselves on their tender kid. If you missed out on the beans and pulses in the first course, you can find hearty dishes cooked in earthenware pots, such as *fave al guanciale* (broad beans with bacon and onions) or *fagioli con le cotiche* or *alla romana* (cooked slowly, with a tomato sauce and pork crackling).

Modern Romans are as adventurous at the table as their classical ancestors, and you'll find a wide choice of ethnic restaurants in the Urbs, but when they want some home cooking they usually want **offal**: a favourite is *pajata*, calves' intestines. Other popular dishes are *fritto misto alla romana* (calves' brains, sweetbreads, liver, artichoke, and bread, all dipped in batter and deep-fried) and *trippa alla romana* (tripe in tomato sauce, flavoured with mint and topped with pecorino cheese). **Veal** is popular, especially in Rome, either in the classic *saltimbocca alla romana* (scallops with ham and sage, cooked in white wine and butter) or *spezzatino alla romana* (sautéed in oil with lemon juice and beaten egg).

Vegetarians need not give in to total despair; besides pasta, minestrone, mozzarella, pizza and salads you may find among the *contorni*: roast potatoes with porcini mushrooms (excellent), aubergine, cardoon, chickory and artichoke *parmigiana*, and in the north *fritto misto alla viterbese*, with artichokes, aubergines, courgettes, broccoli, parsnips and courgette flowers. Roast peppers, wild greens and sautéed garden vegetables are other possibilities. Try the local cheeses; the fresh ones are called *latticini*, and delicious.

Besides the inevitable slices of pizza and sandwiches, the favourite **fast food** in central Italy is *porchetta* (a roast suckling pig, stuffed with herbs, pepper and fennel) sold in stands with slices of bread. In Rome, you'll find *supplì* (rice croquettes filled with tomato sauce and mozzarella, rolled in egg and breadcrumbs and fried).

Specialities of Abruzzo and Molise

Many of the culinary traditions of Lazio's mountain villages are shared by their neighbours in the **Abruzzo**. The region's **pasta** is sold all over Italy, but the great local speciality is the square rather than round spaghetti: *maccheroni alla chitarra* (so called because it is cut with an implement shaped a little like a guitar), served with a meaty sauce of lamb, bacon and pecorino or *ragù all'abruzzese*, in a sauce made of beef, mutton, pork or duck; ravioli filled with ricotta are also popular, along with *orecchie* (pasta shaped a little like ears), *riso e fagioli* (spicy rice and beans) and the

Italian Menu Vocabulary

Antipasti

These before-meal treats can include almost anything; these are among the most common.

antipasto misto mixed antipasto
bruschetta garlic toast (sometimes with tomatoes)
carciofi (sott'olio) artichokes (in oil)
frutti di mare seafood
funghi (trifolati) mushrooms (with anchovies, garlic and lemon)
gamberi ai fagioli prawns (shrimps) with white beans
mozzarella (in carrozza) cow/buffalo cheese (fried with bread in batter)
olive olives
prosciutto (con melone) raw ham (with melon)
salsicce sausages

Minestre (Soups) and *Pasta*

agnolotti ravioli with meat
cacciucco spiced fish soup
cannelloni meat/cheese rolled in pasta tubes
cappelletti small ravioli, often in broth
crespelle crêpes
fettuccine long strips of pasta
frittata omelette
gnocchi potato dumplings
lasagne sheets of pasta baked with meat and cheese sauce
minestra di verdura thick vegetable soup
minestrone soup with meat, vegetables and pasta
orecchiette ear-shaped pasta, served with turnip greens
panzerotti ravioli with mozzarella, anchovies and egg
pappardelle alla lepre pasta with hare sauce
pasta e fagioli soup with beans, bacon, and tomatoes
pastina in brodo tiny pasta in broth
penne all'arrabbiata quill-shaped pasta with tomatoes and hot peppers
polenta cake or pudding of corn semolina
risotto (***alla milanese***) Italian rice (with stock, saffron and wine)
spaghetti all'amatriciana with spicy pork, tomato, onion and chilli sauce
spaghetti alla bolognese with ground meat, ham, mushrooms etc.
spaghetti alla carbonara with bacon, eggs and black pepper
spaghetti al pomodoro with tomato sauce
spaghetti al sugo/ragù with meat sauce
spaghetti alle vongole with clam sauce
stracciatella broth with eggs and cheese
tagliatelle flat egg noodles
tortellini pasta caps filled with meat and cheese
al pomodoro with tomato sauce
con panna with cream
in brodo in broth
vermicelli very thin spaghetti

Carne (Meat)

abbacchio milk-fed lamb
agnello lamb
animelle sweetbreads
anatra duck
arista pork loin
arrosto misto mixed roast meats
bistecca alla fiorentina Florentine beef steak
bocconcini veal mixed with ham and cheese and fried
bollito misto stew of boiled meats
braciola chop
brasato di manzo braised beef with veg
bresaola dried raw meat
capretto kid
capriolo roe-buck
carne di castrato/suino mutton/pork
carpaccio thinly sliced raw beef
cassoeula pork stew with cabbage
cervello (***al burro nero***) brains (in black butter sauce)

famous *virtù* (*see* p.287). The Abruzzo grows plenty of **saffron**, *zafferano di Navelli*, to be precise, which appears in some local rice and polenta dishes, although the bulk is exported to Milan to flavour its famous risotto. The Abruzzesi are also very fond of **hot peppers**, in pasta dishes and meat stews. They grow some sizzlers, like the long red *corne di capra* ('goat's horns'), but, fearing to offend, they use them more at home

cervo venison
cinghiale boar
coniglio rabbit
cotoletta veal cutlet
alla milanese fried in breadcrumbs
alla bolognese with ham and cheese
fagiano pheasant
faraona guinea fowl
alla creta in earthenware pot
fegato alla veneziana liver with filling
lepre (in salmì) hare (marinated in wine)
lombo di maiale pork loin
lumache snails
maiale (al latte) pork (cooked in milk)
manzo beef
osso buco braised veal knuckle
pancetta rolled pork
pernice partridge
petto di pollo boned chicken breast
alla fiorentina fried in butter
alla bolognese with ham and cheese
alla sorpresa stuffed and deep fried
piccione pigeon
pizzaiola beef steak in tomato and oregano
pollo chicken
alla cacciatora with tomatoes and mushrooms, cooked in wine
alla diavola grilled
alla Marengo fried with tomatoes, garlic and wine
polpette meatballs
quaglie quails
rane frogs
rognoni kidneys
saltimbocca veal scallop with prosciutto and sage, cooked in wine and butter
scaloppine thin slices of veal sautéed in butter
spezzatino pieces of beef/veal, usually stewed
spiedino meat on a skewer/stick
stufato beef and vegetables braised in wine
tacchino turkey
trippa tripe
uccelletti small birds on a skewer
vitello veal

Pesce (Fish)

acciughe/alici anchovies
anguilla eel
aragosta lobster
aringa herring
baccalà dried salt cod
bonito small tuna
branzino sea bass
calamari squid
cappe sante scallops
cefalo grey mullet
coda di rospo angler fish
cozze mussels
datteri di mare razor (or date) mussels
dentice dentex (perch-like fish)
dorato gilt head
fritto misto mixed fried delicacies, mainly fish
gamberetto shrimp
gamberi (di fiume) prawns (crayfish)
granchio crab
insalata di mare seafood salad
lampreda lamprey
merluzzo cod
nasello hake
orata bream
ostriche oysters
pesce spada swordfish
polipi/polpi octopus
pesce azzurro various small fish
pesce di San Pietro John Dory
rombo turbot
sarde sardines
seppie cuttlefish
sgombro mackerel
sogliola sole
squadro monkfish
stoccafisso wind-dried cod
tonno tuna
triglia red mullet (rouget)
trota trout
trota salmonata salmon trout
vongole small clams
zuppa di pesce mixed fish in sauce or stew

than in restaurants. If you like it hot, let them know and they can probably fix you up something special.

Inland Abruzzo is mountainous and well-suited to sheep-rearing; you will find plenty of **lamb** dishes (either *agnello* or *castrato*, castrated mutton), grilled or roasted or stewed. Innards are popular, as in *torcinelli* (lamb offal and lights (lungs) roasted on

Contorni (Side Dishes, Vegetables)

asparagi asparagus
alla fiorentina with fried eggs
broccoli broccoli
carciofi (alla giudea) artichokes (deep fried)
cardi cardoons/thistles
carote carrots
cavolfiore cauliflower
cavolo cabbage
ceci chickpeas
cetriolo cucumber
cipolla onion
fagioli white beans
fagiolini French (green) beans
fave broad beans
finocchio fennel
funghi (porcini) mushrooms (boletus)
insalata (mista/verde) salad (mixed/green)
lattuga lettuce
lenticchie lentils
melanzane aubergine/eggplant
patate (fritte) potatoes (fried)
peperoncini hot chilli peppers
peperoni sweet peppers
peperonata stewed peppers, onions, etc. (similar to ratatouille)
piselli (al prosciutto) peas (with ham)
pomodoro(i) tomato(es)
porri leeks
radicchio red chicory
radice radish
rapa turnip
rucola rocket
sedano celery
spinaci spinach
verdure greens
zucca pumpkin
zucchini courgettes

Formaggio (Cheese)

bel paese soft white cow's cheese
cacio/caciocavallo pale yellow, sharp cheese
caprino goat's cheese
fontina rich cow's milk cheese
groviera mild cheese (gruyère)
gorgonzola soft blue cheese
parmigiano Parmesan cheese
pecorino sharp sheep's cheese
provolone sharp, tangy cheese
dolce is less strong
stracchino soft white cheese

Frutta (Fruit, Nuts)

albicocche apricots
ananas pineapple
arance oranges
banane bananas
cachi persimmon
ciliege cherries
cocomero watermelon
datteri dates
fichi figs
fragole (con panna) strawberries (with cream)
lamponi raspberries
limone lemon
macedonia di frutta fruit salad
mandarino tangerine
mandorle almonds
melagrana pomegranate
mele apples
mirtilli bilberries
more blackberries
nespola medlar fruit
nocciole hazelnuts
noci walnuts
pere pears
pesche peaches
pesca noce nectarine
pinoli pine nuts
pompelmo grapefruit
prugna/susina prune/plum
uva grapes

Dolci (Desserts)

amaretti macaroons
cannoli crisp pastry tubes filled with ricotta, cream, chocolate or fruit
coppa gelato assorted ice cream

a skewer pierced with sage leaves; sometimes it's called *matassine*). There are also many **sheep cheeses**, especially fresh or aged pecorino cheese, the latter often served with pasta instead of Parmesan, while the local 'mozzarella' is *scamorza*, a soft cheese of cow's and sheep's milk, often served grilled as a main course. The Abruzzese like their **pancakes**, filled with cheese and ham (*scripelle mbusse*) or in a broth with

crema caramella caramel-topped custard
crostata fruit flan
gelato (produzione propria) ice cream (home-made)
granita flavoured ice, often lemon or coffee
monte bianco chestnut pudding with cream
panettone sponge cake with candied fruit and raisins
panforte dense cake of chocolate, almonds and preserved fruit
saint honoré meringue cake
semifreddo refrigerated cake
sorbetto sorbet/sherbet
spumone a soft ice cream
tiramisù layers of sponge, mascarpone, coffee and chocolate
torrone nougat
torta cake, tart
torta millefoglie layered pastry and custard cream
zabaglione eggs and Marsala wine, served hot
zuppa inglese trifle

Bevande (Beverages)

acqua minerale mineral water
 con/senza gas with/without fizz
aranciata orange soda
birra (alla spina) beer (draught)
caffè (freddo) coffee (iced)
cioccolata chocolate
gassosa lemon-flavoured soda
latte (intero/scremato) milk (whole/skimmed)
limonata lemon soda
succo di frutta fruit juice
tè tea
vino wine
 rosso red
 bianco white
 rosato rosé

Cooking Terms (Miscellaneous)

aceto (balsamico) vinegar (balsamic)
affumicato smoked
aglio garlic
alla brace cooked over embers
bicchiere glass
burro butter
cacciagione game
conto bill
costoletta/cotoletta chop
coltello knife
cucchiaio spoon
filetto fillet
forchetta fork
forno oven
fritto fried
ghiaccio ice
griglia grill
in bianco without tomato
magro lean meat/pasta without meat
marmellata jam
menta mint
miele honey
mostarda candied mustard sauce
olio oil
pane bread
pane tostato toasted bread
panini sandwiches (in roll)
panna cream
pepe pepper
piatto plate
prezzemolo parsley
ripieno stuffed
rosmarino rosemary
sale salt
salmì wine marinade
salsa sauce
salvia sage
senape mustard
tartufi truffles
tavola table
tazza cup
tovagliolo napkin
tramezzini finger sandwiches
umido cooked in sauce
uovo egg
zucchero sugar

chicken livers (*scripelle in brodo*), or in a *timballo*, a mould with *scamorza* and artichokes; another dish, *timballo abruzzese*, has pasta sheets baked in a mould with chicken livers and lights, veal rissoles and *scamorza* cheese.

Some other dishes are *tacchino alla canzanese* (turkey in aspic), *coniglio 'mbriache* (drunken rabbit, in white wine) and pork dishes with funny dialect names such as *'ndocca 'ndocca* ('piece by piece', which includes most conceivable pig parts from ears to trotter) and *cif cin'* or *'ncif 'ncin* (more pork, with garlic and rosemary). The local mortadella, the *mortadella di Campotosto*, is spicier than that of Bologna, flavoured with garlic and nicknamed *coglioni di mulo* (mule's balls) for its shape.

The food of the **Molise** uses many of the same basic ingredients, with plenty of pasta (*zite, bucatini, penne*, and home-made *cavatelli, sagnetelle, cappellacci*, etc.) mixed with a wide variety of fresh vegetables or beans. Only here you're likely to come across even more offal, and virtually everything tends to be flavoured with little **hot red peppers**, called *diavolini* ('little devils') by the Molisani. They favour dishes like stuffed lamb heads (*testine d'agnello*); *capuzzelle e patane* (lamb's head with potatoes, garlic, diavolini); a tripe salad featuring *allullera*, lamb tripe filled with offal, cheese, eggs, herbs and *diavolini*, boiled and served sliced with *fischioni*, pasta tubes boiled in the broth. A winter favourite is **polenta** with red beans, olive oil, hot peppers and garlic (*polenta maritata*). The traditional summer **salad**, *caponata*, contains chopped tomatoes, celery, olives, peppers, boiled eggs and anchovies, served with the traditional hard bread, *tarallo*, to soak up the oil and vinegar. Favourite **light dishes** include salt cod fritters (*frittelle di baccalà*), courgette (zucchini) flowers fried in batter, *cace e ova* (a dish made with ricotta, Parmesan, breadcrumbs, with a sauce of tomatoes and onion) and *pizza con le foglie*, or *mbaniccia*, a kind of thick pizza filled with greens flavoured with boiled pork, ideally baked wrapped in chestnut leaves.

Like all coastal areas of Italy, the Abruzzo and Molise have their own **fish stew** recipes, here generally known as *brodetto*, with different versions as you travel down the coast, using a variety of fish, with garlic, tomato, onion, parsley, as well as their own squid speciality – squid stuffed with anchovies, breadcrumbs and garlic. *Polpi in purgatorio* are cuttlefish in a very spicy sauce. Also good is *scapece* (pickled fried fish with saffron), a speciality of Chieti.

Wine

Italy is a country where everyday wine is cheaper than Coca-Cola or milk, and where many families own some vineyards or have some relatives who supply most of their daily needs – which are not great. Even though they live in one of the world's largest wine-growing countries, Italians imbibe relatively little, and usually only at meals.

If Italy has an infinite variety of regional dishes, there is an equally bewildering array of **regional wines**, many of which are rarely exported because they are best drunk young. Unless you're dining at a restaurant with an exceptional cellar, do as the Italians do and order a carafe of the local wine (*vino locale* or *vino della casa*; in Lazio especially it's often *sfuso*, straight out of the barrel). Most Italian wines are named after the grape and the district they come from. If the label says DOC (*Denominazione di Origine Controllata*) it means that the wine comes from a specially defined area and was produced according to a certain traditional method. DOCG (*Denominazione di Origine Controllata e Garantita*) is allegedly a more rigorous classification, indicating that the wines not only conform to DOC standards, but are tested by government-appointed inspectors. At present few wines have been granted this status, but the number is planned to increase steadily. *Classico* means that a wine comes from the oldest part of the zone of production, though is not necessarily better than a non-Classico. *Riserva*, *superiore* or *speciale* denotes a wine that has been aged longer and is more alcoholic; *Recioto* is a wine made from the outer clusters of grapes, with a higher sugar and therefore alcohol content. Other Italian wine words are *spumante* (sparkling); *frizzante* (pétillant), *amabile* (semi-sweet), *abboccato* (medium dry), *passito* (strong sweet wine made from raisins). *Rosso* is red, *bianco* white; between the two extremes lie *rubiato* (ruby), *rosato*, *chiaretto* or *cerasuolo* (rose). *Secco* is dry, *dolce* sweet, *liquoroso* fortified and sweet. *Vendemmia* means vintage, a *cantina* is a cellar, and an *enoteca* is a wine-shop or museum when you can taste and buy wines.

Wines of Lazio

Wine has been made in Lazio since the 8th century BC; the vines introduced by the Greek colonists just to the south in Ischia and Cumae readily took root in the volcanic soils, finding conditions that are well nigh perfect. Yet 90 per cent of Lazio's wines are scarcely known outside the region – they don't travel well, they tend to be extremely variable, and until very recently no one has bothered to make a concerted effort to change that status quo. Nearly all are white wines, most of them everyday, affordable, and great for quaffing by the carafe.

The Castelli Romani and Alban hills (DOC Colli Albani) keep Rome sloshing happily away, although **Frascati**, Lazio's one oenological household name, still rules as the pick of the bunch – very soft, fruity and easy to drink, reportedly as far away as Buckingham Palace. Although the Romans used to like it a bit sweet (*cannellino*) it's now almost invariably *secco*. Other Castelli wines to look for, often as good as Frascati, are Marino and Velletri (which also produces a very nice young red wine, too). Ask for red wine in the Castelli and you might get a puzzled look. Red wines from southern Lazio tend to come from the Ciociaría, made from the local grape, Cesanese. Agnani is the home of the legendary Torre Ercolano, developed by a musician named Luigi Colacicchi, who blended the local grape Cesanese with a mix of merlot and cabernet to produce a very mellow wine that becomes exquisite as it ages – the 1990 vintage is considered mythic.

Northern Lazio is best known for a wine that tends to be all packaging and mediocre content, Est! Est!! Est!!! (*see* p.222), from Montefiascone near Lake Bolseno. The Est-growing area has recently been expanded, so you might find a decent drink, but much of it tends to be plonk. The opposite is true of Orvieto Classico, of which a large part of its growing area spills over from Umbria into Viterbo province. The excellent and versatile DOC Cervéteri rarely disappoints, and you won't go far wrong with the wines from the Colli Etruschi and Vignanello. Grádoli is famous for its legendary ruddy dessert wine, Aleatico, with a soft musky rose fragrance, heavy but not too sweet, ranging from 14° to 16°, the latter in less sunny years, when the wine has to be fortified. The light red Grechetto di Grádoli has recently won its DOC label. There may be more red wines from the north in the future: new vineyards in Tarquínia, Castiglione in Taverina and Montefiascone have yielded some very promising results in recent years.

Wines of Abruzzo and Molise

The local wines, white and red, make excellent accompaniments both to the local hearty stews and to the more delicate fish dishes of the coast, and in recent years wine growers have made an extra effort to improve their quality. Montepulciano d'Abruzzo is the best-known wine of the area. It's a smooth, dry red which, like many Italian wines, is best drunk within three years. Trebbiano is the best Abruzzo white, a dry, delicate wine, while another, Controguerra ('antiwar') is a good fruity white wine from Téramo. In Molise the Biferno and Pentro wines both come in red, white or rosé. They're not quite as good as the Abruzzo wines, but are excellent with the simple local dishes.

Travel

07

Getting There

By Air from the UK and Ireland

Flying is obviously the quickest and most painless way of getting to central Italy from the UK. There are direct flights to Rome from over half a dozen British airports. Scheduled services are, in the main, more expensive than charters although there are a couple of low-cost airlines whose scheduled flight prices can compete with the very lowest charter fares (*see* below).

Most **scheduled** flights are operated either by the Italian state airline Alitalia, or British Airways. Return fares vary greatly, depending on the season. The best-value deals are usually Apex or SuperApex fares, for which you must book seven days ahead, and stay a Saturday night in Italy – no alterations or refunds are possible without high penalties. Return scheduled fares range typically from around £150 off-season; midsummer fares will probably be well over £250.

You can usually find good **flight deals** on *www.opodo.com*, an online service which is run by several of Europe's biggest carriers including British Airways and Alitalia. Of the 'no-frills' airlines, easyJet offers services to Rome from London Stansted, and Ryanair, *www.ryanair.com*, **t** 0870 333 1231, has flights from London Stansted and Dublin to Rome and from London Stansted to Pescara on the Abruzzo coast.

From **Ireland**, Alitalia and Aer Lingus operate direct flights to Rome. The frequency depends on the time of year.

Early birds get the best seats, so think ahead when booking. If you're prepared to be flexible, last-minute stand-bys can be a snip. Children, young people or bona fide students, and senior citizens may travel for reduced fares.

By Air from the USA and Canada

Rome is the main Italian air gateway from North America, but you may well find a cheaper flight by way of Amsterdam, London or Frankfurt. Alitalia is the major carrier, but from the USA American Airlines, British Airways and Delta also fly from a number of cities. From Canada, Air Canada, KLM and Alitalia operate from Toronto and Montreal.

Summer round-trip fares from New York cost around US$800–1,000. However, British Airways sometimes run special offers when prices may well drop under the $700 mark. Otherwise, it may be worth your while catching a cheap flight to London (New York–London fares are always very competitive) and then flying on from there.

Prices are rather more from Canada, so you may prefer to fly from the States. As elsewhere, fares are seasonal and much cheaper in winter, especially mid-week.

By Train

A train journey from London to Rome used to be something of a nightmare involving ferries and station changes and taking the best part of 24 hours. Thanks to the opening of the Channel Tunnel and the construction of new fast rail networks throughout Europe, you can take a Eurostar to Paris and a high-speed Eurocity train to Italy (none go directly to Rome) in about 12 hours. Prices range from about £220 in second class including a couchette, to upwards of £500 in first class with a sleeper cabin. Train travel has its benefits but, in an age of low-cost airlines, it is not much of an economy. For more information, contact **Rail Europe** or **Eurostar** (*see* box on p.72).

There are dozens of **rail passes** on offer. In the UK, check *www.raileurope .co.uk*; in the US or Canada, check *www.raileurope.com*. **Interail** (UK) passes for unlimited travel in one zone cost from £119 for 12 days to £139 for 22 days. One-month passes are also available for 2 or more zones (from £189–355). If you are travelling just in Italy, the **Euro-domino** pass is available for 3 to 8 days unlimited travel within a one-month period and costs from £94–119 in second class. Eurodomino passes are available to anyone who has lived in Europe for six months.

From the US and Canada, there is a range of passes specifically for travel in Italy. The **Italy Flexi Rail Card** offers 4, 8 or 12 days unlimited

Airline Carriers

UK and Ireland

Aer Lingus, Dublin **t** 0818 365000, or Belfast **t** (0645) 737 747, *www.aerlingus.com*

Alitalia, **t** 0870 544 8259, or **t** (01) 677 5171 (Dublin), *www.alitalia.com*

British Airways, **t** 0845 773377, *www.britishairways.com*

easyJet, **t** 0870 600 0000, *www.easyjet.com*

Ryanair, **t** 0870 333 1231, *www.ryanair.com*

USA and Canada

Air Canada, **t** 1 888 247 2262, *www.aircanada.com*

Alitalia, **t** 800 223 5730 (USA), **t** 800 563 5954 (Canada), *www.alitalia.com*

American Airlines, **t** 1 800 433 7300, *www.americanairlines.com*

British Airways, **t** 800 247 9297, *www.britishairways.com*

Delta, **t** 0800 241 4141, *www.delta-air.com*

KLM, **t** 800 777 5553, *www.nwa.com*

Discounts and Students

UK and Ireland

Besides saving 25 per cent on regular flights, young people under 26 have the choice of flying on special discount charters.

Budget Travel, 134 Lower Baggot Street, Dublin 2, **t** (01) 661 1866, *www.budgettravel.ie*.

Italflights, 125 High Holborn, London WC1V 6QA, **t** (020) 7405 6771.

Italia Nel Mondo, 6 Palace Street, London SW1E 5HY, **t** (020) 7828 9171.

STA, 74 and 86 Old Brompton Rd, London SW7, or 85 Shaftesbury Avenue, London W1V 7AD, Bristol, Leeds, Manchester, Oxford, Cambridge, and many other branches in the UK. One telephone number: **t** 0870 160 6070, *www.statravel.co.uk*.

Trailfinders, 194 Kensington High Street, London W8 6BD, **t** (020) 7937 1234, *www.trailfinders.com*.

USIT Now, Aston Quay, Dublin 2, **t** (01) 602 1600; Cork, **t** (021) 270 900; Belfast, **t** (01232) 324073; Galway, **t** (091) 565177; Limerick, **t** (061) 415064; Waterford, **t** (051) 872601; *www.usitnow.ie*. Ireland's biggest student travel agents.

USA and Canada

Airhitch, 2472 Broadway Suite 200, New York, NY 10025, **t** (212) 736 4470, *www.air-hitch.com*.

Council Travel, 205 E. 42nd Street, New York, NY 10017, **t** 1 8888 COUNCIL, *www.counciltravel.com*.

Last Minute Travel Club, 132 Brookline Avenue, Boston, MA 02215, **t** 800 527 8646.

Mr Cheap's Travel, 74 Varick St, Suite 307, New York, NY 10013, **t** (212) 459 1616.

STA, 48 East 11th Street, New York, NY 10003, **t** 800 777 0112, *www.sta-travel.com*.

Travel Cuts, 187 College Street, Toronto, Ontario M5T 1P7, **t** 1 800 667 2887, *www.travelcuts.com*.

Websites

www.lastminute.com. Last-minute bargains.

www.travelocity.com. Cheap flights.

www.opodo.com. Run by a group of Europe's biggest airlines.

www.eurobookers.com. Flights and holidays.

www.packyourbags.com. City breaks.

www.online-travellers.co.uk. Flights and holidays.

www.holiday-to-rome.co.uk. City breaks.

www.justcities.com. Luxury city breaks.

www.italyfarmholidays.com. Rural holidays across Italy.

www.holidaybank.co.uk. Cultural holidays in Lazio.

www.agriturist.it. Farm holidays in Lazio, Abruzzo and Molise.

www.hotel-holidays.it. Italian company offers holidays in the Abruzzo National Park.

www.giroscopio.it. Hotel booking service in Abruzzo.

train travel in a 1-month period (for fares *see* p.74). There are saver tickets if 2 or more people travel together and other options include a combined France–Italy rail pass, or a **Eurail** pass which offers travel throughout Europe. A 15-day Eurail pass for travel within Italy plus 17 other countries costs US$572; a three-month pass is US$1,606. There are saver tickets for under-26s. If you are just planning to see Italy, inclusive rail passes may not be

Rail Tickets and Information

Eurostar, EPS House, Waterloo Station, London SE1, **t** 08705 186186, *www.eurostar.com.*
Rail Europe, 179 Piccadilly, London W1V OBA, **t** 08705 848848, *www.raileurope.co.uk.*
Wasteels Travel, Adjacent Platform 2, Victoria Station, London SW1, **t** (020) 7834 7066.

CIT Offices Outside Italy

UK: Marco Polo House, 3–5 Lansdowne Rd, Croydon, Surrey CR9 1LL, **t** (020) 8686 5533.
USA: 15 West 44th Street, Fifth Floor, New York, NY 10036, **t** 800 248 7245, **f** 888 FAX CIT.
Canada: 1450 City Councillors, Suite 750, Montreal H3A 2E6, **t** (514) 845 4310.

worthwhile. Fares on FS (Ferrovie dello Stato), the Italian State Railway, are among the lowest, kilometre for kilometre, in Europe.

Convenient pocket-sized **timetables** (£6 plus 50p postage) detailing all the main and secondary Italian railway lines are available from **Wasteels Travel**, adjacent to Platform 2, Victoria Station, London SW1, **t** (020) 7834 7066. If you wait until you arrive in Italy you can pick up the Italian timetable (in two volumes) at any station from about €6 each.

From the USA and Canada, contact **Rail Europe**, central office at 226–230 Westchester Ave, White Plains, NY 10604, **t** (914) 682 2999 or 800 438 7245, *www.raileurope.com*. **Wasteels** also have a USA office at 5728 Major Boulevard, Suite 308, Orlando, FL 32819, **t** (407) 351 2537.

By Bus and Coach

Eurolines is the main international bus operator in Europe, with representatives in Italy and many other countries. In the UK, they can be found at Victoria Coach Station, London SW1, **t** 08705 143 219, *www.gobycoach.com*. Regular services terminate in Rome. Needless to say, the journey is long (36 hours) and the relatively small savings on price (a return ticket from London to Rome costs £125; single £88) make it a masochistic choice in comparison with a discounted air fare, or even rail travel. Within Italy, you can obtain more information on long-distance bus services from any CIT office.

By Car

It's the best part of 36 hours' driving time from the UK to Rome, even if you stick to fast toll roads. The most scenic and hassle-free route is via the Alps, avoiding crowded Riviera roads in summer, but, if you take a route through Switzerland, expect to pay for the privilege (around €25 for motorway use). You can avoid some of the driving by putting your car on the train, though this is scarcely a cheap option. **Express Sleeper Cars** run to Milan from Paris or Boulogne (infrequently in winter).

To bring a GB-registered car into Italy, you need a **vehicle registration document**, **full driving licence**, and **insurance papers** – these must be carried at all times when driving. Non-EU citizens should preferably have an **international driving licence** which has an Italian translation incorporated. Your vehicle should display a nationality plate indicating its country of registration. Before travelling, check everything is in perfect order. Minor infringements like worn tyres or burnt-out sidelights can cost you dear in any country. A **red triangular hazard sign** is obligatory; also recommended are a spare set of bulbs, a first-aid kit and a fire extinguisher. Spare parts for non-Italian cars can be difficult to find, especially Japanese models. Before crossing the border, fill her up; *benzina* is very expensive in Italy.

For more information on driving in Italy, *see* 'Getting Around By Car' (p.75) or contact the motoring organizations: **AA**, **t** 08705 500 600, *www.theaa.co.uk*, or **RAC**, **t** 08705 722 722, *www.rac.co.uk* in the UK, and **AAA**, **t** (813) 289 5000 in the USA.

Entry Formalities

Passports and Visas

EU nationals with a valid passport can enter and stay in Italy as long as they like. Citizens of the USA, Canada, Australia and New Zealand need only a valid passport to stay up to three months in Italy, unless they get a visa in advance from an Italian embassy or consulate. By law you should register with the police within eight days of your arrival in Italy. In practice this is done automatically for most visitors when they check in at their first hotel.

Don't be alarmed if the owner of your self-catering property proposes to 'denounce' you to the police when you arrive – it's just a formality.

If you play to stay in Italy long-term without working, you should register with the police within eight days of arrival and apply for a *permesso di soggiorno* from the local **Questura** (police station) – get there early in the morning as most state offices close in the afternoon. You need a *permesso* in order to open a bank account in Italy, or buy a car. It lasts for three months, after which you will need to renew it. If you can prove you have enough money to live on, permission is usually granted, though non-whites may have a hard time.

Customs

EU nationals over the age of 17 can now import a limitless amount of goods for their personal use.

Arrivals from non-EU countries have to pass through Italian Customs which are usually benign, although how the frontier police manage to recruit such ugly, mean-looking characters to hold the sub-machine guns and drug-sniffing dogs from such a good-looking population is a mystery. However, they'll let you be if you don't look suspicious (sadly, not being Caucasian is often 'suspicious' enough).

Duty-free allowances have now been abolished within the EU. For travellers entering the EU from outside, the duty-free limits are 1 litre of spirits or 2 litres of liquors (port, sherry or champagne), plus 2 litres of wine, 200 cigarettes and 50 grams of perfume. Much larger quantities – up to 10 litres of spirits, 90 litres of wine, 110 litres of beer and 800 cigarettes – bought locally and provided you are travelling between EU countries, can be taken through customs if you can prove that they are for private consumption only and taxes have been paid in the country of purchase. Under-17s are not allowed to bring tobacco or alcohol into the EU. Pets must be accompanied by a bilingual Certificate of Health from your local Veterinary Inspector.

For residents of Britain and other EU countries, the usual regulations apply regarding what you can carry home. Note that you cannot bring fresh meat, vegetables or plants into the UK.

Residents of the USA may each take home US$400-worth of foreign goods without attracting duty, including the tobacco and alcohol allowance. Canadians can bring home $300-worth of goods in a year, plus their tobacco and alcohol allowances.

Getting Around

Italy has an excellent network of airports, railways, highways and byways and you'll find getting around fairly easy – until one union or another takes it into its head to go on strike (to be fair, they rarely do it during the high holiday season). There's plenty of talk about passing a law to regulate strikes, but it won't happen soon if ever. Instead, learn to recognize the word in Italian: *sciopero* (SHO-per-o), and do as the Romans do – quiver with resignation. There's always a day or two's notice, and strikes usually last only a day, just long enough to throw a spanner in the works if you have to catch a plane. Keep your ears open and watch for notices posted in the stations.

By Train

*FS information from anywhere in Italy, **t** 892 021 88088, open 7am–9pm; www.fs-on-line.com, www.trenitalia.com.*

Italy's national railway, the FS (*Ferrovie dello Stato*) is well run and often a pleasure to ride. There are also several private rail lines around cities and in country districts. We have tried to list them all in the Getting Around sections of the Gazetteer chapters in this book. You may find that some of these private companies won't accept Interail or Eurail passes.

Train **fares** have increased greatly over the last couple of years and only those without extra supplements can still be called cheap. Possible FS unpleasantnesses you may encounter, besides a strike, are delays and crowding (especially on Friday nights, weekends and in the summer). Reserve a seat in advance (*fare una prenotazione*). The fee is small and can save you hours of standing. For the upper echelon trains (Eurostars and some Intercities), reservations are mandatory. Do check when you purchase your ticket in advance that the date is correct; tickets are only valid the day they're purchased unless you specify otherwise.

Tickets may be purchased not only at stations, but at many travel agents (and some also on-line) and it's wise to buy them in advance as the queues can be long. Make sure that you ask which **platform** (*binario*) your train leaves from; the big permanent boards posted in the stations are not always correct.

Always remember to **stamp your ticket** (*convalidare*) in the not-very-obvious machine at the head of the platform before boarding the train. Failure to do so may result in a fine. If you get on a train without a ticket you can buy one from the conductor, with an added 20% penalty. You can also pay a conductor in order to move up to first class as long as there are places available.

There is a strict hierarchy of **trains**. A *Regionale* travels short-ish distances, and tends to stop at all the stations. There are only a few *Espressi* trains left in service, but they are in poor condition, and mostly serve the long runs from the south of Italy. No supplement is required. *Intercity* trains link Italian cities, with minimum stops. Some carry an obligatory seat reservation requirement (free in this case), and all have a supplement. The true 'Kings of the Rails' are the super-swish and super-fast (Florence–Rome in 1½ hours) *Eurostars*. These make very few stops, offer both first- and second-class carriages, and carry a supplement that includes an obligatory seat reservation. So, the faster the train, the more you pay. Make sure you check all fares at the time of booking.

The FS offers several **passes**. A flexible option is the **Flexi Card** (also available through CIT or Rail Europe *see* p.72) which allows you unlimited travel either for four days within a month (€144), 8 days within a month (€150) or 12 days within a month (€259), plus supplements and seat reservations on Eurostars. Another ticket, the **Kilometrico**, gives you 3,000km of travel, made on a maximum of 20 journeys, and is valid for two months (2nd class €177, 1st class €181, plus supplements). One advantage is that it can be used by up to five people at the same time. However, supplements are payable on Intercity trains.

Other **discounts**, available only once you're in Italy, are 15% off same-day return tickets and three-day returns (depending on the distance involved), and discounts for families of at least four travelling together. Senior citizens (60 and over) can also get a *Carta d'Argento* ('silver card') for €25, entitling them to a 20% reduction in fares. A *Carta Verde* bestows a 20% discount on people under 26 and costs €25. The *Carto Amicotreno*, €50 for one year, gets you discounts from 10 to 50%.

Refreshments on routes of any great distance are provided by buffet cars or trolleys; you can usually get sandwiches and coffee from vendors along the tracks at intermediary stops. Station bars often have a good variety of take-away travellers' fare; at least consider investing in a plastic bottle of mineral water, since there's no drinking water on the trains.

Italy's stations also offer other facilities. All have a *deposito*, where you can leave your bags for hours or days for a small fee. The larger ones have porters (who charge about €2.50 per piece) and luggage trolleys; major stations have an *albergo diurno* ('day hotel', where you can take a shower, get a shave and haircut, etc.), information offices, currency exchanges open at weekends (not at the most advantageous rates), hotel-finding and reservation services, kiosks with foreign papers, restaurants, etc. You can also arrange a rental car to await you at your destination, through hire firms Avis, Hertz or Maggiore.

By Coach and Bus

Inter-city coach travel is sometimes quicker than train travel, but also a bit more expensive. The system really comes into its own for that small minority of people who want to see the country without the hassles of a car. Italy's system is admirable; coaches reach even the smallest villages; they're reliable and services are usually arranged to make connections possible to more distant points. In many regions they are the only means of public transport and are well used, with frequent schedules. Coaches, generally painted blue, almost always depart from the vicinity of the train station, and tickets usually need to be purchased before you get on; if there isn't a ticket booth, they'll be on sale in one or more of the nearby bars. If you can't get a ticket before the coach leaves, tell the conductor when you get on. The bases for all country bus lines are the provincial capitals – from Rome, you can get a bus to just about anywhere in central Italy from Termini Station or one of the suburban stations.

City buses, which are almost always painted orange, are the traveller's friend. All charge flat fees for rides within the city limits and immediate suburbs, at the time of writing around €0.75. Bus tickets must always be purchased before you get on, either at a tobacconist's, a newspaper kiosk, in bars, or from ticket machines near the main stops. Once you get on, you must 'obliterate' your ticket in the machines in the front or back of the bus; controllers stage random checks to make sure you've punched your ticket. Fines for cheaters are about €50, and the odds are about 12 to 1 against a check, so many passengers take a chance.

By Car

In Rome, a car is the last thing you want or need, but out touring the hill towns and the Apennines it's the most convenient way to go. As Italy becomes a more car-orientated society, more and more good hotels and restaurants are located on the outskirts of towns or in the country. Central Italy also has a wealth of parks and nature reserves, as well as archaeological sites and medieval churches in out-of-the-way locations that can only be reached by car.

If you've got one, there are some drawbacks: first of all, town centres, where **parking** in always a problem. Some areas are marked *zona disco blu* after the blue time discs, obtainable in many shops and fixed inside the windscreen, where you set the hour of your arrival and get an hour or two of free parking. Elsewhere an old gent with a book of receipts will shamble up to your car and hit you for a few euros, or there may be a parking ticket machine; blue stripes on the pavement instead of white always mean pay-parking.

Worse than parking, sometimes, can be simply driving. The Italian *centro storico* was just not made for cars. Often, sensibly, it is closed to them; the red circle sign at the entrance will have a notice underneath explaining hours and vehicles forbidden. You'll notice enforcement isn't very strict, and exceptions are usually made if you are loading or unloading at a hotel. Even when you can get into the centre, finding that the main street soon funnels into a 12ft passage full of pedestrians makes driving lose much of its charm. One false move, and you may be driving down a stairway, or through an alley where your car gets stuck between the walls. Give these fine old towns, and their residents, a break, and leave your beast in the parking areas thoughtfully signposted around the walls.

Another feature of motoring life in towns with too many cars and too little space (in effect, all of them) is the early evening rush-hour, a daily festival of immobility even in villages of 5,000 people. It lasts from about 4.30 to 7 or 8pm, or even later. On the other hand, if you want to look around a town from your car, do it from 1–3pm, when the Italians are dining and digesting; the streets will be utterly deserted.

Be prepared to encounter some of the highest fuel costs in Europe, and face drivers who look at motoring as if it were a video game. The Italians, whether 21-year-old madcaps or elderly nuns, turn into aggressive starfighters once behind the wheel; their mission is to reach their destination in a certain allotted time (especially around lunch or dinner, if they think the pasta is already on the boil) regardless of minor nuisances such as other cars, road signs, traffic signals, solid no-passing lines, or blind curves on mountain roads. No matter how fast you trip along on the *autostrade* (Italy's toll motorways, official

Car Rental Agencies

UK and Ireland:

Avis: **t** 08705 6060100 (UK), **t** (021) 281111 (Ireland), *www.avis.co.uk*

Hertz: **t** 08705 996699 (UK), **t** (01) 676 7476 (Ireland), *www.hertz.co.uk*

National: **t** 0870 400 4502 (UK), *www.nationalcar.com*

USA and Canada:

Avis: **t** 800 230 4898 (USA), **t** 800 272 5871 (Canada), *www.avis.com*

Hertz: **t** 800 654 3001 (USA), *www.hertz.com*

speed limit **130km/80miles** per hour). someone will pass you going twice as fast.

If you aren't intimidated, buy a good road map of Italy or a detailed one of the region you're travelling in (the Italian Touring Club produces excellent ones). Most petrol stations close for lunch in the afternoon, and few stay open late at night, though you may find a 'self-service' one where you feed a machine nice, smooth banknotes. *Autostrada* tolls are high – the website *www.autostrada.it* will help you calculate the cost for your journey. The rest stops and petrol stations along the motorways are open 24 hours. Other roads – from *superstrade* on down through the Italian grading system – are free of charge. The Italians are good about signposting, and roads are almost all excellently maintained. Some highways seem to be built of sheer bravura – suspended on cliffs, crossing valleys on enormous piers – feats of engineering that will remind you, more than almost anything else, that this is the land of the ancient Romans. Beware that you may be fined on the spot for speeding, a burnt-out headlamp, etc; if you're especially unlucky you may be slapped with a *super multa*, or superfine, of €130–260 or more. You may even be fined for not having a portable triangle danger signal (these can be picked up at the border or from an ACI office).

The **Automobile Club of Italy** (ACI) (Via Marsala 8, Rome, **t** 800 313535 or **t** 06 49981, **f** 06 499 82469, *www.aci.it*) is a good friend to

Specialist Tour Operators

A selection of specialist companies are listed below. Not all of them are necessarily ABTA-bonded; we recommend you check before booking.

In the UK

Abercrombie & Kent, Sloane Square House, Holbein Place, London SW1W 8NS, **t** 0845 0700 610, *www.abercrombiekent.co.uk*. Can arrange flights and 5-star accommodation in La Posta Vecchia, Lazio. Also offer villas.

Accessible City Breaks, Avionics House, Naas Lane, Gloucester, GL2 2SN, **t** (01452) 729 739, **f** (01452) 729 853, *www.accessiblecitybreaks.co.uk*. Accessible city breaks to Rome for disabled travellers.

Alternative Travel, 69–71 Banbury Road, Oxford OX2 6PE, **t** (01865) 310399. Tailor-made walking and cycling tours around Rome, led by specialist tour guide leaders.

Andante Travels, The Old Barn, Old Road, Alderbury, Salisbury SP5 3AR, **t** (01722) 713800. An excellent range of luxury tours focusing on archaeology, art and architecture off the beaten track. 'Latium and the Roman Countryside' takes in Hadrian's villa at Tívoli and Tiberius' on the beach at Sperlonga; Early Christianity and the Great Abbeys of Central Italy includes the breathtaking Montecassino Abbey and San Vincenzo al Volturno. All tours are fully inclusive and led by expert archaeologists. Accommodation in 3- or 4-star hotels with character.

Arblaster & Clarke, Farmham Rd, West Liss, Hants GU33 6JQ, **t** (01730) 893 344, *www.winetours.co.uk*. Wine tours around Frascati in the Castelli Romani.

Blair Travel for the Arts, 12–15 Hangar Green, London W5 3EL, **t** (020) 8799 8350. Tailor-made music and opera tours of Rome and Abruzzo; 3- and 4-star accommodation.

Citalia, Marco Polo House, 3–5 Lansdowne Road, Croydon CR9 1LL, **t** (020) 8686 5533, *www.citalia.com*. Can arrange everything: including car hire, flights and hotel, B&B and half-board accommodation. Mainly Rome and Lazio.

Cox & Kings, Gordon House, 10 Green Court Place, London SW1P 1PH, **t** (020) 7873 5000, *www.coxandkings.co.uk*. Deluxe art and architecture tours in assocation with NADFAS (The National Association for Decorative and Fine Arts). Mostly in and around Rome, with lectures in the evenings. Accommodation in central 4-star hotels.

GO-CTE Ltd, 76 Croft Road, Carlisle, Cumbria CA3 9AG, **t** (01228) 526 795, *www.cteitaly.net*. Month-long language, history, music and art workshops for retired people in Abruzzo.

Italia 2000, 8 Timperley Way, Up Hatherley, Cheltenham, Gloucestershire GL51 5RH, **t** (01242) 234 215, *www.italia2000.co.uk*. Tailor-made sports holidays in the Roman countryside: golf, riding, mountain-biking, canyoning and para-gliding.

the foreign motorist. Besides having bushels of useful information and tips, they can be reached from anywhere by calling **t** 116 – also use this number if you have an accident, need an ambulance, or simply have to find the nearest service station. If you need major repairs, the ACI can make sure the prices charged are according to their guidelines.

Hiring a car is fairly simple if not particularly cheap (around €50 a day for a smallish car, €300 for a week). Italian car rental firms are called *autonoleggi*. There are both large international firms through which you can reserve a car in advance, and local agencies, which often have lower prices. Air or rail travellers should check out possible discount packages.

Most companies will require a deposit amounting to the estimated cost of the hire, and there is 19% VAT added to the final cost. Petrol is as expensive as in the UK; diesel is significantly cheaper. Rates become more advantageous if you take the car for a week with unlimited mileage. If you need a car for more than three weeks, leasing is a more economic alternative. The National Tourist Office has a list of firms in Italy that hire caravans (trailers) and campers.

Hitchhiking

It is illegal to hitch on the *autostrade*, though you may pick up a lift near one of the

Italiatour, Unit 9, Whyteleafe Business Village, Whyteleafe Hills, Surrey CR3 OAT, **t** (01883) 621900; 4–5 Dawson St, Dublin 2, **t** (01) 671 7821. Independent tailormade tours staying in country house hotels; can also arrange football tickets, riding holidays and cookery tuition.

Kirker, 3 New Concordia Wharf, Mill Street, London SE1 2BB, **t** (020) 7231 3333. Short breaks, including custom-built packages.

Martin Randall Travel, 10 Barley Mow Passage, Chiswick, London W4 4PH, **t** (020) 8742 3355. Cultural tours in Abruzzo and Lazio for groups up to 22. Emphasizing art, architecture, wines, gardens, music, led by experts.

Prospect Music & Art, 36 Manchester Street, London W1V 7LH, **t** (020) 7486 5705, **f** (020) 7486 5868, *sales@prospecttours.com*. Fully escorted, lavish week-long art, architecture, music and archaeology tours; based in Rome.

Special Tours, 2 Chester Row, London SW1W 9JH, **t** (020) 7730 2297, *info@specialtours.co.uk*. Art, architecture and garden tours run by small private travel company for National Art Collections Fund members. Staying in comfortable hotels in Italy.

Travelsphere, Compass House, Rockingham Road, Market Harborough, Leicestershire LE16 7QD, **t** (01858) 464 818. 8–15-day coach tours.

Venice Simplon-Orient Express, Sea Containers House, 20 Upper Ground, London SE1 9PF, **t** (020) 7928 6000. Travel to Rome in style.

Wallace Arnold, Gelderd Road, Leeds LS12 6DH, **t** (01132) 310 739. Coach-touring holidays through classical Rome.

In the USA/Canada

American Express Travel Service, 250 University Ave, Palo Alto, CA 94301, **t** (650) 327 3711. Prepackaged and tailor-made tours.

Archaeological Tours Inc., Suite 904, 271 Madison Avenue, New York, NY 10016, **t** 1 866 740 5130; led by expert archaeologists, with an ever-changing programme.

Bike Riders, PO Box 130254, Boston, MA 02113, **t** (617) 723 2354, **f** (617) 723 2354, *www.bikeriderstours.com*. Gentle cycle tours through the Roman countryside, also including 'bike and cook' holidays accompanied by professional chefs. For groups of 16 or fewer.

Dailey-Thorp Travel, 475 Park Ave South, New York, NY 10019, **t** (212) 307 1555. Varied programme of music and opera tours throughout Italy. Includes deluxe accommodation, gourmet meals and off-the-beaten-track sightseeing.

Maupintour, 1515 St Andrew's Drive, Lawrence, Kansas 66047, **t** 800 255 4266.

Stay and Visit Italy, c/o Great Travels, 5506 Connecticut Avenue NW, Suite 28, Washington, DC 20015, **t** (202) 237 5220/ **t** 800 411 3728, **f** (202) 966 6972, *www.stayandvisit.com*. Unusual range of highly specialized tours throughout the region, including skiing in the Abruzzi.

toll booths. Don't hitch from the city centres, head for suburban exit routes. For the best chances of getting a lift, travel light, look respectable and take your sunglasses off. Hold a sign indicating your destination if you can. Women should try never to hitch alone. Two or more men may encounter some reluctance.

By Motorcycle and Bicycle

Mopeds, Vespas and scooters are the vehicles of choice for a great many Italians. You will see them everywhere. In the traffic congested towns this is a ubiquity born of necessity; when driving space is limited, two wheels are always better than four. However, in Italy, riding a two-wheeler often seems to be as much a form of cultural and social expression as it does a means of getting from A to B. Stand watching the traffic on a busy town corner for any length of time and certain trends will begin to become apparent. For one thing, there is a clear generational control at work over the individual's choice of machine. Italian youths tend to prefer chic Italian lines, Vespas, Lambrettas and the like, which they parade self-consciously through the town's main drags. Older members of society, in the main, plump for mopeds, the type you can actually pedal should you feel so inclined. Choosing your machine, however, is only the first stage of this cultural process; it then becomes necessary to master the Italian way of riding. This almost invariably means dispensing with a crash helmet, despite the fact that they are compulsory, so as to be better able to perfect the method of riding in as laid-back a style a possible whilst still achieving an alarming rate of speed: riding sidesaddle, whilst on the phone, in sunglasses, whilst smoking, whilst holding a dog or child under one arm; all of these methods have their determined and expert adherents.

Despite the obvious dangers of this means of transport (especially if you choose to do it Italian-style), there are clear benefits to moped-riding in Italy. For one thing it is cheaper than car hire – costs for a *motorino* range from about €20 per day, scooters somewhat more (up to €30), you must be at least 14 – and can prove an excellent way of covering a town's sites in a limited space of time. Furthermore, because Italy is such a scooter-friendly place, car drivers are more conditioned to their presence and so are less likely to hurtle into them when taking corners. Nonetheless, you should only consider hiring a moped if you have ridden one before (Italy's hills and alarming traffic are no place to learn) and, despite local examples, you should always wear a helmet. Also, be warned, some travel insurance policies exclude claims resulting from scooter or motorbike accidents.

Italians are keen cyclists, racing drivers up the steepest hills; if you're not training for the Tour de France, consider the region's topography well before planning a bicycling tour, especially in the hot summer. You can hire a bike in most Italian towns. Prices range from about €12 per day, which may make buying one interesting if you plan to spend much time in the saddle (€120 upwards), either in a bike shop or through the classified ads. Alternatively, if you bring your own bike, do check the airlines to see what their policies are on transporting them. Bikes can be transported by train in Italy, either with you or within a couple of days – apply at the baggage office (*ufficio bagagli*).

Practical A–Z

08

Calendar of Events

There are literally thousands of festivals answering to every description in Italy. Every *comune* has at least one or two honouring patron saints. Carnival, after being suppressed and ignored for decades, has been revived in many places. Holy Week celebrations take on a dirge-like Spanish flavour in the Abruzzo, when robed and hooded penitents haul melodramatic floats through the streets. Whatever the occasion, eating is a primary pastime at all jamborees, and regional specialities are prepared. Check at the local tourist office for precise dates, which alter from year to year.

January

1 Rome's citizens throw old furniture out of their windows, eat sausages, lentils, stuffed pig's foot (*zampone*) and drink *spumante*

5–6 Child-orientated Epiphany celebrations, honouring the good stocking-filling witch La Befana; live *presepio*, with a cast of over 100, **Rivisondoli**

16 Le Farchie, big fires in honour of St Anthony, **Fara Filiorum Petri** (near Chieti)

17 Carnevale, with masks and music, celebrating the return of the sun to the village, **Artena**; Festa di Sant'Antonio Abate, with cowboy parade, **Sutri**; cowboy parades, blessing of animals, **Tuscánia**

20 San Sebastiano, **Ortona**

February

2 Festa delle Stuzze, huge bonfire celebrating a miracle of St Biagio, **Fiuggi**

3 Distribution of anti-sore throat sandwiches, good for a year, at San Biagio church, in **Rome** and **Taranta Peligna** (Chieti)

Carnival Allegorical parade and Sagra dei Fritteloni, **Cívita Castellana**; Piazza Pazza, palio, processions and floats, **Poggio Mirteto**; parades in **Ronciglione**; parades and floats, **Lanciano**; also events in **Francavilla al Mare**

March

19 I Faoni, bonfire festival, **Sermoneta**

21 La Fiaccolata, in honour of St Benedict, **Cassino**; Processione al Sacro Speco, **Subiaco**

Last 10 days Annunciation Fair, **Grottaferrata**

Easter Thurs Procession of Holy Thorn, **Vasto**

Good Friday Procession to Colosseum led by the Pope, **Rome**. Also live tableaux, **Fondi**; Procession of the Dead Christ, **Orte**, and **Lanciano**, Processione dei Sacconi, **Priverno**; enormous procession with tableaux, **Sezze**; procession with figures designed by contemporary artists, **L'Áquila**; Italy's oldest Via Crucis in **Chieti**, with 100 violins and male choirs

Easter Sagra del Casatiello (a local pastry), **Ponza**; medieval procession of the Madonna che Scappa in Piazza, **Sulmona**; traditional Easter blessing by the Pope, **Rome**

April

16 Spring festival, **Vasto**

21 Rome's birthday

23–25 Palio di Sant'Anselmo and Sagra del Biscotto, **Bomarzo**

1st Sun after 23 Oldest Infiorata in Italy (decorating the pavements with pictures made of flower petals), **Gerano**

27–28 San Vitale, **San Salvo** (Chieti)

28 Statua in Mare Aperto, traditional blessing of the sea, **Civitavécchia**

Last Sunday Festa della Madonna del Suffragio, procession with tableaux, at **Monte San Giovanni Campano** (near Arpino)

May

1 Sant'Ambrogio, procession of an equestrian statue, **Ferentino**; Spozalizio dell'Albero sul Monte Fogliano, nature festival, **Vetralla**; Sagra delle Virtù, **Téramo**

First Thursday Festival of Snakes, **Cocullo**

3 Festa di San Biagio, **Francavilla al Mare**

6 Sea procession for St Thomas, **Ortona**

12 San Pancrazio, **Albano Laziale**

14 The Barabbata, a unique semi-pagan procession of elaborate reed floats and the fruits of the earth, **Marta**

15 La Madonna del Fiore, **Acquapendente**, with flower art celebrating the liberation of the city from Frederick I Barbarossa; flower festival, **Téramo**

2nd Sun *Certamen Ciceronianum Arpinas*, competition of Latin students to translate and comment on Cicero, **Arpino**; Carosello storico, tournaments and palio at **Cori**

20 Festa di San Nicola, **Guardiagrele**

Pentecost Madonna della Filetta, **Amatrice**; miracle of the oxen, **Loreto Aprutino**

Mon after Pentecost Festa di San Zopito, traditional carts pulled by oxen, **Loreto Aprutino**

25–27 Festa di San Pardo, **Larino**

Last Sun Festa del Fiore, with local carnations, **Santa Marinella**; *Lu cencialone*, dancing around the bonfire and songs, **Silvi Marina**; narcissus festival, **Rocca di Mezzo**

June

All month Medieval and Renaissance theatre studies, **Viterbo**; strawberry festival, **Nemi**
1st Sun Festa della Madonna dei Sette Dolori, **Pescara**
13 St Anthony, procession of *ceri* in **Rieti**
Corpus Domini Religious procession, **Bolsena**; Sagra dei Misteri di Corpus Domini, **Campobasso**
23–24 San Giovanni, sea processions, **Formia**; festival and market at the Lateran, **Rome**
3rd Sun Boat races and procession for San Silverio, **Ponza**
29 Festa di San Pietro, at the Vatican, **Rome**
June–July Chamber music festival, **Priverno**; Estate Romana, **Rome**

July

All month Classical plays, in the Roman theatre, at **Férento**; jazz festival, **Atina**; Estate Marsia, theatre and music, Alba Fucens, **Avezzano**; jazz festival, **Pescara**; ceramics market, **Guardiagrele**
1–2 17th-century market, **Bassano Romano**
First 10 days Festival della Collina, **Sezze**
3rd Sun Maccarunata collepardese, **Collepardo**; sea festival, **Terracina**
23–24 Misteri di Santa Cristina, **Bolsena**
Last Sun Festa del Sole e Sagra della Fregnaccia e della Panzanella, **Rieti**; art and crafts fair, **Itri**; Festa di Sant'Andrea, **Pescara**
July/Aug Performances at the Roman theatre, in **Minturno**; Festival del Teatro al Tempio di Giove Anxur, **Terracina**; theatre, ballet and concerts at **Tagliacozzo**

August

All month International polyphonic festival, **Palestrina**; antique and modern lace market, **Canzano**; ceramics fair, **Castelli**
1–15 Est! Est!! Est!!! wine *festa*, **Montefiascone**
1st weekend Folklore festival, **Atina**
1st Sun Battle against the 'Turks', **Tollo**
8 Gioco dell'Adriatico, **Vasto**
9–11 San Lorenzo, competitions in **Zagarolo**
mid-month Palio dell'Oca, historic tournament and parade, **Ársoli**
12–15 International Folklore Festival, **Alatri**
14 Corteo Nuziale, re-evocation of traditional wedding, **Scanno**
15 Palio marinaro, boat races, **Civitavécchia**; Inchinata, processions in **Tívoli**; agricultural parade, **Atri**
16 San Rocco, **Ceprano**
16–19 San Franco, **Francavilla al Mare**
2nd and 3rd Sun Lentil festival, **Ventotene**
18 Giostra di Sant'Agapito, historic procession, wines and crafts, **Palestrina**
20–21 Saffron and chickpea festival, **Navelli**
3rd Sun Festa di San Bonaventura, with nocturnal processions, **Bagnoregio**
1st Sun after 15th Palio dei Rioni, **Allumiere** and in **Arpino**; Procession of the Madonna di Porto Salvo, **Gaeta**
28 Festa della Perdonanza, **L'Áquila**
Last Sat Sagra del solco dritto, ox ploughing contest, **Rocca di Mezzo**
31–10 Sept Ottava medievale, **Orte**

September

3 Macchina di Santa Rosa, **Viterbo** (*see* p.212)
4–5 Sagra di Fagioli, **Sutri**
1st Sun Gypsy footrace, **Pacentro**; lentil festival, **S. Stefano di Sessanio**
mid-month Fra' Diavolo e le Olive Nere, celebrating the brigand, and olives too, **Itri**

October

1st Sun Palio dei Rioni e Sagra dell'Uva, races, grapes and wine, **Marino**
2nd Sun Re-evocation of the Battle of Lépanto, with nocturnal procession, **Sermoneta**
Last Sun Chestnut festival, **Arcinazzo Romano**

November

1 All Saints' Fair, **Castel di Sangro**
1st week Sagra delle Zazzichie e Verole, **Gerano**
10 Rural 'New Year' with big fires, **Scanno**
11 San Martino, drinking new wine and joking, throughout the **Abruzzo**
25 Festa di Santa Caterina, **Barisciano**

December

6 San Nicola, in many villages in the Abruzzo and Molise, especially **Pollutri**
8 Festa della Signorina and Sagra del Pangiallo, **Ariccia**; start of Christmas market in Piazza Navona, **Rome**; bonfires at **Atri**
24–26 Re-evocation of St Francis' *presepio*, **Greccio**

Children

Children are still the royalty of Italy: pampered, often spoiled, probably more fashionably dressed than you are, and never allowed to get dirty. If you're bringing your own *bambini* to Italy, they'll be warmly received. Many hotels offer them advantageous rates and have play areas.

If a circus visits town while you're there, you're in for a treat; it will either be a sparkling showcase of daredevil skill or a poignant, family-run, modern version of Fellini's *La Strada*.

In Rome, most children enjoy the Colosseum, Castel Sant'Angelo with its dungeons, a trip to the catacombs, the Trevi Fountain, the Villa d'Este at Tívoli, and racing up to the top of St Peter's dome. The Monster Park at Bomarzo, Northern Lazio (*see* p.217), will also keep them amused.

Climate and When to Go

O Sole Mio notwithstanding, all of Italy isn't always sunny; it rains just as much in Rome every year as in London. **Summer** comes on dry and hot; the high Apennines stay fairly cool, while the coasts are often refreshed by breezes. You can probably get by without an umbrella, but take a light jacket for cool evenings. For average touring, August is probably the worst month to stump through Italy. Transport facilities are jammed to capacity, prices are at their highest, and Rome is abandoned to hordes of tourists while the locals take to the beach.

Spring and **autumn** are perhaps the loveliest times to go; spring for the infinity of wildflowers in the countryside, autumn for the colour of the trees in the hills and the vineyards. The weather is mild, places aren't crowded, and you won't need your umbrella too much, at least until November. From December to March the happiest visitors are probably those on skis in the Apennines, but it's the best time to go if you want the art and museums to yourself. Beware, though, it can rain and rain, and mountain valleys can lie for days under banks of fog and mist. There will usually be snow on the highest peaks of the Apennines until May.

Disabled Travellers

Italy has been relatively slow off the mark in its provision for disabled visitors, although many of its improvements for the Jubilee included upgrading facilities for disabled people. Cobblestones, uneven or non-existent pavements, the appalling traffic conditions, crowded public transport and endless flights of steps in many public places are all disincentives.

Progress is gradually being made, however. A national support organization in your own country may well have specific information on facilities in Italy, or will at least be able to provide general advice. The Italian tourist office and CIT (travel agency) can also advise on hotels, museums with ramps and so on. If you book rail travel through CIT, you can request assistance.

Eating Out

When you leave a restaurant you will be given a receipt (*scontrino* or *ricevuto fiscale*) which, according to Italian law, you must take with you out of the door and carry for at least 60 metres. If you aren't given one, it means the restaurant is probably fudging on its taxes and thus offering you lower prices. There is a slim chance the tax police (*Guardia di Finanza*) may have their eye on you and the restaurant,

Average Temperatures in °C (°F)

	January	April	July	October
Rome	7.4 (44)	14.4 (58)	25.7 (79)	17.7 (63)

Average Monthly Rainfall in Millimetres (Inches)

	January	April	July	October
Rome	74 (3)	62 (3)	06 (½)	123 (5)

Organizations for Disabled Travellers

Italy

Accessible Italy, Promotur-Mondo Possibile, La Viaggeria, Via Lemonia 161, 00174 Roma, **t** 06 7158 2945, **f** 06 7158 3433, *www.tour-web.com/accessibleitaly*. Travel agency which provides valuable, detailed help and information on access in Italy, including detailed coverage of accessible tourist spots, transport and accommodation in Umbria and the surrounding area.

APT (Azienda Provinciale per Il Turismo di Roma), Via Parigi, 5, Roma, **t** 06 4889 9253, or **t** 06 4889 9255. The official tourist information office, which provides some information.

Centro Studi Consulenza Invalidi, Via Gozzadini 7, 20148 Milan. Publishes an annual guide, *Vacanze per Disabili*, with details of suitable accommodation in Italy.

CO.IN (Consorzio Co-operative Integrate), Via Enrico Giglioli 54a, 00169 Rome, **t** 06 2326 7504, toll free in Italy **t** 800 271 027, **f** 06 2326 7505, *turismo@coinsociale.it*, *www.coinsociale.it*. Their tourist information centre (*open Mon–Fri 9–5*) offers advice and information on accessibility. They also offer **COINtel**, **t** 06 2326 7695, a 24-hour information line in English, and can assist with bookings for guided tours with suitable transport, **t** 06 7128 9676.

Vacanze Serene, toll-free **t** 800 271 027. Gives information on accessible travel throughout Italy (*open Mon–Fri, 9–5*).

UK

Access Travel, 6 The Hillock, Astley, Lancashire, M29 7GW, **t** (01942) 888 844, *info@access-travel.co.uk*, *www.access-travel.co.uk*. Travel agent for disabled people with a base in Rhodes: special airfares, car hire and suitable accommodation.

Chalfont Line Holidays, **t** (020) 8997 3799, **f** (020) 8991 2982, *www.chalfont-line.co.uk*. Escorted or individual holidays for disabled people.

Holiday Care Service, Imperial Building, Victoria Rd, Horley, Surrey, RH6 7PZ, **t** (01293) 774535, **f** (01293) 784647, *www.holidaycare.org.uk*. Holiday Care can give up-to-date information on destinations both in the UK and abroad, on transportation and on suitable tour operators.

RADAR (Royal Association for Disability and Rehabilitation), 12 City Forum, 250 City Rd, London, EC1V 8AS, **t** (020) 7250 3222, *www.radar.org.uk*. RADAR publish a range of

and if you don't have a receipt they could slap you with a heavy fine.

Prices quoted for meals are for an average complete meal, Italian-style with wine, for one person. We have divided restaurants into price categories (*see* box below).

When you eat out, mentally add to the bill (*conto*) a bread and cover charge (*pane e coperto*, between €1 and 3), and a 15% service charge. This is often included in the bill (*servizio compreso*); if not, it will say *servizio non compreso*, and you'll have to do your own arithmetic. Additional tipping is at your discretion, but never do it in family-owned and -run places.

Restaurant Price Categories

very expensive over €45
expensive €30–45
moderate €20–30
cheap below €20

For further information about eating in Italy, including local specialities, and an Italian menu decoder, *see* **Food and Drink**, p.57.

Electricity

Your electric appliances will work if you adapt them to run on 220 AC with two round prongs on the plug. American appliances need transformers as well.

Embassies and Consulates

UK: Via XX Settembre 80/a, Rome, **t** 06 4220 0001, *www.britain.it*.

Ireland: 3 Piazza di Campitelli, Rome, **t** 06 697 9121.

USA: Via V. Veneto 119/a, Rome, **t** 06 46741, *www.usembassy.it*.

very useful books, including the titles *Holidays and Travel Abroad: A Guide for Disabled People*.

Royal National Institute for the Blind (RNIB), 224 Great Portland Street, London W1S 5TB, **t** (020) 7388 1266, *www.rnib.org.uk*. Its mobility unit offers 'Plane Easy', an audio-cassette which advises blind or partially-sighted people on travelling by plane. They also advise on accommodation.

Royal National Institute for the Deaf (RNID), 19–23 Featherstone Street, London EC1Y 8SL, Infoline **t** 0808 808 0123, textphone **t** 0808 808 9000, **f** (020) 7296 8199, *www.rnid.org.uk*, *informationline@rnid.org.uk*. Call their information line for help and advice.

Tripscope, Alexandra House, Albany Road, Brentford, Middlesex TW8 0NE, **t** 08457 585641, **f** (020) 8580 7022, *www.justmobility.co.uk/tripscope*. Practical advice and information on travel and transport for elderly and disabled travellers. Information can be provided by both letter and tape.

USA

Access America, Washington DC, DC 20202, USA, *www.accessamerica.gov*. Provides information on facilities for disabled people at international airports. The US government website, *www.dot.gov/airconsumer/disabled.htm*, also details lots of useful information.

Alternative Leisure Co, 165 Middlesex Turnpike, Suite 206, Bedford, MA 01730, **t** (718) 275 0023, *www.alctrips.com*. Organizes vacations abroad for disabled people.

Mobility International USA, PO Box 10767, Eugene, OR 97440, USA, **t/TTY** (541) 343 1284, *www.miusa.org*. International educational exchange programmes and volunteer service overseas for the disabled.

SATH, (Society for Accessible Travel and Hospitality), Suite 610, 347 5th Avenue, New York, NY 10016, **t** (212) 447 7284, *www.sath.org*. Advice on all aspects of travel for the disabled.

Other Useful Contacts

Access-Able Travel Source, *www.access-able.com*. Information on travelling with disabilities, disabled magazines, access guides, mature travel and wheelchair travel.

Access Ability, *www.access-ability.co.uk*. Information on travel agencies catering specifically for disabled people.

Emerging Horizons, *www.emerginghorizons.com*. International on-line travel newsletter for people with disabilities.

Canada: Via GB de Rossi 27, Rome, **t** 06 445 981, *www.canada.it*.

Australia: Via Alessandria 215, Rome, **t** 06 852 721, *www.australian-embassy.it*.

New Zealand: Via Zara 28, Rome, **t** 06 440 2928, *www.nzemb.org*.

Health and Insurance

You can insure yourself for almost any possible mishap – cancelled flights, stolen or lost baggage and health. Check any current policies you hold to see if they cover you while abroad, and under what circumstances, and judge whether you need a special **traveller's insurance** policy for the journey. Travel agencies sell them, as well as insurance companies.

Citizens of EU countries are entitled to **reciprocal health care** in Italy's National Health Service and a 90% discount on prescriptions (bring **Form E111** with you, available from post offices). The E111 does not cover all medical expenses (no repatriation costs, for example, and no private treatment), and it is advisable to take out separate travel insurance for full cover. Citizens of non-EU countries should check carefully that they have adequate insurance for any medical expenses, and the cost of returning home. Australia has a reciprocal health care scheme with Italy, but New Zealand, Canada and the USA do not. If you already have health insurance, a student card, or a credit card, you may be entitled to some medical cover abroad.

In an **emergency**, dial **t** 115 for fire and **t** 113 for an ambulance in Italy (*ambulanza*) or to find the nearest hospital (*ospedale*). Less serious problems can be treated at a *Pronto Soccorso* (casualty/first aid department) at any hospital clinic (*ambulatorio*), or at a local health unit (*Unità Sanitaria Locale* – USL). Airports and main railway stations also have

first-aid posts. If you have to pay for any health treatment, make sure you get a receipt, so that you can make any claims for reimbursement later.

Dispensing **chemists** (*farmacia*) are generally open from 8.30am to 1pm and from 4 to 8pm. Pharmacists are trained to give advice for minor ills. Any large town will have a *farmacia* that stays open 24 hours; others take turns to stay open (the address rota is posted in the window).

No specific **vaccinations** are required or advised for citizens of most countries before visiting Italy; the main health risks are the usual travellers' woes of upset stomachs or the effects of too much sun. Take a supply of **medicaments** with you (insect repellent, anti-diarrhœal medicine, sun lotion and antiseptic cream), and any drugs you need regularly.

Most Italian doctors speak at least rudimentary English, but if you can't find one, contact your embassy or consulate for a list of English-speaking doctors.

Maps and Publications

The maps in this guide are for orientation only; to explore in any detail, invest in a good, up-to-date regional map before you arrive from any of the following bookshops:

Stanford's, 12–14 Long Acre, London WC2 9LP, **t** (020) 7836 1321, *www.stanfords.co.uk*.

The Travel Bookshop, 13 Blenheim Crescent, London W11 2EE, **t** (020) 7229 5260.

Traveler's Choice Bookstore, 111 Greene St, New York, NY, **t** (212) 941 1535.

Excellent maps are produced by **Touring Club Italiano**, **Michelin**, and **Istituto Geografico de Agostini**. They are available at all major bookshops in Italy (e.g. Feltrinelli) or sometimes on news stands. Italian tourist offices are helpful and can often supply good area maps and town plans.

Money

It's a good idea to order a wad of euros from your home bank to have on hand when you arrive in Italy, the land of strikes, unforeseen delays and quirky banking hours (*see* below). Take great care how you carry it, however (don't keep it all in one place). Obtaining money is often a frustrating business involving much queueing and form-filling. The major banks and exchange bureaux licensed by the Bank of Italy give the best exchange rates for currency or traveller's cheques. Hotels, private exchanges in resorts and FS-run exchanges at railway stations usually have less advantageous rates, but are open outside normal banking hours. Weekend exchange offices can be found in most large cities: **Rome**: Banca Nazionale delle Comunicazioni, Stazione Termini; Thomas Cook, Piazza Barberini 21D. In addition there are exchange offices at most airports. Remember that Italians indicate decimals with commas and thousands with full points.

Most British banks have an arrangement with the Italian banking authorities whereby you can (for a significant commission) use your bank card to take money out of Italian cash machines, but check with your bank first. Besides traveller's cheques, most banks will give you cash on a recognized credit card (taking little or no commission), and in big cities such as Rome you can find automatic tellers (Bancomats) to spout cash on a Visa, American Express or Diners card. You need a PIN number to use these. Read the instructions carefully. MasterCard (Access) is much less widely acceptable in Italy. Large hotels, resort area restaurants, shops and car hire firms will accept plastic as well; smaller places may not.

You can have money transferred to you through an Italian bank but this process may take over a week, even if it's sent urgent, *espressissimo*. You will need your passport as identification when you collect it. Sending cheques by post is inadvisable.

Banking hours vary, but core times in large towns are usually Monday to Friday 8.30am–1pm and 3–4pm, closed weekends and on local and national holidays (*see* below).

National Holidays

The Italians have cut down somewhat on their official national holidays, but note that every town has one or two local holidays of its own – usually the feast day of its patron saint. Official holidays, shown on transport timetables and museum opening hours, etc., are treated the same as Sundays.

National Holidays

1 January (New Year's Day)
6 January (Epiphany)
Easter Monday
25 April (Liberation Day)
1 May (Labour Day)
15 August (Assumption, also known as *Ferragosto*, the biggest holiday of them all)
1 November (All Saints' Day)
8 December (Immaculate Conception)
25 December (Christmas Day)
26 December (*Santo Stefano*, St Stephen's Day)

Most museums, as well as banks and shops, are closed on the national holidays (*see* box).

Opening Hours and Museums

Although it varies from region to region, with the north bearing more resemblance to the rest of Europe than the Mediterranean south, most of Italy closes down at 1pm until 3 or 4pm to eat and properly digest the main meal of the day. Afternoon hours are from 4 to 7, often from 5 to 8 in the hot summer months. Bars are often the only places open during the early afternoon. In any case, don't be surprised if you find anything in Italy unexpectedly closed (or open for that matter), whatever its official stated hours.

Shops usually open Monday–Saturday from 8am to 1pm and 3.30 to 7.30pm, though hours vary according to season and are shorter in smaller centres. In some large cities hours are longer. Some supermarkets and department stores stay open throughout the day.

Many of Italy's **museums** are magnificent, many are run with shameful neglect, and many have been closed for years for 'restoration' with slim prospects of reopening in the foreseeable future. With two or three works of art per inhabitant (accounts differ), Italy has a hard time financing the preservation of its national heritage; but they have made a truly impressive effort, in Rome and elsewhere, to get old monuments and museums fixed up and ready for the Jubilee Year of 2000, and you'll see the fruits of this everywhere you go.

To make the most of the sights, you can buy a cumulative ticket called the **Roma Archeologia Card**, valid 7 days, which includes the Palatino, Colosseum, Cripta Balbi, Palazzo Massimo, Palazzo Altemps, Terme di Diocleziano, Baths of Caracalla, Tomb of Cecilia Metella and Villa dei Quintili; the ticket can be acquired at any of these sites and costs €20.

Note that when hiring autoguides at museums, you will always be asked to leave some ID or a credit card as security.

Italy's **churches** have always been a prime target for art thieves and as a consequence are usually locked when there isn't a sacristan or caretaker to keep an eye on things. All churches, except for the really important cathedrals and basilicas, close in the afternoon at the same hours as the shops (1 to 4 or 5pm), and the little ones can be closed permanently. Always have a pocketful of coins for the light machines in churches, or whatever work of art you came to inspect will remain clouded in ecclesiastical gloom. Don't do your visiting during services, and don't come to see paintings and statues in churches the week preceding Easter – you will probably find them covered with mourning shrouds.

In general, Sunday afternoons and Mondays are dead periods for the sightseer – you may want to make them your travelling days. Places without specified opening hours can usually be visited on request – but it is best to go before 1pm. We have listed the hours of important sights and museums, and specified which ones charge admission. Entrance charges vary widely; major sights are fairly steep (€6 plus), but others may be completely free. EU citizens under 18 and over 65 get free admission to state museums, at least in theory.

Packing

You simply cannot overdress in Italy; whatever grand strides Italian designers have made on the international fashion merry-go-round, most of their clothes are purchased domestically, prices be damned. Now whether or not you want to try to keep up with the natives is your own affair and your own heavy suitcase's – you may do well to compromise and just bring a couple of smart outfits for big nights out. It's not that the Italians are very formal; they simply like to dress up with a gorgeousness that adorns their cities just as much as those old Renaissance churches and palaces. The few places with dress codes are the major churches and basilicas (no shorts, sleeveless shirts or strappy sundresses – women should bring a light silk scarf to throw over the shoulders), casinos, and a few posh restaurants.

After agonizing over fashion, remember to pack small and light: transatlantic airlines limit baggage by size (two pieces are free up to 1.5m in height and width; in second-class you're allowed one of 1.5m and another up to 110cm). Within Europe limits are by weight; 20kg (44lbs) in second class, 30kg (66lbs) in first, and considerably less if you are flying with a budget or no-frills airline. You may well be penalized for anything larger. If you're travelling mainly by train, you'll want to keep bags to a minimum: jamming big suitcases in overhead racks in a crowded compartment isn't much fun for anyone. Never take more than you can carry, but do bring the following: any prescription medicine you need, an extra pair of glasses or contact lenses if you wear them; a pocket knife and corkscrew (for picnics), a flashlight (for dark frescoed churches, caves and crypts), a travel alarm (for those early trains) and a pocket Italian–English dictionary (for flirting and other emergencies; outside the main tourist centres you may well have trouble finding someone who speaks English). If you're a light sleeper, consider ear-plugs.

Photography

Film and developing are much more expensive than they are in either the UK or the USA, though there are plenty of outlets where you can obtain them. You are not allowed to take pictures in most museums and in some churches. Most cities now offer one-hour processing if you need your pics in a hurry.

Police Business

There is a fair amount of petty crime in Italy – purse-snatchings, pickpocketing, minor thievery of the white collar kind (always check your change) and car break-ins and theft – but violent crime is rare. Nearly all mishaps can be avoided with adequate precautions. Scooter-borne purse-snatchers can be foiled if you stay on the inside of the pavement and keep a firm hold on your property (sling your bag-strap across your body, not dangling from one shoulder); pickpockets strike in crowded buses or trams and gatherings. Don't carry too much cash, and split it so you won't lose the lot at once. In cities and popular tourist sites, beware groups of scruffy-looking women or children with pieces of cardboard, apparently begging for money. They use distraction techniques to perfection. The smallest and most innocent-looking child is generally the most skilful pickpocket. If you are targeted, the best technique is to grab sharply hold of any vulnerable possessions or pockets and shout furiously. (Italian passers-by or plain-clothes police will often come to your assistance if they realize what is happening.) Be extra careful in train stations, don't leave valuables in hotel rooms, and always park your car in garages, guarded lots or on well-lit streets, with portable temptations well out of sight. Purchasing small quantities of soft drugs for personal consumption is technically legal in Italy, though what constitutes a small quantity is unspecified, and if the police don't like you to begin with, it will probably be enough to get you into big trouble.

Political terrorism, once the scourge of Italy, has declined greatly in recent years, mainly thanks to special quasi-military squads of black-uniformed national police, the *Carabinieri*. Local matters are usually in the hands of the *Polizia Urbana*; the nattily dressed *Vigili Urbani* concern themselves with directing traffic, and handing out parking fines. If you need to summon any of them, dial **t** 112.

Post Offices

Dealing with *la posta italiana* has always been a risky, frustrating, time-consuming affair. It is one of the least competent and slowest postal services in Europe. Even buying the right stamps requires dedicated research and saintly patience. One of the scandals that mesmerized Italy in recent years involved the minister of the post office, who disposed of literally tons of backlog mail by tossing it in the Tiber. When the news broke, he was replaced – the new minister, having learned his lesson, burned all the mail the post office was incapable of delivering. Not surprisingly, fed-up Italians view the invention of the fax machine as a gift from the Madonna. From these harsh judgements, however, we must exempt the Vatican City, whose special postal service (on angelic wings?) knocks spots off the rest of the country for speed and efficiency. If you're anywhere in Rome, be sure to post your mail in the Holy See. You need to buy Vatican stamps, which provide a tidy profit for the papal coffers.

Post offices in Italy are usually open from 8am until 1pm (Monday to Saturday), or until 6 or 7pm in a large city. To have your mail sent *poste restante* (general delivery), have it addressed to the central post office *Fermo Posta* and expect three to four weeks for it to arrive. Make sure your surname is very clearly written in block capitals. To pick up your mail you must present your passport and pay a nominal charge. Stamps (*francobolli*) may be purchased in post offices or at tobacconists (*tabacchi*, identified by their blue or black signs with a white T). Don't try to mail packages at all, if you value your sanity; take the thing home with you if you can.

You can also have money telegraphed to you through the post office; if by chance all goes well, this can happen in a mere three days, but expect a fair proportion of it to go into commission.

Shopping

'Made in Italy' has become a byword for style and quality, especially in fashion and leather, but also in home design, ceramics, kitchenware, jewellery, lace and linens, glassware and crystal, chocolates, bells, Christmas decorations, hats, straw work, art books, engravings, handmade stationery, gold and silverware, bicycles, sports cars, woodworking, a hundred kinds of liqueurs, aperitifs, coffee machines, gastronomic specialities, and antiques (both reproductions, and the real thing).

Non-EU citizens should save all receipts for Customs on the way home; however if you spend over a certain amount (around €90) in a shop you can get a tax rebate at the airport; participating shops have details. If you are looking for antiques, be sure to demand a certificate of authenticity – reproductions can be very, very good. To get your antique or modern art purchases home, you will have to apply to the Export Department of the Italian Ministry of Education and pay an export tax as well; your seller should know the details.

Italians are very fond of weekend flea market/antique fairs. They take place on the following monthly schedule:

First Sunday: **Frosinone** (except in July and Aug)

Second Sunday: **Trevignano Romano** (organic foods, art and crafts); **Monterotondo** (except in Aug); **Bracciano** (antiques and crafts)

Third Sunday: **Farfa**, **Rieti**

Third Saturday and Sunday: **Rieti**

Fourth Sunday: **Véroli** (June–Sept), **Cívita Castellana**

Last weekend: **Viterbo** (exc. July and Aug).

Sports and Activities

Cycling

About three-quarters of Italy is hilly or mountainous, so a cycling holiday is no soft option. It is best to bring your own bike (a mountain bike if possible) and spare parts; cycling is growing fast, but nowhere near as fanatically practised in Italy as, say, in France or Denmark. Facilities for hiring or repairing bikes are less widespread. You can buy a good bike in Italy, however. Most airlines and rail companies will transport bikes quite cheaply. The spring *Giro d'Italia* is Italy's great annual cycling event.

Fishing

You don't need a permit for sea-fishing (without an aqualung), but Italy's coastal waters, polluted and over-exploited, may disappoint. Commercial fishing has depleted stocks to such an extent that the government has begun to declare two- and three-month moratoria on all fishing to give the fish a break. Many freshwater lakes and streams are stocked, and if you're more interested in fresh fish than the sport of it, there are innumerable trout farms where you can practically pick the fish up out of the water with your hands. To fish in fresh water you need to purchase a year's membership card from the Federazione Italiana della Pesca Sportiva, *www.fipsas.it*, which has an office in every province; they will inform you about local conditions and restrictions. Bait and equipment are readily available.

Football

Soccer (*calcio*) is a national obsession, and Lazio (who play in Rome) are one of the top teams. For many Italians *calcio* far outweighs tedious issues like the state of the nation, the government of the day, or any momentous international event. All major cities, and most minor ones, have at least one team of some sort. Modern Italian teams are known for their grace, precision and coordination; rivalries are intense, scandals, especially involving bribery and cheating, are rife. The tempting rewards offered by such big-time entertainment attract all manner of corrupt practices, yet crowd violence is minimal. Big-league matches are played on Sunday afternoons from September to May. For information, contact the Federazione Italiana Giuoco Calcio, Via G Allegri 14, 00198 Rome, **t** 06 84911, *www.figc.it*. Rugby and baseball are also played increasingly; even American football and basketball have their devotees.

Golf

Italians have been slower than some nationalities to appreciate the delights of biffing a small white ball into a hole in the ground, but they're catching on fast. Write or ring beforehand to check details before turning up. Most take guests and hire equipment. Contact the Federazione Italiana Golf, Viale Tiziano 74, 00196 Rome, **t** 06 323 1825, *www.federgolf.it*, for more information.

Hiking and Mountaineering

These sports are becoming steadily more popular among native Italians every year. The Apennines, especially the Abruzzo National Park, now have a good system of waymarked trails and mountain refuges run by the Italian Alpine Club (CAI), *www.cai.it* (with lists of regional offices, but all in Italian), represented in all the hilly provinces. If you are planning to use the more popular routes in summer, write beforehand to reserve beds in refuges. Local tourist offices can put you in touch with the right people and organizations. Walking at high altitudes is generally practicable between May and October, after most of the snow has melted; all the necessary gear – boots, packs, tents, etc. – are readily available in Italy but for more money than you'd pay at home.

The CAI can put you in touch with guides or climbing groups if you're up for some real adventure, or write to the Italian national tourist board for a list of operators offering mountaineering holidays. Some Alpine resorts have taken to offering *Settimane Verdi* (Green Weeks) – good-value accommodation and activity packages for summer visitors similar to skiers' White Weeks.

Hunting

Italy's most controversial sport pits avid enthusiasts against a growing number of environmentalists. The debate is fierce and the start of the season is marked by huge protests. Indiscriminate trapping, netting and shooting is responsible for the decimation of many migrant Mediterranean songbirds, as well as many local species, like thrushes. Less controversial, at least from the conservationists' point of view, is duck-, pigeon- and wild boar-shooting.

Riding Holidays

These are now available in many parts of Italy, particularly in areas where Agriturist (*see* p.94) is well represented, such as Lazio and the Abruzzo, where tours staying at country estates are organized. There are riding stables in most cities and resorts. For more information, contact the local Agriturist office. Rome's International Riding Show in the Villa Borghese draws a big crowd each May.

Skiing and Winter Sports

Italy still lacks the cachet of neighbouring Switzerland or Austria among the skiing fraternity, but has caught up significantly and now has a better reputation for safety and efficiency than it once did, though erratic snow cover is always a problem. The Abruzzo has the snowiest heights in central Italy, with 17 ski stations in the region – Campo Imperatore and Monte Cristo, Campo Felice (a favourite of the Romans), Prato di Tivo, Roccaraso, Scanno and Rivisondoli are the main centres, along with Terminillo near Rieti. A number of others specialize in cross-country skiing. Equipment hire is generally not too expensive, but lift passes and accommodation can push up the cost of a winter holiday, although here it never hits Alpine levels. Prices are highest during Christmas and New Year holidays, in February and at Easter. Most resorts offer *Settimane Bianche* (White Weeks) – off-season packages at economical rates. Other winter sports such as ice-skating and bob-sleighing are available at larger resorts.

Tennis

If soccer is Italy's most popular spectator sport, tennis is probably the game most people actually play. Every *comune* has public courts for hourly hire, especially resorts. Private clubs may offer temporary membership to passing visitors, and hotel courts can often be used by non-residents for a reasonable fee. Contact local tourist offices for information. Italy's big tennis event is the Grand Prix tournament held in Rome in May.

Watersports

All the usual watersports are immensely popular off both coasts. Lazio's main resorts are south of Rome (avoid the Lido di Ostia or anywhere near the mouth of the Tiber for swimming) while the Abruzzo and Molise coasts offer over a hundred kilometres of sandy if sometimes monotonous beach. The many seaside resorts are plagued by that peculiarly Italian phenomenon, the *bagnaio*, or concessionaire, who parks ugly lines of sunbeds and brollies all the way along the best stretches of coast, and charges all comers for the privilege of clean sand and watching your neighbours. You can often find a public beach amidst the concessions, but it will probably be strewn with rubbish. No one bats an eye at topless bathing, though nudism requires more discretion.

The most beautiful area for sailing and diving are the Pontine Islands, off the southern Lazio coast (*see* p.253). Waterskiing is possible on all the major lakes, as well as at many coastal resorts, although boat and equipment hire are often quite expensive. For further information, contact the Italian State Tourist Office or write to the following organizations:

Federazione Italiana Vela (Italian Sailing Federation), Via Odoardo Beccari 28, 00154 Rome, **t** 06 574 8115, *www.federvela.it*.

Federazione Italiana Motonautica (Italian Motorboat Federation, *www.fimconi.it*), and **Federazione Italiana Sci Nautico**, both at Via Piranesi 44b, Milan, **t** 02 701631.

Telephones and the Internet

Public telephones for international calls may be found in the offices of **Telecom Italia**, Italy's telephone company. They are the only places where you can make reverse-charge calls (*a erre*, collect calls) but be prepared for a wait, as all these calls go through the operator in Rome. Rates for long-distance calls are among the highest in Europe. Calls within Italy are cheapest after 10pm; international calls after 11pm. Some call boxes accept €0.10, €0.20, €0.50 and €1 coins (€0.10 should be enough for a short, inter-city call), but most now work with **phonecards** instead: *schede telefoniche* are available from tobacconists for €2.58, €5.16 and €7.75. In smaller villages, you can usually find *telefoni a scatti*, with a meter on them, in at least one bar (a small commission is generally charged). Try to avoid telephoning from hotels; this used to be a major rip-off, but is less so today; small hotels will usually do it without a mark-up, but others might add 25% to the bill or lots more.

Direct calls may be made by dialling the international prefix (for the UK 0044, Ireland 00353, USA and Canada 001, Australia 0061, New Zealand 0064). If you're calling **Italy from abroad**, dial 39 and then the whole number, including the first zero. Many places have public fax machines, but the speed of transmission may make costs very high; a sympathetic hotelkeeper might help.

Internet Cafés

Internet points have popped up at almost every street corner in Rome (*see* below), but finding Internet access in almost any other town in central Italy is virtually impossible. Rates charged will range from €2 to 3 per hour.

Easyeverything, Via Barberini 2, **t** 06 4290 3388, *www.easyeverything.com*

Internet Cafe Excape: Viale Somalia, 227, **t** 06 8632 9492; *www.excape.it*
Internet Point: Corso Vittorio Emanuele II 312, **t** 06 6830 8823; *www.internet-point.com*
Internet Café Stargate: Via dei Marrucini 12, **t** 06 445 4953; *www.internetcafe.it*
The Netgate: Piazza Firenze, 25, **t** 06 689 3445; *www.thenetgate.it*
The Traveller's Friend, Via Crescenzio 41, **t** 06 6821 0410
TreviNet Place, Via in Arcione 103, **t** 06 6992 2320

Toilets

Frequent travellers have noted a steady improvement over the years in the cleanliness of Italy's public conveniences, although as ever you will only find them in places like train and bus stations and bars. Ask for the *bagno*, *toilette*, or *gabinetto*; in stations and the smarter bars and cafes, there may be washroom attendants who expect a small tip for keeping the place decent. You'll probably have to ask them for paper (*carta*). Don't confuse the Italian plurals; *signori* (gents), *signore* (ladies).

Tourist Information

Known under various initials as EPT, APT or AAST, Italian tourist offices usually stay open from 8am to 12.30 or 1pm, and from 3 to 7pm, possibly longer in summer. Few open on Saturday afternoons or Sundays. Information booths can also be found at major railway stations and can provide hotel lists, town plans and terse information on local sights and transport. Queues can be maddeningly long. If you're stuck, you may get more sense out of a friendly travel agency than an official tourist office. The official state tourist website is *www.enit.it*. Nearly every city and province now has a web page, and you can often book your hotel direct through the Internet.

UK: 1 Princes Street, London W1R 8AY, **t** (020) 7408 1254, *italy@italiantouristboard.co.uk*.
USA: 630 Fifth Ave, Suite 1565, New York, NY 10111, **t** (212) 245 4822, *www.italian tourism.com*.
12400 Wilshire Blvd, Suite 550, Los Angeles, CA 90025, **t** (310) 820 1898.
500 N. Michigan Ave, Suite 1046, Chicago IL 60611, **t** (312) 644 1996.
Australia: Level 26, 44 Market St, NSW 2000, Sydney, **t** (02) 926 21666, *enitour@ihug. com.au*.
Canada: 175 Bloor St E, Suite 907, South Tower, Toronto M4W 3R8, **t** (416) 925 4882, *www.italiantourism.com*.

Tourist and travel information may also be available from **Alitalia** (Italy's national airline) or **CIT** (Italy's state-run travel agency) offices in some countries.

Where to Stay

All accommodation in Italy is classified by the Provincial Tourist Boards. Price control, however, has been abandoned since 1992. Hotels now set their own tariffs, which means that in some places prices have rocketed. Good-value, interesting accommodation in cities can be very difficult to find. In general, prices are simply too high right now, in comparison to some of Italy's neighbours. In much of central Italy, especially in parts of Lazio, you'll also find there are not enough rooms; there are murmurings that the hotel owners' associations use their influence to see that the number is kept down; they would rather have a few rooms always filled than a good supply with lower occupancy rates. In general, there are few hotels inland and plenty along the coasts wherever there is a beach. So when you can't find a room and it's getting dark, head for the nearest Lido (or spa town, or mountain resort; if it's August, though, you might end up sleeping in the car).

The quality of furnishings and facilities has generally improved in all categories in recent years. Many hotels have installed smart bathrooms and electronic gadgetry. At the top end of the market, Italy has a number of exceptionally sybaritic hotels, furnished and decorated with real panache. But you can still find plenty of simple, older-style hotels and *pensioni*.

Hotels and Guesthouses

Italian *alberghi* come in all shapes and sizes. They are rated from one to five stars, depending on what facilities they offer (not their character, style or charm). The star

Hotel Price Categories

Prices are for a double room with bath.
luxury over €250
very expensive €150–250
expensive €100–150
moderate €60–100
cheap below €60

ratings are some indication of price levels, but for tax reasons not all hotels choose to advertise themselves at the rating to which they are entitled, so you may find a modestly rated hotel just as comfortable (or more so) than a higher rated one. Conversely, you may find a hotel offers few stars in the hope of attracting budget-conscious travellers, but charges just as much as a higher-rated neighbour. *Pensioni* are generally more modest establishments, though nowadays the distinction between these and ordinary hotels is becoming blurred. *Locande* are traditionally an even more basic form of hostelry, but these days the term may denote somewhere fairly chic. Other inexpensive accommodation is sometimes known as *alloggi* or *affittacamere*, rooms over bars in small towns. You'll never find them by looking; ask around. There are usually plenty of cheap dives around city railway stations; for something more salubrious, head for the town centre or the fringes near a motorway.

If you're picky about hotels and prices, it's essential to stop in at any tourist office and ask for an *elenco degli alberghi*. Nearly every province publishes a complete list of accommodation, with all the necessary information and correct prices – they'll usually only cover that province, so while you are travelling make sure you know where the provincial boundaries are.

Price lists, by law, must be posted on the door of every room, along with meal prices and any extra charges, such as air conditioning, or even a shower in cheap places (they will be so posted about half the time). Many hotels display two or three different rates, depending on the season. Low-season rates may be about a third lower than peak-season tariffs. Some resort hotels close down altogether for several months a year. During high season you should always book ahead to be sure of a room (a fax reservation may be less frustrating to organize than one by post). If you have paid a deposit, your booking is valid under Italian law, but don't expect it to be refunded if you have to cancel. Tourist offices do not generally make reservations for visitors. Major city business hotels may offer significant discounts at weekends.

Main railway stations generally have accommodation booking desks; inevitably, a fee is charged. Chain hotels or motels are generally the easiest hotels to book, though not always the most interesting to stay in. Top of the list is CIGA (*Compagnia Italiana Grandi Alberghi*) with some of the most luxurious establishments in Italy, many of them grand, turn-of-last-century places that have been exquisitely restored. The French consortium *Relais et Châteaux* (not a chain) specializes in tastefully indulgent luxury accommodation, often in historic buildings.

One of the biggest chains in Italy is *Jolly Hotels*; these can generally be found near the centres of larger towns. Many motels are operated by the ACI (Italian Automobile Club) or by AGIP (the oil company) and usually located along major exit routes. These chain hotels are strictly accommodation of last resort; catering to the expense-account crowd, they will always be bland and far more expensive than comparable places run by local owners.

If you arrive without a reservation, begin looking or phoning round for accommodation early in the day. If possible, inspect the room (and bathroom facilities) before you book, and check the tariff carefully. Italian hoteliers may legally alter their rates twice during the year, so printed tariffs or tourist board lists (and prices quoted in this book!) may be out of date. Hoteliers who wilfully overcharge should be reported to the local tourist office. You will be asked for your passport for registration purposes; they should give it back as soon as they fill out the form for the police.

Prices listed in this guide are for double rooms; you can expect to pay about two-thirds the rate for single occupancy, though in high season you may be charged the full double rate in a popular beach resort. Extra beds are usually charged at about a third more of the room rate. Rooms without private bathrooms generally charge 20–30% less, and most offer discounts for children sharing parents' rooms, or children's meals (many older posh hotels still have a room or two without a full bath at cheaper rates; you can always ask about these). A *camera singola* (single room) may cost anything from about €40 upwards. Double rooms (*camera doppia*) go from about €60 to 300 or more. If you want a double bed, specify a *camera matrimoniale*.

Breakfast is usually optional in hotels, though obligatory in *pensioni*. You can usually get better value by eating breakfast in a bar or café. In high season you may be expected to take half-board in resorts if the hotel has a restaurant, and one-night stays may be refused.

And in this beautiful, mountainous country, remember to ask for a room with a view, a *camera con vista*.

Hostels and Budget Accommodation

There aren't many youth hostels (*alberghi* or *ostelli per la gioventù*) in Italy, but they are generally pleasant and sometimes located in historic buildings. The **Associazione Italiana Alberghi per la Gioventù** (Italian Youth Hostel Association, or AIG) is affiliated to the International Youth Hostel Federation (*www.iyhf.org*). For a full list of hostels, contact AIG at Via Cavour 44, 00184 Roma, **t** 06 487 1152; **f** 06 488 0492, *www.ostellionline.org*. An international membership card will enable you to stay in any of them. You can obtain these in advance from:

UK: International Youth Hostel Federation, 1st Floor, Fountain House, Parkway, Welwyn Garden City, Hertfordshire, AL8 6JH, **t** (01707) 324170, **f** (01707) 323980, *iyhf@iyhf.org*, *www.iyhf.org*

USA: American Youth Hostels Inc., 733 15th St NW, Suite 840, Washington DC 20005, **t** (202) 783 6161, *www.hiayhi.org*.

Australia: Youth Hostels Association, 422 Kent St, Sydney, **t** (02) 926 11111, *www.yha.org.au*.

Canada: Youth Hostelling International, Room 400, 205 Catherine St, Ottowa, Ontario, K2P 1C3, **t** 800 663 57777, *www.hihostels.ca*.

Cards can usually be purchased on the spot in many hostels if you don't already have one. You can book youth hostel accommodation online at *www.hostellinginternational.com*.

Religious institutions also run hostels; some are single sex, others will accept Catholics only. Rates are usually somewhere between €10 and 20, including breakfast. Discounts are available for senior citizens, and some family rooms are available. You generally have to check in after 5pm, and pay for your room before 9am. Hostels usually close for most of the daytime, and many operate a curfew. During the spring, noisy school parties cram hostels for field trips. In the summer, it's advisable to book ahead. Contact the hostels directly.

Villas, Flats and Chalets

If you're travelling in a group or with a family, self-catering can be the ideal way to experience Italy. The National Tourist Office has lists of agencies in the UK and USA which

Self-catering Tour Operators

In the UK and Ireland

Citalia, Marco Polo House, 3–5 Lansdowne Rd, Croydon CR9 1LL, **t** (020) 8986 0677, *www.citalia.co.uk*.

Inghams, 10–18 Putney Hill, London SW15 6AX, **t** (020) 8780 4450.

Interhome, 383 Richmond Road, Twickenham, Middx TW1 2EF, **t** (020) 8891 1294.

Magic of Italy, Kings Place, Wood Street, Kingston KT1 UF, **t** (020) 8939 5453, *www.magictravelgroup.co.uk*.

Topflight, D'Olier Chambers, D'Olier Street, Dublin 2, **t** (01) 679 9177.

The Individual Travellers' Company, Manor Courtyard, Bignor, Pulborough, West Sussex RH20 1QD, **t** (01798) 869461, *www.indiv-travellers.com*.

In the USA

CIT, 15 West 44th Street, New York NY 10036, **t** 800 248 8687, **t** (212) 730 2121.

At Home Abroad, 405 East 56th Street, apt 6-H, New York, NY 10022-2466, **t** (212) 421 9165, **f** (212) 752 1591, *athomabrod@aol.com*.

Hideaways International, 767 Islington Street, Portsmouth NH 03801, **t** (603) 430 4433, *www.hideaways.com*.

RAVE (Rent-a-Vacation Everywhere), 135 Meigs Street, Rochester, New York, NY 14607, **t** (716) 256 0760.

rent places on a weekly or fortnightly basis. If you have set your heart on a particular region, write to its tourist office for a list of agencies and owners, who will send brochures or particulars of their accommodation. Maid service is included in the more glamorous villas; ask whether bed linen and towels are provided. A few of the larger operators are listed in the box.

Rural Self-catering

For a breath of rural seclusion, the gregarious Italians head for a spell on a **working farm**, in accommodation (usually self-catering) that often approximates to the French *gîte*. Often, however, the real pull of the place is a restaurant in which you can sample some home-grown produce. Outdoor activities may include riding, fishing and so forth. *Agriturismo*, as they call it, is an idea that has grown tremendously in the last decade. It's the best way to get to know the Italians (just don't expect them to speak any English).

This branch of the Italian tourist industry is run by three organizations, Agriturist, Turismo Verde and Terranostra. It has burgeoned in recent years, but prices of farmhouse accommodation are still reasonable. Local tourist offices will have information on *agriturismo* in their areas; write ahead for their lists: **Agriturist**, Corso Vittorio Emanuele 101, 00186 Rome, **t** 06 685 23337, *www.agriturist.it*; **Turismo Verde**, Via Caio Mario 27, 00192 Rome, **t** 06 326 87430, *www.turismoverde.com*. Not surprisingly, in the mainly rural Abruzzo, *agriturismo* is especially popular, and the region has recently published an extremely useful book in English, *Agriturism in the Land of Abruzzo*, available from Agriturist, Via Stradonetto, 65128 Pescara, **t/f** 085 53051; Terranostra, Viale Regina Margherita 39, 65100 Pescara, **t** 085 421 9416, **f** 085 422 0560; Turismo Verde, Viale Bovio 85, 65124 Pescara, **t** 085 421 6816, **f** 085 422 3819.

Alpine Refuges

The Italian Alpine Club operates refuges (*rifugi*) on the main mountain trails (some accessible only by *funivie*). These may be predictably spartan, or surprisingly comfortable. Many have restaurants. For an up-to-date list, write to the Club Alpino Italiano, Via Fonseca Pimental 7, Milan, **t** 02 2614 1378, *www.cai.it/rifugi*. Charges average €10–20 per person per night, including breakfast. Most are open only from July to September, but those used by skiers are about 20% more expensive from December to April. Book ahead in August.

Camping

Life under canvas is not the fanatical craze it is in France, nor necessarily any great bargain, but there are over 2,000 sites in Italy, particularly popular with holidaymaking families in August, when you can expect to find many sites at bursting point. Unofficial camping is generally frowned on and may attract a stern rebuke from the local police. Camper vans (and facilities for them) are increasingly popular. You can obtain a list of local sites from any regional tourist office; every resort will have at least one. Campsite charges generally range from about €5 to 10 per adult; tents and vehicles additionally cost about €5–12 each. Small extra charges may also be levied for hot showers and electricity. A car-borne couple could therefore spend practically as much for a night at a well-equipped campsite as in a cheap hotel.

To obtain a camping carnet and to book ahead, write to the **Centro Internazionale Prenotazioni Campeggio**, Casella Postale 23, 50041 Calenzano, Firenze, **t** 055 882 381; **f** 055 882 3918 (ask for their list of campsites with the booking form).

The **Touring Club Italiano** (TCI) publishes a comprehensive annual guide to campsites throughout Italy which is available in bookshops for about €20. Write to: TCI, Corso Italia 10, Milan, **t** 02 85261/852 6245.

Rome

09

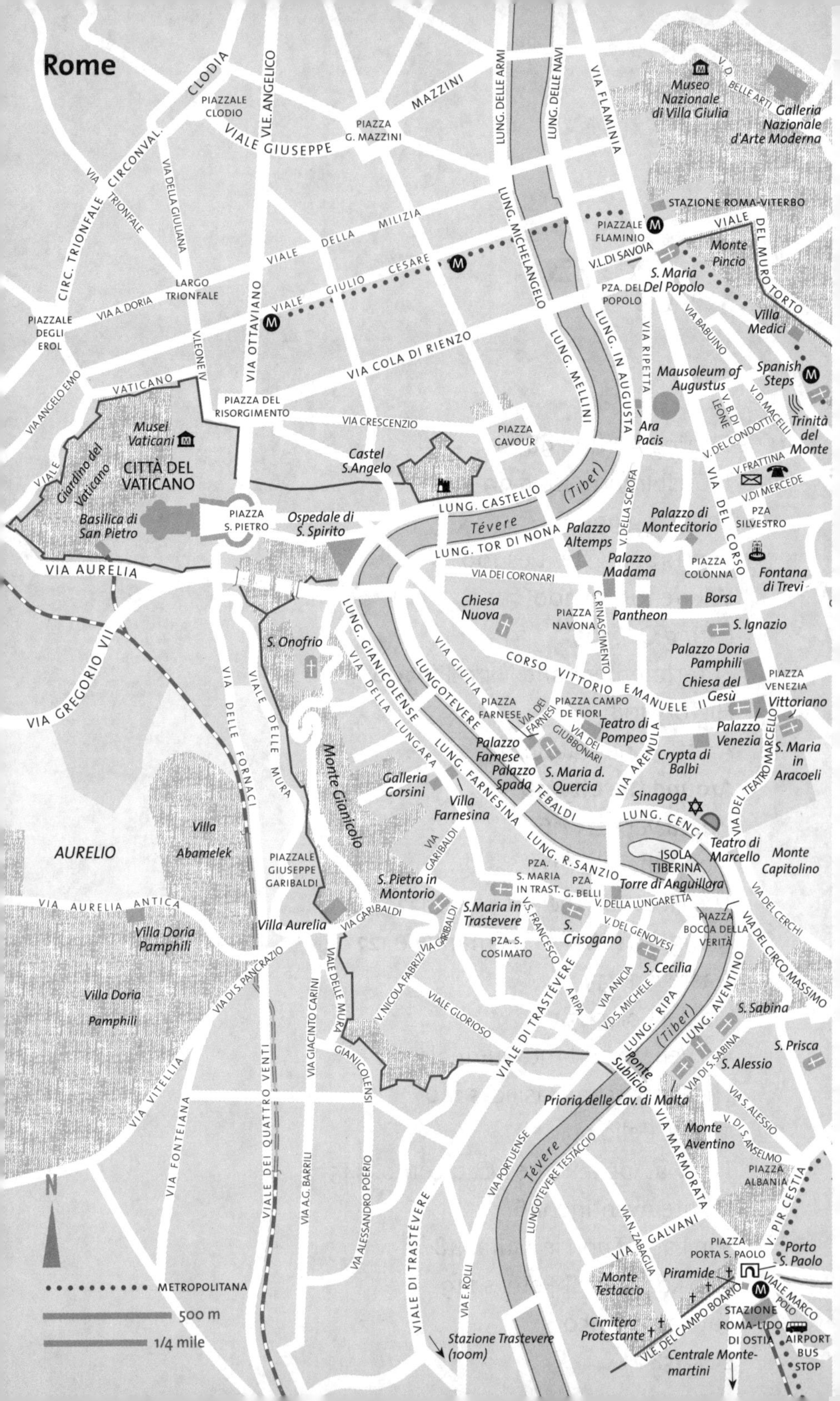
Rome
Clodia
Piazzale Clodio
Vle. Angelico
Viale Giuseppe Mazzini
Piazza G. Mazzini
Lung. delle Armi
Lung. delle Navi
Via Flaminia
Museo Nazionale di Villa Giulia
V. D. Belle Arti
Galleria Nazionale d'Arte Moderna
Via Circonval. Trionfale
Via Trionfale
Via della Giuliana
Circ. Trionfale
Viale della Milizia
Lung. Michelangelo
Stazione Roma-Viterbo
Piazzale Flaminio
Viale del Muro Torto
Monte Pincio
V.L. di Savoia
S. Maria Del Popolo
Pza. del Popolo
Viale Giulio Cesare
Largo Trionfale
Via A. Doria
Piazzale degli Erol
V. Leone IV
Via Ottaviano
Villa Medici
Via Babuino
Via Ripetta
Lung. in Augusta
Lung. Mellini
Via Cola di Rienzo
Mausoleum of Augustus
Spanish Steps
Via Angelo Emo
Vaticano
Piazza del Risorgimento
Via Crescenzio
Piazza Cavour
Ara Pacis
V. B. di Leone
V. D. Macelli
Trinità del Monte
V. del Condotti
Musei Vaticani
Viale
Giardino del Vaticano
Città del Vaticano
Castel S. Angelo
Via della Scrofa
V. Frattina
V. di Mercede
Via del Corso
Lung. Castello
(Tiber)
Tévere
Basilica di San Pietro
Piazza S. Pietro
Ospedale di S. Spirito
Palazzo di Montecitorio
Pza Silvestro
Lung. Tor di Nona
Palazzo Altemps
Piazza Colonna
Fontana di Trevi
Via Aurelia
Via dei Coronari
Palazzo Madama
Borsa
Chiesa Nuova
Piazza Navona
C. Rinascimento
Pantheon
S. Ignazio
S. Onofrio
Lung. Gianicolense
Via della Lungara
Via Giulia
Lungotevere
Corso Vittorio Emanuele II
Palazzo Doria Pamphili
Chiesa del Gesù
Piazza Venezia
Via Gregorio VII
Via delle Fornaci
Viale delle Mura
Piazza Farnese
Via dei Farnesi
Piazza Campo de Fiori
Via dei Giubbonari
Teatro di Pompeo
Vittoriano
Palazzo Venezia
Via del Teatro Marcello
Palazzo Farnese
Palazzo Spada
S. Maria d. Quercia
Crypta di Balbi
Via Arenula
S. Maria in Aracoeli
Monte Gianicolo
Galleria Corsini
Lung. Farnesina
Lung. Tebaldi
Villa Farnesina
Synagoga
Lung. Cenci
Villa Abamelek
Aurelio
Via Garibaldi
Piazzale Giuseppe Garibaldi
Lung. R. Sanzio
Isola Tiberina
Teatro di Marcello
Monte Capitolino
Pza. S. Maria in Trast.
Pza. G. Belli
Torre di Anguillara
S. Pietro in Montorio
V. della Lungaretta
Via del Cerchi
Via Aurelia Antica
Villa Aurelia
S. Maria in Trastevere
V. S. Francesco
S. Crisogano
V. del Genovesi
Piazza Bocca della Verità
Villa Doria Pamphili
Via Garibaldi
Pza. S. Cosimato
Via del Circo Massimo
Via di S. Pancrazio
V. Nicola Fabrizi
Viale delle Mura
Viale Glorioso
Viale di Trastévere
A Ripa
Via Anicia
V. D. S. Michele
S. Cecilia
Lung. Ripa
Lung. Aventino
S. Sabina
Via Giacinto Carini
Gianicolensi
Ponte Sublicio
S. Prisca
S. Alessio
Via di S. Sabina
Via S. Alessio
Via Vitellia
Priora delle Cav. di Malta
Via Marmorata
Monte Aventino
V. di S. Anselmo
Via Fonteiana
Viale dei Quattro Venti
Via A.G. Barrili
Via Alessandro Poerio
Via Portuense
Lungotevere Testaccio
Piazza Albania
Via N. Zabaglia
V. Pir Cestia
Via Galvani
Piazza Porta S. Paolo
Porto S. Paolo
Piramide
Viale Marco Polo
Monte Testaccio
Metropolitana
500 m
1/4 mile
Via E. Rolli
Stazione Trastevere (100m)
Cimitero Protestante
Vle. del Campo Boario
Stazione Roma-Lido di Ostia
Airport Bus Stop
Centrale Montemartini
N

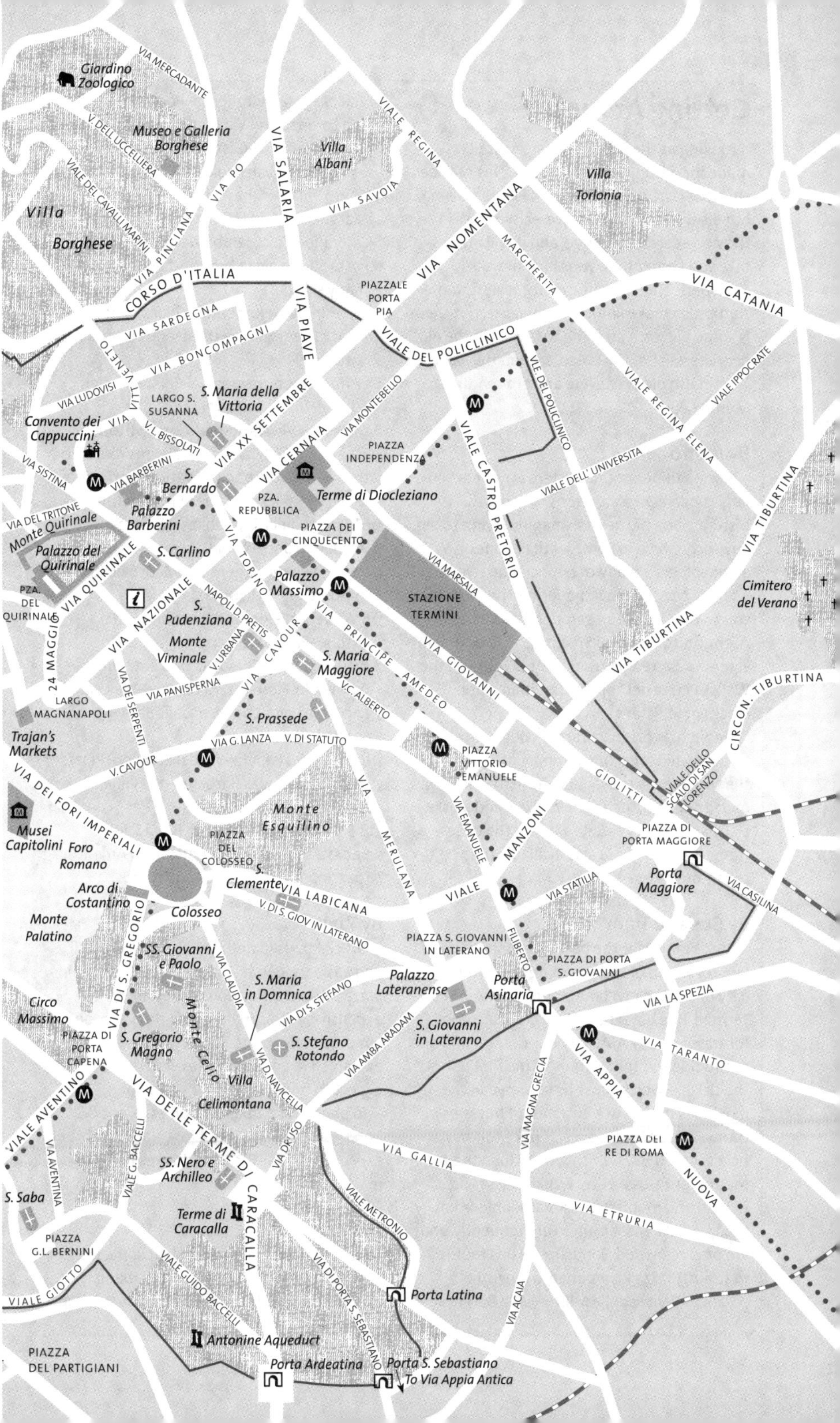
Giardino Zoologico
VIA MERCADANTE
Museo e Galleria Borghese
V. DELL'UCCELLIERA
VIALE DEL CAVALLI MARINI
Villa Borghese
VIA PINCIANA
VIA PO
VIA SALARIA
Villa Albani
VIALE REGINA
VIA SAVOIA
Villa Torlonia
VIA NOMENTANA
MARGHERITA
CORSO D'ITALIA
VIA PIAVE
PIAZZALE PORTA PIA
VIA CATANIA
VIALE DEL POLICLINICO
VIA SARDEGNA
VIA BONCOMPAGNI
VIA VENETO
VIA LUDOVISI
VIA VITT
LARGO S. SUSANNA
S. Maria della Vittoria
VIA XX SETTEMBRE
VIA CERNAIA
VIA MONTEBELLO
PIAZZA INDEPENDENZA
VIALE CASTRO PRETORIO
VLE. DEL POLICLINICO
VIALE REGINA ELENA
VIALE IPPOCRATE
VIALE DELL' UNIVERSITA
Convento dei Cappuccini
V. L. BISSOLATI
VIA SISTINA
VIA BARBERINI
S. Bernardo
Terme di Diocleziano
PZA. REPUBBLICA
VIA TIBURTINA
VIA DEL TRITONE
Monte Quirinale
Palazzo Barberini
PIAZZA DEI CINQUECENTO
Palazzo del Quirinale
S. Carlino
VIA TORINO
VIA MARSALA
Palazzo Massimo
STAZIONE TERMINI
Cimitero del Verano
PZA. DEL QUIRINALE
VIA QUIRINALE
VIA NAZIONALE
NAPOLI D. PRETIS
S. Pudenziana
Monte Viminale
V. URBANA
VIA CAVOUR
VIA PRINCIPE AMEDEO
VIA GIOVANNI
S. Maria Maggiore
24 MAGGIO
VIA DEI SERPENTI
VIA PANISPERNA
V.C. ALBERTO
LARGO MAGNANAPOLI
S. Prassede
CIRCON. TIBURTINA
Trajan's Markets
VIA G. LANZA
V. DI STATUTO
PIAZZA VITTORIO EMANUELE
GIOLITTI
VIALE DELLO SCALO DI SAN LORENZO
V. CAVOUR
VIA DEI FORI IMPERIALI
VIA MERULANA
Monte Esquilino
VIA EMANUELE
MANZONI
Musei Capitolini
Foro Romano
PIAZZA DEL COLOSSEO
PIAZZA DI PORTA MAGGIORE
Porta Maggiore
Arco di Costantino
S. Clemente
VIA LABICANA
VIALE
VIA STATILIA
VIA CASILINA
Monte Palatino
Colosseo
V. DI S. GIOV IN LATERANO
VIA DI S. GREGORIO
SS. Giovanni e Paolo
VIA CLAUDIA
PIAZZA S. GIOVANNI IN LATERANO
FILIBERTO
PIAZZA DI PORTA S. GIOVANNI
Monte Celio
S. Maria in Domnica
Palazzo Lateranense
Porta Asinaria
VIA LA SPEZIA
Circo Massimo
VIA DI S. STEFANO
VIA AMBA ARADAM
S. Giovanni in Laterano
PIAZZA DI PORTA CAPENA
S. Gregorio Magno
S. Stefano Rotondo
VIA TARANTO
VIA APPIA
VIA D. NAVICELLA
Villa Celimontana
VIALE AVENTINO
VIA DELLE TERME DI CARACALLA
VIA MAGNA GRECIA
PIAZZA DEI RE DI ROMA
VIA DRUSO
VIA GALLIA
NUOVA
VIA AVENTINA
VIALE G. BACCELLI
SS. Nero e Archilleo
S. Saba
VIALE METRONIO
VIA ETRURIA
Terme di Caracalla
PIAZZA G.L. BERNINI
VIALE GUIDO BACCELLI
VIA DI PORTA S. SEBASTIANO
VIALE GIOTTO
Porta Latina
VIA ACAIA
Antonine Aqueduct
PIAZZA DEL PARTIGIANI
Porta Ardeatina
Porta S. Sebastiano
To Via Appia Antica

Getting Around

Looking at the map, Rome seems to be made for getting around on foot. This may be so in the *centro storico* around Piazza Navona, but elsewhere it's deceptive – city blocks in the newer areas are huge, and it will always take you longer than you think to walk anywhere. The hills, the outsize scale and the traffic also make Rome a tiring place, but there is some pleasant strolling to be had in the old districts west of the Corso, around the Isola Tiberina, in old Trastevere and around the Monte Celio.

By Metro

Rome's underground system is not particularly convenient as it seems to avoid the historic parts of the city; imagine trying to dig any sort of hole in Rome, with legions of archaeologists ready to pounce. The two lines, A and B, cross at Stazione Termini and will take you to the Colosseum, around the Monte Aventino, to Piazza di Spagna, San Giovanni in Laterano, San Paolo fuori le Mura (outside the Walls), Piazza del Popolo, or within eight blocks of St Peter's.

Single tickets (€0.77), also good for city buses – valid for 75mins from obliteration in the turnstile – are available from machines in metro stations, tobacconists, bars and kiosks. Daily and weekly tickets valid on the buses, trams and metro are also available from tobacconists (*see* below).

By Bus and Tram

Buses are by far the best way to get around. Pick up a map of the bus routes from the **ATAC** (city bus company) booth outside Stazione Termini. Bus tickets cost €0.77, and are good for travel on any ATAC city bus or tram and one metro ride – within 75mins of the first use of the ticket – which must be stamped in the machines in the back entrance of buses or trams. There are also special-price full-day tickets called BIG (which also include the metro) for €3, as well as weekly passes (CIS €12.40) and monthly passes available from tobacconists. Most routes run frequently, and are often crowded. Some useful bus routes:

19 (tram) Piazza Risorgimento (near the Vatican)–Viale delle Milizie–Villa Borghese–Viale Regina Margherita–Porta Maggiore–San Lorenzo and Via Prenestina.

23 Musei Vaticani–Castel Sant'Angelo–Tiber banks–Porta San Paolo–S. Paolo.

3 (tram) Villa Borghese–Viale Regina Margherita–San Lorenzo–S. Giovanni in Laterano– Colosseum–Viale Aventino–Porta San Paolo (a fun trip, taking in many sights).

36 Termini–Via Nomentana (Sant'Agnese).

46 Piazza Venezia–Corso Vittorio Emanuele–Vatican.

63 Largo Argentina–Via del Corso–Via del Tritone–Via Vittorio Veneto.

64 Termini–Via Nazionale–Corso Vittorio Emanuele–Vatican (the main bus route from the *centro storico* to the Vatican and famous for its pickpockets so be extra careful).

116T Piazza della Repubblica–Via Nazionale–Via del Tritone–Via del Corso–Piazza Venezia–Largo Argentina–Mausoleo di Augusto (8pm–1.30am).

116 Via Veneto–Piazza Barberini–Via del Tritone–Piazza del Parlamento–Corso Rinascimento–Corso Vittorio Emanuele – Campo de' Fiori–Piazza Farnese–Via Giulia (a circular minibus, weekdays 8am–9pm, Sat 8am–midnight).

119 Piazza del Popolo–Via del Babuino–Piazza di Spagna–Piazza Barberini–Via Veneto–Porta Pinciana (and back).

218 S. Giovanni in Laterano–Porta San Sebastiano–Via Appia Antica–Via Ardeatina (passing the catacombs and tombs).

By Taxi

Official taxis (painted white) are plentiful, and easier to get at a rank in one of the main piazzas than to flag down. They are quite expensive, with surcharges for luggage, on Sundays and after 10.30pm. Fares are clearly explained in English inside every taxi. Don't expect to find one when it's raining.

To phone for a taxi, call **t** 06 3570, or **t** 06 4994; you don't pay extra for calling a cab, but expect to pay for the time it takes for it to reach you.

By Car

Absolutely not recommended! Rome isn't as chaotic as Naples, but nearly so. Parking is expensive and difficult to find; many areas in the centre are closed to traffic (and the signs for them are hard to spot) and riddled with narrow, one-way streets. Rome and its cars are mortal enemies; sooner or later one or the other will have to succumb.

Tourist Information

Azienda di Promozione Turistica (APT), Via Parigi 11, 00185, **t** 06 488 991, **f** 06 4889 9238. *Open Mon–Fri 9.30–12.30, Mon and Thurs also 2.30–4.30*. The central office, near the Baths of Diocletian and Termini. The APT offices are the best source of information about what's on in Rome and its province.

APT (*Fiumicino airport*), **t** 06 6595 6074. *Open Mon–Sat 8.15–7*. A useful branch office if you arrive by plane.

Comune di Roma Tourist Information Office, Termini Station. *Open daily 8–8*. Inside Rome's main train station. You'll find more information about the city here than at APT. Ask for free city maps and brochures in English about the city's tourist attractions, including museums, archaeological sites and parks. The free ATAC public transport map is very useful.

Comune di Roma helpline, **t** 06 3600 4399 (*select 2 for an English-speaking operator*). *Open daily 9–7.30*. For similar information over the phone, contact the helpful call centre or visit *www.romaturismo.com*.

In addition, there are **tourist kiosks** (*all open daily 9.30–7.30*) at Largo Goldoni, Piazza Pia, Piazza del Tempio della Pace, Piazza delle Cinque Lune, Via Marco Minghetti, Via Nazionale, Piazza Sonnino, Piazza San Giovanni in Laterano, Via dell' Olmata and Stazione Termini.

The Hotel Reservation Service, **t** 06 699 1000 (*open daily 8am–10.45pm*) offers commission-free reservations at several hundred hotels in town.

Enjoy Rome, Via Varese 39, **t** 06 445 1843, also near Stazione Termini, is an efficient privately run English-speaking information service which organizes inexpensive walking tours as well as accommodation. Two weeklies available from news stands, *Romac'è* (with a short English section at the back) and *Time Out* (in Italian) are the best sources of information on what's on in Rome.

24-hour pharmacies: **Piram**, Via Nazionale 228, **t** 06 488 0754; **Arenula**, Via Arenula 73, **t** 06 6880 3278, near Largo Argentina. Lists of duty pharmacists are also posted outside all other pharmacies.

Money: Outside banking hours, money can be changed at **American Express**, Piazza di Spagna 38, **t** 06 67641 (*open Mon–Fri 9–5.30, Sat 9–12.30*); **Thomas Cook**, Via della Conciliazione 23, **t** 06 6830 0435 (*open Mon–Sat 8–6, Sun 8–5*); and numerous money changing shops.

Main post office: Piazza San Silvestro 19, **t** 06 160, *www.poste.it*

Shopping

Rome isn't as exciting for big-game shoppers as Milan, though when it comes to clothing you will find all the major designers and labels well represented. Serious shoppers should check out the website *www.made-in-italy.com*. There is no shortage of shops selling **antiques**, a great number of them clustered together between the Tiber and Piazza Navona; look especially off Via Monserrato, Via dei Coronari and Via dell'Anima. For **old prints**, generally inexpensive, try Casali, Piazza Rotonda 81A; Alinari, Via Alibert 16/a, is a good address for artistic **black and white pictures of old Rome**. **L'Art Nouveau**, Via dei Coronari 221, offers just what its name implies. **Antiques** also show up in the celebrated Sunday morning flea market at Porta Portese, as well as anything else you can imagine, all lumped together in often surreal displays (*open dawn–1*).

The most **fashionable shopping** is on the streets between Piazza di Spagna and the Corso, with Via Condotti still the designer shopping street *par excellence*. Some special items: Massoni, Largo Goldoni 48, near Via Condotti, much frequented by film stars, sells some of Rome's finest **jewellery**; for **menswear**, Testa, Via Borgognona 13 and Via Frattina 42, or Valentino Uomo, Via Condotti 12, or for **custom tailoring**, Battistoni, Via Condotti 61/a. For **women's clothes** try the outlets of the big designers in the same area: Missoni, Via del Babuino 96, Giorgio Armani, Via Condotti 76–7 and Via del Babuino 140, Mila Schöen, Via Condotti 51, or the Rome-based Fendi, Via Borgognona 36/e. For **leather**, the Gucci outlet is at Via Condotti 8, and do not miss Fausto Santini, Via Frattina 120.

Discounted designer fashion may be had at Il Discount dell'Alta Moda, Via Gesù e Maria 16/a; for **high-fashion shoes**, try Barrilà, Via Condotti 29 and Via del Babuino 33; and for **Borsalino hats**, Troncarelli, Via della Cuccagna 15, near Piazza Navona.

For a special bottle of **wine**, try Enoteca Costantini, Piazza Cavour 16, for a wide selection. If you wish to stock up on Italian **coffee**, Tazza d'Oro, Via degli Orfani 84, has special bags of the city's best, the 'Aroma di Roma'.

If you need a good **book**, try the Anglo-American Book Co., Via della Vite 27, the Lion Bookshop, Via dei Greci 36, the Economy Book Center, Via Torino 135/a, near Via Nazionale (which also has second-hand books), or Feltrinelli International, just off the Piazza della Repubblica at Via Orlando 84–6 (this also stocks guides and maps).

For an amazing selection of **fancy kitchen gear**, there's C.U.C.I.N.A., Via Mario dei Fiori 65, while for serious, **professional pans, pots and tools** head to Zucchi, Via Sant'Antonio all'Esquilino 15, near Santa Maria Maggiore. Try Image, Via della Scrofa 67, for **posters, postcards and photographs**; and De Ritis, Via de' Cestari 1, for the latest **ecclesiastical fashions**, along with Madonnas and crucifixes.

Sports and Activities

Rome's main public **swimming pool** is the Piscina delle Rose, Viale America 20, in EUR, **t** 06 5425 2185 (Ⓜ EUR Fermi) (*open June–mid-Sept daily 9–7; adm €10.50*). There is also an attractive private pool at the Centro Sportivo Italiano, Lungotevere Flaminio 55, about a half-mile north of Piazza del Popolo, **t** 06 323 7333 (*open in summer*).

Rome's two top **football** clubs, AS Roma and Lazio, both play on Saturday or Sunday afternoon at the Stadio Olimpico, Viale dei Gladiatori 2 (Ⓜ Linea A to Ottaviano, then bus no.32) during the season (*Sept–May*). Tickets range in price from €18–110 and are put on sale 10–14 days ahead; contact Lazio Point, Via Farini 34, **t** 06 6482 6688; or Orbis, Piazza Esquilino 37, **t** 06 474 4776.

Where to Stay

Rome ✉ 00100

For a city that has been entertaining visitors for the last 2,000 years, Rome has not acquired any special flair for accommodating them. Perhaps it is just the uninterrupted flow of the curious and faithful that keeps prices higher and service and quality lower than elsewhere in Italy. From Belle Époque palaces on Via Veneto to grimy hovels on the wrong side of Stazione Termini, there will always be somewhere for you to stay, although places with a history, a view or quiet gardens are rare. Exceptions exist, but this is probably not the place to make the big splurge. That said, the city went into overdrive building, renovating and sprucing up its hotels for the huge numbers of visitors expected in 2000, and there's more choice now than ever before.

Rooms can be difficult to find at short notice, but the free **Hotel Reservation Service**, **t** 06 699 1000, will do the looking for you. The private **Enjoy Rome** (*see* p.99) will also make commission-free hotel bookings.

Luxury

*******Art** by the Spanish Steps, Via Margutta 56, 00187, **t** 06 421281, **f** 06 3600 3995, *www.hotelart.it*. Very sleek boutique hotel decorated with a fashionable mix of antiques and contemporary design, set in a former *palazzetto* near the Spanish Steps. Extras include a Turkish bath, sauna and jacuzzi.

*******Excelsior**, Via Veneto 125, 00187, **t** 06 47081, **f** 06 482 6205, *www.westin.com/excelsiorroma*. Also located in a choice area, though lacking the aura it had in the 1950s. The reception areas have thicker carpets, bigger chandeliers and more gilded plaster than anywhere in Italy, and most of the rooms are just as good – don't let them give you a modernized one. There are saunas, a famous bar, a tiny cinema (yes, really) and as much personal attention as you could ask for.

*******Hassler-Villa Medici**, Piazza Trinità dei Monti 6, 00187, **t** 06 699340, **f** 06 678 9991, *www.hotelhasslerroma.com, hasslerroma@mclink.it*. One of Rome's best hotels, with a fine location at the top of the Spanish Steps and wonderful views over the city for those who book far enough in advance. Around for over a century, it has regained its position as the élite hotel of Rome, with a beautiful courtyard, rooftop terrace, deferential service, and large wood-panelled rooms.

★★★★**D'Inghilterra**, Via Bocca di Leone 14, 00187, **t** 06 699811, **f** 06 6992 2243, *www.hoteldhinglaterraroma.it*. Another favourite near Piazza di Spagna. Parts of this building date from the 15th century, when it served as a prince's guest house; in its career as a hotel, since 1850, it has played host to most of Europe and America's literati and artists. Don't miss the beautiful roof garden.

★★★★**Columbus**, Via della Conciliazione 33, 00193, **t** 06 686 5435/ **t** 06 6819 9360, **f** 06 686 4874, *www.hotelcolumbus.net*. Staid but reliable, this is slightly geared towards business travellers; attractive, well-equipped rooms, some with views over St Peter's; prices are a bit high.

★★★★**Raphael**, Largo di Febo 2, 00186, **t** 06 682 831, **f** 06 687 8993, *info@hotelraphael.com*, *www.raphaelhotel.com*. Very near Piazza Navona, a vine-covered old charmer, decorated with antiques. Try to get a top-floor room for the views. TV, bar, restaurant, air conditioning and business facilities.

★★★**Carriage**, Via delle Carrozze 36, 00187, **t** 06 699 0124, **f** 06 678 8279, *www.hotelcarriage.net*. Almost at the foot of the Spanish Steps; a sleepy but charming spot with tastefully refubished rooms and welcoming staff. Book well in advance.

Very Expensive

★★★**Celio**, Via del Santio Quattro 35c, **t** 06 7049 5333, **f** 06 709 6377, *www.hotelcelio.com*. A welcoming, idiosyncratic hotel close to the Colosseum; each room bears the name of a famous opera singer and the bathrooms have mosaic-style floors. Prices range from luxury to expensive categories.

★★★**Due Torri**, Vicolo del Leonetto 23, 00186, **t** 06 687 6983, **f** 06 686 5442, *www.hotelduetorri.roma.it*. On a tiny, quiet street, this attractive little hotel was once the home of a famous prelate and offers comfortable, if slightly small, rooms (try for one with rooftop views). Charming service.

★★★**Fontana**, Piazza di Trevi 96, 00187, **t** 06 678 6113, **f** 06 679 0024, *www.fontanahotel.com*. Would be a good hotel anywhere; it is also right across the street from the Trevi Fountain – something to look at out of your window that will guarantee nice dreams. Prices can reach luxury category.

★★★★**Forum**, Via Tor de' Conti 25, 00184, **t** 06 679 2446, **f** 06 678 6479, *info@hotelforum.com*, *www.hotelforum.com*. The only fancy establishment near the ancient Forum; it's somewhat worn, but has unbeatable views from the roof terrace.

★★★**Fontanella Borghese**, Largo Fontanello Borghese 84, **t** 06 6880 9504, **f** 06 686 1295, *www.fontanellaborghese.com*. Set in a 15th-century palazzo, this is a delightful and atmospheric little hotel with tastefully decorated rooms and large bathrooms.

★★★★**La Residenza**, Via Emilia 22, 00187, **t** 06 488 0789, **f** 06 485 721, *www.venere.it/roma/laresidenza*. Near the Via Veneto; stands out as a very pleasant base, with beautifully appointed rooms in an old town house, and some luxuries more common to the most expensive hotels. It's recently opted to become a non-smoking hotel.

★★★**Locarno**, Via della Penna 22, **t** 06 361 0841, *www.hotellocarno.com*. Close to the Piazza del Popolo, this welcoming Art Nouveau-style hotel has plenty of charm. Elegant, well-equipped rooms, some have hi-fi, video and modem connections. There's also a lovely roof terrace. Book well in advance.

★★★**Hotel Sant'Anselmo**, Piazza Sant'Anselmo 2, 00153, **t** 06 574 8119, **f** 06 578 3604, *www.aventinohotels.com*. Up on Monte Aventino, a very peaceful hotel with a garden and comfortable, individually decorated rooms. Ask for one with views of the city.

★★★**Portoghesi**, Via dei Portoghesi 1, 00186, **t** 06 686 4231, **f** 06 687 6976, *www.hotelportoghesi.roma.com*. A small, well-kept hotel in an former mansion on a quiet street north of Piazza Navona, with antique-filled rooms. The suite with a private balcony on the roof is worth splashing out on.

★★★**Teatro di Pompeo**, Largo del Pallaro 8, 00186, **t** 06 6830 0170, **f** 06 6880 5531, *hotel.teatrodipompeo@tiscalinet.it*, *web.tiscali.it/hotel_teatrodipompeo*. A small, very welcoming hotel with plain rooms, which is built on the Teatro di Pompeo by Campo de' Fiori, perfect for peace and quiet.

★★★**Villa San Pio**, Via Santa Melania 19, 00153, **t** 06 574 8119, **f** 06 578 3604, *www.aventino hotels.com*. A glorious Aventine villa with a gorgeous, secluded statue-studded garden. The recently refurbished rooms are quietly elegant and some lead out onto the garden. Linked to Hotel Sant'Anselmo (*see* above).

Expensive

★★**Campo de' Fiori**, Via del Biscione 6, 00186 **t** 06 6880 6865, **f** 06 687 6003, *www. campodefiori.com*. A revamped hotel covered in a sheet of ivy with hall-of-mirrors corridor, and theme-park bedrooms (the kitschest of which boasts a bathroom roofed with hewn logs). Vertiginous views from the roof garden. Bar and air conditioning. Some much cheaper rooms are available with bathroom. Breakfast extra.

★★★**Hotel Scalinata di Spagna**, Piazza Trinità dei Monti 17, **t** 06 679 3006, **f** 06 6994 0598. With a perfect location at the top of the Spanish Steps, this small hotel has just 15 rooms which book up quickly. The price is worth it for the views from the breakfast terrace alone. Prices soar to luxury price category in the high season.

★★★**Lancelot**, Via Capo d'Africa 47, **t** 06 7045 0615, **f** 06 7045 0616, *www.lancelothotel. com*. A charming, family-run hotel full of knick-knacks close to the Colosseum with recently refurbished singles, doubles and triples.

★★**Sole**, Via del Biscione 76, 00186, **t** 06 687 9446, **f** 06 689 3787 *info@solealbiscione*. Near Campo de' Fiori, on the foundations of Pompey's Theatre, rises the not very sunny but still rather endearing 'Sun', a family-run favourite of backpackers, grandparents and everyone else under the sun. Book in advance and request a room facing the pretty enclosed garden overlooked by a church. Cheaper rooms without bath available (*moderate*).

Moderate

★★**Abruzzi**, Piazza della Rotonda 69, 00186, **t** 06 679 2021. Directly across the square from the Pantheon. The rooms in the back without the view aren't so great, but at least they're quiet, and all the rooms are a good size. A bit ragged, but amenable. Showers in the hall. TV, bar, air conditioning.

The City Guesthouse, Viale Opita Oppio 78, 00174, **t** 06 7698 3140, **f** 06 7696 7961, *www.cityguesthouse.com*. Out of the centre, but still only a 20-minute metro ride to Termini or the Spanish Steps. Rooms are individually decorated with trendy bold prints and slick, minimalist furniture. The staff couldn't be friendlier and there are plenty of good restaurants nearby.

★★**Hotel Boccaccio**, Via del Boccaccio 25, **t/f** 06 488 5962, *www.hotelboccaccio.it*. Delightful, simple little hotel (just eight rooms) not far from the Piazza di Spagna. The rooms are plain, but there's a pretty plant-filled courtyard and utterly charming staff. Prices are at the very bottom end of this bracket.

★★**Nardizzi**, Via Firenze 38, **t** 06 488035, **f** 06 4880 0368, *www.hotelnadarzzi.it*. A very reasonably priced, simple option close to Termini. It doesn't ooze charm, but has friendly staff, clean, well-equipped rooms (with air conditioning), and a roof garden. Prices can reach moderate category.

Cheap

The area around **Stazione Termini** offers a wide choice of inexpensive hotels, ranging from plain, family-run establishments – often quite comfortable and friendly – to bizarre dives with exposed plumbing run by Sudanese and Sri Lankans for visiting countrymen.

Accommodation Planet 29, Via Gaeta 29, **t** 06 486520, **f** 06 484141, *cristina@mclink.it*, *www.mclink.it/com/travel*. A friendly place close to Termini train station which has 15 simple rooms – some with kitchenette tucked away in a cupboard – from around €60 per night.

Colors Hotel and Hostel, Via Boezio 31, **t** 06 687 4030, *wwwicolorshotel.com*. One of the few budget places not in the Termini area. It's a popular, bright hotel and hostel close to the Vatican with dorm rooms (€19 per person), doubles (around €75), and self-catering accommodation. Kitchen, terrace, TV lounge and laundry.

Freedom Traveller, Via Gaeta 25, **t** 06 478 23 862, *info@freedom-traveller.it*, *www. freedom-traveller.it*. Big, brash backpacker hostel near Termini with an Internet café, kitchen facilities, common room, terrace and organized pub crawls. Dorm rooms from €18 per person; doubles from €50 per room. Breakfast is included.

****Pensione Primavera**, Piazza San Pantaleo 3, 00186, **t** 06 6880 3109, **f** 06 6880 3109. A little-known *pensione* with eight simple rooms, two minutes' walk from both Campo de' Fiori and Piazza Navona.

***Restivo**, Via Palestro 55, **t** 06 446 2172, **f** 06 445 2629. Immaculate *pensione* run by a sweet Sicilian lady, whose hall is cluttered with gifts from affectionate visitors. If it's full, try the plain, but very cheap **Cervia** (**t** 06 491057, **f** 06 491056, *hotelcervia@wnt.it*) in the same palazzo.

Apartments and Self-Catering

If you are here with family, or spending a couple of weeks in the city, renting an apartment can be a cheaper option.

Aldovrandi Residence, Via U Aldovrandi 11, **t** 06 322 1430, **f** 06 322 2181, *www.aldovrandiresidence.it*. Smart, upmarket flats with all mod cons in an equally smart neighbourhood not far from the Villa Borghese. There's a pool, restaurant and daily maid service. Prices start at around €1,000 for a week for a one-bedroom apartment.

cityapartments.it, Viale Opita Oppio 78, **t** 06 7698 3140, **f** 06 7696 7961, *admin@cityapartments.it*, *www.cityapartments.it*. A selection of apartments in great central locations throughout Rome (and other Italian cities). Charming, very personal service: can organize tours, airport pick-ups, and provide tourist information (*www.cityfacts.it*). Prices range from €80 to €250 per night. Highly recommended.

Bed and Breakfast

'Bed and Breakfast' was almost unheard of in Rome until 2000, when the flood of pilgrims meant that the city had to work out new ways of accommodating them. Now it's becoming increasingly popular and the APT tourist office (*see* tourist information, above, for address) publish a comprehensive list of bed and breakfast establishments. In addition, the Rome Chamber of Commerce provides a free booking service for establishments which have been given its quality award: **t** 06 679 5937, **f** 06 678 6521, *www.hotelreservation.it*.

Eating Out

Unlike many other Italians, the Romans aren't afraid to try something new. Chinese restaurants have appeared in droves, not to mention Arab, Korean and macrobiotic places. This should not be taken as a reflection on local cooking. Rome attracts talented chefs from all over Italy, and every region is represented by a restaurant somewhere in town, giving a microcosm of Italian cuisine you'll find nowhere else. For local specialities, wine, and a menu decoder, *see* **Food and Drink**, p.57. Though you can drop as much as €150 (without wine) if you follow the politicians and the TV crowd, prices somehow manage to keep close to the Italian average.

Very Expensive

La Pergola dell'Hotel Hilton, Via Cadlolo 101, **t** 06 3509 2152. Perched high above the city, this is one of the city's top restaurants for *alta cucina* served in elegant surroundings with all of Rome at your feet. Meals can be enjoyed on the roof terrace. Reserve well ahead. *Open Feb–Dec Tues–Sat 7.30–11.45pm.*

La Rosetta, Via della Rosetta 8, near the Pantheon, **t** 06 686 1002. Rome's best fish-only restaurant, with a Sicilian touch; even if you aren't dining, step in to admire the heap of shiny fish, oysters and sea-urchins arranged on the marble slab in the hall. Service isn't quite up to the standard of the food. Reserve well ahead. *Open Sept–July Mon–Sat 7.45–11.45pm, Thurs–Fri 1–3pm.*

Alberto Ciarla, Piazza San Cosimato 40, **t** 06 581 8668. Some way south of Santa Maria in Trastevere; the French-trained owner, proud enough to put his name on the sign, sees to it that everything is delicately and perfectly done, and graciously served: oysters, seafood ravioli and quite a few adventurous styles of *pesce crudo* (raw fish) are among the most asked for. *Open Mon–Sat 7.30–midnight, except 2 weeks in Jan and 1 week in Aug.*

Il Convivio, Vicolo dei Soldati 31, **t** 06 686 9432. Some of the most innovative cuisine in Rome, prepared with a knowing touch – unbeatable chilled fruit soups, baked *zucchini* flowers and, for dessert, exquisite pastries. Reserve. *Open Tues–Sat 1–2.30 and 8–10.30, Mon 8–10.30 only, exc 1 week in Aug.*

Checchino dal 1887, Via di Monte Testaccio 30, **t** 06 574 3816. Don't pass up a chance to dine at the acknowledged temple of old Roman cooking, owned by the same family for 107 years. Both the fancy and humble sides of Roman food are well represented, with plenty of the powerful offal dishes that Romans have been eating since ancient times, and the setting is unique – on the edge of Monte Testaccio, with one of Rome's best cellars excavated under the hill. *Open Sept–July Tues–Sat 12–3 and 8–11.30; closed Aug and over Christmas.*

Expensive

Il Toscano, Via Germanico 58, **t** 06 397 25717. Perhaps your best option in the tourist-trap Vatican area: family-run and very popular with Roman families, offering well-prepared Tuscan specialities like *pici* (rough, fresh spaghetti rolled by hand) in game sauce, and *fiorentina* steak – and home-made desserts. Reserve. *Open Sept–July Tues–Sat 12.30–3 and 8–11, except last week of Dec.*

Papà Giovanni, Via dei Sediari 4, **t** 06 686 5308. Brick walls, bottles and postcards provide the intimate setting for some of the most heavenly food in Rome, entirely based on availability in the market. This is your chance to dine like Caesar; the chef specializes in reviving old Roman recipes. *Open Mon–Sat 1–4 and 8–12, except first 2 weeks in Aug.*

Piperno, Via Monte de' Cenci 9, **t** 06 6880 6629. There is no better place to try *carciofi alla giudea* than right on the edge of the old ghetto at Rome's most famous purveyor of Roman–Jewish cooking – simple dishes on the whole, but prepared and served with refinement. *Open Sept–July Tues–Sat 12.45–2.30 and 8–10.30, Sun 12.30–3.*

Camponeschi, Piazza Farnese, **t** 06 687 4927. One of the top spots for star-spotting, this fine restaurant has views of the elegant Palazzo Farnese and its beautiful square. Charming, knowledgeable service. *Closed 10–24 Aug.*

Vecchia Roma, Piazza di Campitelli 18, **t** 06 686 4604. Good food, an imaginative seasonal menu and fine wine list in a lovely quiet setting with tables outdoors; not far from Piazza Venezia. *Open Sept–July Thurs–Tues 1–3.30 and 8–11.*

Margutta Vegetariano, Via Margutta 119, **t** 06 3600 1805. One of Rome's few vegetarian restaurants. Rather chic and somewhat overpriced by international vegetarian standards, but it's got a lovely plant-filled terrace on a quiet square. *Open Mon–Sat 12.30–3 and 7.30–11.30.*

Dal Bolognese, Piazza del Popolo 1, **t** 06 361 1426. With tables outside on the grand piazza and a view of the Pincio, this is the place to go to sample Emilian specialities – don't miss the *tortellini* or any other fresh pasta dish, and finish with *fruttini*, a selection of real fruit shells each filled with its own sorbet flavour. *Open Tues 8.15–11, Wed–Sun 12.45–3 and 8.15–11; closed Aug and Christmas.*

Da Paris, Piazza San Calisto 7/a, **t** 06 581 5378. Just beyond Piazza Santa Maria in Trastevere; serves classic Roman–Jewish cuisine; come here for the *minestra di arzilla* (skate soup), *tagliolini con scampi e fiori di zucca* ('little cut' pasta with prawns and pumpkin flowers). *Open Sept–July Tues–Sat 12–3 and 8–11, Sun 12–3.*

The quarters just outside the Aurelian wall and north and east of the Villa Borghese are more good places to look for restaurants:

Al Ceppo, Via Panama 2, **t** 06 841 9696. In the heart of the Parioli neighbourhood, with an open grill and warm, comfortable, elegant décor reminiscent of a bourgeois drawing room. Traditional Italian cuisine with specialities from the Marches, such as *linguine Monte Cónero* (with a clam sauce). Save space for the desserts. Tables outside in summer. *Reserve for Sunday lunch. Open Tues–Sun 1–3 and 8–11, except 3 weeks in Aug.*

Moderate

Less expensive places are not hard to find in the *centro storico*, but chances to eat anything different from Roman cuisine are pretty low.

Albistrò, Via dei Banchi Vecchi 140, **t** 06 686 5274. Sample the lamb with honey sauce or the chicken with leeks in this family-run restaurant. Arrive early to secure a table in the inner courtyard. An unusual treat are the tapas served on Mon, Thurs, Fri and Sat between 5.30 and 7.15. *Open late Aug–early July Thurs–Tues 7.30–11, Sun 12.30–3 and 7.30–11.*

Armando al Pantheon, Salita dei Crescenzi 31, **t** 06 6880 3034. An authentic Roman trattoria famous for *spaghetti cacio e pepe* (with pecorino cheese and black pepper) or *all'amatriciana*, *saltimbocca*, and a delicious ricotta tart. *Open Mon–Fri 12.30–3 and 7–11, Sat 12.30–3 only; closed Aug.*

Checco er Carettiere, Via Benedetta 10, **t** 06 580 0985. One of Trastevere's oldest inns, with well-prepared versions of popular Roman specialities like *coda alla vaccinara* and seafood. Famous for making even tripe taste good. The fish is just right. *Open Mon– Sat 12–3 and 7–12, Sun 12–4.30; closed May.*

La Cantina Tirolese, Via Vitelleschi 23, **t** 06 686 9994. A cheerful cellar in the Tyrolese style, with wooden benches, ironwork chandeliers and more than 30 Tyrolese fabric calendars on the walls – one for each year since the restaurant opened in 1971. Hearty, delicious food from the Alpine region, best enjoyed in winter. *Open Mon 8–1, Tues–Sun 12–4 and 8–1, except 2 weeks in Aug.*

Ditirambo, Piazza della Cancelleria, **t** 06 687 1626. A favourite with young Romans; you'll have to take the noise along with the good food. Home-made pasta and vegetarian dishes such as ravioli with ricotta and almond filling, cabbage leaves stuffed with mozzarella, and potato and mushroom flan with a melted cheese and truffle sauce. *Open Tues–Sun 1–3.30 and 8–11.30, Mon 8–11.30 only; closed 3 weeks in Aug.*

L'Eau Vive, Via Monterone 85, **t** 06 6880 1095. Only in Rome would you find a good French restaurant run by a Catholic lay missionary society – *sole meunière* and onion soup in the well-scrubbed and righteous atmosphere not far from the Pantheon. A nourishing meal at a modest price, served with serenity, will have you joining in a prayer to the Virgin before dessert; the fixed lunch menu is a great bargain. *Open Sept–July Mon–Sat 12.30–3 and 7.30–10.30.*

Café Romana de l'Hotel d'Inghilterra, Via Bocca di Leone 14, **t** 06 699 81500. Another exception: an elegant retreat in the heart of the shopping district at the foot of the Spanish Steps (dinner very expensive).

Grappolo d'Oro, Piazza della Cancelleria 80, **t** 06 689 7080. Near Campo de' Fiori; offers good value traditional Roman cooking. One of the best places to sit outside at night. *Open Sept–July Mon–Sat 12–3 and 8–11.*

Cheap

Africa, Via Gaeta 26, **t** 06 494 1077. A great Ethiopian/Eritrean restaurant that offers spicy meals at very low prices. *Open for breakfast; closed Mon.*

Acchiappafantasmi, Via dei Cappellari 66, **t** 06 687 3462. Rustically decorated trattoria close to the Campo de' Fiori, where you'll find delicious home cooking at reasonable prices. *Closed Tues and 2 weeks in Aug.*

Enoteca Corsi, Via del Gesù 87, **t** 06 679 0821. This buzzy, down-to-earth trattoria in the heart of the city is enormously popular thanks to its economical menu. *Closed Aug.*

Tram Tram, Via dei Reti 44, **t** 06 490416. Busy, trendy restaurant in the arty San Lorenzo neighbourhood east of Termini. *Closed Mon.*

Pizzerias

Roman pizza is crisp and thin, although the softer, thicker Neapolitan-style pizza has now won a fat slice of the market. Most pizzerias are open only for dinner, often until 2am.

Blu, Via dei Sabelli 193, **t** 06 494 0863. Good pizza and pasta at this mellow, candle-lit bistro in San Lorenzo. *Open Tues–Sun 6.30–12, 12–3 and 6.30–12.30; closed 2 weeks in Aug.*

Dar Poeta, Via del Bologna 46, **t** 06 588 0516. Enormously popular pizzeria in Trastevere, which also serves good *bruschette* and salads. Try the famous *calzone* with ricotta and Nutella. *Open Mon, Wed–Sun 12.30–3 and 6.30–12.30, Tues 6.30–12.30; closed Sept.*

La Montecarlo, Vicolo Savelli 12, **t** 06 686 1877. Sit elbow to elbow with your neighbours and duck as brilliant pizzas (€4–8, try the pizza with zucchini flowers), chairs and tables are whipped over your head. *Open May–Oct daily 12–3 and 6.30–1, except 2 weeks in Aug; Nov–April Tues–Sun only.*

PizzaRé, Via di Ripetta 14, **t** 06 321 1468. Proper Neapolitan pizzas – including a '*pizza sostanziosa*' with everything on it. Also good sandwiches. *Open daily 12.45–3.30 and 7.30–12.30; closed 2 weeks in Aug.* Also, **PizzaRé 2**, at Via Oslavia 39, Prati, **t** 06 372 1173.

Frontoni, Viale Trastevere 52, **t** 06 3630 7865. Choose what to put in your pizza sandwich from a large selection of fillings. *Open Mon–Thurs 11am–1am, Fri and Sat 11am–2am.*

Supplì e Pizza al Taglio, Via San Francesco a Ripa, **t** 06 588 0516. Besides slices of pizza and roasted chicken, try the famous *supplì* – deep-fried rice balls with melted mozzarella in the middle. *Open noon–midnight.*

Wine Bars/*Enoteche*

If the thought of a full meal sandwiched between Roman antiquities and Baroque treasures seems a bit much, consider lunch in a **wine bar**, which offers cured meat and cheese, soups, salads and occasional quiches and flans, and desserts (usually) made in-house. Choose from about 20 wines *alla mescita* (by the glass) and hundreds by the bottle:

Semidivino, Via Alessandria 230, **t** 06 4425 0795. A classy and intimate wine bar run by an Iranian expatriate. Good for a first-rate meal based on excellent salads, interesting cheeses, pork-cured meat and comforting soups at reasonable prices. *Open Sept–July Mon–Fri 12.30–2 and 7.30–11.30, Sat 7.30–11.30.*

Trimani, Via Cernaia 37/b, not far from Termini, **t** 06 446 9630. A haven of sanity where business types and intellectuals with demanding tastebuds flock at lunchtime. *Open Mon–Fri 12–12, Sat 8–12, except 2 weeks in Aug.*

Cul de Sac, Piazza Pasquino 73, **t** 06 6880 1094. A tiny – and always crammed – bottle-lined bar with a few tables outside which serves light meals to gastronomes (cured meats, cheeses, salads) as well as home-cooked lasagne and other dishes. *Open daily 12–12.30; closed May.*

Cavour 313, Via Cavour 313, **t** 06 678 5496. A civilized wood-beamed bar which serves delicious, high-quality snacks and light meals, lunchtime and evenings, to accompany whichever of its 500 wines you care to drink. *Open Mon–Sat 12.30–2.30 and 7.30–12.30, Sun 7.30–12.30 only; closed all day Sun between June and Sept.*

Il Cantinere de Santa Dorotea, Via Santa Dorotea, **t** 06 581 9025. Tucked away in Trastevere, this warm and welcoming *enoteca* has delicious soups, pastas and cured meats to accompany its excellent selection of wines.

Entertainment and Nightlife

The best entertainment in Rome is often in the passing cosmopolitan spectacle of its streets; as nightlife goes, it can be a real snoozer compared with other European cities, though if you don't expect too much you'll have a good time. If you're determined, the back streets around the Piazza Navona or Campo de' Fiori swarm with people in the evenings, and these are the places to come to plan your night ahead, as leaflets and free tickets are always being handed out. Another source is *Romac'è* (€1 from news stands, *www.romace.it*), with comprehensive listings and a small section in English, or the weekly *Time Out* with listings and articles (in Italian). The current hip neighbourhoods for going out are San Lorenzo, east of Termini station, and Testaccio, both former working-class areas which are becoming increasingly gentrified and filling up with cool bars and restaurants.

Rome can be uncomfortably sticky in August, but there's plenty going on. The ***Estate Romana*** (Roman Summer, *www.estateromana.caltanet.it*, **t** 06 3600 4399) is a three-month long festival of outdoor events, music, theatre and film (shown on outdoor screens around the city), and most museums run longer hours. Ask at the tourist office for information, check *Romac'è*, and keep an eye out for posters. A far older Roman party is the traditional **Festa de' Noantri** in Trastevere (16–31 July), where you may well find a gust of old Roman spontaneity along with music from all across the spectrum, acrobats, dancing and stall upon stall extending down Viale Trastevere and into the quarter's piazzas.

Opera, Classical Music, Theatre, Film

If you want to go to any events or concerts in Rome, try to get tickets as soon as possible to avoid disappointment. **Orbis**, Pza Esquilino 37, **t** 06 474 4776, *www.ticketone.it*, is a reliable agency for concert, opera and theatre tickets (*open Mon–Sat 9.30–1 and 4–7.30*).

From November until May you can take in a performance at the **Teatro dell'Opera di Roma**, Piazza B Gigli, off Via del Viminale, **t** 800 016665, *www.opera.roma.it*. Other concerts are performed at and by the **Accademia**

Nazionale di Santa Cecilia, in the auditorium on Via della Conciliazione 4, **t** 06 361 1044, and by the **Accademia Filarmonica Romana**, Via Flaminia 118, box office, **t** 06 6880 9222. Medieval, Baroque, chamber and choral music are performed at the **Oratorio del Gonfalone**, Via del Gonfalone 32/a, **t** 06 687 5952.

Traditionally during the summer there has been a range of special seasons, although of late Rome has become noticeably sluggish in organizing programmes. Evening concerts are held outside in the **Teatro di Marcello**, **t** 06 481 4800, or **t** 06 780 4314 (*mid-June–Sept*), and concerts are performed by the Accademia di Santa Cecilia and visiting international orchestras at **Villa Giulia** (*July*). The opera moves outside in the summer – in the **Terme di Caracalla** until a few years ago, when it was feared that the site was being damaged. Every year there's talk of a return to the glorious baths, but meanwhile, the **Villa Borghese** and the **soccer stadium** serve as alternate venues. The listings guide *Romac'è* (*see* above) has a comprehensive list of other one-off venues.

Despite the Italian tendency to dub all foreign films, you can find films in *versione originale* at:

Alcazar, Via Cardinal Merry del Val 14, Trastevere, **t** 06 588 0099 (*Mon*).

Nuovo Sacher, Largo Ascianghi 1, Trastevere, **t** 06 5811 8116 (*Mon and Tues*). One of the best places to see new cinema in Rome.

Quirinetta, Via M Minghetti 4, **t** 06 679 0012.

Pasquino, Piazza Sant'Egidio, near Santa Maria in Trastevere, **t** 06 580 3622 (*daily*).

Cafés and Bars

Caffè Greco, Via Condotti 86, **t** 06 679 1700. When you're tired of window-shopping you can rest your legs at Rome's oldest café (1760) and sit where Keats and Casanova sipped their java – an institution that offers the cheapest chance for a 20-minute dose of *ancien régime* luxury in Rome.

Rosati, Piazza del Popolo 4, **t** 06 322 5859. Another *grand café*: an elegant place founded in 1922, and popular with the Roman intelligentsia, attracted by its extravagant ice creams.

Babington's Tea Rooms, Piazza di Spagna 23. 150 years old; serves scones and tea or a full lunch in the proper Victorian atmosphere.

Sant'Eustachio, Piazza Sant'Eustachio 82, near Piazza Navona. Trendy home of Rome's most famous coffee; tell them to mind the sugar.

Bar della Pace, Via della Pace 5. Another kind of Roman bar is represented by this ultra-hip place frequented by celebrities and a place for serious posing.

Vineria Reggio, Campo de' Fiori 15. A more funky and friendly atmosphere can be found most evenings here at this relaxed traditional wine bar/shop with tables outside.

Il Gelato di San Crispino, Via della Panetteria 42, near the Trevi Fountain. It's not hard to find *gelato* on every corner in Rome, but hold out for the best the city has to offer.

Forno del Ghetto, Via del Portico d'Ottavia 2 (*closed Sat*). Another novelty are these sweets from the Jewish bakery.

Rock, Jazz and Clubs

Rome has a select band of clubs with live music – *Romac'è* will have details.

Il Locale, Vicolo del Fico 3, **t** 06 687 9075. Features hip and trendy Italian bands.

Big Mama, Vicolo San Francesco a Ripa 18, in Trastevere, **t** 06 581 2451, *www.bigmamma.it*. Mainly rock venue.

Alpheus, Via del Commercio, 36, in Ostiense, **t** 06 574 7826. A blues club.

Caffè Latino, Via de Monte Testaccio 96, **t** 06 5728 8556. Dance club with live latin music.

For **jazz** – which has a strong local following – try the following venues. All feature foreign as well as Italian performers:

Alexanderplatz, Via Ostia 9, **t** 06 3974 2171.

Gregory's, Via Gregoriana 54, **t** 06 679 6386, *www.gregorysjazzclub.it*.

For serious **dancing** try the clubs below. All are what Italians call *di tendenza*, meaning they keep up with current UK and US trends. Most indoor clubs and music venues close down completely in late July and August.

Akab Cave, Via Monte Testaccio 69, **t** 06 578 2390. A hip favourite on two levels in Testaccio with live music and DJ sessions.

Alien, Via Velletri 13, near Piazza Fiume, **t** 06 841 2212.

Alpheus, Via del Commercio 36, off Via Ostiense, **t** 06 574 7826.

Gilda, Via Mario de' Fiori 97, close to the Spanish Steps, **t** 06 678 4838. Less juvenile (jacket required).

To know what Rome is, visit the little church of San Clemente, unobtrusively hidden away on the back streets behind the Colosseum. The Baroque façade conceals a 12th-century basilica with a beautiful marble choir screen 600 years older. In 1857 a cardinal from Boston discovered the original church of 313, one of the first great Christian basilicas, just underneath. And beneath *that* are two buildings and a Temple of Mithras from the time of Augustus; from it you can walk out into a Roman alley that looks exactly as it did 2,000 years ago, now some 28ft below ground level. There are commemorative plaques in San Clemente, placed there by a Medici duke, a bishop of New York, and the last chairman of the Bulgarian Communist Party.

You are not going to get to the bottom of this city, whether your stay is for three days or a month. With its legions of headless statues, acres of paintings, 913 churches and megatons of artistic sediment, this metropolis of aching feet will wear down even the most resolute of travellers (and travel writers). The name Rome passed out of the plane of reality into legend some 2,200 years ago, when princes as far away as China first began to hear of the faraway city and its invincible armies. At the same time the Romans were cooking up a personified goddess, the Divine Rome, and beginning the strange myth of their destiny to conquer and pacify the world, a myth that would still haunt Europe a thousand years later.

In our prosaic times, though, you may find it requires a considerable effort of the imagination to break through to the past Romes of the Caesars and popes. They exist, but first you will need to peel away the increasingly thick veneer of the 'Third Rome', the burgeoning, thoroughly up-to-date creation of post-Reunification Italy. Ancient Rome at the height of its glory had perhaps a million and a half people; today there are four million, and at any given time at least half of them will be pushing their way into the metro train while you are trying to get off. The popes, for all their centuries of experience in spectacle and ceremony, cannot often steal the show in this new Rome, and have to share the stage with a deplorable over-abundance of preposterous politicians, with *Cinecittà* and the rest of the cultural apparatus of a great nation, and of course with the tourists, who sometimes put on the best show in town. The old guard Romani, now a minority in a city swollen with new arrivals, bewail the loss of Rome's slow and easy pace, its vintage brand of *dolce vita* that once impressed other Italians, let alone foreigners. Lots of money, lots of traffic and an endless caravan of tour buses have a way of compromising even the most beautiful cities. Don't concern yourself; the present is only one snapshot from a 2,600-year history, and no one has ever left Rome disappointed.

History

The beginnings are obscure enough. Historians believe the settlement of the Tiber Valley began some time about 1000 BC, when an outbreak of volcanic eruptions in the Alban Hills to the south forced the Latin tribes down into the lowlands. Beyond that there are few clues for the archaeologists to follow. But remembering that every ancient legend conceals a kernel of truth – perhaps more poetic than scientific – it would be best to follow the accounts of Virgil, the poet of the Empire, and Livy, the great 1st-century chronicler and mythographer.

When Virgil wrote, in the reign of Augustus, Greek culture was an irresistible force in all the recently civilized lands of the Mediterranean. For Rome, Virgil concocted the story of Aeneas, fleeing from Troy after the Homeric sack and finding his way to *Latium*. Descent from the Trojans, however specious, connected Rome to the Greek world and made it seem less of an upstart. As Virgil tells it, Aeneas' son Ascanius founded Alba Longa, a city that by the 800s was leader of the Latin Confederation. Livy takes up the tale with Numitor, a descendant of Ascanius and rightful king of Alba Longa, tossed off the throne by his usurping brother Amulius. In order that Numitor should have no heirs, Amulius forced Numitor's daughter Rhea Silvia into service as a Vestal Virgin. Here Rome's destiny begins, with an appearance in the Vestals' chambers of the god Mars, staying just long enough to leave Rhea Silvia pregnant with the precocious twins Romulus and Remus.

When Amulius found out he of course packed them away in a little boat, which the gods directed up the Tiber to a spot near today's Piazza Bocca della Verità. The famous she-wolf looked after the babies, until they were found by a shepherd, who brought them up. When Mars revealed to the grown twins their origin, they returned to Alba Longa to sort out Amulius, and then returned (in 753 BC, traditionally) to found the city the gods had ordained. Romulus soon found himself constrained to kill Remus, who would not believe the auguries that declared his brother should be king, and thus set the pattern for the bloody millennium of Rome's history to come.

The legends portray early Rome as a glorified pirates' camp, and the historians are only too glad to agree. Finding themselves short of women, the Romans stole some from the Sabines. Not especially interested in farming or learning a trade, they adopted the hobby of subjugating their neighbours and soon polished it to a fine art.

Seven Kings of Rome

Following Livy's legendary history, Romulus was the first, followed by Numa Pompilius, who laid down the forms for Rome's cults and priesthoods, its auguries and College of Vestals. Tullius Hostilius, the next, made Rome ruler of all *Latium*, and Ancus Martius founded the port of Ostia. The next king, Tarquinius Priscus, was an Etruscan, and probably gained his throne thanks to a conquest by one of the Etruscan city-states. Tarquin made a city of Rome, building the first real temples, the Cloaca Maxima or Great Drain, and the first Circus Maximus.

His successor, Servius Tullius, restored Latin rule, inaugurated the division between patricians (the senatorial class) and plebeians, and built a great wall to keep the Etruscans out. It apparently did not work, for as next king we find the Etruscan Tarquinius Superbus (about 534 BC), another great builder. His misfortune was to have a hot-headed son like Tarquinius Sextus, who imposed himself on a noble and virtuous Roman maiden named Lucretia (cf. Shakespeare's *Rape of Lucrece*). She committed public suicide; the enraged Roman patricians, under the leadership of Lucius Junius Brutus, chased out proud Tarquin and the Etruscan dynasty for ever. The Republic was established before the day was out, with Brutus as first consul, or chief magistrate.

The Invincible Republic

Taking an oath never to allow another king in Rome, the patricians designed a novel form of government, a Republic (*res publica* – public thing) governed by the two consuls elected by the Senate, the assembly of the patricians themselves; later innovations in the Roman constitution would include a tribune, an official with inviolable powers elected by the plebeians to protect their interests. The two classes fought like cats and dogs at home but combined with impressive resolve in their foreign wars. Etruscans, Aequi, Hernici, Volsci, Samnites and Sabines – all powerful nations – were defeated by Rome's citizen armies. Some of Livy's best stories come from this period, such as the taking of Rome by marauding Gauls in 390 BC, when the cackling of geese awakened the Romans and saved the citadel on the Capitoline Hill.

By 270 BC Rome had eliminated all its rivals to become master of Italy. It had taken about 200 years, and in the next 200 Roman rule would be established from Spain to Egypt. The first stage had proved more difficult. In Rome's final victory over the other Italians the city digested its rivals: whole cities and tribes simply disappeared, their peoples joining the mushrooming population of Rome. After 270 it was much the same story, but on a wider scale. In the three Punic Wars against Carthage (264–146 BC) Rome gained almost the whole of the western Mediterranean; Greece, North Africa and Asia Minor were absorbed in small bites over the next 100 years. Rome's history was now the history of the Western world.

Imperial Rome

The old pirates' nest had never really changed its ways. Rome, like old Assyria, makes a fine example of that species of carnivore that can only live by continuous conquest. When the Romans took Greece they first met Culture, and it had the effect on them that puberty has on little boys. After some bizarre behaviour, evidenced in the continuous civil wars (Sulla, Marius, Pompey, Julius Caesar), the Romans began tarting up their city in the worst way, vacuuming all the gold, paintings, statues, cooks, poets and architects out of the civilized East. Beginning perhaps with Pompey, every contender for control of the now constitutionally deranged Republic added some great work to the city centre: Pompey's theatre, the Julian Basilica, and something from almost every emperor up to Constantine. Julius Caesar and Augustus were perhaps Rome's greatest benefactors, initiating every sort of progressive legislation, turning dirt lanes into paved streets and erecting new fora, temples and the vast network of aqueducts. In their time Rome's population probably reached the million mark, surpassing Antioch and Alexandria as the largest city in the Western world.

It was Augustus who effectively ended the Republic in 27 BC, by establishing his personal rule and reducing the old constitution to formalities. During the imperial era that followed his reign, Rome's position as administrative and judicial centre of the Empire kept it growing, drawing in a new cosmopolitan population of provincials from Britain to Mesopotamia. The city became the unquestioned capital of banking and finance – and religion; Rome's policy was always to induct everyone's local god as an honorary Roman, and every important cult image and relic was abducted to the

Capitoline Temple. The emperor himself was *Pontifex Maximus*, head priest of Rome, whose title derives from the early Roman veneration of bridges (*pontifex* means keeper of bridges). St Peter, of course, arrived, and was duly martyred in AD 67. His successor, Linus, became the first pope – or *pontiff* – first in the long line of hierophants who would inherit Rome's long-standing religious tradition.

For all its glitter, Rome was still the complete predator, producing nothing and consuming everything. No one with any spare *denarii* would be foolish enough to go into business with them, when the only real money was to be made from government, speculation or real estate. At times almost half the population of Roman citizens (as opposed to slaves) was on the public dole. Naturally, when things went sour they really went sour. Uncertain times made Aurelian give Rome a real defensive wall in AD 275. By AD 330 the necessity of staying near the armies at the front led the western emperors to spend most of their time at army headquarters in Milan. Rome became a bloated backwater, and after three sackings (Alaric the Goth in 410, Gaiseric the Vandal in 455 and Odoacer the Goth in 476), there was no reason to stay. The sources disagree: perhaps 100,000 inhabitants were left by the year 500, perhaps as few as 10,000.

Rome in the Shadows

Contrary to what most people think, Rome did not ever quite go down the drain in the Dark Ages. Its lowest point in prestige undoubtedly came in the 14th century, when the popes were at Avignon. The number of important churches built in the Dark Ages and the mosaics that embellished them, equal in number if not in quality to those of Ravenna, testify to the city's importance. There was certainly enough to attract a few more sacks (Goths and Greeks in the 6th-century wars, Saracens from Africa in 746).

As in many other Western cities, but on a larger scale, the bishops of Rome – the popes – picked up some of the pieces when civil administration disintegrated and extended their power to temporal offices. Chroniclers report fights between them and the local barons, self-proclaimed heirs of the Roman Senate, as early as 741. It must have been a fascinating place, much too big for its population though still, thanks to the popes, thinking of itself as the centre of the Western world. The forum was abandoned, as were the gigantic baths, rendered useless as the aqueducts decayed. Almost all of the temples and basilicas survived, converted to Christian churches. Hadrian's massive tomb on the banks of the Tiber was converted into a fortress, the Castel Sant'Angelo, an impregnable haven for the popes in troubled times.

The popes deserve credit for keeping Rome alive, but the tithe money trickling in from across Europe confirmed the city in its parasitical behaviour. With two outrageous forgeries, the 'Donation of Constantine' and the 'Donation of Pepin', the popes staked their claim to temporal power in Italy. Charlemagne visited the city after driving the Lombards out in 800; during a prayer vigil in St Peter's on Christmas Eve, Pope Leo III sneaked up behind the Frankish king and set an imperial crown on his head. The surprise coronation, which the outraged Charlemagne could not or would not undo, established the precedent of Holy Roman Emperors having to cross over the Alps to receive their crown from the pope; for centuries to come Rome was able to keep its hand in the political struggles of all Europe.

Arnold of Brescia and Rienzo

Not that Rome ever spoke with one voice; over the next 500 years it was only the idea of Rome, as the spiritual centre of the universal Christian community, that kept the actual city of Rome from disappearing altogether. Down to some 20–30,000 people in this era, Rome evolved a sort of stable anarchy, in which the major contenders for power were the popes and noble families. First among the latter were the Orsini and the Colonna, racketeer clans who built fortresses for themselves among the ruins and fought like gangs in 1920s Chicago. Very often outsiders would get into the game. A remarkable woman of obscure birth named Theodora took the Castel Sant'Angelo in the 880s; with the title of Senatrix she and her daughter Marozia ruled Rome for decades. Various German emperors seized the city, but were never able to hold it. In the 10th century, things got even more complicated as the Roman people began to assert themselves. Caught between the people and the barons, nine of the 24 popes in that century managed to get themselves murdered. The 1140s was a characteristic period of this convoluted history. A Jewish family, the Pierleoni, held power, and a Jewish antipope sat enthroned in St Peter's. Mighty Rome occupied itself with a series of wars against its neighbouring village of Tivoli, and usually lost. A sincere monkish reformer appeared, the Christian and democrat Arnold of Brescia; he recreated the Senate and almost succeeded in establishing Rome as a free *comune*, but in 1155 he fell into the hands of the German emperor Frederick Barbarossa, who sold him to the English pope (Adrian IV) for hanging.

Too many centuries of this made Rome uncomfortable for the popes, who frequently removed themselves to Viterbo. The final indignity came when, under French pressure, the papacy decamped entirely to Avignon in 1309. Pulling strings from a distance, the popes only made life more complicated. Into the vacuum they created stepped one of the noblest Romans of them all, later to be the subject of Wagner's first opera. Cola di Rienzo was the son of an innkeeper, but he had a good enough education to read the Latin inscriptions that lay on the ruins all around him, and Livy, Cicero and Tacitus wherever he could find them. Obsessed by the idea of re-establishing Roman glory, he talked at the bewildered inhabitants until they caught the fever too. With Rienzo as Tribune of the People, the Roman Republic was reborn in 1347. Power does corrupt, however, in Rome more than any spot on the globe, and an increasingly fat and ridiculous Rienzo was hustled out of Rome by the united nobles before the year was out. His return to power, in 1354, ended with his murder by a mob after only two months. Rome was now at its lowest ebb, with only some 15,000 people, and prosperity and influence were not to be completely restored until the reign of Pope Nicholas V after 1447.

The New Rome

The old papacy, before Avignon, had largely been a tool of the Roman nobles; periods when it was able to achieve real independence were the exception rather than the rule. In the more settled conditions of the 15th century, a new papacy emerged, richer and more sophisticated. Political power, as a guarantee of stability, was its goal, and a series of talented Renaissance popes saw their best hopes for achieving this by rebuilding Rome. By the 1500s this process was in full swing. Under Julius II (1503–13) the papal domains for the first time were run like a modern state; Julius also laid plans for the rebuilding of St Peter's, beginning the great building programme that transformed the city. New streets were laid out, especially Via Giulia and the grand avenues radiating from Piazza del Popolo; Julius' architect, Bramante, knocked down medieval Rome with such gay abandon that Raphael nicknamed him 'Ruinante'.

Over the next two centuries the work continued at a frenetic pace. Besides St Peter's, hundreds of churches were either built or rebuilt, and cardinals and noble families lined the streets with new palaces, imposing if not always beautiful. A new departure in urban design was developed in the 1580s, under Sixtus V, recreating some of the monumentality of ancient Rome. Piazzas linked by a network of straight boulevards were cleared in front of the major religious sites; each would eventually be marked with an Egyptian obelisk.

The New Rome, symbol of the Counter-Reformation and the majesty of the popes, was, however, bought at a terrible price. Besides the destruction of Bramante, buildings that had survived substantially intact for 1,500 years were cannibalized for their marble; the popes wantonly destroyed more of ancient Rome than Goths or Saracens had ever managed. To pay for their programme, they taxed the economy of the Papal States out of existence. Areas of Lazio turned into wastelands as exasperated farmers simply abandoned them; the other cities of Lazio and Umbria were set back centuries in their development. The New Rome was proving as voracious a predator as the old. Worst of all, the new papacy in the 16th century instituted terror as an instrument of public policy. In the course of the previous century the last vestiges of Roman liberty had been gradually extinguished. The popes tried to extend their power by playing a game of high-stakes diplomacy between Emperor Charles V of Spain and King Francis I of France, but reaped a bitter harvest in the 1527 Sack of Rome. An out-of-control imperial army occupied the city for almost a year, causing tremendous destruction, while the disastrous Pope Clement VII looked on helplessly from the Castel Sant'Angelo. Afterwards the popes were happy to become part of the Imperial–Spanish system. Political repression was fiercer than anywhere else in Italy; the Inquisition was refounded in 1542 by Paul III, and book burnings, torture of freethinkers and executions became even more common than in Spain itself.

The End of Papal Rule

By about 1610 there was no Roman foolish enough to get burned at the stake; at the same time workmen were adding the last stones to the cupola of St Peter's. It was the end of an era, but the building continued. A thick accretion of Baroque, like coral, collected over Rome. Bernini did his Piazza Navona fountain in 1650, and the Colonnade for St Peter's 15 years later. The political importance of the popes, however, disappeared with surprising finality. As Joseph Stalin was later to note, the popes had plenty of Bulls, but few army divisions, and they drifted into irrelevance in the power politics of modern Europe during the Thirty Years War.

Rome was left to enjoy a decadent but pleasant twilight. A brief interruption came when revolutionaries in 1798 again proclaimed the Roman Republic, and a French army sent the pope packing. Rome later became part of Napoleon's empire, but papal rule was restored in 1815. Another republic appeared in 1848, on the crest of that romantic year's revolutionary wave, but this time a French army besieged the city and had the pope propped back on his throne by July 1849. Garibaldi, the republic's military commander, barely escaped with his life.

For twenty years Napoleon III maintained a garrison in Rome to look after the pope, and consequently Rome became the last part of Italy to join the new Italian kingdom. After the French defeat in the war of 1870, Italian troops blew a hole in the old Aurelian wall near the Porta Pia and marched in. Pius IX, who ironically had decreed papal infallibility just the year before, locked himself in the Vatican and pouted; the popes were to be 'prisoners' until Mussolini's Concordat of 1929, by which they agreed to recognize the Italian state.

A Little Orientation

Two Walls

Of Rome's earliest wall, built by King Servius Tullius before the Republic, little remains; you can see one of the last surviving bits outside Stazione Termini. The second, built by Aurelian in AD 275, is one of the wonders of Rome, though taken for granted. With its 19km length and 383 towers, it is one of the largest ever built in Europe – and certainly the best-preserved of antiquity. In places you can see almost perfectly preserved bastions and monumental gates.

Three Romes

Historians and Romans often think of the city in this way. Classical Rome began on the Monte Palatino, and its business and administrative centre stayed nearby, in the original Forum and the great Imperial Fora built around it. Many of the busiest parts lay to the south, where now you see only green on the tourist office's map. After Rome's fall these areas were never really rebuilt, and even substantial ruins like Trajan's Baths remain unexcavated.

The Second Rome, that of the popes, had its centre in the Campus Martius, the plain west and north of the Capitoline Hill, later expanding to include the 'Leonine City' around St Peter's, and the new Baroque district around Piazza del Popolo and the Spanish Steps.

The Third Rome, capital of United Italy, has expanded in all directions; the closest it has to a centre is Via del Corso.

As capital of the new state, Rome underwent another building boom. New streets like Via Vittorio Veneto and Via Nazionale made circulation easier; villas and gardens disappeared under blocks of speculative building (everything around Stazione Termini, for example); long-needed projects like the Tiber embankments were built; and the new kingdom strove to impress the world with gigantic, absurd public buildings and monuments, such as the Altar of the Nation (Il Vittoriano) and the Finance Ministry on Via XX Settembre, as big as two Colosseums. Growth has been steady; from some 200,000 people in 1879, Rome has since increased twentyfold.

The Twentieth Century

In 1922 the city was the objective of Mussolini's 'March on Rome', when the Fascist leader used his blackshirt squads to demand, and win, complete power in the Italian government, though he himself famously made the journey into town by train, and in his best suit. Mussolini was one more figure who wanted to create a 'New Roman Empire' for Italy. For twenty years Piazza Venezia was the chosen theatre for his oratorical performances. He also had big ideas for the city itself: it was under Fascism that many of the relics of ancient Rome were first opened up as public monuments in order to remind Italians of their heritage, and Via dei Fori Imperiali was driven past the Forum, destroying some of the archaeological sites in the

Seven Hills

Originally they were much higher; centuries of building, rebuilding and river flooding have made the ground level in the valleys much higher, and emperors and popes shaved bits off their tops in building programmes. The Monte Capitolino, smallest but most important, now has Rome's City Hall, the Campidoglio, roughly on the site of ancient Rome's greatest temple, that of Jupiter Greatest and Best. The Palatino, adjacent to it, was originally the most fashionable district, and got entirely covered by the palaces of the emperors.

The plebeian Aventino lies to the south of it, across the Circus Maximus. Between the Colosseum and the Stazione Termini, the Esquilino, the Viminale and the Quirinale stand in a row. The Quirinale was long the residence of the popes, and later of the Italian kings. Finally, there is the Monte Celio south of the Colosseum, now an oasis of parkland and ancient churches. Rome has other hills not included in the canonical seven: Monte Vaticano, from which the Vatican takes its name, Monte Pincio, including the Villa Borghese, and the Gianicolo, the long ridge above Trastevere, which the ancients called the Janiculum.

Fourteen Regions

Ancient Rome had neither street lights nor street signs; modern Rome has plenty of both. Being Rome, of course, the street signs are of marble. In the corner, you will notice a small number in Roman numerals; this refers to the *rione*, or ward. In the Middle Ages, there were 14 of these, descendants of the 14 *regii* of the ancient city; even after the fall of Rome they maintained their organization.

process. His greatest legacy was the EUR suburb, the projected site of a world exhibition for 1942, and a showcase of his preferred Fascist–classical architecture. At the end of the war it was only half built, but the Italians, not wishing to waste anything, decided to finish the project, and it now houses a few of Rome's museums and sports venues.

Since the war Rome has continued to grow fat as the capital of the often ramshackle, notoriously corrupt political system thrown up by the Italian Republic, and the headquarters of the smug *classe politica* that ran it. Rome has been accused by Lombard regionalists of drawing off wealth from the productive areas of Italy in much the same way that it once demanded to be fed by the Empire; nevertheless, Romans joined in Italy's 'Moral Revolution' of the 1990s, abusing the old-style political bosses, despite the fact that a great many in this city of civil servants themselves benefited from the system.

Today's visitors to the city enjoy the benefits of substantial improvements made for the Holy Year 2000, including over 700 public works projects (restorations, refurbished museums, upgraded transportation and additional car parks). Among the highlights for those who have not been to Rome for a few years are the Domus Aurea, Musei Capitolini, the façade of Saint Peter's, the Vittoriano monument on Piazza Venezia, and Trajan's Markets.

Around the City

Piazza Venezia

This traffic-crazed, thoroughly awful piazza may be a poor introduction to Rome, but it makes a good place to start, with the ruins of old Rome on one side and the boutiques and bureaucracies of the new city on the other. The piazza takes its name from the **Palazzo Venezia**, built for the Venetian Cardinal Pietro Barbo (afterwards Pope Paul II) in 1455, but long the Embassy of the Venetian Republic. Mussolini made it his residence, leaving a light on all night to make the Italians think he was working. His famous balcony, from which he would declaim to the 'oceanic' crowds in the square (renamed the Forum of the Fascist Empire in those days) still holds its prominent place, a bad memory for the Italians.

Nowadays the palazzo holds a **museum of Renaissance and Baroque decorative arts** (***t** 06 679 8865; open Tues–Sun 8.30–7.30; adm*), with an impressive collection that runs from Byzantine ivories to Renaissance bronzes; the vast Sala del Mappamondo was Mussolini's office. The palace complex was built around the ancient church of **San Marco** (***t** 06 679 5305; open 9.30–1 and 4.30–6.45; no entry during services*), with a 9th-century mosaic in the apse. Parts of the building are as old as AD 400, and the façade is by the Renaissance architect Benedetto di Maiano.

Long ago the southern edge of this piazza had approaches up to the Monte Capitolino. The hill is still there, though it's now entirely blocked out by the **Altar of**

the Nation (also known as **Il Vittoriano**, the 'Wedding Cake' or the 'Typewriter'), Risorgimento Italy's own self-inflicted satire and one of the world's apotheoses of kitsch (***t*** *06 699 1718; open Tues–Sun 10.30–6.30, last adm 5.30*). Its size and its solid marble walls are explained by the 1880s prime minister who commissioned it; he happened to have a marble quarry in his home district of Brescia. Recounting its sculptural allegories would take pages – but of the two big bronze imperial-style *quadrigae* on top, one represents Italian Liberty and the other Italian Unity. In the centre, the modest virtues of Vittorio Emanuele II have earned him a 38ft bronze equestrian statue, perhaps the world's largest. Beneath him, Italy's Unknown Soldier sleeps peacefully with a round-the-clock guard. It's worth the climb to the top terrace for staggering views across the city (without the blight of the Typewriter itself to spoil them). Il Vittoriano is home to a pair of **exhibition galleries** (*times depend on exhibition; adm*), another temporary exhibition space, and two military museums: the **Sacrario Militare della Bandiera** (a flag museum, *open Tues–Sun 9–1*) and the **Museo Centrale del Risorgimento** (*open Tues–Sun 10.30–6.30, last adm 5.30*). On the left-hand side of the monument you can see the remains of the republican Roman tomb of C. Publius Bibulus.

Monte Capitolino (The Capitoline Hill)

Behind the Vittoriano, two stairways lead to the top of the hill. This is a fateful spot; in 121 BC the great reformer Tiberius Gracchus was murdered here by what today would be called a 'right-wing death squad'. Almost a millennium and a half later Cola di Rienzo was trying to escape Rome in disguise when an enraged mob recognized him by the rings on his fingers and tore him to pieces. Rienzo built the left-hand staircase, and was the first to climb it. It leads to **Santa Maria in Aracoeli** (*Scalinata d'Aracoeli;* ***t*** *06 679 8155; open 6.30–5.30*), begun in the 7th century over the temple of Juno Moneta – the ancient Roman Mint was adjacent to it. The Aracoeli, which in Rienzo's time served as a council hall for the Romans, is one of the most revered of churches; legend has it that one of the Sibyls of Tivoli prophesied the coming of Jesus and told Augustus to build a temple here to the 'first born of God'. Inside you can seek out frescoes by Pinturicchio (*San Bernardino of Siena*) and Gozzoli (*San Antonio of Padua*), and a tombstone by Donatello, near the entrance.

The second stairway takes you to the real heart of Rome, Michelangelo's **Piazza del Campidoglio**, passing a rather flattering statue of Rienzo set on a bronze pedestal. Bordering the piazza, a formidable cast of statues includes the Dioscuri, who come from Pompey's Theatre, and Marforio (in the Musei Capitolini courtyard), a river god once employed as a 'talking statue', decorated with graffiti and placards commenting on current events. The great 2nd-century AD bronze equestrian statue of the benign and philosophical Emperor **Marcus Aurelius**, that stood on the plinth in the middle of the piazza from the 16th century until 1981, has been fully restored and regilded and is now in the Musei Capitolini – fortunately enough, since it was an old Roman saying that the world would end when all the gold flaked off. The Christians of old only refrained from melting him down for cash because they believed he was not Marcus Aurelius, but Constantine. A faithful copy now stands in the piazza.

The Musei Capitolini

Michelangelo's original plans may have been adapted and tinkered with by later architects, but nevertheless his plan for the Campidoglio has come out as one of the triumphs of Renaissance design. The centrepiece, the **Palazzo Senatorio**, Rome's city

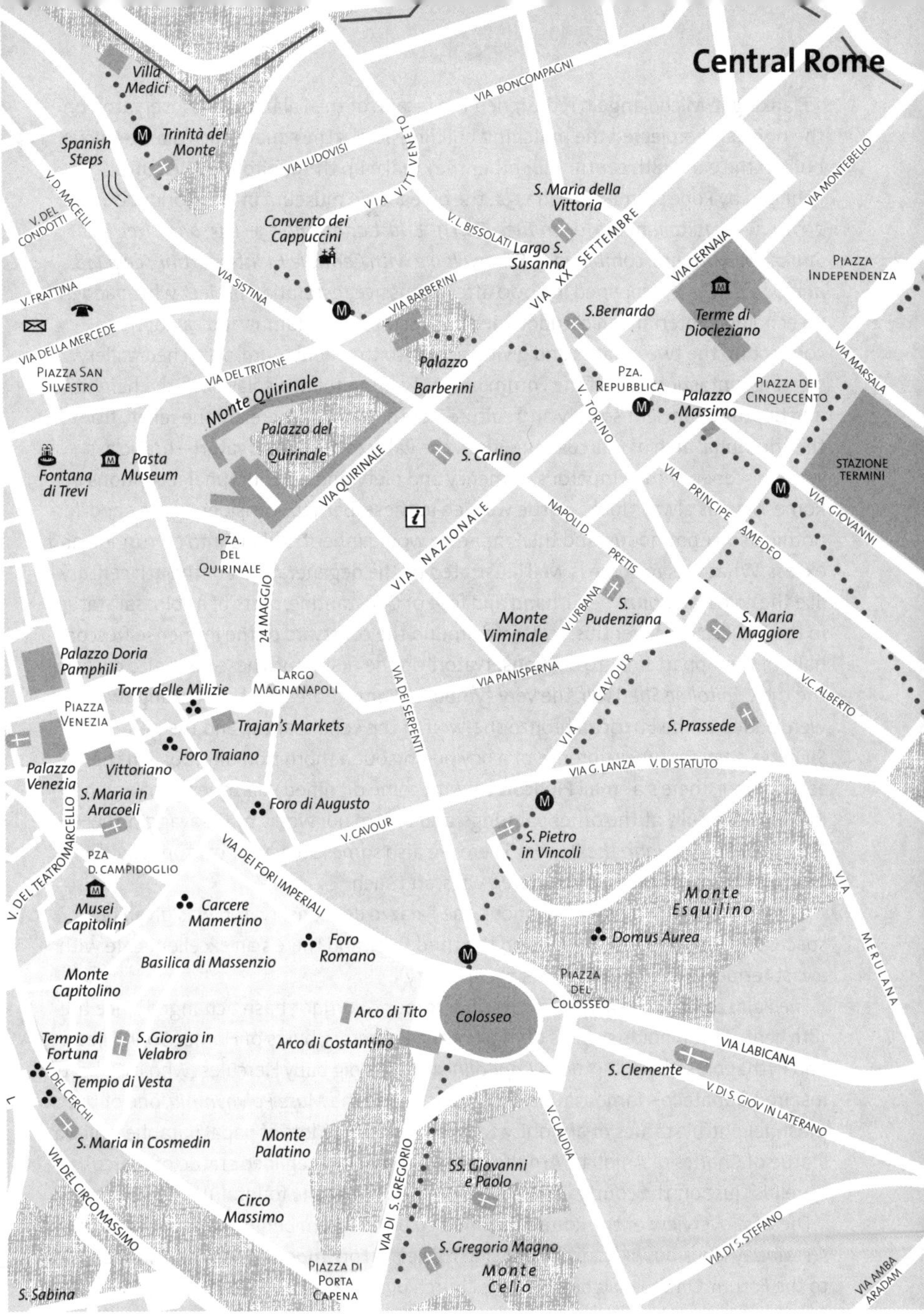

hall, with its distinctive stairway and bell tower, is built over the ruins of the Roman *tabularium*, the state archive.

At the base of the stair, note the statue of Minerva, standing guard proudly in her aspect as the allegorical goddess Roma.

Flanking it, Michelangelo redesigned the façade of the Palazzo dei Conservatori on the right, and projected the matching building across the square, the Palazzo Nuovo, built in the early 18th century. Together they make up the **Capitoline Museums**. Founded by Pope Clement XII in 1734, the oldest true museum in the world (***t*** *06 6710 2071, www.capitolium.org; open Tues–Sun 9–8, last adm 7, hols 9–1.45; adm, free last Sun of every month; combined ticket available with Centrale Montemartini, see p.148, audioguide €3.50*) reopened in 2000 after a massive restoration project which added an echoing subterranean corridor lined with sculpture, columns and sarcophagi, connecting the two palaces and giving access to the Tabularium, an arched gallery offering fantastic views of the Forum below. The Capitolini display both the heights and depths of ancient society and culture. For the heights there are the reliefs from the triumphal arch of Marcus Aurelius in the **Palazzo dei Conservatori** – first-class work in scenes of the Emperor's clemency and piety, and his triumphal receptions in Rome. Marcus always looks a little worried in these, perhaps considering his good-for-nothing son Commodus, and the Empire he would inherit, sinking into corruption and excess. What was to come is well illustrated by the degenerate art of the 4th century, like the colossal bronze head, hand and foot of Constantine, parts of a colossal statue in the Basilica of Maxentius, scattered around the courtyard or the immense frescoed halls of the 'Appartamento dei Conservatori' on the first floor. These halls also contain the the *Capitoline She-Wolf*, the very symbol of Rome (note that the suckling twins were added to the Etruscan bronze she-wolf in the Renaissance), and the gentle *Spinario*, a 1st-century BC bronze of a boy pulling out a thorn from his foot. On the second floor, there's a small **Pinacoteca**, with some dignified Velázquez gentlemen, looking scornfully at the other paintings, and two major works by Caravaggio, the *Fortune Teller* and *John the Baptist*. There are also some lovely 18th-century porcelains – orchestras of monkeys in powdered wigs, and such.

As part of the millennial renovations, the Palazzo dei Conservatori was given new spaces for temporary exhibitions on the third floor, and there's an excellent café with a vast terrace and beautiful views over the city.

The **Palazzo Nuovo**, reached via the underground corridor, hasn't changed since the 18th century and holds statues of most of the emperors, busts of Homer, Sophocles and Pythagoras; the voluptuous *Capitoline Venus*; a big baby Hercules (who may have inspired Donatello's famous *Amor* in Florence); and the *Muse Polyhymnia*, one of the most delightful statues of antiquity. Later works include lots of papal paraphernalia, a statue of Charles of Anjou by Arnolfo di Cambio, and the regilded statue of Marcus Aurelius (just off the courtyard with its enormous Neptune fountain).

The best overview of the Roman Forum is to be had from behind Palazzo Senatorio. A stairway leads down from the left side to Via dei Fori Imperiali and the entrance to the Forum. On the way, beneath the church of San Giuseppe Falegnami, you can visit the **Carcere Mamertino** (*Via del Carcere Tulliano; open 9–12 and 2.30–5; donation requested*), the small calaboose used by the ancient Romans for their most important prisoners – the Catiline conspirators, Vercingetorix (the Gaulish chief captured by Caesar), and finally St Peter. The southern end of the Capitol, one of the quietest corners of Rome, was the site of the temple of Jupiter Optimus Maximus (Greatest and Best), built originally by the Etruscan kings. At the time it was the largest in Italy, testimony to Rome's importance as far back as 450 BC. Along the southern edge of the hill, the cliffs you see are the somewhat reduced remains of the **Tarpeian Rock**, from which traitors and other malefactors were thrown in Rome's early days.

Along the Tiber

The early emperors did their best to import classical Greek drama to Rome, and for a while, with the poets of the Latin New Comedy, it seemed the Romans would carry on the tradition. Great theatres were built like the **Teatro di Marcello** (*open by prior arrangement only, send a fax to* ***f*** *06 689 2115*), begun by Caesar and completed by Augustus. By the second century AD, however, theatre had already begun to degenerate into music hall, lewd performances with naked actresses and grisly murders (condemned prisoners were sometimes butchered on stage), and shows by celebrity actors probably much like some of today's unseemly spectacles. Marcellus' theatre survived into the Middle Ages, when the Orsini family converted it into their palace-fortress, the strongest after the Castel Sant'Angelo. You can still see the tall arches of the circumference surmounted by the rough medieval walls, a dramatic backdrop for occasional concerts.

The streets to the west contain a mix of some of Rome's oldest houses with new buildings; the latter have replaced the old walled **ghetto**. There has been a sizeable Jewish community in Rome since the 2nd century BC; after conquering the Jews at the end of the 1st century AD, Pompey and Titus brought them to Rome as slaves. They helped finance the career of Julius Caesar, who would prove to be their greatest benefactor. For centuries they lived near this bend in the river and in Trastevere. Paul IV took time off from burning books and heretics to wall them into the tiny ghetto in 1555; at the same time he forced them to wear orange hats, attend Mass on Sunday, and limited them to the rag and old iron trades. Tearing down the ghetto walls was one of the first acts of the Italian kingdom after the entry into Rome in 1870. The exotic, eclectic main **synagogue** was built in 1904; there are guided tours, and a small **museum of the Jewish Community** (*Museo Ebraico, Lungotevere dei Cenci,* ***t*** *06 6840 0661; open Mon–Thurs 9–7.30, last adm 7pm, Fri and Sun 9–1.30, closed Jewish hols; adm*), which includes a wrenching section on the Holocaust.

Opposite the synagogue, the **Isola Tiberina** is joined to both sides of the river by surviving ancient bridges. In imperial times the island was sacred to Aesculapius, god of healing; a legend records how serpents brought from the god's shrine in Greece escaped and swam here, choosing the site by divine guidance. Now, as in ancient times, most of the lovely island is taken up by a hospital, the Ospedale Fatebenefratelli; in place of the Temple of Aesculapius, there is also the church of **San Bartolomeo** (***t*** *06 687 7973; open 9–10.30 and 4–6.30*), most recently rebuilt in the 1690s.

The **Velabrum**, in the earliest days of Rome, was a cattle market (interestingly, in the Middle Ages, the Roman Forum itself was used for the same purpose). In this area, east of the Isola Tiberina, is **San Giorgio in Velabro** (*Via del Velabro 19; open 9–1 and*

3–6.30), in parts as old as the 7th century; there is a Cosmatesque altar, and early Christian fragments on the left wall. The lovely portico has been completely restored after a Mafia bombing in 1993. Of the two ancient arches outside, the **Arco degli Argentari** was erected by the moneychangers in honour of Septimius Severus. The larger, the unfinished, four-sided **Janus Quadrifons**, dates from the time of Constantine.

Piazza Bocca della Verità

Tourists almost always overlook this beautiful corner along the Tiber, but here you can see two well-preserved Roman temples. Both go under false names: the round **Temple of Vesta**, used as an Armenian church in the Middle Ages, and the **Temple of Fortuna Virilis** – it now seems almost certain that they were actually dedicated to Hercules Victor and Portunus (the god of harbours) respectively. Some bits of an exotic Roman cornice are built into the brick building opposite, part of the **House of the Crescenzi** (*Via Luigi Petroselli*), a powerful family in the 9th century, descended from Theodora Senatrix. Look over the side of the Tiber embankment here and you can see the outlet of the **Cloaca Maxima** (*Lungotevere Pierleoni*), the sewer begun by King Tarquin. Big enough to drive two carriages through, it is still in use today.

Just upstream, past the Ponte Palatino, a single arch decorated with dragons is all that remains of the Pons Aemilius. Originally built in the 2nd century BC, it collapsed twice and was last restored in 1575 by Gregory XIII, only to fall down again 20 years later. Now it is known as the 'broken bridge', or **Ponte Rotto**.

Across from the temples, the handsome medieval church with the lofty campanile is **Santa Maria in Cosmedin** (***t** 06 678 1419; open 10–6.30, in winter until 5*), built over an altar of Hercules in the 6th century and given to Byzantine Greeks escaping from the iconoclast emperors in the 8th. The name (like 'cosmetic') means 'decorated', but little of the original art has survived; most of what you see is from the 12th century, including some fine Cosmatesque work inside. In the portico, an ancient, ghostly image in stone built into the walls has come down in legend as the **Bocca della Verità** – the Mouth of Truth. Medieval Romans would swear oaths and close business deals here; if you tell a lie with your hand in the image's mouth he will most assuredly bite your fingers off. Try it.

The Heart of Ancient Rome

In the 1930s Mussolini built a grand boulevard between the Vittoriano and the Colosseum to ease traffic congestion and show off the ancient sites. He called it the Via del Impero, coinciding with his aspirations of returning Rome to greatness through a new empire in Africa. After Mussolini's demise the road was re-christened **Via dei Fori Imperiali**, after the Imperial Fora which it part covers.

The **Imperial Fora** of Augustus, Nerva and Trajan were built to relieve congestion in the original Roman Forum. **Trajan's Forum** (*Foro di Traiano*), built with the spoils of his conquest of Dacia (modern Romania), was perhaps the grandest architectural and planning conception ever built in Rome, a broad square surrounded by colonnades, with a huge basilica flanked by two libraries and a covered market outside (the world's first shopping mall). A large part of **Trajan's Markets** (*Mercati di Traiano*) still stands and has recently been expensively converted into a massive and very striking exhibition space (*entrance on Via IV Novembre;* ***t*** *06 679 0048; open Tues–Sun 9–5; adm*), and the network of surrounding paths and viewing points which pick over the ruins are due to be expanded. Behind it, you can see Rome's own leaning tower, the 12th-century **Torre delle Milizie**. All that remains of Trajan's great square is the paving and its centrepiece, **Trajan's Column** (*Colonna Traiana*). The spiralling bands of reliefs, illustrating the Dacian Wars, reach to the top, some 96ft high. They rank with the greatest works of Roman art; plaster casts are on display at eye level in the Museo della Civiltà Romana at EUR. Behind the column, **Santa Maria di Loreto** (*Piazza Madonna di Loreto; open 7.30–12 and 4–6*) is a somewhat garish High Renaissance bauble, built by Bramante and Antonio da Sangallo the Younger. The Romans liked the church so much that in the 1730s they built another one just like it next door, the **Santissimo Nome di Maria**. Scanty remains of **Caesar's Forum** (*Foro di Cesare*) and **Augustus' Forum** (*Foro di Augusto*) can be seen along the boulevard to the south.

The Roman Forum

The entrances are on Via dei Fori Imperiali at Via Cavour, and at the end of the ramp that approaches the Forum from the Colosseum side; ***t*** *06 699 0110; open daily 9–1hr before sunset. There's a new visitors' centre for the Fori Imperiali on the Via dei Fori Imperiali.*

For a place that was the centre of the Mediterranean world, there is surprisingly little to see; centuries of use as a quarry have seen to that. The word *forum* originally meant 'outside' (like the Italian *fuori*), a marketplace outside the original Rome that became the centre of both government and business as the city expanded.

The **Via Sacra**, ancient Rome's most important street, runs the length of the Forum. At the end of it beneath the Capitoline Hill you will be facing the **Arch of Septimius Severus** (AD 203), with reliefs of some rather trivial victories over the Arabs and Parthians; conservative Romans of the time must have strongly resented this upstart African emperor planting his monument in such an important spot. The arch also commemorated Septimius' two sons, Geta and Caracalla; when the nasty Caracalla did his brother in, he had his name effaced from it. In front of it, the **Lapis Niger**, a mysterious stone with an underground chamber beneath it, is the legendary tomb of Romulus (*closed to the public*). The inscription down below – a threat against the profaning of this sacred spot – is one of the oldest ever found in the Latin language. The famous Golden Milestone also stood here, the 'umbilicus' of Rome and the point from which all distances in the Empire were measured. To the right is the **Curia** (the Senate House), heavily restored after centuries' use as a church (the good Baroque church behind it is **SS. Luca e Martina** (*Clivo Argentario; closed for restoration*), built by Pietro da Cortona in the 1660s). To the left of the arch the remains of a raised stone area were the **Rostra**, the speakers' platform under the Republic, decorated with ships' prows (*rostra*) taken in a sea battle in about 320 BC. Of the great temples on the Capitol slope only a few columns remain; from left to right, the **Temple of Saturn**, which served as Rome's treasury, the **Temple of Vespasian** (three standing columns) and the **Temple of Concord**, built by Tiberius to honour the peace – so to speak – that the emperors had enforced between patricians and plebeians.

In front of the Rostra, in the open area once decorated with statues and monuments, the simple standing **column** was placed in honour of Nikephoros Phocas, Byzantine Emperor in 608 – the last monument ever erected in the Forum; the Romans had to steal the column from a ruined building. Just behind it a small pool once marked the spot of one of ancient Rome's favourite legends. In 362 BC, according to Livy, an abyss suddenly opened across the Forum, and the sibyls predicted that it would not close unless the 'things that Rome held most precious' were thrown in. A consul, Marcus Curtius, took this as meaning a Roman citizen and soldier. He leapt in fully armed, horse and all, and the crack closed over him.

This section of the Forum was bordered by two imposing buildings, the **Basilica Aemilia** to the north and the **Basilica Julia** to the south, the latter built by Caesar with the spoils of the Gallic Wars. The **Temple of Caesar** closes the east end, built by Augustus as a visual symbol of the new imperial mythology.

The adjacent **Temple of the Dioscuri** is a good example of how temples were used in ancient times. This one was a meeting hall for men of the equestrian class (the knights, though they were really more likely to be businessmen); they had safe-deposit boxes in the basement, where the standard weights and measures of the empire were kept. Between them, the round pedestal was the foundation of the small **Temple of Vesta**, where the sacred hearth-fire was kept burning by the Vestal Virgins; ruins of their extensive apartments can be seen next door.

Two more Christian churches stand in this part of the Forum. **SS. Cosma e Damiano** (*open daily 9–1 and 3–6.30*) was built on to the **Temple of Antoninus Pius and Faustina** in the 6th century; most of the columns survive, with a fine sculptural frieze of griffons on top. **Santa Francesca Romana** (*open daily 9.30–12 and 4–7*) is built over a corner of Rome's largest temple, that of **Venus and Rome**. Built by Hadrian, this was a curious, double-ended shrine to the state cult, one side devoted to the Goddess Roma and the other to Venus – in the imperial mythology she was the ancestress of the Caesars.

The church entrance is outside the Forum, but the adjoining convent, inside the monumental area, houses the **Antiquarium Forense**, a tired collection of Iron-Age burial urns and other paraphernalia from the Forum excavations. Between the two churches the mastodontic **Basilica of Maxentius**, finished by Constantine, remains the largest ruin of the Forum, its clumsy arches providing an illustration of the ungainly but technically sophisticated 4th century.

Near the exit, the **Arch of Titus** commemorates the victories of Titus and his father Vespasian over the rebellious Jews (AD 60–80), one of the fiercest struggles Rome ever had to fight. The reliefs show the booty being carted through Rome in the triumphal parade – including the famous seven-branched golden candlestick from the holy of holies in the Temple at Jerusalem.

South of the arch a path leads up to the **Monte Palatino** (*__t__ 06 3996 7700; open daily 9–1hr before sunset; adm. A cumulative ticket called the Roma Archeologia Card, valid 7 days, includes Palatino, Colosseum, Crypta Balbi, Palazzo Massimo, Palazzo Altemps, Terme di Diocleziano, and Baths of Caracalla, Tomb of Cecilia Metella and Villa dei Quintili; this ticket can be acquired at any of these sites and currently costs €20*). Here, overlooking the little corner of the world that gave our language words like *senate, committee, rostrum, republic, plebiscite* and *magistrate*, you can leave democracy behind and visit the etymological birthplace of *palace*. The ruins of the imperial *Palatium* once covered the entire hill. As with the Forum, almost all the stone has been cannibalized, and there's little to see of what was once a complex half a mile long, to which a dozen of the emperors contributed.

There are good views across the Circus Maximus from just above what was once the portico from which the emperor could watch the races. Don't miss the chance to take a stroll through the gardens planted by the Farnese family (*currently closed for renovation*) over what were the imperial servants' quarters – one of the most peaceful spots in the city. The one modern building on the Palatino houses the Museo Palatino (*adm included in ticket for Palatine*), a good little collection of relics found within a stone's throw of the building, plus a history of the hill with models of the huts built by its first inhabitants.

The Colosseum

Piazza del Colosseo; open daily 9–1hr before sunset; adm; see cumulative ticket p.86; audioguide in English €4. Daily guided tours in English at 3pm, plus 4.15 and 5.15 in summer, €3.50.

Its real name was the Flavian Amphitheatre, after the family of emperors who built it, beginning with Vespasian in AD 72; Colosseum refers to the *Colossus*, a huge gilded statue of Nero (erected by himself, of course) that stood in the square in front. There doesn't seem to be much evidence that Christians were literally thrown to lions here – there were other places for that – but what did go on was perhaps the grossest and best-organized perversity in all history. Gladiatorial contests began under the Republic, designed to make Romans better soldiers by rendering them indifferent to the sight of death. Later emperors introduced new displays to relieve the monotony – men versus animals, lions versus elephants, women versus dwarfs, sea-battles (the arena could be flooded at a moment's notice), public tortures of condemned criminals, and even genuine athletics, a Greek import the Romans never much cared for. In the first hundred days of the Colosseum's opening, 5,000 animals were slaughtered. The native elephant and lion of North Africa and Arabia are extinct thanks to such shenanigans.

However hideous its purpose, the Colosseum ranks with the greatest works of Roman architecture and engineering; all modern stadia have its basic plan. One surprising feature was a removable awning that covered the stands. Sailors from Cape Misenum were kept to operate it; they also manned the galleys in the mock sea-battles. Originally there were statues in every arch and a ring of bronze shields around the cornice. The concrete stands have eroded away, showing the brick structure underneath. Renaissance and Baroque popes hauled away half the travertine exterior – enough to build the Palazzo Venezia, the Palazzo Barberini, a few other palaces and bridges and part of St Peter's. Almost all of the construction work under Vespasian and Titus was performed by Jewish slaves, brought here for the purpose after the suppression of their revolt.

Just outside the Colosseum, the **Arch of Constantine** marks the end of the ancient Triumphal Way (now Via di San Gregorio) where victorious emperors and their troops would parade their captives and booty. The arch, with a coy inscription mentioning Constantine's 'divine inspiration' (the Romans weren't sure whether it was yet respectable to mention Christianity), is covered with reliefs stolen from older arches and public buildings – a sad commentary on the state of art in Constantine's day.

Domus Aurea and the Monte Esquilino

When Nero decided he needed a new palace, money was no object. Taking advantage of the great fire of AD 64 (which he apparently did *not* start), he had a huge section of Rome (temporarily renamed Neropolis) cleared to make a rural estate in the middle of town. The **Golden House** (*Colle Oppio;* ***t*** *06 3996 7700; open Wed–Mon 9–7.45; advance booking essential; adm; audioguide €2 recommended if you want to know what you are looking at*) was probably the most sumptuous palace ever built in Rome, decorated in an age when Roman art was at its height, but Nero never lived to see it finished – he committed suicide during an army coup by Spanish legions. When the dust settled the new Emperor Vespasian realized that this flagrant symbol of imperial decadence had to go. He demolished it, and Titus and Trajan later erected great bath complexes on its foundations; Nero's gardens and his enormous lake became the site of the Colosseum.

In the 1500s some beautifully decorated rooms of the Domus Aurea were discovered underground, saved for use as the basement of Titus' baths. Raphael and other artists studied them closely and incorporated some of the spirit of the fresco decoration into the grand manner of the High Renaissance (our word 'grotesque', originally referring to the leering faces and floral designs of this time, comes from the finds in this 'grotto').

The **Monte Esquilino** is better known today as the Colle Oppio. Much of it is covered with parks; besides the Domus Aurea there are very substantial ruins of the **Terme di Traiano**, still unexcavated. On the northern slope of the hill, **San Pietro in Vincoli** (***t*** *06 488 2865; open daily 7–12.30 and 3.30–6*) takes its name from relics supposed to be the chains Peter was locked in before Nero had him crucified. They are kept over the main altar, though the real attraction of this church for non-Catholics is the famous, ill-fated **tomb of Julius II** which tortured Michelangelo for many years. Of the original project, planned as a sort of tabernacle with 40 individual statues, the artist completed, as well as the statues of *Leah* and *Rachel*, the powerful figure of *Moses*, perhaps the closest anyone has ever come to capturing prophetic vision in stone, even if he bears a striking resemblance to Charlton Heston. All the other statues on the tomb are the work of Michelangelo's students.

San Clemente

Via San Giovanni in Laterano; ***t*** *06 7045 1018; open weekdays 9–12.30 and 3–6, weekends and hols 10–12.30 and 3–6; adm to the excavations.*

This church, a little way to the east of the Colosseum, is one of the more fascinating remnants of Rome's many-layered history. One of the first substantial building projects of the Christians in Rome, the original basilica of *c.* 375 burned along with the rest of the quarter during a sacking by the Normans in 1084. It was rebuilt soon afterwards with a new Cosmatesque pavement, and the 6th-century choir screen – a rare example of sculpture from that ungifted time – saved from the original church. The 12th-century mosaic in the apse represents the *Triumph of the Cross*, and the chapel at the entrance contains a beautiful series of quattrocento frescoes by Masolino. From a vestibule, nuns sell tickets to the **Lower Church**. This is the lower half of the original San Clemente, and there are remarkable, though deteriorated, frescoes from the 900s and the 12th century. The plaque from Bulgaria, mentioned on p.108, commemorates SS. Cyril and Methodius, who went from this church to spread the Gospel among the Slavs; they translated the Bible into Old Slavonic, and invented the first Slavic alphabet (Cyrillic) to do it.

From here, steps lead down to the lowest stratum, 1st- and 2nd-century AD buildings divided by an alley; this includes the **Mithraeum**, the best-preserved temple of its kind after the one in Capua. The larger, neighbouring building was filled with rubble to serve as a foundation for the basilica, and the apse was later added over the Mithraeum. Father Mulhooly of Boston started excavating in the 1860s, and later excavations have revealed a Mithraic antechamber with a fine stuccoed ceiling, a Mithraic school with an early fresco, and the temple proper, a small cavern-like hall with benches for the initiates to share a ritual supper.

Mithraism was a mystery religion, full of secrets closely held by the initiates (all male, and largely soldiers) and it is difficult to say what else went on down here. Two altars were found, each with the usual image of the Persian-import god Mithras despatching a white bull, including a snake, a scorpion and a crow, and astrological symbolism. Underneath all this, there is yet a fourth building level, some foundations from the republican era. At the end of the 1st-century building you can look down into an ancient sewer or underground stream, one of a thousand entrances to the surreal sub-Roma of endless subterranean caves, buildings, rivers and lakes, mostly unexplored and unexplorable. A century ago a schoolboy fell in the water here; they found him, barely alive, in open country several kilometres from the city.

Along Corso Vittorio Emanuele

This street, chopped through the medieval centre in the 1880s, still hasn't quite been assimilated into its surroundings; nevertheless, this ragged, smoky traffic tunnel will come in handy when you find yourself lost in the tortuous, meandering streets of Rome's oldest quarter. Starting west from Piazza Venezia, the church of **Il Gesù** (1568–84) (*Piazza del Gesù;* ***t*** *06 697 001; open 7–12 and 3–7.30*) was a landmark for a new era and the new aesthetic of *cinquecento* Rome. The transitional, pre-Baroque fashion was often referred to as the 'Jesuit style', and here in the Jesuits' head church architects Vignola and Della Porta laid down Baroque's first law: an intimation of paradise through decorative excess. It hasn't aged well, though at the time it must have seemed to most Romans a perfect marriage of Renaissance art and a reformed, revitalized faith. St Ignatius, the Jesuits' founder, is buried in the left transept right under the altar, Spanish-style; the globe incorporated in the sculpted Trinity overhead is the biggest piece of lapis lazuli in the world.

Further west the street opens into a ghastly square called Largo Argentina. Remains of several Republican-era temples, unearthed far below ground level, occupy the centre. The square teems with cats: tucked beneath the square at one end is the **Roman Cat Sanctuary** (***t** 06 687 2133, www.romancats.com*), which is always looking for volunteers and donations. Take a short detour around the corner, halfway down Via delle Botteghe Oscure at No.31, to find the newest addition to the Museo Nazionale d'Arte Romana: the **Crypta Balbi** (*open Tues–Sun 9–7.45; adm, or part of Roma Archeologia Card, see p.86, or the Museum Card, see p.131*). This modern, glassy museum is built over the ruins of a theatre, which was almost as large as the huge theatres of Pompey and Marcellus. A medieval church grew up on the ruins, before becoming submerged by the modern street. Interesting, well-considered exhibitions give a fascinating glimpse into Rome's many layered history.

Back up on Via Corso Emanuele, just beyond the Largo Argentina, is another grand Baroque church, **Sant'Andrea della Valle** (***t** 06 686 1339; open 8–12 and 4.30–7*), with the city's second-tallest dome. Maderno, one of the architects of St Peter's, did most of the work. The curving façade across the street belongs to **Palazzo Massimo alle Colonne** (*open 16 Mar only 7–1; adm*), the masterpiece of the Renaissance architect Baldassare Peruzzi; he transplanted something of the Florentine style of monumental palaces, adding some light-hearted proto-Baroque decoration. If you can, have a look at the adjacent church of **San Pantaleo de Parione** (*opposite Via dei Baullari; open, rarely, for Mass*), with its outlandish sculptural frieze of shields, trays and popes' hats piled like a rubbish heap. The sumptuous Palazzo Braschi next door houses the **Museo di Roma** (*Piazza San Pantaleo 10; **t** 06 8207 7384; open Tues–Sun 9–7, guided tours Sat and Sun, call for times; adm, audioguide €3.62*), which reopened in 2002 after a decade of restoration, but has a thin and disappointing collection of artefacts, which are virtually meaningless without the help of the audioguide to place them in context. The views over the Piazza Navona are good, though.

Right across the street is one of the earliest and best of the palaces on Corso Vittorio Emanuele, the delicate **Piccola Farnesina** by Antonio da Sangallo the Younger. It houses another little museum, a collection of ancient sculpture called the **Museo Barracco** (***t** 06 6880 6848; open Tues–Sun 9–7; adm*). A third museum – not a well-known one – is just around the corner from Sant'Andrea: the **Burcardo Library and Theatre Collection**, Via Sudario 44 (***t** 06 6819 471; open Sun–Fri 9–1.30, closed hols*) gathers together theatrical costumes, texts, scene and stage sketches, and has a famous library with over 40,000 volumes.

The biggest palace on the street, attributed to Bramante, is **Palazzo della Cancelleria** (*t 06 6989 3405; open for visits by reservation at least one month in advance*), once the seat of the papal municipal government. St Philip Neri, the gifted, irascible holy man who is patron saint of Rome, built the **Chiesa Nuova** (*open 8–12 and 4.30–7*) near the eastern end of the Corso (1584). Philip was quite a character, with something of the Zen Buddhist in him. He forbade his followers any sort of philosophical speculation, but made them sing and recite poetry; two of his favourite pastimes were insulting popes and embarrassing initiates – making them walk through Rome with a foxtail sewn to the back of their coat to learn humility. As was common in those times, sincere faith and humility were eventually translated into flagrant Baroque. The Chiesa Nuova is one of the larger and fancier of the species. Its altarpiece is a *Madonna with Angels* by Rubens. Even more flagrant, outside the church you can see the curved arch-Baroque façade of the **Oratorio dei Filippini** by Borromini. The form of music called the *oratorio* takes its name from this chapel, a tribute to St Philip's role in promoting sacred music.

Campo de' Fiori

Few cities can put on such a variety of faces to beguile the visitor; depending on where you spend your time in Rome, you may come away with the impression of a city that is one great Baroque stage set, a city of grimy early 1900s palazzi and bad traffic, or a city full of nothing but ruins and parks. Around Campo de' Fiori, one of the spots dearest to the hearts of Romans themselves, you may think yourself in the middle of some scruffy south Italian village. Rome's market square, disorderly, cramped and chaotic, is easily the liveliest corner of the city, full of market barrows, buskers, teenage bohemians and the folkloresque types who have lived here all their lives – the least decorous and worst-dressed crowd in Rome. The best time to see the square is during the morning market (*Mon–Sat dawn–1*) or at night along with the adjacent Piazza Farnese. During papal rule the old square was also used for executions – most notoriously the burning of Giordano Bruno in 1600. This well-travelled philosopher was the first to take Copernican astronomy to its logical extremes – an infinite universe with no centre, no room for Heaven, and nothing eternal but change. The Church had few enemies more dangerous. Italy never forgot him; the statue of Bruno in Campo de' Fiori went up only a few years after the end of papal rule.

Just east of the square, the heap of buildings around Piazzetta di Grottapinta is built over the cavea of **Teatro di Pompeo**, ancient Rome's biggest. This complex included a curia, the place where Julius Caesar was assassinated in 44 BC. Walk south from Campo de' Fiori and you will be thrown back from cosy medievalism into the heart of the High Renaissance with the **Palazzo Farnese** (*open for group visits by arrangement with the cultural section of the French Embassy*), one of the definitive works of that Olympian style. The younger Sangallo began it in 1514, and Michelangelo contributed to the façades and interiors. The building is now the French Embassy, and the square it overlooks is one of the most romantic in the city.

Most of the palaces that fill up this neighbourhood have one thing in common – they were made possible by someone's accession to the papacy, the biggest jackpot available to any aspiring Italian family. Built on the pennies of the faithful, they provide the most outrageous illustration of Church corruption at the dawn of the Reformation. Alessandro Farnese, who as Pope Paul III was a clever and effective pope – though perhaps the greatest nepotist ever to decorate St Peter's throne – managed to build this palace 20 years before his election, with the income from his 16 absentee bishoprics.

Palazzo Spada, just to the east on Via Capo di Ferro 13, was the home of a mere cardinal, but its florid stucco façade (1540) almost upstages the Farnese. Inside, the **Galleria Spada** (*t 06 6880 9814; open Tues–Sat 9–7.30, Sun 9–6.30; adm*) is one of Rome's great collections of 16th- and 17th-century painting. Guido Reni, Guercino and the other favourites of the age are well represented. Don't miss the courtyard, which has decoration similar to the façade, and a glass window with a view through the library to one of Rome's little Baroque treasures: the recently restored *trompe l'œil* corridor, designed by Borromini to appear four times its actual length (the statue at the end of the path is actually less than a yard in height). To the south, close to the Tiber, **Via Giulia** was laid out by Pope Julius II: a pretty thoroughfare lined with churches and palazzi from his time. Many artists (successful ones) have lived here, including Raphael.

Piazza Navona

In 1477 the area now covered by one of Rome's most beautiful piazzas was a field full of huts and vineyards, tucked inside the imposing ruins of the Stadium of Domitian. A redevelopment of the area covered the long grandstands with new houses, but the decoration had to wait for the Age of Baroque. In 1644, the Pamphili family won the papal sweepstakes with the election of Innocent X. Innocent, a great grafter and such a villainous pope that when he died no one – not even his newly wealthy relatives – would pay for a proper burial, built the ornate **Palazzo Pamphili** (now the Brazilian Embassy) and hired Borromini to complete the gaudy church of **Sant'Agnese in Agone** (*open Tues–Sun 10–7 and for Mass*), begun by Carlo and Girolamo Rainaldi.

Borromini's arch-rival Bernini got the commission for the piazza's famous fountains; the Romans still tell stories of how the two artists carried on. Borromini started a rumour that the tall obelisk atop the central **Fontana dei Fiumi** was about to topple; when the alarmed papal commissioners arrived to confront Bernini with the news, he tied a piece of twine around it, secured the other end to a lamppost, and laughed all the way home. The fountain is Bernini's masterpiece, Baroque at its flashiest and most lovable. Among the travertine grottoes and fantastical flora and fauna under the obelisk, the four colossal figures represent the Ganges, Danube, Rio de la Plata and Nile (with the veiled head because its source was unknown). Bernini also designed the smaller **Fontana del Moro**, at the southern end. The third fountain, that of *Neptune*, was an empty basin until the nineteenth century, when the statues by Giacomo della Porta were added to make the square seem more symmetrical. Off the southern end of the piazza, at the back of Palazzo Braschi, **Pasquino** is the original Roman 'talking statue', embellished with placards and graffiti ('*pasquinades*') since the 1500s – one of his favourite subjects in those days was the insatiable pigginess of families like the Farnese; serious religious issues were usually too hot to touch, even for a statue.

Piazza Navona seems mildly schizoid these days, unable to become entirely part of high-fashion, tourist-itinerary Rome, yet no longer as comfortable and unpretentious as the rest of the neighbourhood. One symptom will be readily apparent should you step into any of the old cosy-looking cafés and restaurants around the piazza: they're as expensive as in any part of Rome. The best time to come to Piazza Navona is at night when the fountain is illuminated – or, if you can, for the noisy, traditional toy fair of the **Befana**, set up between just before Christmas and Epiphany. **Palazzo Altemps**, on Piazza Sant'Apollinare, now contains part of the excellent **Museo Nazionale Romano** (***t*** *06 683 3759; open Tues–Fri 9–7.45, Sun 9am–11pm; adm; admission included with the Roma Archeologia Card, see p.86, or with the Museum Card, which is valid 7 days, costs €9 and covers the four sites run by the Museo Nazionale Romano: the Palazzo Altemps, the Palazzo Massimo, Baths of Diocletian and the Crypta Balbi*). The beautiful palace makes a stunning setting for the busts and statues: the *piano nobile* still contains fragments of 16th-century frescoes and there's a glorious painted loggia lined with busts of the Caesars, as well as a tiny, forlorn gilded theatre in the basement. Some of the churches in the area are worth a look, such as **Santa Maria della Pace** (*Vicolo del Arco della Pace 5;* ***t*** *06 686 1156; open Tues–Sat 10–12 and 4–6, Sun 9–11*), with Raphael's series of *Sibyls and Prophets* on the vaulting and a cloister by Bramante. **San Luigi dei Francesi** (***t*** *06 688 271; open Mon–Wed and Fri–Sun 8.30–12.30 and 3.30–7; Thurs 8.30–12.30 only*), the French church in Rome, contains the great *Life of St Matthew* by Caravaggio in a chapel on the left aisle. Towards the Pantheon, **Sant'Ivo alla Sapienza** (*Palazzo della Sapienza, Corso del Rinascimento 40,* ***t*** *06 686 4987; open Sun am for Mass*) once served the English community in Rome. Borromini built them one of his most singular buildings (1660), with its dome and spiralling cupola.

The Pantheon

Piazza della Rotonda, ***t*** *06 6830 0230;*
open Mon–Sat 8.30–7.30, Sun 9–6.

When we consider the fate of so many other great buildings of ancient Rome we begin to understand what a slim chance it was that allowed this one to come down to us. The first Pantheon was built in 27 BC by Agrippa, Emperor Augustus' son-in-law and right-hand man, but was destroyed by fire and replaced by the present temple in 119–128 by Emperor Hadrian, though curiously retaining Agrippa's original inscription on the pediment. Its history has been precarious ever since. In 609 the empty Pantheon was consecrated to Christianity as 'St Mary of the Martyrs'.

Becoming a church is probably what saved it, though the Byzantines hauled away the gilded bronze roof tiles soon after, and for a while in the Middle Ages the portico saw use as a fish market. The Pantheon's greatest enemy, however, was Gian Lorenzo Bernini. He not only 'improved' it with a pair of Baroque belfries over the porch (demolished in 1887), but he had Pope Urban VIII take down the bronze covering on the inside of the dome to melt down for his *baldacchino* over the altar at St Peter's. Supposedly there was enough left over to make the pope 60 cannons. (Urban was of the Barberini family, and Pasquino's comment about this act was, 'What the barbarians didn't do, the Barberini did.')

You may notice that the building seems perilously unsound. There is no way a simple vertical wall can support such a heavy, shallow dome (steep domes push downwards, shallow ones outwards). Obviously the walls will tumble at any moment. That is a little joke the Roman architects are playing, for here they are showing off as shamelessly as in the Colosseum, or the aqueduct with four storeys of arches that used to run *up* to the Monte Palatino. The wall that looks so fragile is really 23ft thick and the dome on top isn't a dome at all; the real hemispherical dome lies underneath, resting easily on the walls inside. The ridges you see on the upper dome are courses of cantilevered bricks, effectively almost weightless. The real surprise, however, lies behind the enormous original bronze doors: an interior of precious marbles and finely sculpted details, the grandest and best-preserved building to have survived from the ancient world. The movie directors who made all those Roman epics in the 1950s and '60s certainly took many of their settings from this High Imperial creation, just as architects from the early Middle Ages onwards have tried to equal it.

Brunelleschi learned enough from it to build his dome in Florence, and a visit here will show you at a glance what Michelangelo and his contemporaries were trying so hard to outdo. The coffered dome, the biggest cast concrete construction ever made before the 20th century, is the crowning audacity, even without its bronze plate. At 141ft in diameter it is probably the largest in the world (a little-known fact – but St Peter's dome is 6ft less, though much taller). Standing in the centre and looking at the clouds through the 28ft *oculus*, the hole at the top, is an odd sensation you can experience nowhere else.

Inside, the niches around the perimeter held statues of the Pantheon's 12 gods, plus those of Augustus and Hadrian; in the centre, illuminated by a direct sunbeam at midsummer noon, stood Jove. All these are gone, of course, and the interior decoration is limited to an *Annunciation*, attributed to Melozzo da Forlì, and the tombs of eminent Italians such as Raphael and kings Vittorio Emanuele II and Umberto I. The Pantheon simply stands open, with no admission charges, probably fulfilling the same purpose as in Hadrian's day – no purpose at all, save that of an unequalled monument to art and the builder's skill.

Just behind the Pantheon, the big church of **Santa Maria sopra Minerva** (***t*** *06 679 1217; church open daily 7am–7.30pm, cloister open Mon–Sat 8–1 and 4–7*) is interesting for being one of the few medieval churches of Rome (*c.* 1280) to escape the Baroque treatment; its Gothic was preserved in restoration work in the 1840s. Two Medici popes, Leo X and Clement VII, are buried here, as is Fra Angelico. Santa Maria's Florentine connection began with the Dominican monks who designed it; they also did Florence's Santa Maria Novella. A work of Michelangelo, *Christ with the Cross*, can be seen near the high altar; the Carafa Chapel off the right aisle, where you can pay your respects to Pope Paul IV, has a series of frescoes (1489) on the *Life of St Thomas* by Filippino Lippi, his best work outside Florence.

Trastevere

So often just being on the wrong side of the river encourages a city district to cultivate its differences and its eccentricities. Trastevere isn't really a Left Bank – more of a pocket-sized Brooklyn, and as in Brooklyn those differences and eccentricities often turn out to be the old habits of the whole city, preserved in an out-of-the-way corner.

The people of Trastevere are more Roman than the Romans. Indeed, they claim to be the real descendants of the Romans of old; one story traces their ancestry back to the sailors who worked the great awning at the Colosseum. Such places have a hard time surviving these days, especially when they are as trendy as Trastevere is right now. But even though such things as Trastevere's famous school of dialect poets may be mostly a memory, the quarter remains the liveliest and most entertaining in Rome. The young crowd that Trastevere attracts now provides much of the local colour, their colourful trendy clothes somehow a perfect match for the medieval alleys.

Just over Ponte Garibaldi is Piazza Sonnino, with the **Torre degli Anguillara**, an uncommon survival of the defence towers that once loomed over medieval Rome, and the 12th-century church of **San Crisogono** (***t** 06 581 8225; open Mon–Sat 7am–7.30pm, Sun 8–1 and 4.15–7.30*), with mosaics by Pietro Cavallini (master of the Roman 13th-century school) built over the remains of an earlier church. Near the bridge, the dapper statue in the top hat is Giuseppe Gioacchino Belli, one of Trastevere's 19th-century dialect poets.

Turn left on to one of the narrow streets off Viale di Trastevere and make your way to the church of **Santa Cecilia in Trastevere** (***t** 06 589 9289; open daily 9.30–1 and 4–7.15*), founded over the house of the 2nd-century martyr whom centuries of hagiography have turned into one of the most agreeable of saints, the inventor of the organ and patroness of music. Cecilia was disinterred in 1599, and her body was found entirely uncorrupted. Clement VIII commissioned Maderno to sculpt an exact copy from sketches made before her body dissolved into thin air; this charming work can be seen near the altar, beneath an altarpiece by Giulio Romano.

Nearby there is a *Tabernacle* by Arnolfo di Cambio similar to the one in St Paul's, and 9th-century mosaics in the apse. The church has other treasures: Renaissance tombs, including one of a 14th-century cardinal from Hertford; frescoes by the school of Pinturicchio in a chapel on the right; and a crypt built in the underlying Roman constructions, thought to be Cecilia's home (*adm*). Up in the singing gallery (*visits to Cavallini's frescoes Sun 11.15–12, Tues and Thurs 10–12; adm*) are the remains of the original church wall decoration – a wonderful fresco of the *Last Judgement* by Cavallini.

Across Viale di Trastevere – an intrusive modern boulevard that slices the district in two – lies the heart of old Trastevere, around **Piazza Santa Maria in Trastevere** and its church. Most of this building dates from the 1140s, though the original church, begun perhaps in 222, may be the first anywhere dedicated to the Virgin Mary. The medieval building is a treasure-house of Roman mosaics, starting with the frieze with the Virgin breast-feeding Christ flanked by ten female figures on the façade, and continuing with the remarkable series from the *Life of Mary* by Cavallini in the apse, a bit of the early Renaissance 100 years ahead of schedule (*c.* 1290). Above them are earlier, more glittering mosaics from the 1140s. The piazza, and the streets around it, has been for decades one of the most popular spots in Rome for restaurants; tables are spread out wherever there's room, and there will always be a crowd in the evening.

Via del Corso

The Campus Martius, the open plain between Rome's hills and the Tiber, was the training ground for soldiers in the early days of the Republic. Eventually the city swallowed it up and the old path towards the Via Flaminia became an important thoroughfare, *Via Lata* (Broad Street). Not entirely by coincidence, the popes of the 14th and 15th centuries laid out a new boulevard almost in the same place. **Via del Corso**, or simply the Corso, has been the main axis of Roman society ever since. Goethe left a fascinating account of the Carnival festivities of Rome's benignly decadent 18th century, climaxing in the horse races that gave the street its name. Much of its length is taken up by the overdone palaces of the age, such as the Palazzo Doria (1780), where the **Galleria Doria Pamphili** (*Piazza del Collegio Romano 2,* ***t*** *06 679 7323, www.doriapamphili.it; open Fri–Wed 10–5; adm, includes audioguide in English*), still owned by the Pamphili, has a fine painting collection – with Velázquez' *Portrait of Innocent X*, Caravaggio's *Flight into Egypt*, and works by Rubens, Titian, Brueghel and more. Guided tours of the apartments (in English by request) give an idea of the lifestyle a family expected when one of its members hit the papal jackpot.

Continuing northwards, the palaces have come down in the world somewhat, tired-looking blocks that now house banks and offices. Look on the side streets for some hidden attractions: **Sant'Ignazio** (*Piazza di Sant'Ignazio; open 7.30–12.30 and 4–7.15*) is another Jesuit church with spectacular *trompe l'œil* frescoes on the ceiling; a block north on Piazza di Pietra, columns of the ancient **Temple of Hadrian** are incorporated into the north side of the city's tiny Stock Exchange. **Piazza Colonna** takes its name from the column of Marcus Aurelius, whose military victories are remembered in a column (just like those of Trajan); atop stands a statue of St Paul. The obelisk in adjacent Piazza di Montecitorio once marked the hours on a gigantic sundial in Emperor Augustus' garden; **Palazzo di Montecitorio** (***t*** *06 67601; open to the public late Sept–July on first Sun of every month 10–6. For admission to parliamentary sessions or tours, apply at the rear, Piazza del Parlamento No.24. Visitors must be at least 14 years old and smartly dressed; non-EU visitors must bring a letter from their country's embassy in Rome*), begun by Bernini, now houses the Italian Chamber of Deputies.

A little way east of Piazza Colonna is the **Fontana di Trevi**, into which you can throw your coins to guarantee your return trip to Rome. The fountain, completed in 1762, was originally planned to commemorate the restoration of Agrippa's aqueduct by Nicholas V in 1453. The source was called the 'Virgin Water' after Virgo, a young girl who had shown thirsty Roman soldiers the hidden spring. It makes a grand sight – enough to make you want to come back; not many fountains have an entire palace for a stage backdrop. The big fellow in the centre is Oceanus, drawn by horses and tritons through cascades of travertine and blue water. Across from the fountain, little **SS. Vincenzo and Anastasio** (*t 06 678 3098; open 7–9am*) has the distinction of caring for the pickled hearts and entrails of dozens of popes; an odd custom. They're kept down in the crypt.

Just a short walk from the Trevi Fountain is the **Museo delle Paste Alimentari**, on Piazza Scanderbeg 117 (*t 06 699 1119; open daily 9.30–5.30; adm*), where a small, modern display traces the history of Italy's most famous food.

Further north, the Corso reaches close to the Tiber and the dilapidated and overgrown **Mausoleo di Augusto** (*closed to the public*), a cylinder of shabby brick once covered in marble and golden statues. All the Julian emperors except Nero were interred here, in the middle of what were Augustus' enormous gardens. After the centuries had despoiled the tomb of its riches the Colonna family turned the hulk into a fortress.

Further indignities were in store. Until 1823, when the pope forbade them, bullfights were popular in Rome, and a Spanish entrepreneur found the circular enclosure perfect for the *toreros*. After that the tomb was used as a circus, before Mussolini, wishing to afford the founders of Imperial Rome due respect (and perhaps intending to be buried there himself), declared it a national monument and had trees planted around it. Even so, no one quite seems to know what to do with it; it sits locked and empty.

Across the street, Augustus' **Ara Pacis**, Altar of Peace (*Via di Ripetta, t 06 6710 3819; closed for restoration*), has had a better fate. Bits and pieces of the beautiful sculpted reliefs, dug up in 1937, were joined with casts of others from museums around Europe to recreate the small building almost in its entirety, one of antiquity's noblest (and least pretentious) conceptions. Among the mythological reliefs, note the side facing the river, with the emperor and his family dedicating a sacrifice. At the time of writing it's shrouded in scaffolding while Richard Meier's glassy new visitors' centre takes shape around it.

Piazza di Spagna

The shuffling crowds of tourists who congregate here at all hours of the day are not a recent phenomenon; this supremely sophisticated piazza has been a favourite with foreigners ever since it was laid out in the early 16th century. The Spaniards came first, as their embassy to the popes was established here in 1646, giving the square and the steps their name. Later, the English Romantic poets made it their headquarters in Italy; typical mementoes – locks of hair, fond remembrances, death masks – are awaiting your inspired contemplation at the **Keats–Shelley Memorial House** at No.26 (*t 06 678 4235; open Mon–Fri 9–1 and 3–6; Sat 11–2, and 3–6; adm*). Almost every artist, writer or musician of the last century spent some time here, but today the piazza often finds itself bursting at the seams with refreshingly Philistine gawkers and wayward youth from all over the world, caught between the charms of McDonald's (the first one built in Rome) and the fancy shops around nearby Via Condotti.

All these visitors need somewhere to sit, and the popes obliged them in 1725 with the construction of the **Spanish Steps** (*Scalinata di Trinità dei Monti*), an exceptionally beautiful and exceptionally Baroque ornament. The youth who loll about here are taking the place of the hopeful artists' models of the more picturesque centuries who once crowded the steps, striking poses of antique heroes and Madonnas, waiting for some easy money. At the top of the stairs the simple but equally effective church of **Trinità dei Monti** (***t*** *06 679 4179; open 9–8*) by Carlo Maderno (early 16th century) was paid for by the king of France. At the southern end of Piazza di Spagna, a Borromini palace housed the papal office called the *Propaganda Fide*, whose job was just what the name implies. The column in front (1857) celebrates the proclamation of the Dogma of the Immaculate Conception. Via del Babuino, a street named after a siren on a fountain so ugly that Romans called her the 'baboon', connects Piazza di Spagna with Piazza del Popolo. Besides its very impressive antique shops, the street carries on the English connection, with All Saints' Church, a sleepy neo-pub and an English bookshop just off it.

Piazza del Popolo

If you have a choice of how you enter Rome, this is the way to do it, through the gate in the old Aurelian wall and into one of the most successful of all Roman piazzas, copied on a smaller scale all over Italy. No city has a better introduction, and the three diverging boulevards direct you with thoughtful efficiency towards your destination. Valadier, the pope's architect after the Napoleonic occupation, gave the piazza the form it has today, but the big obelisk of Pharaoh Ramses II, punctuating the view down the boulevards, arrived in the 1580s. It is 3,200 years old but, like all obelisks, it looks mysteriously brand-new. Augustus brought it to Rome from Heliopolis and planted it in the Circus Maximus; it was transferred here by Pope Sixtus V. The two domed churches designed by Rainaldi, set like bookends at the entrance to the three boulevards, are from the 1670s, part of the original plan for the piazza to which Bernini and Fontana may have contributed.

Nero's ashes were interred in a mausoleum here, at the foot of the Monte Pincio. The site was planted with walnut trees and soon everyone in Rome knew that Nero's ghost haunted the grove, sending out demons – in the form of flocks of ravens that nested there – to perform deeds of evil. In about 1100 Pope Paschal II destroyed the grove and scattered the ashes; to complete the exorcism he built a church on the site, **Santa Maria del Popolo** (***t*** *06 361 0636; open Mon–Fri 6–1 and 5–7.30, Sat–Sun 8–1 and 5–7.30*). Rebuilt in the 1470s, it contains some of the best painting in Rome: Caravaggio's stunning *Crucifixion of St Peter* and *Conversion of St Paul* (in the left transept), and frescoes by Pinturicchio near the altar. Raphael designed the Chigi Chapel, off the left aisle, including its mosaics.

Villa Borghese

From Piazza del Popolo a winding ramp leads up to Rome's great complex of parks. Just by coincidence this was mostly parkland in ancient times. The **Monte Pincio** once formed part of Augustus' imperial gardens, and the adjacent **Villa Medici** (*Viale della*

Trinità dei Monti 1, ***t*** *06 676 1305, www.villamedici.it; open for guided tours of the gardens 1 Mar–31 May and 6–25 Oct, Sun every half-hour 10–12.30*) occupies the site of the Villa of Lucullus, the 2nd-century BC philosopher and general who conquered northern Anatolia and first brought cherries to Europe. Now the home of the French Academy, the Villa Medici was a posh jail of sorts for Galileo during his Inquisitorial trials. The Pincio, redesigned by Valadier as a lovely formal garden, offers rare views over Rome. It is separated from the **Villa Borghese** (*open dawn–sunset*) proper by the Aurelian wall and the modern sunken roadway that borders it; its name, Viale del Muro Torto (crooked wall), refers to a section that collapsed in the 6th century and was left as it was because it was believed to be protected by St Peter.

Exploring the vast spaces of Villa Borghese, you will come across charming vales, woods and a pond (rowing boats for hire), an imitation Roman temple or two, rococo avenues where the bewigged dandies and powdered tarts of the 1700s came to promenade, bits of ancient aqueduct and a **zoo** (*Piazzale del Giardino Zoologico,* ***t*** *06 360 8211, www.bioparco.it; open daily Mar–Oct 9.30–6, Oct–Mar 9.30–5; adm*), which is finally becoming more eco-friendly and has rechristened itself the Bioparco. On the northern edge of the park is a ponderous boulevard called **Viale delle Belle Arti**, where academies have been set up by foreign governments to stimulate cultural exchange. The **Galleria Nazionale d'Arte Moderna** (***t*** *06 322 981; open Tues–Sun 8.30–7.30; adm; guided tours in English by reservation, Sun 11am, €4 extra*) makes its home here in one of Rome's most inexcusable buildings (1913), but the collection includes some great works of Modigliani and the Futurists, as well as a fair sampling of 19th- and 20th-century artists from the rest of Europe.

From there, gingerly skirting the Romanian Academy, you come to the **Museo Etrusco Nazionale di Villa Giulia** (***t*** *06 321 7224; open Tues–Sun 8.30–7.30; adm, entrance on Piazzale di Villa Giulia*). If you cannot make it to Tarquínia, this is the place to get to know the Etruscans. Some of their best art has been collected here, as well as laboriously reconstructed terracotta façades to give you some idea of how an Etruscan temple looked. As usual, the compelling attraction is the Etruscans' effortless, endearing talent for portraiture: expressive faces that bridge the gap between the centuries can be seen in terracotta ex-votos (some of children), sarcophagi and even architectural decoration. Serious art is often more stylized; fine examples are the charming couple on the *Sarcophago dei Sposi* from Cervéteri, and the roof statues from the Temple of Portonaccio at Veii – these by Vulca, the only Etruscan artist whose name has survived along with his work. The museum building and its courts and gardens are attractions in themselves; Julius III had Vignola and Ammannati build this quirky Mannerist villa in 1553, and Vasari and Michelangelo may also have helped.

The fantastic trove of ancient relics and late-Renaissance and Baroque painting and sculpture – including masterpieces by Bernini and Caravaggio – at the **Museo e Galleria Borghese** (***t*** *06 32810; open Tues–Sun 9–7; adm, advance booking (€1 fee) recommended and essential in summer; guided visits of museum at 9.10 and 11.10, €5; guided tours of the Villa's Secret Gardens Sat at 10.30, free, call to reserve,* ***t*** *06 8107 7304*) is testimony to the legendary greed and avarice of Cardinal Scipione Borghese, nephew of Pope Paul IV. He amassed, by any means available, one of the great private collections of the 17th century and built a magnificently decorated palace on the family's property to hold it. The display today is all the more impressive because a descendant of the Cardinal 'sold' many pieces to his brother-in-law, Napoleon Bonaparte, who put them in the Louvre.

The Museo Borghese (ground floor) offers an intriguing mix of great art and Roman preciosity. Often the two go hand-in-hand, as with the sensuously charged show-pieces of Bernini: *Apollo and Daphne*, *The Rape of Proserpina* and especially his *David*, which the artist modestly chiselled in his own image. Canova, the hot item among sculptors in Napoleon's day, contributes a titillatingly languorous statue of Pauline Borghese (Napoleon's sister) as the *Conquering Venus*. Even the ancient world joins in the fun, with such works as the famous Hellenistic *Sleeping Hermaphrodite*. Also downstairs are several Caravaggios, including the *Madonna of the Palafrenieri*, *David with the Head of Goliath* and *St Jerome*.

No less impressive are the paintings in the gallery upstairs (entrance through the café in the basement), representing many of the finest 16th- and 17th-century painters: Titian's *Sacred and Profane Love*, *St Sebastian* and *Christ Scourged*, two Bernini self-portraits, Raphael's *Deposition*, Correggio's *Danae* and Rubens' *Deposition*.

Via Veneto and the Quirinale

This chain of gardens was once much bigger, but at the end of the last century many of the old villas were lost to the inevitable expansion of the city. Perhaps the greatest loss was the Villa Ludovisi, praised by many as the most beautiful of all Rome's parks. Now the choice 'Ludovisi' quarter, it has given the city one of its most famous streets, Via Veneto, the long winding boulevard of grand hotels, cafés and boutiques that stretches down from Villa Borghese to Piazza Barberini. A promenade for the smart set in the 1950s, it wears something of the forlorn air of a jilted beau now that fashion has moved on.

Pull yourself away from the passing show on the boulevard to take in the unique spectacle provided by the **Convento dei Cappuccini** at the southern end of the street, just up from Piazza Barberini (*entrance halfway up the stairs of Santa Maria della Concezione; open daily 9–12 and 3–6; adm*). Unique, that is, outside Palermo, for, much like the Capuchin convent there, the Roman brethren have created a loving tribute to our friend Death. In the cellars 4,000 dead monks team up for an unforgettable *Danse Macabre* of bones and grinning skulls, carefully arranged by serious-minded Capuchins long ago to remind us of something we know only too well.

On the other side of Piazza Barberini, up a gloomy Baroque avenue called Via delle Quattro Fontane, you'll find the Palazzo Barberini, one of the showier places in Rome, decorated everywhere with the bees from the family arms. Maderno, Borromini and Bernini all worked on it, with financing made possible by the election of a Barberini as Pope Urban VIII in 1623. Currently it houses the **Galleria Nazionale d'Arte Antica** (***t*** *06 481 4591; open Tues–Sun 8.30–7.30; adm*) – a misleading title, since this is a gallery devoted to Italian works of the 12th–18th centuries. Often the original decoration steals the show from the pictures: Bernini's Great Hall, for example, with a ceiling fresco by Pietro da Cortona, the *Triumph of Divine Providence*, or the ceiling in Room 7, with a fresco by Andrea Sacchi where the enthroned Virgin looking down on the round earth seems like a Baroque attempt to create a new Catholic astronomy. Works present include a Bernini self-portrait, Raphael's famous portrait of his beloved mistress *La Fornarina*, the 'baker's girl', more portraits by the Genoese artist Baciccio, lots of Caravaggios, Lippi's *Madonna* and two rather sedate pictures by El Greco. A large section of 15th-century artists not from Tuscany proves that not all the action was happening in Florence.

San Carlino (*t 06 488 3261; open Mon–Fri 9–1 and 3–4, Sat 9–12.30, Sun 10.30–1*), on the corner of Via delle Quattro Fontane and Via Quirinale, is one of Borromini's best works – and his first one (1638), a purposely eccentric little flight of fancy built exactly the size of one of the four massive pillars that hold up the dome in St Peter's. Just down the street, his rival Bernini counters with **Sant'Andrea al Quirinale** (1658–70), a small, richly decorated elliptical church that is one of the great architectural *tours de force* of the Baroque. Continue down **Via Quirinale** and you'll reach the summit of that hill, covered with villas and gardens in ancient times, and abandoned in the Middle Ages. Then even the name Quirinale had been forgotten, and the Romans called the place 'Montecavallo' after the two big horses' heads projecting above the ground. During the reign of Sixtus V they were excavated to reveal monumental Roman statues of the **Dioscuri** (Castor and Pollux), probably copied from Phidias or Praxiteles. Together with a huge basin found in the Forum, they make a centrepiece for Piazza del Quirinale. Behind it, stretching for a dreary half-kilometre along the street is the **Palazzo del Quirinale** (*t 06 46991; open late Sept–early July, Sun 8.30–12.30; adm*), built in 1574 to symbolize the political domination of the popes, later occupied by the kings of Italy, and now the official residence of the country's president.

Around Stazione Termini: Terme di Diocleziano and Museo Nazionale Romano

Rome's great big station takes its name from the nearby **Terme di Diocleziano** (*t 06 3996 7700; open Tues–Sun 9–7; adm; adm included with Roma Archeologia Card, see p.86, and Museum Card, see p.131*), just on the other side of Piazza dei Cinquecento, which is part of the **Museo Nazionale Romano**, the greatest Italian collection of antiquities after the museum in Naples. Until the popes dismantled the baths for building stone this was by far Rome's biggest ruin; its outer wall followed the present-day lines of Via XX Settembre, Via Volturno and Piazza dei Cinquecento, and the big semi-circular **Piazza della Repubblica**, with its mouldering, grandiose 1890s palazzi and huge fountain, occupies the site of the baths' exercise ground, or *palaestra*. All together the complex covered some 11 hectares. Michelangelo, not on one of his better days, converted a section of the lofty, vaulted central bathhouse into the church of **Santa Maria degli Angeli**, conserving some of the building's original form and adding a broad new cloister. The cloister and the adjoining building now house part of the Museo Nazionale Romano's enormous collection.

Across the street, you can see more of the Museo Nazionale's holdings at the unmissable **Palazzo Massimo alle Terme** (*t 06 3996 7700; open Tues–Sun 9–7; adm;*

adm included with Roma Archeologia Card, see p.86, and Museum Card, see p.131). The basement, courtyard and first floor contain coins, jewellery, busts and statuary, but it's the delicate frescoes and mosaics from the Villa di Livia, the Villa della Farnesina and other aristocratic homes which really stand out (*visits by guided tour only because of the fragility of the collection; the time will be marked on your admission ticket. Tours start on the second floor*). There's a shimmering sea-green forest of fruit trees and exotic birds which once covered the dining room of the Villa di Livia, and a lively fresco from the old fish market with boats and fishermen grinning among shoals of ludicrously outsized fish – an advertisement for what was on offer at the market stalls.

A block north of the baths, Piazza San Bernardo has two interesting churches: **San Bernardo**, built out of a circular library that once occupied a corner of the baths' walls, and **Santa Maria della Vittoria** (***t** 06 482 6190; open 7–12 and 4.30–7*), home to one of the essential works of Baroque sculpture, the disconcertingly erotic *St Teresa in Ecstasy* by Bernini (in a chapel off the left aisle).

The Patriarchal Basilicas

Besides St Peter's there are three Patriarchal Basilicas, ancient and revered churches under the care of the pope that have always been a part of the Roman Pilgrimage. Santa Maria Maggiore, San Paolo Fuori le Mura (*see* p.148) and San Giovanni in Laterano are all on the edges of the city, away from the political and commercial centre; by the Middle Ages they stood in open countryside, and only recently has the city grown outwards to swallow them once more.

Santa Maria Maggiore

Santa Maria Maggiore, on Monte Esquilino, was probably begun about 352, when a rich Christian saw a vision of the Virgin directing him to build a church; Pope Liberius had received the same vision at the same time, and the two supposedly found the site marked out for them by a miraculous August snowfall. The church (***t** 06 483 195; open 7–7; call for info on guided visits to the Loggia delle Benedizioni, which has 13th-century mosaics depicting the legend of the church's foundation*) took its current form in the 1740s, with a perfectly elegant façade by Fernando Fuga and an equally impressive rear elevation by other architects; the obelisk behind it came from the Mausoleum of Augustus. Above everything rises the tallest and fairest **campanile** in Rome, an incongruous survival from the 1380s. Inside, the most conspicuous feature is the coffered ceiling by Giuliano da Sangallo, gilded with the first gold brought back from the New World by Columbus, a gift from King Ferdinand and Queen Isabella of Spain. In the apse there are splendid but faded mosaics from 1295 of the *Coronation of the Virgin*; others, from the 5th century, decorate the nave and the 'triumphal arch' in front of the apse. Santa Maria Maggiore has a prize relic – nothing less than the genuine manger from Bethlehem, preserved in a sunken shrine in front of the altar; in front, kneeling, is a colossal, rather grotesque statue of Pope Pius IV added in the 1880s.

In 822, two decades after Charlemagne visited Rome, Pope Paschal I found the money and the talent to build works he hoped would be compared to the magnificent

Santa Maria Maggiore

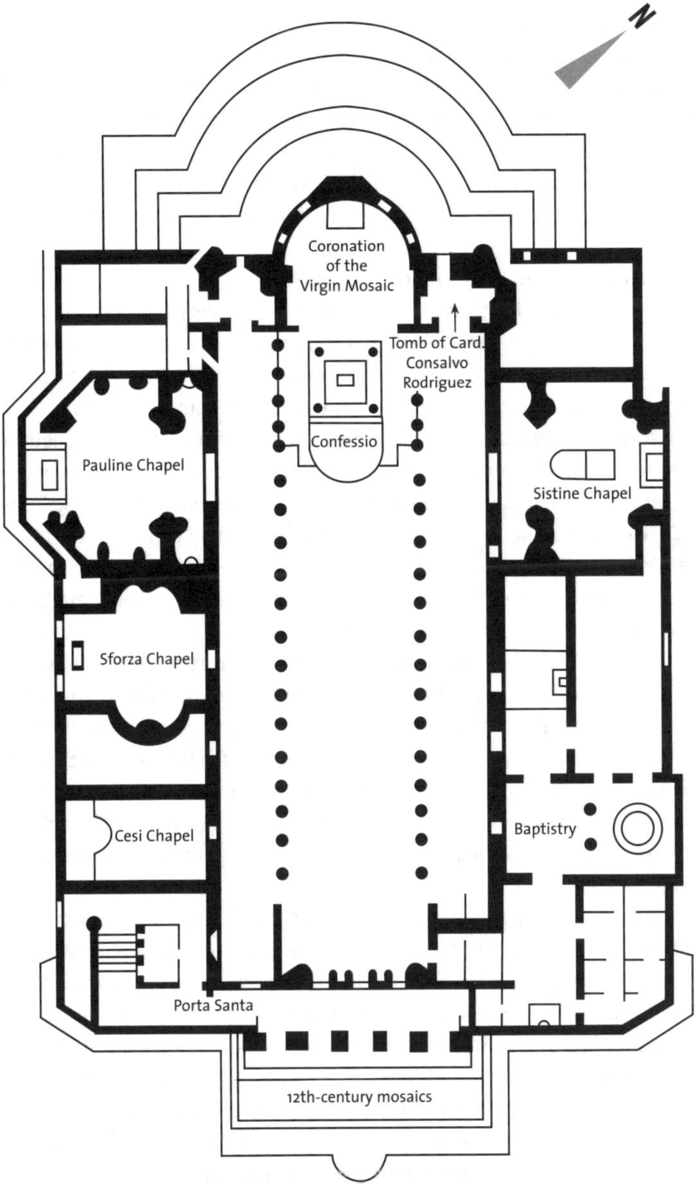

ruins that lay on every side. The churches he had rebuilt near Santa Maria Maggiore commemorating two sisters, early Christian martyrs of the 1st century, were not large, but they were a start, and to embellish them he imported Byzantine artists who originated a rebirth of mosaic work and painting in Rome. **Santa Pudenziana** (*Via Urbana 160;* ***t*** *06 481 4622; open 7–7*) conserves a mosaic of *Christ and the Apostles* from the

4th century, a thoroughly classical work from the very beginnings of Christian art. At **Santa Prassede** the mosaics reveal a different world: the shadowy Rome of the not-entirely Dark Ages. The jewel of Santa Prassede (*Via Santa Prassede 9/a, **t** 06 488 2456; open 7–12 and 4–6.30*) is the small San Zeno Chapel, which Paschal intended as a mausoleum for his mother. The square vaulted chamber is entirely covered with gold-ground mosaics of Christ Pantocrator, saints and some very dignified, classical angels who look as if they never heard anything about the fall of Rome. The 9th-century mosaics around the altar are even better, if less golden.

San Giovanni in Laterano (St John Lateran)

Where is Rome's cathedral? It isn't St Peter's, and never has been. The true seat of the Bishop of Rome, and the end of a Roman Pilgrimage, is here in the shadow of the Aurelian wall, a church established by Constantine himself (***t** 06 6988 6433; open daily 7–6.45; Museo Sacro and cloister open 9–6*). The family of Plautius Lateranus, according to ancient records, had their property here confiscated after a failed coup against Nero in AD 66. It eventually became part of the imperial real estate and Constantine and his wife Fausta (whom he later executed) once kept house in the Lateran Palace. Later he donated it to Pope Miltiades as a cult centre for the Christians of Rome. Almost nothing remains of the original basilica; the sacks of the Vandals and Normans, two earthquakes and several fires have resulted in a building made up of bits and pieces from each of the last 16 centuries.

Like Santa Maria Maggiore, this church has an 18th-century exterior that is almost miraculously good considering other Italian buildings from that age, with a west front by Alessandro Galilei (1736) that confidently and competently re-uses the High Renaissance architectural vernacular. The equally fine north façade is older, done by Domenico Fontana in 1586, and incorporates the twin medieval bell towers. Entering at the west front you pass an ancient statue of Constantine, found at the baths he built on the Quirinale; the bronze doors in the central portal once graced the Senate House in the Forum.

Inside, the nave is dominated by giant statues of the Apostles (*c.* 1720), glaring down like Roman emperors of old. There is some carefree and glorious Baroque work in the side chapels – also remains of a fresco by Giotto, behind the first column on the right. Near the apse, decorated with 13th-century mosaics (of a reindeer worshipping the cross, an odd conceit probably adapted from older mosaics in Ravenna), the Papal Altar supposedly contains the heads of Peter and Paul. Below floor level is the tomb of Pope Martin V; pilgrims drop flowers and coins on him for good luck.

Rome in the later Middle Ages had evolved an architectural style entirely its own, uninterested in Gothic or reviving classicism, or, for that matter, in anything else that was going on in the rest of Italy. Sadly, almost all of it disappeared in the Renaissance and Baroque rebuildings. The towers of Santa Maria in Cosmedin and Santa Maria Maggiore are good examples of it, as well as the expressive mosaics of Pietro Cavallini and his school and the intricate, geometrical Cosmatesque pavements in this church and so many others. Perhaps the most striking survival of this lost chapter in art is the Lateran **cloister** (*open daily 9–6, until 5 in winter; adm*), with its pairs of spiral columns and 13th-century Cosmatesque mosaics; it completely upstages everything else in the church. All around the cloister walls, fragments from the earlier incarnations of the basilica have been assembled, a hoard of broken pretty things that includes an interesting tomb of a 13th-century bishop, which may be the work of Arnolfo di Cambio.

The Lateran's **baptistry** (*open daily 8–12.30 and 3.30–7*) is no ordinary baptistry – nothing less than the first one in Christendom, converted from an older temple by Constantine; its octagonal form has been copied in other baptistries all over Italy. Inside there are unusual pairs of bronze doors on either side: one from 1196 with scenes of how the Lateran basilica appeared at that time, and the other from the Baths of Caracalla, 'singing' doors that make a low, harmonic sound when you open them slowly. Built around the baptistry are three venerable chapels with more mosaics from the early Middle Ages. The entrance to the baptistry is in Piazza San Giovanni in Laterano, behind the **Lateran Palace** (***t** 06 6988 6452; open Mon–Sat 8–1; adm*) rebuilt in 1588 over the original building that had served as home for the popes from the 4th to the 14th centuries.

Across the piazza, which has the obligatory obelisk at its centre, you will see the **Scala Santa** (***t** 06 6988 6392; open daily 6.15–12 and 3.30–6.45, in winter 3–6*), supposedly the stairs of Pilate's palace in Jerusalem, ascended by Christ on his way to Judgement and brought to Rome by Constantine's mother, St Helena. Serious pilgrims ascend them on their knees. The Chapel of San Lorenzo at the top, a part of the medieval Papal Palace, contains two miraculous portraits of Jesus, painted by angels. While you're here, you have a good opportunity to explore the Aurelian Wall. The stretch of it behind the Lateran Palace probably looks much as it did originally, and the nearby **Porta Asinara** (next to Porta San Giovanni) is one of the best-preserved monumental ancient gateways.

Monte Celio

South of the Colosseum you can see nothing but trees, but, on every inch of this vast tract of parkland, ancient neighbourhoods wait just a few feet beneath the surface. Modern Rome never expanded in this direction, and almost the whole of it has been preserved as open space. It's a fascinating place to walk around, if you can avoid the traffic thundering down the big boulevards towards the southern suburbs. The Monte Celio is only a small part of it, but it is one of the least known and most delightful corners of Rome. Have a picnic in the **Villa Celimontana** (*behind Piazza della Navicella; open daily 7am–sunset*) and you may have only squirrels for company.

Some of Rome's most ancient churches repose in quiet settings here, all worth a look inside if they are open. **Santo Stefano Rotondo** (*Piazza della Navicella, at Via de Santo Stefano Rotondo, **t** 06 7049 3717; open Tues–Sat 9–1 and 3.30–6, Mon 3.30–6 only*), the oldest circular church in Italy, was built around 470 over the ruins of a market-place of Nero's time; across the street more mosaics from the age of Paschal I (*c*. 820) can be seen in **Santa Maria in Domnica** (***t** 06 700 1519; open 9–12 and 3.30–7, in winter until 6*) standing in **Piazza della Navicella**, with a fountain made in the form of an ancient Roman ship. Take the narrow road (just downhill from the church) that cuts down into the hill to **SS. Giovanni e Paolo** (*open 8.30–12 and 3–6.30*), built in the 4th century in the top floor of three Roman houses, which have just emerged from restoration and can be visited (*adm*). Down the western slope you reach **San Gregorio Magno** (***t** 06 5526 1617; open 8–12.30 and 4–6.30*), begun by Pope Gregory the Great in 590. St Augustine lived here before being sent by Gregory to convert the Angles and Saxons of Britain. Adjacent to the church are several chapels with remarkable frescoes by Guido Reni, Domenichino and Pomarancio.

Circus Maximus and Terme di Caracalla (Caracalla's Baths)

Piazza Porta Capena, at the foot of the Monte Celio, has an odd decoration, an obelisk erected by Mussolini to commemorate his conquest of Ethiopia – he stole it from the Ethiopian city of Axum, although at long last it is scheduled to be returned to its rightful owner. The piazza itself is a vortex of Mussolinian pretensions; the dictator built himself a new Triumphal Way (now Via San Gregorio) along the route of the original one, to celebrate his piddling triumphs in Roman imperial style. A huge building that was to house the Ministry of Africa to administer Mussolini's colonies found a more agreeable use after the war – as home of the United Nations Food and Agricultural Organization (FAO). To the west, a broad green lawn is all that's left of the **Circus Maximus**. Archaeologists have estimated that as many as 300,000 Romans could squeeze in here and bet on the chariot races. Founded by King Tarquin and completed by Trajan, the stadium proved simply too convenient a quarry; the banked, horseshoe-shaped depression, however, still follows the line of the grandstands.

The **Terme di Caracalla** (AD 206–220), in a large park south of Porta Capena, rank with those of Diocletian as the largest and most lavish (***t** 06 975 8626; open Tues–Sun 9–1hr before sunset, Mon 9–2; adm, or with Roma Archeologia Card, p.86; guided tours Sat and Sun 10.30, audioguide €4*). Roughly 1,000ft square, with libraries and exercise courts, the baths probably boasted more gold, marble and art than any building complex in Rome; here the Farnese family dug up such masterpieces as the *Hercules* and the *Farnese Bull*, now in the Naples Museum. In the 1700s these baths were one of the obligatory sights of the Grand Tour; their lofty, broken arches and vaults appealed to the Romantic love of ruins like no other. Much of the central building survives, with its hot and cold rooms, great hall and swimming pool, all decorated with mosaics. A large tunnel connects the baths with the area around Palazzo Venezia, a mile away; its purpose was to transport the vast amounts of wood needed to keep the baths hot. Mussolini initiated the custom (now provisionally discontinued owing to the frailty of the ruins) of holding summer operas here; he liked to drive his roadster through the tunnel and pop out dramatically on stage at the beginning of the festivities.

Behind the baths a stretch of the **Antonine Aqueduct** that supplied it can still be seen. On the other side, facing Via Terme di Caracalla, **SS. Nereo e Achilleo** (*open daily 10–12 and 4–6; ring for custodian*) has more mosaics from the time of Leo III (*c.* 800), a Cosmatesque floor and choir and some gruesome 16th-century frescoes of the martyrdoms of the saints.

The Via Appia: Rome's Catacombs

The hop-on, hop-off 'Archeobus' minibus departs from the Piazza Venezia and heads down the Via Appia all the way to the Villa dei Quintili. There are hourly departures, and tickets (available on the bus) are valid all day, priced €7.75.

Rome's 'Queen of Roads', the path of trade and conquest to Campania, Brindisi and the East, was begun in 312 BC by Consul Appius Claudius. Like most of the consular roads outside Rome, over the centuries it became lined with cemeteries and the elaborate mausolea of the wealthy, since ancient Roman practice, inherited from the Etruscans, prohibited any burials within the *pomerium*, the sacred ground of the city itself. Later the early Christians built extensive catacombs here – the word itself comes from the location, *ad catacumbas*, referring to the dip in the Via Appia near the suburban Circus of Maxentius. The Via Appia Antica (as distinguished from the modern Via Appia Nuova) makes a pleasant excursion outside the city, especially on Sundays when the road is closed to traffic all the way back to Piazza Venezia.

The road passes under the Aurelian wall at **Porta San Sebastiano**, one of the best-preserved of the old gates. It houses the **Museo delle Mura** (***t** 06 7047 5284; open Tues–Sun 9–7, in winter until 5.30; adm*), admission to which also gives you access to a well-preserved section of the 4th-century wall alongside it. Continuing along the road, after about ½km, with some ruins of tombs along the way, there is the famous church of **Domine Quo Vadis?** (***t** 06 512 0441; open 7.30–6.45*), on the spot where Peter, fleeing from the dangers of Rome, met Christ coming the other way. 'Where goest thou, Lord?' Peter asked. 'I am going to be crucified once more,' was the reply. As the vision departed the shamed Apostle turned back, to face his own crucifixion in Rome.

Another kilometre or so takes you to the **Catacombe di San Callisto**, off on a side road to the right (*open for guided tours only, summer Thurs–Tues 8.30–12 and 2.30–5; winter 8.30–12 and 2.30–5, closed Feb; adm*). Here the biggest attraction is the 'Crypt of the Popes', burial places of 3rd- and 4th-century pontiffs with some well-executed frescoes and inscriptions. A word about catacombs: popular romance and modern cinema notwithstanding, these were never places of refuge from persecution, but simply burial grounds. The word 'catacombs' was only used after the 5th century; before that the Christians simply called them 'cemeteries'. The burrowing instinct is harder to explain. Few other places have ancient catacombs (Naples, Syracuse, Malta and the Greek island of Milos are among them). One of the requirements seems to be tufa, or some other stone that can be easily excavated. Even so, the work involved was tremendous, and not explainable by any reasons of necessity. Christians were still digging them after they had become a power in Rome, in Constantine's time. No one knows for certain what sort of funeral rites were celebrated in them, just as no one knows much about any of the prayers or rituals of the early Christians; we can only suspect that a Christian of the 4th century and one of the 16th would have had considerable difficulty recognizing each other as brothers in the faith.

Most catacombs began small, as private family cemeteries; over generations some grew into enormous termitaries extending for miles. Inside, most of the tombs you see will be simple *loculi*, walled-up niches with only a symbol or short inscription. Others, especially the tombs of popes or the wealthy, may have paintings of scriptural scenes, usually very poor work that reflects more on the dire state of the late Roman imagination than on the Christians.

You can detour from here another ½km west to the **Catacombe di Santa Domitilla** (*Via delle Sette Chiese 283; **t** 06 511 0342; open Feb–Dec for guided tours only, Wed–Mon 8.30–12 and 2.30–5.30; adm*). She was a member of a senatorial family and, interestingly, the catacombs seem to incorporate parts of earlier pagan hypogea, including a cemetery of the Imperial Flavian family; the paintings include an unusual *Last Supper* scene, portraying a young and beardless Jesus and Apostles in Roman dress. There is an adjacent basilica, built about the tombs of SS. Nereus and Achilleus, on Via delle Sette Chiese. Not far away on Via Ardeatina 174 is a monument to martyrs of a very different sort, the **Mausoleum of the Fosse Ardeatine** (***t** 06 513 6742; open Mon–Fri 8.15–6.45, weekends 8.15–3.30*), dedicated to the 335 Romans massacred by the Nazis on this spot in 1944 in retaliation for a partisan attack. Back on the Via Appia Antica, there are several catacombs near the corner of Via Appia Pignatelli, including a Jewish one (*closed*); the largest are the **Catacombe di San Sebastiano** (***t** 06 788 735; open for guided tours only Fri–Wed 8.30–12 and 2.30–5.30, closed Nov; adm*). This complex, too, began as a pagan cemetery and has intriguing paintings and incised symbols throughout. The place had some special significance for the early Christians, and it has been conjectured that Peter and Paul were originally buried here, before their removal to the basilicas in Constantine's time.

Further south, by now in fairly open country, there are the ruins of the **Circus of Maxentius** (***t** 06 780 1324; open April–Sept, Tues–Sat, 9–7 and Sun 9–1; Oct–Mar Tues–Sat 9–5, Sun 9–1; adm*), built in the early 4th century, and then the imposing cylindrical **Tomb of Cecilia Metella** (***t** 06 780 2465; open Tues–Sun 9–7; adm, or with Roma Archeologia Card, see p.86*), from the time of Augustus. In the Middle Ages the Caetani family turned the tomb into a family fortress, guarding the road to the south; at other times, before and since, it was a famous rendezvous for *banditti*. The road continues, flanked by tombs and stately pines, with stretches of the original paving, for 16km beyond the walls of Rome. Further out still are the extensive, marble-strewn remains of the **Villa dei Quintili** (*open 9am–one hour before sunset; adm, or with Roma Archeologia Card, see p.86*), built in the 2nd century AD by the Quintilius brothers and once the largest villa outside the city walls.

Monte Aventino

Every now and then, when left-wing parties walk out of negotiations, Italian newspapers may call it an 'Aventine Secession', an off-the-cuff reference to events in Rome 2,500 years ago. Under the Republic, the Monte Aventino was the most solidly plebeian quarter of the city. On several occasions, when legislation proposed by the senate and consuls seriously threatened the rights or interests of the people, they retired *en masse* to the Aventino and stayed there until the plan was dropped. Rome's unionists are probably unaware that their ancestors had the honour of inventing the general strike.

The Aventino had another distinction in those times. In its uninhabited regions – the steep, cave-ridden slopes towards the south – Greek immigrants and returning soldiers introduced the midnight rituals of Dionysus/Bacchus. Though secret, such goings-on soon came to the attention of the senate, which rightly saw the orgies as a danger to the state and banned them in 146 BC. They must not have died out completely, however, as in the Middle Ages the Aventino had a reputation as a haunt of witches. The early Christian community also prospered here, and their churches are the oldest relics on the Aventino today.

Coming up from the Circus Maximus along Via Santa Sabina, **Santa Sabina** (*Piazza Pietro d'Illiria; open daily 6.30–12 and 3.30–7*) is a simple, rare example of a 5th-century basilica, with an atrium at its entrance like a Roman secular basilica, and an original door of cypress carved with scriptural scenes. This has been the head church of the Dominicans ever since a 13th-century pope gave it to St Dominic. Both Santa Sabina and the church of **Sant'Alessio** (*open daily 8.30–8*) down the street have good Cosmatesque cloisters.

At the end of this street, one of the oddities only Rome can offer stands on its quiet square, oblivious of the centuries: the **Priorato dei Cavalieri di Malta** (*open for guided tours by prior arrangement; call **t** 06 577 9193*), a fancy rococo complex designed by Giambattista Piranesi. The Knights of Malta – or more properly, the Knights Hospitallers of St John – no longer wait for the popes to unleash them against Saracen and Turk. Mostly this social club for nobles bestirs itself to assist hospitals, its original job during the Crusades. The Order's ambassadors to Italy and the Vatican still live here. You can't go inside, but the gate is the most visited in Rome for the intriguing view through the keyhole.

Elsewhere on the Aventino, **Santa Prisca** (***t** 06 3996 7700; open by appointment only*) has beginnings typical of an early Roman church; its crypt, the original church, was allegedly converted from the house of the martyr Prisca, host to St Peter; the Apostle must have often presided over Mass here. **San Saba** (*Via San Saba; open 7–12 and 4–7*) was founded in the 7th century by monks fleeing the Arabs in Jordan and Syria, with a 1205 rebuilding, including some Cosmatesque details, a superb mosaic floor and a crypt with 7th–11th-century frescoes.

Rome's Pyramid and Monte Testaccio

Porta San Paolo stands in one of the best-preserved sections of the Aurelian wall. The gate itself looks just as it did 1,700 years ago, when it was the *Porta Ostiense*; its change of name came about because Paul passed through it on the way to his execution. Near the gate is something unique: the 92ft **Pyramid of Caius Cestius** (AD 12) may seem a strange self-tribute for a Roman, but at least Cestius, who had served in Egypt, paid for the tomb himself.

Behind it, inside the walls, the lovely **Cimitero Protestante** (*Via Caio Cestio 6; **t** 06 574 1900; open Tues–Sun 9–5.30, in winter until 4.30; ring the bell at the gate; donation expected*) is a popular point of Romantic pilgrimage. The graves of Shelley and Keats are there, recently joined by 400 British soldiers who died during the march on Rome in 1944. Just to the west is the youngest of Rome's hills, **Monte Testaccio**, made up almost entirely of pot-shards. In ancient times, wine, oil, olives and nearly everything else were shipped in big *amphorae*; here, in what was Rome's port warehouse district, all the broken, discarded ones accumulated in one place. The hill, now grassed over, is 115ft at its highest point – there is a big cross on top – and it covers a large area. The vast cellars the Romans left beneath it are now used as workshops, wine cellars and nightclubs that make Testaccio a swinging area after dark.

San Paolo Fuori le Mura (Outside the Walls)

***t** 06 541 0341; basilica open 7–6.30, cloister 9–1 and 3–6.*

Paul was beheaded near the Ostia road; according to an old legend, the head bounced three times, and at each place where it hit a fountain sprung up. The Abbazia delle Tre Fontane, near EUR, occupies the site today. Later, Constantine built a basilica alongside the road as a fitting resting place for the saint. Of the five patriarchal basilicas this one has had the worst luck. Today it sits in the middle of factories, gasworks and concrete flats. Once St Paul's was the grandest of them all; 9th-century chroniclers speak of the separate walled city of 'Giovannipolis' that had grown up around it, connected to the Aurelian wall by a 1½km-long colonnade built by Pope John VIII in the 870s. The Norman sack of 1084, a few good earthquakes, and finally a catastrophic fire in 1823 wiped Giovannipolis off the map, and left us with a St Paul's that for the most part is barely more than a century old. Still, the façade of golden mosaics and sturdy Corinthian columns is pleasant to look at, and some older features survive – the 11th-century door made in Constantinople, a Gothic *baldacchino* over Paul's tomb by Arnolfo di Cambio, a beautiful 13th-century Cosmatesque cloister (almost a double of the one in the Lateran), and 5th-century mosaics over the 'Triumphal Arch' in front of the apse, the restored remains of the original mosaics from the façade, contributed by Empress Galla Placidia. Art Deco is not what you would expect from those times, but Americans at least will have a hard time believing these mosaics were not done by President Roosevelt's WPA. The apse itself has some more conventional mosaics from the 13th-century Roman school, and the nave is lined with the portraits of all 263 popes. According to one Roman legend, when the remaining eight spaces are filled, the world will end.

On the same road as San Paolo (Via Ostiense), is the **Centrale Montemartini** (*open Tues–Sun 9.30–7; adm; combined ticket available with Musei Capitolini (see p.120); metro to Garbatella and cross the flyover towards the Via Ostiense, or take a bus to the Via Ostiense*). The Capitoline Museums have found an unusual home for the overflow of their great hoard of ancient art; this converted power station makes a dramatic setting for busts, mosaics and statuary which are arranged around two enormous power generators. There's a peaceful café on the top floor where you can gaze out across the mosaics and statue gallery below.

Two Roads to St Peter's

One is broad and straight, the route of the many; the other is tortuous and narrow, and after it but few enquire. **Via della Lungara**, the route of the slothful from Trastevere, takes you past **Villa Farnesina** (*open Mon–Sat 9–1; adm*), an early 1500s palace built for the Chigi family. Inside are some of the best frescoes in Rome: the *Galatea* by Raphael and the *Cupid and Psyche Gallery*, designed by Raphael and carried out by his pupils, a prospect of the constellations and a room of false perspectives by Baldassare Peruzzi, who also designed the building; and works of Sodoma. Across the street, the **Palazzo Corsini** (*t 06 6880 2323; open Tues–Sat 8.30–6.30, Sun 9–1; adm*) contains an exceptional collection of 16th- and 17th-century art, including works by Caravaggio, Van Dyck, Guido Reni, Salvatore Rosa and many others – it's out of the way, but this may be the best of all Rome's many small state picture galleries.

The other road may be more difficult to find, but repays the effort with lovely gardens and views over Rome from the Gianicolo, the ancient *Janiculum*. First find Via Garibaldi, in the back streets behind Ponte Sisto, and continue up to the Renaissance church of **San Pietro in Montorio** (*t 06 581 3940; open 9–12 and 4–6; if closed, ring bell at door to right of church*), once erroneously believed to be the spot of St Peter's upside-down crucifixion. A popular church for weddings, it has several fine paintings in the shallow chapels, including a marvellous *Flagellation* by Sebastiano del Piombo – but the real draw here is Bramante's famed **Tempietto** in the adjacent courtyard. In so many Renaissance paintings – Perugino's *Donation of the Keys* in the Sistine Chapel or Raphael's *Betrothal of the Virgin* in Milan – the characters in the foreground take second place in interest to an ethereal, round temple centred at the perspectival vanishing point. These constructions, seemingly built not of vulgar stone but of pure intelligence and light, could stand as a symbol for the aspirations of the Renaissance. Bramante was the first actually to try to build one; his perfect little Tempietto (1502), the first building to re-use the ancient Doric order in all of its proportions, probably inspired Raphael's painting two years later.

Via Garibaldi continues up the *Janiculum* to the gushing **Acqua Paola Fountain**, where you should turn right along the Passeggiata del Gianicolo. The **Garibaldi Monument** stands at the summit, overlooking the Botanical Gardens and the rest of Rome. At the other end of the hill, going towards the Vatican, the road curves downwards, passing the Renaissance church of **Sant'Onofrio** (*open daily 9–1*), with frescoes by Peruzzi in the apse. After descending the Passeggiata del Gianicolo, cross the modern Piazza della Rovere into the Borgo district. On your right is the hospital of Santo Spirito and the church of **Santo Spirito in Sassia** (*open daily 7.30–12 and 3–7.30*). This name may ring a bell for antiquarians. 'Sassia' refers to the Saxons of England, who upon their conversion became among the most devoted servants of the Church. English princes founded this hospital in the 8th century – astounding enough when you think about it. The Angles and Saxons who settled in Rome made up almost a small village unto themselves at this bend of the Tiber, and their 'burgh' gave its name to the neighbourhood called the Borgo today.

Castel Sant'Angelo

Lungotevere Castello 50, **t** *06 3996 7600; open Tues–Sun 9–8; adm; audioguide in English €4. Guided visits, by reservation (extra charge), of the castle in English Tues–Fri 10.30am, Sat–Sun 10.30, 12.15 and 4.30; and of the prisons in English Sun 2.30pm. Note that times of guided tours change, so call in advance to confirm.*

Though intended as a resting place for a most serene emperor, this building has seen more blood, treachery and turmoil than any in Rome. Hadrian designed his own mausoleum three years before his death in 138, on an eccentric plan consisting of a huge marble cylinder surmounted by a conical hill planted with cypresses. The marble, the obelisks and the gold and bronze decorations did not survive the 5th-century sacks, but in about 590, during a plague, Pope Gregory the Great saw a vision of St Michael over the mausoleum, ostensibly announcing the end of the plague, but perhaps also mentioning discreetly that here, if anyone cared to use it, was the most valuable fortress in Europe.

There would be no papacy, perhaps, without this castle – at least not in its present form. Hadrian's cylinder is high, steep and almost solid – impregnable even after the invention of artillery. With rebellions of some sort occurring on average every two years before 1400 the popes often had recourse to this place of safety. It last saw action in the sack of 1527, when the miserable Clement VII withstood a siege of several months while his city went up in flames. The popes also used Castel Sant'Angelo as a prison; famous inmates included Giordano Bruno, Benvenuto Cellini and Beatrice Cenci (better known to the English than the Italians, thanks to Shelley's verse drama). Tosca tosses herself off the top at the end of Puccini's opera.

Inside, the recently restored spiral ramp leads up to the **Papal Apartments**, decorated as lavishly by 16th-century artists as anything in the Vatican. The **Sala Paolina** has frescoes by Perin del Vaga of events in the history of Rome, and the **Sala di Apollo** is frescoed with grotesques attempting to reproduce the wall decorations of Nero's Golden House. Above everything, a mighty statue of Michael commemorates Gregory's vision. As interesting for its structure as anything on display inside, Castel Sant'Angelo makes a great place to rest after the Vatican. The views from the roof are some of the best in Rome, and there's a café on the 4th floor. The three central arches of the **Ponte Sant'Angelo** were built by Hadrian, although the statues of angels added in 1688 steal the show; at once dubbed Bernini's Breezy Maniacs, they battle a never-ending Baroque hurricane to display the symbols of Christ's Passion.

Vatican City

The world's smallest country contains the world's largest museum, piazza, and church. It is next to impossible to see the Vatican Museums, St Peter's and Castel Sant'Angelo all in one day, let alone the **Vatican Gardens**, easily Rome's most beautiful park, with a remarkable Renaissance jewel of a villa inside: the Casino of Pius IV (1558–62) by Pietro Ligorio and Peruzzi (*morning tours May–Sept Mon–Tues and Thurs–Sat; Oct–April on Sat; €9 per person; reserve a few days in advance with the*

Vatican Practicalities

The **museums** are *open Mar–Oct Mon–Fri 8.45–2.20, Sat 8.45–12.20, Nov–Feb Mon–Sat 8.45–12.20; adm; also open (and free) the last Sun of each month 8.45–12.20*. Times are subject to change so confirm in advance. The entrance is on Viale Vaticano, to the north of Piazza San Pietro.

St Peter's is *open daily Nov–March 7–6, April–Oct 8–7*; the basilica is closed when there are official ceremonies in the piazza, although visitors are allowed during Mass. The **dome** is *open summer 8.30–5.45, winter 8.30–4.45* and the **Treasury**, *9–6.15*. The dress code – no shorts, short skirts or sleeveless dresses – is strictly controlled by the papal gendarmes. Free guided visits to St Peter's in English on Sun at 2.30, Mon, Wed–Sun at 3pm.

The **Vatican Information Office**, t 06 6988 1662, in Piazza San Pietro (*open daily 8.30–7*) is very helpful, and there are Vatican post offices on the opposite side of the square and inside the Vatican Museums for distinctive postcards home. The information office arranges 2hr-long morning tours of the **Vatican Gardens**, The rest of the Vatican is strictly off limits, patrolled by Swiss Guards (still recruited from the three Catholic Swiss cantons).

For tickets to the Wednesday morning **papal audience**, usually held at 10.30am in the piazza (*May–Sept*) or in the Nervi Auditorium (*Oct–April*), apply in advance at the Papal Prefecture – through the bronze door in the right-hand colonnade of Piazza San Pietro (*open Mon–Sat 9–1.30*, **t** *06 6988 3114*, ***f*** *06 6988 5863; collect tickets Mon–Sat 3–8 at the Portone del Bronzo on Piazza San Pietro*).

Vatican information office). Nor will you fit in the afternoon tour of the ancient **necropolis** under St Peter's – underneath the crypt, archaeologists in the 1940s discovered a street of Roman tombs, perfectly preserved with many beautiful paintings (*open by appt only for 1½-hour guided visits (in English); adm €8. Call the Ufficio degli Scavi, to the left of St Peter's,* **t** *06 6988 5318, for information; then fax them,* ***f*** *06 6988 5518, with your name, nationality, the language you want a tour in, the dates you are in Rome, and email address and a contact number in Rome – they will confirm a date and time*).

Michelangelo also designed the **wall** that since 1929 has marked the Vatican boundaries. Behind it are things most of us will never see: several small old churches, a printing press, the headquarters of L'Osservatore Romano and Vatican Radio (run, of course, by the Jesuits), a motor garage, a 'Palazzo di Giustizia' and even a big shop – everything the world's smallest nation could ever need. Modern popes, in contrast to their predecessors, do not take up much space. The current **Papal Apartments** are in a corner of the Vatican Palace overlooking Piazza San Pietro; John Paul II usually appears to say a few electrically amplified words from his window at noon on Sundays.

St Peter's

Along Borgo Sant'Angelo, leading towards the Vatican, you can see the famous **covered passageway**, used by the popes since 1277 to escape to the castle when things became dangerous. The customary route, however, leads up **Via della Conciliazione**, a broad boulevard drilled by Mussolini through the tangled web of medieval streets. Critics have said it spoils the surprise, but no arrangement of streets and buildings could really prepare you for Bernini's Brobdingnagian **Piazza San Pietro**. Someone has calculated there is room for about 300,000 people in the piazza, with no crowding. Few have ever noticed Bernini's little joke on antiquity; the open space almost exactly meets the size and dimensions of the Colosseum. Bernini's **Colonnade** (1656), with 284 massive columns and statues of 140 saints, stretches around it like 'the arms of the Church embracing the world' – perhaps the biggest cliché in Christendom by now, but exactly what Bernini had in mind. Stand on either of the two dark stones at the foci of the elliptical piazza and you will see Bernini's forest of columns resolve into neat rows, a subtly impressive optical effect like the hole in the top of the Pantheon. Flanked by two lovely fountains, the work of Maderno and Fontana, the Vatican **obelisk** seems nothing special as obelisks go, but is actually one of the most fantastical relics in all Rome. This obelisk comes from Heliopolis, founded as a capital and cult centre by Akhnaton, the half-legendary Pharaoh who, according to Sigmund Freud and others, founded the first monotheistic religion, influencing Moses and all that came after. Caligula brought it over to Rome in AD 37 to decorate the now-disappeared Circus Vaticanus (later referred to as the Circus of Nero) where it would have overlooked Peter's martyrdom. In the Middle Ages it was placed to the side of the basilica, but Sixtus V moved it to where it now stands in 1586.

It may be irreverent to say so, but the original St Peter's, begun over the Apostle's tomb by Constantine in 324, may well have been a more interesting building: a richly decorated basilica full of gold and mosaics with a vast porch of marble and bronze in front and a lofty campanile, topped by the famous golden cockerel that everyone believed would some day crow to announce the end of the world. This St Peter's, where Charlemagne and Frederick II received their imperial crowns, was falling to pieces by the 1400s, conveniently in time for the popes of the Renaissance to plan a replacement. In about 1450 Nicholas V conceived an almost Neronian building programme for the Vatican, ten times as large as anything his ancestors could have contemplated. It was not until the time of Julius II, however, that Bramante was commissioned to demolish the old church and begin the new. His original plan called for a great dome over a centralized Greek cross. Michelangelo, who took over in 1546, basically agreed, and if he had had his way St Peter's might indeed have become the crowning achievement of Renaissance art that everyone hoped it would be.

Unfortunately over the 120 years of construction too many popes and too many artists got their hand in – Rossellino, Giuliano da Sangallo, Raphael, Antonio da Sangallo, Vignola, Ligorio, Della Porta, Fontana, Bernini and Maderno all contributed something to the hotchpotch we see today. The most substantial tinkering came in the early 17th century, when a committee of cardinals decided that a Latin cross was desired, resulting in the huge extension of the nave that blocks the view of Michelangelo's dome from the piazza. Baroque architects, mistaking size and virtuosity for art, found perfect patrons in the Baroque popes, interested in the power and majesty of the papacy. Passing through Maderno's gigantic façade seems like entering a Grand Central Station full of stone saints and angels, keeping an eye on the clocks overhead as they wait for trains to Paradise. All along the nave, markers showing the length of other proud cathedrals prove how each fails to measure up to the Biggest Church in the World. This being Rome, not even the markers are honest – Milan's cathedral is actually 63ft longer.

The best is on the right: Michelangelo's *Pietà*, now restored and kept behind glass to protect it from future madmen. Sculpted when he was only 25, it helped make Michelangelo's reputation. Its smooth and elegant figures, with the realities of death

St Peter's

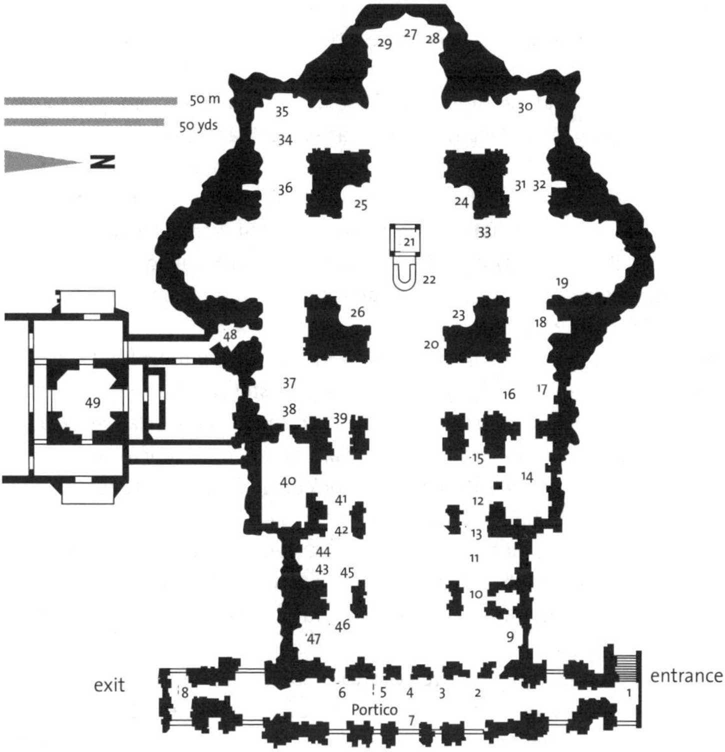

1 Statue of Constantine/ Scala Regia
2 Holy Door
3 Crocetti Door
4 Filarete Door
5 Manzù Door
6 Minguzzi Door
7 Giotto's Navicella
8 Statue of Charlemagne
9 Michelangelo's *Pietà*
10 Queen Christina Monument
11 Cappella di San Sebastino
12 Countess Matilda Monument
13 Innocent XII Monument
14 Cappella del Santissimo Sacramento
15 Gregory XIII Monument
16 Cappella Gregoriana
17 Madonna del Soccorso
18 Lift up to Dome
19 Altar of St Wenceslas
20 Statue of St Peter
21 High Altar/Bernini Baldacchino
22 Confessio
23 St Longinus/Entrance to Grottoes
24 St Helen
25 St Veronica
26 St Andrew
27 Tribune/Cathedra of St Peter
28 Urban VIII Monument
29 Paul III Monument
30 Guercino's St Petronilla
31 Altar of the Navicella
32 Clement XIII Monument
33 St Bruno
34 Cappella della Colonna
35 Leo the Great Tomb
36 Alexander VII Monument
37 Cappella Clementina
38 Pius VII Monument
39 Leo XI Monument
40 Cappella del Coro
41 Innocent VIII Monument
42 Pius X Monument
43 Cappella della Presentazione
44 John XXIII Monument
45 Clementina Sobieska Monument/stairs and down lift from Dome
46 Monument to the last Stuarts
47 Baptistry
48 Pius VIII Monument/entrance to St Peter's Treasury
49 Sacristy

and grief sublimated on to some ethereal plane known only to saints and artists, were a turning point in religious art. From here the beautiful, unreal art of the religious Baroque was the logical next step. Michelangelo carved his name in small letters on the band around the Virgin's garment after overhearing a group of tourists from Milan who thought the *Pietà* the work of a fellow Milanese. Not much else in St Peter's really stands out. In its vast spaces scores of popes and saints are remembered in assembly-line Baroque; the paintings over most of the altars have been replaced by mosaic copies. The famous bronze statute of St Peter, its foot worn away by the touch of millions of pilgrims, is by the right front pier. Stealing the show, as he knew it would, is Bernini's great, garish ***baldacchino*** over the high altar, cast out of bronze looted from the Pantheon roof.

Many visitors head straight for Michelangelo's **dome** (*open summer 8.30–5.45, winter 8.30–4.45; adm €5 with lift, €4 without. There are still 320 steps AFTER the lift to get right up to the cupola viewing terrace*). To be in the middle of such a spectacular construction is worth the climb itself. You can walk out on to the roof for a view over Rome, but even more startling is the chance to look down from the interior balcony over the vast church 250ft below. In the **treasury** (*open 9–6.15; adm*), built in the 18th century, there are a number of treasures – those the Saracens, the imperial soldiers of 1527, and Napoleon couldn't steal. The ancient bronze cockerel from the old St Peter's is kept here, along with ancient relics, Baroque extravaganzas and a gown that belonged to Charlemagne.

Do not pass up a descent to the **Sacred Grottoes** (*same hours as basilica, see p.151*), the foundation of the earlier St Peter's converted into a crypt. Dozens of popes are buried here, along with distinguished friends of the Church like Queen Christina of Sweden and James III, the Stuart pretender. Perhaps the greatest work of art here is the bronze tomb of Sixtus IV, a definitive Renaissance confection by Pollaiuolo, though the most visited is undoubtedly the simple monument to John XXIII.

The Musei Vaticani (Vatican Museums)

The admission (*currently €10, audioguides €5*) may be the most expensive in Italy, but for that you get 10 museums in one, with the Sistine Chapel and the Raphael rooms thrown in free. Altogether almost 7km of exhibits fill the halls of the Vatican Palace, and unfortunately for you there isn't much dull museum clutter that can be passed over lightly. Seeing this infinite, exasperating hoard properly would be the work of a lifetime. On the bright side, the pope sees to it that his museum is managed more intelligently and thoughtfully than anything run by the Italian state. A choice of two colour-coded itineraries, which you may follow according to the amount of time you have to spend, will get you through the labyrinth in two or four hours.

Near the entrance, the first big challenge is the large **Museo Egizio** – one of Europe's best Egyptian collections – and then some rooms of antiquities from the Holy Land and Syria, before the **Museo Chiaramonti**, full of Roman statuary (including famous busts of Caesar, Mark Antony and Augustus) and inscriptions. The **Museo Pio Clementino** contains some of the best-known statues of antiquity: the dramatic *Laocoön*, dug up in Nero's Golden House, and the *Apollo Belvedere*. No other ancient

The Vatican Museums

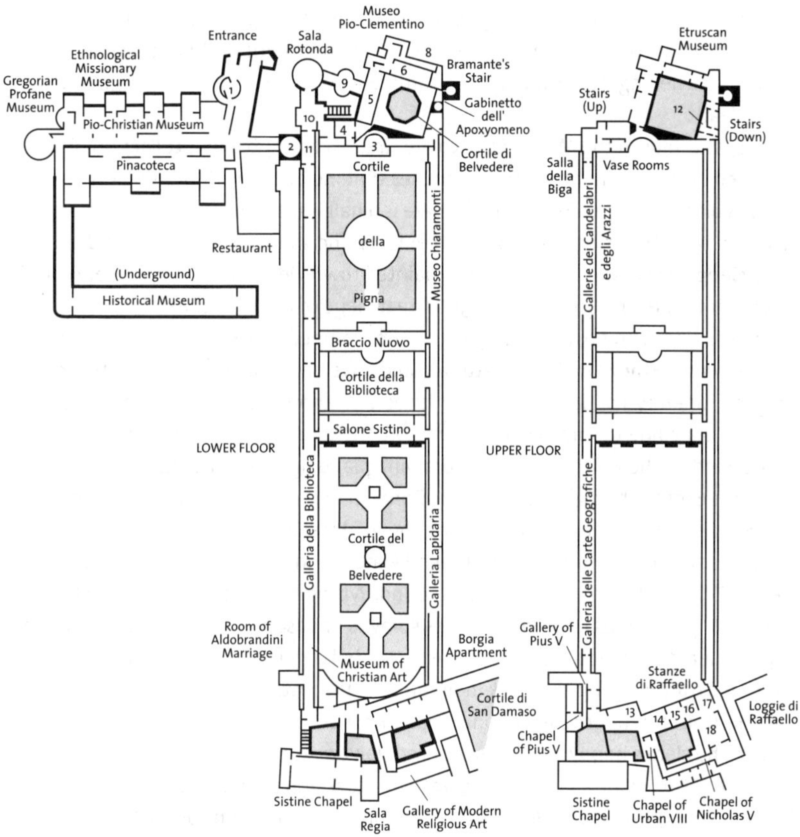

1 Spiral
2 Quattro Cancelli
3 La Pigna
4 Egyptian Museum
5 Room of the Animals
6 Gallery of Statues
7 Mask Room
8 Gallery of Busts
9 Hall of the Muses
10 Hall of the Greek Cross
11 Museum of Pagan Antiquities
12 Rooms of Greek Originals
13 Hall of the Immaculate Conception
14 Stanza dell'Incendio
15 Stanza della Segnatura
16 Stanzi di Eliodoro
17 Sala di Costantino
18 Sala dei Chiaroscuri

works recovered during the Renaissance had a greater influence on sculptors than these two. A 'room of animals' captures the more fanciful side of antiquity, and the 2nd-century 'Baroque' tendency in Roman art comes out clearly in a giant group called 'The Nile', complete with sphinxes and crocodiles – it comes from a Roman temple of Isis. The bronze papal fig-leaves that protect the modesty of hundreds of nude statues are a good joke at first – it was the same spirit that put breeches on the saints in Michelangelo's *Last Judgment*, ordered by Pius IV once Michelangelo was safely dead.

The best things in the **Museo Etrusco** are Greek, a truly excellent collection of vases imported by discriminating Etruscan nobles that includes the famous picture of *Oedipus and the Sphinx*. Beyond that, there is a hall hung with beautiful high-medieval tapestries from Tournai (15th century), and the long, long **Galleria delle Carte Geografiche**, lined with carefully painted town views and maps of every corner of Italy; note the long scene of the 1566 Great Siege of Malta at the entrance. Anywhere else, with no Michelangelos to offer competition, Raphael's celebrated frescoes in the **Stanza della Segnatura** would have been the prime destination on anyone's itinerary. The *School of Athens* is too well known to require an introduction, but here is a guide to some of the figures: on Aristotle's side, Archimedes and Euclid surrounded by their disciples (Euclid, drawing plane figures on a slate, is a portrait of Bramante); off to the right, Ptolemy and Zoroaster hold the terrestrial and celestial globes. Raphael includes himself among the Aristotelians, standing between Zoroaster and the painter Sodoma. Behind Plato stand Socrates and Alcibiades, and to the left, Zeno and Epicurus. In the foreground, Pythagoras writes while Empedocles and the Arab Averroes look on. Diogenes sprawls philosophically on the steps, while isolated near the front is Heraclitus – really Michelangelo; Raphael put him in at the last minute after seeing the work in progress in the Sistine Chapel.

Across from this apotheosis of philosophy, Raphael painted a Triumph of Theology to keep the clerics happy, the *Dispute of the Holy Sacrament*. The other frescoes include the *Parnassus*, a vision of the ancient Greek and Latin poets, the *Miracle of Bolsena*, the *Expulsion of Heliodorus*, an allegory of the triumphs of the Counter-Reformation papacy, the *Meeting of Leo I and Attila* and, best of all, the solemn, spectacularly lit *Liberation of St Peter*.

Nearby, there is the **Loggia** of Bramante, also with decoration designed by Raphael, though executed by other artists (*only visitable with written permission*), and the chapel of **Nicholas V**, with frescoes by Fra Angelico. The **Appartamento Borgia**, a luxurious suite built for Pope Alexander VI, has walls decorated by Pinturicchio. These run into the **Opere d'Arte Religiosa Moderna**, a game attempt by the Vatican to prove that such a thing really exists.

The Sistine Chapel (*Cappella Sistina*)

To the sophisticated Sixtus IV, building this ungainly barn of a chapel may have seemed a mistake in the first place. When the pushy, despotic Julius II sent Michelangelo up, against his will, to paint the vast ceiling, it might have turned out to be a project as hopeless as the tomb Julius had already commissioned. Michelangelo spent four years of his life (1508–12) on the Sistine Ceiling. No one can say what drove him to turn his surly patron's whim into a masterpiece: the fear of wasting those years, the challenge of an impossible task, or maybe just to spite Julius – he exasperated the pope by making him wait, and refused all demands that he hire some assistants.

Everywhere on the Sistine Ceiling you will note the austere blankness of the backgrounds. Michelangelo always eschewed stage props; one of the tenets of his art was that complex ideas could be expressed in the portrayal of the human body alone. With sculpture, that takes time. Perhaps the inspiration that kept Michelangelo on the ceiling so long was the chance of distilling out of the Book of Genesis and his own genius an entirely new vocabulary of images, Christian and intellectual. Like most Renaissance patrons, Julius had asked for nothing more than virtuoso interior decoration. What he got was the way the Old Testament looks in the deepest recesses of the imagination.

The fascination of the Sistine Ceiling, and the equally compelling ***Last Judgment*** on the rear wall, done much later (1534–41), is that while we may recognize the individual figures we still have not captured their secret meanings. Hordes of tourists stare up at the heroic Adam, the mysterious *ignudi* in the corners, the Russian masseuse sibyls with their longshoremen's arms, the six-toed prophets, the strange vision of Noah's deluge. They wonder what they're looking at, a question that would take years of inspired wondering to answer. Mostly they direct their attention to the all-too-famous scene of the Creation, with perhaps the only representation of God the Father ever painted that escapes being merely ridiculous. One might suspect that the figure is really some ageing Florentine artist, and that Michelangelo only forgot to paint the brush in his hand. The restoration of the ceiling and *Last Judgment*, paid for by a Japanese television network, have accurately revealed Michelangelo's true colours – jarring, surprise colours that no interior decorator would ever choose, plenty of sea-green, with splashes of yellow and purple and dramatic shadows. No new paint was applied, only solvents to clean off the grime.

Most visitors overlook the earlier frescoes on the lower walls, great works of art that would have made the Sistine Chapel famous by themselves: scenes from the *Exodus* by Botticelli, Perugino's *Donation of the Keys*, and Signorelli's *Moses Consigning his Staff to Joshua*.

More Miles in the Big Museum

There's still the **Vatican Library** to go, with its seemingly endless halls and precious manuscripts tucked neatly away in cabinets. The brightly painted rooms contain thousands of reliquaries and monstrances, medieval ivories, gold-glass medallions from the catacombs, and every sort of globe, orrery and astronomical instrument. If you survive this, the next hurdle is the new and beautifully laid out **Museo Gregoriano**, with a hoard of classical statuary, mosaics and inscriptions collected by Pope Gregory XVI. Then comes a museum of **carriages** (*closed for restoration*), the **Museo Pio-Cristiano** of early-Christian art and, finally, one of the most interesting of all, though no one has time for it: the museum of **ethnology**, with wonderful art from every continent, brought home to Italy by missionaries over the centuries.

By itself the Vatican **Pinacoteca** would be by far the finest picture gallery in Rome, a representative sampling of Renaissance art from its beginnings, with some fine works of Giotto (*Il Redentore* and the *Martyrdoms of Peter and Paul*) and contemporary Sienese painters, as well as Gentile da Fabriano, Sano di Pietro and Filippo Lippi. Don't overlook the tiny but electrically surreal masterpiece of Fra Angelico, the *Story of St Nicolas at Bari*, or the *Angelic Musicians* of Melozzo da Forlì, set next to Melozzo's famous painting of Platina being nominated by Sixtus IV to head the Vatican Library – a rare snapshot of Renaissance humanism. Venetian artists are not well represented, but there is a *Pietà* by Bellini and a *Madonna* by the fastidious Carlo Crivelli. Perhaps the best-known paintings are the *Transfiguration of Christ*, Raphael's last work, and the *St Jerome* of Da Vinci.

EUR

By the late 1930s Mussolini was proud enough of his accomplishments to plan a world fair. Its theme was to be the Progress of Civilization, measured no doubt from the invention of the wheel up to the invention of the Corporate State. A vast area south of Rome was cleared and transformed into a grid of wide boulevards broken by parks and lagoons. Huge Mussolini-style pavilions were begun, and a design was accepted for an aluminium arch – forerunner of the famous one in St Louis but many times bigger – that would overarch the entire fairground. War intervening, the arch never appeared, and the Esposizione Universale di Roma never came off.

After 1945 the Italians tried to make the best of it, turning EUR into a model satellite city and trade centre, on the lines of La Défense in Paris. The result will derange your senses as much as it does the average Roman's: a chilly nightmare of modernism with Boulevards of Humanism, Electronics and Social Security.

Still, for those who can appreciate the well-landscaped macabre, EUR can be fun. Some of the older corners reveal giant Fascist mosaics of heroic miners, soldiers, assembly-line workers and mothers, and at the end of the Boulevard of Civilization and Labour you can have a look at the modest masterpiece of Mussolini architecture – a small, elegantly proportioned **Palazzo della Civiltà del Lavoro**, nicknamed the Square Colosseum. Liberal, post-war Italy has rarely, if ever, been able to conceive anything with such a sure sense of design and a feeling of history.

EUR is also home to a few good museums. The **Museo della Civiltà Romana**, Piazza G Agnelli 10 (***t** 06 592 6041; open Tues–Sat 9–6.45, Sun 9–1.30; adm*), a collection of antiquities and exhibits including a huge scale-model of ancient Rome with every building present, is a great place to seed your imagination with visions of the old city's splendour. Others in the area include a **museum of prehistory and ethnography**, nearby in Piazza Marconi 14 (***t** 06 549921; open Tues–Sun 9–8; adm*), covering civilizations before classical Rome, and a **museum of the early Middle Ages**, at Viale Lincoln 3 (***t** 06 5422 8199; open Tues–Sat 9–8; adm*).

Around Rome

10

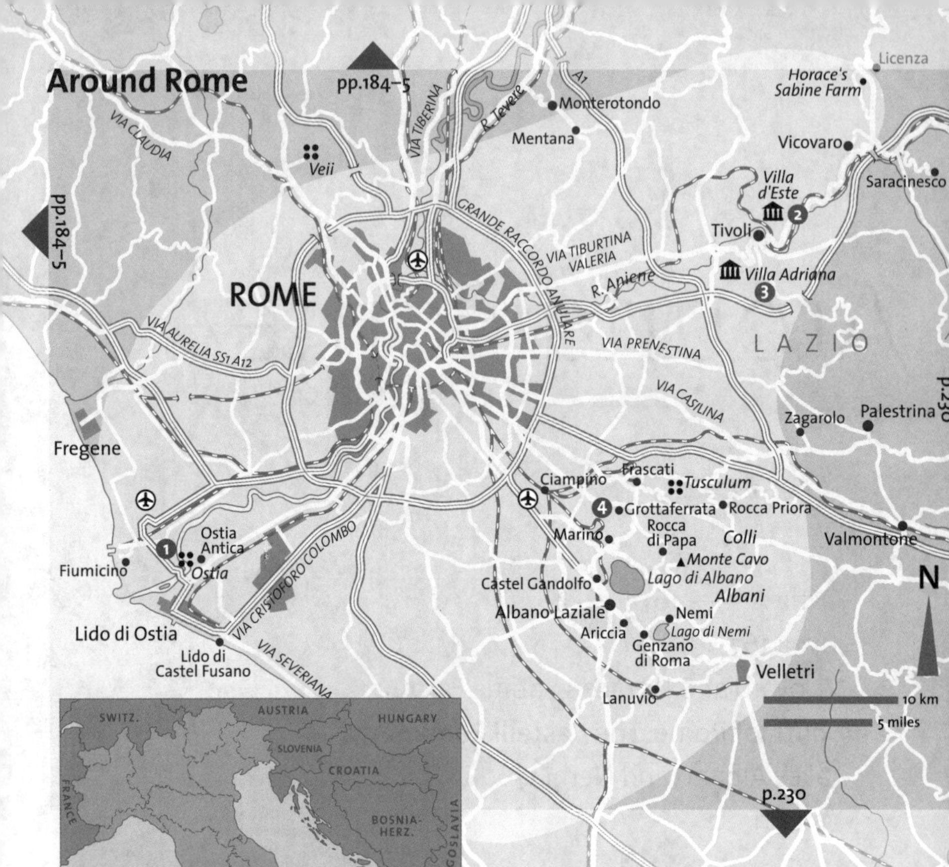

Highlights

1 Ancient Rome's port, Ostia Antica
2 Fantastical fountains of the Villa d'Este, Tívoli
3 Hadrian's villa, the most opulent residence of antiquity
4 The unique, Byzantine–Roman Abbazia di Grottaferrata

The Campagna Romana – the beautifully idyllic countryside around Rome, with its parasol pines, low hills and majestic crumbling ivy- and creeper-clad ruins so beloved of 18th- and 19th-century landscape painters – hasn't been obliterated in the 20th, only nearly so. But if you're looking for an easy day's excursion from Rome there are still plenty of possibilities. Tívoli, with its sumptuous gardens, everyone knows. Ostia, on the other hand, gets lost in the shadows of Rome, but it is one of the few lost cities where the ruins are sufficient to make the ancient world come alive. But the best thing you can do from Rome is take the short hop south to the Castelli Romani in the Alban Hills, a bit of authentic old Rome in a small-town setting; even in Italy, few places can boast so much beauty and interest concentrated in a small area.

Ostia Antica, the Port of Empire

After Pompeii and Herculaneum, **Ostia Antica** is the best-preserved Roman town in Italy, just down the Tiber and a fascinating lesson on everyday life in ancient Rome itself. Set amid parasol pines and wild flowers, it is as lovely as it is interesting, its brick walls festooned with garlands of ivy, its ruined temples home to scores of sunning lizards and tiny blue butterflies.

History

According to legend, Ostia was founded in the 6th century BC by the fourth king of Rome, Ancus Martius, although archaeological evidence prefers a 4th-century date. Its name derives from *Ostium*, or river mouth, for it was here 'that the waters of the Mediterranean mingled with the Tiber', as the Romans used to joke. Originally built as a walled *castrum* – perhaps the prototype for all subsequent 'camps' that in the next four centuries would stretch from Britain to the Near East – Ostia guarded the main entrance to Rome and produced salt from the surrounding marshes. Rome's growing sea trade soon made it a thriving port; the First Punic War made it of necessity a naval base as well. Its major setback came from its own mother's hands, when the Romans under Marius sacked it; Sulla immediately rebuilt it, with the wall that still bears his name (the Cinta Sillana).

By the 1st century AD the port of Ostia could no longer handle Rome's insatiable demand for more and more goods, and Claudius began a new port at Portus. But still Ostia grew. After Rome's great fire of AD 64, Nero sent tons of debris down the Tiber

Getting There and Around

Ostia Antica is very easy to reach: **trains** run from the Roma-Lido station next to the Ⓜ Pyramide (Linea B). It takes 30 minutes, and the excavations are only a five-minute walk away. By **car**, from Porta San Paolo drive out 23km along Via del Mare, which runs parallel to the ancient Via Ostiense. The most agreeable way to get to Ostia Antica is on a boat trip down the Tiber; contact **Tourvisa**, Via Marghera 32, **t** 06 446 3481 (*open Mon–Fri 9–1 and 2–6; evenings and w/e*, **t** *06 445 4741*).

Where to Stay and Eat

Lido di Ostia ✉ 00121

Ostia is convenient for the airport, too.

*****Sirenetta**, Lungomare Toscanelli 46, **t** 06 562 2720, **f** 06 562 2310 (*moderate*). Central, very well run and welcoming; the hotel also has one of Ostia's more popular restaurants, specializing in seafood (*also moderate*).

*****Kursaal** 2000, Via Isabella di Castiglia 7, **t** 06 5647 0616, **f** 06 5647 0547 (*low moderate*). Further down the beach; has a roof terrace and roof garden.

Vecchia Pineta, Piazzale dell'Aquilone 4, **t** 06 5647 0255 (*expensive*). In a Mussolini-era building, but with an inspired young chef who knows what to do with fresh home-made pasta and seafood. *Closed Tues eve.*

Fiumicino ✉ 00054

*****Mach 2**, Via Portuense 2465, **t** 06 650 7149, **f** 06 650 5855, *www.hotelmach2.it* (*moderate*). Less than a mile from the airport.

Molo, Via Torre Clementina 312, **t** 06 650 5358 (*very expensive*). Renowned restaurant with all kinds of seafood and vegetable dishes, and dreamy creamy desserts. *Closed Mon.*

Perla, Via di Torre Clementina 214, **t** 06 650 5038 (*expensive*). Denizens of the deep also rule here, prepared in traditional and surprising ways – try turbot with caramelized lemon. *Closed Tues, and part of Aug–Sept.*

to reclaim the surrounding swamplands. Hadrian poured money into the town, rebuilding it as a 2nd-century garden suburb for middle- and working-class families. Although many businesses had relocated to nearby Portus, Ostia's warehouses, *horreae*, had the task of managing Rome's enormous dole, the *annona*. Ostia's worst enemy proved to be Constantine, who conferred all of its ancient rights as a city to Portus, perhaps because the residents had little use for his new religion – 18 *mithraea* have been uncovered so far, in contrast to only a handful of Christian buildings. Still, the city survived as a residential backwater; new, more splendid *domus*-style homes were built, until the 5th century brought total decadence and, even worse, malaria. Ostia was neglected, looted, and covered with sand; the silt of the Tiber moved the coastline a few miles west, and in 1575 a flood altered the course of the Tiber.

The Excavations

The excavations are open summer 9–4, winter 9–6, closed Mon; adm. The museum (same ticket) closes at 1.

The excavations of Ostia, begun in the 19th century, have so far uncovered two-thirds of the city. Earlier shovels and chisels were at work along the **Via delle Tombe**, at the entrance to the site; fortune-hunters have left only a few *columbaria* and sarcophagi undamaged. The road from Rome, **Via Ostiense**, its flagstones deeply grooved by ancient cart wheels, leads up to the Republican-era **Porta Romana**, Ostia's main gate. Emperor Domitian added two winged Minerva Victories to flank the gate, one of which, a weird-looking creature, survives in the **Piazza della Vittoria**.

The Decumanus Maximus

Once through the gate, Via Ostiense becomes the main street, the **Decumanus Maximus**. On the right it passes a series of ***horreae***, or warehouses, one of which was converted in the 1st century AD into a bath complex, known as the **Baths of the Cisiarii**; a mosaic in the *frigidarium* shows the guild members at work, carting passengers about in wagons. The fancier **Baths of Neptune**, still on the right side of the Decumanus, were built by Hadrian and decorated with elaborate mosaics of frolicking sea gods and a *palaestra* for gymnastics. Just before the baths, Via dei Vigili leads back to a fine *Mosaic of the Winds*; on the left Hadrian built **Police and Firemen's Barracks**, marked by a curious, steeply inclined ramp (an early version of a firemen's pole?). The mosaic in the centre, of men leading a bull to sacrifice, was part of the barracks' shrine to the deified emperors, or *Augusteum*. On the narrow lane behind the barracks is a well-preserved row of *insulae*, with their shops on the ground floor and stairs leading up to the flats (the average *insula* at Ostia had four floors). The shop at the end of the lane, facing the Decumanus, was the **Tavern of Fortunatus**, with perhaps history's first example of advertising: 'Fortunatus says: if you're thirsty, drink a bowl of wine.'

The Theatre and Forum of the Corporations

Beyond stands the much-restored **Theatre**, built by Agrippa, who included shops in the arcades under the seats, one now selling souvenirs, another a bar, and a third the

WC. Three marble masks, once part of the stage decoration, have been set up on tufa columns. In front of the theatre is the fascinating **Forum of the Corporations**, a quadrangle where 61 of Ostia's various maritime concerns had their offices around a quadrangle. The temple in the centre was dedicated either to Ceres or 'Annona Augusta', the Divinity of Imperial Provisions, to which each firm was devoted, heart and soul. Black and white mosaics indicate the special business of each (most depict cargo ships; those with elephants and reindeer dealt in land transport), its trademark, and the nationality of its merchants and fitters. Ponder them, as Jérôme Carcopino wrote,

> *And suddenly you see the throngs of people, strangers to each other, born in far distant lands, rowing to meet each other here in answer to the needs of Rome, and you feel that there gravitates forever round this unforgettable enclosure not only the mass of goods which Rome appropriated for herself in every corner of the earth, but the cortège of docile nations whom she had consecrated to her service.*

Or picture Rome as a queen termite, too bloated to move, with scores of tiny servants whose sole job is to bring food to drop in her insatiable maw.

Further along the Decumanus: Warehouses and a Snack Bar

Next to the Forum is the **House of Apuleius**, a *domus* with a peristyle, like many of the houses of Pompeii; adjacent, along the Decumanus, is the **Mithraeum of the Seven Spheres**, named for the seven semicircles shown on the mosaic floor, symbolizing the seven stages of initiation and/or the seven planets. Its neighbour, the **Great Horrea**, the largest warehouse in Ostia, has a porticoed court surrounded by some 60 small rooms for storing corn. Across the Decumanus, the **Seat of the Augustales** was the headquarters of the priests in charge of the official emperor-worship.

Via dei Molini and Via Semita dei Cippi mark the eastern limits of the original *castrum*. Via dei Molini is named for the **Apartment of the Millstones** (still containing mills and olive presses). The adjacent **Casa di Diana**, one of the more posh *insulae*, was originally four storeys, with taverns and shops on the ground floor and spacious flats above, with its own latrine, balconies, cistern and pool in the court, and its own private mithraeum. Across Via di Diana, don't miss the **Thermopolium**, or snack bar, which wouldn't look out of place in Rome today, with its shiny marble bar and shelf to display the various snacks, these illustrated by a surviving fresco; it has a small wine cellar, vessels set in the floor for storing oil, and an area for sitting outside in good weather, complete with a little fountain. Next to the Casa di Diana, the **Casa dei Dipinti** was equally large, and the most luxurious *insula* ever found, once entirely covered on the outside with festoons and paintings; through the gate you can see a colourfully frescoed room. Take the stairs to the top floor for a view of the excavations.

Museo Ostiense

Open daily 9–1, closed Mon; same ticket as the excavations.

This museum stands just to the north, in a converted 15th-century salt deposit. Among the most interesting items are the bas-reliefs in the first room, portraying daily life in ancient Ostia (including a birth scene) and, beyond, a 1st-century BC round relief of the twelve gods, statues of Mithras stabbing the bull, Trajan in a cuirass (looking very uncomfortable with a slice of his abdomen missing), also Perseus with Medusa's head, Julia Domna (Septimius Severus' wife), dressed as Ceres; the headless but very virile *Hero in Repose*; Maxentius as Pontifex Maximus; a beautifully carved sarcophagus of a boy from Portus' necropolis at Isola Sacra, and what is believed to be a portrait of Christ, a beautiful polychrome *opus sectile* pavement. Strangest of all are the marble footprints, facing in opposite directions. Found in the temple of the war goddess Bellona, they were probably a soldier's votive offering of thanks for returning safely from war.

The Forum

From the museum, Via Tecta leads past the **Piccolo Mercato**, an amazingly well-preserved grain warehouse, and continues into Ostia's **Forum**, with its two temples facing each other across the square: nearest, with the broad stairway, is the **Capitolium**, a temple dedicated to the Etruscan/Roman trinity of Jupiter, Juno and Minerva, rebuilt by Hadrian. Throughout the centuries its high walls have always been visible, and were used by local farmers as a sheep pen. Across the Forum stands the older **Temple of Rome and Augustus**; marble fragments of both temples that escaped the busy medieval lime kilns lay near each. Much less has survived of the other Forum buildings, the **Curia**, seat of Ostia's Senate, the **Basilica** (the courts), and the **Round Temple**, probably dedicated to emperor worship; its ruined spiral staircase once led up to the dome. Next to the Temple of Rome and Augustus the **Casa Triclini** is named for the dining couches found in the rooms along the right; built into this *insula*'s right-hand corner is the public lavatory, or **forica**, a 20-holer once equipped with a revolving door and a constant flow of water. The only thing lacking was paper; the Romans used mussel shells, or swabs on the end of sticks (hence the expression 'to get the wrong end of the stick'). Across from the loo were the **Forum Baths**, Ostia's largest (2nd century AD, but remodelled many times). You can make out the furnaces used for heating the steam baths and *caldarium*, and the ornate *frigidarium* for cooling off. Just to the south is another bath complex contributed by Hadrian, the **Terme del Faro**, named for its mosaic of Ostia's lighthouse surrounded by sea creatures; it also has a fresco of a bull-riding nereid.

Along the Cardo Maximus

Across the Cardo Maximus is the **Casa di Giove Fulminatore**, decorated with a relief of a foot-long phallus, like an arrow pointing to the door (as at Pompeii, these are good luck charms). The **Domus delle Colonne**, named for the white marble columns in the courtyard, is the next building south; in the adjacent lane, the 3rd-century AD **Caupona del Pavone** was one of Ostia's nicer inns, perhaps even the one mentioned by St Augustine in his *Confessions*, where he had his famous conversation with his mother St Monica before their departure for Africa – though as Monica fell ill and died before they set sail, the inn may not have been so nice after all. Near the **Porta Laurentina** is the triangular sacred precinct of the **Campo della Magna Mater**, most of which was strictly off-limits for women. Against the gate is the **Temple of Bellona** and its college of adepts, the **Schola of the Hastiferii**; here, too, flanked by two *telamones* of Pan, is the **Sanctuary of Attis**, part of the **Temple of Cybele**, the Great Mother. A slight detour from the gate up Via Semita dei Cippi will take you to the **Domus of the Vestibule**, with a fine polychrome mosaic, and the **Domus of Fortuna Annonaria**, with a mosaic of the she-wolf, a *nymphaeum*, and a one-hole *forica*.

Via Epagathiana

Returning to the Forum, walk beyond the Curia to Via Epagathiana, a street marking the western limits of the *castrum* – a puny place compared to Ostia's later size. On the right is **Horrea Epagathiana**, a private warehouse, with the two owners' names still inscribed over the door and a large swastika in the floor mosaic (one of the most ancient sun symbols, though once its religious meaning was forgotten it became a lucky charm if the arms bent to the right, and bad luck if they went to the left). Across the lane stands the **House of Cupid and Psyche**, an attractive 4th-century *domus* named for the statue group discovered within; it has a lavish *opus sectile* pavement, and is believed to have been owned by a wealthy merchant who preferred Ostia even in its decline to dense and noisy Portus. The adjacent **Baths of Buticosus** is named for a bath attendant whose portrait in mosaic was discovered here, along with another rollicking mosaic of sea monsters.

Via della Foce

South of here the Decumanus Maximus forks; the branch called Via della Foce continues towards the Tiber. On the right are the **Baths of Mithras**, especially good for exploring the subterranean plumbing if it's not flooded by ground water; note the marks left by the water wheel, which filled the lead pipes running into the boiler. Next door is the **Hall of the Wheat Measurers**, with a mosaic illustrating their tasks.

Heading back along Via delle Foce, note the high-walled group of buildings on the right, nearly all built by Hadrian in what may have been a kind of ancient self-sufficient estate complex, with condominiums, baths, a *mithraeum*, and shops. First on the right is the **House of Bacchus** and the **House of Serapis**, a pair of *insulae* with one of Ostia's finest mosaics, of Bacchus and Ariadne; next are Hadrian's **Baths of Trinacria**, with more fine mosaics and plumbing fixtures underground. Then come the **Baths of the Sette Sapienti**, or Seven Sages, though here you'd call them the seven wise guys: each is frescoed with a caption with advice on how to wash your rude bits. Don't miss the beautiful mosaic of a hunting scene in the circular hall. Adjacent to the baths is the **Insula Aurigi**, or House of the Charioteers, named for its fresco of two jockeys; its high, upper level of arches gives a fair idea of what the *insulae* looked like.

The Decumanus to the Porta Marina

Heading back to the fork of the Decumanus Maximus and wedged between the two streets is a presumed **Christian Basilica**, while across the Decumanus is the **Macellum**, or meat market, complete with mosaics and marble counters and basins that once held live fish. The **Schola di Traiano**, headquarters of a corporation (of shipbuilders?), was a monumental complex with a long niched pool. Further down and across the Decumanus stands the **Insula of the Painted Vaults** (*usually closed, but you could try asking for access at the museum*), an apartment house built by Hadrian and later converted into a *lupanare*, or bordello, as the traces of fresco and graffiti bear witness. Evidence suggests that the ancient sex business was fairly specialized; a mosaic nearby that the tour groups never get to see depicts the services offered by male dwarfs. This is right next to Ostia's high rent district, another complex of *insulae* built by Hadrian, luxurious and most innovative in style, the perfect home for an upper-crust Roman. First, there's the **Casa delle Muse**, with a restored roof and wall paintings of Apollo and the Muses (though again only visible through a gate); the **Casa dei Giardini**, the Garden Homes, which looked onto their private garden like a Bloomsbury square; and the **Domus of the Dioscuri**, embellished with beautiful polychrome mosaics of the 4th century.

The Decumanus leaves Ostia by the **Marine Gate**, which by the time of Hadrian had been built over by citizens who felt no threat from a sea they called their own. One of the old towers was converted into an inn, the **Caupona of Alexander Helix**, whose name may be read on the floor mosaic; other mosaics in the tavern show Egyptian contortionist-dancers, Venus, and two wrestlers. Beyond the gate, towards the ancient beach, stood funerary monuments, including the imposing travertine **Monument of C Cartilius Poplicola**, along with some seaside villas and the **Baths of Marciana**. Four tall columns with composite capitals are all that remains of the **Synagogue** (1st century AD), which stood right on the beach; some of the mosaic floor remains, as well as the apse that once held the ark of the Torah, and an adjacent oven probably used to bake unleavened bread.

Modern Ostia

The excavations are on the edge of the sleepy hamlet of **Ostia**, founded in 831 as 'Gregoripolis' by Pope Gregory IV, to defend Rome after the Saracens captured Sicily. Pope Julius II, while he was still Ostia's cardinal, built the huge brick **Castello**, Ostia's 1483 landmark sample of Renaissance fortifications. It frightened the Turks and would-be marauders up the Tiber until the river itself moved; now it holds a humble historical collection. Within the walls of Ostia are Renaissance-era attached houses built for workers in the papal salt pans, and the small Renaissance church of **Sant'Aurea**, built over the 5th-century basilica of Ostia's first martyr. Ask if the **Episcopio** or bishop's palace is open, to see the unusual decorations by Baldassare Peruzzi, 1511–13, recently discovered under layers of whitewash. Julius at the time was trying to kick the French out of Italy, and the 15 grisaille frescoes, adaptations of scenes from Trajan's Column, painted to look like reliefs, are pure Renaissance flattery, comparing wars of the Pope to conquests of the Emperor.

Portus and the Isola Sacra

Remains of **Portus**, Emperor Claudius' new port, were found during the construction of Fiumicino Airport. In ancient times its most spectacular feature was its lighthouse, the **Pharos of Portus**, built on an artificial island, created by sinking the massive ship that transported the Vatican obelisk from Egypt. Trajan later added a canal linking the port to the Tiber, creating an island known as the **Isola Sacra**. Isola Sacra was the necropolis of ancient Portus until the 4th century, discovered excellently preserved under layers of sand. The inhabitants of Portus, unlike many Romans, had to work for a living and couldn't afford big fancy monuments. Instead the dead were laid out in simple barrel-vaulted tombs or 'trunk tombs' shaped like 19th-century travelling trunks, or had their ashes deposited in *columbaria*. Many opted for fine terracotta, stucco or mosaic decoration, often depicting the deceased's trade; one Egyptophile lies under a baby brick pyramid.

Of **Portus** itself only a small village remains, though the ancient ports of Claudius and Trajan are being excavated. The latter's hexagonal docks have survived as a little inland lake, **Lago Traiano**, on Via Portuensis; you may see it when flying into Fiumicino Airport. The **Museo delle Navi Romane** near the airport (*open 9–1.30, Tues and Thurs also 2–4.30;* ***t*** *06 652 9192; adm*) contains seven ships uncovered during the construction of the airport in 1961, and offers guided tours of the Portus excavations on the last Sunday of each month at 9.30am (*adm included in museum entrance*).

From the seaside town of **Fiumicino**, take bus 020 north to the relatively clean pine-shaded beach of **Fregene**, surrounded by reclaimed marshlands and industry, or bus 02 back past Ostia Antica to Rome's own beach, at **Lido di Ostia**. Romans too lazy to travel any further frequent the endless broad beaches here, but Lido di Ostia is really a typical slice of middle-class Rome transported to the seaside. It's a surprisingly likeable neighbourhood, with two lovely Mussolini Deco buildings from the '30s: the **post office** on the main drag, Via del Mare, with a striking curved portico, and the **Vigili del Fuoco** two streets to the south, a little jewel of a fire station.

A monument at Idroscalo, near the mouth of the Tiber, marks the spot where film director Pier Paolo Pasolini was murdered in 1975; if you swim here the pollution will kill you, too. The sea gets a bit cleaner the further south you go, near the pine forests of **Castel Fusano** and beyond.

Tívoli

East of Rome, Tívoli offers both natural beauty and some of the more unbridled efforts of the Renaissance imagination – the unique gardens of the Villa d'Este, the ruins of Hadrian's country retreat, the size of a small city, and the plunging artificial waterfall of the Villa Gregoriana. Ancient *Tibur*, set on a cliff with a beautiful view over the Roman *campagna*, became a sort of garden retreat for the senatorial class in the early days of the Empire. Its spa, the Bagni di Tivoli, was celebrated by Strabo and Pausanius. But a town with a view is also usually easily defensible, and by the early Middle Ages, despite all the dirty work of Goths and Huns, Tibur had changed its name to Tívoli and managed a successful transition from posh resort to gutsy, independent hill town. Once, in its struggles with Rome, it even defeated its bossy neighbour and captured a pope. But pachydermic Rome never forgets a grudge, and in the 1460s Pope Pius II built a castle, the Rocca Pia, at the town's door to keep Tívoli in line.

Getting There

Tívoli (31km) is most easily reached from Rome by COTRAL **buses**, departing every 15mins from the bus station at Ⓜ Ponte Mammolo on metro line B. By **car**, take the A24 to avoid the long sprawl along the Via Tiburtina. Although the Aniene Valley is most easily reached by car, COTRAL buses from Ⓜ Ponte Mammolo (metro line B) go to Vicovaro, Licenza, Antícoli Corrado and Subiaco.

Tourist Information

Largo Garibaldi, **t** 0774 311 249, **f** 0774 331294.

Where to Stay and Eat

Tívoli ✉ 00019

★★★★**Sirene**, Piazza Massimo 4, **t** 0774 330605, **f** 0774 330608 (*expensive*). Next to the Villa d'Este; occupies an 19th-century villa and is in the record books as the first one in the world to have electric lights. Offers satellite TV, hairdryers, and more; there's parking, and pretty views from the terraces.

★★★**Adriano**, Via Villa Adriana 194, **t** 0774 382235, **f** 0774 535122 (*moderate*). 6km from the centre, near Hadrian's villa, this lovely little hotel has a garden and an excellent restaurant (*expensive*). *Closed Sun eve.*

★★★★**Grand Hotel Duca d'Este**, Via Tiburtina Valeria 330, **t** 0774 3883, **f** 0774 388101 (*very expensive–moderate*). In Bagni di Tívoli, 8km from Tívoli, this is a big spa hotel with all the trimmings – luxurious, stylish rooms, indoor and outdoor pools, sauna, hammam, gym, beauty treatments, and three restaurants.

Accommodation less grand than these is in very short supply:

★★**Delle Rose**, Via Tiburtina 186 near Hadrian's Villa, **t** 0774 357930, **f** 0774 531382 (*moderate*). Basic.

★★★**Padovano**, Via Tiburtina Valeria 130 on the outskirts of Tívoli, **t** 0774 530807 (*moderate*). Equally basic, with a good simple pizzeria/restaurant.

Antica Hosteria dei Carrettieri, Via D Giuliani 55, **t** 0774 330159 (*moderate*). For excellent traditional cuisine.

Sibilla, next to the 'Temple of the Sibyl' on Via della Sibilla. Fun, unabashedly touristy, and serves good grilled trout. *Closed Mon.*

Villa d'Este

Open Tues–Sun, summer 8.30–1½hrs before sunset; adm. Some days the fountains are not running – check with the tourist office.

Wealth returned to Tívoli in the late Renaissance in the form of moneybags cardinals; one in particular, Ippolito d'Este, son of Lucrezia Borgia and Duke Ercole I of Ferrara, created in 1550 perhaps the most fantastically worldly gardens Italy had seen since antiquity. The musty villa itself, designed by Pirro Ligorio and heavily coated with Mannerist frescoes, was rented by Franz Liszt from 1865 until his death in 1886 (it was the inspiration for his *Fountains of the Villa d'Este*). The residence is entirely upstaged by the gardens, set on a descending series of terraces. Among the palms and cypresses water shoots and cascades from an incredible hydraulic fantasy land, weaving intricate patterns of water: the *Fountain of Glass* by Bernini, the stuccoed *Grotto of Diana*, the *Fountain of Dragons*, the *Fountain of the Owl and Birds*, a favourite water trick that no longer warbles or moves; nor has the cardinal's *Water Organ* worked for donkey's years. One of the most curious features is *Little Rome*, a pint-sized replica of the Tiber Island in Rome, with models of ancient buildings.

Tívoli Town

Tívoli has an interesting Romanesque church with early medieval frescoes, **San Silvestro**, located on steep and narrow Via del Colle (just north of the Villa d'Este); at the bottom, just beyond the gate, are the remains of the vast **Sanctuary of Hercules** (2nd century BC), once the office of the Sibyl of Tívoli. Like Cumae near Naples, Tibur had a college of Sibyls (pictured so memorably on the Sistine Chapel ceiling and elsewhere, for the story that they prophesied the birth of Christ). The presence of these oracular ladies, cousins to the oracle at Delphi, shows the influence of Greek thought and religion in Latium from the earliest times. The stiff climb up Via del Colle leads eventually to Tívoli's gaudy 17th-century **Cathedral** at the corner of Via del Duomo, containing a moving, 13th-century wooden sculpture of the *Deposition from the Cross*.

Villa Gregoriana

Open 10am until 1hr before sunset; adm.

From here, Via del Colle becomes Via Valerio and crosses the Aniene on its way to the nearly vertical gardens of the Villa Gregoriana. The gardens were named in honour of Pope Gregory XVI, who in 1831 put an end to the regular flooding of the Aniene with the construction of a vast double tunnel through Mt Catillo. The river then emerges with dramatic flair high up in a natural chasm, forming a 400ft pluming mist of rainbows called the **Grande Cascata**. Shady paths wind down past various viewpoints over the waterfall; if you can trick yourself into forgetting about the awful climb back up, descend past the rather scanty remains of a Roman villa to the artificial **Cascata Bernini** and the limestone cavern called the **Grotta della Sirena**, where the waters are squeezed into an abyss. From the bottom a path leads up the other lip of the chasm, the acropolis of *Tibur*, where stand two remarkably well-preserved Roman temples, the famous circular **Temple of Vesta** and the rectangular **Temple of the Sibyl**, as fancy has named them (they can also be reached from above, on Via della Sibilla). Both temples date from the Republican era; the Temple of Vesta, with its beautiful frieze and Corinthian columns, was a favourite of romantic tourists.

Along the Via Tiburtina towards Rome are the strange, sheer-sided travertine quarries that have helped Tívoli make a living since ancient times. Almost all of Rome is built of it; one solemn grey variety went into the Colosseum, the city gates, and most of the other ruins. The other, streaked with beige and black, is the material Mussolini used for scores of railway stations all over Italy. Demand is still great, and Tívoli ships travertine all over the world.

Hadrian's Villa (Villa Adriana)

The COTRAL bus from Rome leaves you a 20min walk away at the Bivio Villa Adriana; local buses from Tívoli will take you much nearer the entrance; open daily 9–1½hrs before sunset; adm.

Just outside Tívoli on the plain, signs direct you to the quiet residential neighbourhood that has grown up around Hadrian's Villa, a 180-acre spread that was nothing less than one man's personal World's Fair and the largest villa ever built in the entire Roman Empire; the Villa d'Este is a mere anthill in comparison.

To get some idea of the scale on which a 2nd-century AD emperor could build, stop first at the room-sized model of the villa near the entrance. Made entirely of marble

Hadrian's Villa

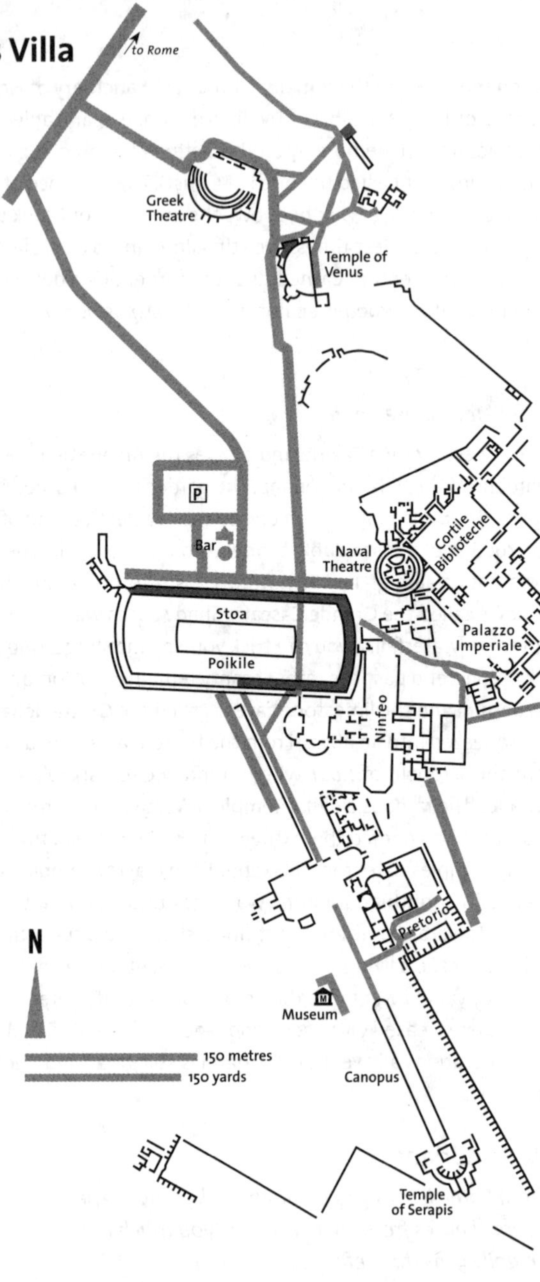

and travertine, and about the same size as the monumental centre of Rome – the Imperial Fora included – Hadrian's dream 'house' clearly shows the excess that even the most intelligent and useful of emperors was capable of. Archaeologists have found features that would surprise even a Californian – a heated beach with steam pipes under the sand, and a network of subterranean service passages for horses and carts (a private Underground!). Other emperors used the villa until Constantine, unable to create anything as fine, plundered it to embellish Constantinople; lime burners, invaders and builders gnawed at it until Pope Alexander VI began the first excavations. Yet despite the depredations many of the finest Roman statues in Europe's museums were discovered here.

Hadrian fancied himself as an architect, contributing to the Pantheon, the Temple of Venus and Rome, and the urban redevelopment of Ostia Antica; but unlike most dilettantes he had the resources of the Roman Empire at its peak at his disposal. Hadrian especially wanted to remember famous buildings he had seen on his travels, and helped design reproductions: the **Stoa Poikile** of Athens, near the entrance, a rectangular peristyle with a massive fishpond in the centre; the **Canopus**, or Temple of Serapis near Alexandria, complete with a canal reproducing the Nile and decorated with Egyptian statues (now mostly restored; a nearby **museum** contains finds from the most recent excavations); the **Platonic Academy** in an ancient olive grove, with an Odeion, a round Temple of Apollo, and, beyond this, the entrance to an underground rectilinear hell, or **Hades**. Baths, libraries, an imperial palace, nymphaea, temples, Praetorian barracks and a reproduction of the Valle di Tempe with a Greek theatre are among the other buildings discovered in the ongoing excavations. But the most charming corner of the complex is the so-called **Naval Theatre**, actually a little circular palace on an island in an artificial lagoon, attainable only by a retractable bridge on rollers; it may have been Hadrian's private retreat, where he could escape the cares of empire to write poetry and paint.

Vicovaro and Horace's Sabine Farm

Just up the Aniene valley from Tívoli is **Vicovaro** (46km east of Rome), noted for its little octagonal Renaissance **Tempietto di San Giacomo** (1450), a work by two Dalmatian architects, Domenico da Capodistria and Giovanni Dalmata, who designed the charming porch. Just beyond Vicovaro, a road turns left up a lovely valley towards Licenza for **Horace's Sabine Farm** (*always open; tip the custodian. Bus riders should ask the driver to stop at the unpaved lane leading to the Villa d'Orazio*). No farm has ever enjoyed as many poetic musings as this 12-room country estate Maecenas gave to Horace in 33 BC, which was all the poet asked for in the world: 'a portion of land, not so big, a garden and near the house a spring of never-failing water, and a little wood beyond. It is well. I ask no more.' The spring still flows; the lovely mosaics, pavements, garden swimming pool, and some of the lead pipes and the pretty surroundings survive to complete Horace's picture of an idyllic retreat. The custodian of the site has a roomful of small finds from the excavations; the more interesting items are in the little **Antiquarium** (*open 9–6*) 8km up the road in the castle of **Licenza**, one of Lazio's handsomest hill towns.

Most of the hill towns in the Aniene valley have escaped the worst of modern tourism, like lovely **Antícoli Corrado** on its steep cliff, famous for producing the most beautiful artists' models in Rome. The town has had an art colony of its own for almost 200 years, whose works fill the town museum. Recently discovered frescoes by their predecessors in the 1100s may be seen in the well-preserved church of **San Pietro**, in the piazza with a fountain of Noah's Ark. Another striking town, **Saracinesco**, was founded on a crag by Saracen raiders in the 9th century; the present townspeople are their direct descendants.

South of Rome: The Castelli Romani

In the Museo Civico at Albano you can see some photos of Lazio taken from space, and they reveal a startling sight. Landscapes that look delicious from ground level can be deceiving; look at the region from a hundred miles up, and you will see Rome sitting on the Tiber with one colossal volcano to the north of it, and another to the south. Though each is about 60 miles across, they are extremely low (in fact they look quite like the shallow volcanoes on the surface of Mars). The one to the north has Lake Bracciano for a crater, while the one to the south rises to the peaks and crater lakes of the Alban Hills.

'Extinct' may be one of the dirtiest words of the 20th century, but with volcanoes it usually translates into lovely scenery, romantic lakes, and fertile soil for vines. Such are the charms of the *Colli Albani*. Rome was still a twinkle in the god Mars' eye when the ancient Latins found these hills a convivial place to settle, and their villages, the foundations of the small towns called the Castelli Romani, grew to become some of the strongest members of the Latin League. Since being pounded into submission 2,200 years ago, their role has been reduced to that of providing the capital with wine, flowers, and a pleasant place to spend summer weekends. Heavy bombing in 1944 during the battle for Rome wrecked many fine old churches, villas and artworks in the Castelli, and though the damage has been repaired, much is new; some of the nearer Castelli are becoming strangled in Rome's suburban tentacles. Still, the countryside, especially around Lake Nemi, is beautiful. Another attraction is the numerous old-fashioned wine cellars; so old that one in Marino, along the lake road, was formerly used as an underground Mithraeum, and has a fine fresco of the god inside.

Frascati

Frascati, the nearest of the Castelli (21km, on Via Tuscolana) and one of the most visited, began as a refuge for the people of the ancient city of Tusculum; when Pope Paul III rebuilt and enlarged the city in the 1500s, he called it *Tusculum Novum*. Ancient Tusculum was famous for its magnificent villas, most famously one of Cicero's, and Frascati inherited the tradition on its refreshing hillside. Unfortunately Field Marshal Kesselring liked it as well, and 80 per cent of the town was destroyed in the bombing to squeeze him out of his headquarters. Frascati's main attractions these days are its wine and trattorias, and its imposing late Renaissance and Baroque villas. The magnificent 17th-century **Villa Aldobrandini**, celebrated for its views over Rome (*gardens open Mon–Fri 9–1 and 3–6, in winter till 5*), is notable for its grand fountain by Carlo Maderno called the Theatre of Waters. The swish new **Museo delle Scuderie Aldobrandini** (*open Tues–Fri 10–6, Sat and hols 10–7*) houses the Museo

Getting There

All the Castelli and Velletri can be reached by COTRAL **bus**, from the depot at the Anagnina Metropolitana A station; there's also a little **train** to Frascati departing from Termini Station. While connections between the towns are frequent, the links are not always convenient; with a car you can easily see the highlights in a day, if the traffic permits. That's a big 'if'; congestion on the narrow roads within and between the Castelli can be as bad as Rome itself, with backups liable to occur at any time of day.

The roads around Frascati are the worst, along with the Via Appia through Castel Gandolfo, Albano and Genzano.

Tourist Information

Frascati: Piazza Marconi, **t** 06 942 0331.
Marino: Pro-loco, Piazza Lepanto, **t** 06 938 5555, *www.romacastellionline.com*.

Where to Stay and Eat

Everywhere you go in the Castelli, look for the old-fashioned *vino e cucina* establishments, where you can mull over a glass of Frascati with snacks on offer, or pasta or even a full dinner. These used to be common in Rome, and all over Italy. The Castelli are a bastion of authenticity; their people are more like the Romans of a century ago than the Romans themselves. The fashionable dish these days is the hearty *pappardelle al cinghiale*, wide strips of pasta with stewed boar in tomato sauce.

Frascati ✉ 00044

***__Villa Tuscolana__, a mile out of the centre on the Via del Tuscolo, **t** 06 942900, **f** 06 942 4747, *www.villatuscolana.com* (*very expensive–expensive*). Occupying an 18th-century villa on top of a hill, with rooms containing many original features, this hotel also has two restaurants, a games room and shuttle bus to Frascati.

***__Giadrina__, Via A Diaz 13, **t** 06 941 9415, **f** 06 942 0440 (*moderate*). Central, has pretty views and an excellent breakfast. It shares quarters with Frascati's most famous restaurant, **Cacciani**, **t** 06 942 0378 (*moderate*), in business for over 75 years, serving classic and Roman dishes; home-made desserts, too. *Closed Sun eve and Mon.*

****__Flora__, Via Vittorio Veneto 8, **t** 06 941 6110, **f** 06 941 6546, *www.hotel-flora.it* (*expensive*). A charming hotel set in a beautifully refurbished mansion, with a roof garden and extras including jacuzzis in some rooms.

__Il Pinocchio__, Piazza del Mercato 20, **t 06 941 7883 (*inexpensive*). A good budget choice, with big, old-fashioned rooms overlooking the market and a pretty square.

__Eden Tuscolano__, Via Tuscolano 15, **t 06 940 8589, **f** 06 940 8591, *www.edentuscolano.it* (*moderate–cheap*). Just out of town, a quiet, family-run place which is set in large gardens and has simple, bright rooms.

Zarazà, Via Regina Margherita 21, **t** 06 942 2053 (*moderate*). A traditional trattoria, with a delightful laid-back atmosphere. *Closed Mon, Aug, Sun eves in winter.*

San Martino Il Vicolo, Via San Martino 6, **t** 06 941 6102 (*moderate*). A delightful and romantic little restaurant tucked down a side street with tables outside in summer.

Tuscolano on the ground floor, with a small gathering of discoveries from ancient Tusculum (*see* below), and a huge, light-filled gallery devoted to changing exhibitions of modern and contemporary art on the first floor. On either side of the Villa Aldobrandini are the **Villa Lancelotti**, and the shady **Villa Torlonia**. The area around Frascati has several other grandiose palaces, none open to the public, but testimony to its position as the leading country retreat of the Roman families who ran the church in the 16th–18th centuries. The regular commuter train service from Frascati to Rome was the first train built in the Papal States; it opened in 1856. It was supposed to go south of the Castelli to Naples, but so many influential cardinals lived around Frascati that it came here instead.

Charming staff and excellent local cuisine including very fine *pappardelle al cinghiale.*

Zapata Bar, Via Risorgimento 4, no tel (*cheap*). Here you can eat decent trattoria-style food with trendy young locals surrounded by photos of moustachioed rebels and murals.

Rocca Priora ✉ 00040

★★★★**Villa La Rocca**, Via dei Castelli Romani 1, **t** 06 947 1594, **f** 06 947 1750 (*expensive*). Modern and comfortable. Its restaurant, **La Lanterna**, **t** 06 947 1750 (*expensive*), is excellent, featuring wild mushrooms and truffles.

Grottaferrata ✉ 00046

Grottaferrata has some of the most charming places to stay in the Castelli.

★★★★**Park Villa Grazioli**, Via U. Pavoni 19, **t** 06 945401, **f** 06 941 3506, *www.villagrazioli.com* (*very expensive*). Built in the the 1500s, and beautifully positioned, with magnificent views over Rome and the hills. Public rooms have lovely frescoes, and bedrooms have every comfort. The hotel has a shuttle bus into Rome and Fiumicino airport.

★★★★**Grand Hotel Villa Fiorio**, Viale Dusmet 28, **t** 06 9454 8007, **f** 06 9454 8009, *www.villafiori.it* (*very expensive*). An elegant Liberty-style hotel with plenty of character, especially in its salon; outside there's a beautiful pool in a lush English garden.

★★★**Villa Ferrata**, Via Tuscolana 287, **t** 06 9454 8049, **f** 06 9454 8050 (*moderate*). Doesn't have the tone of the other two, but is modern and welcoming, and has a pool and gazebo for dining out in its pretty park, and shuttles to Frascati and Rome.

★★**Centro**, Via 1 Maggio, **t** 06 941 5151 (*cheap*). In the town centre; cheap and simple.

Taverna dello Spuntino, Via Cicerone 22, **t** 06 9431 5704 (*expensive*). The vaulted dining room of this taverna features solid country cooking and home-made pasta. *Closed Wed and most of Aug.*

Fico Vecchio, Via Anagnina 257, **t** 06 945 9261 (*expensive*). Classic and *autentico*, built in the ruins of an ancient aqueduct; traditional cooking, featuring meat or fish. *Closed Tues.*

Fico Nuovo, Via Anagnina 134, **t** 06 9431 5390 (*expensive*). Owned by Claudio Ciocca, whose face you may recognize from a score of Fellini films; good fish and dishes from other corners of Italy; outdoors in summer. *Closed Wed and a week in Aug.*

Antica Osteria del Corso, Piazza Cavour. Less expensive; has outside tables and a two-sided menu: *low moderate* for the usual dishes and a bit more for the house specialities, such as *strangolapreti* with rocket, or a *filetto* with wild mushrooms.

La Briciola, Via G D'Annunzio 12, **t** 06 945 9338 (*moderate*). Excellent cod and pheasant dishes, and plenty of porcini mushrooms in season. *Closed Sun eve, Mon, Aug.*

Marino ✉ 00047

★★★★**Helio Cabala**, Via Spinabella 13/15, **t** 06 9366 1235, **f** 06 9366 1125 (*expensive*). The best hotel here, with its beautiful belvedere, fountain and garden, offering a touch of class as well as large rooms, a pool, and tennis and golf. The restaurant is up to snuff, and on summer nights you can dine outside.

Cantina Colonna, Via G Carissimi 32, **t** 06 9366 0386 (*moderate*). Don't resist the antipasti at this evocative restaurant; *spaghetti alla carbonara* here achieves a kind of epiphany. *Closed Wed, Aug, and lunchtimes.*

In the centre of Frascati, Piazza San Pietro has a pretty fountain and a **cathedral** with a wonderfully overdone late Baroque façade, much restored after bombing; beyond the fountain, the church of the **Gesù** is a smaller version of the Gesù in Rome, designed by Pietro da Cortona and decorated with perspective *trompe l'œil* dome frescoes by Andrea Pozzo and Antonio del Colli; a black disc on the floor marks the spot from where the illusion is perfect. The **Museo Etiopico**, in the Convento dei Cappuccini, Via Cardinal Massaia 26, is a small collection of art and objects from Ethiopia, brought by missionaries in the 19th century (***t*** *06 942 86601; open daily 9–12 and 3.30–6*).

Five kilometres east, on a minor road from Villa Aldobrandini, you can find **Tusculum**, Frascati's predecessor. Reputedly founded by Telegonus, the son of Odysseus and

Circe, the city indeed seems to have been unaccountably Greek for much of its early history; archaeologists confirm that its inhabitants followed Greek religious practices, and they minted images of Zeus on their coins; further complicating things is the name, which seems to suggest the Etruscans were involved here too. Tusculum was the birthplace of the sourball arch-conservative Cato and later fief of Senatrix Theodora, whose family took the name of Counts of Tusculum and ran Rome like a brothel for much of the 11th century. They became so hated by rival factions that when a Roman army conquered the town in 1197, they razed it so thoroughly that it was never rebuilt, but you can still pick out the ruins of the 'Villa of Cicero' and have a picnic in the well-preserved Roman theatre. Climb up to the former citadel (760m) for one of the finest views over the Alban Hills. The highest of all the hill towns, **Rocca Priora**, lies just to the east, surrounded by chestnut forests and crowned by an eccentric reconstruction of a medieval castle.

Grottaferrata and Marino

Grottaferrata, another Castelli town only 3km south of Frascati, was built around an 11th-century abbey, the well-fortified Basilian **Abbazia di Grottaferrata**, founded by SS. Nilus and Bartholomew, Greek monks from Calabria who came here as refugees from Saracen raids. The Abbey is still home to a congregation of Basilian monks of the Greco-Byzantine rite (*open daily 7–6.30*). Not many abbeys are so well protected; this one owes its impressive walls to Cardinal Giulio della Rovere, later Pope Julius II, who commissioned Giuliano da Sangallo to fortify the town; the abbey just happened to stand on the key spot in the defences.

Inside the walls, the **Basilica di Santa Maria**, consecrated in 1025, must be the most artistically ecumenical church building in Christendom. It has a colourful 12th-century campanile and a wonderfully carved marble portal of the same period, both in the Roman medieval style, topped by a Byzantine mosaic (all of these were heavily restored in 1910). The entrance is through a narthex, with a delightful 10th- or 11th-century baptismal font carved with scenes of fishermen. Inside, above the Cosmatesque floor, rococo Roman frippery frames a Greek mosaic inscription. The best part is the triumphal arch over the altar, with 13th-century mosaics of Nilus and Bartholomew, and the twelve Apostles flanking the empty throne of Christ (representing the Ascension – but this is an ancient Greek motif; in classical Greek art the empty throne was Zeus's). The paintings around the mosaics, of angels and the life of Moses, were done at approximately the same time. Off the right aisle, in the **Chapel of St Nilus**, Domenichino painted what his partisans claim are his best frescoes (and in the 18th and 19th centuries he was considered one of the greatest of all painters), a cycle on the *Life of SS. Nilus and Bartholomew*; one scene shows the visit of Emperor Otto III, another the legend of how Nilus miraculously caught a falling column during the construction of the basilica.

The monastery's **museum** (*open for tours Sat and Sun at 5pm (May–Sept), 4pm (Oct–April); other days ring* **t** *06 340961 9736, www.abadiagreca.it*) contains some beautiful classical sculpture, as well as frescoes, vestments and icons. The abbey also has one of the greatest libraries of rare and antique books in Italy, a centre of Greek learning for nearly a thousand years. The monks no longer copy manuscripts; now they run an important laboratory for the preservation and restoration of old books.

A few kilometres from Grottaferrata towards Rome on the SS511, the **Catacombs of Ad Decimum** (at the tenth milepost from Rome, hence the name) contain burials of the 3rd and 4th centuries (***t** 06 945 94244; open Sun only, 10–12.30, also 4–7pm in summer, 3–5 in winter; guided tours; adm*). South of Grottaferrata, the SS216 will take you to **Marino**, like Frascati a famous wine town that suffered seriously during the war. Marino's topers are devoted to the local stuff; on any sleepy afternoon the old-fashioned wine shops will be the only establishments open. The liveliest time to visit is the first Sunday in October, during the merry *Sagra dell'Uva* when the last year's vintage flows through the **Fountain of the Moors** in Piazza Lépanto; this commemorates the many natives who fought in the Battle of Lépanto – a Turkish shield taken as a trophy still hangs in the **Basilica di San Barnaba**, Marino's landmark with its lofty dome, and a richly appointed interior full of 17th-century paintings and sculpture.

Lakes Albano and Nemi

In the loveliest part of the Castelli, the Via Appia follows the volcanic rim around two crater lakes, Albano and Nemi, formed by huge explosions three or four million years ago. Along the way it passes the Pope's summer retreat at Castel Gandolfo, the remarkable ancient relics of Albano Laziale, and some architectural flash from the Baroque master Bernini.

Lake Albano: Rocca di Papa and Monte Cavo

From Marino you can continue along the occasionally panoramic **Via dei Laghi** (SS217) which overlooks the elliptical **Lake Albano**. Romans, whose taste for vicarious battles followed them even on holiday, used to come to watch mock sea fights from their lakeside villas. Beyond the lake there's a turn-off for **Rocca di Papa**, a dramatically sited town built around a castle, with a picturesque medieval citadel called the *Quartiere dei Bavaresi* after the Bavarian troops of Emperor Ludwig stationed here in the 1320s. A private toll road leads up from Rocca di Papa to the second highest of the Alban Hills, **Monte Cavo** (948m; or you can walk up from town). Monte Cavo, the ancient *Mons Albanus*, was the sacred mountain of the Latin tribes. Aeneas' son Anchises founded *Alba Longa*, their most ancient city and political centre, nearby (no one knows its exact site for sure), while at the summit was the sanctuary of Jupiter Latiaris, the cult centre of all Latium. Sir James Frazer writes how one of the ancient kings of *Alba Longa* considered himself the equal of Jupiter, inventing machines that mimicked thunder and lightning, banging and sparking enough to drown out the real storm. Jupiter did not take kindly to the competition, and blasted the impudent king with a thunderbolt, followed by a cloudburst that drowned his very palace under the waters of Lake Albano, traces of which, legend says, are visible when the water is low.

Despite this setback, *Mons Albanus* remained the political and religious centre of the Latin League until the Romans did steal Jupiter's thunder by building him a

Tourist Information

Albano Laziale: Viale Risorgimento 1, **t** 06 932 4081, **f** 06 932 0040, *turismoalbano@tin.it*.
Nemi: Piazza Muncipio, **t** 06 936 8001.
Castel Gandolfo: Piazza Libertà 7, **t** 06 936 1241.
Velletri: Pza Garibaldi, **t** 06 963 0896.

Where to Stay and Eat

Rocca di Papa ✉ 00040

*****Europa**, Piazza della Repubblica 20, **t/f** 06 9474 9361 (*moderate–cheap*). In a refurbished old palazzo; bright rooms with views.

****Villa Ortensie**, Via Ariccia 19, **t** 06 9474 9108, **f** 06 949 5155 (*moderate*). Out of the centre, by the woods and overlooking Lake Albano; simple, quiet, and relaxing.

La Foresta, Via del Laghi km12, **t** 06 9474 9392 (*moderate*). Enormous and rather grand, but it offers some of the best local cuisine in the area, with a fine wine list to match and excellent traditional desserts.

Castel Gandolfo ✉ 00040

******Castelvecchio**, Viale Pio XI 23, **t** 06 936 0308, **f** 06 936 0579, *www.itlayhotel.com/lazio/c.gandolfo/c.vecchio* (*luxury*). Have a holiday with the Pope for your neighbour at this modern hotel next to the papal gardens.

Pagnanelli, Via Antonio Gramsci 4, **t** 06 936 0004 (*expensive*). The best restaurant in town for a long time; serves a good *zuppa di frutti di mare* and 'burn-your-fingers' lamb (*abbachio alla scottadito*). *Closed Tues.*

Albano Laziale ✉ 00041

*****Miralago**, Via dei Cappuccini 12, **t** 06 932 1018, **f** 06 932 5335, *miralagoemail@libero.it* (*moderate*). Outside the centre and offering serenity and enough modern comforts to make for a relaxing stay. *Closed May.*

Antica Abbazia, Via S. Filippo Neri 19, **t** 06 932 3187 (*moderate*). An 18th-century English monastery now contains this delightful restaurant, where the menu stars the freshest local ingredients – try the *orecchiette* with wild chicory. *Closed Mon.*

Ariccia ✉ 00020

Behind the Palazzo Chigi, under the bridge, there's a happy collection of *vino e cucina* places and *porchetta* stands along Via Borga San Rocco, where everybody goes at night.

La Fiaschetta de Sora Ines (*cheap*). Here you get a plate of *pappardelle al cinghiale* or whatever else is on that night, preceded or followed with choosing what you like from the antipasti on display – artichokes, various salads, prosciutto and other good things.

Lanuvio ✉ 00046

L'Anfiteatro, Piazza Centuripe 4, **t** 06 937 5753 (*moderate*). A pretty setting near the Roman Theatre, and besides pizza offers solid favourites such as *pappardelle al cinghiale*, and *abbacchio scottadito*. *Closed Tues.*

Velletri ✉ 00049

*****Benito al Bosco**, Via Contrada Morice 20, **t** 06 963 3991, *www.benitoalbosco.com* (*moderate*). Set in a leafy old park,this hotel has a pool and adequate rooms, although the big attraction is the top-quality restaurant (*expensive*) especially in mushroom season. *Closed Tues.*

Benito, Via Lata 241, **t** 06 963 2220 (*expensive*). Under the same management; specializes in game and mushrooms as well, and desserts as rich as Bill Gates. *Closed Mon, Aug.*

superior temple on the Capitol. But the importance of his first sanctuary was never forgotten, and it became the practice for any conquering hero whose victories weren't momentous enough for the Forum to be given a second-class triumph here, along Monte Cavo's Via Triumphalis. The footpath from the upper reaches of Rocca di Papa follows its route beyond the **Campi d'Annibale**, the hollow of an ancient crater where Hannibal and his elephants are said to have camped, to the top where there are fabulous views in all directions. No trace of a temple of Jupiter Latiaris has ever been discovered here; as god of sky, thunder, and oaks he was apparently worshipped outdoors in a sacred grove. Tarquin the Proud built a wall to define the sacred precinct, and when Cardinal Henry, Duke of York, built a Passionist monastery here (since converted into a hotel) he reused some of its blocks. The people of Rocca di Papa used to collect snow in the winter in wells here, to sell to the Romans in summer. Where the ancient pagans and not so ancient Passionist fathers worshipped, there is now a forest of television transmitters.

Castel Gandolfo

Castel Gandolfo is a happy little village, perched 1,400ft above Lake Albano, and famous as the Vatican enclave where the pope spends the dog days of summer. The discovery of an Iron Age necropolis used in the 9th to 7th centuries BC strengthens Castel Gandolfo's claim that it was the site of *Alba Longa*. Interestingly, the graves were found coated with a thin layer of lava, supporting the old, discredited legend that volcanic eruptions forced the early inhabitants down from these hills to Rome. Finds from the cemetery are in EUR's Museo Preistorico. Castel Gandolfo is named for the Gandolfi family of Genoa, who built a castle here in the 12th century. The **Papal Palace** was constructed on its ruins by Carlo Maderno in 1624, and was much remodelled by Pius IX. To attend the Pope's general audience on summer Wednesdays at 11am you need tickets from the Vatican (*see* Vatican Practicalities, p.151), though on Sundays in the summer John Paul II appears at noon to give a homily to the crowd in the palace courtyard. The Palace, with its huge gardens that contain ruins of a Roman imperial villa, is officially part of the Vatican state, along with the **Villa Barberini** and the nearby **Vatican Observatory**. The little domed church of **San Tommaso di Villanova** (1661) was the first church designed by Gianlorenzo Bernini (at the age of 59), and he handles it with unaccustomed gravity and restraint. Bernini also did the two fountains in the village, and there are fine views from behind the theatrical **Piazza della Libertà** (also known as the Piazza del Plebiscito).

The other thing to do in Castel Gandolfo is walk down the track below the rail station to the cave entrance of the **Emissarium**, a tunnel nearly 1½km long, carved by the Romans in 397 BC. At the time the war with Veii seemed endless, and they asked an oracle what it took to win. 'Drain the lake,' replied the sibyl, and so they did in their literal Roman way; to this day, the Emissarium is still used to control the level of the lake. The prettiest route from Castel Gandolfo on to Albano is the upper of Urban VIII's two roads, called the **Galleria di Sopra**, or upper tunnel, for its roof of interwoven ilex branches – the lower 'tunnel', the **Galleria di Sotto**, is the busy main road. The Upper Road begins above Albano's Piazza San Paolo and follows the rim of Monte Cavo's crater, with views of the lake and the surrounding country.

Albano Laziale

Alba Longa may have been located at Castel Gandolfo, but its name lingers on in **Albano Laziale**, the next important town up the Via Appia. In AD 199, Septimius Severus created a large permanent camp for the 2nd Legion here, called *Castra Albano*, the first time any emperor had based a legion within Italy. Severus' short-lived predecessor, Didianus Julius, had purchased the Imperial crown at auction from the Praetorian Guard, and Severus, a serious-minded African general who had to defeat two rivals to gain his throne, wanted to put a stop to such shenanigans. He replaced the greedy Praetorians with his own trusted veterans, and for extra security deployed a legion here to keep an eye on them – and also to give the other legions a central reserve, which could move anywhere quickly via the road system or by sea.

Any emperor who wanted to keep his head on his shoulders in this era had to make sure his soldiers were happy, and Severus built them a camp fit for heroes, a city in itself, with gardens, baths and temples. Most of it was destroyed after the fall of the Empire, and the town grew up over the ruins later. But enough remains to make Albano a treasurehouse of antique curiosities. The modern town centre, shaped like a wedge on the slope of Monte Cavo's crater, just about fills the space of the legion's huge camp, with the main Corso Matteotti following the track of the ancient Via Appia, along what was the camp's western wall. The church of **San Pietro** was built over a bath complex in the 6th century and has a fine Romanesque campanile, and fragments of ancient architectural decoration and medieval frescoes inside. On the next street up, Via Don Minzoni, you can see the mighty ruins of the three-arched **Porta Praetoria**, the camp's principal gate, rediscovered in 1944 after a bomb fell nearby.

From here, a walk up Via Saffi and left on the next street takes you to **Santa Maria della Rotonda**, a remarkable miniature Pantheon, built inside a *nymphaeum* from the camp's baths. At the entrance, a mosaic of sea-monsters gives away the church's origins, leading to a grand interior, a cylinder of Roman brick underneath a concrete dome with an oculus. More of the original mosaics survive, in the eight *exedrae* around the walls; and, in a chamber to the left of the altar, fragments of reliefs and decorations – including a fine relief of Mithras and the bull (*see* box, p.180).

Further up Via Saffi is a perfectly preserved underground reservoir, or **Cisternone**, carved into the living rock on the order of Septimius Severus to supply the troops, and still used today to hold Albano's water (*to see it, ask at the Museo Civico*). Ruins of the **Amphitheatre** lie behind the church in genteelly dilapidated Piazza San Paolo; the very presence of this huge amphitheatre, built for soldiers in the mid-3rd century, in the middle of the biggest military and economic crisis Rome had yet known, says a lot about the priorities of the late Empire. Behind it, from the top of the hill, you can see Lake Albano shimmering far below.

Where Corso Matteotti turns into Viale Risorgimento, at the southern end of Albano, the 19th-century Villa Ferrajoli houses the **Museo Civico**, set in a pretty garden (*open daily 9–1; Wed and Thurs 4–7pm; adm; ask them about guided tours of the Cisternone, Catacombs of San Senatore and the other ruins of Albano*); besides a relentlessly thorough grounding in the town's geology and prehistory, the museum has a collection of Roman finds, including an ingenious device for measuring and mixing wine.

Just down the street, beneath the end of the viaduct that carries the Via Appia to Ariccia, are the five truncated cones of the so-called **Tomb of the Horatii and Curiatii**, built in an Etruscan style. Roman legend has it that three Roman Horatii and three Latin Curatii fought in single combat to end the war between Alba Longa and Rome during the reign of Tullus Hostilius – but Alba Longa's tyrant proved deceitful, resulting in its total destruction by the Romans. Arguments over this tomb have been flying around for over 400 years. Some guessed it was really a monument erected in

Rise and Fall of a God

As Mitra, Mithras is mentioned in the Hindu Vedas as early as 1400 BC. In Persia he was one of the important gods of the old pantheon, and his cult came into the west with the returning soldiers of Alexander the Great. The Greeks never cared much for Mithras; he was after all the god of their arch-enemies. But the Persian cult found a home in various places around the Mediterranean, and made a spectacular upsurge in the 2nd and 3rd centuries AD. Historians can't explain it, but it seems imperial patronage had a lot to do with it. Emperors such as Commodus, Caracalla and Albano's founder Septimius Severus were initiates. Mithras was a god of light, but also associated with friendships, bonds and contracts of all kinds, the patron of loyalty to one's sovereign and brotherhood on the battlefield: altogether a perfect deity for the imperial service and the army. Its practice seems a kind of freemasonry. Only men took part, and there were seven levels of achievement, corresponding to the seven planetary spheres, each with its initiation. Like its competitor, Christianity, and in contrast to all the other cults of the day, Mithraism carried with it a big dose of morality and ethics; the Seven Deadly Sins were originally a Mithraic concept (one for each planetary sphere, of course).

Imperial Romans saw nothing amiss with combining religion with pleasure, and their *mithraea* were often parts of bath complexes like Albano's, or the famous one discovered under the Baths of Caracalla in Rome. Often they were taken over by the Christians, as at Sutri (*see* p.203) or at Rome's San Clemente. *Mithraea* are always underground, and the major feature is always a fresco or relief of Mithras sacrificing the sacred white bull. He didn't want to do it, and the sorrow on his face is often skilfully portrayed in the cult images. But Mithras was literally born with the knife in his hand. It was his destiny, and his father the sun god ordered him to make the sacrifice – it meant the creation of our world. The bull's blood poured out and formed all the plants and trees, while his sperm created men and animals. Its body was transformed into the moon, while Mithras' cloak became the firmament of stars. Usually the icons in *mithraea* show a serpent, or scorpion, underneath the bull. They are the origin of evil, attracted from the depths by the sacrifice to lick up the bull's spilled blood.

In the 3rd century, Mithraism probably had more adherents than Christianity, and it came very close to becoming Rome's state religion. But when Constantine became Emperor he took the first fateful steps toward converting the Empire to Christianity.

honour of Pompey, or else the tomb of Arruns, son of Lars Porsenna, the Etruscan chief of Clusium who reoccupied Rome after the fall of the Tarquins. The unusual form with the five cones is Etruscan; it appears in funeral reliefs found in Volterra, and is said to be the style of Porsenna's own tomb. Most likely it was erected in the 3rd century BC or later by a local noble family of Etruscan origins. The intact parts of the tomb are largely reconstructions, done by the famed sculptor Canova and the architect Valadier when Napoleon ruled Italy.

Albano has yet more curiosities, which you can only see by asking at the Museo Civico: the **Catacombs of San Senatore**, across from this tomb under the church of Santa Maria della Stella, contains a medieval painting of a crazed-looking Christ

Pantocrator and Madonna, and other frescoes from as early as the 5th century. On Via Olivella are the remains of a **Villa Imperiale**, one of 14 great villas that stood in or around Albano. This one was built by Pompey, with his spoils from the wars against Mithridates in Asia Minor. He was buried somewhere here, though if his remains still exist no one's yet found them.

Aríccia

From here the Via Appia crosses a series of viaducts on its way south, passing by way of **Aríccia**, a village immersed in trees, with summer villas all around. It boasts two works by Bernini, who was employed by the Chigi to beautify the village. Within Aríccia, he did the façade of **Santa Maria del Galloro**, at the northern entrance to the town, and restored the **Palazzo Chigi**, set in front of a gorgeous park at the southern end, while across the Appia his round, domed **Santa Maria dell'Assunzione** was his second church project. The simple cylinder and dome recall the Pantheon, although the curved arms on each side are pure Bernini, as are the short twin steeples (a Bernini trademark, like the twin belfries he installed on the Pantheon, demolished later, that his numerous critics called 'Bernini's asses' ears'; perhaps to hide them from the critics, here he puts them behind the dome). The interior provides a demonstration of the scenographic revolution of Baroque architecture Bernini helped inspire. The church honours the Assumption of Mary into heaven, and Bernini makes the building a kind of stage to emphasize it – the interior of the cylinder, lined with Corinthian columns, is the earthly level, while above it the dome is almost literally the dome of heaven where Mary is bound, decorated with carved angels and flowers.

Some Renaissance prints show the ancient Temple of Diana at Nemi, only two miles away, as looking something like this church. It didn't at all – that was just the artist's fantasy, but it's fascinating to think that Bernini might have been trying to reproduce the temple here. Note the building to the left of the church; under the portico is a fountain which, as an inscription explains, was built from remains of the tomb of Simon Magus, the pagan nemesis of St Peter.

Lake Nemi: Genzano di Roma, Lanuvio and Nemi

Next along the Via Appia is the big and busy town of **Genzano di Roma**, overlooking Lake Nemi. Genzano is best known for the *infiorata* on the Sunday after Corpus Christi, when the streets are covered with patterns made from over 8,000lbs of flower petals. Little **Lanuvio**, further south, makes a natural balcony on the edge of the *Colli Albani*, with views over the Roman Campagna and the sea. Lanuvio was the birthplace of Antoninus Pius, one of the best of emperors (AD 138–61), whose reign was so peaceful and prosperous that no one remembers his name, and it was also the home of a famous sanctuary of Juno, now partly underneath the Salesian convent and partly on the grounds of the town library. If Aríccia is Bernini's, Lanuvio belongs to the late Baroque architect Carlo Fontana, who contributed the **Collegiata di Santa Maria Maggiore** (1675) and the **Fontana degli Scogli**. There is also a **Museo Comunale**, on Via Roma (***t** 06 9378 9228; open Wed 10–1 and 5–7, Thurs–Sun 10–1 and 4–7; adm*) with a collection somewhat smaller than it was before the bombers blew it up in

1944, as well as remains of a Temple of Hercules, and a Republican-era Roman bridge, the **Ponte Loreto**. Sample Lanuvio's *Colli Lanuvini* wines at its **Enoteca Comunale**.

From Genzano, you can go down to the magical 'Mirror of Diana', the round, deep, blue **Lake Nemi**, its still waters encompassed by dripping forests and plastic-coated strawberry farms. As it descends, the road passes the meagre ruins of the **Temple of Diana Nemorensis**, the celebrated sanctuary of Diana of the woodlands, in whose forest, known as the 'grove of Ariccia', were held the barbaric rites that inspired Sir James Frazer's *The Golden Bough* (*see* p.48). New excavations are under way, but the temple is occasionally open to visitors (ask at the Roman Ships museum).

Caligula, who had a special mad devotion to this cult, built two magnificent ships to ferry visitors across the lake to the temple. These ships, which featured marble-columned pavilions and mosaic floors, sank during the reign of Claudius, and although they were discovered in 1446 by Leon Battista Alberti, who tried to raise one but only succeeded in breaking its keel, they remained in a remarkable state of preservation at the bottom of the lake until 1932, when Mussolini had them brought up. It's a shame that they didn't stay there a little longer, for as a last act of gratuitous spite in 1944 the retreating Germans set a fire in the lakeshore **Museum of Roman Ships**, near the Temple, and burnt them to cinders. This mournful, half-empty hangar (*open daily exc Mon; 9 until 6 in April, 6.30 in May, 7.30 July and Aug, 5.30 in Sept; 9–2 the rest of the year; all Sundays 9–1; adm*) is still worth a visit, with bronze figurines and bits salvaged from the fire, and models of the ships one-fifth the size of the originals. One of the ships is currently being reconstructed, using the ancient methods and materials, and the immense prow sits at the entrance to the museum.

From the opposite side of the lake you can climb up to **Nemi**, a picturesque little village wrapped around its 9th-century castle, famous for its wild strawberry festival.

Velletri

After Genzano and Lanuvio, the Castelli are done, and there's nothing left but to climb down to **Velletri** (*40km from Rome, the last COTRAL stop*), an ancient Latin and Volscian city that has managed to keep its character in the shadow of Rome. Velletri was the childhood home of Augustus, and like the Castelli it became a favoured spot for the villas of the Roman élite; after nearly disappearing in the Dark Ages, Velletri came back as a flourishing free city in the Middle Ages until it fell into the clutches of the Church in the papacy of Boniface VIII. Today, like the Castelli towns, it is a leading wine producer. Although bombed to smithereens in the war, its landmark **Torre del Trivio**, a leaning 148ft needle-like campanile from 1353, has been restored. The **museum** in the Palazzo Comunale (*open Tues–Fri 9–11.30, Thurs also 4–6.30; adm*) contains a collection of Volscian sarcophagi, while the crazy quilt of a **cathedral**, built over a Roman basilica, has artworks from the Cosmati to the 1950s, with nearly every style in between. Under the portico is the entrance to a small **museum** (***t*** *06 962 7217, www.museovelletri.com; open 10–1 and 3–7; adm*), with Madonnas by Gentile da Fabriano and Antoniazzo Romano and a Byzantine reliquary from the 12th century.

Northern Lazio

11

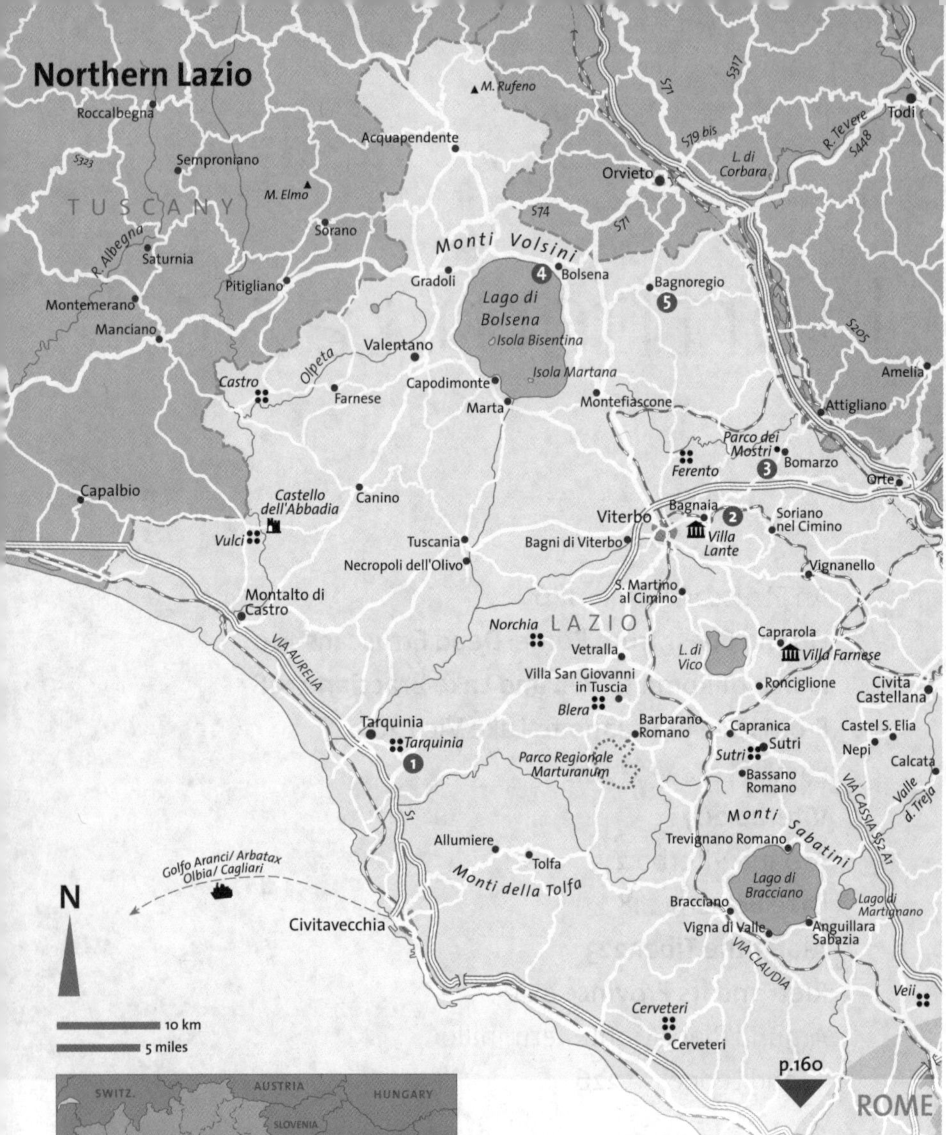

Highlights

1 Frescoed Etruscan tombs of Tarquínia
2 Lovely Renaissance gardens of the Villa Lante, Bagnaia
3 The Monster Park of Bomarzo
4 Pristine Lake Bolsena and medieval Bolsena town
5 Lazio's ghost city, Cívita di Bagnoregio

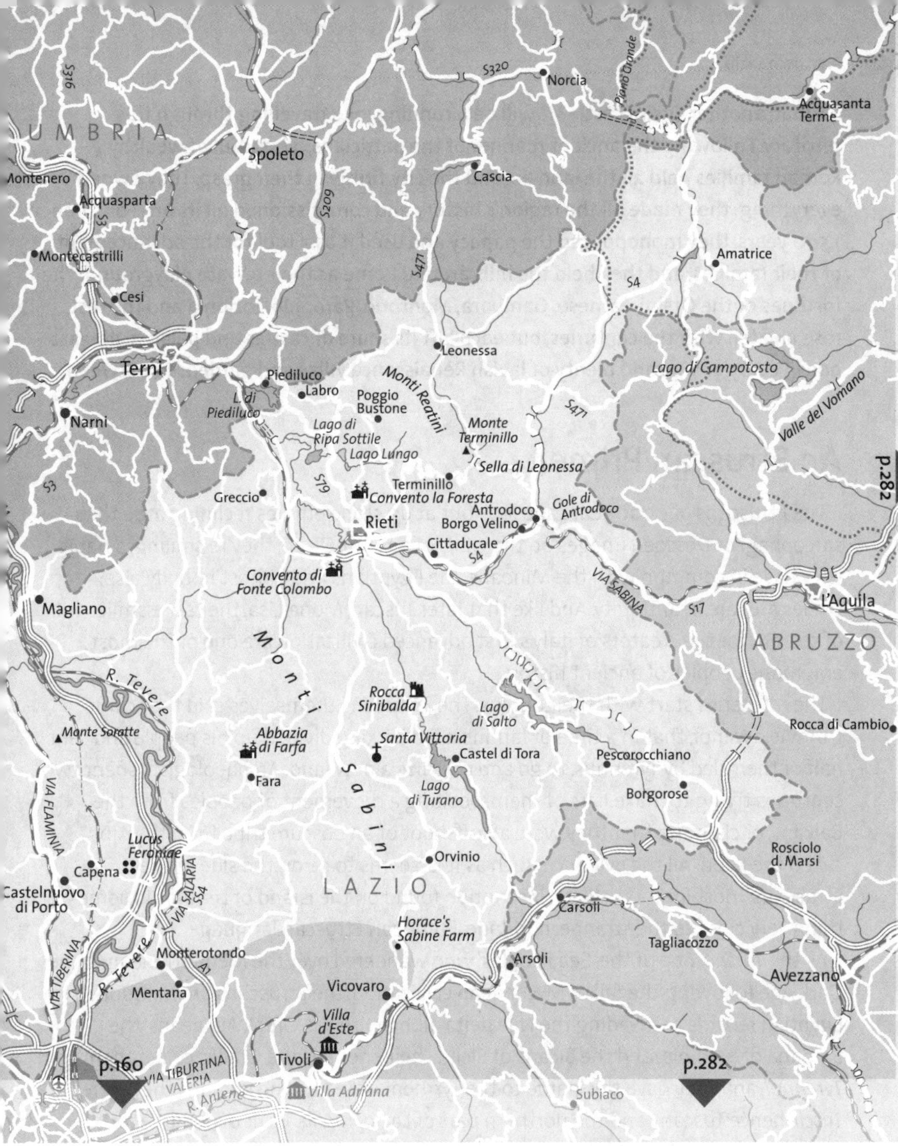

In the time of the Etruscans this region was called *Tuscia*, and in recent years both the name and the region have been making a comeback. The landscapes are some of Italy's most distinctive; its coastline may not be much to speak of, but inland a chain of long-dead volcanoes has graced the countryside with patches of pretty hills and a chain of volcanic lakes. Long ago, the Etruscans made it the richest and most densely populated corner of the peninsula, but it has known mostly hard times since. Some great capitals create rich and prosperous regions around themselves; Rome, the eternal predator, sucks its hinterlands dry. Under the misrule and neglect of caesars and popes, the old Etruscan heartland became a wasteland; even a century ago its western half was populated mostly by lonely shepherds and bandits. One thing it does possess in abundance – castles.

What, another Orsini castle? It will be a running joke travelling through this territory. Following the ancient manner of the patricians, a handful of wealthy Roman families held all the land around the city firmly in their grasp. They owned everything; they made all the region's history and commissioned all its art. For some 1,500 years, they monopolized the papacy and used it as a tool for the advancement of their families, and they held the hills around Rome as their private playground. The fortunes of the Orsini, Farnese, Gambara, Montorio, Pamphili, Torlonia and the rest rose and fell with the centuries, but each left its share of castles and palaces: at least one in every village and plenty of lavish Renaissance villas and gardens in between.

An Etruscan Primer

The Etruscans of 2,700 years ago look out at us, stone effigies reclining atop their sarcophagi or frescoed images on the walls of a tomb. Often, they're smiling, a habit they have in common with the Minoans, the Egyptians and almost nobody else; smiles are rare in antiquity. And like that later Tuscan, Mona Lisa, theirs are smiles full of secrets, for the creators of Italy's first advanced civilization are one of the most enigmatic peoples of ancient history.

The mysteries start with their origins. The Etruscans themselves said they came from Asia Minor, that in a time of famine a Lydian king divided up his people and sent half of them, led by Tyrennus, to go and colonize a new land. Archaeologists spent two centuries trying to make liars of them, positing a movement of peoples from the Balkans, or claiming that they were an offshoot of an obscure tribe from the Alps called the Raeti. All the evidence, such as it is, seems to be on the side of the Etruscans, most importantly an inscription found on the island of Lemnos in something very close to the strange, non-Indo-European Etruscan language.

As the *Tursha*, one of the 'Sea Peoples' who wandered over the Mediterranean in the Dark Age following the fall of Mycenaean civilization, the Etruscans are mentioned in Egyptian records as invading the Nile delta along with the Greek Achaeans, the Sardana of Sardinia, and the Sicans of Sicily. Their enemies the Greeks called them *Tyrennoi*, and they gave this name to the Tyrrhenian Sea; to the Romans they were *Tuscii*, hence Tuscany and the northern part of Lazio, *Tuscia*. Their own name for themselves, discovered from inscriptions, was *Rasena*.

They probably came by sea, settling either as colonists or a conquering military élite on both the Adriatic and Tyrrhenian shores. The oriental transplant thrived on the Tyrrhenian side, where they took over many of the Villanovan settlements, and developed new cities of their own in northern Lazio and Tuscany, almost always in defensible hilltop sites. There was wealth to be gained in the new land, and the Etruscans made the most of the chance. Their considerable skill in waterworks, land reclamation and irrigation helped create a prosperous agriculture, but even greater opportunities came from trade and industry. Greek writers spoke of the Etruscan 'thalassocracy'; commerce and seapower went hand in hand, and in the 6th century BC they were the bosses of the Tyrrhenian, establishing bases at what is now Genoa, and at Aleria in Corsica. This naturally led to conflict with those other thalassocrats, the Greeks, and in the power politics of the era the Etruscans usually found themselves allied with the Carthaginians against the Greek cities of southern Italy and Sicily. Etruscan kings also ruled at Rome. In the 6th century BC the dynasty of the Tarquinii made this rough-and-ready settlement into a proper city, and gave it its first imposing temples.

Like the Greeks, the Etruscans never achieved, or perhaps even imagined, any kind of political unity. The basic unit was the city-state, with the cities linked in a loose federal organization, a 'dodecapolis' or league of twelve cities, the importance of which was largely religious rather than political. There were three such leagues, one in the Po valley of northern Italy, one in Campania, of which the leading city was Capua, and one in the Lazio–Tuscany constellation of city-states. Of these the last was the first and by far the richest and strongest. To understand the sudden prominence of any ancient people, follow the money – and the source of sudden wealth is usually a mine. Alexander the Great financed his armies from a new gold mine in Macedonia, and Athens bullied its way to power after it found silver at Laurion. In the Etruscans' case, the windfall was the island of Elba and its mountains of iron ore, along with other mines on the Tuscan coast.

According to Etruscan myths, their religious practices were defined by Tages, a mythical child prophet who sprang miraculously from a ploughed furrow. Tages must have taught them well, for the Etruscans are undeniably one of the most god-haunted peoples of antiquity, obsessed with the art of divination. The basic principle was the unity of all creation, and they took it to extremes. The heavens, the earth, and everything in them were in a sense identical. Each was divided into zones governed by different influences and embodying different properties; thus an Etruscan priest could find news about the future on earth from watching the sky (which they divided into 16 'temples', not a 12-sided zodiac), observing the flight of birds, or inspecting the liver of a sacrificed animal, performed by a priest called a *haruspex*; near Piacenza, a bronze model of a sheep's liver has been discovered, divided into zones each marked with its significance. Almost anything, in fact, could be interpreted as a message from the gods – it isn't surprising that the Etruscans had a well-deserved reputation for superstitiousness. This, like so many other things, they passed on to the Romans, especially a healthy fear of lightning, the weapon of their chief god Tinia, the equivalent of Zeus or Jupiter.

Tinia ruled over Etruscan destinies as part of a trinity, along with Uni (Juno) and Minerva (often equated with Athena, though Minerva was more concerned with fertility and childbirth); the most important temples were usually dedicated to these three together, in three separate *cellae*. Many other Etruscan gods – and there are over forty of them – seem to be largely borrowed from the Greeks, or at least a Greek personality superimposed on some older form, such as Hercle (Herakles) and Apulu (Apollo). We also hear of Nethuns (Neptune), Maris (Mars), and Turan (Venus). One important, somewhat shadowy figure is Vertumna, a god of vegetation and the principal object of worship at the federal sanctuary, the *Fanum Voltumnae*, in a sacred wood which was probably located somewhere between Bolsena and Viterbo. The

Etruscans took death seriously; almost all of their surviving architectural works are tombs, and most of the art you will see in the museums came from inside them. We don't know whether their deceased were supposed to make use of these in the afterlife, or what they expected to find there; all we have are the puzzling figures of the *caronti*, painted on the tombs, carrying great hammers or double-axes and leading the dead in procession to the world beyond.

The Greeks started building temples only in the 8th century BC, and the Etruscans followed. They built in wood, with the structural beams strongly expressed, and their constructions seem an unusual cross between the classical Greek and the Japanese. Usually, the wooden parts were covered with plates of decorative sculpted friezes in terracotta, and more terracotta figures adorning the rooflines, all brightly painted; often these portray scenes from Greek mythology. In the other arts the Etruscans leave a mixed record: striking originality and slavish copying, works of exceptional skill and power next to childish scrawling. As soon as they had the money, they began importing Greek vases in great numbers; the museums of Etruria are full of them, another testimony to the tremendous influence of Hellenic culture. In the 7th century, they began copying these for themselves (an economic as well as artistic enterprise, since painted ceramics were status items, and an important component of trade), and became quite skilled at it. Another of their specialities, for everyday use, was the lustrous black *bucchero* ware.

The Etruscans also learned fresco painting from the Greeks; because they painted in tombs, some of their work has survived, while the Greeks' did not. The famous painted tombs of Tarquínia may in fact be our best clue to what Archaic Greek frescoes actually looked like (many writers have also noticed intriguing similarities between Etruscan painting and the art of the ancient Minoans). Sculpture was a particular talent, especially in the expressive terracotta portrait busts, and in the figures of the deceased on sarcophagus lids, where they show an interest in human personality and character that was beyond even the Greeks. They also excelled in casting bronze; a few spectacular examples have survived in the museums of Florence, Rome and Volterra. For all that, we might be forgiven for thinking that their hearts were really in the luxury items of the 'minor arts' – jewellery most of all; the Etruscans created some of the most elegant and intricate gold filigree work of all time, along with plenty of big garish bits that wouldn't look out of place in Las Vegas.

And no culture anywhere ever left archaeologists so many mirrors, cosmetics cases and perfume burners. They say that no two hairdos in portraits of Etruscan women are ever alike, and that these ladies often dyed it blonde. Sarcophagi and tomb paintings show an equal lavishness in dress. Perhaps the Italians of today get their talent for making shoes from the Etruscans, who exported theirs around the Mediterranean; in the 5th century BC, the fashion was curling pointed toes. Etruscan men were peacocks too, but this fashion-consciousness may be related to one of the most significant differences between the people of Etruria and their contemporaries: the role of women. While Greek and Roman women stayed locked up at home under the tedium and oppression of their patriarchies, their Etruscan counterparts kept their surnames after marriage, enjoyed considerable legal rights, and had some role in cultural and political life. There are plenty of hints in ancient writers that Etruscan women drove the Romans crazy; they just didn't know their place.

The reasons why are unclear, but after about 550 BC everything started to fall apart for the Etruscans. The Greeks of Cumae defeated them in 524, putting an end to their expansion in Campania. Fifteen years later the Etruscan kings were booted out of Rome, and for the next two centuries, one disaster followed on another: the Syracusans and their allies wrested control of the Tyrrhenian; the Samnites came down from the mountains and conquered all of the Etruscan cities in Campania, and in 406, the Romans began their long struggle with Veii, their first Etruscan victim. Roman weakness in the early 4th century, after the city was sacked by the Celts, gave them some breathing space, but meanwhile the Celts were also gobbling up the northern dodecapolis in the Po valley. Now only Tuscany and northern Lazio were left, and the recovering Romans snatched up the Etruscan cities one by one; almost all of Etruria was at the mercy of the Romans by 250, though the last holdout, Volterra, lasted until 79.

Throughout this dismal period, trade and manufactures showed a steady decline. The archaeologists find that goods in the tombs were being made less skilfully, from cheaper materials; they note how the serene processions into the afterlife in older art give way to more unsettling, sometimes horrific conceptions. One key to this remarkable collapse may be strains in the social structure of Etruscan society. Revolts of the lower classes became common; at Volscinii such a revolt succeeded, and the nobles invited the Romans in to help them regain control.

Which brings us back to those Etruscan smiles, and the secrets they continue to conceal. Some scholars paint them as an effete, somewhat decadent nation that simply didn't have what it takes to survive against such dangerous neighbours. Others suggest a darker picture, of an oppressive slave-based society that perished because so few of its people had an interest in defending it. The simple lack of political unity among the city-states may provide a more prosaic answer, but whatever the reason, when the Etruscans fell they fell hard. Under Roman rule, their culture disintegrated and their cities decayed. In the civil wars of the 1st century BC many Etruscan towns chose the wrong side and were punished by the victorious dictator Sulla, while vast areas of Etruria were confiscated and granted to wealthy Romans and army veterans. Finally even their language disappeared; the last men to understand it were the *haruspices*, the diviners, whose services were still in demand until the Empire became Christian.

The Romans had one talent and one delight: making war. Almost everything else we associate with them they got from the Etruscans: their religious practices and art, togas, concrete, sewers and drainage projects, rectilinear town planning and road building, races and gladiators (from Etruscan funeral games); even the very symbol of Rome, the famous bronze she-wolf (now in the Capitoline Museum) was the work of an Etruscan artist. The Etruscan nation may have disappeared from the face of the earth, but many of its achievements and much of its way of life went on to become the common property of the Mediterranean world.

Up the Coast from Rome: Dead Etruscans

It will seem hard to believe, but this phenomenally empty stretch of coast north of Rome was the richest and most heavily populated part of ancient Etruria. Today, the defunct Etruscans have the territory pretty much to themselves. You'll find them good company, though, and they put on a good show in the necropoli and museums of Tarquínia, Cervéteri and Vulci. Tarquínia especially, with its spectacular collection of painted tombs, and Cervéteri with its unique city of the dead, are the two sites in all of Etruria where this lost civilization really comes, so to speak, back to life.

Cervéteri

Locally famous for its artichokes, **Cervéteri** (*Caere Vetere*, 'Old Caere') is a mostly modern town built over the site of Caere, the Etruscans' richest city. Caere also had the closest cultural ties to Greece; according to Herodotus, it was the only non-Greek city with a sanctuary at Delphi. It had three seaports (for a population of 25,000) and mined the Tolfa mountains for the metals it exchanged for Attic vases and other luxury goods. Decline began when the Greek cities in southern Italy defeated the Etruscan fleet in 474 BC, ending their naval supremacy. Caere then turned to agriculture and became an ally of Rome, even sheltering Roman refugees when the city was sacked by the Gauls in 370. A falling out came in the 3rd century BC, when Caere

Getting Around

From Lépanto terminus in Rome there are frequent **buses** to Cervéteri, as well as about ten departures a day to Tarquínia. Civitavécchia is linked to Rome by train, and has several COTRAL buses a day to Tolfa, Viterbo, Tarquínia, Ladispoli and Bracciano. Civitavécchia is the main port for Sardinia: the offices of Tirrenia or the FS, the two ferry concessionaries, are both at the harbour near the docks if you feel a sudden desire to bolt there (Tirrenia: **t** 199 123199, *www.tirrenia.it*, with ferries to Olbia, Arbatax and Cagliari; FS runs 2 ferries). To reach Vulci, take the train to Montalto di Castro and catch a taxi or bus from there.

Tourist Information

Cervéteri: Pro Loco, Piazza Risorgimento 1, **t** 06 896301, *www.comune.cerveteri.rm.it*.

Civitavécchia: Viale Garibaldi 42, **t** 0766 25348, **t** 06 21834.

Tarquínia: Piazza Cavour 1, **t** 0766 856384 (*open Mon–Sat 8–2*).

Tuscánia: in Teatro il Rivelleno, Piazza Basile, **t** 0761 436371 (*open 10–1, 3–6; closed Mon*).

Where to Stay and Eat

Cervéteri ✉ 00052

Trattoria Roma, near the museum on Via Roma, **t** 0699 994040 (*moderate*). A wide choice of pizza, *bruschetta*, pasta and seconds, with an outdoor garden.

Antica Locanda le Ginestre, also in the centre on Piazza Santa Maria, **t** 0699 40672 (*moderate*). A fine place to try seasonal dishes, home-made pasta, and game dishes. *Closed Wed.*

Sora Lella, Pza Alessandrina 1, **t** 0699 204251 (*cheap*). Situated nearby, at Ceri. *Closed Wed.*

Civitavécchia ✉ 00053

The nicest places to stay are south of the centre, by the beach.

********Sunbay Park**, Via Aurelia Sud, km 68, **t/f** 0766 22801 (*expensive*). Relatively luxurious, this hotel has its own little port, a pair of pools and a squash court, as well as some moderately priced rooms in the annexe; the restaurant is an added bonus.

rebelled and was put in its place, minus the rights of full Roman citizenship. Like the other southern Etruscan cities, Caere languished under Roman rule; its remaining inhabitants finally abandoned it after the fall of the Empire, moving to what is now the nearby village of Ceri. Old Caere had a brief renaissance in the 13th century; the Orsini later added a small castle in the piazza, now the **Museo Nazionale di Cervéteri** (*open Tues–Sun 9–7*), which has a well-arranged display of tomb finds from the 8th–1st centuries BC, including a magnificent collection of Greek and Greek-style vases, and some very lively and expressive terracotta portrait busts found in the sanctuary at Manganella, the valley that separates old Caere from the Banditaccia necropolis. A wooden model near the museum entrance shows old Caere as it might have looked, with a peculiarly Etruscan skyline of round houses and pointy cypresses.

It's a 2km drive or walk up from here to the round tufa mound of the **Banditaccia Necropolis** (*turn right from the piazza, and then right again on the narrow branch lane; open May–Sept Tues–Sun 9–7; Oct–April Tues–Sun 9–4; adm same ticket as museum*). This is only one of Cervéteri's four cemeteries (which cover three times the area of the city for the living), but it's the most interesting, in a park setting of cypresses and parasol pines. The tombs were laid out in the form of a town, an Etruscan Model Tumulus Show where you can see every style available, from the early grave trenches carved in the tufa to 'cube' tombs resembling lines of terrace houses, to the round structures with *hypogea* carved into the rock below – heavy stone

****La Medusa**, nearby on Via Aurelia Sud, **t** 0766 24327, **f** 0766 22775 (*cheap*). Nine rooms near the new marina, nearly all with sea views. *Closed during Christmas.*

New Port, Riva di Traiano, off Via Aurelia Sud, **t** 0766 580 410 (*moderate*). Dine well in the same area.

Scaletta, Lungoporto Gramsci 66, **t** 0766 24334 (*expensive*). In town, the excellent Scaletta has tables on the Renaissance bastions, and waiters bringing an array of seafood dishes – if you like it spicy, try the *gamberoni al diavolo*, then cool off with a home-made sorbet. *Closed Tues, exc in summer.*

Tarquínia ✉ 01016

*****Velacamare**, Via degli Argonauti 1, at Tarquínia Lido, **t** 0766 864380, **f** 0766 864024 (*moderate*). Luminous modern rooms and a summer piano bar in the garden, where you can lounge Etruscan-style; the hotel restaurant (*expensive*) is the best around and specializes in the freshest of seafood. *Closed Tues exc in summer; both hotel and restaurant closed Nov, Dec.*

****San Marco**, in the centre opposite the museum at Piazza Cavour 20, **t** 0766 842306, *info@san-marco.com* (*cheap*). A small, well-run hotel with pleasant double rooms; there's also a restaurant.

Due Orfanelle, Vicolo Breve 4 (off Via di Porta Tarquínia), **t** 0766 856307 (*moderate*). Local food and good grilled meat. *Closed Tues.*

Trattoria Prassede, in Piazza Trento e Trieste (*inexpensive*). A reasonable lunch menu with a lot of choices; also pizza in the evening.

Tuscánia ✉ 01017

*****Al Gallo**, hidden in the medieval centre at Via del Gallo 22, **t** 0761 443388 (*moderate*). Plush, antique-filled, comfortable rooms, some in the back with nice views over the town; also a Michelin-starred restaurant attached. *Closed Mon.*

Bar Rinaldi, by the entrance gate on Via Roma, **t** 0761 435021. Cheap rooms above the bar.

Locanda di Mirandolina, Via del Pozzo Bianco 40, **t** 0761 436595 (*cheap*). Simple, but welcoming rooms and a restaurant (*moderate*) with a lovely outdoor terrace on the town walls. *Closed Mon.*

Le Sette Cannelle, Largo Sette Cannelle by the fountain, **t** 0761 435739 (*moderate*). For outdoor terraces, at least, this runs a close second; good pizza and a wide variety of local dishes. *Closed Wed.*

domes, set low to the ground, that look more like modern defence bunkers than ancient tombs. The largest measure over 130ft in diameter, with as many as four *hypogea* built into them, and in these you can see the forerunners of the Etruscan-style mausolea of Augustus and Hadrian in Rome.

Not all of the tombs are lit; the site is quite large, and you may want to buy the map on sale at the entrance to find your way. For serious exploration, ask a guide to unlock and light the more distant tombs for you, though in winter and early spring these may well be flooded. Don't miss the **Tomba dei Capitelli** near the entrance, carved from tufa to resemble Etruscan houses, or the **Tomba delle Cornici**, with unusual military decoration; another, even stranger, the **Tomba dei Rilievi**, is covered with painted stone reliefs of cooking utensils and other household objects. Two of the real giants are at the far end of the necropolis: the **Tumulo del Colonello** and the never-completed **Tumulo Mengarelli**.

Civitavécchia

Further up the coast, you'll pass Civitavécchia, modern Rome's commercial port, the gateway for ferries to Sardinia, and Italy's second largest passenger port. Designed for Trajan in 106, probably on a design by his favourite architect, Apollodorus of Damascus, the town was named *Centumcellae* ('the hundred rooms') for Trajan's enormous villa, of which only parts of the baths remain. In the 2nd century it was converted into a prison especially for Christians. It became a Byzantine stronghold in the 6th century, but was destroyed by the Saracens in 829. Although the refugees were settled by Pope Leo IV in a new fortified *Centumcellae*, legend has it that in 889 a sailor named Leandro gave such a nostalgic discourse under an oak tree about the ruined old town, now called the Old City or *Civitavécchia*, that everyone returned. It was at this moment that the city adopted its arms: an oak with the letters OC, standing for Leandro's *Ottimo Consiglio*, or Best Advice. And Leo IV's *Centumcellae* is now the ruined castle and walls of **Cencelle**, 15km away up in the Tolfa mountains.

Papal interest in the port grew with the discovery of alum (essential in dyeing, tanning and papermaking) in the Tolfa hills just behind Civitavécchia, and in the 15th century a number of civic improvements took place. Leonardo da Vinci was sent to make a detailed study of the port, and its restoration was assigned to Bramante and Baccio Pontelli. The mighty **Forte Michelangelo** overlooking the harbour was begun by Bramante and Antonio da Sangallo in 1508 and, at least according to tradition, finished by Michelangelo, who designed the outer walls to withstand the new artillery. For three centuries major improvements were added by the popes, designed by their greatest architects (including Bernini, who designed an extraordinary fan-shaped arsenal modelled on his colonnade in St Peter's Square). Nearly everything was blasted to bits in the aerial bombardments of 1943–4, and rebuilt since. The **Museo Nazionale Archeologico**, a block west of the fortress on Largo Plebiscito (*open Wed, Sat–Sun 9.30–12.30; Aug and Sept daily exc Mon 9–2; adm*) occupies the 18th-century customs house, and contains Attic vases, Roman reliefs, and copies of Greek statues.

Inland, the **Monti della Tolfa**, where the Etruscans mined their copper, iron and lead, are part of a nature preserve populated by Maremma horses and cows. After alum was found here in the 1400s, the mines at **Allumiere** paid a lot of papal bills for the next two centuries and enriched the popes' bankers, the House of Medici. This village has an unusual Renaissance complex of miners' housing, the **Fabbricone**, and a **Museo Civico** with archaeological finds and exhibits on the mines.

Tarquínia

Further up the coast, **Tarquínia** is the most important of the Etruscan sites in Lazio, famous for the painted tombs in its necropolis, the largest collection of pre-Roman painting anywhere in the Mediterranean. The city takes its name from the legendary King Tarchuna, or Tarchon, the son or brother of the Lydian King Tyrrenus, who led his people across the sea to Italy and inaugurated the Etruscan rituals of divination. Etruscan finds here go back to the 9th century BC, and the city of *Tarxna* became one of the richest and most powerful members of the Dodecapolis. It provided the kings of the 'House of the Tarquinii' who ruled over Rome in the 6th century before the establishment of the Republic; soon after that the tides turned, and Rome took control of *Tarxna* after a battle in 407. The city survived, just barely, under Roman rule, and in the Dark Ages its remaining population moved to a more defensible site on the next hill. Under a new name, *Corneto*, it did well for itself as a free trading city from the 10th century AD onwards, finally coming under the rule of the popes in the 1500s; the name was changed back to Tarquínia in 1922.

Many of the finest discoveries from the Etruscan city and its necropolis have been assembled for the **Museo Nazionale Tarquínia** (***t*** *0766 856036; open Tues–Sun 8.30–7.30; adm; combined ticket with tombs also available*). The museum is housed in the 15th-century Palazzo Vitelleschi, built by Giovanni Vitelleschi, who played an important role in consolidating papal power in these parts after the popes returned from Avignon; Giovanni started out as a *condottiere* and ended up a cardinal in 1437, the year after this palace was begun. The stars of the collection (on the top floor) are the famous **Winged Horses** from the 'Altar of the Queen' temple on the acropolis, beautiful beasts, but made of terracotta like most Etruscan temple decorations, which explains why so few have survived. Well-carved sarcophagi are present in abundance – fellows named Vel, Varth or Arnth, reclining on their tombs over long inscriptions detailing their services to the city-state (you can't miss the Sarcophagus of the Obese Man, clearly an Etruscan bon viveur) – and there is a collection of Greek vases by some of the greatest 6th–5th-century Attic painters. The Etruscans were talented at ceramics, too, as seen by the fine samples of *bucchero* ware, black pottery incised or painted with puzzling Etruscan images. Some images, in later Greek and Greek-influenced work, aren't puzzling at all – red-figure kylixes (used for drinking wine) feature scenes of flirting, both gay and straight, and there are a few that were once probably relegated to the locked room Italian museums used to call the *sezione pornografica*. Like any good Etruscan museum, this one has a fair helping of the baubles and imported luxuries that belonged to Vel and Arnth and their fancy women: Sardinian bronzes, jewellery, a carved Egyptian scarab, even a painted ostrich egg.

Some painted tombs from the necropolis, discovered only in 1958, have been relocated here for their protection, including a rare view of an Etruscan ship in the *Tomba della Nave*, and scenes of chariot-riding and athletics in the *Tomba delle Olympiade*. You can see the origins of the Roman gladiator in the Etruscan *phersu* from the funeral games pictured here, one fighting with a club, the other with the aid of a fierce dog (*phersu* originally referred to the masks the gladiators wore; the word passed into Latin as *persona*, and our word 'person' is probably only one of many in English with a secret Etruscan heritage). Almost any subject is likely to turn up on Etruscan tomb walls; the *Tomba del Triclinia* with its dancers is one of the most beautiful.

There is more to see in Tarquínia than departed Etruscans. From the museum, Via Vittorio Emanuele leads to the centre of town, Piazza Trento e Trieste, with the **Palazzo Comunale**, parts of which go back to the 11th century, and the 18th-century **Chiesa del Soffraggio**, with a simple but exceptionally elegant rococo façade. Behind the museum, Via Porta Castello leads up to the highest part of the town, a quiet quarter of very old houses built among the walls of the **Castello**. Here, the church of **Santa Maria di Castello** has a wealth of Cosmatesque work, including the portal, choir screen, and a well-preserved pavement. Just outside the city, on the site that was *Tarxna*'s acropolis, you can see the ruins of the so-called **Ara della Regina**, the 'Altar of the Queen' where the Winged Horses in the museum once held pride of place. This was the largest temple ever built by the Etruscans, and it may have been their federal sanctuary before the creation of the *Fanum Voltumnae*.

Painted Tombs: the Monterozzi Necropolis

A 15-minute walk from Via Porta Tarquínia in town; ***t*** *0766 856036; open Tues–Sun 9–1hr before sunset; adm (combined ticket with museum).*

Unlike Cervéteri, it does not seem a very impressive site at first, only some holes in the ground with sheds built over the entrances; and there isn't enough staff to keep open all the tombs. The few you can see on any given day, however, rank among the finest examples of Etruscan painting. The 'Grotte Cornetane', as they used to be called, were discovered in the Renaissance; many artists visited, including Michelangelo, who made a sketch of one of the figures. Works like those of the **Tomba degli Auguri** and the **Tomba delle Leonesse**, with their beautiful 'Ionic' style paintings, seem remarkably close to the art of ancient Crete. These began to appear in the 6th century BC, and only in the tombs of the richest Etruscans; more typical of the rest is the **Tomba degli Scudi**, carved simply out of the tufa and hung with arms and trophies. The **Tomba dei Leopardi** is decorated with fascinating scenes of an Etruscan feast.

The guards may forget to remind you that there is a separate part of the necropolis, about 100 yards down the road from the main entrance. Still under excavation, this includes a street of Roman-era tombs cut into the tufa, of which the largest is the **Tomba degli Anina**, with a funeral scene of *Vanth* and *Caronti* painted in the weird manner of the last stage of Etruscan painting, and some sarcophagi left in place.

Vulci

On the Lazio–Tuscan border, off the coastal highway (the Roman Via Aurelia), truly dedicated Etruscophiles may detour into the hills to Vulci, a member of the

Dodecapolis and an important and wealthy town in the 9th–1st centuries BC, one that controlled the rich mines of Monte Amiata in Tuscany. Vulci was renowned for its bronze-working and ceramics, inspired by its precocious contacts in the 8th century BC with the cities of Magna Graecia to produce its own versions of the most fashionable pots of the day. Later, many painters in Vulci were Greek immigrants; the city may have also been the first in the region to plant the crops introduced by the Greeks: olives and vines. The luxury trade thrived, then began to decline when the Etruscan fleet was defeated by Syracuse off Cumae in 474 BC. Vulci never got along with other members of the Etruscan league, and was defeated by Rome in 280 BC. Afterwards a Roman *municipium*, it was wiped off the map in the 9th century by the Saracens.

Vulci's most striking monument is its 13th-century **Castello dell'Abbadia**, next to its magnficent single-arch bridge, the **Ponte dell'Abbadia**. The bridge, over 100ft above the bed of the river Fiora, is a medieval construction built on Roman and Etruscan foundations, while the castle was begun as a fortified monastery by the Cistercians; the popes later rebuilt it as a customs house, when the Fiora marked the border between the Grand Duchy of Tuscany and the Papal States. Today the castle houses a small **museum** (*t 0761 437787; open Tues–Sun 9–4 in winter, 9–5 in March, 9–6 in April; May–Sept 9–7, Oct 9–5; adm*) with some good painted vases and a reproduction of a Villanovan-era house; Vulci would have more to show, but when the necropolis was discovered in 1828 it was part of the estate of Lucien Bonaparte, Napoleon's little brother, who thanks to the Pope was then 'Prince of Canino' (*see* p.197); Bonaparte worked the necropolis like a mine, selling the choice bits to the museums and private collectors of Europe and trashing the rest. Vulci's large **necropolis**, with some 15,000 tombs (some choice paintings, detailing early figures of Roman history, are now in Rome's Museo Torlonia), has been incorporated into the **Parco Naturalistico Archeologico di Vulci** (*open daily 9–7; adm; combined ticket with museum also available*). The museum can also let you in to see the site at **La Civitá**, with ruins of a Roman temple and patrician villa. Around the area there are scant bits of the city walls, more Roman remains, and another impressive if more ruinous bridge, the 279ft **Ponte Rotto** from the the 1st century BC.

There are some impressive arcades of a Roman aqueduct, the **Archi di Pontecchio**, at **Montalto di Castro**, though this town is better known as the site of Italy's only nuclear power plant, a source of controversy since the day it was conceived. If you're headed that way, there are more promising attractions just over the border in Tuscany: the resorts of **Monte Argentario** and the island of Giglio, and a genuine surprise practically on the border itself, just north of the SS 1 Via Aurelia, the **Giardino dei Tarocchi** at Capalbio – a park with 22 colossal sculptures covered in brightly coloured tiles, representing the major arcana of the tarot deck, the work of the noted French artist Niki de Saint-Phalle (*open May–Oct daily 2.30–7.30; times change annually so ring for details, **t** 0564 895700*).

Tuscánia

Tuscánia stands alone at the centre of one of the emptiest, eeriest corners of Italy, a region of low green hills where you will find Etruscan ruins, old castles and religious shrines, but few people. According to legend, the town was founded by Ascanius, son of Aeneus, who was told by the god Mars to found a city on the spot where he discovered a bitch with twelve puppies, hence *Tus-cana*, 'twelve dogs'. The 'twelve dogs' may well have been a confederacy of twelve villages – so far twelve necropoli (630–470 BC) have been discovered, with their administrative and religious centre on San Pietro hill. Roman control seems to have occurred peacefully around 280 BC, and after the Social Wars in 90 BC Romanization was complete, and villas, granaries (this was always a major agricultural centre) and baths were built. Tuscánia regained its importance for a while, first under the Lombards and then as a free *comune*. The popes claimed it under the 'Donation of Charlemagne', and Tuscánia's history was largely a matter of trying to keep the popes at bay until the city's final submission in the 1300s. Papal misrule, aided by a thorough sacking from the French in 1494, nearly made Tuscánia disappear; the city only started getting back on its feet after Italian unification. A horrific earthquake in 1971 did considerable damage, nearly destroying its two famous medieval monuments, San Pietro and Santa Maria Maggiore. But with their accustomed doggedness and skill, the Italians got all the pieces put back together again, and visiting today you would hardly know there had been an earthquake at all.

As Tarquínia seems a smaller version of Viterbo, so is Tuscánia a sort of miniature Tarquínia: a sombre grey medieval centre with a wall around it, a handful of old churches and square tower-fortresses inside and a sprinkling of Etruscan necropoli in the surrounding hills. Tuscánia has shrunk considerably since its medieval heyday; the old centre, **Piazza Basile**, is now at the southern end of town, a beautiful ensemble of medieval buildings that includes the Palazzo Comunale, the 13th-century San Leonardo, and the **Fontane delle Sette Cannelle** – 13th century, but a fountain has been flowing on this spot since Etruscan days.

Etruscan sarcophagi from the nearby necropolis are on display at the excellent **Museo Archeologico** in the former Santa Maria del Riposo convent (***t*** *0761 436209; open Tues–Sun 8.30–7.30*); best among them are the complacent bon vivants of the Curunas family, reclining lazily on their urns, as if in a family gallery. Five generations of the Vipinana family, from 320–190 BC, are in the last room. Masks, figures of actors, a mirror and a helmet are among the grave goods, and there's a mysterious Etruscan rebus from the 6th-century BC 'tomb of the Dado' at Pescheria. To visit any of the Etruscan necropoli around Tuscánia, including the **Necropoli dell'Olivo**, with its labyrinthine 'Tomba della Regina', ask at the museum. The convent church of Santa Maria del Riposo contains paintings by Pastura and Perin del Vaga, while there are fragmentary 14th-century frescoes in two other churches nearby, Santa Maria della Rosa and San Silvestro.

The real attractions are on a hill above the town – originally, they were inside it. **San Pietro** and **Santa Maria Maggiore** (*both open daily 9–1; in summer also 3–7; in winter also 2–5*), two of the finest Romanesque churches in central Italy, were both begun in the 8th century, with additions in the 11th and 12th centuries. Besides their carved altars, pulpits and bits of painting from the 8th–14th centuries, both churches' best features are their unusual sculpted façades – San Pietro's especially, with colourful Cosmati work, fragments of ancient sculpture and outlandish carved grotesques.

Note the famous 'green men', three-faced heads with foliage growing out of them, keeping company with sirens, lions, griffins and bulls. Probably nothing in the sculpture of a Romanesque church is merely decorative, and these fellows have had scholars wondering for centuries; they seem to tap the same lost vein of medieval mysticism that stretches from the legendary *Khidr* of Muslim tales to the story of *Sir Gawain and the Green Knight*. Santa Maria Maggiore has a wonderful *Last Judgment* painted on the east wall: a medieval devil tossing souls down into the mouth of hell on the left (hell is always on the sinister side in Last Judgements, but it's Jesus' left, not yours), while cute naked virtuous folk rise out of their coffins opposite.

Canino and Castro

One of the most charming towns in the province, **Canino** sits proud among its celebrated olive groves west of Tuscánia. Named for one of the noblest Etruscan families, the *gens Caninia* of Vulci, its shadowy Etruscan history has recently been complicated by the discovery of a large temple found at the entrance to town, adding to speculation that it may have been one of the lost Etruscan cities: Maternum, or else Vetulonia. Canino reappears in history in Pope Leo IV's bull of 847 as *Mausoleum Canini*. Later it was ruled by Viterbo, and then Tuscánia (a scholarly place, that – it demanded from Canino an annual tribute of ten books) and then the Farnese. Pope Paul III was born here, and his nephew Cardinal Alessandro Farnese lavished money on its embellishment. After Napoleon made himself an emperor and his sister Elisa the Queen of Etruria, another sibling began to buy up land here – Lucien Bonaparte, who got on very well with Pope Pius VII despite being the only real revolutionary in the Bonaparte family; in 1814 the Pope made him 'Prince of Canino and Musignano'. When Napoleon arrested and imprisoned the Pope, Luciano, as he is known here, beat a hasty retreat with his family to America, was captured at sea by the British, and returned four years later. The locals remember him fondly as a benefactor who took care of the poor and improved local agricultural techniques. The Torlonia family later bought Canino, and held on all the land until 1950, when the state redistributed it to the local farmers.

The oldest part of Canino, **Le Buche**, where the narrow streets still have their original paving, has a great public *lavatoio* in the centre built by Alessandro Farnese. Pope Paul was born in the tower of the **Castello Farnese**, near the gate. The **Palazzo Bonaparte** at the end of Via Roma belonged originally to the Farnese and was redecorated for the Prince of Canino by the neoclassical architect Valadier. In Piazza Vittorio Emanuele, there's a fine fountain and the beautiful arcaded Renaissance **Palazzo Miccinelli** of 1475, while further along in Piazza Costantino de Andreis you'll find Vignola's twelve-sided **Fontana del Cane**, 'dog fountain' decorated with Farnese and Canino emblems (continuing the Tuscánia canine theme; Canino means 'puppy'). It shares the square with the **Collegiata** (1793), with a neoclassical Bonaparte chapel, with monuments to Carlo (father of the famous family), Luciano and his first wife Cristina, in cool marble statuary attributed to Canova. Much of the other art in the Collegiata was donated by Luciano, including a curious, anonymous 15th-century *Nativity*. On the edge of town, the church of the **Annunziata** dates from the 10th century; St Francis came here to pray and plant trees, and in 1484 a Farnese built the Franciscans from Isola Bisentina a new convent here, **San Francesco**, with frescoes by the school of Perugino.

Further north, along the Tuscan border, lies **Farnese**, centre of the ancestral lands of that famous family, with one of their palaces and the richly furnished Renaissance church of **San Salvatore**. The Farnese's real capital was in the larger town of **Castro**, just up the road. An Etruscan site, and an important town in the Middle Ages, Castro was gained by the Farnese when one of them seized and destroyed it at the request of Pope Clement VII. Paul III, the Farnese pope, made plans to have it entirely rebuilt, hiring the great Antonio da Sangallo the Younger to design a pentagonal fortified palace, a huge *osteria* for guests, walls, churches and piazzas. Not all of this ambitious programme was finished, but Castro nonetheless would be one of the showpieces of the Renaissance – if there were anything left of it. In 1649, Castro gained the honour of being the only town to be twice completely annihilated by popes. This time it was Innocent X of the Pamphili family, one of the vilest creatures ever to grace St Peter's throne. Innocent hated the Farnese, and used a slight pretext to attack the town; after tricking the last Duke into surrendering, he ordered the entire place blown to bits, and forced the former inhabitants and neighbouring villages to pay the expense; for 200 years after, anyone even entering the site risked excommunication. It's an eerie, remarkable place today, with only scattered hints of what had been a town among the vegetation, along with an inscribed column erected by Innocent, bearing the legend *Qui fu Castro* – 'Here was Castro'.

North of Rome to Veii and Lake Bracciano

From the 8th to the 6th century BC Veio, or *Veii*, was the largest city in the Etruscan federation and Rome's most bitter rival. From the ruins of Veii this route continues to Lake Bracciano, a favourite weekend resort of modern-day Romans, who often use its storybook castle for film sets. Don't go on Monday; everything's closed.

Veii

The excavations are open daily except Mon, 9am–1hr before sunset; adm.

The sparse, scattered remains of ancient **Veii**, once enclosed in walls 11km around, make it the most difficult Etruscan site to visit, with more of the country ramble to it than archaeological thrill. Compensating for the meagre ruins, however, is Veii's striking position, on a sheer tufa plateau over a moat formed by two streams – exactly the sort of site Etruscans loved for founding a city. But these natural defences were not enough for the ancient Veians; they wanted a port, and managed to muscle in a fortified trading post on the Tiber – defying the claims of both Cervéteri and the Latins of Alba Longa. In 753 BC the Latins, according to the legends under the leadership of Romulus, united with Cervéteri to oust Veii from its Tiber port, founding in its place *Rumon*, which as any Etruscan will tell you really means 'city on the river'.

Getting There

ATAC **bus** 201 from Piazza Mancini (across the Tiber from the Foro Italico) will take you to La Giustiniana, where you can pick up bus 032 to Isola Farnese and Veii; COTRAL bus from Via Lépanto (Metro A) or train from Termini for Lake Bracciano. If you're **driving** to Veii, take Via Cassia (N2) to La Storta; after another kilometre you'll see a sign for Isola Farnese and the excavation. From here, Via Braccianese Claudia continues to the lake.

Tourist Information

Bracciano: Piazza IV Novembre 5, **t** 06 9984 0062, *turismo@comunedibracciano.it*, *www.comunedibracciano.it*.

Anguillara Sabazia: Piazza del Lavatoio, **t** 06 996 8415.

Where to Stay and Eat

Bracciano ✉ 00062

****__Villa Clementina__, Via Traversa Quarto del Largo 12, **t/f** 06 998 6268, *www.charmerelax.it/villaclementina* (*expensive*). The most sumptuous hotel in Bracciano, the delightful Villa Clementina has just seven quirkily decorated rooms in a whitewashed country house surrounded by beautiful gardens. There's a pool, tennis and an excellent restaurant. *Closed Nov–Feb except for a fortnight over Christmas and New Year.*

There are innumerable places to eat along Bracciano's shores, but all seem designed to exploit the weekend exodus of Romans.

Vino e Camino, Via delle Cantine 11, **t** 06 9980 3433 (*cheap*). Pay above the odds for an average meal, or concentrate on wine, accompanied by bean soup, *porchetta*, or octopus couscous. *Eves only, closed Mon.*

Taverna degli Orsini, Via Arazzeria 27, near the Castello Orsini-Odescalchi. Offers a €15 menu: a wide choice and a good price, for everything from *scalloppine* to roast boar.

Trevignano Romano ✉ 00069

***__Albergo Nuovo Torrione__, Viale Garibaldi 127, **t/f** 06 999 9046 (*moderate*). Family-run; has large comfortable rooms, some with enormous terraces with views of the lake, a little garden and a pizzeria-restaurant (*inexpensive*) downstairs.

Archetto, Via San Sebatiano 26, **t** 06 999 9580 (*moderate*). Overlooks the lake; a good place to try the perch and other lake fish, and game in season. *Closed Tues.*

Osteria La Cantinella, Piazza V Emmanuele III, **t** 06 999 9580 (*cheap*). Typical local dishes including very tasty grilled lamb in a stone-vaulted dining room or out on a minuscule terrace in summer. *Closed Thurs.*

Anguillara Sabazia ✉ 00061

****__I Due Laghi__, Loc. Le Cerque, **t** 06 9960 7059, **f** 06 9960 7068, *www.iduelaghi.it* (*expensive*). With views over both Bracciano and Lake Martignano, this is a former *agriturismo* villa, and has maintained all its sporting facilities (riding, tennis, basketball, mountain bikes, pool and private beach on Lake Bracciano). The restaurant makes good use of ingredients grown on the farm.

Bastioni, Piazza dei Bastoni 2, **t** 06 996 8133 (*moderate*). Family-run and situated above the lake. One of the best places to try the lake fish; dining outside in the summer. *Closed Wed, exc in summer.*

Veii, minus a port and the precious salt pans of Ostia, nevertheless continued as one of the strongest and most powerful Etruscan cities, famed for its artisans' skill in terracotta sculpture. It may well have been bossing Rome around throughout the 7th and 6th centuries, but the city on the river was getting stronger. When Rome's Fabii clan took it upon themselves to patrol and harass Veii, the Veians ambushed and massacred all but one (475 BC). Some 25 years later, neither city could tolerate the other, and a fight to the finish became inevitable; of all Rome's wars, this was the most crucial, for its very existence was at stake. Veii called upon its fellow Etruscan cities for aid. None came, and the Romans under M. Furius Camillus began a siege that ended only when the Romans unblocked one of Veii's drainage tunnels leading under the walls. Veii was thus surprised, captured and thoroughly destroyed; the Romans carted off its chief deity, Juno, to a new temple on the Aventine. Julius Caesar and Augustus tried to plant a colony on the site, but it never prospered.

Among the scanty remains to be seen are the Temple of Portonaccio, dedicated to Apollo (where the Villa Giulia's beautiful Apollo of Veio was found), cisterns, a tunnel in the rock (where Camillus led the Romans?), and best of all, the 7th-century BC **Tomba Campana**, containing some of the oldest Etruscan paintings ever discovered, of strange Etruscan animals, and the *caronti* escorting the dead to the underworld. Seven kilometres from Veii towards Lake Bracciano are the picturesque ruins of the **Castle of Galéria**, with the pretty hamlet of **Santa Maria di Galéria** below.

Bracciano and its Lake

All of the lakes of northern Lazio, surrounded by circular ranges of hills, are the craters of long-dead volcanoes. They are also the most ingratiating features in the Lazio landscape, with a few narrow, sleepy beaches here and there; not exactly off the main tourist track, and popular with the Romans. For swimming, watersports and sailing they are often more pleasant than any of the coastal beach resorts near Rome.

Bracciano's broad sheet of water sloshes about in the round volcanic crater of Mt Sabatini, and it is best known for its eels, whose babies sometimes get sucked into the fountains in St Peter's Square and clog the pipes. It is one of Rome's most popular swimming holes, still remarkably clean and beautiful even though Rome's suburbs are already lapping up against its southern shores. There is little of monumental interest around the lake – from June to Sept you can take boat tours from the town of **Bracciano**, but the best view of it is from the ramparts of the five-towered **Castello Orsini-Odescalchi** (*open Tues–Sun 10–12 and 3–5, daily in Aug; tours every hour on the hour; adm exp*) built by the Orsini, stronghold of the bearish clan from 1470 to 1696, when they ceded castle and town to the Odescalchi.

Although the Orsini were usually supporters of the papacy against their nemesis, the Colonna, they knew the Roman pot could boil over at any time, and so they built this castle as one of their many private bunkers close to Rome. Built in the retro style of a medieval castle, not very useful against Renaissance artillery, it was intended more as a residence than a fortress. Nevertheless, it served them in good stead, fending off the attack of the entire papal army of Alexander VI in 1494, when the Orsini were caught fraternizing with the French invader, Charles VIII. They managed to hold out here for seven more years, against the Pope and the rest of the Borgias, in an unusual little war that featured Orsini–Borgia naval battles on the lake.

As Roman castles go, this one is in very good condition, with a beautiful setting overlooking the lake; it has been used as a set for a score of films, most recently Kenneth Branagh's *Othello*. Frescoes and painted ceilings by Antoniazzo Romano in the 1490s, later frescoes by the two Zuccari and busts of the Orsini by Bernini decorate the interior, along with another fresco cycle by an unknown hand on the *Labours of Hercules*. There is a wonderful view of the lake from the upper terrace, and plenty of endearing castle clutter, from a good collection of arms and armour to a pair of

Just Your Typical Renaissance Happy Family

Pope Sixtus IV fled Rome to wait out a spell of plague here, and King Umberto I of Italy dropped in for a stay, but probably the most notorious inhabitant of the Castello Orsini was Vittoria Accoramboni, the centre of a scandal that had all Renaissance Europe talking. Vittoria, a beautiful Roman girl, married a fellow named Francesco Peretti in 1573. Though only sixteen, she almost immediately started a liaison with Paolo Giordano Orsini, Duke of Bracciano. The Duke had already made a name for himself by strangling his wife, Isabella de' Medici, for similar behaviour (and on the castle tour they'll show you the trap door in her bedroom for her lovers). In 1581, the Duke seems to have had Peretti murdered, and he and Vittoria were married soon after. The Pope, Gregory XIII, annulled the marriage and locked up Vittoria in Rome's Castel Sant'Angelo; later he relented, and sent her off to confinement in her parents' house. She didn't stay long; as soon as the stir died down, she sneaked back to the safety of Bracciano and married the Duke once again. The real problems started in 1585, with the election of Pope Sixtus V – none other than Francesco Peretti's uncle. The couple had to flee to Venice, and the Duke died a few months later. He left much of his fortune to Vittoria, which did not sit well with the other Orsini, but the Duke's cousin Lodovico solved the problem neatly by sending a gang of ruffians after Vittoria; they brought her eventful life to an end at the ripe old age of 28.

For the rest of Europe it was just further proof of the decadence and depravity of the Italians. Though the details and the characters of the principals differ widely in every version of the story, Vittoria does not seem to have been as naughty a girl as her papal accusers made out. Nevertheless, the story eventually made its way to the closest equivalent the Renaissance world had to our tabloids – the London stage. John Webster's play *The White Devil*, based on Vittoria's life, appeared in 1608.

French neo-Gothic toilets. Parts of the complex actually date back to an earlier castle of the 1100s; these the Orsini turned into kitchens, with ovens seemingly large enough to roast a few whole cows at a time.

Around the Lake

After the unpleasantness between the Orsini and Alexander VI, the family squared things with the popes by helping roust the piratical Anguillara family from their eyrie of **Anguillara Sabazia**, rising on a sheer spur over the south shore of the lake. The family took their name from the town ('the eel-ery') and decorated their coat of arms with erect eels. The steep *centro storico* has a gate and **Palazzo Baronale** (now the Municipio) built by the Orsini, the latter containing some good Mannerist frescoes (including one of a hermaphrodite) which it's possible to see if the town council isn't in session. Anguillara has another Orsini **castle**; this one houses a museum of Italian sporting heroes. If you have the puff to make it to the **church of the Assunta** at the top of the town, the reward is a lovely view over the lake.

In Mussolini's day, Lake Bracciano was Italy's dirigible and seaplane base, and a refuelling stop for the first British airliners on their way to Asia and Australia. Two old hangars in **Vigna di Valle**, 6km south of Bracciano, were converted in the 1970s to hold the **Historical Museum of the Italian Air Force** (*open Oct–May 9.30–4.30, June–Sept 9.30–5.30; adm*). Exhibits include a model of Leonardo da Vinci's wing-flapping machine, fighter planes, racing planes, seaplanes, the first plane purchased for the Italian air force, a body organized by Wilbur Wright in 1909, planes that went to the North Pole and the world's first operational jet fighter – an Italian innovation of 1942. Most curious of all is a hot air balloon launched from Paris to Rome in 1804 in honour of Napoleon's coronation, bearing instead of a basket a large glass replica of the little emperor's crown. The glass crown fell into Lake Bracciano before reaching Rome, a neat augury that water, from island exiles to Waterloo and Wellington, would bedevil Napoleon to the end.

North and east of Lake Bracciano are the Monti Sabatini, named not for the Sabines but an even more obscure nation, the Sabatines – hence Bracciano's original name, *Lacus Sabatinus*. The jewel of the hills is hidden away east of the lake, surrounded by Roman suburban sprawl off the SS2 (Via Cassia): the perfectly idyllic little crater **Lake of Martignano**, privately owned though accessible to walkers, but not their cars. The Sabatine headquarters was **Trevignano Romano** on the north shore of Bracciano, a very pretty village of cobbled streets and expensively restored second homes belonging to smart English and American families based in Rome. Only ruins remain of its 15th-century castle, but by all means make the walk up to see the **church of the Assunta**, for its views over the lake and beautiful fresco of the *Dormition, Assumption and Coronation of the Virgin* (1517) by the school of Raphael, with scenes of Lake Bracciano in the background, including the castle of Trevignano. Trevignano also has a small **Museo Civico**, with remains from nearby Etruscan tombs.

From Lake Bracciano to Lake Vico

From Bracciano, the Via Claudia (SS493) sweeps around the west shore of Lake Bracciano and heads north to **Barbarano Romano**, inhabited by the Villanovans and later by the Etruscans; their vast **Etruscan Necropolis of San Giuliano**, in Marturanum Natural Park, has an unusual variety of tomb architecture, including the Costa tomb, with a richly carved ceiling (***t** 0761 4144531; open Thurs–Fri 10–1, Sat–Sun 10–1 and 3–6; adm*). In Barbarano, the **Museo Civico** (*open Tues–Thurs 9–1, Sat and Sun 10–1 and 3–6; adm*) has sarcophagi and funerary urns, red and black figure vases, and other finds, both from San Giuliano and Villanoviano.

The hills to the north of here, and west of Lake Vico, conceal no less than 12 minor Etruscan sites; all you'll see of these vanished cities, however, are the usual rock-cut tombs, some with temple-like carved façades, as at **Blera** and **Norchia**. Blera has three different necropoli: Pian del Vescovo, La Casetta and San Giovenale, all open and unguarded and all containing some unusual tombs for determined Etruscophiles; at San Giovenale a small part of the Etruscan town has been excavated. Norchia, accessible on a back road 12km from the town of Vetralla, is one of the most isolated and melancholy of all Etruscan sites, built on a defensible plateau which now has some ruins of the failed medieval town that took its place. The necropoli are all around, including some tombs with badly eroded mythological reliefs. There is also a strange 1,200ft avenue, cut deeply into the easily worked tufa.

Sutri

Tourist office: Piazza del Comune 31, ***t*** *0761 600330.*

The Via Cassia (SS2), the old main Roman road to the north, snakes westwards to fit between Lake Bracciano and Lake Vico, passing on the way two pretty hill towns: Sutri and Capránica. Sutri is famously old – perhaps as early as 1000 BC; legends place its founding back with the mysterious 'Pelasgians' (pre-Greek inhabitants of the eastern Mediterranean) and its name may come from the god Saturn, like nearby Saturnia in southern Tuscany. It's a strategic spot, the 'gateway to Etruria' for the Romans. Sutri used to belong to Veii, and the Romans grabbed it after Veii fell, in 383 BC. In AD 728, Sutri became the first temporal possession of the popes, the nucleus of the future Papal States, when the Lombard King Liutprand granted it to Pope Gregory II. The town itself is high on the hill, but it has left some fascinating relics from its earlier incarnations down by the Via Cassia. These are now the **Parco Archeologico Preistorico-Paesaggistico** (*open summer 4–7pm, plus 10–1 at weekends; winter 10–1 and 3–6.30; adm*) with a variety of tombs, and a curious elliptical **amphitheatre**, which may date back to the Etruscans, cut into the tufa. The little medieval church of the **Madonna del Parto** (the Pregnant Madonna) is a cave that started as an Etruscan tomb and later served as a Roman-era temple to Mithras. Inside are frescoes of the legend of St Michael from his famous shrine at Monte Sant'Angelo in Puglia.

Sutri's last moment in the spotlight came in 1046, when Emperor Henry III presided over a Church Council in the **cathedral** here to sort out three wacky guys who were running around Rome calling themselves pope. One of these was Benedict IX, often listed as the worst pope ever, a libertine hoodlum who was also the only man to attain to the papal see three times – the first time, he was thrown out by a Roman insurrection, and the second, he sold the papacy to his godfather. Breaking with tradition, in a time when the papacy was little more than a plaything of the brawling Roman nobles, Henry understandably deposed all three unworthy contenders and put a good solid German bishop in the chair: Suidgerius of Bamberg, who became Clement II (he only lasted two years; they said Benedict had him poisoned). Besides memories of the Council and Clement II, the cathedral has a campanile from the 1200s, a simple Cosmatesque pavement and a good Lombard-style crypt. Also in the town centre is the **Museo del Patrimonium** (*open Sat only, 10.30–1; sometimes open by request,* ***t*** *0761 600867*), with finds ranging from bits of Etruscan fresco to Renaissance paintings.

Lake Vico and Caprarola

The smallest and perhaps loveliest of the lakes, Vico is ringed by the rugged Monti Cimini; unspoiled marshes line some of its shore, a favourite stop for migratory birds and now a wildlife reserve. At the northern edge this ancient crater has a younger volcano (also extinct) poking up inside it: **Monte Venere**. Its shady banks are a perfect place for a picnic and to gird one's loins for the next attraction just over the hills: the **Villa Farnese** at **Caprarola**, one of Italy's most arrogantly ambitious Renaissance spreads, incongruously set in one of Lazio's poorest and most bedraggled villages (***t*** *0761 646052; open daily 8.30–6.45; guided tours; adm*).

When Alessandro Farnese, member of an obscure Lazio noble family, set his sister Giulia up as mistress to Pope Alexander VI, his fortune was made; Alessandro later became Pope Paul III, a great pope who called the Council of Trent, rebuilt Rome and kept Michelangelo busy – but also a rotten pope, one who oppressed his people, reinvigorated the Inquisition, and became the most successful grafter in papal history. Before long the Farnese family ruled Parma, Piacenza and most of northern Lazio. With the fantastic wealth Alessandro accumulated, his grandson, also named Alessandro, built this family headquarters; Giacomo da Vignola, the family architect, turned the entire town of Caprarola into a setting for the palace, ploughing a new avenue through the town as an axis that led to a grand stairway, then a set of gardens (now disappeared), and then another stairway up to the huge pentagonal villa, built over the massive foundations of an earlier, uncompleted fortress. The palace is empty today; the Farnese lost everything in later papal intrigues (*see* 'Castro', p.198), and someone, some time, was forced to sell the furniture.

Nevertheless it is still an impressive place; some of the highlights of the guided tour include Vignola's elegant central courtyard, a room with uncanny acoustical tricks that the guides love to demonstrate, one with frescoes of the *Labours of Hercules*, another with a wonderful ceiling painted with the figures of the constellations, and an incredible **spiral staircase** of stone columns and neoclassical frescoes, Vignola's decorative masterpiece. The best part, however, is the 'secret garden' in the rear, an extensive park full of azaleas and rhododendrons leading up to a sculpture garden of grotesques and fantastical *telamones* that recall the Monster Park (*see* p.217; there is a connection, as one of the Orsini of Bomarzo was Alessandro Farnese's secretary). Finally there is a delightful, smaller villa, the **Palazzina del Piacere**.

East of Lake Vico

A Visit to the Faliscans: Cívita Castellana

In ancient Italy, people thought of geography with a twist we might find hard to understand. In a mountainous country largely covered in forest, the most important feature to a practical Latin mind was the patch of cleared, farmed land, the *ager*, as in the *Ager Romanus* of the Tiber valley around Rome (Italians still think this way, only with other words, as in the Roman *Campagna*, or the fertile patch around Naples called the 'Land of Work', the *Terra di Lavoro*). To the old Romans, the land east of Lake Vico, as far as the Tiber, was the *Ager Faliscus*, home to a quiet little nation that did its best to keep out of the struggles of their troublesome neighbours, aided by thick protecting forests on all sides.

The Faliscans spoke a language related to Latin, though they were heavily influenced by the more advanced Etruscans. They liked to portray horses and fish on their

Where to Stay and Eat

Caprarola ✉ 01032

★★★**Bella Venere**, Località Scardenato, Caprarola, **t** 0761 612342, **f** 0761 612344, *bellavenere@labellavenere.it* (*moderate*). On the eastern shore, a rare find: a lovely small hotel with gardens, beach, tennis courts and a large restaurant (*moderate*). *Closed Nov.*

Other Lake Vico hotels can be found nearby at Ronciglione Lago, at the southeastern corner of the lake:

★★★**Sans Soucis sul Lago**, **t** 0761 612052, Via delle Nocciolette 18, Punta del Lago, near the road to Ronciglione (*moderate*). Also with a beach and garden, and views over the lake. *Half-board mandatory in Aug.*

★★★**Il Cardinale**, **t/f** 0761 604051 (*moderate*). Further down the road and slightly cheaper.

Cívita Castellana ✉ 01033

★★★★**Palace Hotel 'Relais Falisco'**, Via Don Minzoni 19, **t** 0761 54981, **f** 0761 598432, *palacehotelrelaisfalisco@katamail.com* (*expensive*). The only place to stay in the centre of town; set in a grandly refurbished palace, it offers all comforts including a smart restaurant and a pool.

★★★**Aldero**, **t** 0761 514757, **f** 0761 514756 (*moderate*). 6km from Cívita at Fabrica di Roma; a comfortable place, with a high-tech feature or two, a piano bar and restaurant.

★★**Hotel Sassacci**, Loc. Sassacci km56 Via Flaminia, **t** 0761 542007 (*inexpensive*). A battered but friendly place with a popular scruffy bar just off the main road about 6km from the centre of town. Rooms are larger and quieter than you might think.

L'Altra Bottiglia on Via delle Palme, **t** 0761 517 403 (*expensive*). If you're in the mood for a splurge, this *enoteca*-restaurant has the most formidable wine list in the area, and some marvellous versions of simple country dishes. *Eves only exc Sun, closed Wed and Aug.*

Ristorante Mignolo, **t** 0761 513465, in the *centro storico* on Via Ferretti (*moderate*). A quiet outdoor garden where you can enjoy grilled meats or seafood, as well as game dishes in season. *Closed Thurs.*

Calcata ✉ 01030

Circolo Vegetariano, Piazza Roma 23, **t** 0761 587200, *www.vegetus.net/calcata*. Calcata's a trendy place, offering anything from tea rooms to the 'experimental cuisine' of this eaterie, where as in a monastery instead of asking for a bill you leave an offering.

La Piazzetta, Via San Giovanni 47, **t** 0761 588708 (*moderate*). For something more traditional: local dishes and lots of porcini mushrooms. *Closed Mon.*

painted vases, until they started copying the Greek style in the 5th century – which they did pretty well. They made their fatal mistake by siding with Veii in that city's death struggle with Rome. The victorious Romans burned the Faliscan capital, Falerii, in 395 BC, a year after they wrecked Veii. In the years that followed the Faliscans revolted repeatedly against Roman exploitation, a problem the Romans solved once and for all by levelling Falerii to the ground in 241 BC.

To replace it, the Romans founded a new city, Falerii Novi. With the coming of the Dark Ages, however, its people gravitated back to the old town, on a more defensible site. Thus was Falerii reborn as **Cívita Castellana**, a distinguished and lovely town that few tourists go out of their way to see. One of the things they miss is the spectacular façade of its **cathedral** (*open summer 9–12 and 4.30–7.30, winter 9–12 and 3.30–6.30*), possibly the greatest work of the Cosmati family outside Rome. Plenty of gold is still glittering in the mosaic trim, and you can still read the inscription of how Master Jacopo and his son Cosma made it in the year 1210. Especially noteworthy are the sculpted reliefs (of the Four Evangelists), done in the sharp, stylized manner popularized in the reign of Emperor Frederick II. The interior, redone in the 1700s, still has the Cosmati's pavement and altar rails, and the original medieval crypt (find the mermaid).

People in these parts still call themselves *Falisci*, and it's uncanny how similar the faces on the street are to the ancient terracotta busts in the **Museo Archeologico dell'Agro Falisco** (*open Tues–Sun 8–7; free*). The museum is housed in the **Rocca**, one of the most elegant of all Renaissance castles, begun for Pope Alexander VI by the Florentine Giuliano da Sangallo and finished by his nephew Antonio da Sangallo, the greatest military architect of his time. Intended as much a papal residence as a fortress, it includes a monumental courtyard with a marble fountain; inside, some chiaroscuro ceiling frescos by the Zuccaris survive. Of the museum collections, the best part is the painted terracotta relief decorations from one of Falerii's Etruscan-style temples, a nearly complete set that makes Etruscan architecture come alive. When the Romans destroyed Falerii, they spared its important religious sanctuaries; one of these must have had some association with healing, for the museum has a bizarre collection of terracotta ex-votos of parts of the body – ears, eyes, even vaginas.

Cívita still makes a living from its clay, though not for vases and temples, but bathroom tiles. Nevertheless, the town was a noted artistic centre for ceramics from the Middle Ages onwards, and you can see some of its works at the **Museo della Ceramica** in the Palazzo Petrosi-Andosilla (*open Tues–Sun summer 10–12.30 and 4–7, winter 10–12.30 and 3–6.30*).

Calcata, Monte Soratte and Nepi

Elsewhere in the *Ager Faliscus*, the ruins of the Roman town, ***Falerii Novi***, 5km west on the road to Caprarola, include a well-preserved city wall, and the Romanesque church of Santa Maria dei Falleri. **Calcata**, a striking hill village in the exceptionally pretty Valle del Treja south of Cívita, was nearly abandoned when it started filling up with artists from Italy and around the world. Now it's the New Age centre of central Italy, home not only to artists and galleries (and a school of 'telematic' artists looking for new performance tricks to play with modern telecommunications) but occultists and even vegetarians. The **Opera Bosco/Museo d'Arte e della Natura** (*guided tours, Sun and hols, must be booked in advance on* ***t*** *0761 588 048; adm exp*) is an open-air excursion through a series of artworks made from natural materials and intended to draw attention to the processes of nature.

The territory east of Cívita stands in the shadow of dramatic **Monte Soratte** (Mount Soracte) a favourite subject of Romantic-era poets and landscape painters. Though only 2,267ft, it stands alone, and changes its aspect strangely as you travel around it – from some angles it looks like a giant Egyptian pyramid. In ancient times Soracte was a holy mountain, home to a sanctuary of Apollo where the priests were famous for walking over hot coals like Indian fakirs. Apollo was replaced by the little chuch of **San Silvestro** near the summit; built with stones and columns from Apollo's temple, it may be as old as the 6th century.

West of Cívita, **Castel Sant'Elia** has two interesting churches. The cave-church of **Santa Maria ad Rupes** isn't as old as it looks; an 18th-century hermit spent 37 years cutting it out of the tufa. It now houses a collection of medieval church gear (ask at the adjacent Polish convent for admittance). On the outskirts of the village, the **Basilica di Sant'Elia** was built in the 11th century over a ruined temple of Diana. It contains a Cosmatesque pavement and furnishings, and some fine Byzantine-style frescoes from the 12th century.

Nepi, which supplies much of the mineral water in Lazio restaurants, is just down the road from Castel Sant'Elia. It's a lovely village; you wouldn't know Napoleon's army burned it all down in 1798. A section of the Etruscan wall still stands, and the **Castello** (*currently under restoration*) used to belong to Lucrezia Borgia, a present from her dad the Pope. The rebuilt **cathedral** has a portico full of fragments from the medieval original; there are some good paintings, including a triptych by Giulio Romano, and down in the crypt is an altar from the temple of Jupiter over which the cathedral was built. Few villages of 6,000 have such a grandiose **Palazzo Comunale**. Antonio da Sangallo the Younger took time off from building the Rocca at Cívita Castellana to create it, and the memorable fountain in front, built in the form of a castle with water pouring through the gate, is attributed to Bernini. Inside, Nepi's **Museo Civico** (*open Wed–Fri 11–1 and 4–6; Sat and Sun 10–1 and 4–7*) has Etruscan and Roman finds from the area; ask at the museum for admission to the **Catacombs of Santa Savinilla**, at the cemetery, and to the Etruscan necropolis at **Cerro**.

Viterbo

Viterbo ought to be visited. Where else in Italy can one rest a while in a café on Death Square, or stroll over to the Piazza of the Fallen to pay one's respects to Our Lady of the Plague? Surrounded by grey, forbidding walls and the ghastly modern districts beyond them, the city is actually rather cute inside, full of grand churches and palaces, and well-preserved medieval streets brightened everywhere with fountains and flowers. The population seems evenly divided between teenagers on scooters, as bejewelled and trendy as their counterparts in Rome, and blasé young soldiers from Italy's biggest army base.

Like the rest of Lazio, Viterbo has had more than its share of troubles, most of them traceable to the proximity of Rome. That geographical necessity, however, also gave Viterbo its greatest period of glory. For much of the 13th century Viterbo, and not Rome, was the seat of the popes.

History

Although a small city in both Etruscan and Roman times, Viterbo's modern history begins with its fortification by the Lombard King Desiderius in the 8th century. It was an attempt to build a strong base close to Rome, to overawe or perhaps even capture the city – a dream spoiled when Charlemagne came over the Alps in 778 and put an end to the Lombards' Kingdom of Italy. By 1100, it was a free *comune*, one of the few cities in Lazio strong and energetic enough to manage it, and a big programme of building was under way, including churches, palaces and the city's impressive walls.

Viterbo was usually an enemy of Rome, but it often provided the popes with a convenient refuge from the thuggish Roman nobles. When Arnold of Brescia's revolution made Pope Eugenius III a refugee in 1145, he moved his court here. Emperor

Frederick I Barbarossa soon restored the popes to Rome, but again in 1257, Alexander IV found Viterban hospitality gratifying when the Guelph–Ghibelline wars made Rome too hot for him. In this most confusing period of Italian history, over a dozen popes were crowned, died or at least spent time here, in short stays on their way to or from France, Tívoli – and sometimes even Rome. Viterbo's finest hour came in 1243. Emperor Frederick II, the 'Wonder of the World', had occupied the city, and was building a palace for his incredible court, with his Muslim bodyguard, his astrologers, poets, dancing girls and elephants. In his absence the Viterbans chased out the German garrison, and under the leadership of their bishop they withstood a determined siege when Frederick came back, a severe blow to the Ghibelline cause in Italy.

In 1309, when the 'Babylonian Captivity' began and the papacy was carted off to Avignon, Viterbo could only decline; the Black Death of 1348 helped it along, carrying off over half the population. Viterbo still ruled over most of northern Lazio, but the city stagnated under the rule of a dynasty of tyrants, the di Vico family, and finally lost its independence in the 1360s courtesy of Cardinal Albornoz, a strong-willed veteran of campaigns against the Moors in Spain who pacified much of central Italy, built castles everywhere (including Viterbo's Rocca), and did much to make possible the return of the popes. A papal army captured and executed the last of the di Vico in 1431. When the popes came back to Rome once more, the city that had once been Rome's strongest rival found itself a mere provincial town of the Papal States. Its population, which had risen as high as 60,000 in the Middle Ages, dropped by two-thirds (it's back to the medieval level today, and growing). Viterbo is an important railway junction, and during the Second World War the Allies bombed it as intensively as any city in Italy. Their aim might have been better; some 70 per cent of its buildings were destroyed, including many monuments in the medieval centre.

Piazza del Plebiscito

In Viterbo's centre, two not-so-fierce-looking lions, the city's ancient symbol, gaze out over the typical pair of buildings representing the often conflicting imperial and local powers: the **Palazzo del Podestà** of the 1460s (*closed to the public*), with its tall clock tower, and the 13th-century **Palazzo dei Priori** (now the city hall, and often called *Palazzo Comunale*). The politicians won't mind you looking around the building and its fine Renaissance courtyard, and its worth the trouble to see the *Sala Regia* where the city council meets (*open Mon–Sat 9–1.30, Tues and Thurs also 3–6*), decorated with fanciful frescoes on the history of Viterbo from Etruscan times, inspired by the tall tales of Annius of Viterbo (*see* p.214). Across the square is the church of **Sant'Angelo in Spatha**, the façade of which has for centuries incorporated a Roman sarcophagus (lately removed for restoration and replaced by a copy) containing the body of a medieval lady of incomparable virtue named Galiena; accounts of her fatal charm and sad demise vary from one Viterban to another; some say, however, that the sarcophagus was placed here only to commemorate the destruction of Férento in 1172, or some Viterban victory over the Romans.

Viterbo
N
200 metres
200 yards
Porta Fiorentina Station
Roma-Nord Station
To Bagnaia & La Quercia
VIALE TRIESTE
VIALE TRENTO
VIA DELLA PALAZZINA
Prato Giardino
PIAZZALE A. GRAMSCI
PORTA FIORENTINA
Rocca Albornoz
San Francesco
PIAZZA S. FRANCESCO
PORTA MURATA
VIALE RANIERO CAPOCCI
VIA SAN BONAVENTURA
V. BRACCIA DI S. FRANCESCO
VIA GIACOMO MATTEOTTI
PIAZZA DELLA ROCCA
VIA DEL PILASTRO
V. G. AMENDOLA
PIAZZA GIUSEPPE VERDI
VIA FRATELLI ROSSELLI
VIA DI SANTA ROSA
Santa Rosa
SAN FAUSTINO
PIAZZA S. FAUSTINO
VIA DE PAVONE
V. S. LUCA
VIA G. SIGNORELLI
VIA CAIROLI
VIA EMILIO BIANCHI
VIA GUGLIELMO MARCONI
TRINITA
VIA MARIA SS. LIBERATRICE
SANTA ROSA
CROCETTA
VIA GIUSEPPE MAZZINI
Madonna della Peste
PZA DELLA REPUBBLICA
PIAZZA DEI CADUTI
CORSO ITALIA
SS. Trinità
PIAZZA DELLA TRINITÀ
DECOLLATO
S. Giovanni Battista
PIAZZA MARTIRI D'UNGHERIA
VIA F. ASCENZI
GIOVANNI
Bus Station
PIAZZA D'ERBE
VIA ROMA
VIA OROLOGIO VECCHIO
V. DELLA MARROCCA
PORTA DELLA VERITÀ
PIAZZA F. CRISPI
Museo Civico
S. Maria della Verità
Palazzo dei Priori
S. Angelo in Spatha
VERITA
VIA DELLA VERITÀ
VIA SAN
Valle di Faul
PIAZZA DEL PLEBISCITO
VIA S. ANTONIO
VIA FAUL
Casa Poscia
VIA CAVOUR
VIA DELLA PACE
VIA DEI MILLE
CENZIALE OVEST
Gesù
PIAZZA DEL GESÙ
VIA SAN LORENZO
Palazzo Papale
PIAZZA SAN LORENZO
Duomo
S. Maria Novella
PZA. DON MARIA GARGIULI
RADA BAGNI
llicame
PIAZZA DELLA MORTE
VIA CARDINALE LA FONTAINE
Fontana Grande
V. GIUSEPPE GARIBALDI
San Sisto
PORTA ROMANA
V. DEL MEONE
PIAZZA S. CARLUCCIO
Museo della Macchina
Palazzo degli Alessandri
V. SAN PELLEGRINO
V. VALLEOUNA
PIAZZA S. PELLEGRINO
VIA GROTTI
V. S. PIETRO
V. S. LEONARDO
S. Pellegrino
V. SANTA MARIA DI GRADI
To Soriano nel Cimino
SAN PELLEGRINO
V. S. TOMMASO
VIA SAN PIETRO
VIA DELLE FORTEZZE
DIAZ
VIA SAN PAOLO
VIA DI PIANOSCARANO
ARMANDO
Palazzo Pamphili
Porta Romana Station
PORTA SAN PIETRO
VIA VICO SQUARANO
V. DI PORTA FIORITA
VIALE

Getting Around

Viterbo actually has three **railway** stations, all just outside the city walls. Regular FS trains north to Orvieto and Florence stop at Stazione Porta Fiorentina, north of the walls on Viale Trento. Most trains for Rome usually leave from here, too, also stopping at Stazione Porta Romana, on Viale Raniero Capocci, the big boulevard east of the walls. In addition there is a local line run by COTRAL, which rattles along a separate route from its station next door to Porta Fiorentina, by way of Bagnaia, Soriano nel Cimino and Cívita Castellana, to Roma-Nord station in Rome. However, the fastest way to reach Viterbo from Rome is by COTRAL **bus**, leaving roughly every thirty minutes from Saxa Rubra Station. More buses for Tarquínia, Bolsena, Civita-vécchia and other provincial towns leave from Piazza Martiri d'Ungheria, next to Piazza dei Caduti in the town centre.

Tourist Information

Piazza San Carluccio 5, **t** 0761 304795 (*open Mon–Sat 9.30–1.30 and 3–7*).

Where to Stay

Viterbo ✉ 01100

Viterbo doesn't offer a lot of choice, but try Via della Cava near Piazza della Rocca, where there are hotels in every price range.

*****Leon d'Oro**, at No.36, **t** 0761 344444, **f** 0761 344447 (*moderate–cheap*). Quiet; a bit staid.

****Roma**, Via della Cava 26, **t** 0761 226474 (*cheap*). Almost next door; tattier and slightly cheaper, with private parking.

*****Milano**, Via San Luca 17 in the *centro storico*, **t** 0761 303367, **f** 0761 303425, *info@hotelmilano2.com* (*moderate*). Recently redone with modern décor (a/c optional).

*****Tuscia**, Via Cairoli 41, **t** 0761 344400, **f** 0761 345976 (*moderate*). Off the Piazza dei Caduti, comfortable and carpeted, and with very friendly staff. Parking available.

******Niccolò V Terme dei Papi**, Strada Bagni 12, Bullicame, **t** 0761 3501, **f** 0761 352 4510, *info@termedeipapi.it, www.termedeipapi.it* (*very expensive*). A small, luxurious spa in Bullicame, offering marble baths, large airy rooms, a winter garden and an enormous naturally heated outdoor pool – the water

Quartiere San Pellegrino

From Piazza del Plebiscito, Via San Lorenzo takes you into the heart of Viterbo's oldest quarter. Three streets down and off to the left, **Santa Maria Nuova** is the best-preserved of the city's medieval churches. On the façade is an ancient image of Jupiter set into the portal, and a small outdoor pulpit in the corner where St Thomas Aquinas once preached. On the other side of Via San Lorenzo, Viterbo's old market square faces the 11th-century church of the **Gesù**, a medieval tower-fortress, one of several left in the city, and a palazzo that long ago was the town hall (*usually closed; but the custodian of Santa Maria might open it for you*). To the south, trailing down from the aforementioned **Piazza della Morte** – ironically one of the lovelier squares in Viterbo – the **San Pellegrino** quarter hangs its web of alleys, arches and stairs along Via San Pellegrino with a romantic and thoroughly medieval air. Lately, some of the quarter's old buildings have been restored, notably the elegant 13th-century **Palazzo degli Alessandri** and adjacent **Torre Scacciaruca** on Via San Pellegrino. The **Museo della Macchina di Santa Rosa**, Via San Pellegrino 60 (*open Fri 3–5.30, Sat/Sun 10–1 and 3–5.30*) chronicles Viterbo's festival with photos and models of past *macchine* (*see* p.212).

The Papal Palace and Cathedral

From Piazza della Morte, a bridge on Roman and Etruscan foundations called the **Ponte del Duomo** carries over to Piazza San Lorenzo and the **Palazzo Papale**, begun in 1266 and now the home of Viterbo's bishops, and a conference centre. This squarish, comes out of the ground at 58°C (*pool open to non-residents Mon–Fri 9.30–4.30, Sat–Sun 9.30–5; also open eves in summer*).

Eating Out

Restaurants around here are often very good, with a determined adherence to traditional Viterban dishes: slender *fettuccine* called *fieno* (hay) or fat *spaghetti* called *lombrichelle*, roast baby lamb, eels and lake fish: *lattarini, coregone* (whitefish) or *persico* (perch).

Enoteca La Torre, Via della Torre 5, **t** 0761 226467 (*expensive–moderate*). A wine bar and smart restaurant set in a stone palace; at the restaurant, you can dine on immaculate Viterban dishes washed down with some fine regional wines; or snack on some delicious local cheese and ham at the bar.

Il Richiastro, Via della Marrocca 18, **t** 0761 228 009 (*moderate*). Occupies the courtyard and cellars of a medieval palace, inside the walls near the Museo Civico. At bargain prices you can dine on smoked trout, roast lamb, polenta and some unusual home-made desserts, with everything fresh according to the season. *Open Thurs–Sat and Sun lunch only; closed 2 months in summer.*

Il Labirinto, Via San Lorenzo 46, **t** 0761 307026 (*moderate–inexpensive*). An excellent friendly trattoria, with a limited menu but good cooking. *Closed Tues.*

Il Portico, Via C la Fontaine 28, near Santa Maria Nova, **t** 0761 321143 (*moderate*). A good choice for seafood – *vongole*, scallops and grilled fish.

Scaletta, Via Marconi 45, **t** 0761 340003 (*moderate*). Another old favourite, with traditional cooking, and pizza in the evening if you don't feel like a big dinner. *Closed Mon.*

Antica Taverna Marcus, on Via San Lorenzo 61, **t** 0761 304383, south of Piazza del Plebiscito (*cheap*). Ideal for snacks or a light lunch: a wide variety of designer *bruschette* (with salmon, or pumpkin flowers) as well as sandwiches and antipasti.

Pino, in the centre of San Martino al Cimino at Via Abate Lamberto 2–4, **t** 0761 379242 (*moderate*). Not well marked but worth a trip for the home-made pasta and the absolutely exquisite mushroom dishes in season. *Closed Tues and May.*

battlemented building, in the style of a medieval city hall or private palace, is a finer building than the Pope's present address in Rome, though admittedly much smaller. On the best part, the open Gothic loggia, you will see lions (for Viterbo) interspersed with the striped coat of arms of the French Pope Clement V, who finished the building.

Popes and cardinals did not always have an easy time in Viterbo. The first to settle into the the new palace, Alexander IV, died 17 days after his arrival. Five later popes were elected in conclaves held in the Great Hall, among them Urban IV, who was chased out by the Imperial army of Frederick II's son Manfred, and then Clement IV, who died two weeks after his coronation. In selecting his successor, arguments between the French and Italian factions led to a two-year deadlock among the cardinals. The exasperated Viterbesi tried to speed up the conclave, first by locking the cardinals in the palace, and then by tearing off the roof; somehow, according to the story, the churchmen got around this by making tents in the Great Hall. Finally the people decided to starve them out, and before long the Church was blessed with the rather undistinguished compromise of Gregory X. He had the roof fixed, but maybe skimped on the materials, for the whole thing came down six years later on the head of his successor, John XXI, who was quickly entombed next door in the **Duomo**. That was the last straw; the cardinals high-tailed it back to Rome before Viterbo ruined the Church altogether. Behind its late Renaissance façade, tacked on by Cardinal Gianfrancesco Gambara (the same fellow who built Villa Lante at Bagnaia), this hodgepodge cathedral has suffered many indignities over the centuries, most

The *Macchina di Santa Rosa*

Viterbo is the city where the most distinguished title a man can have is 'porter'. Not just any *facchino*, of course, but a *Facchino di Santa Rosa*, one of the 90 stout citizens in white caps and red sashes who carry the *macchina* across Viterbo every year at 9.30pm on Santa Rosa's feast day, 3 September. The *macchina* is an impossibly tall and slender portable steeple, surmounted by an image of the saint; the current model is about 120ft and weighs five tons. Local artists and construction firms create a new *macchina*, money permitting, every five years (the last model was modernistic and startlingly attractive; the current one, built in 1998, looks more traditional). The festival is similar to the 'Dance of the Lilies' in Nola and other towns down in Campania where people like to carry heavy objects. According to local legend, Viterbo started it in 1656, a vow made during a time of plague. The procession, however, has been documented to at least 1512, and they may have been at it even earlier.

Santa Rosa was a little girl who did little but pray and preach from the age of three. Her preaching helped inspire the Viterbesi to defeat the siege by Emperor Frederick II in 1243 (which is undoubtedly how she got to be a saint). The annual trip of the *macchina* commemorates the moving of the saint's body in 1258 to what was then the church of San Damiano, now rededicated in her honour. It seems a rather slender pretext for a city's biggest festival, but don't try telling that to people in Viterbo.

The *macchina*'s progress begins at the church of San Sisto, passing down Via Garibaldi and Via Cavour to Piazza del Plebiscito, where it does a turn for the assembled dignitaries, then up Via Cavour and Corso Italia. Finally comes the fun part, when the exhausted *facchini* have to schlep the thing uphill – at a trot – to the church of Santa Rosa. If you're in Viterbo on 3 September, camp on a good viewing place two hours in advance (Piazza Fontana Grande and Piazza Verdi are best; bring folding chairs and sandwiches as the Viterbesi do). The *macchina* is brilliantly illuminated, and when it approaches everyone turns off all the lights on the street; anyone with a window overlooking it who doesn't douse theirs is likely to get something thrown at them. Often the thing seems ready to topple over, though it never does; the *facchini*'s greatest embarrassment came in 1967, when a new *macchina* proved too top-heavy and had to be abandoned midway. You'll know it's getting close when the Viterbesi start screaming; watching an illuminated steeple walk down the street, with little Santa Rosa floating above the rooftops, can be a strangely transcendant moment.

recently the Allied bombing in 1944. A 14th-century campanile survives, and the Romanesque interior has some finely carved capitals (some with sphinxes), and a painting of the *Marriage of St Catherine* by the Viterban artist Pastura. The **Museo del Colle del Duomo** (*open Tues–Sun 9–12; adm*) next door contains a patchy collection of religious treasures – manuscripts, vestments, reliquaries and some dull painting and sculpture.

North of Piazza del Plebescito

Via Ascenzi, under the arch of the Palazzo dei Priori, leads to the northern end of Viterbo, towards Piazza dei Caduti and **San Giovanni Battista**, a church of 1511 now used for art exhibitions. Across the piazza, **Madonna della Peste** is an octagonal Renaissance church built to commemorate the end of a plague, and now coverted into a war memorial – because of its long involvement with the popes, Viterbo has more churches than it can use.

Beyond that, by the walls, is the **Rocca** Cardinal Albornoz built in 1354 to keep watch on the Viterbesi. This squat palace-fortress, much rebuilt and restored (most recently since the bombings of 1944), is now home to the **Museo Archeologico** (*open Tues–Sun 8.30–7.30; adm*). It's a relentlessly didactic museum, but one where you can learn a good deal about everyday life among the Etruscans; there's a diorama of an Etruscan dining room, for example, showing how they ate dinner seated three to a *kline* (couch). That's a Greek custom; not content with copying Greek art, the Etruscans from the 6th century BC or so aped nearly everything else from the East. And before you try the 'Etruscan cuisine' attempted by some restaurants in these parts, consider that one of their greatest culinary delights was dormouse; they raised them in jars. The museum's outstanding find is a nearly complete terracotta portico from a temple at *Aquarossa* (Férento: *see* p.215), one of the many Etruscan sites in the vicinity, with reliefs portraying the *Labours of Hercules*; some of the original paint is still present – done in red, black and white, just like a Greek vase. The second floor is mostly Roman, with finds from the Roman theatre in Férento, including nine beautiful, unfortunately headless statues of the muses.

Two of Viterbo's 13th-century popes are buried in the 13th-century **San Francesco** church, near Porta Murata at the northern end of the walls. Clement V's tomb is probably the work of Arnolfo di Cambio; Clement IV's was done by Pietro Oderisio, the artist who travelled up to England to do Edward the Confessor's tomb in Westminster Abbey. Off Piazza Verdi, the late 19th-century church of **Santa Rosa**, goal of the *macchina* each 3 September, houses the considerable remains of Viterbo's 13th-century patroness, too holy to decompose and usually on display for all to see.

Santa Maria della Verità and the Museo Civico

East from Piazza del Plebiscito, Via Cavour takes you to the **Casa Poscia**, an interesting 13th-century house (*still a private residence; closed to the public*) on a stairway to the left, and then the **Fontana Grande**, the best of Viterbo's many fountains. Via Garibaldi leads on further east to the Porta Romana and **San Sisto**, an imposing church in parts as old as the 9th century, with two campanili, one of them built into the city wall. The oldest part, the nave, was rebuilt with the original columns after the bombings of 1944; it leads to a tremendous space at the crossing, with a tall flight of steps leading to the elevated choir and an altar made of ancient sculptural fragments from the Roman temple that previously occupied the site.

Outside the walls and up Viale Capocci, **Santa Maria della Verità** from the 13th century suffered terrible vandalism at the hands of 18th-century redecorators, and worse from the American bombers; the frills and plaster frosting are gone now, and only a few fragments have survived of the Renaissance frescoes by Melozzo da Forlì. The **Cappella Mazzatosta**, behind an iron grille, has the best painting Viterbo can offer: frescoes of the *Marriage of the Virgin* and the *Presentation at the Temple* by

Lorenzo of Viterbo (1469). Little is known about the life of this hometown artist, whose other surviving work is one painting in Rome, but it was a pity he died young. His work shows the strong influence of Piero della Francesca, whose great fresco cycle at San Francesco in Arezzo was finished four years previously; there's some science in his art, a close study of the new method of perspective and a great attention to light and forms in space. In the *Marriage of the Virgin*, note the 'ideal temple' in the background, a popular theme in early Renaissance art; later, architects would be building real ones, as at Prato and Montepulciano in Tuscany, or Todi in Umbria, or Bramante's Tempietto in Rome. Viterbo's own Madonna della Peste is a very modest example.

Annius of Viterbo

Every good city deserves a devoted historian, a man of letters who chronicles its antiquities and recounts its glories, as Livy did for ancient Rome. It is not clear, however, what Viterbo did to deserve Fra Giovanni Nanni, a 15th-century Dominican writer, alchemist and astrologer who went under the name of Annius of Viterbo. *Campanilismo*, the 'worship of one's bell-tower', is a common passion in this land of beautiful cities, but Annius may be the most extreme example in recorded history. For him, Viterbo was *umbilicus universi*, the navel of the universe. In a time when Viterbo was losing the last vestiges of its independence to the pope, he must have thought the city's cause needed all the intellectual ammunition it could get. He wrote numerous books about its history, and scholars may still be searching them in hopes of finding a single statement that is not a howling whopper.

According to Annius, Viterbo was founded by none other than Hercules, who built a castle on the hill where the Duomo stands now. The Greek hero made some other contributions to the landscape, notably Lake Vico, which he created by whacking the ground with his club. After the flood, the first thing Noah did was refound Viterbo, making it the oldest city in the world. Annius goes on to explain how Viterbo became the capital and greatest city of the Etruscans, and he uses a fabricated etymology to show how the city was the original home of a dynasty of Byzantine emperors, the Palaeologi. Behind the Duomo and the Palazzo dei Priori is an open space within the city walls, the Valle di Faul; Annius used the name to invent an ancient mystic alphabetical device, like Rome's SPQR: FAUL meant *Fanum Auguste Volturne Lucumonum*, 'Volturnia (according to Annius, the city's Etruscan name), the august temple of the Lucumones'. The Viterbesi, of course, were completely taken in by Annius's wonderful stories, and they commissioned artists to portray them on the walls of their city hall.

Not content with his writings, Annius also created some fascinating fake monuments to support them. Some of these have survived in the Museo Civico. One, the 'Decreto di Desiderio', is a marble tablet supposedly engraved by the Lombard King Desiderius, declaring Viterbo the 'Once and Present Capital of the Etruscans'. The best is an uncannily beautiful stone called the *Marmo Osiriano*; supposedly an ancient work, it is really a medieval relief of birds in their nest, with trim and an inscription carved by some of Annius's co-conspirators, detailing how the Egyptian god Osiris voyaged to Viterbo, and killed some giants there.

The adjacent cloister, full of roses, is an oasis in this gritty part of Viterbo; it houses the **Museo Civico** (*open Tues–Sun 9–7; in winter until 6; adm*), with a small archaeological section and a picture gallery, starring a beautiful *Pietà* by Sebastiano del Piombo. This is only one of a wealth of winsome Madonnas here, including one by Viterbo's other artist of note, Antonio del Marsaro, known as Il Pastura (d. 1513), a follower of Pinturicchio; you'll see other works of his in many of Viterbo's churches. Upstairs, the museum has old views of the city (full of medieval tower-fortresses as late as the 1700s; there are still quite a few left) and plans of *macchine* going back to the 1690s. The best things in this museum, however, are absolute frauds... (*see* box, opposite).

Near Viterbo: Hot Mud and a Theatre

West of the city, some of the Etruscans' and Romans' favourite thermal springs still carry on doing whatever it is they do that makes Italians so happy. At the ancient **Springs of Bullicame** you can stop by the roadside for a dip in a sulphurous pool, check into a hotel spa, or visit the municipally run baths for an aerosol inhalation to help your sinuses, and a frosting with hot mineral mud to calm your nerves.

Eight kilometres north from Viterbo, along the Bagnoregio road, stood the Roman town of **Férento**, which replaced an Etruscan town and considered itself in the 2nd century BC a *splendidissima civitas*. In the 1170s it challenged Viterbo for local supremacy, lost, and was razed to the ground. Little is left, save a well-preserved **Roman theatre**, where concerts are held in summer; the theatre survived through the Middle Ages because its arches were used as shop stalls (*open Tues–Fri and Sun 9–1, Sat 9–1hr before sunset*). Another lonely side road, southwest from Viterbo, will take you 9km to **Castel d'Asso**, another open site inhabited solely by Etruscan ghosts. It's a beautiful spot, full of wild flowers and scrub that conceal endless tombs and bits of a medieval fortress, the 'Ace Castle' that stands on the acropolis of the town the Romans called *Axia*.

South of Viterbo, if you're heading for Lake Vico take a detour into the hills for the lovely town of **San Martino al Cimino**, a summer retreat of the Viterbesi for centuries. San Martino is built around a fine 13th-century abbey, built in the French Gothic style by Cistercians from Pontigny and featuring inside a painting of *St Martin* dividing his cloak, by Mattia Preti. The town itself is an unusual example of Baroque planning, full of trees and half-surrounded by a single curving lane of terraced houses.

Around Viterbo

East of Viterbo: the Villa Lante

East of Viterbo, the road for Orte (SS204) enters the old suburb of La Quercia, passing in front of a landmark of late Renaissance architecture: **Santa Maria della Quercia**, built in the late 1470s. The distinctive 1509 façade has a carved oak tree (*quercia*) and lions, and lunettes by Andrea della Robbia over the doors. Inside, the beautiful marble tabernacle contains a miraculous painting of the Virgin, and there is also a fine Gothic cloister; ask the custodian to let you in to the **Museo degli Ex-Voto** (*visits on request, call* **t** *0761 303430*), a collection of some 200 devotional plaques

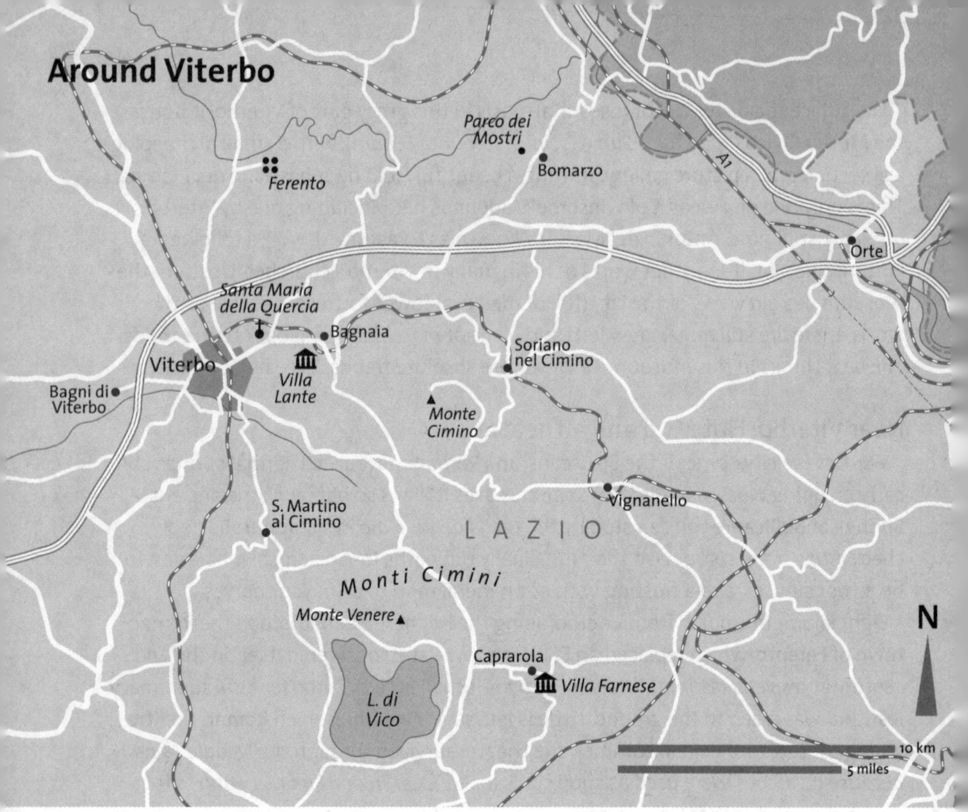

brought to this shrine over the centuries, painted with fascinating scenes of miracles attributed to the Madonna.

Six kilometres further east is **Bagnaia**, an old hill village expanded by wealthy Viterban bishops into a residence town. In the 1570s Cardinal de Gambara, the fellow who carved his name on the front of Viterbo's cathedral, commissioned the architect Vignola to create the theatrical **Villa Lante** (*gardens open Tues–Sun 9–1hr before sunset; guided tours of the gardens and villa every half-hour; adm*), with one of the most striking of all Renaissance gardens. Gambara was a relative of the Farnese, and the Villa Lante was an attempt to equal their great villa at Caprarola; he may not have had as much money as his cousins, but he certainly had a head swelled to Farnese proportions; his name is carved on everything here, or else a relief of a prawn (*gambara*), the family symbol. Besides the two villas, the *palazzine*, there is a large public park and a classic 'Italian garden', geometrically arranged on a series of sloping terraces full of groves and statuary; the water is the real show, descending through carved stone channels, disappearing under walkways and then reappearing in pools and fountains on each terrace. The entrance to the gardens is at the bottom, though they are meant to be experienced from the top, beginning with a lovely grotto where tree roots mingle with the stones, artfully hung with curtains of maidenhair fern. From there it passes two pavilions, down to a peculiar wedding-cake fountain, and then through the most famous feature, a gracefully carved 100ft stone channel, which was lined with tables for outdoor banquets. Next come two huge sculptures of

Where to Stay and Eat

Soriano nel Cimino ✉ 01038

***__La Bastia Residence__, Via Giovanni XXIII, **t** 0761 745 383, *info@labastia.it* (*moderate*). Near the woods; attractive apartments.

Bomarzo ✉ 01020

***__Le Querce__, Loc. Fossatello, **t** 0761 924299, **f** 0761 343049, *info@querce.com*. This is the only place to stay in Bomarzo, but it's a good and inexpensive, and also has a decent restaurant.

river gods, representing the Arno and the Tiber. The features get bigger and more grandiose with each terrace, culminating in the totally over-the-top **grand fountain** at the bottom – a huge basin navigated by stone boats, with a central island where four Moors hold up the coat of arms of Gambara's successor, Cardinal Montorio, who completed the gardens. Of the matching bookend ***palazzine***, one is open to visitors (at the entrance) with frescoes by Cavalier d'Arpino and others, including views of the gardens as they were originally, with some features, including a labyrinth, that have since disappeared.

Through the Monti Cimini to Orte

The Viterbo–Bagnaia road continues into the beech forests of the Monti Cimini, north of Lake Vico. The next town, **Soriano nel Cimino**, is crowned by the mighty mass of the well-preserved medieval **Castello Orsini** (*open by appointment,* ***t*** *0761 748398*), begun by Pope Nicholas III and until recently a prison. The 16th-century **Palazzo Chigi-Albani**, a Mannerist confection designed by Vignola, consists of two wings united by the extraordinary **Fontana Papacqua**, decorated with eleven *mascheroni* and other figures, and a sculptural group featuring Moses in the central niche. Soriano has an extinct volcano, 3,422ft **Monte Cimino**, for a neighbour, the highest point in northern Lazio. **Vignanello**, further east, has a citadel or *rocca*, founded by Benedictines in the 9th century. It has gone through countless changes, lastly in 1610; now the **Palazzo Rusponi**, its classical gardens and parterres of intricate geometric designs are among the best in Italy (*private, but open April–Oct, Sun and hols, 10–1; adm €6.20*).

Orte, in the Tiber valley on the Umbrian frontier, is known to most Italians as a place to wait for train connections, but there is more to it than that: from the 6th century BC onwards its river port, Seripola, was one of the most important on the Tiber. Orte's *centro storico* on its tufa heights is a well-preserved medieval hill town of tiny lanes and palaces; its Romanesque church of San Silvestro is now a **Museo Diocesano d'Arte Sacra** (*to visit, ring* ***t*** *0761 493276*), housing tryptychs and polyptychs (one from 1282 on the *Life of St Francis*, a *Madonna* by Taddeo di Bartolo, a 7th-century Byzantine mosaic from old St Peter's, and more). At Piana de Lucignana, down on the Tiber, in the remains of the **Porta Seripola** (*always open*), you can trace out the remains of docks, shops and houses, some with mosaic pavements.

The Monster Park at Bomarzo

t *0761 924029; open daily 8am–sunset; adm exp.*

Some of the same sculptors who worked on St Peter's in Rome made this extravagant little nightmare, hidden away in the hills between Viterbo and the Tiber. The two works seem somehow related, opposite sides of the coin that may help in explaining the tragic, neurotic atmosphere of late 16th-century Italy. Vicino Orsini, a distant member of that ancient and powerful Roman family, was a *condottiere* who served in the endless wars of that period, witnessing more than his share of atrocities before retiring to this estate in the 1550s. Here, Piero Ligorio laid out gardens for him before returning to Rome and St Peter's. Over the next 30 years, Orsini commissioned a collection of huge, strange sculptures for them, many carved out of rocky outcrops on the site; he called it his Sacro Bosco – sacred wood – and in its present state it is impossible to tell whether it was the complex allegory it pretends to be, or just a refined joke.

The **Parco dei Mostri** lies just outside the village of Bomarzo. Long neglected and almost forgotten, the park has been gradually, painstakingly restored over the last few decades by its owners, Giovanni Bettini and his family. Near the entrance is the ***casetta inclinata***, a pavilion built at a rakish angle; walking its tilted floors seems to have been intended as a kind of purposeful disorientation to prepare you for what is to come. Next comes the impressive though dilapidated **Tempietto**, a domed 'ideal temple' attributed to Vignola, and dedicated to Orsini's wife. From there you wander the ill-kept grounds, encountering at every turn colossal monuments and eroded illegible inscriptions: a 6m-tall screaming face, where you can walk inside the mouth, under an inscription that reads 'every thought flees', and find a small table and benches, apparently waiting for a dinner party; a life-size elephant, perhaps one of Hannibal's, crushing a terrified Roman soldier in its trunk; a giant wrestler, in the act of ripping a woman in two from the legs. In every corner decayed Madonnas, mermaids, sphinxes, nymphs and harpies wait to spook you. Most are done in a distorted, almost primitive style. It would be almost too easy to read too much into these images: a cry of pain from the degraded, humiliated Italy of the 1560s, half-pretending madness as the only way to be safe from the Spanish and the Inquisition, an exaggerated expression of the over-heated mentality of Mannerism – or perhaps merely a symbol for the loss of mental balance that followed too many centuries of high culture and over-stimulation. Whatever, the Monster Park will make you feel like an archaeologist, discovering some peculiar lost civilization. Vicino's home, the **Palazzo Orsini**, is now Bomarzo's town hall, with terraces offering views over the park.

Lake Bolsena

Occupying over a dozen craters in the Monti Volsini, Bolsena at 44 square miles is the fifth largest lake in Italy and the largest crater lake in Europe. It has one inexplicable peculiarity, called the *sessa* – every few weeks, the lake rocks gently to and fro, creating a tide of about a foot and a half; it may have to do with some very slight seismic vibrations. Mostly spring-fed, with a deep outlet near Marta, Bolsena is one of the cleanest and most transparent lakes you'll find anywhere – already pristine, the installation of a new state-of-the-art collection and drainage system has made it,

Tourist Information

Bolsena: Piazza Matteotti, t 0761 799902.

Where to Stay and Eat

Bolsena ✉ 01023

******Ai Plantani Hotel Moderno***, Via Roma 2, t 0761 799079, f 0761 798468, *info@bolsena.com* (*moderate*). Between the castle and the lake; well-equipped rooms with disabled access, parking and a restaurant.

*****Lido**, Via Cassia km 115, t 0761 799026, f 0761 798479, *www.atihotels.it* (*moderate*). Smaller and right on the lake; private beach, restaurant, and access to tennis courts.

There are many fish restaurants around Lake Bolsena, serving seafood as well as fresh lake fish – try the local fishermen's soup, *sbroscia*, using not only the lake fish but the lake water.

Trattoria da Picchietto, Via Porta Florentina 15, t 0761 799158 (*moderate*). An old favourite, since 1927, with a garden. *Closed Mon.*

Antica Ristorante-Pizzeria del Corso, Corso della Repubblica. Another old favourite, right in the centre, is good for *coregone* and other lake fish at inexpensive rates.

Gino al Miralago, Lungolago Marconi 58, t 0761 870910 (*moderate*). In Marta; a very pleasant waterfront trattoria. *Closed Tues.*

Montefiascone ✉ 01027

****Dante**, Via Nazionale 2, t 0761 826015 (*inexpensive*). A modest hotel with a good honest trattoria attached: a €15 lunch menu with a wide choice of pasta, and *secondi* such as eels, lake fish or stuffed pigeon. *Closed Tues.*

*****Altavilla**, Via del Pino 9, t 0761 820123, *altavillahotel@isa.it* (*moderate*). A modern, quieter and more expensive hotel, with its own restaurant and bar.

literally, clean enough to drink. Its whitefish, perch, bass and eels are highly regarded; one pope, Martin IV, died from a surfeit of Bolsena eels, and was condemned by Dante to hell for his gluttony.

Bolsena Town

The lake's elegant capital, **Bolsena** town, makes a bold sight on the north shore of the lake, its castle and walled old quarters set on various terraces descending to the lake. This was the important Etruscan city of *Velzna*, or *Volsinium* as the Romans called it, founded in 264 BC by refugees fleeing the Roman destruction of the original *Velzna* – modern Orvieto (*Urbs Vetus*) just 10km over the border in Umbria. Old *Velzna* had been the last important town in southern Etruria to resist Rome; it fell after a revolt of recently freed slaves. The noble families called in the Romans to crush them, and some of these, the Larcii, Aconii and Cominii, retained their wealth and power under Roman rule. After flourishing in early Christian times, the city was abandoned in the 6th century with the arrival of the Lombards.

Bolsena revived in the Middle Ages; in 1398 Pope Boniface IX gave the town to the Mondaleschi family, who built the medieval **Castello Mondaleschi**. Although it was almost destroyed by the locals in 1815 to keep Napoleon's brother Luciano from getting it, it was pieced back together and now houses the **Museo Territoriale del Lago di Bolsena** (*open summer Tues–Sun 9.30–1.30 and 4–8; winter Wed–Fri 10–1, Sat and Sun 10–1 and 3–6; adm*). It's a stiff climb up lovely medieval streets to the castle; the best way is under the vaults and arches of **Via delle Piagge**. The museum has a tremendous view over the lake from its roof, and also a fine archaeological collection, including frescoes from the Poggio Moscini villas and a 2nd-century BC 'Throne of Dionysos' decorated with panthers; these were often used in theatres, though this one came from a house that may have been used as a cult centre to the god's Italian equivalent, Bacchus. Don't overlook the *oscillum*, a carved stone disc that was hung in a tree or between columns to mark a sacred space (and used for the same purpose on theatre stages). Like the one here, these *oscilla* are some of the most haunting and beautiful relics of the ancient world.

The ongoing excavations of Etruscan–Roman Volsinii are at **Poggio Moscini**, just behind the museum along the Orvieto road (*open Tues–Sun 9–1.30*) and include a dry stone tufa wall that once measured 5km, a large forum, two fancy villas and a basilica converted to Christian use in the 4th century. The outline of the amphitheatre, still unexcavated, can be seen 500 yards further along the road.

In the 1490s, when he was 17, Cardinal Giovanni de' Medici, son of Lorenzo il Magnifico of Florence (whose money would some day make him Pope Leo X), was governor of Bolsena. He began work on what is now the **Palazzo del Drago**, a work continued by his successors, and containing fine Mannerist frescoes by the school of Perin del Vaga. Cardinal Giovanni also built the **Fontana San Rocco** under the palace complex. The story goes that in the 14th century, St Rocco (or Roche, a native of Montpellier) was on his way to Rome when he arrived in Acquapendente (*see* p.223) which was decimated by the Black Death, although Rocco was able to cure victims with the sign of the Cross. By the time he reached Bolsena, however, he himself had a bubonic sore above the knee, and hid in a cave in the countryside, surviving thanks to a local dog, who brought him *ciambelle* (ring-shaped rolls) from its master's table. Rocco eventually came to Bolsena and bathed his sore in the water, and was cured, although his sufferings had so disfigured him that when he finally returned to Montpellier he was thrown in prison as a supicious vagrant.

Basilica di Santa Cristina

Open Easter–Sept 7.45–12.45 and 3.30–7.45, Oct–Easter 7.15–12.30 and 3–5.45.

But Bolsena, once sacred to the principal Etruscan god Voltumna and site of a national gathering of the *lucumoni*, or priests, is a place used to miracles. The town's patron is the 12-year-old daughter of a Roman prefect, who took the name Cristina as a daughter of Christ, and was martyred under Diocletian, with a good deal of difficulty – she was practically invulnerable, facing the wheel, snakes, and all kinds of nasty tortures until she was struck by that old Etruscan nemesis, a bolt of lightning. Her various torments are re-enacted every 23–24 July, in ten silent *misteri* or living tableaux, in a tradition dating from the Renaissance, the various roles passed down in some families for generations. Cristina was buried on the island of Martana, and her body was brought back in the 1070s by Pope Gregory VII and his most powerful ally, the Countess Matilda of Tuscany, and buried in the **Basilica di Santa Cristina**, built over a palaeo-Christian church. Most of the bones were stolen in the 12th century and sold to the Count of Molise, who left them in Palermo Cathedral.

Giovanni de' Medici paid for a new façade for the Basilica, a design by Benedetto and Francesco Buglioni that is said to have been a loser in the competition for a façade for Florence cathedral, while the façade of the adjacent **Chapel of the Miracle** (or Chiesa

The Miracle of Bolsena

In the 13th century, the popes were having a hard time putting over the doctrine of transubstantiation, an archaic, genuinely pagan survival that many in the Church had difficulty in accepting. Among these was a Bohemian priest named Peter, who in June 1263 was making the pilgrimage to Rome when he was asked to celebrate Mass in the church. Father Peter had long been sceptical that the Host became in truth the body of Christ, but during the service the Host itself answered his doubts by dripping blood on the altar linen. Marvelling, Peter took the linen to Pope Urban IV, then living in Orvieto, and Urban declared it a miracle and instituted the feast of Corpus Christi. Thomas Aquinas, also in Orvieto at the time, was asked to compose a suitable office for the new holy day, while the pope promised Orvieto – and not poor Bolsena – one of Italy's greatest cathedrals to house the relic. All through Italy (most spectacularly here and in Genzano di Roma, *see* p.181) the day is celebrated with *infioriti* – pavements decorated with flower pictures, over which processions of the Host are borne.

d'Oro) was added in 1863. This is entered from the church through a lovely marble doorway funded by Pope Gregory and Countess Matilda, and now has a 17th-century interior. It seems hard on Bolsena, losing both the relics of Cristina and the holy linen (*see* box), but here you can at least see miraculous stones – the stones on which the blood fell – three out of sight in the fancy altar and one in a reliquary of 1980. Off this is the rock-cut chapel with a beautiful terracotta statue dedicated to Santa Cristina by Benedetto Buglioni.

The **Grotto di Santa Caterina**, part of the Paleolithic church, has a 9th-century baldachin made with Roman columns, and another statue by Buglioni, while behind the screen is the altar of the miracle and the millstone that Cristina was tied to when she was tossed in the lake (like a motorboat, it pulled her to safety). The 'millstone', made of basalt and marked with small footprints, may really have come from a Neolithic solar temple – similar ones have been found elsewhere in Europe. Further back, in a chilly cavern redone in the 19th century, is a rather lovely and serene effigy of the saint by Buglioni, while steps lead down to an extensive series of 4th-century **catacombs** (*open summer 9–12 and 3.30–5.45, winter 9–12.30 and 3–5.30; adm*), that go on for at least two miles and preserve inscriptions and traces of painting in its *loculi*.

Around Lake Bolsena

Most of the shore near Bolsena town has been discreetly developed with campsites and such, but the rest still offers plenty of opportunities for a picnic, and even some small quiet beaches: on the west shore, just beyond Capodimonte, and near **Grádoli**, a village in the hills above the lake that has another **Palazzo Farnese**, with remains of frescoes by Perin del Vaga; it now houses the town council and the **Museo del Costume Farnesiano**, with a collection of ceramics and Renaissance costumes (*open Tues–Sun 10–1, also Sat afternoons 3–6; in summer Wed 5–7pm, Fri–Sun 10–1 and 5–7; adm*). Along the eastern side of the lake, at a place called **Gran Carro**, lie the remains of a 9th-century settlement of the Villanovan people, predecessors of the Etruscans; it was a lake village, built on piles over the water for defence, like many in Italy in that era. Right now it's only in the planning stage, but in the near future Bolsena means to create a unique three-storey floating museum over it.

From Bolsena town, you can take an excursion on the lake to the delightful **Isola Bisentina** (*a private residence, but they offer guided tours; several boat companies, including Navigazione Alto Lazio,* **t** *0761 798033, offer a boat tour plus guided visit*). The island takes its name from the Etruscan–Roman town of *Bisentium*, which has left some scant ruins on the shore nearby; its people seem to have used the island as a necropolis. It later became a favoured retreat of popes, and then the Farnese in the 1500s, when the family was just beginning its spectacular career. The Farnese commissioned Antonio da Sangallo the Younger to build them a palace and a large domed church, **SS. Giacomo e Cristoforo**, as well as seven little **Calvary chapels** on Mount Tabor, some with frescoes, where one could obtain a plenary indulgence. The island's current owners have restored its beautiful Italian gardens, long neglected, and hold evening concerts in the summer. The cruise boats and the regular lake ferry will also take you to the smaller **Isola Martana**, with steep granite cliffs and woods above, a celebrity prison in the days of the Gothic Kingdom of Italy; the tragic Amalasunta, widow of the great king Theodoric, was locked up and eventually assassinated here by her cousin Theodahad in the year 535. The island has ruins of a castle and a 9th-century church. There are two ports on the southern end of the lake: **Capodimonte** on a small promontory with beaches and **Marta**, where there is a pretty park on the water's edge with a view of the islands. A nice reason to linger in either is try the local *Cannaiola* wine, a slightly sparkling, slightly sweet red wine that is rarely sold anywhere else.

This, perhaps unfortunately, is not true of **Montefiascone**, 11km east of Marta on the southeast shore of Bolsena. A big, lively town topped by its **Rocca dei Papi**, this is the home of *Est! Est!! Est!!!* wine and the legend that it has travelled on for 880 years: in the year 1111, a German abbot, Giovanni Defuc, and his servant Martin were on their way to Rome for the coronation of Emperor Henry V. The good abbot liked his wine, and Martin's job was to keep ahead of him and act as a roving sommelier, testing the plonk in each cellar; if it was good, he would write *Est* ('there is') on the door; if it was exceptional, Martin would write *Est, Est*. When he tried the muscatel at Montefiascone, he was overwhelmed. *Est! Est!! Est!!!* he wrote. His master agreed, and after the coronation he and Martin returned and drank, until Defuc dropped dead, leaving Martin to write his epitaph '*per il troppo Est qui morì il mio signore*' which still graces his tomb in the ancient Benedictine church of **San Flaviano**, facing the Via Cassia. Founded in the 6th century, it was rebuilt in the 11th century and then completely changed in the 13th, resulting in an unusual structure with a façade that seems like a French Gothic cathedral gone wrong, and where what seems to be a *matroneum*, or women's gallery, reveals itself as an entire upper church. Bits of fresco are everywhere, including a freshly restored painting of San Flaviano over the altar, and a pair of big feet that could only have belonged to a St Christopher (in legend he was a giant; also it was good luck to see him before starting a journey, so they painted him extra large so you wouldn't miss him). Montefiascone's landmark is the stately dome of its **cathedral** (1764), designed by the late-Baroque architect Carlo Fontana.

East of Lake Bolsena, you'll see signs everywhere inviting you to visit *La Città chi Muore*, at **Bagnoregio**. The 'dying city' isn't Bagnoregio itself, though the town has undoubtedly seen better days, but its near neighbour **Cívita di Bagnoregio**, the famous medieval ghost town. Follow the signs to the convent of the Minori. From there it's a 1km walk, most of it over a pedestrian bridge; the still and sombre city makes an unforgettable sight over the bizarrely eroded Etruscanish landscape. Cívita's long decrepitude was mightily accelerated by tufa erosion and an 18th-century earthquake that made it nearly inaccessible. Two decades ago it was almost completely abandoned, but today such places in Italy inevitably fill up with second-home people; Germans have bought up many of the houses still standing, and restoration work is under way on the church of **San Donato**, which was a cathedral until 1699, and on shoring up the cliffsides to keep Cívita from getting even smaller. Some of the walls still stand; the arch of the main gate goes back to the Etruscans – some scholars hold that the Etruscans invented the arch. Cívita's, along with others in Volterra and Perugia, are the only surviving examples.

North of Bolsena, **Acquapendente** is the northernmost town in Lazio, abutting the province of Siena. An elegant town tucked on a cliff, its chief glory is its **cathedral**, damaged and patched up in the last war, with a 9th-century crypt, a copy of the Holy Sepulchre in Jerusalem with some stout columns with sculpted capitals. Upstairs, the cathedral has some fine art, including reliefs and marble screens and a *tempietto* in the right transept with a terracotta altarpiece by Iacopo Beneventano (1522). On the Sunday after 15 May the town celebrates its liberation from the rule of Frederick Barbarossa in 1149 with ox carts and *pungoli* (ox goads) bearing political messages made out of flowers, which are placed afterwards in the cathedral until they completely wither. Flowers, wild this time, are also the focus of a nature reserve on nearby Monte Rufeno; in its confines is a **Museo del Fiore** (*open May–Sept 10–1 and 3.30–7, Oct–April 10–5; adm*), a didactic exhibit dedicated to flowers and their secrets.

Along the Tiber

Lucus Feroniae

Up the Tiber, along the ancient Via Tiberina, near the Castello di Scorano, you can visit one of the 'newest' archaeological sites in Lazio, discovered in 1953. **Lucus Feroniae** (*open Tues–Sun 9–1; adm*) was once a prosperous town of the people most famous for having its women rustled by the early Romans – the Sabines. The name recalls its famous sanctuary dedicated to the goddess Feronia, worshipped equally by the Sabines, Etruscans and Latins, and linked to crops and fertility. The impious Hannibal razed it to the ground, and afterwards the town and shrine were rebuilt on a grand scale. You can trace the forum, arcades of the shops, one of Italy's smallest amphitheatres, and the temple with a beautifully carved Hellenistic altar; the votives to Feronia, as at Cívita Castellana, are nearly always body parts or internal organs. On the outskirts of the site, the massive late-Republican era **Villa dei Volusii** (*for admission ask at Lucus Feroniae*) might not quite match Hadrian's, but it was no country shack either: today its chief glory is its 7,000 sq ft of black, white and colour mosaics, and copies of Greek statues. There is a huge Sabine necropolis nearby at Civitucola, 3km from **Capena**, a medieval town now best known for its DOC white wine.

Closer to Rome, and across the Tiber, are two towns made illustrious from the campaigns of Garibaldi, **Monterotondo** and **Mentana**. In 1867, all of Italy had been unified save only Rome and some territory around it, where a French army had been keeping the pope in power since Mazzini and Garibaldi's revolt of 1849. The new Italian kingdom could do nothing against the French (at least until 1870, when the Franco-Prussian War forced them to withdraw), but Garibaldi came out of retirement and raised a force of volunteers to try and put the Papal States out of their misery. He beat the French at Monterotondo, but lost decisively at Mentana – and was arrested for his troubles when his force made it back into Italian territory. Mentana remembers the events with a small **Museo del Risorgimento** in its town hall.

Rieti and its Province

This comes as something of a digression, but this seldom-visited strip of land reaching over the Apennines to touch the borders of the Marche is also a part of Lazio. Before the Roman conquest in 290 BC by Curius Dentatus, it was the land of the Sabines, sometime allies but often fierce enemies of Rome. The Romans pushed their Via Salaria through here on its way to the Adriatic, generally following the route of the modern SS4 to Ascoli Piceno, and made it an important staging post. The tranquillity of the mountains appealed to St Francis, and they've scarcely changed since then.

Rieti and the Valle Santa

Rieti, the ancient capital of the Sabines and now the provincial capital, likes to think of itself as the 'Navel of Italy'. The town will never make the television travelogues, but it has a pleasant medieval centre enclosed in about a kilometre of well-preserved and very medieval-looking walls. In the centre there's a 12th-century **cathedral**, a grand Gothic **Palazzo Vescovile** behind it, and a **Museo Diocesano** in the separate baptistry (*open Sat 10–12 and 4–6, Sun 11–1 and 4–6*). There's a small picture collection in its **Museo Civico**, housed in the town hall (*open Tues–Thurs 8.30–1.30, Fri–Sat 8.30–1.30 and 3–6, Sun 10.30–1.30 and 3–6*).

St Francis loved the isolated mountains north of Rieti, the '*conca reatina*' bordering on his native Umbria, and he attracted a number of followers among the locals. In 1217 he lived in a hut on top of deeply wooded Monte Lacerone, occasionally descending to preach to the people of **Greccio**. They begged him to stay closer to them, and Francis relented; he asked a boy from Greccio to stand on the mountain and toss a flaming coal down, saying he would live where it landed: it fell to the rock below, and here Francis founded the **Convento di Greccio** on a lovely mountain site west of Rieti, with views stretching across the green plain below. In 1223, Francis was in Greccio again, where he made the very first Christmas crib, or *presepio*, using the locals as models, as a visual aid to the Christmas Mass, emphasizing the humility and poverty of the Holy

Getting There and Around

Rieti is on the **rail** line between Terni, L'Áquila, and Sulmona, with connections for Rome (infrequent service). There are lots of **buses** to Rome: generally one every half-hour (to Tiburtina Station), also to L'Áquila, and other towns in the Abruzzo, and all the villages of Rieti province from Piazza Mazzini; **t** 0746 256750 for information.

Tourist Information

Rieti: Piazza Vittorio Emanuele II, **t** 0746 203220, *www.apt.rieti.it* (*open Mon–Fri 9.30–1 and 4–6*).

Terminillo: Via dei Villini 33, Pian de' Valli, **t** 0746 261121 (*open summer daily 9–1 and 4–8; winter daily 9–1 and 4–6*).

Leonessa: Pro Loco, Corso San Giuseppe 48, **t** 0746 923380.

Amatrice: Pro Loco, Corso Umberto I 98, **t** 0746 826344.

Where to Stay and Eat

Rieti ✉ 02100

★★★★**Quattro Stagioni**, Piazza C. Battisti 14, **t** 0746 271071, **f** 0746 271090, *grandealbergo quattrostagioni@tiscalinet.it* (*moderate*). With a few Liberty-style touches in its public rooms, this elegant hotel near the cathedral has comfortable rooms, housed in a 19th-century palazzo. Excellent breakfast buffet.

★★★★**Miramonti**, a short walk from the station at Piazza Oberdan 5, **t** 0745 201333, **f** 0745 205790 (*moderate*). An excellent hotel in an even older building, with lovely views; pretty modern rooms and some jacuzzis.

★★★**Cavour**, Piazza Cavour 10, **t** 0746 485252, **f** 0746 484072 (*cheap*). A pleasant little hotel on the river Velino; cosy, quiet rooms.

Oro, Via Marchetti 10, **t** 0746 204271 (*moderate*). The classic, elegant place to dine; offers the best *bollito misto* in the province, good wines and excellent desserts. *Closed Mon.*

Pecora Nera, Via del Terminillo 33, **t** 0746 497669 (*moderate*). This gracious, happy restaurant features beautifully presented, imaginative dishes and a highly acclaimed lemon tart. *Closed Sun, Aug and late Dec.*

Bistrot, Piazza San Rufo 25, **t** 0746 498798 (*moderate*). An adventurous menu draws local foodies to this family-run restaurant; the *menu degustazione* is packed full of delicious surprises and daily specials. *Closed Sun, and Mon lunchtime.*

Il Grottino, Piazza C. Battisti 4, **t** 0746 497683 (*moderate*). Traditional regional menu. *Closed Tues.*

La Palazzina, Via Ricci 107, **t** 0746 271111 (*moderate*). Excellent regional dishes and grilled meat. *Closed Tues.*

Family. The Italians have been gaga about *presepi* ever since, although the poverty angle takes a back seat in the typical *bella figura* display in painted wood, ceramics or marble, ranging from life-size to the teeny-tiny ones squeezed in a walnut shell. Some feature a cast of hundreds, in which Mary, Joseph and Jesus are swamped by splendidly outfitted Turks, Neapolitans, frolicking children, pizza-makers and sausage-sellers (there's a good if somewhat sober one in Leonessa, *see* p.226). In Greccio, however, Francis' original version is re-created on 24 and 26 December. Other times of year, visit the convento (*open summer 9–12.40 and 3–6.40, winter 9–12.40 and 3–6*) to see the chapel of the Presepio, carved out of the rock, and the dormitory and oratory of St Francis, with a curious painting of the saint, crying (a copy of the lost original).

At the time, Francis had been staying at the **Convento di Fonte Colombo** (*open summer 8–12 and 3.30–8, winter 8–12 and 3–7*) on a hill covered with holm oaks just southwest of Rieti. Here he had his vision of Christ, who came to confirm the rule of absolute poverty, service and itinerant preaching that he had just devised for his Order. Five kilometres north of Rieti, at the **Convento La Foresta** (*open summer 8.30–12 and 2.30–6, winter 8.30–12 and 2.30–6*) he wrote the *Canticle of Brother Sun* and performed a miracle – making wine out of vines trampled by the crowds who came to see him while he stayed at the simple church of San Fabriano. The tub where he made the wine can be seen in the little cloister, built in the 15th century around the little room where Francis stayed. Lastly, on the east side of the *conca*, near **Poggio Bustone**, you can visit another Franciscan shrine, the **Convento di San Giacomo**, founded in 1235, where Francis had another retreat on the mountains.

Along the SS79 north, the main road into Umbria, two little lakes, Lago di Ripa Sottile and Lago Lunga, survive in the centre of the swamps of yore, now part of the **Riserva Naturale dei Laghi Reatini**; you can swim in them but keep an eye peeled for snakes. To the north, the pale hill town of **Labro** overlooks the larger, lofty lake of Piediluco just over the border in Umbria: Labro, a former nest of noblemen on the run, has since been colonized by Belgians. The medieval **castle** has recently been restored (*guided tours summer 10–12, 3–7, winter 10–12 and 3–6; adm*). The mountain valleys here were once swampy and uninhabitable. If you want see what the Romans did to suck all the excess water out of the *conca*, it's a 20-minute drive from Piediluco to the **Cascata delle Marmore**, a 413ft waterfall, the highest in Europe, created by Curius Dentatus in 271 BC, who dug the channel to divert the once swollen river Velino into the Nera (*they let the waters flow Jan–Feb Sat and hols 12–1 and 3–6; March Sat and hols 11–1 and 4–9, weekdays 12–1 and 5–7; April Sat and hols 10–1 and 4–9, weekdays 12–1 and 4–5; May Sat and hols 10–1 and 3–10, weekdays 12–1 and 4–5; June–Aug Sat and hols 10–1 and 3–10, weekdays 11–1 and 4–6; Sept Sat and hols 10–1 and 3–9, weekdays 12–1, 4–5 and 8–9; Oct Sat and hols 11–1 and 3–7, Fri 3–5; Nov–Dec Sat and hols 12–1 and 3–5; after dark they are illuminated; www. marmore.it*).

Around Rieti: Monte Terminillo and Leonessa

The province's biggest attraction is its mountain scenery: from Rieti take the SS4 bis to the dome of 7,270ft **Monte Terminillo**, with a modest ski resort on the slopes of its peak. In summer the road around it makes a panoramic drive to **Leonessa**, an attractive medieval town that is one of the quietest, most out-of-the-way places in Italy, a favourite for summer *villeggiatura*, as well as winter sports on the slopes of Monte Tilia. Controlled at various times by the Angevins, Aragonese and Charles V's daughter, Margherita of Habsbourg, and then the Regno, Leonessa's porticoed streets are lined with medieval houses and two Abruzzese-style churches: **Santa Maria del Popolo**, with its *quattrocento* façade and rose window, and an 18th-century interior, and the nearby **San Francesco**, with octagonal pilasters in the nave, decorated with 14th-century votive frescoes and a chapel with a fine 16th-century *presepio* in painted terracotta by Abruzzese artists.

South of Rieti

South of Rieti, there are the hills around the artificial lakes of **Salto** and **Turano**, dammed in the 1930s to control the waters flowing into the *conca*. On the way to the latter you will see an impressive castle called the **Rocca Sinibalda** (*open Sat, Sun and hols for guided visits at 10, 11, 12, in summer also at 3 and 6, in winter also at 3 and 4;*

Where to Stay and Eat

Terminillo ✉ 02017

★★★★**Cristallo**, Via dei Licheni, Pian de' Valli, **t** 0746 26112, **f** 0746 261392, *www.apt.rieti.it/hotelcristallo.htm* (*expensive*). A well-equipped, sporty hotel, with studio flats as well as rooms; riding, tennis, archery and mountain bike facilities nearby. *Open winter and summer only.*

★★★**La Lucciola**, **t** 0746 261138, **f** 0746 261370 (*cheap*). A reasonable budget choice, with basic rooms and its own restaurant and bar.

Ostello della Neve, Anello Campoforgna 1, **t** 0746 261169. A large youth hostel, convenient for skiiers or walkers. *Open Dec–mid May, 15 June–Aug.*

Leonessa ✉ 02046

★★★★**La Torre**, Via F. Crispi 2, **t** 0746 922166, **f** 0746 923157 (*moderate*). Pool and tennis, well-equipped rooms and a restaurant. *Closed Oct, Nov.*

★★★★**Leo Hotel**, Largo Gonesse 1, **t** 0746 922 908, **f** 0746 922602 (*expensive–moderate*). Slightly posher, with everything you need, plus pool, tennis, gym and Turkish bath.

★★★**Da Mosé**, Loc. Fontenova, **t/f** 0746 922214 (*cheap*). Above the centre, on the northern slopes of Terminillo; 8 simple rooms and a good restaurant, open to non-guests. Try the ricotta – *fiore molle* – flavoured with saffron.

Amatrice ✉ 02012

★★★**Roma**, Via dei Bastonini 29, **t** 0746 85777, **f** 0746 85779 (*cheap*). Tranquil with views over the mountains; a good restaurant starring the dish that put Amatrice on the map.

★★★**Il Castagneto**, Via del Castagneto 9, **t** 0746 85722, **f** 0746 824028 (*cheap*). Welcoming hotel with spacious modern rooms with plenty of wood and mod-cons for the price.

★★**Conca**, Via della Madonnella 24, **t** 0746 826791 (*cheap*). A fine place, surrounded by trees, with a good restaurant serving excellent antipasti, lamb and a good house wine.

adm) designed by Baldassare Peruzzi in 1530, with three courtyards and three mighty towers. The medieval village of **Castel di Tora**, overlooking the lake, stands on the site of the Sabine city Tiora.

South of the large Lago del Salto, the main village is **Borgorose**, site of a Sabine settlement with walls from the 4th century BC; polygonal walls remain on Monte Frontino, and a monumental earthen tumulus, Montariolo, some 180ft in diameter, has been found to contain over a hundred tombs from the 6th and 5th century BC, including many warriors buried with their arms; other tombs are from a Roman colony founded in the early years of the 3rd century BC. More 'cyclopean' walls, standing 18ft high, are just west in **Pescorocchiano**.

The Via Salaria/SS4, from Rieti to Rome, passes through the heart of the ancient Sabine lands, an area still known as *Sabina* today. The Sabines have been pretty quiet since the Romans stole their womenfolk; it would be hard to find a corner of Italy so utterly lacking in history and art. The area's one attraction is the once-mighty **Abbazia di Farfa** (*t 0765 277315/217065; open Tues–Sat 9.30–1 and 3.30–6.30, Sun 10–1 and 3–7.30; adm by guided visit; adm*), near the village of Fara in Sabina. Farfa was founded in the 6th century, and soon became the richest and most powerful monastery in central Italy. A rude interruption in its career came in 898, when a Saracen army took the monastery after besieging it for seven years. The Italians never liked to remember it, but this stretch of the Apennines, so close to Rome, was dominated by Muslims for most of the 9th century (west of Tívoli there's a village called Saracinesco where their descendants still live). The band that took Farfa used it as a base for years, raiding all over central Italy. When the monks finally got it back, they made Farfa one of Italy's most renowned centres of book copying and illumination. After a gradual decline over the centuries, Farfa became abandoned in the 1870s, and was re-seeded with monks from Rome only in 1919. The **abbey church**, last rebuilt in 1492, contains frescoes by the Zuccaris and Orazio Gentileschi; off in a room on the side there is an interesting *Last Judgment* by an unknown Flemish painter. Farfa has two cloisters, the medieval **Chiostrino Longobardo**, and the larger **Chiostro Grande** from the 1600s; steps here lead down to the crypt surviving from the original church, with a lovely Roman sarcophagus for an altar. There is also a **museum**, with some choice archaeological finds and medieval art (*same hours as Abbazia*).

Way Out East: Up the Valle del Velino to Amatrice

From Rieti, look for the SS4 and the town of **Cittaducale**, founded in 1309 by Charles II d'Anjou and named in honour of his son, Duke Robert of Calabria. Laid out in a neat rectangular grid and still preserving its walls, it has all the air of a typical medieval 'new town', modelled on the *bastides* of southern France, with a defence tower on one end of the walls, and its main church in the central square: **Santa Maria del Popolo**, with a handsome late Romanesque façade in the Abruzzo style. Note, too, the late Gothic portal of the nearby **Sant'Agostino** (1450). Up the Velino, **Borgo Velino** is a little medieval centre on the riverbank, with a watchtower and a Romanesque church, **Sant' Antonio**, made of bits of older buildings; the 18th-century parish church of **San Matteo** is lavishly decorated with stuccoes. There's a small **Museo Civico**, in Piazza Umberto I (*open Mon–Sat 8–2*) with paintings, old weapons and antique agricultural tools.

Antrodoco is the result of several centuries' mispronunciation of the Roman *Interocrium*, 'between the mountains'. It sits at the crossroads of the Via Sabina (SS17, with its narrow gorge) and the Via Salaria, which passes through an even longer gorge, the **Gole del Velino**. Its most important monument is **Santa Maria extra Moenia**, a church founded in the 5th century, on the road towards Borgo Velino: redone in the 12th century (the period of its campanile) its Romanesque portal now graces Antrodoco's cathedral, but inside it has kept its 16th-century *Pietà*, by a German sculptor, and its hexagonal baptistry from the 9th century, with Renaissance frescoes on the life of St John the Baptist and scenes from the Old Testament.

Amatrice

Saying 'Amatrice' to an Italian usually conjures up a visions of spaghetti or *bucatini* in a pungently delicious *all'amatriciana* sauce of fresh tomatoes, chopped bacon, onion and garlic, topped with tangy grated pecorino. Students of Renaissance art may recognize the name Cola d'Amatrice (Nicola Filotesio, 1489–1559), a so-so painter and architect who was influenced by the Umbrians and spent much of his career in the Marche. He didn't leave anything in his home town, although it has compensated with reproductions of his work on display in the **Centro Culturale di Sant'Emidio** in Via Cola (*open summer 5–8pm, winter Sat 5–8, Sun 11–1 and 4–8*). There are two good churches to look at: **Sant'Agostino**, on the northeast edge of town, with a late Gothic door and 15th-century frescoes, and the Romanesque–Gothic **San Francesco**, with a beautiful marble portal and a pretty Gothic reliquary on the altar.

Southern Lazio

12

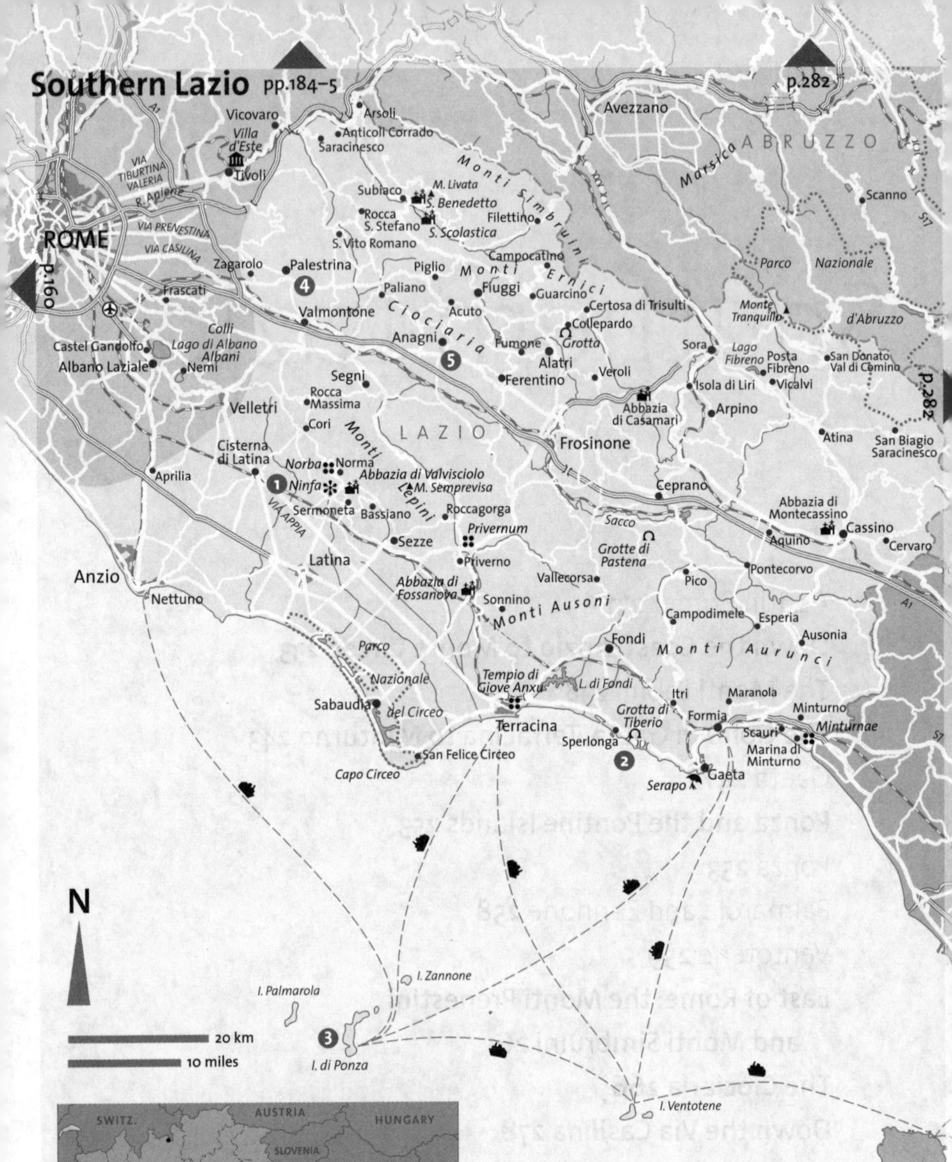

Highlights

1 Botanical gardens and medieval ruins of Ninfa

2 Romantic, whitewashed Sperlonga and the Grotto of Tiberius

3 Ponza, one of Italy's most beautiful islands

4 Palestrina, built inside a gigantic Roman Temple of Fortune

5 The 'Medieval Sistine Chapel' in Anagni cathedral

On a map, the territory seems to be a hopeless muddle, with little patches of mountains scattered randomly, and rivers that take their own sweet time about finding their way to the sea. When you're on the ground it will start to make sense. Those are the Monti Ernici over there, where Fiuggi is, and those rugged bare ones are the Monti Lepini – so Rome must be that way...

And after a spell in southern Lazio, you'll start to wonder how there could be such a perfectly amenable corner of Italy where no one ever goes. The secret is that the region comes in second, or close to it, in nearly everything: there are gracious hill towns not quite so packed with art as those of Tuscany, a stretch of coastline (the Gulf of Gaeta), not quite as spectacular as Liguria's or Amalfi's, and a mini-archipelago of lovely islands that are just a little further out of the way than the famous ones in the Bay of Naples.

The coastline, at least, was popular enough in ancient times; the nabobs of ancient Rome have left it littered with the ruins of their seaside villas and temples. Before them, this was the homeland of the Latins, the Volsci and various other people who did their best to see that we never want for archaeological remains. Like northern Lazio, the region's later history is bound up with the great families of Rome and their popes, who contributed most of the art, including the wonderful medieval frescoes of Anagni and Subiaco.

A Latin Primer

The nation that would one day set all the world to conjugating wandered into Italy some time in the 2nd millennium BC, one of a group of similar Indo-European peoples who get lumped together in the histories as 'Italics'. The record is murky at best; some claim that the Latins, or 'proto-Latins', spread themselves all over Italy at first, and were gradually beaten back after that, finally finding a safe home in the fertile and easily defensible Alban hills south of the Tiber, later adding some territory to the south as far as Monte Circeo. Their closest cousins seem to have been the Veneti, who lived up in the Veneto, and the Siculi of Sicily.

Like the Etruscans (and many other Italian peoples) the Latins were organized in a loose federal league of city-states, the importance of which was more religious than political. Its centre was the sanctuary of Jupiter in *Alba Longa*; besides Alba and Rome, the leading cities were Tusculum, Tívoli, Praeneste, Gabii, Lavinium and Ardea. The Latins were bound together by a common language and culture; they intermarried freely between the city-states, and when a Latin moved to a new town – or even visited – he had the right to vote and to bring legal actions. These, of course, were two of their favourite pastimes; the passion for politicking, orating and litigating that eventually made the Roman Republic the most remarkable state of antiquity was something the Latins had in the blood.

One feature that distinguished them from most of their neighbours was their practice of burial by cremation, leaving the ashes in a little urn shaped like the house in which the deceased had lived. No doubt about it, to these Latins there was no place like home. The household gods, the *lares* and *penates*, were probably more important to their religion in these early days than any high-flown cults of Jupiter or Diana, and the households they protected were among the most tightly controlled patriarchal tyrannies of all time. *Paterfamilias* was an absolute ruler, who had the right of life and death over wife and children. Sons did not even reach their legal majority until their father died.

When ancient historians considered Latins, Romans and their spectacular rise, they wrote that the most remarkable quality of this people was their piety. Early Latin religion is a curious and little-understood business, with its shadowy pantheon and infinity of taboos – not to mention the occasional human sacrifice. As for the embellishments of civilization, these were not their strong point. Such art and architecture as they had came from the more advanced Etruscans and Greeks, along with their alphabet.

Almost from the founding of Rome in the 8th century BC, that city began to diverge sharply from its Latin neighbours. Though Latin in language and customs, Rome from the start seems to have been a place where people from many nations settled; its location at the intersection of many trade routes, and its position on the border of Etruria, helped give the new city a more cosmopolitan outlook. Under the Etruscan kings, the Tarquins of the 6th century, Rome appears to have dominated its Latin neighbours at a time when the strength and influence of Etruscan civilization was at its height.

The expulsion of the Etruscans from Rome in 509 BC, and the subsequent defeats at the hands of the Latins and Greeks that led to the end of Etruscan power in Latium, paradoxically made both Romans and Latins poorer and weaker than before. Under the Tarquins, Rome had lorded it over the other Latin cities; now they were able to break free, and formed the Latin League under the leadership of Tusculum to keep Rome at bay. Latin territory, already small enough, got even smaller, as the Volsci came down from the Apennines and conquered Ánzio, Cori, Terracina and Velletri. Even with such embarrassments as the sacking at the hands of the Gauls in 390, Rome was growing inexorably stronger. In 358 the city signed a treaty with the Latins under terms of relative equality; by 340, however, they were at war again, and the total victory of Rome two years later meant the end of the Latin League and the freedom of its city states. From then on the Latins had a new destiny, as part of Rome.

Under the *jus Latii*, they held rights just slightly inferior to those of Roman citizens, but, as with Etruria to the north, getting sucked into the Roman military machine meant the depopulation of Latium, and the sharp decline of its cities. Many Latins found new homes in Rome itself, though many others were transplanted to the Latin colonies Rome founded in all the new lands it conquered. Southern Lazio was, along with Etruria, the proving ground for this exceptionally effective method of empire-building, by which the Latins, along with their language and customs, were spread across the Mediterranean.

To complete the *dramatis personae* for southern Lazio, we should mention some of the other occupants of the region in historic times: the **Ausoni** and **Aurunci** do not count for much, both small tribes of the coastal mountains who were thoroughly squashed and assimilated by more aggressive neighbours; little is known about either, or about the **Aequi**, who occupied the area around the Monti Simbruini and get a brief role in ancient histories as enemies of Rome. The **Rutuli**, in Virgil's *Aeneid* the most powerful members of the anti-Trojan coalition under their legendary leader Turnus, were really a branch of the Latins, with their capital at Ardea.

The Latins' most powerful enemies were the **Volsci**, who started out in the upper valley of the Liri and were pushed into southern Lazio by the Samnites. There they formed a strong state around their capital Privernum, and warred fitfully against Rome for over two centuries. For a while, after the sack of Rome by the Gauls, the Volsci seemed to be getting the upper hand, but when Rome recovered it dispatched the Volsci once and for all, annexing their lands in 304. After that, the Volsci became Romanized so completely that they lost their original language and customs; consequently very little is known about them either.

The **Hernici**, who figure prominently in the *Aeneid*, were later generally allies of the Romans, as their local enemies, the Aequii to the north and the Volsci to the south, were against them. Their territories stretched from the Sacco to Lake Fucinus in the Abruzzo, and their capital was Anagni. In the mid-4th century they fell out with the Romans and suffered the usual fate, succumbing in 306 when Anagni was taken; like the Volsci they soon lost their language and cultural identity. Finally there are the **Samnites**, long one of the most powerful nations of Italy, with their base in the southern Apennines. These tough and rather uncouth (to hear the Romans tell it, anyhow) mountaineers occupied only a small part of the present Lazio, the mountains of the southeastern corner, but they controlled much of southern Italy, and were to prove the toughest foes the Romans ever had to face, not completely succumbing until the 1st century BC. Most scholars believe that the **Sabines** of the mountains northeast of Rome (now in Rieti province) were a branch, and perhaps the original stock, of the Samnites.

Down the Coast: Ánzio to Monte Circeo

Ánzio

The coastal road from Ostia, the SS601 Via Severiana, passes plenty of beaches, including those around the promontory of **Ánzio**, the main feature of the coast between the Tiber and Monte Circeo. Originally its port, *Caenon*, was a favourite base for ancient pirates. The Volsci occupied it in the early 5th century BC, and made *Antium* a redoubtable adversary of Rome. The legendary patrician Gnaeus Marcus Coriolanus, named and famed for his courage at the siege of Coriolo, came here when he was banished from Rome by the tribunes of the people in 491 BC for demanding the elimination of their office during a famine. As Shakespeare's tragedy relates, he took refuge with the king of the Volscians, and took command of his troops against Rome, only turning back at the pleas of his mother and wife. Rome's war with the Volscians ended in 338 BC with the destruction of Antium, a triumph the Romans celebrated by tearing the *rostra*, or prows, off their ships and using them to decorate

Getting There and Around

The main Rome–Naples **rail** line runs parallel to the coast a few kilometres inland. For Terracina and Sabaudia, get off at Priverno; for Sperlonga, at Fondi; for Gaeta, at Fórmia, and take local buses. There are regular COTRAL **buses** to all towns, including direct connections between Ánzio to Latina (weekdays only) and to Velletri. For connections to the Pontine Islands, *see* p.254.

Latina's station is down by the sea at Latina Scalo, and is linked once an hour by bus to Latina, Cori, Norma, Rocca Mássima, Bassiano, and Sermoneta. The main COTRAL station in Latina is on Viale Giulio Cesare, **t** 0773 664067, and also has connections to the above villages and Rome (Anagnina and EUR), Frosinone, Fossanova, Terracina and all the other towns in the province.

Tourist Information

Ánzio: Piazza Pia 19, **t** 0698 45147, **f** 0698 48135.
Latina: Via Duca del Mare 19, **t** 0773 695404, **f** 0773 661266, *www.aptlatinaturismo.it*.
San Felice Circeo: Piazza Lanzuisi, **t** 0773 547770 (*open daily 10–12 and 5–8; in winter closed Sat and Sun pm*).

Where to Stay and Eat

Ánzio ✉ 00042

★★★★**Grand Hotel dei Cesari**, Via Mantova 3, **t** 06 987901, **f** 06 780835 (*expensive*). Julius and Co. would have liked this large, comfortable establishment with an annexe right on the sea, fitness centre, private beach, pool, palestra, and piano bar too. *Open all year*.

★★★**Lido Garda**, Piazza G. Caboto, **t** 06 987 0354, **f** 06 986 5386, *www.lidogarda.com* (*moderate*). Half the size, this amiable hotel is by the Ánzio Colonia station and the sea. It has a pool and private beach; rooms are attractive and modern. *Closed Nov–Feb*.

A favourite of Roman day-trippers, Ánzio has some of the finest seafood restaurants along the coast.

Romolo al Porto, Via Porto Innocenziano 19, **t** 06 984 4079 (*expensive*). This famous, family-run restaurant is not the prettiest in town, but the food is prepared just so to bring out the full flavour of the fish and shellfish – the *tartare di triglie* (red mullet) and *minestra di pesce* are superb. *Closed Wed*.

Sbarco di Ánzio, **t** 06 984 7675 (*expensive*). Its elegant near neighbour and rival is just as good, and takes special pride in the quality of its fish, plucked fresh from the sea, and served in all the traditional Italian styles. *Closed Tues, Nov*.

the Tribunes' public speaking platform in the forum – hence our *rostrum*. Like elephants, the Romans never forgot.

Antium was wasted again, during the civil war in 87 BC by Marius, when it supported Sulla, but after that it settled down to its career as the closest and most popular seaside resort of ancient Rome. Cicero, Maecenus and Augustus were the first to build themselves villas in the area; Augustus' **Imperial Palace** (*open 10–1, July–Aug also 6–9pm; guided visits on request in July–Aug Thurs–Sun, call* **t** *06 9849 9407*) on the promontory overlooking the sea would be one of the most favoured retreats of the Caesars. Caligula liked it so much he wanted to move the capital to Ánzio, while Nero, who was born here, was its greatest benefactor, filling it full of statues such the *Apollo Belvedere* (in the Vatican) and *The Maid of Ánzio*, believed to be an original Greek Hellenistic work, in Rome's National Museum. Above the beach of Arco Muto, 'the mute arch', its ruins stretched along the cliffs for 800 yards – walls, mosaics, the *cryptoporticus* (or Domitian's Library) and *thermae* can be seen, although nothing remains of the famous temple of Fortune, mentioned by Horace. Nero also commissioned Antium's **harbour** just below, an ancient feat of maritime engineering; his

Pierino, Piazza C Battisti 3, **t** 06 984 5683 (book; *expensive*). This fashionable restaurant overlooks the town hall rather than the sea, but has a pretty summer terrace as well; here the seafood is prepared with a deft, light touch – try the spaghetti with anchovies and pecorino. *Closed Mon, and afternoons in summer, mid-Nov, Feb.*

Latina ✉ 04100

★★★★**Victoria Residence Palace**, Via V. Rossetti 24, **t** 0773 663966, **f** 0773 489592 (*moderate*). Just south of the centre; with comfortable if business-like rooms, but it's also the only hotel in town with a pool in the garden, as well as tennis and a gym, and Latina's most reputed restaurant, **L'Abaco**.

★★★★**Cami Hotel**, Via Canova 12, **t** 0773 661281, **f** 0773 661153 (*expensive–moderate*). In the same part of town but less expensive, the Cami offers comfortable, functional, soundproofed rooms and buffet breakfast.

If you're just looking for a place to stop for the night, there are plenty of hotels just 7km to the south at Capo Portiere on Latina's Lido:

★★★**Miramare**, right on the beach, Lungomare Capoportiere, **t** 0773 273470, **f** 0773 273862 (*moderate–cheap*). Friendly and comfortable.

Enoteca l'Orologio, Piazza del Popolo 20, **t** 0773 692037 (*moderate*). Latina's best-known restaurant features fine wines and cuisine to match. *Closed Sun, Mon lunch and Aug.*

In Latina Lido, dozens of seafood restaurants with terraces line the Via Lungomare: try **Il Tarantino**, Via Lungomare 150, **t** 0773 272253 (*moderate, closed Wed*), or the smaller but no less classic **Risacca**, Via Lungomare 93, **t** 0773 273223 (*moderate, closed Thurs*).

San Felice Circeo ✉ 04017

If you're looking for a resort hotel with all the creature comforts, San Felice comes up with the goods.

★★★★**Punta Rossa**, right out on the promontory 5km away from the centre at Quarto Caldo, **t** 0773 548 085, **f** 0773 548 075 (*very expensive–expensive*). Mediterranean-style hotel with indoor and outdoor pools to go with its beach; rooms are very comfortable and most have lovely views.

★★★★**Circeo Park Hotel**, Lungomare Circe 49, **t** 0773 548815, **f** 0773 548028 (*very expensive–expensive*). Sits on the sea in its garden, with a pool, tennis and beach, and well-equipped rooms, a private dock and good restaurant. *Open July, Aug.*

★★**Giardino degli Ulivi**, Via XXIV Maggio 13, **t** 0773 548034 (*moderate–cheap*). A pretty, simple little hotel in the centre of town with a sunny terrace.

★★**Capo Circeo**, Lungomare Viale Europa, **t/f** 0773 540408 (*moderate–cheap*). Down by the beach; the best rooms have sea views. *Open Easter–Sept.*

piers, two of his jetties and the grotto-warehouses are still visible. He may also have built the intimate **Roman Theatre**, now a wistful ruin on Antium's acropolis (near the modern church of S. Teresa). **Villa Spigarelli** marks the traditional site of Coriolanus' tomb and a villa built under Nero's reign; the lawyer who built the current villa in the 1920s tried to reproduce an ancient Roman one, incorporating many original features.

Ánzio's fortunes began to improve again in 1700, when Pope Innocent XII built another harbour next to Nero's. Cardinals began building summer villas where the pagans once frolicked, and Pius IX came here each summer to the **Villa Albani**. At the turn of the 19th century Liberty-style villas went up, along with the opulent, elliptical **Paradiso sul Mare** with its silver cupolas, designed as a casino by Cesare Bazzini and decorated inside with frescoes and statues of the seasons, although its career as a gambling den was short-lived – Pius X found it far too close to the Vatican and closed it down. Fellini turned it into Rimini's Grand Hotel in *Amarcord* – you can take in the lovely frescoed interior when an exhibition is on.

On 22 January 1944 the British and American forces found its beaches an ideal spot for a landing, a bloody, somewhat bungled, but ultimately successful end-run that forced the Germans to abandon their Gustav Line at Montecassino and opened the way for the liberation of Rome; near the station is the **Museo dello Sbarco di Ánzio**, founded on the 50th anniversary of the event in the Villa Adele (*open Tues, Thurs–Sat, 9.30–12 and 3.30–6; Mon, Wed, Sun 9.30–12*): not 'a cold conglomeration of junk' as the prospectus says, but a rather charming home-made effort with fashion dummies modelling army uniforms. The villa itself is one of Ánzio's most splendid, built by a cardinal in 1620 and owned at various times by the Pamphili, Borghese and Aldobrandini; part of it became a hotel, and in 1937 it served as the seat of the Secretary of Fascism Abroad. Large military cemeteries surround Ánzio.

Latina and the Pontine Marshes

> *...nowhere else has the creative power of Fascism left a deeper mark. The immense works can be summed up in the lapidary phrase of Il Duce: 'You redeem the land, you found some cities.'*
>
> from a 1939 Italian guidebook

You wouldn't have been travelling this way 70 years ago, when the broad plain of the Pontine Marshes was the biggest no man's land in Italy, racked by malaria and healthy only for the water buffalo. Under the Romans, canals were dug to reclaim the swamps, but they became blocked up in the Dark Ages when no one had the money to keep them cleared. Once again during the 13th century some of the marshes were drained, but a few centuries of papal rule had the area back to its pristine emptiness when Mussolini decided to make it one of the showpieces of his regime. It wasn't as heroic a gesture, or as expensive, as Fascist propaganda of the day made out. The Papal States, in a rare burst of activity in the 1770s, had started the job (and, more typically, abandoned it half-finished), and Mussolini, as in all of his big projects, was able to draw on free 'volunteer' labour from convicts, conscripted labourers and the Fascist youth groups. But at least it got done; today, except for the small corner preserved as a park and wildlife refuge, the Pontine Marshes no longer exist, and brand-new towns like Aprilia, Pomézia, Pontinia and Sabaudia sit amid miles of prosperous farms as curious monuments to the more constructive side of Fascism.

Aprilia is nothing to look at, and **Pomézia** is surrounded by American-style sprawl that has made it perhaps the most hideous town in all Italy. But **Latina**, largest of the Pontine foundations and Italy's youngest provincial capital (1932), is a bright and busy place. As the most ambitious project of 20th-century Italian architecture and planning, it's worth some attention; our century has done far worse. The city (originally named *Littoria*) is built on an octagonal plan, centred on what after the war was renamed Piazza del Popolo; it reminds everyone who has ever written about it of some vaguely unsettling scene from a de Chirico painting, with plenty of open spaces and chunky Mussolini travertine palazzi – today these attract a lot of rude graffiti. The piazzas are built into the plan in an irregular fashion, an attempt to translate something of the picturesque asymmetricality of the old Italian urban design into a modern form. The Mussolini Deco architecture – smooth, clean lines, stucco painted in earth tones, creative uses of fenestration and buildings tied together with simple, open travertine porticos – is rather restrained here, though it lapses briefly into the absurd with a government office block on Corso della Repubblica called the **Palazzo M**, draped with heroic statuary and built in the shape of every good Fascist's favourite initial.

Monte Circeo and the National Park

Between Ánzio and Capo Circeo the coast is almost a solid stretch of beaches and dunes (we would bet Fellini shot part of *La Strada* along the coastal Via Severiana/ SS601). Behind it you'll find the **Agro Pontino**, the prosperous agricultural area reclaimed from the marshes: a broad plain with long, die-straight roads branching off the Appian Way, lined with pines and drainage canals. Punctuating the end of the former marshes, **Monte Circeo** was an island in ancient times, one of many candidates around the Mediterranean for Homer's Isle of Circe from the *Odyssey*. Ruins of a temple to Maga Circe at Picco di Circe, at the 177ft summit of the promontory, are evidence that this claim was taken pretty seriously – Circe and Odysseus' son, after all, gets credit for founding towns in the area, as part of the ancient Italian obsession with Homeric legitimacy. The acropolis of the ancient town of **Circeii**, a stiff hike up from San Felice Circeo, has impressive polygonal walls (especially to the west), a main gate with traces of the door jambs (a bit difficult to get to), and a stone hypogeum.

San Felice Circeo, on the slopes, was a Templar town, and still has a tower and cloister built by the knights, as well as a series of Martello towers built by Pope Pius IV in 1562 to defend this coast from Saracen pirates. In its most recent incarnation, San Felice is a growing resort, offering boat trips around the big rock and its many caves, many of which were inhabited in Palaeolithic times – in the case of the Grotta Guattari, right in San Felice, 100,000 years ago. Specialized guided tours are offered through the tourist office; the **Museo Homo Sapiens e Habitat** (*open summer daily exc Mon 5.30–8pm, winter by appointment only,* ***t*** *0773 5221*) in the Templars' tower has displays on the human and environmental history of the area. Since 1934 most of this area has been included in the Circeo National Park, a beautiful and unspoiled expanse of watery landscape. Migratory birds of all kinds stop here twice a year, and besides a wealth of wild flowers and primeval pine forests you may see woodpeckers, buzzards, peregrine falcons and herons – maybe even that most overdressed of sea birds, the Cavaliere d'Italia. The Visitor Centre for the **Circeo National Park** is on the outskirts of Sabaudia (***t*** *0773 511385; open 9–1 and 3–8, 3–7 in winter*), and has a museum devoted to the park with exhibits on the archaeological remains and the wildlife you might encounter – including more than 250 species of bird. There are two more **park information offices** in San Felice Circeo (***t*** *0773 549038*) and at the Associazione Pro in Sabaudia (***t*** *0773 351 5146*), and all three organize accompanied visits across the lake in a boat to the **Villa of Emperor Domitian**, but you must book well in advance.

Sabaudia, adjacent to the park in a lovely setting of beaches and pine groves, is another of Mussolini's new towns, a smaller version of Latina built by some of the same planners and architects. This was a major propaganda show for the Fascists; as the florid inscription on the town hall explains, Sabaudia (named for the Royal House of Savoy) was built entirely in 253 days, starting on 5 August 1933, to 'redeem this land from its deathly sterility and the lethargy of millennia'.

The Monti Lepini

Before the Pontine Marshes were drained, people could only live as close as the nearest hills where the malaria couldn't reach them; some farmers would have to descend daily to the plains to tend gardens and orchards, or check on their buffalo. From the old days, there is left a string of hill towns on the southern slopes of the **Monti Lepini**; the main attractions are one ancient town that has survived, Sermoneta, and one that hasn't, the lost city of Ninfa.

The northernmost of these towns, set in a sea of olives and vineyards, is **Cori**. Like Rome and so many other Latin towns, Cori likes to trace its founding to Trojan refugees. It may well be 3,000 years old, though the Cyclopean **walls** that link the lower and upper parts of town are 5th century BC; these may have been built either by the Latins or the Volsci, who were contending for the city at that time. There are also many Roman remains, including an intact bridge, the **Ponte della Catena**, at the entrance to town, an enormous well, the **Pozzo Dorico** and, at its very top, the so-called **Temple of Hercules** (really a temple of Jupiter), a small 1st-century BC Doric building complete except for its roof. The centre of town is still resolutely medieval: the partially covered **Via del Porticato** leads to the church of **Santa Oliva**, with good medieval and Renaissance frescoes; nearby are ruins of another temple, dedicated to Castor and Pollux. The oldest church, **Santa Maria della Pietà**, was built over a temple of Fortune.

Interesting towns all beginning with 'N' lie 10km further south. **Norma**, built on the edges of a steep, curving spur over the Pontine plain, seems almost like a city suspended in the air, and on fine weekend days, as often as not you'll see hang-gliders floating down from its pinnacle. Norma's name comes from **Norba**, the 'stone town' a kilometre away, which in spite of 2.3km of Cyclopean walls was besieged and destroyed by the legions in the Social Wars in 89 BC, never to be rebuilt. To help you

Where to Stay and Eat

Norma ✉ 04010

***__Villa del Cardinale__, Via dei Colli, t 0773 354 611, f 0773 354442, *villa.cardinale@flashnet.it* (*moderate–cheap*). In the upper town, in a former seminary, surrounded by gardens. Not as austere as it sounds: all rooms are en suite, there's a restaurant, and the owner can arrange horse-riding from nearby stables.

Sermoneta ✉ 04010

***__Principe Serrone__, Via del Serrone 1, t 0773 30342, f 0773 30336 (*moderate–cheap*). This one hotel makes Sermoneta the best base for touring around this region. Set in the medieval centre, in a building dating from the 11th century, it has only 13 rooms, assured tranquillity and pretty views over the valley.

Al Castello, Via della Fortezza 7, t 0773 30404 (*moderate–inexpensive*). This nearby restaurant's good home cooking features *tagliatelle* with wild mushrooms, and the Italian version of shish kebab: *spiedini di pecora*. *Closed Thurs.*

imagine what it was like, however, Norma has virtually reconstructed it in the **Museo Virtuale** (*open Tues–Fri 9.30–12.30, Sat–Sun 4–7 only; adm*); it also contains more usual archaeological finds, incluing a beautiful sarcophagus from the 2nd century BC. Norma also turns its attention to one of the sweetest of subjects in the **Museo del Cioccolato**, Via Colle Catilina 1 (*open Sept–May 9–12 and 3–6*), with displays on the history of chocolate from Meso-America to the present, and a fine collection of 20th-century chocolate advertisements.

Ninfa, the 'Pompeii of the Middle Ages'

***t** 0773 695404; open April–Oct, first Sat and Sun of each month, April–June also on the third Sun of each month, 9–12 and 3–6; 45min guided tour only; adm exp. Limited number of tickets available, from the site, the Latina tourist office, or at Rome's Palazzo Caetani porter's lodge, Via Botteghe Oscure 32, **t** 06 6880 3231.*

On the plain below Norma, the town of Ninfa grew up in the early Middle Ages next to a romantic spring-fed lake. At various times it belonged to a Byzantine emperor, the popes and the counts of Tusculum, and like any town close to Rome it had its share of historical intrigues linked to the squabbles of popes and emperors. Two popes were in fact elected here, and Frederick Barbarossa sacked the town in 1171. At the end of the 13th century, when Boniface VIII was using the Church's money to buy up much of southern Lazio for his family, Ninfa became the possession of Boniface's nephew Pietro Caetani. Later, the family split up into spiteful factions, one based in nearby Sermoneta and supporting the popes, the other down in Fondi (*see* p.245), partisans of the Kings of Naples. The Fondi crew got the upper hand in the late 14th century, and they sacked and burned Ninfa in 1382. The town never recovered; as the cultivated land around it reverted to swamp the site became increasingly unhealthy, and by the 1600s Ninfa was abandoned and nearly forgotten.

If the Caetani were the death of Ninfa, they also occasioned its resurrection. In 1921, Gelasio Caetani, a skilled engineer, began to reclaim the land and plant the gardens, a project taken up by his English wife Ada Wilbraham, and then by an American daughter-in-law, Marguerite Chapin. Decades of loving care have made it one of the great botanical gardens of Europe, with plants from all over the world that give it something to show off in every season of the year, in an exceptionally romantic setting laced with water: the lake, the little river Ninfa, and the moat of the medieval walls. A great many of the medieval buildings survive, at least in ruins, with beautiful plantings all around to keep melancholy at bay. The **castle**, with its tall tower of the 1300s, is Ninfa's landmark, next to the intact medieval **Municipio**. Some of the town walls and defence towers survive, along with the imposing ruins of its most important church, **Santa Maria Maggiore**.

Ninfa is run by the Roffredo Caetani Foundation (the last member of the Caetani family died in 1977) and the WWF, in a protected zone covering nearly 2,000 acres. The foundation is more interested in maintaining Ninfa than showing it off; if they open it at all, it is only to meet expenses.

Sermoneta

Ninfa lies in the *comune* of **Sermoneta**, a hill town in a lovely setting with the best-preserved medieval centre of all the towns on the Monti Lepini, still entirely closed within its walls and guarded by the restored **Castello Caetani** (*guided tours daily exc Thurs; Oct–Mar weekdays at 10, 11, 12, 2, 3, 4, also at 5pm on weekends; April–Sept 10, 11, 12, 3, 4, 5 and 6; adm*). Parts of it are early medieval, but Antonio da Sangallo built most of what you see for the Borgias; they stole it from the Caetani, and Lucrezia Borgia spent some time here. The Caetani got it back in 1504 and held it ever after, with an unpleasant Napoleonic interlude – the thieving French made off with all the furniture and 36 cannons, though the Caetani bedrooms have been redone with furnishings from the 1500s, sharing the space with frescoed allegories of virtues and vices. The most interesting part is the 1400s *scuderia* and adjacent soldiers' quarters, including a prison covered with graffiti; in the Renaissance this was a little more civilized than today:

S'ingiustmente per sii carcerato,
Ricordati di qualch'altro peccato.
(Though you're locked up unjustly, reflect on your other sins.)

This part of the castle belongs to a ghost, still occasionally seen and even photographed. He's a 20-year-old Caetani duke, who was killed in the soldiers' mess by the Borgia troops while defending the castle.

In summer, the guided tours are sometimes extended to include the **Loggia dei Mercanti** (town hall) and some of Sermoneta's medieval tower houses. The 12th-century **Collegiata di Santa Maria** has a very Roman medieval campanile, Romanesque and Gothic frescoes, including a fine but badly damaged *Last Judgment*, an *Annunciation* by Guido Reni, and best of all a glittering *Madonna* by the quattrocento Florentine Benozzo Gozzoli; surrounded by angels, birds and flowers, she is one of the most transcendent Madonnas you'll ever see.

Between Sermoneta and Ninfa is one of Lazio's three Cistercian Gothic foundations, the little sister of the famous abbeys at Fossanova and Casamari: the **Abbey of Valvisciolo** (*open daily 9–12 and 3.30–6; no entry during Mass*) is in fact the oldest of the three, founded by Greek monks in the 700s and later the property of the Templars before they passed it on to the Cistercians, who rebuilt it as a simple Gothic church with a fine cloister.

Another hill town immersed in chestnut woods, **Bassiano** makes a cool retreat in the summer. Built in the form of a spiral up its hill, and enclosed by 12th-century walls, Bassiano has several churches with frescoes – those in **San Nicola di Bari** go back to the 11th century. The great 16th-century editor and publisher Aldus (Aldo Manunzio) may have made his fame and fortune in Venice, but he was born in Bassiano: the **Museo dell'Opera Aldina** (*open June–Sept 9.30–12.30 and 5.30–7, Oct–May 9.30–12.30 and 3.30–5.30; adm*) is devoted to his works and the lovely *aldini* type he invented. Aldus' dolphin-and-anchor colophon was the symbol of the first and finest of all publishing houses. No one has ever spread so much learning around; he's as important a part of the Renaissance as Michelangelo. Three kilometres away at Selvascura, the **Santuario del Crocifisso** has a wooden *Crucifix* sculpted by Fra Vincenzo Pietrosanti, another native son and one of the 17th century's masters of the genre. Bassiano is by the highest of the Monti Lepini, the 5,039ft **Monte Semprevista**, the 'always seen'; from its summit, which can be reached by a difficult road up from Bassiano, you can see Vesuvius, the Alban Hills, and the Pontine Islands.

Sezze, another town under Semprevisa, predates even Cori; in a cave called Riparo Roberto, drawings in ochre dated 3000 BC were discovered on the wall. Like the other towns in the Monti Lepini, Sezze belonged to the Volsci; the Roman castrum was built right over the top, and the medieval town on top of that. The **Antiquarium** (*open Tues–Sat 9–1 and 4–7, Sun 9–1*) contains bits from all eras: prehistoric artefacts, mosaics, Roman coins, ceramics and Baroque paintings. After that you may clear your head of archaeology with something unexpected – a toy museum. The **Museo del Giocattolo** (*open by request,* **t** *0773 803797*) has a small collection of traditional toys from the region and around Italy.

Priverno and Fossanova

In Book VII of the *Aeneid*, Virgil conjures up a vision:

Besides all these there came from the Volscian nation Camilla
Leading a cavalry column, squadrons petalled with bronze:
A warrior maid, her woman's hand unaccustomed to womanly tasks –
lines 773–6; trans. C. Day Lewis

Camilla, the legendary Volscian princess who grew up in the woods and was nourished by a wild mare, was the daughter of King Metabo of *Privernum*; in the *Aeneid*, she led the Volsci into battle, shooting the Trojans full of arrows before finally succumbing in Book X. Her city, the capital of the Volsci, was eventually destroyed by the Romans and refounded on the plains. After the vicissitudes of the centuries, *Privernum* migrated upwards in the Dark Ages to become the hill town of **Priverno**, one that maintained its independence in the Middle Ages and lorded it over neighbouring towns, including Sezze and Terracina.

Today it isn't capital of anything, but Priverno still has a resolute civic pride, exemplified by the stout 13th-century **Palazzo Comunale** on the central Piazza Giovanni XXIII; it faces the **cathedral**, mostly 17th century, with only a pointed-arch portico to betray its Gothic origins – the French Cistercians were busy here too. A long flight of steps behind the cathedral takes you to the former bishop's palace, now an exceptionally well-laid out and informative **Museo Archeologico** (*open Tues–Fri 9–1, Sat–Sun 9–1 and 3–8; adm*). The prize exhibit is a mosaic of that popular Roman theme, a passage along the Nile with crocodiles and hippos, fellahs and ducks (like the more famous one at Palestrina), though this museum really shines at insights into everyday life in Roman times, with copious explanations (only in Italian): lead pipes, kitchen gear, a nine-man-morris board carved on a stone (always a popular game: there's one carved into a step in the Roman Forum), a glass windowpane (1st century AD, when it was a new invention). There are also reconstructed parts of an early temple, with narrow gables, projecting eaves and terracotta decoration, showing the strong influence of the Etruscans. Part of the museum's collection is kept in the nearby church of **Santa Chiara**, wrecked by Napoleon and only recently restored.

Some of Priverno's old churches have intriguing medieval frescoes done by local artists, particularly **San Giovanni Evangelista**, a few streets south of the museum, with a 1300s scene of the *Martyrdom of St Catherine*, and **San Benedetto**, near the walls at Porta San Benedetto, with the *Madonna della Misericordia* (*if they aren't open, try ringing the Ufficio Cultura Priverno,* **t** *0773 903088*).

The archaeological site of Roman **Privernum** (*same hours as the museum*) is by the river at Mezzagosto, amid fields of artichokes, modern Priverno's bread and butter. Considerable remains have been excavated, including part of the wall, the baths, the Capitolium, and a nearby peristyle house where the mosaic in the museum was discovered. Just south of Priverno, on the road to Fossanova, the 1569 **Palazzo Tolomeo Gallio** stands in a beautiful wooded park. It houses a new museum of mathematics designed by the University of Florence, the **Garden of Archimedes** (*open mid-Sept–May Tues–Fri 9–1, Sat–Sun 9–1 and 3–6; June–mid-Sept Tues–Fri 4–8, Sat–Sun 10–1 and 4–8; Aug daily 10–1 and 4–8; guided visits; adm; www.math.unifi.it/archimede*), with plenty of interactive exhibits and child-friendly activities.

Five kilometres south of Priverno, **Fossanova** is a lovely hamlet of old red ochre-painted houses covered in vines, with one of the finest Gothic buildings in Italy for a centrepiece: the 12th-century **Cistercian abbey** (*currently closed for restoration*). The monastery was actually founded by Benedictines in the 800s; and they handed it over to the Cistercians about 1130. These dour, austere monks, followers of the puritanical St Bernard of Clairvaux, were the medieval experts in reclaiming waste land and making a profit from it. The stretch of the Pontine Marshes granted to them by Pope Innocent III was one of their biggest challenges, and they set up a string of monasteries along the hills on its edge, of which the most important were Casamari, Valvisciolo and this one, which gets its name from the Cistercians' drainage canal, the 'new ditch'. Besides their skills at draining swampland, the French monks also brought with them the new Gothic architecture from France. The Italians, on the whole, weren't interested (in the Renaissance they would in fact invent the term 'Gothic', implying that the greatest architectural advance in a thousand years was somehow barbaric), and Fossanova survives along with San Martino nel Cimino near Viterbo, Casamari (*see* p.275), Santa Maria Maggiore in Ferentino and a few others as perhaps the purest examples of the northern style on this side of the Alps. After the 1400s both wealth and talent deserted Fossanova, and after centuries of decadence the monastery was expropriated in 1873, and its treasures dispersed.

This is an abbey of cathedral proportions, a fine, sedate Burgundian Gothic work with a beautiful rose window. Don't expect much sculptural decoration in any Cistercian building; St Bernard wouldn't have approved. Consequently, there is little to look at inside, except the stately rows of piers and pointed arches, bare and harmonious – in a sense Cistercian austerity allows the unadorned Gothic form to make a stronger impression. The vaulted refectory and infirmary are also striking, along with the **cloister**, graced by a little pavilion called the *edicola* that could be the backdrop for some fantasy on a medieval tapestry; the gargoyle cat above it is the only bit of whimsy in the whole abbey. Fossanova's most famous moment came when Thomas Aquinas died here on his way to the Council of Lyon in 1274; his room is now a chapel in the **foresteria**, or hostel, behind the abbey, and has a relief of the saint explaining the *Songs of Songs* to the monks as he passed away. The handsome new **Museo Medievale** (***t*** *0773 905065; open Tues–Fri 9–1, Sat–Sun 9–1 and 2.30–6.30; adm*) is set in one of the cathedral's outbuildings, and has engaging and beautifully presented exhibits depicting life for a Cistercian monk during the Middle Ages (ask for the English-language text at the entrance).

From Fossanova, you can take a dead-end 8km road up to **Sonnino**, an attractive hill town high in the Monti Ausoni; Sonnino was the birthplace of Gasparone, one of Lazio's most celebrated bandits a century ago, and they commemorate him and his colleagues in the **Museo del Brigante** (*open on Sat and Sun by request,* ***t*** *0773 98039*).

The Golfo di Gaeta: Terracina to Minturno

Back on the coast, beyond Monte Circeo the marshes gradually give way to two small coastal ranges, the Monti Ausoni and Monti Aurunci, which combine to frame the most beautiful coastline in Lazio, the Golfo di Gaeta. The precocious trading city of Gaeta was big news here in the Middle Ages, and in later years this coast became contested land between the popes and the kings of Naples. Nowadays it's all about holidays and seafood, and an excellent spot for both. The Monti Aurunci, ever looming in the background, seem bare and dreary from the coast, but their inner strongholds conceal beautiful forests of beech and pine. They are famous for their wild orchids, including the *Ophrys Aurunca*, which grows only here and nowhere else in the world.

Terracina

The Ausonian Mountains begin to crowd against the sea at Terracina, a city perhaps founded by the Etruscans and later a major city of the Volsci, who called it *Anxur*. Emperor Trajan built a great harbour here that made the town the most important port between Rome and Naples; sailors knew they were close when they saw the familiar landmark of the great Temple of Anxurian Jove on the rock above. The Via Appia (called Via Roma in town) runs a straight course through Terracina, with an unremarkable modern town on one side, towards the sea, and on the other, up on the heights, a strangely magical, tiny *centro storico* where great age is almost tangible.

The Capitolium

From Via Roma, Via Annunziata climbs up to the centre of the old town, **Piazza del Municipio**, where an incongruous modern town hall stares across at the ruins of the ancient Capitolium, a 1st-century BC **temple** with three *cellae* – Etruscan style – in a pretty checkerboard pattern of *opus reticulatum* stonework, dedicated to Jove, Juno and Minerva. Ruins are everywhere, including the original paving from the forum and a stretch of the original Appian Way under an undecorated arch just off the piazza on

Getting Around

The bus station next to Fórmia's train station is the central node for the area, with departures for all the mountain villages as well as Cassino, Frosinone, Rome and the coastal towns. For schedules, ring **t** 8488 88088.

Tourist Information

Terracina: Via Leopardi, **t** 0773 727759, **f** 0773 727964.
Sperlonga: Piazza della Rimembrenza, **t** 0771 54796, **f** 0771 549798.
Gaeta: Piazza Traniello, **t** 0771 462767, **f** 0771 465738. Summer tourist office, in Piazza XXIV Maggio, **t** 0771 461165.
Fórmia: Viale Unità d'Italia, **t** 0771 771490, **f** 0771 771386.
Minturno-Scauri: Via Marconi 23, **t** 0771 683788, **f** 0771 683400.

Where to Stay and Eat

In August, expect at least half-board requirements at the resorts – it's an old Italian tradition, when they can get away with it.

Terracina ✉ 04019

★★★★**Grand Hotel Palace,** Via Lungomare Matteotti, **t** 0773 709523, **f** 0773 709623 (*very expensive–moderate*). On the western Lungomare; has beach facilities, well-equipped air-conditioned rooms, a garage and roof garden.
★★★**L'Approdo Grand Hotel**, Lungomare Circe, **t** 0773 726221, **f** 0773 723598, *www. approdohotel.com* (*expensive–moderate*). In an ideal location; also has a private beach and dock, cosy rooms with views, and a babysitting service.
★★**Piccolo**, Viale Circe 224, **t** 0773 730690 (*cheap*). Stylish in a boxy kind of way, and has 20 adequate rooms near the beach.
Trattoria la Magnatora, with outside tables on Piazza della Repubblica, **t** 0773 702417 (*moderate*). A popular place for seafood. *Closed Tues.*
Rifugio Olmata, Via Olmata 88, **t** 0773 700821 (*moderate*). If you've had enough fish for a while, head for some wonderful country cooking with wild mushrooms, wild asparagus and game dishes in season. *Closed Tues.*

Fondi ✉ 04022

La Cantina di Galba, Via Filzi 11, **t** 0771 500058 (*moderate*). An old house built into Fondi's walls that specializes in seafood, with a tasty *risotto marinaro*, and *orate* among other grilled fish. *Closed Tues.*

Sperlonga ✉ 04029

Sperlonga has some nice spots around the beaches:
★★★**La Playa**, in Via C Colombo at Località Fiorelle, **t** 0771 549496, **f** 0771 54106 (*expensive–moderate*). Modern, with pool, tennis courts and a bit of a beach.
★★★**Parkhotel Fiorelle**, **t/f** 0771 548092 (*moderate*). Very close by and slightly less expensive.
★★**Amyclae**, Via C. Colombo 77, **t** 0771 540 8051 (*moderate–cheap*). Further down the strip, this venerable hotel has doubles with balconies right on the beach.
★★**Corallo**, Corso S. Leone, **t/f** 0771 548060 (*moderate*). The place to go if you don't need a beach, and would prefer to watch the people come and go in the pedestrianized centre; welcoming, very well run and has its own restaurant.

There are plenty of relatively inexpensive fish restaurants around the beaches; in town, try **La Siesta**, Viale Ortichello, **t** 0771 54617, good for grilled prawns and lobster (*moderate*, except for the lobster of course), or **La Bisaccia**, Via Romita 25, **t** 0771 54576 (*moderate*), a charming little place serving only fish and pasta dishes. *Closed Nov and Tues in winter.*

Via San Francesco. All these ruins were thoughtfully excavated by Allied artillery and bombers in the war; before that they were all covered with buildings.

Next to the town hall, the medieval Torre Frumentaria is home to Terracina's **Museo Civico** (*open May–Sept 9.30–1.30, Tues–Sat 9–1.30 and 3–9, Sun 10–1 and 5–9, in Aug*

4–10; winter Mon 9.30–1.30, Tues–Sun 9–7; adm), with statues and other finds from the postwar excavations. And next to that is the lovely hotchpotch **Cathedral of San Cesareo**, a building that began its career as a temple of the personified goddess Rome and the deified Augustus – go around the side and you can see the Roman columns showing in the wall. In the 11th century, a Romanesque portico with a mosaic frieze was tacked on; inside this note the big granite Roman bathtub, with a wonderfully preposterous inscription explaining how Christians were 'tortured and butchered in it before the idol of Apollo'. The cathedral has a Moorish-looking 13th-century brick **campanile** similar to Gaeta's. Inside are medieval mosaics in the apse and on the floor, and a Cosmatesque pulpit and paschal candlestick.

Ruins on the Plain

A Capitolium, in which Roman provincial towns imitated the great Capitol in Rome, was often the same as the acropolis of an ancient Greek city. The rest of Roman Terracina, abandoned under the pressure of Muslim pirate raids and malaria, lies under the modern town below: ruins of an **amphitheatre** on Via Martucci, and **baths** close by on Via Leopardi; more baths, part of the ancient spa called the **Terme Nettunie**, are on Piazza della Repubblica. Right on Via Roma, the French neoclassical architect Valadier designed the impressive church of **San Salvatore** (1796) and the semicircular Piazza Garibaldi in front of it. A canal runs through the town, the outlet of the **Canale Pio V** begun by that pope to drain the Pontine Marshes. **Lungomare Circeo** runs along the seaside, flanking an enormous beach that makes Terracina a popular resort today. Beyond Porta Napoli, the southern entrance to the town on Via Roma, you can see an impressive bit of Roman engineering from Emperor Trajan's day: the **Pisco Montano**, a passage cut through the mountainside to accommodate the Appian Way.

Take the Strada Panoramica from Piazza della Repubblica up to the top of Monte Sant'Angelo, to enjoy the views and visit the ruins of the **Temple of Anxurian Jove**, built on a mighty stone platform that survives intact from the 1st century BC (the snack bar has plans of the complex inside, and a model). Built into it is a 200ft arcaded *cryptoporticus*. The mountain gets its name from the early monastery that replaced the temple, dedicated to St Michael; ruins of this too lie scattered about. The mountaintop is now used for a summer theatre festival.

Fondi

From Terracina, you can continue on the coast road or allow yourself to be seduced by the modest charms of **Fondi**, 17km inland on a plain between the Monti Ausoni and the Monti Aurunci decorated with idyllic semi-salt lakes, of which the largest is the **Lago di Fondi**. There'll be plenty of tractors to get in your way, for Fondi is the market for one of the richest fruit and vegetable areas in Lazio. Founded according to legend by Hercules, Fondi became a Volscian town, and was gobbled up by the Romans in 338 BC. Even with good walls – and Fondi has a fine medieval set, built in parts over an ancient Cyclopean circuit – a town on a level site near this coast was bound to see some trouble. They have had their share, worst of all in 1534 when the

Turkish pirate Barbarossa arrived in search of the Countess Giulia Gonzaga, tales of whose beauty had reached the ears of Sultan Suleyman; having been warned, La Gonzaga fled, and in a fury Barbarossa sacked the town and decimated the population, killing many and dragging the rest off to slavery.

At one end of the walls is the bluff and businesslike **Castello** (1329), built from the stones of a ruined amphitheatre, with powerful round towers in the style of the Castel Nuovo in Naples. It houses the **Museo Civico** (*open Mon and Fri 9.30–12.30, Tues and Sat 9.30–12.30 and 5–7, Sun 9.30–1, closed Wed; adm*), with an archaeological collection of mostly Roman finds. Just inside the walls, the **Duomo** recalls Fondi's brief moment in the historical spotlight – in 1387, when an assemblage of cardinals here elected the Antipope Clement VII and started the Great Schism. This 12th-century cathedral has a fine Gothic portal with a bust of St Peter above it by Arnolfo di Cambio. Inside is one of the best of all Cosmatesque pulpits, Clement's antipapal throne, and a 4th-century Byzantine cross with portraits of Emperor Constantine and his mother, St Helen.

Fondi's streets still follow their Roman grid plan without much change; some of them are paved with lava – volcanic basalt – like towns in Sicily. Off Corso Dante, you can find one of the oldest parts of town, a nest of narrow alleys still called the **Giudea**. Fondi had an important Jewish population as early as the 4th century, and it lasted through the Middle Ages. In the centre of town, the 15th-century **Santa Maria Assunta** has a wealth of Renaissance furnishings and Neapolitan-school frescoes.

Sperlonga and the Grotto of Tiberius

Back on the coast road, **Sperlonga** is a perfect small resort, with a romantic, whitewashed medieval quarter high on its steep promontory and miles of fine beaches to either side. Like the rest of the coast, it was attacked numerous times, most memorably in 1534 by the pirate Barbarossa, who treated it to a brutal sacking on his way to Fondi. Sperlonga's name comes from *spelunca*, or cave. South of the town, the coastal Via Flacca passes directly over the seaside **Grotto of Tiberius** (*entrance through the museum, both open daily 8.30–7.30; adm*), once fitted out as a sort of pleasure dome for that imperial hedonist when he tired of his home on the island of Capri. His seaside villa (now partly submerged) is mentioned in Suetonius and Tacitus, owing to an incident when a rockslide occurred during a dinner party, killing some of the guests. The cave was dedicated to the muses, a *musaeum*, with a circular tank for raising fish (wealthy Romans kept goldfish in particular as pets; some would embellish them with jewels, or teach them to bob up and eat out of their hands). Tiberius kitted his grotto out with some extravagant, larger-than-life statuary, starting with the *Rape of Ganymede* over the entrance, a mythological nudge-wink to hint at the goings-on inside – for all the dirt on this devoted pederast, perhaps the kinkiest of all Roman emperors, consult Suetonius' tell-all *Lives of the Caesars*.

Other sculptures, signed by Athanadoros, Agesandros and Polydoros, famous Hellenistic sculptors of Rhodes, were set in the surrounding niches, or on their own artificial islands in the fish pond; they were discovered during road works in 1957, in a thousand pieces. Now reassembled from such pieces as survived, the statues are displayed in the adjacent **Museo Archeologico Nazionale**. The largest composition is the *Blinding of Polyphemos*, related to the *Laocoön* in the Vatican. Contemporaries mention that Tiberius had a warm spot in his heart for Odysseus and his cunning, and the other groups show Odysseus rescuing the Palladium (a statuette of Athena) from Troy and lifting the dead Achilles from the battlefield. The most dramatic of them all shows his ship attacked by the monster Scylla, with the face of a beautiful woman and nine dog-headed serpents issuing from her waist (this one was actually in the water, in the centre of the grotto). The museum building itself is also worth a look, designed by architects Vicenzo Piccini and Giuseppe Zander, evident followers of Frank Lloyd Wright.

Gaeta

In the middle of this scenic stretch of coast, Gaeta stands behind its medieval walls on a narrow peninsula, the grandest sight before the Bay of Naples. Virgil wrote that it was named for Caieta, Aeneas' nurse, although Strabo begged to differ and said it came from the Greek word for 'cavity', for the great gap formed by its gulf. For a while in the early Middle Ages, when it was the only safe refuge on this coast, Gaeta was an important Mediterranean trading centre, a little maritime republic allied to the Byzantines and a rival to Amalfi and Pisa. Its naturally defensible site made it a valued stronghold for centuries after, for the Normans of the south, the Angevins, Aragonese and Bourbons of Naples, and finally NATO; a big American cruiser or two will usually be lolling offshore. Gaeta has often been a last redoubt; in 1848 the Pope held court here during Garibaldi and Mazzini's revolt, and in 1861 the last King of Naples and his palace guard briefly withstood a siege from the army of the new Italy, hoping for help from France that never came.

That grand view, as seen from the Fórmia side, is a little deceptive. Gaeta is really a kind of beautifully painted stage set; the old houses rise up almost perpendicularly from the harbour, but there's nothing behind but a sheer cliff on the other side. It's a tiny place, full of evocative, crumbling old streets and alleys, especially around the **cathedral** with its lofty tower. Consecrated in 1106, it was redone in the 18th century; bits of the ancient columns used in the original still peek out in places from under the rococo frosting. The redecorating created an impressive interior, with some rich *pietra dura* work in the chapels, but the most remarkable thing in it is still an impressive **paschal candlestick** from the 13th century, a sort of miniature Trajan's Column, much more antique in manner than medieval, sculpted with scenes from the Lives of Christ and St Erasmus; note the views of Gaeta at the bottom. The remains of St Erasmus (*see* below) are down below in the crypt; other treasures from the medieval building are kept in the adjacent **Museo Diocesano** (*open by request*, ***t*** *0771 461234*), including medieval exultet rolls, paintings, and such curiosities as the entire *Divina Commedia* written on a single sheet of paper. For all that, the most memorable part of the cathedral is the 185ft **campanile**, Gaeta's landmark and one of the most spectacular medieval towers of Italy. Begun in the 11th century, at the height of Gaeta's career as a merchant city, its interlaced arches and splashes of coloured tile betray the strong influence of the minarets of Spain and North Africa.

Where to Stay and Eat

Gaeta ✉ 04024

★★★★**Villa Irlanda**, Lungomare Caboto 6, **t** 0771 712581, **f** 0771 712172, *www.villairlanda.com* (*very expensive*). Consists of four historic buildings in the garden of a Roman villa from the 1st century BC – the reception occupies the ruins, while the restaurant is in the refectory of a convent of 1930 with hand-painted decoration; rooms are in the convent or a neoclassical villa, built in 1912. All are set in a beautiful park, with a pair of swimming pools, one Olympic-size; rooms all have air conditioning, TV and mini bar.

★★★**Gajeta**, Lungomare Caboto 6, **t** 0771 45081, **f** 0771 450 8236 (*moderate*). In the centre, overlooking the harbour, the friendly, comfortable Gajeta has terraces with sea views, and air-conditioned rooms – but no restaurant. It has a few apartments with kitchenettes and is a favourite with US families from the military base opposite.

★★★**Summit**, on the coastal Via Flacca, km 23, **t/f** 0771 741741 (*moderate*). Near Gaeta; a fine modern resort hotel in a good location, if a bit on the large side. *Open April–mid-Nov.*

★**Da Civitina**, Salita del Leone 8, **t** 0771 461748 (*cheap*). A modern, functional place in the heart of the old town, with en suite rooms.

Masaniello, Piazza Commestibili 6, **t** 0771 462 296 (*expensive*). Perhaps Gaeta's oldest restaurant, with succulent fish specialities prepared with Neapolitan flair. *Closed Mon.*

La Saliera, Piazza Traniello 30, **t** 0771 465651 (*moderate*). Less expensive choices can be found along the Lungomare, including this place,with outdoor tables in a pretty setting by the park. Good pizza, and also a full menu including seafood. *Closed Thurs.*

Fórmia ✉ 04023

★★★★**Grande Albergo Miramare**, **t** 0771 320 047, **f** 0771 320050 (*moderate*). One of the best places (and best bargains) on the coast. On the Via Appia on the southern edge of the town, a beautiful old villa with Spanish fittings and extensive gardens on the shore, a beach and a pool, and modernized but pleasant rooms with air conditioning, as well as an elegant restaurant in a pavilion.

★★★**Villa Maria Teresa**, Viale Unità d'Italia, **t/f** 0771 770557 (*cheap*). This white, turn-of-last-century hotel overlooks the sea near the

Nearby in Piazza De Vio 9, the **Permanent Exhibition of the Historic Centre** (*open 4.30–7.30*) has the pennant that flew over the ship of Marcantonio Colonna in the Battle of Lépanto, and paintings, including some by local Baroque painter Sebastiano Conca. The 13th-century **castello** on the heights above the town was built by Emperor Frederick II and enlarged by the Angevins (the two cone-shaped towers and sheer seaside tower) and Aragonese (the upper, rectangular castle with cylindrical towers). The narrow stairs and alleys of old Gaeta hold a number of medieval houses with bifora windows and high arches reminiscent of Venice, some of which have had restorations in recent years. The churches are still waiting for theirs. **San Giovanni a Mare**, with its Siculo-Norman cupola, is the most interesting, but like the others it's never open. One that is can be visited in Via Annunziata, the church of the **Annunziata** with a 17th-century wooden choir, and a separate, richly decorated chapel called the **Grotta d'Oro** (*open 9–12 and 3–6*), with paintings by Sebastiano Conca and contemporaries.

Gaeta has a second historic centre, **Il Borgo**, which grew up in the 16th century towards Fórmia when Charles V extended the walls and made life difficult for the town's sailors, farmers and craftsmen. To this day it solidly maintains the atmosphere of an old-fashioned popular quarter, with shambolic little alleys and lanes branching off from main **Via Indipendenza** ('the Gut'); here and there you can see remains of the Roman villas.

centre; it has a pretty garden and pool and immaculately clean if rather spartan rooms looked after by nuns.

Europa, Via Appia on the southern edge of town, **t 0771 723896, **f** 0771 722121 (*cheap*). Sometimes it can be fun to find a hotel of some pretensions that has entirely abandoned them: this '60s skyscraper has settled into a niche as a modest budget hotel, but it's still well kept, and has rooms with balconies, a pool and a stretch of beach.

Del Golfo, Piazzale della Stazione 1, **t 0771 790037, **f** 0771 771874 (*cheap*). Your basic central hotel by the station, with some en-suite rooms and parking.

For dinner in Fórmia, look no further than Via Unità d'Italia, the name the Via Appia takes as it passes through the town. Most of the best restaurants are on or near it – though the road has become so busy the sea view is no longer much of an attraction:

Sirio, **t** 0771 772705 (*moderate*). A classy restaurant that prides itself on the quality of both sea- and land-food, and prepares them with a Tuscan touch. *Closed Mon eve, Tues*.

Rivabella, **t** 0771 26556 (*moderate*). Not far from the street; an unpretentious and convivial place with outdoor seating, a wide choice of pizzas in the evening and good seafood. *Closed Wed*.

Zì Anna Mare, on Largo Paone facing the harbour, **t** 0771 771063 (*moderate*). Serves more seafood classically prepared, and a surprisingly large choice of what comes out of this part of the Tyrrhènian, but also memorable *primi piatti*. *Closed Tues*.

Il Tartufo, Via Appia 237 on the southern edge of Fórmia, **t** 0771 22615. For something different, this is one of the few places where truffles from the Ciociaría find their way to the sea: truffles on the pasta, in omelettes, even in seafood dishes (*moderate*, though too many truffles and the price can go out of sight). *Closed Mon*.

Minturno-Scauri ✉ 04028

If you're stopping over anywhere in Lazio's southwestern corner, this humble but pleasant lido provides the widest choice of places to stay.

***Villa Eleonora, Via Italo Balbo, **t** 0771 683243, **f** 0771 614371, *www.giroscopio.com* (*moderate–cheap*). The best of the bunch – a classic pre-war resort hotel on the beach.

The hill above Gaeta is now the **Monte Orlando Regional Park** (*closed to cars, but there is a regular shuttle bus from the strip of hotels on Via Firenze, on the western side*) where you can enjoy the views and visit the rich and well-preserved cylindrical **Mausoleum of Munatius Plancus**, the Roman general who founded Lyon in France (*open Sat and Sun 9–1 and 2–6*). Measuring 40ft in diameter, rimmed by a Doric frieze sculpted with military emblems, it was originally topped with a statue of the deceased. In the Middle Ages, it was impressive enough that people began to think it was the tomb of Charlemagne's legendary nephew Roland (Orlando). Under Ferdinand of Spain and his grandson, Emperor Charles V, the promontory was heavily fortified, some of the walls seeming to imitate the Roman tomb.

Pretty beaches, tucked between rocks and under cliffs, dot the coast to the west – the broad **Spiaggia di Serapo** is the most popular, named for an ancient temple of Serapis that was connected to a villa of Emperor Hadrian. It begins on the western end of Monte Orlando, near the **Santuario della Montagna Spaccata**, founded in the 11th century at a fissure in the rock said to have been caused by an earthquake at the moment when Christ died. The current church is Baroque. From here a Via Crucis leads to a chapel and then to the impressive crack; below is a giant sea cave, the **Grotta del Turco** (*both open 9–12.30 and 2 til dusk; adm for the Grotta*).

Much of the sea around Monte Orlando, as well as an area around the Grotto of Tiberius at Sperlonga, has been set aside as a unique sort of underwater park, managed by the World Wide Fund for Nature and called **l'Oasi Blu**; in summer they offer 'guided dives' around the park as well as a glass-bottom boat tour (*for information, ring the WWF at* **t** *0771 683850*).

Fórmia

Over the last century these towns have grown together; where Gaeta stops, **Fórmia** begins. At the foot of the Monti Aurunci, ancient *Fórmiae* was, at least according to Strabo, founded by Laconians and given the Dorian name *Hormiai*, 'landing place'. Other writers claimed it as the land of the Lastrygonians from the *Odyssey*, but there is no real evidence that Greeks of any kind were ever here. Fórmia was a town of the obscure Italic tribe called the Aurunci, and later the Volsci; under the Romans it was an important stop on the Via Appia famous for its climate (*O temperatae dulce Fórmiae litus*, wrote Martial) and it enjoyed a blessed past as one of the gilded resorts of Imperial Rome, like Capri or Baiae. Scipio Africanus, Lepidus and Nerva were among the bigwigs who basked here, but the best known is the virtuous but infinitely tedious orator Cicero, whose seaside villa may well have been on the site of the now privately owned **Villa Caposele**, overlooking the marina.

The villa's park, littered with statues and inscriptions, descends to the sea on terraces; a *nymphaeum* has been identified, along with the baths where in 43 BC, after the assassination of Caesar, Mark Antony's men caught up with the 'father of orators' and knifed him; as a typical Roman touch, they brought his head back with them to the Forum, placing it on the rostrum where he so often spoke, and pierced the tongue with a pin. A large tomb at Fórmia's western gate, by the crossroads of Via Flacca and the Via Appia, has long been known as the **Tomba di Cicerone**, a 75ft concrete conical cylinder (once covered with marble) on a stone base, with two chambers inside (*open Sat and Sun, summer, in winter Sunday only or by request,* **t** *0771 770382*). Further uphill, the smaller, less well-preserved **Tomba di Tullia** is where Cicero buried his beloved daughter – a mummy, in fact, with her name on it, was found there in the 1470s. Nearby along the ancient Via Appia, a late imperial **fountain** can be seen.

Little of ancient Fórmia survived a Saracen attack in 846; it even lost its name for over a thousand years, and was known only as the 'Castellone e Mola di Gaeta' until 1863. The new Fórmia was three-quarters destroyed in 1944; despite the miserable postwar planning only the Italians could have managed the feat of rebuilding it as the cheerful, likeable town it is today. One landmark is the seaside **Castello di Mola**, with its tall cylindrical donjon built in 1200 by Charles of Anjou as part of his defences of Gaeta. The oldest neighbourhood, the **Quartiere Sant' Erasmo**, managed to stay intact, including the **Cancello**, a picturesque Roman theatre in Via Gradoni del Duomo, its curved *cavea* converted into an apartment house where laundry flaps in the arches; an inscription found here, now in Piazza della Vittoria, refers to the gladiatorial games that took place. It was also here that Fórmia's bishop Erasmus met his distinctly unpleasant martyrdom in 303, having his intestines wound around a windlass. Patron of sailors as well as Fórmia, he was known as St Elmo in Britain, giving his name to the mysterious fire that alights on masts. The church of **Sant'Erasmo** was built over his tomb, and served as the seat of the local bishopric from the 4th century until the Saracens wiped Fórmia off the map (the saint's body was removed to safety in Gaeta). The church became a monastery in the Renaissance, and a barracks in the mid-19th century, and is now a simple parish church. In Piazza Sant'Erasmo, the **Torre di Castellone** was built in 1377 on a Roman foundation which defended the Appian Way; originally the castle had twelve similar towers. Part of the megalithic walls can be seen nearby – in their day, according to Livy, they were strong enough to repel Hannibal himself.

A recently discovered statue from the tomb of Tullia, a statue of *Ganymede*, a *Leda and the Swan*, and an impressive collection of heroic male nudes and demurely draped females found during the laying out of Via Vitruvo in 1920 are in Fórmia's **Museo Archeologico Nazionale**, Via Vitruvo (*open daily 9–7; adm*). Other ancient bits are incorporated into the buildings in Piazza della Vittoria.

Itri and the Madonna della Cívita

Inland from Gaeta, **Itri** is near a pretty stretch of the ancient Via Appia. Its hill wears a round medieval tower known as the **Torre del Coccodrillo**, although what exactly a crocodile has to do with it is for them to know and you to find out. Bombs in the war blasted its pretty 13th-century church of **Santa Maria Maggiore**, leaving only the Byzantine-style campanile; the other church, **San Michele Arcangelo**, founded in the 11th century, is an impressive sight on top of its stair, with its bell-tower built into the façade. These days Itri is most famous for its black olives, and for the daring patriot bandit Michele Pezza, born here in humble circumstances in 1771 and better known as Fra' Diavolo, for his devilish ability to get out of jams. He was something of a Robin Hood, if you can imagine the subjects of the King of Naples in the role of the honest Saxons and the French as the villains. Fra' Diavolo joined the Bourbon army at a tender age, and fought Napoleon's men so heroically at Gaeta that he was made a colonel and a duke, briefly, before the French captured him at last in 1806 and hanged him in Naples. His career inspired an operetta which was made into a film in the '30s, though unfortunately for his reputation it was made by Hal Roach, and starred Laurel and Hardy.

Twelve kilometres north of Itri, the hilltop **Santuario della Madonna della Cívita** (*open 7.30–12.30 and 3–7.30*) is one of Italy's oldest Marian shrines, although it's currently housed in a 19th-century church. The icon of the Madonna and Child is believed to have been brought to Italy by Greek monks in the 8th century, during the iconoclast struggles; there's been a church on this site since at least the 11th century, when according to legend, a deaf-mute cowherd, in search of a lost bull, found the beast kneeling in front of the icon hanging in a holm oak. The church has an impressive gallery of votive offerings, and from its porch there are lovely views over the Pontine Islands.

Further up in the Monti Aurunci, the tiny hill town of **Campodimele**, 'honey field', is stalwartly defended by its walls and twelve cylindrical towers. They even help keep the Grim Reaper at bay; Campodimele is 'the village of long life', where it's not uncommon for natives to live a century or more. The locals, however, credit the quantity of beans they eat, and their famous kid-flavoured ragù served with pasta. In the centre of the village grows a liberty tree, planted by local progressives in 1889 for the centenary of the French Revolution.

Above Fórmia on the south slopes of the Monti Aurunci, the medieval hill town of **Maránola** is an atmospheric place, and has good 14th- and 15th-century frescoes and a 16th-century presepio from Puglia in its church of **Santa Maria dei Martiri**. Another church, **Sant'Antonio**, contains a miracle-working statue of the Archangel Michael. Every July, the statue is solemnly taken up the Scalata San Michele in a communal pilgrimage to the 8th-century **Cenobio di San Michele**, built under a mighty overhang in the rock 3,400 ft up, where offerings of bread and cheese are made, a pastoral custom dating back to goodness knows when. A neo-Gothic façade has been built over the entrance to the cave and its miraculous spring. For even grander views, continue up to the top, where a 2.3-ton cast-iron **statue of the Redeemer** – one of twenty in Italy – was erected in 1901 to welcome in the 20th century. Not surprisingly, it took forty days to get it up the hill and put it in place.

Scauri and Minturno

South of Fórmia, in the confines of a nature preserve, the **Parco Gianola-Monte di Scauri**, you'll find the remains of another impressive Roman holiday home from the 1st century BC, this one, if the verses of Catullus are to be believed, belonging to Mamurra, a fabulous wealthy friend of Julius Caesar. Mamurra built on the same scale as Tiberius, on a spread covering 22 acres: terraces and cisterns remain (one, nearly intact, has 36 columns), although unfortunately his artificial sea grotto *musaeum*, carved in the shape of an octagon, was destroyed in 1944. The villa's octagonal reservoir is known as the Temple of Janus; in 1930 the villa's extensive fish farms were converted into a little port, and there's also a pretty beach set in a steep pine wood. A second villa in the park belonged to a member of the same family, Marcus Emilio Scauro, who built the Via Emilia in 115 BC and gave that region of northern Italy its name, while leaving his other name to **Scauri**, now a busy beach resort built over the ancient city of *Pirae*.

Lazio's last coastal town is **Minturno**, founded as a safe refuge by the survivors of old Minturnae after it was destroyed by the Lombards in 590. In 795 Pope Leo III made it a strongpoint, the *Castrum Leopolis*, although it failed to do the job and was occupied by the Saracens for some 70 years before a Christian alliance finally defeated them in 915. Minturno's **Castello Baronale** stands in the panoramic Piazza Portanova; peek in to see the pretty loggia if the gate is open. The main street leads back to the 12th-century church of **San Pietro**, made of Roman bits and bobs; inside, its three naves support pointy arches on Roman columns. The pulpit, made of 13th-century pieces cobbled together in 1618, is a very peculiar piece of work, complete with a plaque of a dragon swallowing a man head-first. Minturno's other landmark is the **Ponte Borbonico** over the Garigliano (1832), one of the first suspension bridges ever built.

Ancient **Minturnae** (*site open daily 8–sunset*), on the right bank of the Garigliano, was an Auruncian town, allied with the Samnites against Rome until it was defeated in 314 BC; two years later the Via Appia was run through its centre to become the decumanus of a new Roman colony, which prospered by transferring goods between its sea and river ports. A frequent visitor, apparently, was Apicius, the 1st-century cookery book writer, who loved the local seafood. In the 6th century it was abandoned for the safer site of the modern town. The excavations have revealed all the essentials of a Roman colony, given that every Roman citizen, no matter where, needed a forum to conduct business, a capitolium with temples of Jove, Juno and Minerva, and a temple to Rome and Augustus to fulfil one's state religious obligations; a theatre and amphitheatre for entertainment; baths for hygiene; and an aqueduct to fill them. Minturnae's **theatre**, with a capacity of 4,500, has been rebuilt for summer performances; here a small **antiquarium** (*same hours as the excavations*) has inscriptions and coins found in the river, where sailors would toss them hoping for a safe and lucky voyage. Lastly, if you've ever wondered what a Roman urinal was like, there are ruins of one near the aqueduct along the Via Appia, down in Marina di Minturno.

Above Minturno, in the Monti Aurunci on the way to Cassino, **Ausónia** was an important fortress town in the Middle Ages. Besides its ruined castle, it has two interesting churches: **San Michele**, built over a temple of Hercules, where the old altar carved with scenes of the hero was pressed into service as a baptismal font (St Michael was often the successor to the earlier dragon-slaying hero in holy sites); and **Santa Maria del Piano**, a Renaissance building below the town on the SS630 with 12th-century frescoes in its crypt.

Ponza and the Pontine Islands

A mini-archipelago, the five Pontine Islands are scattered like buckshot across the Gulf of Gaeta. Only Ponza and Ventotene are inhabited: Ponza is as perfect as a little Italian island can get, while minute, peaceful Ventotene has its modest charms and famous lentils. All owe much of their colour and eccentricities to their fiery volcanic birth, although they belong to two different chains: Ponza, Palmarola and Zannone are part of the volcanic substructure extending from Ánzio, while Ventotene and Santo Stefano belong to the busier volcanic chain in the Bay of Naples. The transparent sea, the rock formations, big eels and shipwrecks make all the Pontine Islands favourites with divers.

Ponza

Our next landfall was on Aiaia, island
of Kirke, dire beauty and divine...

Odyssey, Book X, trans. by Robert Fitzgerald

The journey by sea to Ponza from Fórmia is a charming prelude to one of Italy's loveliest islands. From the sea Gaeta is an enchanting sight. Beyond, Ponza rises on the horizon, and an impressive mountainous place it looks too. But as you pass Zannone and the islet of Gavi, you realize that Ponza, like a child's drawing, isn't quite all it appears to be: the island is merely the upper rim of a volcano shaped like a

Getting There

Note that, while you can take your vehicle on the ferry, driving (and parking) on Ponza and Ventotene is limited, and forbidden in the summer. For information on mainland garage parking, call **t** 0771 771 493. **Fórmia** is the main year-round port for both islands, with daily departures on Caremar ferries (2½–3hrs) and hydrofoils (1hr 20mins): **t** 0771 122710, *www.caremar.it*, and Vetor hydrofoils, **t** 0771 267 098, *www.vetor.it*. There are also ferries that run between Ponza and Ventotene. In the summer you can also catch a ferry from **Ánzio** (Caremar, **t** 199 123 199 (call centre), or SNAV, **t** 0698 45085, *www.snavali.com*, or hydrofoil (Vetor, **t** 0698 45085 running from April to Dec); there's a year-round ferry from **Terracina** (Mazzella ferries, **t** 0773 725536) and in summer a motorlaunch from **San Felice Circeo** (Hipponion Princes, **t** 0336 540264).

Both islands have minibuses and taxis, and hire out boats and motorbikes, or will take you on a tour of the coasts or nearby islands. On Ponza, book the night before for the 10.30am tours of Palmarola and Zannone.

Tourist Information

Ponza: The Pro-loco, Molo Musco (on the quay near the lighthouse), **t** 0771 80031, *prolocopon@ libero.it, www.isolaponza.com*.

Ventotene: Loc. Porto Romano 1, **t** 0771 85257.

Where to Stay and Eat

Ponza ✉ 04027

Note that most of the price categories listed here plunge a peg or even two in the off season. Call hotels in advance: in summer they are often booked up and in winter they often close unexpectedly. Prices soar in August.

★★★★**Grand Hotel Santa Domitilla**, **t** 0771 809951, **f** 0771 809955, *grandhotelsantadomitilla@yahoo.it* (*luxury*). The island's only four-star accommodation, a huge, plush villa with pretty rooms tiled in pastel colours, many with marble bathrooms. There's an outdoor pool, a Roman pool in a grotto, a tennis court, a charming garden and a fine restaurant with outdoor seating under the vines (restaurant open to non-residents). It's a 5min walk to the port or beach.

★★★**Chiaia di Luna**, Via Chiaia di Luna, **t** 0771 80113, **f** 0771 809821 (*very expensive*). With spectacular views over Ponza's most famous beach and cliffs. Designed in a *domus* style with low domes, on a series of terraces and a pool at the bottom; candlelight suppers

crescent moon, ranging from a mile to 600ft wide, decorated with romantic wind-sculpted cliffs, beaches, grottoes, and crags and needle-like pinnacles standing in the sea (the Italians have a lovely name for them – *faraglioni*).

Ponza knew its first prosperity in Neolithic times exporting obsidian, the prized volcanic glass used to make blades for tools and weapons; mined on the island of Palmarola, it was worked at Fieno on Ponza, and then shipped to Cuma on the mainland. In the 8th century BC, the Phoenicians and Greeks (who had just established their first western colony on nearby Ischia) visited the island and called it variously Eèa, Aiaia, Aurora or Eeus, but the first historic inhabitants were the Ausonians, who left a few Cylopean walls. The Romans picked up the little archipelago in 313 BC, and built an aqueduct from Le Forna, Cala Inferno to Santa Maria, dotted with cisterns. Augustus had a villa overlooking the port. Later Caesars used it to stow away pesky relatives; Tiberius, based in nearby Capri, started the trend, while Caligula packed off his brothers, his wife Orestilia and his sister Agrippina to Ponza; liberated after his assassination, she returned to Rome with baby Nero.

After the fall of Rome, the islands were occupied by the Byzantines and a group of monks at Santa Maria in Ponza, where an exiled Pope, the future San Silverio, was make it a good bet for romantics. The hotel bus links it to the port. *Open April–Oct.*

★★★**Bellavista**, Via Parata 1, **t** 0771 80036, **f** 0771 80395 (*expensive*). Small and modern; juts out over the sea, with a little beach just below. *Open April–Oct.*

★★★**La Torre dei Borboni**, Via Madonna 1, **t** 0771 80135, **f** 0771 809884 (*expensive*). Right on the port; a third of the rooms are in an 18th-century castle with wonderful views once enjoyed by Augustus, whose villa was built on this site; many rooms are on two levels and have terraces. *Closed Oct–Easter.*

★★★**Gennarino a Mare**, **t** 0771 80071, **f** 0771 80140 (*expensive*). Recently modernized and right on the port; enchanting views near Sant'Antonio beach and has a good restaurant, open to non-guests as well, with a few tables on a floating platform. *Closed Thurs out of season.*

★★**Feola**, Via Roma 2, **t/f** 0771 80617 (*moderate*). Only 12 rooms and a friendly family-run atmosphere.

★★**Luisa**, Via Chiaia di Luna, **t/f** 0771 80128 (*moderate–cheap*). Up a pedestrian street at the top of the town. *Closed Oct–Easter.*

★★**Ortensia**, 5km from the port in Le Forna, overlooking the Cala Féola and natural pools, **t** 0771 808922, **f** 0771 808365 (*moderate*). Airy white rooms with frigo bars, air conditioning, lovely views and simple restaurant. *Closed Oct–Easter.*

If you don't mind a landlord, you can contact the Pro-loco for a list of ***affittacamere***.

The specialities of Ponza include *coniglio alla cacciatora* (rabbit with onions, tomatoes and so on) and lobster dishes. There's a wonderful Neapolitan pastry-shop on the main drag selling delicious *sfogliatelle ricce* (warm and crisp pastry filled with a ricotta-based cream, spices and candied orange peel) and *torta caprese* (chocolate and almond cake).

Acqua Pazza, Piazza C Pisacane 10, **t** 0771 80643 (*moderate*). You won't do better for exquisitely prepared seafood; features delights from the sea from the antipasti onwards, and a lovely choice of wines to match. *Open eves only, closed winter.*

O'Restorante, with enchanting views over the bay at Via dietro la Chiesa 4, **t** 0771 80338 (*expensive–moderate*). A cheerful place where all the dishes are based on Ponzese tradition, and on the day's catch; home-made desserts too. *Open eves only, closed winter.*

Ristorante da Antonio, Via Dante, **t** 0771 809832 (*moderate*). Friendly, upmarket wooden hut with huge shutters which open onto the sea. It's set right on the beach of San Antonio by the port and serves up fresh seafood platters, and tasty, if rather over-priced, pasta dishes.

lodged in 537. The monks, however, were no match for the Saracens. The lords of Gaeta later gave the islands to the Benedictines, who maintained a presence there until the pirate Barbarossa wiped them out in 1533. Abandoned, the island passed to the Farnese, who occasionally sent expeditions over to see if there was anything to grab; they also cut down all the trees. The last Farnese, Isabelle, who became Queen of Spain, handed the islands over to her stepson Charles III of Naples, in 1731, one of the few Bourbons with a sense of civic responsibility. He encouraged the colonization of Ponza, where settlers – mostly from Ischia – received generous tax incentives to develop the island, plant vineyards, fish and dive for coral. They famously joined forces with the fleets of Rome and Naples to defeat the Barbary pirates at Palmarola in 1757.

The settlers of Ponza may have wondered what they had got into, when an earthquake knocked off a whole peninsula in 1821, and a fierce hailstorm in 1835 destroyed all the crops and half the houses. But they persevered, and by the time of the unification of Italy (1860) they were enough Ponzesi to export. Some went to South America, but the largest colony went to New York (this would later prove a blessing in disguise, when Romans began to look around for holiday houses: it was next to impossible to buy property on the island, as some of the owners' family were always in America).

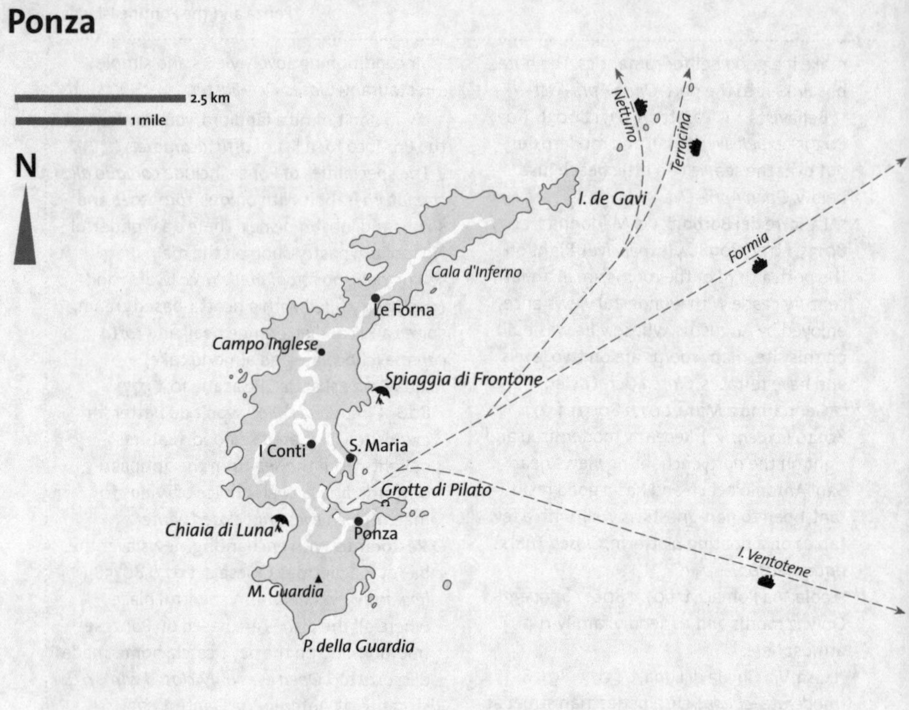

Under the Fascists, Ponza once more became an island of exile, first for anti-Fascists and then for the deposed Duce himself, who spent six days there while the Badoglio government decided what to do with him.

Ponza Town

Ponza town is the archetypal Tyrrhenian port, its pastel houses arranged in an artistic amphitheatre around a picture-perfect curving harbour, with its oddly shaped sea rocks, arches and coves. Man-made landmarks include the Torre dei Borboni, now a hotel, and the lighthouse at Punta della Madonna. The parish church, dedicated to the island's patron saint, Pope San Silverio, dates from the 17th century, although the most prominent building is the arcaded Municipio. Tunnels link the port with the suburbs of **Sant'Antonio** (with a small but clean beach) and **Santa Maria**. In the vicinity are numerous Roman cisterns, remains of the aqueduct, a subterranean reservoir, the *Piscina Limarae*, and the small pension that hosted Mussolini during his brief sojourn. From here the road rises steeply to **I Conti**, with lovely views, then continues past the **Campo Inglese**, named for a small fort built by the English during the Napoleonic Wars.

Ponza's only other settlement is **Le Forna**, named for its lime kilns. A few of the older houses here are built in the North African *domus* style (with low domes), many with their individual tufa cisterns designed to hold the maximum amount of precious rainwater. There are lovely views over the vineyards and cliffs; paths and steps from the Hotel Ortensia lead down to the **Piscina Naturale**, a pool separated from the sea by a narrow strip of land pierced by a tunnel.

Besides waterworks, the Romans dug several tunnels on Ponza. One leads from the port to the loveliest of the island's small bays, the **Chiaia di Luna**, a beautiful crescent-shaped beach, beneath 1,000ft-high pale cliffs. Fellini filmed the last droll cannibal scenes of *Satyricon* here. Although technically across the island, Ponza is so thin that it's within easy walking distance. Just north of the beach is the **Grotta di Circe**, residence of Odysseus' enchantress. *Pace* Monte Circeo, but the Homeric name Eea fits it, and both Virgil and Strabo strengthened Ponza's claim by calling the island Circide.

Ponza's Pope

Silverius of Frosinone, elevated to the pontificate in 536, was the only pope who was the legitimate son of another pope, in this case Hormisdas, who took vows after the death of his young wife. Times were tough: the Monophysite heresy (which considered that Christ had a single, instead of the Orthodox double divine–human, nature) was raging, along with the Greek–Gothic wars – Byzantine Emperor Justinian's General Belisarius had just taken Naples from the Arian Goths and everyone knew he was on his way to Rome, still held by a small Gothic garrison. Belisarius' reputation was such that Silverius knew he could take the city without much trouble, and he hoped to spare the city a siege by opening the gates of Rome to the Byzantines in December. But Belisarius knew the Goths would be back in force, and prepared Rome for the first of three long sieges that would lead the Eternal City to one of its lowest ebbs.

Meanwhile Justinian's wife Theodora – a strong supporter of the Monophysite heresy, and a much tougher cookie than the emperor himself – made a secret deal with Constantinople's Papal legate Vigilius: Belisarius would depose Silverius (who refused to restore a Monophysite bishop to the see of Constantinople), strip him of his robes and tiara and replace him with Vigilius, and Vigilius would do as Theodora wished. But Vigilius reneged, and was himself kidnapped a few years later by Justinian's agent – and this was back when the Eastern and Western churches were still one. Meanwhile, Roman bishops in support of Silverius rallied around him on Ponza, inveighing against Theodora's antipope. Seeing that a schism was in the making, the Empress sent assassins after Silverius, and he was murdered on 20 June 537 as he attempted to flee to Palmarola.

Belisarius, hearing of his death, repented of the role he played in the affair, and founded the church of Santa Maria de' Crociferi in Rome, while Silverius was canonized and has been Ponza's patron ever since. Every 20 June he gets a three-day *festa* – the houses are given a lick of paint or whitewash, and his statue, adorned with coral and gold, is carried in procession, either by land or water; there are fireworks and everyone eats ring-shaped *casatiello* pastries, unique to the island, while the young swains participate in the *palo della gallina*, a contest of apparently pagan origin – a hen is tied to a pole, extended over the sea, and the contest is to see who can pluck a feather without falling into the drink.

Around Ponza by Sea

Ponza's jagged shores are best seen from sea level; there are small motor launches to hire in the port and at Santa Maria, and the tours, stopping at various beaches along the way, take between five and six hours. Near the port, the **Grotte di Pilato**, only accessible by boat, have nothing to do with Pontius Pilate, but everything to do with an imaginative Neapolitan compiler centuries ago, who associated Ponza with Pontius. The three grottoes were connected by tunnels built in Republican times as part of a luxury villa, and were used to store live fresh fish and moray eels in a rock-cut pool, with something resembling an apse carved in the back and four corridors. Augurs, according to some, would come down here and study the entrails of sea eels.

If you were to circle the island clockwise from here, you'd pass a pair of sea rocks with the odd name **Calzone Muto**, 'Silent Trouser', and the lighthouse at the point under Ponza's highest point, **Monte Guardia** (there's also a path from the port); **Punta del Fieno**, on the west coast, was the site of Ponza's Neolithic obsidian works. Beyond lies the aforementioned Chiaia di Luna, and more *faraglioni*; the ones to the north are named after Lucia Rosa, daughter of one of the first colonists, who refused to let her marry a man with beautiful moustaches, so Lucia leapt over the cliff; her name is also attached to the beach. The next beach, **Cala di Féola**, with its natural pools, is easiest reached by boat, while the next promontory, the **Punta Papa**, is named for a watch-tower built by the Farnese Pope, Paul III. Ponza's best-known shipwreck lies just off shore, an American Liberty ship taking German prisoners from Ánzio in 1944 that crashed against the rocks. Both crew and prisoners survived, while the now over-grown wreck, filled with fish, has become a focal point for divers.

At its northeasternmost point, Punta dell'Incenso, Ponza is dotted like an 'i' with the islet of **Gavi**, while around on the east side is a natural arch and the dramatic white cliffs of the **Cala d'Inferno**; just east a number of ships have come to grief. There are more sheer cliffs at Punta Bianca, and a fine beach of **Cala Frontone** (canoes to hire).

Palmarola and Zannone

The westernmost and second largest of the Pontine islands, **Palmarola**, like Ponza, is rugged, sliced by sheer cliffs of white and gold, especially the spectacular Cala dei Briganti, and surrounded by all sorts of picturesque volcanic debris, *faraglioni* and sea grottoes, a favourite of divers – the sea here is crystal-clear. Beautiful as it is, Palmarola has brought bad luck to many: in 303 the Romans abandoned 300 Christians here to die of thirst and hunger; an English cargo ship blew up here; an aeroplane crashed into it. Today a few people have summer houses and rent out a handful of rooms, and there are two *ad hoc* summer trattorias – it may not be your completely paradisaical desert island, but it comes close.

The less dramatic island of **Zannone**, north of Ponza, has remains of its rock-cut Roman fish and eel tanks (near the Varo landing), and a ruined 11th-century Benedictine monastery. Unlike the other Pontine islands, Zannone was never cultivated or deforested, and is covered with its original Mediterranean *macchia*; now the island is ruled by a herd of shy, curved-horn wild sheep. Part of the Parco Nazionale del Circeo since 1981, the island takes about 40 minutes to walk around, and there's an exhibit on the island's environment on top of Monte Pellegrino, near the lodge of the park guardian.

Ventotene

The other inhabited Pontine island, tiny Ventotene (the *Pandataria* of the Romans) resembles a green billiard table floating on a reddish-black tufa platform on the surface of the sea. With no trees or hills to shelter it, Ventotene deserves its windy name, and the islanders are relieved that St Paul of the Cross personally came over in the 18th century and anchored their home with basalt to the seabed. Minuscule gourmet lentils prosper here, as do capers and prickly pears. Another extraordinary thing is that the highest part of the island, the Montagnozzo (all of 452ft above sea level) is covered with sand blown over from the Sahara. It's especially deep around the northwest coast, at Parata Grande and Cala Nave, where the roots of ancient trees have been petrified in the fine loose layers of sand.

The success of the colony on Ponza encouraged Charles III (by now King of Spain, and a close student of Rousseau) to try an experiment on Ventotene; in 1768 he took 300 prostitutes, thieves and other riffraff from the prisons and gutters of Naples and sent them to Ventotene, to prove that, once removed for the evils of society, they would become models of virtue. Within a few years, however, the island was the Sodom and Gomorrah of the Tyrrhenian, and armed forces had to be sent in to round up the failed guinea pigs. They were replaced by good eggs from Torre del Greco near Naples, who later found themselves hosting political prisoners, in a penal colony on Ventotene and a prison built on arid little Santo Stefano.

Julia's villa on Punta d'Eolo, the scene of all this unhappiness, has been nearly scoured clean by the Bourbon colonists and the wind god Aeolus. Clambering over the rocks, however, you can make out ruined walls, sections of mosaic floors, traces of the baths and *odeion*, steps leading down to the sea, and the fish tanks by the light-house, even more complex than the Grotto di Pilato on Ponza, supplied by a subterranean aqueduct or *condotto*. A small head of Julia's favourite goddess Venus was discovered here and is now in the Naples Museum; all the other statues were

Where to Stay and Eat

Ventotene ✉ 04020

Most of Ventotene's seven little hotels have restaurants, all serving the island's famous lentil soup and salads of wild rocket.

****Mezzatorre**, Piazza Castello, **t** 0771 85294, **f** 0771 85315 (*expensive–moderate*). Central hotel with en-suite rooms, minibars and a restaurant.

****Lo Smeraldo**, Via Olivi 4, **t** 0771 85350, **f** 0771 85315 (*expensive–moderate*). A 5-minute walk from the village, and similar to the Mezzatorre.

***Il Cacciatore**, **t** 0771 85055 (*cheap*). In the centre of the island at Montagnozzo; one of Ventotene's oldest, with a restaurant.

***La Vela**, Via Olivi 37, **t** 0771 85185, **f** 0771 85300, *www.ciraloventotene.it* (*cheap*). Another long-time favourite, with simple rooms and nature courses for the kids.

Imperial Indiscretions

Like Ponza, Ventotene saw its share of imperial celebrities come and go – on holiday, in disgrace, or in pieces. The first was Julia, only child of Augustus, who in 25 BC built a grand summer villa at Punta d'Eolo, on the north tip of the island. This became her pleasure palace, far from the wagging tongues of Rome, and such was the respect that she – or her father – commanded that even 200 years later the fishermen of Gaeta refused to divulge the names of the men their great-great-grandfathers had ferried in the night to her villa. Detested by her third husband, Tiberius, Julia found her scandalous behaviour eventually caught up with her and Ventotene became her rock of exile instead of a bower of bliss; for five years, on her father's orders, she languished here without men or wine, and with only her mother Scibonia for company. Although the Romans interceded for Julia's return, Augustus was adamant that she should never enter the Urbs again, although he eventually relented and sent her to more cosy surroundings down by Reggio Calabria.

Later emperors found the little island, so remote and yet so conveniently close to Rome, a useful place indeed to do their dirty work; Julia's daughter, Agrippina, one of the few decent characters in the imperial soap opera, was framed in a conspiracy against her stepfather Tiberius, who sent her into exile here. When she dared to protest, he had her beaten; and when she realized rage was futile she starved herself to death. Tiberius later passed a bill in the Senate praising himself for not having had her strangled. These were among the formative years for Agrippina's son, the future emperor Caligula, who piously retrieved his mother's ashes from Ventotene before he went loco.

Agrippina's grandson Nero (son of Caligula's no-good sister, another Agrippina) outdid them all when he exiled his 20-year-old but unwanted wife Octavia here to please his new mistress Poppaea Sabina. When the people of Rome clamoured for Octavia's return and knocked over the statues of Poppaea, Poppaea convinced the Emperor to have her rival permanently removed. Nero sent his henchmen to the villa, where they slit the veins of the young empress, and when in sheer terror the girl took too long to die, they scalded her in a hot bath, after which they lopped off her head and brought it to Poppaea.

spirited away by the Farnese and Sir George Hamilton. The second of Julia's three husbands, her father's great admiral Agrippa, probably designed the island's artificial port, the **Porto Romano**: a 71,800-square-foot basin carved out of the tufa, with its little storerooms carved in the cliff and ancient bollards, still used every day by the island's little fishing fleet after 2,000 years.

Life in the 18th-century village of **Ventotene** still centres around the central Piazza Castello. There's a **Museo Archeologico** in the Municipio (*open 9–1 and 6–8.30pm, in summer 9.30pm–midnight, closed Mon*), displaying items found in Julia's villa and a Roman ship found offshore in 1981, loaded with building materials, a box of *stylae* (Roman pens) and amphorae holding grapes, nuts and spices. The simple pink Baroque church of **Santa Candida** honours the island's patroness, who was martyred in Carthage with iron combs (don't ask how) and whose body, set adrift in a small boat, ended up in a sea grotto here. The statue on the altar was donated by a couple of woodcutters who were kidnapped while on the island and ransomed, hence the little figures at her side. On 20 September her feast day is celebrated with the release of handmade paper balloons. The prison in town once held many of the 800 political prisoners Mussolini sent to the island, and it was this anti-Fascist climate in the middle of the Second World War that inspired two prisoners, Rossi and Spinelli, to write the *Manifesto di Ventotene* (1942), formulating the idea of a united Europe – one of the precursors of the Treaty of Rome and the European Union: yes, as the Ventotenesi are proud to tell you, written just here, on this lentilly little Lilliput.

You can walk around the whole island in less than an hour on foot; here and there little paths wind towards the sea, the cliffs and beaches – the two nicest ones are by the village, **Cala Rossano** and cliff-lined **Cala Nave**. Since 1997, Ventotene and Santo Stefano have been declared a natural marine reserve, to preserve one of Italy's most diverse and interesting underwater environments.

Santo Stefano

Boats from Ventotene make the excursion over the channel to this little Italian Alcatraz, which is scarcely more than a cliff in the sea. In 1795, the Bourbons built a prison here to house political enemies and criminals serving life sentences, among them Luigi Settembrini, founder of the 'Sons of Young Italy' and the model for the character in Thomas Mann's *The Magic Mountain*, and in more recent years future president Sandro Pertini and other opponents of Mussolini. The prison, **La Citadella**, is a fantastical Baroque pile designed in the form of a horseshoe, with 99 cells facing inwards. Its architect was Francesco Carpi, who no sooner finished it before, in a typically Neapolitan irony, he himself was locked inside for the rest of his life. In 1857, Carlo Pisacane and his band of 26 *Garibaldini* attacked the island and liberated the prisoners, but the new Italian state still found occupants for the cells until 1965. There are no names in the graveyard – only a worn inscription reading: 'Here ends the justice of man, here begins that of God.' There are some striking views from the cliffs, towards Ventotene and Ischia in the Bay of Naples.

East of Rome: The Monti Prenestini and Monti Simbruini

Leaving Rome on the old Via Prenestina or Via Casilina, it won't be long before you're facing some fairly serious mountains. Nowadays the Monti Prenestini are left to the shepherds, in lonely mountain pastures under the grey peaks, and the lofty Monti Simbruini on the Abruzzo border form a regional park. In former days these mountains cast a somewhat longer shadow. Palestrina, ancient *Praeneste*, was like nearby Tívoli (for which *see* p.167), an ancient rival of Rome, and preserves fascinating remains of the ancient Temple of Fortune, mother of the gods. And after the fall of Rome, St Benedict made Subiaco in the Monti Simbruini the first great centre of western Christian monasticism.

Getting There and Around

COTRAL buses from Ⓜ Anagnina (metro line A) or from Ponte Mammolo travel to Palestrina, Zagarolo, Subiaco (these are very regular, usually one each half-hour) and many of the smaller towns. On the bus you can doze through the gruesome eastern suburbs that go on endlessly along Via Casilina. From Subiaco there are also several buses a day to Palestrina, Tivoli, Frosinone and other towns. Palestrina and Zagarolo are also stops for local trains on the Rome–Frosinone line.

Tourist Information

Palestrina: Piazza S. Maria degli Angeli, **t** 06 957 3176.

Subiaco: Via Cadorna 59, **t/f** 0774 822013.

Zagarolo: Pro-loco, Via Tre Cannelle, **t** 06 957 5780.

Where to Stay and Eat

Palestrina ✉ 00036

★★★**Stella**, Piazza della Liberazione 3, **t** 06 953 8172, **f** 06 957 3360 (*cheap*). Next to the big trees in the Parco Barberini; a very simple family-run hotel of long standing, although all rooms do have satellite TV to keep you company. The hotel restaurant is open to all.

Taverna degli Anici, via Anici 39, **t** 06 9531 0061 (*moderate*). Stylish, welcoming and as well known for its impeccable service as its distinctive regional cuisine: try the ravioli stuffed with ricotta and pecorino and finish up with a fabulous home-made dessert.

Antonello Colonna, Via Roma 89, 9km south in little Labico, **t** 06 951 0032, **f** 06 951 1000 (*very expensive, reservations essential*). One of Lazio's top restaurants, which brings out the Romans in droves. The innovative maestro in the kitchen offers a short but exquisite menu with six antipasti, six *primi* and six *secondi*, all beautifully prepared using top ingredients. The cheese cart is mouse heaven, and you can round things off with a glass of brandy and a cigar. *Closed Sun eve and Mon and Aug.*

Subiaco ✉ 00028

A couple of simple choices here:

★★**Roma**, Via F. Petrarca 38, **t** 0774 84609, **f** 0774 822288 (*cheap*). Conveniently located on the edge of the medieval centre.

★**Miramonti**, Via Giovanni XXIII, **t/f** 0774 83243, (*moderate–cheap*). Plain, brick hotel with an excellent restaurant, **La Botte di Bacco**, featuring a seasonal menu of regional dishes – if it's on the menu, try the saffron risotto with truffles and famous Aniene trout. *Closed Tues, except in Aug.*

Locanda Mamma Peppina, **t/f** 0774 826100, (*cheap*). A chalet-style hotel and restaurant right at the foot of Monte Livata's ski slopes. The restaurant serves local products – including truffles and wild boar – with a huge panoramic terrace and just six rooms (full board obligatory).

Zagarolo

If you're starting from Rome along the Via Casilina, the great inland high road of southern Lazio, the beginning of this excursion couldn't be less auspicious. Lost in the sprawl as you leave Rome is the tomb of St Helen, mother of Constantine, called the **Tor Pignattara**, built in 330, and further on, the dried-up site of **Lake Regillus**, near Pantano Borghese, where Castor and Pollux helped the Romans defeat the Latins in 496 BC. To the north, the parallel Via Prenestina passes the very scanty ruins of **Gabii**, a Latin city that was another of Rome's early rivals, in the days of the Tarquins.

Beyond these forlorn memories of the past, the scenery perks up with woodlands and vineyards around **Zagarolo**, a half-medieval, half-Baroque town of churches, theatrical squares and palaces, and a thoroughly strange Baroque gate, the **Porta di San Martino**, decorated with reliefs of armour in curling ribbons. The 13th–18th-century **Palazzo Rospigliosi** (also called Palazzo Pallavicini) has frescoes by the

Zuccari and period furnishings (*open for tours on request; contact the EPT tourist office in Rome,* **t** *06 4889 9255*).

Palestrina

Another 5km leads up to **Palestrina**, ancient *Praeneste*, the birthplace of the composer Giovanni Pierluigi da Palestrina (1524–94), who invented the polyphonic Mass in the nick of time, just when the Council of Trent, dismayed with melodies straight from popular love songs and the tavern, was about to ban church music altogether. But Praeneste was on the map long before there was such a thing as a church. One of the oldest Latin towns, traditionally founded by Telegonus, son of Odysseus and Circe, it predates Rome and long battled against that upstart on the Tiber before making an alliance, rebelling, submitting, etc. But it had something even Rome couldn't match – the greatest Hellenistic temple in Italy, dedicated to Fortune, the mother of the gods: the **Sanctuary of Fortuna Primigenia**. When Palestrina was bombed in the war, it revealed that the sanctuary was as large as the entire modern town. Like many ancient temples, it was built into the side of a hill, neatly combining nature with architecture – though here on a scale previously unheard of. No one is sure when it was built, but in 80 BC it was partially burned during the Social Wars, and rebuilt by Sulla; it was revolutionary in its use of the Romans' special high-silica concrete that would later top the Pantheon and vault a hundred public baths.

Remains of the ancient sanctuary stretch from the bottom to the top of Palestrina in a series of wide artificial terraces. Along Via degli Arcioni, you can see the first level of arches that supported the town core; from the COTRAL bus stop, near the top of Via degli Arcioni, a road curves up to the 17th-century **Porta del Sole** and the remains of pre-Roman *Praeneste's* Cyclopean polygonal walls. Continue up to Via Anicia and turn left for Piazza Regina Margherita, on the terrace of the ancient Forum. Like squares in Rome, it has a certain spontaneous cubism, embellished with a pizza shop, a statue of Giovanni Pierluigi, a section of the ancient road and steps, and the unique, brick collage façade of the **cathedral** (*open 7–12 and 4–7*), built in the 5th century on the foundations of an ancient temple, perhaps dedicated to Jupiter. The nave is lined with a frieze of portraits of Palestrina's cardinals, under florid ceiling frescoes of the triumph of the Cross over paganism; in the left aisle is a copy of the *Palestrina Pietà*, sometimes attributed to Michelangelo (the original was carted off to Florence).

Adjacent to the cathedral are Corinthian columns embedded like fossils in the side of the former Seminary. This was built around *Praeneste*'s sacred area and is not always open to the public; try ringing the Seminario bell, and if they want to let you in, they will. Within is the so-called **Apsidal Hall** (perhaps a temple of Isis) where the famous Barberini mosaic was discovered (*see* below); the **Aerarium**, or treasury, containing the remains of an obelisk, busts and votive offerings; and the **Antro delle Sorti**, formerly believed to be the home of an oracle, and now thought to be the temple of Serapis, decorated with a beautiful mosaic of Alexandria.

Above rise the great steps of terraces leading to the main sanctuary of Fortune. To get there, continue up the steep streets and stairways to the top of Palestrina – if you're driving, begin with Via delle Monache from Piazza S. Maria degli Angeli and zigzag up to **Piazza della Cortina**. This, the highest terrace, was once the courtyard of the sanctuary's theatre; the *cavea* of seats was restored in 1640 to form the steps of the Palazzo Colonna-Barberini, built around the highest temple in the sanctuary. It now houses the **Museo Nazionale Archeologico Prenestino** (*open daily 9–one hour before sunset; adm, which includes access to the excavations*).

The museum contains a model of the sanctuary, a fine bas-relief of a triumph with a slave whispering in the *triumphator*'s ear, pine cone-shaped tombstones, eroded busts, the *cistae*, or bronze vanity cases with etched pictures (a local speciality), and, most splendiferous of all, on the top floor, the exquisite **Barberini mosaic of the Nile**, a brilliantly coloured Hellenistic masterpiece of the 2nd century BC, showing the Nile in flood, with all of Egypt's flora and fauna on islands in the stream, a lovers' banquet, a religious procession, the Canopus of Alexandria, obelisks, a towered city, etc.

Opposite the museum is the excavated area of the sanctuary; from the large rectangular courtyard steps descend to a colonnaded terrace, and then down again to the **Terrazza degli Emicicli**, or hemicycles, lined with Doric columns high up on a huge wall and the famous oracle of Fortune in the centre. This was the heart of the sanctuary, where the Sibyl of Palestrina responded to queries with *sorti*, or small wooden lots with letters carved in them, some of which were discovered in a well. From here there is a splendid view reaching to the sea, and it is said that in ancient times, until the temple was disbanded in the 4th century, two fires would be lit every night from here as beacons for sailors – though the coast is 30 miles away.

To the left of the museum is the pretty little church of **Santa Rosalia** (1660), and beyond it, on the road up to Palestrina's citadel, the ruined **Castel San Pietro** (3.5km), once the property of the Colonna. Pietro da Cortona made the altarpiece in its little church, but the magnificent view steals the show.

Subiaco

Few towns in Lazio can claim as wild and beautiful a setting as **Subiaco**, 74km from Rome at the head of the Aniene valley, where in the troubled late 5th century a certain Benedict of Norcia (480–547) wrote his *Rule* – a much gentler rule than the original, rather austere brand of desert and Irish monasticism designed only for saints. Benedict's Rule was for real men, and it set Christian monasticism on its way. All through the dark centuries his monasteries provided a haven for learning and piety, and retained so much standing in the 1460s that the first printing press in Italy was brought here by two monks from Germany.

As his reputation spread, Benedict became abbot of twelve monasteries in the Aniene valley; those not destroyed by the Lombards fell to earthquakes and the worldly ambition of the monks – although his Rule was relatively relaxed it seemed harsh to the locals; one priest sent him a poison loaf of bread (a raven stole it in the nick of time) and then sent a bevy of dancing girls to seduce his monks. Today only the two original monasteries in Subiaco remain, 2.5km above town, reached by road or footpath, both passing by way of the dismal remains of Nero's once grand **Villa Sublaqueum** ('under the lake'), by one of his long-disappeared artificial lakes. The first monastery, the **Convento di Santa Scholastica** (Benedict's twin sister), is open daily

(9–12.30 and 3.30–7; closed during Sun Mass, 10–11.30). A feudal abbey in the Middle Ages, it was later governed by princely cardinals appointed by the pope – famous inquisitor Torquemada was the first, followed by Rodrigo Borgia, the future Pope Alexander VI. S. Scholastica remains a holy bulwark of the faith, guarded by a stout Romanesque campanile. It has three cloisters, the first that you see built in 1580, incorporating columns from Nero's villa; the second an early Gothic cloister of 1052; the third, beautifully decorated in the 13th century by the Cosmatis. The library contains the first two books printed in Italy. Apparently the Germans and their newfangled contraption put the noses of the monastery's scribes out of joint, and after printing these two tomes the Germans went off in a huff to Rome.

Further up, built in the sheer rock of Monte Taleo, is the monastery of **San Benedetto**, often called the *Sacro Speco* for the cavern where Benedict lived and meditated for three years, having food lowered to him by ropes, and where he later attracted his first disciples (*open daily 9–12.30 and 3–6*). Partly natural, and partly built into the mountainside, the monastery is a monkish enchanted grotto, covered with wonderful medieval and early Renaissance frescoes. The labyrinthine complex, winding through various chapels, corridors and stairs cut into the rock, begins with a long passage lined with faded Renaissance frescoes that leads to the 14th-century **Upper Church**, with a wealth of Cosmati work including altar, paschal candlestick and a gorgeous pavement, under fine Sienese frescoes of the *Passion of Christ*, and a 15th-century Umbrian school cycle of the *Life of St Benedict*.

A stair leads down to the 13th-century **Lower Church**, built on several levels to incorporate St Benedict's Holy Grotto, now lined with marble from Nero's villa and a statue of the saint by Bernini's student Antonio Raggi. The frescoes illustrating the saint's life are by one of the first artists in these parts to have a name – a 13th-century Benedictine known as Master Consulus. In the adjacent **Chapel of St Gregorio Magno**, an anonymous monk in 1210 painted a *Portrait of St Francis*. It may well be the first live portrait done in Italy since Roman times, proof positive of the powerful effect that Francis had on his contemporaries; the artist portrays him as thin, bearded, quite handsome and romantically pensive, and he shares the chapel with some Byzantine works, sinister-looking six-winged seraphs. Below this is Benedict's hermitage, the **Sacro Speco**, hung with lamps to enhance the Aladdin's cave effect. Another stair, the Scala Santa, is painted with Sienese frescoes of the *Triumph of Death* and the *Life of the Virgin*; this leads to the **Grotta del Pastore**, where Benedict preached to the shepherds, containing a rare Byzantine fresco from the 700s. From here you can see what was an ancient bramble where Benedict had lain to mortify his flesh, but which turned into a rose tree at the touch of St Francis.

Subiaco was badly bombed in the Second World War: a pretty 11th-century **campanile** from the church of San Pietro survived, along with the **Rocca Abbaziale**, or Rocca dei Borgia, restored by Rodrigo Borgia in the 15th century. Cesare and Lucrezia Borgia were born here. The **Concattedrale di Sant'Andrea** was built in 1789 by Pius VI, another former Subiaco cardinal; restored after the war, it has rich polychrome marble altars, made from the remains of Trajan's villa at Arcinazzo. Best of all, just south of the town off Via Vittorio Veneto, a lovely humpback medieval bridge over the

Aniene, the **Ponte di San Francesco**, leads to a quiet chestnut grove and the church of **San Francesco** (1327; *open daily 9–12 and 3–7*) with a handsome carved walnut choir and frescoes attributed to Pinturicchio, Sodoma and Sebastiano del Piombo, while on the altar there's a triptych by Antoniazzo Romano.

Below Subiaco, at the bottom of the gorge of the Aniene, there's a little lake with a waterfall; it may have been one of the three mentioned by Tacitus in connection with Nero's villa. Subiaco and its monasteries stand on the edge of the **Parco Naturale Regionale dell' Appennino Monti Simbruini**, a haunt of eagles, beech and chestnut forests and newly introduced bears, with ten big mountains including **Monte Livata** (4,347–6,096ft), known as the *Montagna della Capitale*; it has the nearest skiing to Rome, especially cross-country, with lifts and schools. There is another ski area further east in the park, Campo Staffi at **Filettino**. There are **park information offices** in Livata (***t** 0774 826554*) and Filettino (***t** 0775 58788*) with maps and leaflets detailing excursions and walking trails. There are 13 ski runs at Monte Livata (six blue, five red and two black), and you can get up-to-date snow reports at *www.skiinfo.it*.

The Ciociaría

This humble corner of Lazio, filling up most of the province of Frosinone, is known as the Ciociaría, after the *ciocie*, or bark sandals, worn by the countrymen not so long ago, when this was one of the backwaters of Italy. As they were the first outsiders to come to Rome to seek work, Romans tend to call all new arrivals *Ciociari*, and rarely in a flattering vein – you may have seen the 1960 Vittorio de Sica film *La Ciociara* (*Two Women*) with a virtuoso performance from Sophia Loren. There are corners of the region, perhaps, where everything the Romans say is true, in the backwoods mountainous areas east of Frosinone. But the Ciocaría is also a land of gracious hill towns – Alatri and Ferentino, Arpino, Fiuggi and Anagni, among many others – a lovely and on the whole undiscovered part of Italy just an hour from Rome.

Anagni, and the Great Slap

I see the Lily storm Alagna's paling
and in Christ's vicar, Christ a captive made.
I see once more the mockery and the railing
I see renewed the vinegar and gall
Twixt two live thieves
I see his deadly nailing.

Dante, Purgatory, Canto XX, trans. by Dorothy L. Sayers

Anagni was the capital and holy city of the Hernici, yet another Italic tribe who proliferated in these parts before the Romans came along and made ancient history so much easier to follow. As small as it is, Anagni held centre stage in European politics on several occasions during the Middle Ages. Four 14th-century popes were born here, and several others made it their summer home. Greatest among them was the

Getting Around

Southern Lazio may be a mountainous place, but the broad valley of the Sacco, running through the middle of it, allows for quick travelling by way of the A1 Autostrada del Sole, on its way from Rome to Naples.

A **rail** line follows it too, with main stops and frequent connections at Frosinone and Cassino. Most are local trains, also stopping at Colleferro, Anagni (with bus connections to Fiuggi), Ceprano and Aquino. From Cassino there is also a train or two each day over the Apennines to Avezzano, via Isola dei Liri and Sora, and one to Térmoli in the Molise.

Frosinone, the provincial capital, is the centre for COTRAL **buses**, with connections everywhere; buses from Rome to Frosinone leave from Rome's Anagnina Station, while for Fiuggi they leave from Termini.

Tourist Information

Anagni: Pro-loco, Piazza Innocenzo III, **t** 0775 727852.

Fiuggi: Via Gorizia 4, **t** 0775 515446, **f** 0775 515766, and Piazza Frascara, **t** 0775 515019, *www.fiuggi@apt.frosinone.it*.

Frosinone: Via Aldo Moro 465, **t** 0775 833836, **f** 0775 833837, *info@apt.frosinone.it*, *www.apt.frosinone.it*.

Alatri: Pro-loco, Via Cesare Battisti 7, **t** 0775 435318.

Arpino: Piazza Municipio, **t** 0776 848535.

Cassino: Piazza De Gasperi 6, **t** 0776 21292, **f** 0776 25692.

Where to Stay and Eat

Anagni ✉ 03012

★★★★**Villa La Floridiana**, Via Casilina km63, **t** 0775 769960, **f** 0775 774527 (*expensive–moderate*). Converted from a 19th-century country villa, this welcoming hotel is located just outside the centre; the nine rooms are furnished with antiques and frescoes on the ceiling, and the restaurant is excellent (*but closed Sun eve, Mon lunch and Aug*).

Le Mimose, on the road to Fiuggi, **t** 0775 726491 (*moderate–inexpensive*). For a pizza or full meal in a pretty setting in the country. *Closed Wed.*

Lo Schiaffo ('the Slap'), Strada Vittorio Emanuele, **t** 0775 39148 (*moderate*). In town, near the cathedral; serves up pasta with truffles, filling steaks and chops. *Closed Tues.*

Fiuggi ✉ 03015

You can nearly always find a room in one of Fiuggi's 220 hotels – which makes it a good base, as the rest of the area doesn't have many.

★★★★★**Grand Hotel Palazzo della Fonte**, Via dei Villini 7, **t** 0775 5081, **f** 0775 506752, *www.palazzodellafonte.com* (*luxury*). For plushness and luxury, you can't beat this magnificent Liberty-style hotel, built in 1911, when the newly named Fiuggi decided to aim its waters at a fashionable clientele. Public rooms are sumptuous, bedrooms are fitted with every comfort, and there are indoor and outdoor pools, a fitness centre, beauty farm, and more, all run by knowing pros. Add an excellent restaurant and delicious breakfast buffet, and you really should feel better when you leave, if somewhat poorer. *Open mid-Mar–early Dec.*

son of a local baron who became Boniface VIII, a nasty intriguer who had the poor timing to proclaim loudly the temporal supremacy of the popes long after anyone else took the idea seriously; he also had the bad judgement to excommunicate Philip IV of France. Captured in Anagni in 1303 by the redoubtable warrior Sciarra Colonna and 300 French knights, Boniface dressed in all his insignia and sat waiting on his throne, expecting to be killed. Philip's emissary Guillaume de Nogaret and Colonna strode into the hall, and Colonna gave the pope a resounding slap in the face – a symbolic slap heard around Europe, putting a temporary end to papal dreams of world domination. Boniface's ordeal didn't last long. He had only been captured because the leaders of Anagni had allowed it; three days later they changed their

******Fiuggi Terme**, Via Prenestina 9, **t** 0775 51212, **f** 0775 506566, *hotelfiuggiterme@libero.it* (*very expensive–expensive*). Light and airy, in a park outside Fiuggi Fonte, but there's a shuttle bus to transport you to the centre; pool and tennis are other pluses.

******Villa Igea**, Corso Nuova Italia 32, **t** 0775 515435, **f** 0775 515438 (*expensive–moderate*). A classic Italian spa hotel from the turn of last century, with lovely rooms and a small garden. *Closed Nov and Dec.*

But Fiuggi is hardly a luxury spa, and the area around the baths also has some less expensive choices – the biggest collection of tolerable cheap hotels in central Italy, perhaps:

*****Europa**, Via Gorizia 35, **t** 0775 515002, **f** 0775 515536 (*moderate*). A fine old-fashioned green-shuttered establishment. *Closed Dec.*

****Touring**, Via Nuova Fonte 6, **t** 0775 507000, *info@hoteltouringfiuggi.it* (*cheap*). Similar to the Europa. *Closed Nov, Dec.*

***Gorizia**, Via Fiume 8, **t** 0775 515029 (*cheap*). Tidy and spartan. *Closed Dec.*

La Torre dal 1961, Piazza Trento e Trieste 18, in the *centro storico*, **t** 0775 515382 (*expensive*). A citadel of great wine and imaginative cuisine, making good use of fresh Ciociaría-grown ingredients: pasta in basil and crayfish sauce, or breast of duck with porcini mushrooms. *Closed Tues exc in summer.*

La Locanda, Via Stanislao da Fiuggi, **t** 0775 505855 (*moderate–inexpensive*). Just around the corner from La Torre, this *enoteca* serves strictly fresh pasta, and lots of roast lamb, rabbit, and unusual dishes like oxtail – *coda vaccinara*. *Closed Mon.*

Il Rugantino, 326 Via Armando Diaz, **t** 0775 515400 (*moderate–inexpensive*). Halfway up the road between the spa and the centre; offers both pizza and a full menu with some gratifying choices such as steaks with truffles or wild mushrooms. *Closed Wed.*

Ferentino ✉ 03013

No hotels (nor many restaurants) in or near the centre, unfortunately.

*****Bassetto**, on the SS6 Via Casilina, **t** 0775 244931, **f** 0775 244399 (*moderate*). A comfortable stay in a modern roadside hotel; it also has the best restaurant in town (*moderate*).

*****Fontana Olente**, **t** 0775 24181, **f** 0775 241 8500, *www.hotelfontanaolente.com* (*moderate*). A crisp, modern hotel near the Bassetto with plush rooms and all kinds of therapies on offer at the adjoining spa.

Alatri ✉ 03011

Two choices here, and both basic ones:

***Saturno**, on the SS155 to Fiuggi, **t** 0775 443261 (*cheap*). With an equally basic restaurant.

***La Rosetta**, in a pleasant, quiet location up in the acropolis, Via Duomo 35, **t** 0775 434568 (*cheap*).

Dining's pretty basic too:

La Conca, in the centre on Via Roma, **t** 0775 434650 (*moderate–inexpensive*). Pizza and a full menu in a shady garden. *Closed Mon.*

Acuto ✉ 03010

Colline Ciociare, Via Prenestina 27, **t/f** 0775 56049 (*expensive*). One of the top restaurants in all Lazio is in the otherwise unassuming hill village of Acuto: open by reservation only. Panoramic views and beautiful dining room converted from an old house, with all of six tables. Settle in, and expect to be spoiled rotten at the hands of experts. *Closed Mon, Tues lunch, Nov, mid-Aug.*

minds and freed him, though he and the medieval papacy were never the same again. One of Boniface's ideas has had a longer shelf-life: he proclaimed the first Jubilee or Holy Year in 1300 (it wasn't his idea really; crowds started descending on Rome spontaneously from all over Europe before New Year, repeating a legend that some past pope had declared a Jubilee a century earlier, and Boniface could only play along).

The Cathedral

Open April–Oct 9–1 and 4–7, Nov–Mar 9–1 and 3–6.

Anagni's principal monument is its stout and squarish **cathedral**, begun in 1077 and one of the finest in central Italy, sharing a little of the genius of the Tuscan and

Apulian churches of the same period. The massive Lombard-style apses at the rear give it a fortress aspect, while there is a more graceful loggia on the side for papal ceremonials; Boniface had the statue of himself erected on it shortly after his election in 1294 (Boniface's foes accused him of idolatry from his habit of planting statues of himself everywhere; he also invented the bizarre beehive-shaped triple tiara, designed to show papal supremacy over mere kings and emperors, that popes wore until the 19th century).

In front, behind the imposing 12th-century campanile, the façade is Romanesque, while a rebuilding in the 1300s left it tentatively Gothic within, decorated with a Cosmatesque pavement and a wonderful 13th-century gilded stone *baldacchino* over the altar. The imposing episcopal throne (1263), curiously decorated with a Star of David, wasn't commissioned by Boniface, but it does reveal something of the clerical pretensions of the age, flanked by big marble lions just like the imperial throne in Constantinople. Off the left aisle, the **Cappella Gaetani** contains the Cosmatesque tombs of Boniface's family, with bits of recently discovered 13th-century fresco. When not causing trouble around Europe, Boniface devoted his papacy to enriching his family (usually spelled Caetani) with lands and benefices; by his death they had swallowed much of southern Lazio, and survived as one of Rome's most powerful families for centuries.

Crypt of San Magno: 'the Medieval Sistine Chapel'

Hours same as cathedral; in any case, you may have to wait for someone with the key; adm.

The highlight of the cathedral is the recently restored **crypt of San Magno**. They'll give you a guided tour of about fifteen minutes, which isn't anywhere near enough, but they'll only put the lights on for a little at a time to preserve the colours. Caution raised to the point of absurdity perhaps, but then these are some of the finest medieval frescoes in Italy, blue and gold Byzantine-style painting from the 12th and 13th centuries; the vaulted, three-aisled crypt is completely covered by them, above one of the most richly detailed Cosmati pavements anywhere, signed in stone by Master Cosma himself.

Scholars debate tirelessly over the attributions and dates of the paintings, but the greatest number seem to be the work of three hands. The 'Pittore delle Traslazioni', least Byzantine, most Gothic of the three in style, and especially skilful in the use of colour, did some of the most intriguing paintings. In the left apse are portraits of *Hippocrates and Galen*, alongside fascinating visions of the philosophical cosmology of the Middle Ages: a *Macrocosmos* with man at the centre, a *Zodiac*, and a diagram of the *Four Elements* and their interrelationships. To sum up the world from beginning to end, this painter adds a tremendous vision of the *Apocalypse* in the central apse and adjacent vaulting, with all the demons and cherubim, the 24 elders, the opening of the seals, the Four Horsemen. Some art historians claim this painter actually worked much earlier, about 1100 – it was he, most likely, who painted the seated portrait of *St Peter of Anagni*, the bishop who began this crypt as the first part of the cathedral programme in 1063, and later took part in the First Crusade.

Between them, the 'Pittore Ornatista' and the third painter, a Benedictine monk named Frater Romanus, collaborated on the series of vault paintings that tell the story of the *Ark of the Covenant*. Both are more Byzantine in style, and more precise in their drawing. They also collaborated on the series of the *Life of San Magno* (except for the part on the central apse, the *traslazione* of the saint's body that gave the other painter his name); the latter two also contributed most of the saints, prophets and Madonnas on the walls of the crypt. According to some, Frater Romanus was also one of the artists of the Sacro Speco at Subiaco.

San Magno, the martyr of Anagni to whom all this is dedicated, has a little secret: he never existed. Apparently he is a confusion with the Greek Saint Andrew the Tribune; somewhere, some monk copying a list of saints slipped a rogue comma into the phrase *Andreas Tribunus Magnus Martyr*, and a new saint was born.

The **cathedral treasury** (*open summer 9–3 and 4–7, winter 9–1 and 3–6; adm*) contains a wealth of church gear, some of it from Boniface's time, including an English-made chasuble with the story of St Nicholas and a 13th-century casket showing the martyrdom of St Thomas à Becket, made in Limoges. Thomas' cult appeared everywhere on the continent after his murder – think of him as a key propaganda figure in the papal struggle against secular powers. The cathedral has a separate **chapel** dedicated to him, with more 13th-century frescoes; it lies under the left aisle of the cathedral, and may actually have been built as a *mithraeum* in Roman times.

Around the Town

Just a bit down Strada Vittorio Emanuele, Anagni's main street, is the **Palazzo di Bonifacio VIII** (*open daily summer 9–1 and 3–7, winter 9–1 and 3–6; adm*), actually built by Gregory IX in 1295. Ironically, the last pope to spend time here was Martin V in 1428, who kissed the ground for pardon when he arrived – he was a descendant of Sciarra Colonna. The palace contains a historical and archaeological collection that is mostly clutter and old photos. Some rooms retain their frescoes, including the Great Hall where the Slap was administered, painted with simple decorative frescoes including, oddly, an entire wall of geese.

Take some time for a walk around Anagni, a medieval time-capsule with its walls, towers and palaces; the 14th-century **Casa Barnekow**, further down Vittorio Emanuele, was restored by a 19th-century Swedish painter named Albert von Barnekow to look more medieval than the Middle Ages themselves, with faded, fanciful exterior frescoes. Nearby, where the town park meets the walls, an arcade called the **Arcazzi di Piscina** survives from the Roman baths.

Five kilometres to the south, **Segni** (ancient *Signia*), like so many of its neighbours, was girded by Cyclopean walls from the 6th or 5th century BC; some of these remain, especially a lower stretch pierced by a monumental gate known as the **Porta Saracena**, with a ten-foot-long, monolithic architrave (it's a ten-minute panoramic walk, signposted off the road up to the centre). Segni's 17th-century **cathedral**, built in a Greek cross over a Romanesque original, has paintings by Pietro da Cortona. Take the beautiful **Passeggiata Pianillo** up to the top of the town, where a walled enclosure of the 3rd-century BC temple contains a *cella* now supporting the Romanesque church of **San Pietro**, with 13th- and 16th-century frescoes. Behind it, don't miss the massive **cistern**, from the same period as the temple.

Fiuggi

Up in the wooded mountains above Anagni, **Fiuggi** has been a famous spa for centuries, although until 1911 it went under the name of Anticoli di Campagna. Michelangelo came here to take the waters for his kidney stones after the strain of working on the Sistine Chapel. It originally belonged to the Caetani, and then to the Borgias, and from 1517 to the Colonna; the old town that they knew is still intact on its hill, while down below the two busy spas, the Fonte Bonifacio VIII and Fonte Anticolana, still do the business on kidney stones, and help treat arthritis and gout, and all the complaints of the overworked Italian liver. There's enough water left over to provide one of central Italy's most popular brands of *acqua minerale*.

Fiuggi comes in two parts. Down below, **Fiuggi Fonte** has the spas, the fancy shops, and an infinity of hotels surrounded by forests. With its winsome *belle époque* air, it is gay and pleasurable as only an Italian spa town can be. Via Armando Diaz leads up to the old medieval centre, **Fiuggi Città**, blessed with a grand ensemble of buildings from the 1900s at **Piazza Trento e Trieste**. Here, besides the obligatory Grand Hotel and a fanciful Municipio, the Art Nouveau **Casino** has recently been restored as a municipal theatre; next to it a miniature version of the Louvre Pyramid has been created as an entrance to the town's unusual underground library.

Just west of Fiuggi, **Acuto** gets its name from the sharpness of its hill; the bishops of Anagni had a castle there, and there are superb views down on Anagni and the Sacco valley. At nearby **Piglio**, stop for a glass of Cesanese, the local red wine; they also make a very good white.

Ferentino

Ferentino (ancient *Ferentinum*) and its neighbour Alatri have a lot in common. Both still retain the same form they had in ancient times, with Cyclopean-walled centres and walled acropoli inside, and both are quiet and exceedingly pleasant Lazio-style hill towns. Ferentino was probably founded by the Hernici, but at some point the Volscians snatched it, and it belonged to them until 413 BC, when the Romans captured it and handed it back to their faithful allies. The ancient centre is wrapped in a nearly intact ring of Cyclopean walls, which formed a base for later additions: several of the gates still have their Roman arches intact, including on the south wall the Porta Santa Croce, the Porta Maggiore and the 4th century BC **Porta Sanguinaria** (the bloody gate), the best place to see the ancient Roman and medieval layers on top. Follow the walls outside to the left of this gate to see the **Posterula**, an unusual pointed-arch postern gate in the Cyclopean walls that makes archaeologists wonder about a cultural inheritance from Mycenaean Greece, where similar walls and gates are found (for what it's worth, the ancient Hittites of Turkey built them too). Just inside Porta Sanguinaria, on Via Sabina, is the uncovered half of a 2nd-century BC **Roman theatre**. Nearby stands the Cistercian Gothic church of **Santa Maria Maggiore**, begun in 1150.

This was not an abbey church like the others, but the centre of a small community of monks looking after a *grancia* (a storehouse for grain, from the French *grange*) that belonged to the Abbey of Casamari; the building still stands, hidden by the houses across from the church. There was more to the Cistercian effort in Lazio than just reclaiming land. They must also have had a finger in the rough-and-tumble Church–State conflicts of the time, for Ferentino's Cistercians were twice run out of town by the local Ghibellines, who also wrecked their buildings. In 1255 they were back to stay, and rebuilt Santa Maria Maggiore in its present form, a little Gothic jewel in an improbable setting, a smaller version of Fossanova or Casamari, with an octagonal cupola like Fossanova's over the crossing. As always in a Cistercian building, the paucity of decoration highlights the grace of the architecture, though there is a lovely rose window in the nave, and some good details inside.

On the northern side of town, on Via XX Settembre, the 13th-century **San Francesco** was built under the Gothic influence of the Cistercians; the adjacent convent houses Ferentino's **Museo Archeologico** (*open Tues–Thurs 9–1, Fri–Sun 9–12 and 4–7; adm*).

The **acropolis** of Ferentino stands on a mighty terrace of ancient masonry; Cyclopean below, Roman and medieval above. From Piazza Mazzini, where the Pro-loco occupies the old town hall, the medieval **Palazzo Consolare**, take Via Regina Margherita up the stairs to see the acropolis' massive supporting structures. The **Palazzo Vescovile** sits on top, replacing the palace of the Roman prefects. More stairs lead through the walls up to the cathedral; note the badly eroded phallic symbol on the keystone of the arch; similar phalluses have been discovered on reliefs dug up around the acropolis; it's a little Ferentinese mystery.

At the top, Piazza del Duomo offers great views over the valley of the Sacco. The stones of an ancient temple were recycled to make the handsome Romanesque **cathedral**, begun in 1106. Though remarkably austere outside, it has an interior fit for a pope: in this case Innocent III, most powerful of all medieval popes, who favoured Ferentino and spent much time here. He provided most of the cathedral's complete set of Cosmatesque furnishings, including a very well-preserved pavement, a fine ciborium and transenna, and a virtuoso marble candlestick, carved like a twisted rope. The 1900s Art Nouveau golden frescoes on the apse fit right in. On the frame of the sacristy door, note the heads of Emperor Frederick II and John of Brienne, King of Jerusalem, who visited on their way to a crusade in 1223; inside the sacristy are parts of the 9th-century ciborium from the original church here, now reassembled as an altar. To the right of the cathedral lie the ruins of a grandiose Baroque cathedral that was to replace the medieval one; they abandoned the project when it was scarcely begun, and left the stones sitting to this day.

From Piazza del Duomo, Via Don Morosini curves outside the acropolis walls and runs alongside them, passing along the way Ferentino's unique ancient monument, the **Mercato Romano** (*open April–Sept 9–12 and 4–7; in winter ring the Pro-loco,* **t** *0775 245775*). This, too, is part of a platform supporting the acropolis, but the 1st-century AD Roman architects used the opportunity to create a covered market underneath, with five vaulted chambers for shops and stands; originally it had frescoed decoration, though only hints of this have survived. Following Via Don Morosini to the end takes you to two palaces of the 1200s, the **Palazzo di Innocenzo III** and the more imposing **Palazzo dei Cavalieri Gaudenti**, with an elegant Gothic arcade over the street that was later walled in. Just outside the walls, on the steps leading down from Porta Maggiore, is the **Testament of Quintilius**. This takes the form of an inscription in a niche from the time of Trajan, recording the magistrate's donation of his rents to his home town. North of the centre, near Collepero, are the ruins of a Roman aqueduct and a Roman bridge, the **Ponte Sereno**, still in good nick after 1,700 years.

Nearby **Fumone**, like most hill towns of the Ciociaría, wears a fortified sombrero. This 11th-century **castello** (*open winter 10–12.30 and 3.30–6, summer 10–12.30 and 3–7; adm exp*) was a little prison of the Papal States, chiefly notorious as the place where Boniface VIII imprisoned his predecessor, the gentle, rather simple hermit-pope Celestine V, after the poor monk abdicated (Boniface's enemies claimed that, when Celestine was staying at the Egg Castle in Naples, Boniface whispered into his chamber through a secret tube, pretending to be the voice of God commanding him to abdicate). Another inmate, anti-Pope Gregory VIII, is said to be buried secretly in the walls. The halls are still full of medieval atmosphere, and you can take a walk around the walls and visit the hanging gardens *all'italiana*.

Alatri

Alatri, 2,400 years ago, was another of the main cities of the Hernici, and a firm ally of Rome, a wise policy that spared Alatri the destruction that befell many of the other ancient cities of Lazio. Consequently Alatri, along with its near-twin Ferentino, remains the best example we have of a pre-Roman Italian town, with an almost complete circuit of Cyclopean walls from about the 6th century BC. In the centre, roughly where the old forum stood, is Piazza S. Maria Maggiore, with a pretty fountain, the 19th-century **Fontana Pia**, and the church of **Santa Maria Maggiore** (*open on request,* ***t*** *0775 450280*), built over a temple of Jupiter. It's a cheerful, flower-filled church, like so many dedicated to the Virgin; the current building started out Romanesque in 1137 and ended up with pointed arches before it was done, along with a fine rose window and a slightly tipsy campanile. A chapel on the left aisle is dedicated to the *Madonna di Costantinopoli*, a medieval icon with that genuine faraway Byzantine look in her eyes – though she's really believed to be a French or Italian work. Around her are 12 polychromed wood scenes of the *Lives of Jesus and Mary* from the 13th century, probably by an artist from Campania, as well as a triptych by the local 15th-century artist Antonio di Alatri. The Madonna of Constantinople has her charms, but the Alatrini are fonder of another icon, the *Madonna della Libera*, with a very expressive *trecento* face. They like to think she is a work of Giotto, and they have detatched her from the pier where she was painted and given her her own chapel.

Another set of ancient walls at the top of Alatri marks the boundaries of the **acropolis**, similar to Ferentino's. Inside is a quiet park where the cathedral and the Bishop's Palace stand over the sites of the Hernician temples. The **Duomo** is a curious one; a spooky image of a pope in gold and silver haunts the left transept, while the right aisle contains Cosmatesque relics, perhaps a disassembled pulpit, along with a strange relief of Jonah being gobbled up by the whale. The right transept contains perhaps Lazio's newest church frescoes (1979), colourful scenes of traditional life by an artist named Venere Cerini that commemorate Alatri's medieval miracle. Back in 1228, they say, a young man doubted the Church dogma of the Transubstantiation of the Host. Encouraged in his disbelief by a loose woman, he secretly wrapped the host in a handkerchief one Sunday and slipped it in his pocket. When he looked at it later, it had indeed turned into a hunk of bloody meat. The story reached the ears of Pope Gregory IX, who wrote back (in a letter reproduced here as an inscription) recommending only light punishments for both, and reminding us that anything that increases the faith is a miracle. Medieval sceptics must not have been sufficiently impressed, for the Church was forced to come up with another such miracle in 1264 (*see* 'Bolsena', p.221).

There is more that's peculiar about old Alatri, and next to the Duomo, on a spot that was the highest point of the old acropolis, the town has erected signboards with a detailed explanation of it. It seems that several of the gates in the ancient wall are precisely equidistant from this spot, and aligned with the sunrises and sunsets on the equinoxes and solstices, making the entire town a kind of astronomical observatory. Perhaps these old Italic tribes were more clever than the archaeologists give them credit for. From the opposite wall of the acropolis, you can look down on the **Piagge**, Alatri's quarter of narrow medieval alleys and stairs. The 11th-century **San Silvestro**, at the edge of the Piagge on Via Facchini, has a crypt with medieval frescoes.

The Hernici left their name to the surrounding Monti Ernici, famous since antiquity for their variety of curative herbs – one Roman writer described them as 'the garden of the centaur Chiron, the master of Aesculapius'. You can see them first hand at the WWF's **Giardino Botanico Flora** in **Collepardo**, north of Alatri (*open April–Sept, Sat 3.30–7.30, Sun 10–1 and 3–7.30*), with labels in Latin and English. The town has a small **Herb Museum** (*open by request,* **t** *0775 47012*), but perhaps the most interesting place to learn about them is the **Certosa di Trisulti**, 7km further up into the mountains (*open 9.30–12, 3–5.30, summer 4–6.30*). This is a Carthusian Charterhouse founded in the early 13th century by Innocent III, though most of what you see today dates from the 1700s, when the Certosa was given its lavish Baroque church and grandiose porticoes that took over a century to build. The monks (Cistercians since 1949) have long been famed for their herbal remedies and liqueurs made from the centaur's garden, and inside the Certosa the main attraction is the delightful 18th century **pharmacy**, with its ornate cabinets, ceramics jars and Pompeii-style frescoes, and others by an imaginative Neapolitan painter named Filippo Balbi, who worked here from 1857 to 1865. The monks' *aperitivi* and *digestivi*, still prepared to traditional recipes, are on sale in the Certosa's *Liquoreria*.

Two kilometres from Collepardo centre, the stalactite **Grotte di Collepardo** are famous for their human-shaped formations (*open summer 8am–8pm, winter Sat, Sun and hols only 10–5; adm*); a combined ticket is available to visit the **Pozzo d'Antullo** (*open same hours*), a rare carstic 'well' shaped like a cone measuring 1,000ft in circumference – the floor is covered with lush vegetation.

Frosinone

Along the old Via Casilina, ambitious little **Frosinone** serves as the capital for the Ciociaría, and the centre for all bus lines in the region. One of the candidates for the title of most obscure provincial capital in Italy, Frosinone will nevertheless seem formidable enough when you get there. It's a sprawling, modern town that even boasts its own skyscraper, and its streets wind aimlessly about like a plate of malicious tagliatelle; no town in Lazio works harder to get you lost and keep you lost. There is a tiny *centro storico* on the hilltop, if you can find it, with nice views from Piazza Vittorio Veneto and a hotchpotch cathedral. Frosinone does try to sort out its province's complicated ancient history in the **Museo Archeologico**, in the old governor's palace on Via XX Settembre 32 (*open Tues–Thurs 9–1, Fri–Sun 9–12 and 4–7; adm*).

Véroli and Casamari

East of Frosinone, a side road off the SS214 for Sora will take you to **Véroli**, where the Concattedrale di Sant'Andrea, a 17th-century work that replaced the original after an earthquake, has an interesting **Museo del Tesoro** (*open on request; **t** 0775 237020*) with five ivory coffers of Arab–Sicilian work (9th–13th centuries), Palaeochristian fragments, and a vast collection of parchments from the 10th to the 15th century. Next to the co-cathedral, **Santa Maria Salome** has a colourful interior redone in the 1700s, with Renaissance frescoes and paintings by the Cavaliere d'Arpino and others. The *comune* has a **Museo delle Erbe**, a collection of 1,250 herbs found on the lush slopes of the Monti Ernici, and an exhibit of how drugs were compounded from them in the old days; to visit, ask at the town hall (*mornings are best; **t** 0775 238254*). The back streets of old Véroli have some fine medieval and Renaissance palaces, including the **Casa Reali**; here, displayed on one of the walls, you can see a genuine calendar from the time of Augustus called the *Fasti Verulani*, carved in stone and discovered only in 1922 (the first Emperor's astronomers, who redesigned the calendar and invented the month of August, are also the fellows who thought up the imperial census that sent Joseph and Mary to Bethlehem). The oldest part of Véroli, the ruggedly medieval **Borgo di San Leucio**, leads up to the town's Hernician acropolis, with polygonal walls and a ruined medieval castle.

East of Véroli the SS214 continues to the **Abbey of Casamari** (*open daily 9–12 and 3–6*). The abbey itself was founded in 1005, but what you see is mostly 13th-century Cistercian, similar to the complex at Fossanova, although here the sharp French Gothic arches have been gently tempered by the Italian builders. After a long decline, the abbey was put out of business, ironically enough by the French; Napoleon's men gave it a good sacking in 1798. One thing sets Casamari apart from its Cistercian sisters: a complete set of alabaster windows, giving a warm glow to the interior. The near-total lack of decoration reflects St Bernard's strict rule; only the high altar in polychrome marble, donated by Pope Clement XI in 1711, provides a note of colour. The flower garden in the lovely cloister offers another. Though the church now belongs to the local parish, the monastery is occupied by a *sui juris* Benedictine-style community; they'll sell you some of their monkish liqueurs (and monkish shampoo) in a room filled with a wildlife collection that includes a stuffed anteater. They also have a

Where to Stay and Eat

Frosinone ✉ 03100

All modern and rather plain here, but there are some places to rest your weary head – and you'll certainly never starve.

*****Astor**, Via Casilina Nord 220, **t** 0775 270132, **f** 0775 270135, *astor@fr.flashnet.it* (*moderate*). The nicest place, and recently refurbished. A comfortable businessman's hotel with a restaurant that makes one want to take back all the unkind things one has said about Frosinone. They've got a seriously good cook back there, turning out dishes like *orecchiette* with porcini mushrooms, or *tagliolini* with black truffles, with superb seafood to follow (*moderate*).

*****Palombella**, Via Maria 234, **t** 0775 872163, **f** 0775 270402 (*moderate–cheap*). In a garden setting off the *autostrada*; good buffet breakfast, and another fine restaurant.

Hostaria Tittino, Vic. Cipresso 2, **t** 0775 251227 (*moderate*). An age-old restaurant offering a varied choice of *primi*, including ravioli filled with ricotta and spinach, and the usual suspects for *secondo*, but doesn't try at all with the desserts. *Closed Sun, most of Aug.*

Casamari ✉ 03029

****Caio Mario**, Loc. Casamari, Veroli, **t** 0775 282300, **f** 0775 283311 (*cheap*). The nearby monastery is in a pleasant country setting, and the main attraction here. Nice inexpensive rooms and also a big restaurant popular with the locals (*inexpensive*). *Closed Wed.*

Isola del Liri ✉ 03036

****Scala**, in the centre on Piazza Boncompagni, **t** 0776 808584, **f** 0776 808384 (*cheap*). The only hotel here; basic and well kept.

Ratafià, Vic. Calderoni 8, **t** 0776 808033 (*moderate–inexpensive*). Book to make sure of a table at this intimate restaurant, to feast on such delights as rocket with mushrooms and fresh pecorino and veal *involtini* wrapped in crinkly green cabbage leaves; good desserts and wines. *Closed Mon.*

Arpino ✉ 03033

Nothing special here either, but the ****Bel Sito**, Via Caio Mario, **t** 0776 848272, and the *****Sunrise Crest**, up at Civitavécchia, **t** 0776 848901, will do at a pinch (*both cheap*), and both have restaurants.

Sora ✉ 03039

*****Motel Valentino**, Viale S. Domenico 1 (on the SS82 south), **t** 0776 31071, **f** 0776 824442, *www.arcmedia.it/hotel.valentino* (*moderate*). The last-chance hotel in town for visiting salami salesmen; it's not bad, and the restaurant is an essential part of the Sora experience, with its 200 sq ft television screen and homicidal dissipated waitress; the food ain't bad either. Still, if you have ever been to Oklahoma you're liable to hallucinations that tell you you've died and gone back there. *Closed Sat.*

Olimpus, Viale S. Domenico (on the SS382), **t** 0776 854048, *www.olimpussora.it* (*moderate*). This vast, villa-style place combines a restaurant and disco-bar for salami salesmen with big expense accounts.

Alvito

*****Villa Grancassa**, Via Roma 8, **t** 0776 508915, **f** 0776 508914, *villagrancassa@libero.it* (*expensive–moderate*). Ten kilometres above Alvito, a bishop's palace in medieval San Donato Val di Comino has been refitted as a charming hotel; its 27 perfectly quiet rooms make a good base for the southern part of the Abruzzo National Park. *Closed Nov, and part of Jan, Feb.*

museum, the **Museo Cereate Mariano** (*open by request*, **t** *0775 237020*) with paintings by Annibale Carracci, Guercino, Solimena and others, and an archaeological collection; as the name Casamari suggests, the great general Marius, a man of the people who ran Rome for a while in the 1st-century BC period of civil wars, lived or was born in a villa here, according to inscriptions found on the site.

Isola del Liri is literally an island, where the river Liri creates a little cascade on one side and a dramatic 100ft waterfall on the other. One might expect an Italian town to make good use of such an exceptional setting; Isola del Liri doesn't manage it. In ancient times, this was part of the territory of Arpino; the exact birthplace of the silver-tongued Cicero, in 106 BC, is believed to be just north of Isola del Liri on the Sora road, near the church of San Domenico, where the remains of a Roman villa have been found.

Arpino

No culture in the Ciociaría? The tidy hill town of Arpino, famous cradle of great men, begs to differ: the aforementioned Marius and Cicero were from its territory, along with Agrippa, Augustus' admiral, son-in-law, and builder of the Pantheon. The mothers of Arpino didn't stop there: they went on to give birth to Giuseppe Cesari, better known as the Cavaliere d'Arpino (b. 1568, the stupefyingly mediocre painter of the dome of St Peter's in Rome), and Carlo Conti, teacher of the opera composer Bellini, among many others. This far corner of the Ciociaría, east of (and including) Frosinone, does have a dishevelled hillbilly air to it, but even today Arpino is a distinguished exception.

The main square, **Piazza Municipio**, occupies the old Roman forum; here, besides a statue of Cicero vehemently orating to the pigeons, you'll find the solemn church of **San Michele**, built some time before the first millennium over an ancient Roman temple of the Muses. Remade in the Baroque era, it offers a chance to get a close look at the efforts of the Cavaliere d'Arpino, as well as a beautiful Tuscan *Crucifixion* from the 16th century. The handsome Renaissance palace of the local lords, the Boncompagni, restored in the 1800s, houses the **Centro Internazionale Umberto Mastroianni** (*open Mon, Wed, Thurs 8.30–1.30; Tues, Fri, Sat, 8.30–1.30 and 3.30–6; Sun 9–12; adm*) where you can examine sculptures by the prolific uncle of the late great Marcello (who was born 12km to the southwest, in Fontana Liri). For centuries, Arpino was famous worldwide for its lutes and mandolins; the piazza also has an exhibit of their masterworks, along with other mementoes, including a letter from a tsarina ordering a lute, in the **Mostra della Bottega dei Maestri Liutai Embergher e Cerrone** (*open Mon–Sat 10–1 and 4–7; adm; will also organize guided tours of Arpino if booked in advance, **t** 0776 849241*). The castle on top of Arpino dates from the early 1400s; when the army of Pope Pius II captured it from the Dukes of Alvito, he ordered that Arpino be spared for the sake of the great men she produced. The hill just northeast of Arpino, **Civitavécchia**, was the original site of Arpino, with a monumental ring of megalithic walls, even older than Alatri's. Note the gate, a rare pointed arch similar to the Posterula in Ferentino.

North of Arpino, **Sora** is what happens when a backwoods Ciociaría town turns into a minor industrial centre. Old Sora was a stronghold of clerically inspired resistance against Napoleon, and the French did a good job of smashing it up. A **cathedral** survives, built on the podium of a Roman temple, along with some fine *quattrocento* frescoes in the church of **San Francesco**. Really, the most remarkable thing about Sora is the Bruni Furniture showroom, a brassy concern that spreads its banners all over southern Lazio; its colossal headquarters in the miasmic SS82 sprawl add a tacky *frisson* to a landscape that is half Fellini, half Los Angeles.

Beyond Sora, you're in the wilds on the edge of Lazio, bordering on the Abruzzo National Park. In this mountainous region there are beautiful lakes at the **Riserva Naturale Lago Fibreno** and **Biagio Saracinesco**, and ruins of a 12th-century castle at **Vicalvi**. The lake at Posta Fibreno got a mention in Pliny for its peculiar floating island of algae, which nourishes the lake's many fish, some of which are caught by fishermen in boats built according to an ancient Samnite design.

Atina is the most important town in this district, and has been since the days of the Samnites; relics from its past (Roman and Samnite votive offerings, little bronzes, coins, funeral goods) are preserved in the **Museo Civico** (*open 9–12.30 and 3–6*) housed in the recently restored Palazzo Visocchi. Atina is home to an international folklore festival, and keeps a collection of costumes and other items, both from the region and around the world, in its **Museo del Folklore e della Civiltà Contadina** (*open by request, **t** 0776 610647*).

North of Sora, the area around **Cámpoli Appennino** is famous for truffles, some of the southernmost truffles in Europe; they're featured in all the local restaurants. The SS509 over the **Forca d'Acero** to Pescasséroli and Scanno in the Abruzzo offers spectacular views on the Lazio side, and majestic primeval beech forests when you get over to the Abruzzo.

Down the Via Casilina

Ceprano and Aquino

Ceprano, east of Frosinone overlooking the valley of the River Sacco, is the modern successor to ancient *Fregellae*. There is a good **archaeological museum** (*open weekdays 8–2, hols on request, **t** 0775 914002; adm*) with finds from the ruined town, including most of the façade of a temple of Aesculapius. In the mountains to the south, the 50-million-year-old **Grotte di Pástena** *(open daily in summer 9–7, winter 10–4; adm exp)* offer a chance to plunge into the limestone heart of the Monti Ausoni, with paths taking in nearly two miles of stalactites and stalagmites, underground rivers and lakes; the unusual formations include what seems to be a hill with three crosses, dubbed the 'Monte Calvario'.

Further down the Via Casilina/SS6 (a notorious speed trap; *rallentare, vi raccomando*), **Aquino** was the seat of the counts who produced St Thomas (hence Aquinus, although the Angelic Doctor was actually born in nearby Roccasecca); it was also the birthplace of the poet Juvenal, and is full of Roman-era ruins, including a small Roman arch, the **Arco di Marcantonio** near the village church, **Santa Maria della Libera**, built from the ruins of a Roman temple, with a 12th-century mosaic over the portal.

Cassino and Montecassino

Cassino, though a large and prosperous town these days, isn't much to look at. Hurriedly rebuilt after its near-total destruction in the Second World War (*see* p.50), it still bears some scars, and some reminders, like the bizarre, battered tank beached in

Where to Stay and Eat

Ceprano ✉ 03024

★★★★**Villa Ferrari Relais**, Via Casilina km103, **t/f** 0775 912852 (*expensive*). This romantic *seicento* hotel is one of the most civilized places to stay in southern Lazio, with only six spacious and stylish rooms and marble baths; also a little frescoed chapel, delicious breakfast buffet served out on the terrace, and excellent restaurant (open to non guests). *Closed Nov, Aug.*

Cassino ✉ 03043

★★★**Alba**, Via G Di Biasio 53, **t/f** 0776 270000, *hotelalba@officine.it* (*moderate*). In the centre, modern and comfortable, and has a good restaurant featuring local recipes.

★★★**Rocca**, Via Sferracavalli, **t** 0776 311212, *hotel.rocca@flashnet.it* (*cheap*). If you're driving, this is a simple relaxing place in a quiet setting north of town, with a pool, tennis and watersports on a lake for the kids.

Beyond these, most of Cassino's hotels are newer buildings out on Via Ausonia towards the motorway:

★★★**Silvia Park**, Via Ausonia 47, **t** 0776 300021, **f** 0776 302555 (*cheap*). Nothing special, but a good bargain.

★★★**Al Boschetto**, Via Ausonia 54, **t** 0776 39131, **f** 0776 301315 (*cheap*). Another bargain.

Colombaia, Via G Di Biasio 200, **t** 0776 300892 (*expensive–moderate*). Come here for fresh and well-prepared seafood; the tank of live lobsters is the main attraction. The pasta with *frutti di mare* is especially tasty. *Closed Sun eve and Mon.*

La Tinaia, Piazza Marconi 579, **t** 0776 22736 (*inexpensive*). For a simple lunch in the town centre, this will do nicely. *Closed Sun.*

La Fazenda, Via Chiesa Nuova 81, just north of town, off the SS509 in Sant'Elia, **t** 0776 429695 (*inexpensive*). A simple country restaurant in a walled garden, worth the drive from Cassino for good home cooking and a bargain €12 lunch menu. *Closed Mon.*

front of the rail station. But wherever you go in it, your attention is drawn upwards, to the great bulk of **Montecassino**, crowned by the most famous monastery in Italy.

If divine guidance led St Benedict from Subiaco to found a monastery here, as the old legend states, perhaps God just wasn't thinking clearly that day. Montecassino certainly owns the most dramatic site a monastery could ask for, high on a mountaintop over the Garigliano valley, but that very location has caused the honest monks nothing but trouble over the centuries. They were essential in keeping alive the traditions of letters and scholarship through the Dark Ages – 'Medieval Athens in the night of many centuries' as the historian Gregorovius described it. But it is all the more remarkable when you consider that Montecassino has been utterly destroyed five times. Benedict came in 529, but the Lombards wrecked the place only 50 years later. The Saracens and the Normans repeated the scene in the 9th and 11th centuries, and an earthquake finished off what must have been one of Italy's treasures of medieval architecture in 1349. Each time the place has been rebuilt, but the reason why Montecassino attracts so much strife was demonstrated again during the Italian campaign of 1944. The rock happens to be the most strategically important spot in central Italy, the key to either Rome or Naples, depending on which way your army is walking.

The Benedictines began rebuilding on 15 March 1945, salvaging everything they could from the rubble, and the new Italian Republic made the rebuilding of the **monastery** one of its first priorities. Despite all that was lost for ever, it is still an impressive sight (*open daily 8.30–12 and 3.30–5; until 6 in summer; ask at the office for guided tours. A modest dress code is enforced – no shorts or vests*). The monastery occupies the acropolis of ancient *Casinum*, where Benedict converted a temple of Apollo into his first oratory. Today the entrance is by way of three connecting cloisters that run along the south, with the reconstructed Renaissance **Loggia del Paradiso** offering wonderful views over southern Lazio. From here a grand staircase leads to the centrepiece of the monastery, the **Chiostro dei Benefattori**, designed most likely by Antonio da Sangallo the Younger, and the **basilica**. The interior of the church reproduces the 17th-century design by the Neapolitan maestro Cosimo Fanzago, with lavish gilded mouldings framing modern frescoes by Pietro Annigoni. The tomb of Pietro de' Medici, by Antonio and Francesco da Sangallo, and a painting of the *Pietà* by Francesco Solimena are the only two works of art to survive the bombs, along with the **crypt**, decorated with a remarkable set of glittering **mosaics** from 1913, the work of German monks from Beuron, around the tombs of SS Benedict and Scholastica. A small **museum** (*same hours; adm*) off the left side of the church contains fragments of destroyed works, including reliefs and bits of the church's Cosmatesque pavement, along with gold, silver and enamel reliquaries, illuminated missals, fine works in coral, and paintings by Sebastiano Conca, Luca Giordano and Palma il Giovane among others, while the Archives and Library – its precious contents were packed off by the Germans to Rome for safekeeping before the siege – contain the *placito di Montecassino*, a decree written in 960 and one of the very first texts written in vernacular Italian.

On the lower slopes of Montecassino, the road to the monastery passes the site of ancient *Casinum*. The site, and the mountain, have been inhabited for a long time; finds in the **Museo Archeologico** (*open daily 9–1hr before sunset; adm*) go back to the Palaeolithic. Casinum was a Volscian and Samnite possession before the Romans took it and made it into an important and wealthy city. It withered quickly at the fall of the Empire though, and was almost abandoned when St Benedict arrived. From the museum, you enter the **Zona Archeologica**, with remains of the theatre, a barbaric-looking **amphitheatre** in *opus reticulatum*, a stretch of the Via Latina and the **Tomb of Ummidia Quadratilla**, made into a chapel called the **Cappella del Crocefisso** in the 10th century.

Further up the mountain you'll see a ruinous medieval castle, the **Rocca Ianula** (*currently under restoration*), and the **Polish Military Cemetery**, with a monument near the spot where some of the heaviest fighting took place. There is also a **British Military Cemetery** south of Cassino on the road for Sant'Angelo in Theodice.

Abruzzo and Molise

13

Abruzzo and Molise

pp.184–5

p.230

Highlights

1 Atri, a delightful medieval hill town
2 Frescoes of Santa Maria in Piano, at Loreto Aprutino
3 Gran Sasso d'Italia, the highest peak of the Apennines
4 The distinctive and refined city of L'Áquila
5 Mountain forests of the Abruzzo National Park

In Italy's long and narrow peninsula, dense with cities and great monuments, *autostrade* and pizzerias, sultry sunglassed *signorinas* and Vespa-wrangling dudes, Abruzzo and Molise come as a breath of fresh air. Sparsely populated, historically marginal to the great affairs of state, these two regions (made administratively independent of each other in 1963) stand out for their majestic natural beauty and vast tracts of unspoiled wilderness, encompassing the highest peaks of the Apennines and the habitat of Italy's unique species of bear. With its four national or regional parks, three of them recently established, Abruzzo has fully one-third of its land reserved for nature: the most, they claim, of any region in Europe.

Because of the harsh and rugged terrain, with only small pockets suitable for agriculture, the region's economy has been traditionally pastoral, but with an emphasis on crafts such as pottery and ceramics, gold-, wood-, and iron-working, weaving and lace-making. And though many Abruzzo towns wear the proud badges of progress and modernity, the Abruzzesi have little care to compete with Milan and Rome – instead, like Candide, they tend their own garden and hone their traditional skills. Yet from this mountain-bound land of country tradition came two of Italy's most urbane, sophisticated and passionate poets, Ovid and Gabriele D'Annunzio, and its greatest modern philosopher, Benedetto Croce. It is also, somehow fittingly, the region most passionately enthusiastic about rugby.

Beyond Abruzzo, there's Molise, an atavistic and introspective *banlieu* that formed a county of its own back in the 13th century, which is when its name, of unknown derivation, was first used. This rather charming patch of the Abruzzi that got away in 1963 has its own customs and dialect – a direct result of its impossible geography, and the large settlements established there in the 15th and 16th centuries by Slavs and Albanians. Molise is one of the last regions in Italy where women still don their traditional costumes to please themselves and not the shutter-happy hordes.

History

In prehistoric times the Abruzzo formed part of the little-known Bronze Age culture, sometimes known as the Middle Adriatic, that produced the enigmatic Warrior in Chieti's archaeology museum (*see* p.298). The different Italic tribes who emerged into the first historical records – the Piceni, Praetutii, Vestini, Paeligni, Marsi and others, of whom almost nothing is known beyond their names – formed a formidable challenge to Roman expansion before being overwhelmed by the legions in the Social Wars of 91–82 BC. The Lombards ruled what is now Abruzzo under their Duchy of Spoleto, and Molise as part of the Duchy of Benevento. The Normans, under King William I of Sicily, picked up the region from the English Pope Adrian IV, and Emperor Frederick II, who inherited the Norman possessions in Italy, made the Abruzzi an independent province. In the Middle Ages, this region hit its modest heights; you'll notice that its towns and monuments are on the whole stoutly medieval.

Frederick had grand plans for the region, but they died with him as the Abruzzo was swallowed up by the Angevins, then kings of Naples. Like Umbria, Lazio and most of the Marches, Abruzzo and Molise then began to stagnate, with a few exceptions – the only difference being that these regions stagnated under the Aragonese, Spaniards and the Bourbons on the throne of Naples, rather than under the popes. It was the Bourbons who divided Abruzzo into four administrative territories – Abruzzo Citeriore, Ulteriore Primo, Ulteriore Secondo and Molise – which is why you'll often see the region's name in the plural (the Abruzzi). But if Abruzzo was neglected and sucked dry by the Neapolitans, its lot under the kings of Italy was scarcely better, and thousands of people migrated to North America, Britain and other parts of Europe – among them the father of Dante Gabriel Rossetti, and the ancestors of Madonna. Only after the Second World War, with the small boom of its compact seaside resorts, the development of small-scale industries and the building of new roads, financed by the Cassa per il Mezzogiorno, and the growing interest in the unsullied charms of its landscape, has the tide of emigration been stemmed. Today, Abruzzo is learning that being passed over by history isn't all bad. The region knows where its future lies – in the delights of an unspoiled land that means an attractive lifestyle, and tourism.

Northern Abruzzo

Seaside resorts, jam-packed with Italian families in the summer, line the Adriatic coast; you can expect difficulty finding undeveloped stretches of beach. The real attractions of this northern end of the region are inland: the excellent hill towns of Penne, Loreto Aprutino, and best of all Atri, the little artistic capital of the Abruzzo in Renaissance times. From the tops of these towns you'll have a good view of the Gran Sasso d'Italia, inviting you further inland to the quiet mountain villages of its eastern slopes, and the famous painted ceramics of Castelli.

Giulianova, Roseto and the Lower Vomano Valley

North of Pescara, the Adriatic is lined with the same kind of small, Italian family beach resorts you'll find in the Marches to the north; places like Alba Adriática, Giulianova, Roseto degli Abruzzi, Silvi and Pineto all offer big beaches, modern hotels, amusement arcades and playgrounds. The most interesting of the resorts is **Giulianova**, with its medieval old town set back behind the beachfront sprawl. It was known in Roman times as *Castrum Novum*, and within the old walls you can see the town's monument, the Romanesque **Santa Maria a Mare**, with unusual bas-reliefs on its façade (*currently closed for restoration*), and the Renaissance **cathedral**. There is a small **Pinacoteca Comunale** inside the public library on Corso Garibaldi, with mostly Abruzzese and south Italian works of the last two centuries. The SS80 road turns inland here for Téramo.

Roseto degli Abruzzi, another resort out of the same mould, lies near the mouth of the Vomano, one of the principal rivers coming down from the Gran Sasso, and has fine views up the valley to the limestone peaks of the Gran Sasso. **Pineto**, another little resort, with a pretty pine-lined beach, has for its landmark the **Torre di Cerrano**, built by Charles V against the Ottoman threat and now a marine research station.

From Roseto you can head up the valley (on the SS150) to see two Romanesque gems. One is the church and abbey of **Santa Maria di Propezzano**, near Morro d'Oro,

Getting Around

Services by both train and bus are better and more frequent between the various towns along the coast than to just about any of the inland destinations in the region. The length of the coast is served by the north–south **rail** line between Bologna and Lecce. ARPA, **t** 06 442 33928, the Abruzzo **bus** company, connects towns along the coast with Pescara and L'Áquila, via Téramo. Giulianova is the major hub, and services are frequent, especially in summer when the resorts are packed.

Téramo is fairly easily reached by train, on a spur from the coastal line at Giulianova. As provincial capital, Téramo has connections to Atri and everywhere else in the province; buses on both the *autostrada* and local roads also link Téramo quickly to the coast, to Ascoli Piceno and to L'Áquila.

Tourist Information

Giulianova: Via Mamiani 2, **t** 085 800 3013.
Roseto degli Abruzzi: Piazza della Libertà 37, **t** 085 899 1157.
Pineto: in the Centro Polifunzionario on Via Mazzini, **t** 085 949 1745.
Téramo: Via del Castello 10, **t** 0861 244222, *turismo@provincia.teramo.it, www.provincia.teramo.it*.
Loreto Aprutino: Via dei Normanni 8, **t** 085 829 0484.
Penne: Piazza Luca da Penne, **t** 085 827 0436.

Where to Stay and Eat

Giulianova ✉ 64022

******Gran Hotel Don Juan**, Lungomare Zara 97, **t** 085 800 8341, **f** 085 800 4805 (*very expensive–moderate*). Perhaps the smartest hotel on this stretch of coast, with contemporary Mediterranean styling. Located right on its own beach, it has a pool, tennis courts and garden, and comfortable air-conditioned rooms, including some with wheelchair access. Minimum 3-day stay required. *Closed Oct–April*.

******Riviera**, Lungomare Zara 47, **t** 085 800 6413, **f** 085 800 3022 (*moderate*). Well equipped, with beach, pool, hammam, games room, bikes to borrow, and comfortable rooms with balconies.

*****Promenade**, Lungomare Zara 119, **t** 085 800 3338, **f** 085 800 5983, *www.hotelpromenade.com* (*moderate–cheap*).

where the Abruzzese fondness for simple forms has created a handsome asymmetrical façade and a charming two-storey cloister. The church walls are embellished with 12th- and 13th-century frescoes, the cloister with scriptural scenes by the 17th-century Polish artist Sebastiano Majewski. The other, just up the road, is **San Clemente a Vomano**, whose builders made good use of Roman ruins lying about, fitting them in here and there like a jigsaw. The church houses some rustic medieval frescoes, and an unusual and lovely 12th-century ciborium, with finely carved men and beasts entwined in the foliage; unlike most Romanesque artworks, this one is signed, by 'Master Ruggiero' and his son Robert. Some of the pavement has been replaced with glass, allowing us to see foundations of the 9th century church underneath, while under the choir is a Lombard-style crypt. A side road to the north leads to **Canzano**, famous for the *tacchino alla canzanese*, probably the only turkey speciality in Italy.

Téramo

Northern Abruzzo's modest provincial capital, Téramo lies on a small plain between two rivers, the Vezzoli and the Tordino, midway between the coast and the Gran Sasso. Originally a city of the Umbri and Piceni, Téramo knew its happiest days in the

Smaller; has some of the same amenities if not so much style. *Closed Oct–mid-May.*

★★★**Europa**, Lungomare Zara 57, **t** 085 800 3600, **f** 085 800 0091, *www.htleuropa.it* (*moderate–cheap*). Good value, with optional air conditioning.

Beccaceci, Via Zola 28, **t** 085 800 3550 (*expensive*). Giulianova's – and indeed, all of the Abruzzo's – most celebrated seafood restaurant, where the menu features its own long-established seafood and pasta inventions, so good they've been copied elsewhere – try the *linguine alla giuliese* or the squid stuffed with prawns. *Closed Sun evenings, Mon and 27 Dec–10 Jan.*

Moro, Lungomare Spalato 74, **t** 085 800 4973 (*moderate*). Serves only the day's catch – the baby squid are a speciality. *Closed Wed lunch, Mon, Tues, Sat and mid-Sept to mid-Oct.*

Osteria della Stracciavocc, Via Trieste 124, **t** 085 800 5326 (*moderate–cheap*). One of the best trattorias in town for traditional regional cuisine, with excellent pasta and seafood. *Closed Mon, Tues lunch and 2 weeks in Oct.*

Téramo ✉ 64100

★★★★**Sporting**, Via De Gasperi 41, **t** 0861 414723, **f** 0861 210285 (*moderate*). The nicest of Téramo's handful of hotels because of its garden, although it's located on the outskirts of town; also has a good restaurant.

★★★**Michelangelo**, on the edge of the centre at Via Coste S. Agostino, **t** 0861 413668 (*moderate*). With a covered pool.

★★★**Gran Sasso**, in the centre at Via Vinciguerra 12, **t** 0861 245747 (*moderate*). Very modest; will do if you're passing through.

★**Castello**, Via del Castello 62, **t** 0861 247582 (*cheap*). Another basic but adequate choice, with 7 rooms, all with shared bathrooms.

Il Duomo, Via Stazio 9, **t** 0861 241 774 (*moderate*). Local specialities are served up throughout the year, such as *maccheroni alla chitarra* (so named because the pasta is cut by pushing the dough through a tool with guitar-like strings), and fine meat dishes, including grilled kid. *Closed Mon and part of Jan.*

Sotto Le Stelle, Via Nazario Sauro 50, **t** 0861 247126 (*moderate*). Another excellent choice in the centre of town; concentrates the best of local recipes and ingredients, including an excellent *virtù* and *mazzarelle* (lamb's intestines rolled up in endives) and tamer dishes, too. *Closed Sun, part of Jan.*

★★★★**Miramonti**, Località Prati di Tivo, **t** 0861 959621, **f** 0861 959647 (*moderate*). In Prati di Tivo; a comfortable, modern resort hotel with a garden, pool and tennis courts. *Open 20 Dec–10 April and 20 June–10 Sept.*

14th century under its prince bishops, after which it became the northernmost town of the Kingdom of Naples. In truth, this town has done a wonderful job of avoiding history altogether, aided by the rugged mountains that surround it.

In the centre of Téramo, Piazza Martiri della Libertà, the **cathedral** stands out with its remarkable 14th-century portal, decorated with earlier Romanesque statues of saints; around them a miscellany of lions, collected from here and there, lend feline elegance to the façade, which is simple, square and ungabled, as is typical of churches in Abruzzo. The cathedral's swallowtail Ghibelline crenellations recall the days when Téramo was the fief of its bishop, who still possesses the title of 'Prince of Téramo', though he no longer makes much use of a special papal dispensation from rougher days that allowed him to wear armour under his robes, and keep his sword handy by the altar. The pretty campanile got its brick lantern, decorated with circles of coloured tile, in the 15th century. Campanili like this one, modelled after Atri's, are the architectural trademark of the northern Abruzzo; you'll see one in almost every town. Inside, there is a silver altar frontal with 30 scenes from the Bible, a masterpiece by Nicola da Guardiagrele (1448), who also made the silver statues of Mary and Gabriel by the main door. The 15th-century polyptych in the left chapel is by the Venetian Jacobello del Fiore.

The Virtù of Téramo

Téramo has its own particular culinary speciality, a powerful stew called *virtù* that's customarily cooked on the first of May. Judging from its ingredients, it began as a way of using up whatever was left of the winter stocks and adding the first of the new season's goodies – traditionally local women each contributed an ingredient. It's really a cross between a soup and a stew – a type of minestrone, in fact – based on a stock to which are added seven different kinds of dried peas, beans and lentils, along with seven different kinds of fresh vegetables, and seven kinds of meat (sausage, pig's trotters and ears, and so on), all well salted and seasoned with herbs.

Near the cathedral lie the ruins of the **Roman theatre**, on Via Irelli, and you can trace the city's history since pre-Roman times at the well laid-out **Museo Archeologico**, recently established in a former palazzo on Via Delfico 30 (*open Tues–Sun 9–1 and 3–7; adm*). A short distance further on is the original cathedral, **Sant'Anna** (also called Santa Maria Interamnensis; *Interamna*, 'between the rivers', was Téramo's original Roman name). Sant'Anna was begun by the Byzantines in the 6th century, built over a Roman house (6th–12th-century); this is Téramo's attic of odds and ends, incorporating bits of Roman columns, Lombard carvings, a 6th-century triforium and ancient angelic frescoes. Another block or so east is a well-preserved house built in the 14th century during the Angevin era, the **Casa dei Melatini**. In the Franciscan convent of **Madonna delle Grazie**, to the east near Piazza della Libertà, is a Romanesque cloister and a painted wooden statue of the *Madonna and Child* by one of the Abruzzo's best sculptors, Silvestro dell'Áquila (15th century). More 15th-century Abruzzese works of art are on display in the **Museo Civico e Pinacoteca**, in an elegant 15th-century villa surrounded by parkland on the Via Borio (*open Mon–Sat 10–1 and 3–7; adm*). If you're driving, take the road to the **Osservatorio Astrofisico** for good views of the Gran Sasso.

North of Téramo: Campli

Heading north from Téramo towards Ascoli Piceno on the SS81, the road passes **Campli**, just to the east, a rather distinguished old hill town that is just waking up from a very long nap and starting to restore some of its Romanesque and Gothic monuments. The graceful, porticoed **Palazzo del Comune** (also called Palazzo Farnese) was built in the 14th century but much altered in the 1880s; it faces the church of **Santa Maria in Platea**, its 19th-century façade hiding a wealth of Renaissance painting and sculpture inside. Campli's main street, Corso Umberto, has changed little in centuries, including a lovely Renaissance house with a loggia called the **Casa della Farmaccia**. Just down the street, the plain Romanesque church of **San Francesco** is a fine embodiment of the Abruzzese ideal that less is more; inside are some good 14th-century frescoes, and two works of Cola dell'Amatrice. Its former convent next door now houses an **Archaeology Museum** (*open daily 9–8; adm*), containing artefacts from the 6th to the 3rd-century BC Italic necropolis at Campovalano, 1km away back on the main road. Behind it, on the edge of town, is something few places can boast, a **Scala Santa** with florid frescoes. Going up on your knees on 18 or 19 September will win you a plenary indulgence from Purgatory (and a good bargain; there are only 28 steps).

In **Campovalano**, the excavations aren't much to look at, but nearby there's the interesting abbey and church of **San Pietro**, founded in the 8th century and rebuilt in the 13th; the frescoed figures on the piers inside, common in the Abruzzo, were designed to seem part of the congregation. Part of an early Christian sarcophagus may be seen along the wall (*to visit both the necropolis and San Pietro, call the owner of the Alimentari in Campovalano's main square,* ***t*** *0861 56306, during business hours*).

Going any further into the wilds of Téramo province will take you through some of the most rugged landscapes in all Italy. There's a surreal flair to all this stretch of the Apennines, from the southern Marches to as far south as Chieti, in fact: peculiarly shaped peaks with disorientating rollercoaster roads to carry you up and down. A few kilometres north of Campli rises the superbly positioned Renaissance town of **Civitella del Tronto**, crowned by an impregnable castle that was the last redoubt of the Kingdom of Naples; the Bourbons managed to hold it right to the bitter end in 1861. First built around the year 1000, it has a travertine walled terrace a half-kilometre in length, lending it its distinctive crew-cut skyline. If you've made it this far, there's no excuse not to continue on to **Ascoli Piceno** in the Marches, ancient capital of the Piceni and one of central Italy's most distinguished art towns.

South of Téramo: Towards the Gran Sasso

South of Téramo the SS150 runs inland along the Val di Vomano, heading for the Gran Sasso, the tallest patch of mountains in peninsular Italy. The main road joins up with the SS80 from Téramo and continues up the increasingly narrow Val di Vomano to the north – the most scenic road in the region, which will eventually take you to L'Áquila (for this route, *see* p.306). Of course if you're in a hurry you can take the A24 motorway, with a 10km tunnel right under the 9,464ft **Corno Grande**, highest peak of the Gran Sasso, but this is no place for hurrying. Another route, the SS491, follows the higher Valle di Mavone to the south. The latter route won't get you around the mountains, except by a stretch of unpaved back roads, but it is nearly as beautiful, and offers a number of worthwhile detours.

Along the SS491, near **Castel Castagna** ('chestnut castle') there's **Santa Maria di Ronzano**, an ancient three-nave church embellished with rare frescoes dated 1181; another attraction is panoramic views of the Corno Grande. Between Montorio al Vomano and Isola del Gran Sasso on the SS491 you can take in the village of **Tossicia**, with a pretty medieval nucleus lying between two mountain streams; the tiny church of **Sant'Antonio Abate** has a 1471 Renaissance portal by the Venetian Antonio Lombardo. The scenery is stunning as the road reaches Isola del Gran Sasso, a fine stone village and a good base for mountain hikes.

Castelli and its Ceramics

To the southeast, dramatically positioned at the foot of the great wall of Monte Camicia, is **Castelli**, another good mountain base and a village worth visiting in its own right. Castelli is the great centre in the Abruzzo for ceramics, a local industry that achieved art and glory in the 17th-century workshops of the Grue and Gentili families, veritable dynasties of the art where techniques were handed down over the generations. The ceramic tradition is still continued in various workshops in the town and in the August ceramics fair, where part of the fun is tossing reject plates over the river. Castelli's **Chiesa Madre** contains an unusual majolica *pala* by Francesco Grue, as well as 12th-century wooden statues. More of the Grues' work (as well as that of other local artists) may be seen in the **Museo della Ceramica Abruzzese** (*open June–Sept Tues–Sun 10–7; Oct–May Tues–Sun 10–1, Sun also 3–5; adm*). The museum also serves as a tourist office, **t** 0861 979398, and organizes guided tours around Castelli. Most splendiferous of all, however, is the rural church of **San Donato**, which Carlo Levi dubbed 'The Sistine Chapel of Italian Majolica' for its ceiling of a thousand ceramic tiles (visible from the outside through a grate) – the only ceiling like it in Italy, an impressive 360 square feet covered with a patchwork of different folk motifs (plenty of rabbits, skulls, portraits, notices of various kinds, geometric patterns and so on) made in 1615–17. Also on the outskirts is the derelict Romanesque church of **San Salvatore**, with a charming medieval pulpit.

Atri

Climbing up to Atri will not give you the most cheerful first impression. The two roads that reach it pass once-inhabited caves, eroded rock formations called *calanchi*, and what locals like to call 'Danteesque pits'. But when you get there you'll find one of the most attractive hill towns of the Abruzzo, calm and kind and gracious up in its rarefied air, 8km from the sea and 1,400ft above it. Visible from most of the province on its lofty height, Atri stands on the site of the ancient Piceni city and Roman colony of *Hatriaticum*, founded under the sign of the woodpecker, the bird of Mars and the totem (*picus*) of the Piceni. Atri disputes with Adria in the Veneto the honour of having lent its name to the Adriatic Sea, a controversy that raged among ancient

Where to Stay and Eat

Atri ✉ 64032

★★★**Du Parc**, Viale Umberto I 6, **t** 085 870260, **f** 085 879 8326 (*moderate*). A modern, peaceful place on the outskirts of town, with a pool and good restaurant.

★**San Francesco**, Corso Adriano 38, **t** 085 87287 (*cheap*). An interesting alternative, in the historic centre; a tidy, ancient establishment.

Taverna Adranus, Via A Probi 10, **t** 085 878 0034 (*moderate*). In the old centre, off the Corso near San Francesco. Good for local dishes; they're fond of hot peppers but too shy to put them on the menu – if you like it hot, let them know.

Alla Campana d'Oro, Piazza Duomo 23, **t** 085 870177 (*cheap*). An enjoyable trattoria/pizzeria (pizzas eves only). *Closed Sun lunch and Mon.*

Penne ✉ 65017

★★★**Dei Vestini**, on the outskirts of town at Via Caselli 37, **t** 085 827 8200 (*moderate*). The only hotel here: modern and comfortable, with a pool, tennis, gym and sauna.

Hosteria del Lago, Contrada Colle Formica, **t** 085 827 9474 (*moderate*). Outside town, at Lago di Penne; good cooking and a terrace with a view over the lake. *Closed Mon.*

Loreto Aprutino ✉ 65014

★★★★**Castello Chiola**, Via degli Aquino 12, **t/f** 085 825 0690 (*expensive*). Built into Loreto's Castello; a peaceful setting with beautiful views, pool and restaurant.

★★★**La Bilancia**, Contrada Palazzo 11, **t/f** 085 828 9610 (*cheap*). 5km outside the centre; adequate rooms, but best known for its restaurant, serving regional specialities prepared with the town's famous olive oil; good soups and roast goose. *Closed Mon.*

scholars including Pliny, Livy and Strabo; Atri tried to boost its claim by engraving the fact on its singular coins – the heaviest ever minted in western Europe, guaranteed to put a hole in the pocket of any toga, if togas had any.

The Roman sites that have been excavated in the town include the remains of some ancient baths, in the crypt of Atri's majestic 13th-century **cathedral**. The building itself has an austerely elegant square façade and another striking campanile in brick with round majolica tiles; this one was the original, designed by an architect named Antonio di Lodi. The excellent carved portals on the front and right side are by a 14th-century local artist, Rainaldo d'Atri. Any number of stone lions from earlier churches have been cemented into the side wall; as in much of southern Italy, people in the Abruzzo have always believed that one of the most important things for a church is plenty of lions. Inside, the choir has the finest frescoes in the Abruzzo, remarkable scenes of the *Life of the Virgin, St Joachim and St Anne*, by Andrea de Litio, a great, late-quattrocento painter totally unknown outside the Abruzzo whose work is similar in many ways to that of Piero della Francesca, with exquisite attention to detail, and backgrounds with dream landscapes of knobby hills and imaginary towers. He also did the *Four Evangelists* on the vaulting; note St Luke, the painter, working away while his assistant hangs fruit from strings to study perspective. Part of the choir pavement is a mosaic replaced from the Roman baths. Other works in the cathedral include a 1503 baptismal font in the left aisle, and frescoed saints on the piers of the nave. The right transept leads to the separate church of Santa Reparata, with a gaudy Baroque ciborium in imitation of Bernini's in the Vatican.

The cathedral cloister houses the **Museo Diocesano** (*open daily exc Wed; Oct–May 10–12 and 3–5, June–Sept 10–12 and 4–8; adm*). There are ivories, paintings and some fine carved wood statues, including a 16th-century Neapolitan *Annunciation*, along with an excellent collection of 17th–18th-century majolica from Castelli (*see* p.288) and some mosaics and architectural fragments from the 9th-century church that preceded the cathedral; underneath the museum is the Roman **cistern** that supplied water to the baths. Across Piazza del Duomo from the cathedral is the **Teatro Comunale**, a scaled-down copy of La Scala in Milan; around the back is another black and white **Roman mosaic** from the baths, cemented on to the wall.

Corso Adriano, Atri's main street, leads westwards from the cathedral, passing the little Renaissance church of **Sant'Agostino**, and shops selling the town's specialities, liqueurs and *panducale*, a cake made with almond paste and candied fruit. During the Middle Ages and Renaissance Atri was controlled, off and on, by the Acquaviva dukes, whose frowning 14th-century **Palazzo Acquaviva** (now the town hall and post office) contains a cheerful courtyard. Atri is a fine place to wander down the medieval alleys; it isn't very big, and any of them will soon take you to the belvederes on the edges of town, along Via della Circonvalazione and Via Pomerio, elegantly appointed with stone balustrades and offering wide views over the countryside.

Penne

South of Atri, you can pick your way over the bewildering mountain roads to another fine hill town, stalwart, sleepy, brick-built **Penne**. It started as an important town of an Italic people called the Vestini, and grew in the Middle Ages into an important centre, if a somewhat schizophrenic one: Penne was really two separate towns, one built around the now-demolished castle, the other around the cathedral. One was Ghibelline and the other Guelph, and naturally they didn't get along.

The centre is **Piazza Luca di Penne**, named for a medieval legal scholar and statesman at the court of Charles of Anjou (Penne remembers all its old citizens of distinction, however obscure, and the town does its best to keep up the torch of culture; they even give out an annual literary prize). The piazza separates the two hills of the medieval town, and it contains the **Palazzo Comunale**, the church of **San Domenico**, with one memorably overdone Baroque chapel, and the **Palazzo Aliprandi**, seat of government in Penne's days as a Ruritanian aristocratic capital (the city and surrounding lands, including Atri, somehow fell into the hands of Emperor Charles V, who gave it to his daughter Margaret of Habsburg to play with in 1538; she married a Farnese of Lazio, and they ran a little court here). Corso dei Vestini leads into the castle side of town, with the churches of **San Giovanni Evangelista** and **Santa Croce**, both grab-bags of mixed medieval, Renaissance and Baroque art; just outside the centre here is the **Madonna del Carmelo**, with gloriously decorated Baroque chapels, and a fountain called the **Acqua Ventina**, noted since Roman times (Vitruvius mentions it) for its healthy waters.

From the opposite side of Piazza Luca di Penne, Corso Alessandrini, lined with old *palazzi*, will take you into the 'Colle Sacro' side of town; the highest point is occupied by the **cathedral**, almost completely destroyed in Second World War bombings. Only the crypt survives in its original state, and this has been incorporated into the **Museo Civico** (*open daily 10–1 and 3–6; adm*), with some exceptional medieval sculptural works, many of them fragments from the cathedral. One is a relief of a squatting Adam and Eve (the card says that they have lost everything, and have become symbolically sunk in the material world, but it looks like something quite different); another a strange, beautiful relief of a buck devouring a snake, and being devoured in turn by a wolf. There is also an emotional 14th-century wood *Crucifixion*, the Renaissance *Teca di San Biagio*, a reliquary illustrating the story of Paris from the *Iliad*, a collection of Baroque paintings of saints important to the Knights of St John, who had a chapter here (note the Maltese crosses), and an old whale bone that folks used to think was the rib of a giant. The main attraction of this museum is missing: the *Uomo d'Argento*, a solid silver statue of San Massimo made by the eccentric, virtuoso Neapolitan sculptor Giuseppe Sammartino. Penne managed to hide him from Napoleon, but not from the thieves who broke in in 1982; there remains only the silver model of Penne that the saint was holding in his hand.

A 15-minute walk east from the centre takes you to the old monastic church of **Santa Maria in Colleromano** (*ring the bell if closed*), with a fine medieval portal and other decorations done by sculptors from Atri; the unusual bestiary portrayed in the sculptures has long intrigued scholars, and some have speculated they are a kind of alchemical allegory. More relics are displayed inside in a small museum. Colleromano takes its name from the camp established here by the Romans when they were besieging Penne during the Social Wars. Underneath the hill, the **Riserva Naturale**

Lago di Penne is run by the WWF, around a lake that is home to otters and a wide variety of waterfowl (including a few storks, who pass through in the spring and autumn); there are nature trails and a visitors' centre.

Loreto Aprutino and Santa Maria in Piano

Only seven twisty kilometres to the east, **Loreto Aprutino** spills down its steep hill-side like a waterfall. Loreto was a busy town in the 19th century; after a brave decade of resistance to Napoleon, this little medieval village bestirred itself to become for a time the intellectual heart of the Abruzzo, with libraries, academies and printing presses, a bastion of free thinking and modernism in the woebegone Kingdom of Naples. The very quiet, very clean centre (don't even think of driving a car into this one) possesses few monuments: a huge **Castello**, built in various eras and now home to a fine hotel, and the church of **San Pietro Apostolo**, with a plain nave, some Renaissance–Baroque chapels and ceramic pavements. These, of course, came from Castelli (*see* p.288), and you can see some of the best of this famous town's production in the nearby **Museo delle Ceramiche** (*open Sat–Sun 10.30–12.30 and 3.30–5.30*), housed in the palace of the 19th-century collector who assembled the works on display. Loreto also has a small **Museo Archeologico**, and a **Museo Civico della Civiltà Contadina**, a collection of agricultural implements, traditional craft work and rather naïve tableaux of peasant life. Loreto is famous for its *extra vergine* olive oil, and they take the subject so seriously they have opened a **Museo dell'Olivo** (*same hours as above*) in Piazza del Mercato Vecchio.

Loreto's greatest attraction, **Santa Maria in Piano**, is as its name implies down on the plain just to the south (*follow the 'Pianella Stazione' signs from the Pescara road; open summer 9–7, winter 9–4*). This was a Benedictine monastery church, and the plain around it was the site of an important medieval fair. It contains a spectacular fresco, the largest in the Abruzzi, called the *Giudizio Particolare*, portraying Heaven's elect marching to the pearly gates on a bridge the width of a hair – this is Allah's bridge of *al-Sirat*, mentioned in the Koran, which found its way into a few Last Judgment scenes; oddly enough, they did so via the visions of a seven-year-old. The child's name was Alberico da Settefrati, and when he later became a monk at Montecassino, in 1127, his vision was printed in a book that became popular across Europe, inspiring many artists including the one here. Across the bridge, St Michael waits to weigh the souls, while others climb trees to get into heaven. Hell is missing, the only part of the fresco not to have survived – so obviously all the Loretini go to heaven.

There are more 14th–15th-century frescoes on the side walls, including the *Life of St Thomas Aquinas*; Thomas' noble family, from Aquino in Lazio, was for a time lords of Penne. If the saint is painted looking a little green in the scene of his death, it is probably because of the legend that he was poisoned by Charles of Anjou. The chapel to the right of the altar has frescoes too, but here the interest is not so much the pictures as the **graffiti** scratched into them. Most of it dates from the 1500s, though it's still easy to read, providing a wonderful running chronicle of events of the time: *14 July; God darkened the sun* (an eclipse in fact occurred on this date in 1590). Others read: *arrival of the Spaniards in Loreto; snowed all day; the Germans arrive in Naples; miracle of the Virgin – emitted tears and blood, and gave a blind man back his sight.*

In the empire of olive trees that surrounds Loreto, there are a few more villages with attractions worthy of a detour; naturally, they're all medieval churches. At **Moscufo**, to the east, it's **Santa Maria del Lago**, another Benedictine church, little more than a brick barn, but with a rare treasure inside: an excellent 12th-century pulpit adorned with painted reliefs of Jonah and the whale, among others, and a 13th-century *Last Judgment* painted in the apse. Moscufo's people are strangely devoted to the mandolin; everyone with any talent plays one, and they have a famous guitar and mandolin band called the 'Filarmonica'. At **Pianella**, the next village to the south, the Benedictines gave **Santa Maria Maggiore** an equally fine pulpit, this one by north Italian sculptors. There's a third at Santo Stefano in **Cúgnoli**, to the southwest, done by the same artist as at Moscufo, a fellow named Nicodemo.

Back Down the Coast: Pescara to Térmoli

Ah, the Adriatic Coast – long sandy beaches and resorts, and more sandy beaches and resorts. It doesn't change much from Pescara all the way to Venice. It's a geological mystery; how do these Apennines go bouncing all this way to the east, and then suddenly decide to stop all at the same time, leaving such a long, smooth, drab arc of coastline? If you're not into Italian-style seaside holidays, where you pay for a beach chair and umbrella in neat little rows and watch everyone else do the same, you may find it difficult to find an undeveloped beach where you can just sit on the sands under the pines. South of Pescara at first promises more of the same, but gradually you'll see a hint of something that's been absent for a hundred miles – features. A kink here, a rocky cliff there makes all the difference, with some real towns, and quite interesting ones – Ortona, Vasto, Térmoli – to replace the look-alike postwar lidos.

Pescara and its Endless Sands

Pescara is both Abruzzo's biggest city and its most popular resort, a fishing port and provincial capital. In ancient times it was a modest port, shared by several Italic tribes and later by the Romans. But despite its long history Pescara never made much of itself until 1927, when the government merged the little fishing village with the equally inconsequential Castellammare Adriática across the river Pescara, and started pumping money into it. They also invented a new province for Pescara to be capital of, carved out of Chieti and Téramo. Much of this sudden good fortune was due to the influence of the city's most famous son, Gabriele d'Annunzio (*see* below). Growth still didn't take off until after the Second World War, but Pescara today is the metropolis of the central Adriatic, with a population of 120,000. It isn't the most charming of cities, but its splendid Lungomare and miles of broad beaches make up for the monotonous streets behind.

Pescara's golden egg is its 16km-long sandy **beach**, broad and safe for the youngest child, almost solid with hotels, cafés and fish restaurants between the Pescara River and Montesilvano; whatever old buildings it had were decimated in the fierce fighting that took place along the coast in the Second World War. Still, this is no Rimini; families bake together in the day, and stroll about eating ice cream in the evening. If you need some excitement, there are riding stables, go-kart tracks, tennis courts, fishing and, for some real thrills, the **Museo delle Meraviglie Marine** (Museum of Marine Marvels) (*open Tues and Fri 8.30–1 and 3.30–5.30; Wed, Thurs and Sat 8.30–1; adm*) in Pescara's bustling fish market where Lungomare Matteotti ends at the Pescara river. Founded in 1949, it offers aquariums, fish fossils and the skeleton of a sperm whale that wandered into the Mediterranean and beached itself on the coast. From here Via Paolucci follows the river to **Piazza Italia**, Pescara's Mussolinian civic centre, where the government buildings are concentrated. The original plans called for something more exciting but, as was often the case with Fascist-era projects, the builders and architects were under so much political presssure to finish it in a hurry that the results are a disappointment.

Getting There and Around

Pescara's **airport** (**t** 085 432 4200), on the Via Tiburtina between Pescara and Chieti, now has daily flights to Milan and Turin (Air One, **t** 085 421 3022), in addition to charter connections with other European destinations. Ryanair (*www.ryanair.com*) fly from London Stansted and Frankfurt direct to Pescara. Pescara's main **rail** station is right in the centre on the main Via E Ferrari (information **t** 89 20 21, *www.trenitalia.it*). There are five trains or so each day to Rome, via Chieti, Sulmona, Celano, Avezzano, Tagliacozzo and Tívoli, and a separate, regular service to Sulmona via Manoppello and Bussi, near Pópoli; some of these go on to Terni in Umbria, with connections for Rome. Another line runs up the coast to Giulianova and then inland to Téramo. ARPA **buses** (**t** 085 421 5099) for the main towns of the Abruzzo and everywhere in Pescara province leave from the depot in front of the rail station; there are also eight direct buses a day to Rome, via Avezzano.

Tourist Information

Via Paolucci 3, **t** 085 421 9981; Piazza Maggio 3, **t** 800 502520 (toll free), *presidio.pescara@abruzzoturismo.it*, *www.regione.abruzzo.it*.

Where to Stay and Eat

Pescara ✉ 65100

Pescara has by far the most hotels and restaurants on the coast, but be aware that tranquillity is rare in summer, and full board is bound to be required in July and August.

★★★★**Esplanade**, Piazza I Maggio 46, **t** 085 292141, **f** 085 421 7540, *www.esplanade.net*, (*expensive*). The fanciest hotel in town: an imposing Belle Epoque mansion on the sea.

★★★★**Carlton**, Viale Riviera 35, **t** 085 373125, **f** 085 421 3922 (*moderate*). A very comfortable resort palace on the sea, with a private beach that almost absorbs the racket.

★★★**Bellariva**, Viale Riviera 213, **t** 085 471 2641 (*moderate*). An unpretentious 33-room hotel that's good for families.

★★★**Salus**, Lungomare Matteotti 13/1, **t** 085 374 196 (*cheap*). Central; good standard rooms and private beach. *Closed Christmas hols.*

★★★**Ambra**, Via Quarto dei Mille, 28/30, **t** 085 378247, **f** 085 378183 (*cheap*). Another bargain, only a few steps from the station, quiet with double-glazed windows and optional air conditioning.

Since Pescara is a working town as well as a resort, it has good restaurants that are not attached to hotels.

Guerino, Viale della Riviera 4, **t** 085 421 2065 (*very expensive*). The city's classic seafood

The original fishing village of Pescara lies on the southern bank of the river, now completely spoilt by an elevated motorway. Here you will find the regional folk museum, the **Museo delle Genti d'Abruzzo** (*open winter Sun, Mon and Wed 9–1, Tues and Thurs 9–1 and 2.30–5; summer Mon–Fri 9–1 and 9pm–midnight, afternoons and weekends on request,* **t** *085 451 0026; adm*), on Via delle Caserme, a comprehensive and recently modernized collection, reopened in 1991, dedicated to everyday life and popular traditions in the Abruzzo over the ages. There's another museum, the delightful **Casa Cascella**, in Viale Marconi (*daily 9–1, in summer also 4.30–6.30pm; adm*), with works by the Cascella family of artists and sculptors; one of them made the ship fountain, the **Nave**, along the Lungomare at Piazza 1 Maggio.

Close by and facing the sea is Pescara's newest museum, the **Museo d'Arte Moderna 'Vittoria Colonna'** (*times vary depending on the exhibition; the tourist office has details*), which opened with a big crowd-pulling show featuring Picasso, Léger and Matisse in 2002 and hosts temporary exhibitions of modern and contemporary art.

You can see where the dark angel (*see* box on p.296) got his start in life, at the **Casa D'Annunzio** on Corso Manthoné (*open Mon–Sat 9–1.30, Sun 9–1; adm*); it has a

choice: serving the tasty Adriatic speciality of fillets of John Dory with prosciutto; outdoor seafront terrace. *Closed Tues, exc in July and Aug, and 22 Dec–5 Jan.*

Cantina di Jozz, Via delle Caserme 61, **t** 085 690383 (*moderate*). Near central Piazza Italia; serves daily specials that rarely disappoint in its little vaulted dining rooms; come on Friday for the *maccheroni al sugo di pesce*. *Closed Sun eve, Mon, and two weeks in Jan.*

Duilio, Via Regina Margherita 11, **t** 085 378278 (*moderate*). Seafood in nearly every delicately prepared dish. *Closed Sun eve, Mon, and Aug.*

Ristorante-Pizzeria Marechiaro da Vittorio, Lungomare Matteotti 70, **t** 085 374248 (*moderate for seafood, cheap for pizzas*). A good choice right on the seafront, where yellow-waistcoated waiters serve up excellent, very fresh seafood on the terrace (try the octopus antipasti, or risotto with prawns and asparagus). The pizzas are good too.

La Terrazza Verde, Via Temperi 4–8, **t** 085 413239 (*moderate*). One of Pescara's best restaurants, and it doesn't feature fish at all. In a panoramic setting up in the hills behind the city, it serves delicious gnocchi and duck, a popular dish in Abruzzo. *Closed Wed.*

Trattoria Roma, tucked away at Via Trento 86, **t** 085 295374 (*cheap*). A good place to find hearty Abruzzese cooking. Very popular with locals; the menu changes daily. *Closed Sun.*

Taverna 58, near D'Annunzio's house at Corso Manthoné 58, **t** 085 690724 (*cheap*). Good news for vegetarians: a delicious menu 'for herbivores' as well as dishes for their meat- or fish-eating friends. *Closed Sun, Aug.*

Montesilvano Marina ✉ 65016

★★★★**Serena Majestic**, Viale Kennedy 12, **t** 085 83699, **f** 085 836 9859, *info@serenamajestic.it* (*moderate*). A large, modern and comfortable hotel in Pescara's posh northern suburb of Montesilvano, situated on the beach, with gardens, tennis courts and a pool.

★★★**Piccolo Mondo**, Via Marinelli 86, **t** 085 445 2647, **f** 085 445 2186, *www.hotelpiccolomondo.com* (*cheap*). One of the best-value hotels on the coast. It has just 20 rooms, and a roof terrace and garden; a good choice for a family holiday.

★★★**Albergo Antagos**, Via Lago Trasimeno 8, **t** 085 73870 (*moderate*). Plain and even institutional, this is nonetheless a good option if you are on a budget, not least because it's tucked away on a quiet side street; large rooms with terraces, and friendly owners. Prices drop a category out of season.

Carlo Ferraioli, Via Aldo Moro 52, **t** 085 445 2296 (*expensive*). The best restaurant here has a terrace on the sea: one of the specialities is *rana pescatrice*, 'frog fish', plentiful off the coast and better than it sounds, baked in the oven with spuds. *Closed Mon, half of Jan.*

Pescara's Superman

This otherwise resolutely normal town must have a bit of kryptonite in it somewhere to have produced, in 1864, Gaetano Rapagnetta, the son of a modest local merchant, who after his studies left Pescara for Rome and France, and then disappeared into the phone booth of his ego and imagination, emerging as nothing less than the 'Angel Gabriel of the Annunciation', or Gabriele D'Annunzio. With his new name, D'Annunzio went on to become the greatest Italian poet of his generation, and a master of lavishly sensual language who managed to get nearly every one of his works on the Pope's Index. But D'Annunzio scoffed at the idea that the pen is mightier than the sword. A fervent right-wing nationalist, he clamoured for Italy to enter the First World War. When it was over, he became so furious when Fiume (modern Rijeka) was promised to Italy, then ceded by the Allies to Yugoslavia, that he took matters into his own hands, and invaded Fiume with a band of volunteers (September 1919). In Italy D'Annunzio was proclaimed a hero, stirring up a diplomatic furore before he was forced to withdraw in January 1921.

Luigi Barzini described D'Annunzio as 'perhaps more Italian than any other Italian' for his love of gesture, spectacle and theatre – what can you say about a man who would boast that he had once dined on roast baby? Yet for the Italians of his generation, no matter what their politics, he exerted a powerful influence; he seemed a breath of fresh air, a new kind of superman, hard and passionate yet capable of writing exquisite, intoxicating verse, the spiritual father of the technology-infatuated Futurist movement, ready to destroy the old bourgeois *Italia vile* of museum curators and parish priests and create in its stead a great modern power, the 'New Italy'.

D'Annunzio lived a life of total exhibitionism – extravagantly, decadently and beyond his means, at every moment the trend-setting, aristocratic aesthete, with his borzois and melodramatic affairs which included Italy's best-known actress, the 'Divine' Eleanora Duse. He thought all Italians should be as flamboyant and clever, and disdained the Corporate State of the Fascists. For Mussolini, the popular old nationalist was a loose cannon and an embarrassment (not to mention a potential political rival) and he pensioned him off to a gilded retirement on Lake Garda.

charming little courtyard, and memorabilia and photos on the poet and his family. In the *pineta* 2km south, Pescara has built an outdoor theatre in D'Annunzio's honour, the venue for the Pescara Jazz Festival, a one-week event which usually takes place in the first half of July. On a hill above town, the **Madonna dei Sette Dolori** was built in 1757 to shelter the most famous Madonna of the Abruzzo, who gets her share of pilgrims.

Chieti to Vasto

Chieti

For something a bit weightier than egomaniac poets and beachballs, head up to **Chieti**, about 13km up the Pescara river. Pescara's artificial promotion in the 1920s has made these the only provincial capitals in Italy within sight of each other. Chieti is really only an overgrown hill town, though a rather elegant one, ocupying a 1,000ft-high eyrie above the coast. It began as the citadel of an Italic people called the Marrucini; under the Romans it was called *Theate Marrucinorum*, a name that its bishop, Pietro Carafa, made use of when founding the Theatine Order, in 1524. Bishop Carafa went on to become Paul IV, the most vicious and intolerant of popes, and patron of the Inquisition, but it's no reflection on Chieti; Carafa was a Neapolitan.

If Chieti has a dramatic Gothic **cathedral** it's thanks to Charles of Anjou; the period in the 12th to 14th centuries when the Angevins ruled at Naples was a prosperous time for Chieti and much of the Abruzzo. The architects didn't go too far in accepting French styles; this is a good squarish Abruzzese building, with another Atri-style campanile, oddly placed at an angle in front of the façade, and a strong Puglian influence shown in its shallow gable and side loggia. The present church was actually begun in the 1100s, when Puglian Romanesque architecture was at its height. Angevin additions and remodellings changed its appearance later on, and the interior is all pastel Baroque. The highlight is a statue of Chieti's patron, San Giustino, by Giuseppe Sammartino. There is a crypt, used for Masses, with Renaissance and medieval frescoes. Behind the cathedral, **San Francesco della Scarpa** has more fluffy Baroque inside.

From San Francesco, **Corso Marrucino** runs its unwavering course through the heart of the city; the rectilinear streets here give away their origins in the Roman castrum of *Theate Marrucinorum*. All that survives is the remains of three little **temples** from the 1st century AD, on Via Spaventa, behind the post office, with *cella* walls in patterns

Getting There and Around

Chieti's **rail** station is down in the valley at Chieti Scalo, with regular connecting buses for the town centre, as well as ARPA **buses** to all points in Chieti province. All the trains from Pescara eastwards stop here, though it's only 5mins away.

Tourist Information

Via B. Spaventa 29, Palazzo INAIL, **t** 0871 63640, *presidio.chieti@abruzzoturismo.it*.

Where to Stay and Eat

Chieti ✉ 66100

★★★★**Dangio'**, Strada Solferino 20, Località Tricalle, **t** 0871 347356, **f** 0871 346984 (*moderate*). A towering, modern hotel 2km out of town, with comfortable rooms and a gourmet restaurant, **La Regine** (*expensive*). *Closed Sun evenings and Mon lunch.*

★★★**Grand Hotel Abruzzo**, Via Asinio Herio 20, **t** 0871 41940, **f** 0871 41960, *www.albergoabruzzo.it* (*moderate*). On the edge of the *centro storico*, with fine views, adequate rooms and affable staff – just make sure your room is on the side with the views, not the one facing the busy traffic.

Ristorante Akileas, Via Asinio Herio 20, **t** 0871 41940 (*moderate*). Attached to the Grand Hotel Abruzzo, offering local dishes with wild mushrooms, and good seafood on Tues and Fri, including Sicilian swordfish *involtini*.

Venturini, Via De Lollis 10, **t** 0871 330663 (*cheap*). A fairly priced, fairly cooked meal at this old institution; the speciality is a mushroom risotto with mozzarella. *Closed Tues.*

Caffè Vittoria, Corso Marrucino. This classy old *caffè* is the place to stop for a coffee; you can also get a taste of sweet yellow Corfinio, Aurum, or any of the other liqueur specialities that are so popular in these parts.

Nonna Elisa, Località Brecciarola, Via Per Popoli 265 (take Viale Maiella a bit out of town), **t** 0871 684152 (*cheap*). A delicious, strictly *abruzzese* experience. *Closed Mon, one week in July and one week in Sept.*

of multicoloured stone. Not far to the south, on Via Asinio Herio, stands the **Roman Theatre** (*to visit, ask the staff at the Museo Archeologico*, **t** *0871 331668*). On the eastern flank of Chieti's hill are the **baths** (*open 9–3*), of which a mighty cistern is the most impressive feature. Best of all in this town are the lovely views, stretching from the sea to the Gran Sasso and Maiella Mountains.

The National Museum and the Warrior

The **Museo Nazionale Archeologico di Antichità** (*open daily 9–6.30; adm*) is Chieti's star attraction, and one of the region's most important museums. It occupies a stately mansion in the **Villa Comunale**, a leafy park on the southern edge of the town. The museum is the chief repository of pre-Roman and Roman artworks unearthed in the Abruzzi, including a fellow who has become a symbol for the region: the shapely **Warrior of Capestrano** from the 6th century BC, dressed like a Mexican bandit and accompanied by an inscription in the language of the Middle Adriatic Bronze Age Italics. Its recent translation proved something of a disappointment: 'Animi made this beautiful image for King Neveo Pompuledeio'. There is a room of other items found in Bronze Age tombs, and others, including the bizarrely decorated bronze discs that were the status embellishments of any proto-Abruzzan gentleman (the Warrior of Capestrano wears one). There are also some good Hellenistic and Roman sculptures, tombs, portraits, bronze figurines, vases and votive offerings, many of them discovered in *Alba Fucens*, in the Abruzzo National Park, and Amiternum, near L'Áquila (*see* p.306). Two fascinating rooms house collections of everyday objects: one with dice, combs, toys jewellery, lamps and such; the other with coins – you would be surprised how much coins tell about ancient economic history, and this room gives a graduate-level course in the subject.

Inland: Along the Via Valeria

Inland from Chieti, the old Roman Via Valeria (SS5) accompanies the A25 up the Pescara valley to Sulmona. There is certainly no shortage of medieval churches along the way. In the 10th and 11th centuries there was plenty of empty land for hard-working Benedictines to put to use, and the Lombard dukes were favourable; consequently this valley, along with the hills on either side, developed one of the greatest concentrations of monasteries in Italy, most of them branch offices of the great Benedictine mother house at Montecassino.

At Manoppello Scalo you'll see a steep, prominent hill overlooking the river that once bore a sanctuary and altar (*ara*) to the *Dea Bona*, the 'Good Goddess'. Naturally there is a church in its place, and a particularly delightful one, the early 13th-century **Santa Maria Arabona**. This is a Cistercian Gothic building with lofty vaulting, an Abruzzo offshoot of the great Cistercian colony centred at Fossanova in Lazio (*see* p.242). They never finished the nave, and much of the church's charm is due to the big glass walls that have been installed under the last arches, looking out on a garden cloister. The Cistercians must not have held it for long; they never would have approved of such decorations as the frescoes by Antonio d'Atri (1373).

Manoppello Scalo is only the rail station for the little hill town of **Manoppello**, 5km to the south where they have something you can't see anywhere else – the face of Jesus. Manoppello's holy icon, the Volto Santo, mysteriously appeared here about 1600, at about the same time that one of the greatest relics of St Peter's in Rome dropped out of sight: the veil of Veronica, on which the image of Jesus was impressed when he wiped his face on it during the carrying of the cross. Manoppello is convinced they have the genuine article, and to accommodate the large numbers of pilgrims who come to visit they have built the impressive **Santuario del Volto Santo** on a height overlooking the town, with a *Via Crucis* following the road up.

And beyond Manoppello, on the tortuous SS539 that skirts the northern edge of the Montagna della Maiella, stands perhaps the finest of all the Benedictine churches in the Abruzzo, in one of the loveliest settings. **San Liberatore a Maiella**, on a wooded height above the village of Serramonacesca (*open usual church hours*), was begun in 1080 by monks from Montecassino, in a style that shows influences from both Puglia and Lombardy. Inside is another fine carved pulpit, a geometrically patterned pavement that seems a mountain version of the Roman Cosmatesque, and fragments of 12th-century frescoes including a portrait of Charlemagne, who was said to have founded the first monastery on this site. There are some beautiful walks from the church, including an easy botanical walk along the river bank.

Further up the Via Valeria, there are sulphurous springs at the **Parco dei Sorgenti** south of Scafa along the Torrente Lavino and, near the village of **Torre de' Passeri**, more Romanesque awaits at **San Clemente a Casáuria**, founded by Emperor Louis II (Charlemagne's great-grandson) in 871 over the temple of Jupiter Urios (hence the name 'Casa Urii'). Louis owed the Church a favour, for when he was captured by the Lombard Duke of Benevento, Adelchi, a bishop helped arrange his release. He had a rare treasure to offer the Church in return: the relics of Clement, the third pope, which had recently been found in the Crimea.

The Benedictines rebuilt the church in the 12th century, endowing it with a magnificent three-arched porch, and three stunning portals with reliefs, some of the finest medieval sculpture in central Italy: St Michael on the left, a bemused Madonna on the right and, best of all, in the centre the *Life of St Clement* and the *Funding of the Monastery*; underneath are the original bronze doors, made in 1192, with ornate panels of geometric patterns. The same sculptors may also have carved the decorations inside: a paschal candlestick, intricately carved capitals and a pulpit – but not the wonderful ciborium, with strange human-headed griffins or sphinxes, over the Roman sarcophagus pressed into service as an altar; this is a *quattrocento* replacement for a destroyed original. To the right is the ancient alabaster urn (3rd century Greek), originally containing bones of Peter and Paul before Louis II came and dropped in Clement's too. The original Carolingian-era crypt was preserved in the reconstruction of the church, and is reached by steps from the aisles.

Pópoli stands at the confluence of the Aterno and the Sagittario, where they meet to form the River Pescara. It's also a strategic junction where the roads to L'Áquila, Pescara and Sulmona meet, the 'Key to the Three Abruzzi'. The town's largest church, **San Francesco**, boasting an elegant Romanesque façade, is topped with statues and an unusual rose window. The 14th-century **Taverna Ducale**, decorated with a row of escutcheons, was not where Pópoli's Cantelmi dukes drank, but where they stored the tithes from their subjects. It has survived in better shape than their ruined **castle** which looms over Pópoli. **Corfinio**, to the west, was called *Pentima* until renamed by Mussolini as part of his campaign to restore geographical names from antiquity – for here stood the Paeligni capital *Corfinium*, famous in history as the united headquarters of the rebellious Italic peoples in the Social War of the 1st century BC. They renamed the city *Italia*, the first time the name was used in history to signify a union of the peninsula's peoples, and hoped it would soon take over from Rome as capital. In the tiny centre, there's a small museum on Via di Zambecca, the **Museo delle Antichità Corfiniesi** (*open Tues–Sun 9–1 and 3–5*). Ancient Corfinio's ruins aren't much, only a small area of excavated houses, in open country near the road to Raiano; nearby is the large 12th-century **Basilica di San Pelino** (*open summer 8–12 and 2–6.30, winter 8.30–12 and 2–5*), with fine architectural details and yet another carved pulpit inside.

Ortona

South of Pescara, beyond the suburban resort of **Francavilla al Mare**, lies Abruzzo's largest port, **Ortona**. Over the years Ortona has taken more than its share of lumps, earthquakes and battle wounds, particularly in the Second World War; in the autumn of 1943 the Germans were well-entrenched along the eastern end of the Gustav Line, north of the River Sangro, and they made Ortona a fortified strongpoint. Thousands of lives were lost in the six-week Battle of the Sangro and Moro Rivers before they were rooted out, and Ortona was taken at the end of December. There are two large British military cemeteries in the vicinity, one near the River Moro, about 3km south of Ortona, and the other just south of Torino di Sangro Marina, between Ortona and Vasto; the Canadian cemetery is on the coast just south of Ortona.

Most of Ortona was destroyed in the process, and most of the pieces were too small to put back together; it's poignant to see the old photos in shops and restaurants that people hang to remind themselves of how things once looked. The old part of town, called 'Terravecchia', stands on a cliff with views over the busy port and down the coast. Here, on Piazza San Tommaso, stands the **cathedral**, completely rebuilt after the war, with only sad fragments of its decoration remaining; the beautiful fountain that stood in front was entirely lost. One thing that survived inside is a chapel with sculptures in high relief by a local artist named Vicenzo Perez, dated 1875. People are just starting to fix up some of Terravecchia's old houses now, and reconstruction work is being done on the bombed-out **Castello Aragonese** that hangs over the coast.

An Inland Tour: Guardiagrele and Lanciano

From Ortona, you can take a narrow-gauge local train for an inland loop (the FAS line, with a station on Via Rapino, although admittedly the bus is much faster), seeing Guardiagrele and Lanciano on the way. **Guardiagrele**, a sweet and peaceful hill town on the edge of the Montagna della Maiella section of the Abruzzo National Park, was a famous centre for metalwork and bell-founding in the Renaissance, the birthplace of the renowned Nicola da Guardiagrele, a student of Lorenzo Ghiberti of Florence

Tourist Information

Ortona: Pza della Repubblica 9, **t** 085 9063841.
Vasto: Piazza del Popolo, **t** 0873 367312.

Where to Stay and Eat

Ortona ✉ 66026

Most hotels are at Lido Riccio, outside town.

★★★★**Mara**, Lido Riccio 4, **t** 085 919 0416 (*expensive*). A holiday complex on the beach with a pool, tennis and all the amenities.

★★★**Ideale**, Corso Garibaldi 65, **t** 085 906 3735 (*moderate*). In the centre.

★★**Moderno**, Via della Libertà 147, **t** 085 906 3630 (*cheap*). Central, less expensive, basic.

Cantina Aragonese, Corso Matteotti 88, **t** 085 906 3217 (*moderate*). In the centre; *the* place for an all-seafood feast, and the best Abruzzo wines. *Closed Sun night and Mon.*

Guardiagrele ✉ 66016

★★★**Villa Maiella**, Via Sette Dolori 30, **t** 0871 809362, *info@maiella.it* (*moderate*). A fine place to stay, attached to one of the most popular restaurants in the area (*also moderate*): an imaginative menu based on traditional preparations (some interesting home-made pasta: wide squarish *toccole* and *trenette di farro* made with spelt, also excellent mountain trout), and very tempting desserts. *Closed Mon and last 2 weeks of July.*

★★**Bocca di Valle**, Loc. Bocca di Valle, **t** 0871 808002 (*moderate*). A small hotel, just up the road in a beautiful setting at the edge of the Maiella National Park, with 12 comfortable rooms and a decent restaurant (*cheap*).

Lanciano ✉ 66034

There are a couple of good choices here:

★★★★**Excelsior**, Viale della Rimembranza 19, **t** 0872 713013, **f** 0872 712907 (*expensive–moderate*). Central; well-furnished rooms and a terrace with views of the Gran Sasso.

★★★**Anxanum**, Via San Francesco d'Assisi 8, **t** 0872 715142, **f** 0872 715054 (*low moderate*). Modern and well equipped, with a pool.

La Ruota, Via Fossacesia 62, **t** 0872 44590 (*moderate*). Excellent fish and *abruzzese* lamb. *Closed Sun and 2–3 weeks in July.*

Fossacesia ✉ 66020

This quiet village near San Giovanni in Venere has two possibilities if you're stopping along the coast.

★★★**Giardino**, Via Marina 69, **t** 0872 607359 (*moderate*). Pleasant and simple.

who produced some of the 15th century's finest works in gold and silver, including the silver crucifix in the church of **Santa Maria Maggiore**, on Via Roma. This church has a lovely Gothic façade, and porticos on the sides (rebuilt after wartime bombings) where the town holds its market. It was also famed for its huge exterior fresco of St Christopher by Andrea de Lito, which brought good luck to any traveller who saw it; though faded, it still survives on the north wall. The crucifix is kept in the adjacent **Museo del Duomo** (*open July–Sept, Sat and Sun 10–12.30 and 5–8; daily in Aug, same hours; at other times call ahead,* **t** *0871 82117*). Guardiagrele is still known for its metalwork, though it isn't quite as elaborate as back in the Renaissance: everything from cooking pots to decorative medallions to wrought-iron bedsteads. The town's craftsmen display their work around the main gate, the picturesque **Porta San Giovanni**, and besides metalwork they also sell glass and ceramics. Guardiagrele may not be the most convenient base for seeing the Maiella; the mountains turn a blank wall to it, with no easy roads through. But the countryside is still beautiful, and from the edge of the park just west of town at **Bocca di Valle** there is a hiking path that leads up to a pretty waterfall. North of Guardiagrele, the village of **Rapino** has been a centre for painted ceramics since the 1700s, and its artisans still produce some fine pieces today.

Lanciano, 23km east of Guardiagrele, was a medieval market town that attracted merchants from all over the Mediterranean to its wool and cloth fairs. The commercial

***Golfo di Venere, in a garden next to San Giovanni, Via S. Giovanni 40, t 0872 60541 (*moderate*). This one has a good restaurant next door, the **Parco dei Priori**, t 0872 608171 (*moderate*), located in a well-restored 18th-century villa, and serving lovely seafood, including excellent lobster. *Closed Mon.*

Vasto ✉ 66054

Like Ortona and Térmoli, Vasto has plenty of room in all price categories along the lidos (except at the height of the season in August).

***La Panoramica, Via Smargiassi 1, t 0873 367700 (*moderate*). A pleasant alternative in the town centre, in a tranquil setting on the edge of the old centre near the Belvedere, with views over the coast.

*****Villa Vignola, Marina di Vasto, on the SS16c, t 0873 310050, f 0873 310060, *villavignola@abruzzocitta.it* (*expensive*). 6km from the centre, in Vignola; five charming, spacious rooms in an enchanting seafront villa, surrounded by citrus and olive trees, with a private beach and an excellent restaurant (*expensive*). *Closed Christmas.*

**San Marco, Via Madonna dell'Asilo 10, t 0873 498 2099, f 0873 69952 (*cheap*). The rooms at this slightly battered hotel are decorated in startling shades of pink and green, but it's got a central location on the edge of the old town and you won't find anything cheaper.

**Lido, t 0873 8014107, f 0873 801069, *hotel lido@libero.it* (*cheap*). The best of the cheaper hotels along the seaside strip, with flowers spilling across the balconies (try to get rooms facing the sea) and a reasonable restaurant (*cheap*).

Vasto is a bit of a gastronomic capital.

All'Hostaria del Pavone, Via Barbarotta 15, t 0873 60227 (*moderate–cheap*). Here you can taste a wonderful *scapece* (tiny fishes, first fried then marinated in saffron and vinegar – a dish that has nourished generations of sailors) – as well as many other fish specialities. *Closed Tues and several weeks between Jan and Feb.*

Osteria del Borgo, Via F Crispi 24, t 0873 60505 (*moderate*). There's fresh seafood and charming service at this cosy restaurant, but choose carefully from the menu; the risotto is disappointing but the grilled seafood is usually excellent. There's an interesting selection of wines on offer, including a couple of local organic wines.

La Tana, Piazza Pudente, t 0873 362722. Near the Palazzo d'Avalos; good for pizza and also for reasonably priced seafood antipasti and grilled fish (*cheap*).

advantages of this isolated mountain setting may not be readily apparent, but Lanciano is still doing well today as a minor industrial centre. Its medieval core, urban and urbane, is surprisingly large, consisting of four separate quarters on four hills. The four corners meet at **Piazza del Plebiscito**, built over what once was the valley of a stream. The **cathedral** is uniquely sited atop a Roman bridge, which was restored in the 11th century to support the church; it is dedicated to the 'Madonna del Ponte' after a statue of the virgin that stood on the bridge, and now has pride of place on the main altar. Across the piazza, the church of San Francesco, better known as the **Santuaro del Miracolo Eucaristico**, is an important pilgrimage site (John Paul II came here as a pilgrim when he was still bishop of Cracow). The attraction is the relic of an 8th-century miracle – some drops of blood and a little piece of human heart – when the bread and wine of the Mass supposedly really did turn into flesh and blood, to quiet the doubts of a sceptical monk. The blood and flesh, kept in a silver Neapolitan reliquary of 1713 (*displayed daily, 6.30–12.45 and 3–8*), were tested in 1971; Jesus's blood type was AB. When it happened, this was a Greek church in a partly Greek town; the Franciscans took it over in 1252, and the present church was begun six years later, though the interior is thoroughly Baroque.

From the opposite side of the piazza, Via dei Frentani leads up to the northern end of town, passing some old houses with shop fronts from the days of the medieval fairs, and also the 13th-century church of **Sant'Agostino**, with a silver bust by Nicola da Guardiagrele inside; it ends at the **Porta San Biagio**, Lanciano's only surviving medieval gate. West of Piazza del Plebiscito, you'll find yourself in the straight and narrow alleys of the **Civitanova**, a medieval addition designed on a grid plan. Here, on Via S. Maria Maggiore, is the outstanding French Gothic church of the Abruzzo, **Santa Maria Maggiore**. An existing church, itself built over a temple of Apollo, was rebuilt in 1227 and given a beautiful façade with two great rose windows and a fine portal (added in 1317). Inside, you'll notice the church's little secret – it was built backwards, with the altar under an octagonal apsidal vault right behind the façade. There is another work of Nicola da Guardiagrele here, a fine silver crucifix.

Not far away on Via Madrigale, the **Museo Civico** (***t*** *0872 703701; open Mon 4–8, Tues–Sun 9–1.30 and 4–8*) has a small collection of archaeological finds from the Bronze Age to when Lanciano was Roman *Anxanum*. Part of the Civitanova was once **La Sacca**, the Jewish ghetto, created after Jews were allowed back into the Abruzzi by the Hohenstaufen Emperors in 1191. At the southern end of the quarter are surviving parts of the town walls, along with the 11th-century fortress of the **Torri Montanare**, from which there are great views of the surrounding hills and the mountains further inland; outside the walls, on Via Sant'Egidio is an impressive medieval fountain, the **Fontana Grande di Civitanova**.

Lanciano is also the starting point for one of the most spectacular drives in the Abruzzi – the SS84 to Roccaraso (*see* p.322), near the Abruzzo National Park.

San Giovanni in Venere

Back on the coast, above the railway station of the small resort of **Fossacesia Marina**, stands one of Abruzzo's most remarkable monuments – **San Giovanni in Venere**. 'Venere' refers to the goddess Venus, over whose temple this church was erected; temples to Venus were often placed high over the sea. Begun as early as the 8th century, the church was rebuilt in 1015 and converted into a Cistercian abbey in 1165. There are several Puglian–Sicilian touches in the church – in the decoration of the narrow windows, the bicoloured geometric medallions in stone and blind arches, the robust figures of the bas-reliefs, and the name and design of the magnificent *Portale della Luna*, the marble 'Portal of the Moon' (1230), with scenes from the life of John the Baptist; next to this is an unusual monument to the founder, Abbot Oderisius. Walk around the church to see the arcaded apses. The large crypt, entered from the aisles, contains ancient columns from the temple of Venus and some well-preserved 12th-century frescoes, including a very Byzantine enthroned Madonna on the central apse, flanked by St Nicholas and St Michael modelling the latest in Byzantine court fashions.

Vasto

The next town along the coast is **Vasto**, home of Gabriele Rossetti, poet and father of Dante Gabriel and Christina Rossetti. Vasto stands on a low natural terrace above its port and beaches, which attract large numbers of French as well as Italian tourists, and vacationers from eastern Europe. Beginning as a settlement of the Frentani, it became the Roman *Histonium*, and the medieval *Guasto* – which only coincidentally means 'broken' in Italian. Perhaps a fitting name, but for a town that has been destroyed several times (by the Romans, Franks, Spaniards, Turks and earthquakes) Vasto's in pretty good shape; in fact it is one of the most attractive towns on the Adriatic coast, full of palm trees and old *palazzi* with iron balconies.

The further south you go in Italy, the greater honour accrues to poets; Vasto is far enough south to name its main square **Piazza Rossetti**, along with a grandiose memorial. On one side stands the 15th-century **Castello**, and on the other the **Torrone**, or Torre Bassano, a bastion of the now-demolished walls. Vasto used to be a lot smaller; the medieval centre was only the few streets between here and the sea cliffs. Inside it, on Piazza Pudente, is the **cathedral**, undoubtedly one of the tiniest in Christendom, with a 13th-century portal, and a little further on the Palazzo d'Avalos, home to one of the many feudal families who controlled Vasto and now the home of the **Musei Civici** (*open June – Sept 10.30–12.30, 6.30–10.30, July and Aug until 12 midnight, Oct–May 9.30–12.30 and 4.30–8; adm*). There are three museums: one of archaeological finds, another devoted to local painters including Filippo Palizzi (1818–99), and a brand new third, a museum of modern art. The main church in the medieval centre is the 11–13th-century **Santa Maria Maggiore**; stairs behind it lead down to the **Belvedere**, a lovely garden on the side of the cliff. North of the Palazzo d'Avalos, along Via Adriática, you can see the damage done by another Vasto nemesis: landslides. The last one, in 1956, carried off a few blocks here, along with the medieval church of **San Pietro**, leaving only the façade.

Términoli and the Tremiti Islands

Crossing over the River Trigno, you enter Molise, which is even more rural and unspoiled than Abruzzo, although this may not be immediately apparent from the busy beaches along the coast. **Térmoli** is this region's only port, a bright little fishing town on a promontory, with a long sandy Blue Flag beach, palms and oleanders.

With Térmoli's recent tourist prosperity quite a number of buildings in the old town are getting fixed up. The diva of the old town, or at least the part that survived the Turkish raid of 1566, is the 12th-century **cathedral**, which has just emerged from restoration. The 'Puglian Romanesque' contributed some of the most sophisticated and beautiful styles of medieval architecture and sculpture anywhere in Europe, and this little church makes a fitting introduction to the great works you can see further south. The façade, with its rose window, low gable and blind arcades, contains much precise and elegant stonecarving, unfortunately damaged; note the horseshoe arches, an influence of the mosques of Africa and Spain. Inside a colourful mosaic floor shows mythological beasts twisting and swallowing one another.

From the old town, Via Roma leads off to Piazza Sant'Antonio, with the town hall and the old church of Sant'Antonio, now deconsecrated and used as the **Galleria Civica d'Arte** (*in summer open daily 6–10pm; in winter by request*, **t** *0875 712265; adm*). Térmoli has a competition for contemporary art every two years, and the best works end up here. After enjoying the view from the castle and poking around the old lanes

Getting to the Islands

Though part of the region of Puglia, the islands can be reached by ferry from Térmoli or Vasto. In winter, the only service is from the closest point, Vieste, in Puglia.

From Vasto, there's a hydrofoil daily from 20 June–12 Sept; it's a one-hour ride, and the return is in the afternoon so you can make it a day trip. Tickets at the Agenzia Massacesi, Piazza Diomede 3 in Vasto, **t** 0873 362680.

From Térmoli, hydrofoils and faster *idrogetti* are more frequent; there are boats from the beginning of April through Sept, and in summer you'll have a choice of several daily; each way takes 1½hrs, 50mins on the *idrogetto*. Tickets and information for the Navigazione Libero del Golfo line at the dock, **t** 0875 703937; Adriática Navigazione at the dock, **t** 0875 705343 (run services year-round); and Navigargano, at the dock, **t** 0875 707197.

Tourist Information

Térmoli: Piazza M Bega, **t** 0875 706754, **f** 0875 704956.

Where to Stay and Eat

Térmoli ✉ 86039

******Corona**, Corso M. Milano 2/A, **t** 0875 84041, **f** 0875 84947 (*moderate*). A medium-sized traditional hotel in the centre of town. There's a good restaurant with a Liberty-style dining room. *Closed Sun.*

*****Rosary**, Lungomare C Colombo 24, **t** 0875 84944, **f** 0875 84947 (*cheap*). Also central, on the beach, this '60s-style hotel has balconies and nice old-fashioned rooms.

*****Cian**, Lungomare Colombo 48, **t** 0875 704436 (*cheap*). A good budget hotel with nine rooms, located on a rock above the coast, but it's close to the main road.

Z'Bass, Via Oberdan 8, **t** 0875 706703 (*expensive*). Prepares some of the finest freshest seafood around. Near the old fish market. *Closed Mon, exc in summer.*

Da Noi Tre, Corso Fratelli Brigida 34, **t** 0875 703 639 (*moderate*). Following the grand old Italian trattoria tradition, there is a television set in the dining room, and fish is served exclusively. *Open daily in summer; in winter closed Mon and most of Dec and Jan.*

Il Battello Ebbro, Via Vico VI Duomo, **t** 0875 703219 (*cheap*). For something different – a cheerful Greek restaurant behind the cathedral overlooking the bay.

Il Nuovo Mangiatoio, Via Antonio d'Andrea, **t** 0875 714104 (*cheap*). You can get snacks and sandwiches here; also with outdoor dining on a pedestrian street.

Torre Saracena, 5km north from the centre of Térmoli, on the SS16 Adriática Highway, **t** 0875 703318 (*expensive–moderate*). Located in an ancient watchtower on the beach, and features the freshest of fish, prepared in some surprising ways. *Closed Mon and Nov.*

inside the walls, there's nothing more demanding to do than relax on the beach and try to decide which seafood restaurant to try in the evening. If Térmoli's too crowded, there's another modest resort down the coast, **Campomarino**.

The two **Tremitis** are Italy's only islands in the Adriatic. In winter they have a population of 50; in August, however, they crawl with some 100,000 holidaymakers who buzz over for the day from the resorts. They are made up of well-scoured limestone and the sea around them is remarkable clean. Historically they have been a place of exile – Augustus sent his adulterous granddaughter, Julia the Younger, and Charlemagne sent his pesky Italian father-in-law Paolo Vinifrido, minus his hands and eyes, though he nevertheless managed to escape somehow and make it to Montecassino. The only historic sight, on the smaller island of **San Nicola**, is a huge, half-ruined fortress monastery begun by the Benedictines in the 11th century.

Local boats link San Nicola to the larger island of **San Domino**, where the ferries dock, and where you'll find the only beach and all the hotels. It's a beauty of an island, set in a translucent blue-green sea, well forested and surrounded by coves and lagoons. If you can avoid coming in August, the Tremitis can be a prefect spot to let your watch run down. Any time in the summer, however, come prepared to face hungry mosquitoes.

The Gran Sasso and L'Áquila

The Upper Vomano Valley

Coming over the mountains from Téramo, at **Montorio al Vomano** the SS150 joins the main SS80, the scenic road which, like the more efficient but less panoramic *autostrada*, links Téramo with L'Áquila. Montorio, topped by its grand but never-completed Spanish castle, has an eclectic church, the **Collegiata di San Rocco**, with a façade that has been tinkered with whenever funds were handy; within, the carved Baroque altar and tapestries are the main attraction.

Further up the valley the twin blunt, snow-shrouded peaks of the Due Corni del Gran Sasso look over the shoulder of **Fano Adriano**, an old village that's now a small winter and summer resort, with skiing and hiking at **Prato Selva**. The village's name translates as 'Hadrian's Temple', although nothing of this remains; the 12th-century **San Pietro** is modern Fano's finest church, with a Renaissance façade from 1550. **Pietracamela**, even higher up in the lap of the Gran Sasso (3,262ft), is a base for hikes over the Sella dei Due Corni to the Campo Imperatore, and for skiing at the Gran Sasso's biggest resort, the **Prati di Tivo**, a lofty meadow of beech forests. During the peak season a helicopter takes expert skiers up to otherwise inaccessible runs.

The SS80 towards L'Áquila continues past the **Lago di Campotosto**, an irregular man-made lake richly stocked with fish, and popular with birdwatchers and hang-gliders, with the Gran Sasso for a striking backdrop. From there it winds around the western flank of the Gran Sasso; about 10km before L'Áquila it comes to **Amiternum**, the ruins of a Sabine city mentioned in the *Aeneid*, and later a Roman colony that was the birthplace of the poet Sallust. A small theatre, amphitheatre and foundations of houses were brought to light in 1978, all accessible in an open field. The nearby medieval village of **San Vittorino** has, underneath its 12th–16th-century church of

Where to Stay and Eat

Gran Sasso ✉ 67100

*******Albergo di Campo Imperatore**, t 0862 400000, f 0862 400004 (*moderate*). At the top of the cable car route, the Duce's hotel-prison has been renovated, and has very comfortable facilities.

******Fiordigigli**, by the lower funicular station at Fonte Cerreto in Assergi, t 0862 606171, f 0862 606674 (*moderate–cheap*). Another hotel that was used to hold Mussolini in 1943, it is now a pretty, friendly hotel that makes a good base for visiting the mountains and L'Áquila, 16km east.

******La Villetta**, t 0862 606171, f 0862 606674 (*moderate–cheap*). Sister hotel to the nearby Fiordigigli, with colourful pointy turrets like a witch's castle, comfortable rooms and a snack bar and shop (for picnic supplies).

Elodia, at Camarda, on the SS17 bis towards L'Áquila, t 0862 606219 (*moderate*). All manner of tasty local dishes, using saffron, wild mushrooms and local cheeses. *Closed Sun eve, Mon and two weeks in July.*

San Michele, something out of the ordinary in this part of the world: catacombs. Unlike the great ones in Rome, these don't go very far, but they do have some sculptural fragments from Amiternum and bits of medieval frescoes. A procession is held through them on the last Sunday in May.

The Big Rock of Italy, and the Campo Imperatore

The Gran Sasso offers Alpine grandeur only an hour by motorway from Rome, and as such is an immensely popular ski and hiking resort. The entire area, including the Monti della Laga to the north, was set aside in 1995 as the **Parco Nazionale del Gran Sasso e Monti della Laga**. If you plan to do any hiking pick up a map either from the tourist office or from the Italian Alpine Club (CAI) in L'Áquila, at Via del Mulino, **t** 0862 24342 (*open daily 7am–8pm*). You can also visit the **park information office** (*Via Roio 10–12, L'Áquila,* **t** *0862 401903, www.gransassolagapark.it*); for information on ski facilities in the park, *see* p.310. Among the wildlife to be found are chamois (reintroduced after being hunted to the point of extinction), deer, bears and the Apennine wolf, as well as more than 100 species of bird, including golden eagles and peregrine falcons.

To reach the Gran Sasso from L'Áquila, catch the bus from Corso Vittorio Emanuele to the *funivia* (cable car) at Fonte Cerreto, near **Assergi**, the village at the mouth of the Gran Sasso Tunnel and the most popular base for visiting the mountains – alternatively, if you have a car and the roads are clear, drive up the SS17bis by way of **Bazzano** (site of an interesting 12th-century church, Santa Giusta). The *funivia* is an impressive trip, climbing over 3,000ft in seven minutes (*in winter, and from 20 July–25 Aug, it runs every half-hour from 8.30–4.45; in summer, every hour from 8.30–5*). Both the funivia and the road (the SS17bis) will take you to the **Campo Imperatore**, a beautiful, gentle upland meadow 20km long and 6,910ft above sea level, filled with flowers in the late spring and ski bunnies in the winter. The **Museo Giardino Alpino** (*open May–Oct 8–7*) has exhibits on the flora and fauna of the mountains.

Many of the trails through the Gran Sasso begin at Mussolini's hotel (*see* box below), including one up past the Duca degli Abruzzi refuge to the **Corno Grande**

Mussolini's Least-Favourite Hotel

Near the upper funicular station stands the Albergo di Campo Imperatore, which once sheltered a real would-be emperor. After the King and the ad hoc Italian government of Marshal Badoglio had deposed Mussolini and begun to seek peace with the Allies in 1943, there remained the delicate question of what to do with the former Duce. After being shuttled off for a while to Ponza, he was brought to this hotel, which set the stage for SS Commando Otto Skorzeny's rescue on 12 September 1943. German paratroopers slipped in and out with the aid of a Fieseler Storch – an aeroplane with a very short takeoff and a cockpit the size of the average refrigerator – into which Skorzeny somehow managed to squeeze the portly Mussolini before escaping. Hitler then set up a new headquarters for his associate on Lake Garda.

This episode fooled the Allies, and has fooled historians for decades. Only recently has it been established that Skorzeny's exploit wasn't necessary at all. No one was guarding the Duce, perhaps intentionally, and the Germans still controlled the area; they could have carried him off in a pram. It was all a publicity stunt, part of Hitler's campaign to glorify the SS at the expense of the regular German army, which was getting beaten on all fronts, and the political loyalty of which it was already suspect.

(9,464ft), a spectacular 8-hour walk. There are three ski lifts in the Campo Imperatore and four at Monte Cristo.

L'Áquila

L'Áquila in Italian means 'the eagle', the symbol of empire, and it's not surprising to learn that the city was founded by Emperor Frederick II. He meant it not only to increase trade and commerce, but also to gain a measure of control of a wild territory full of battling feudal barons, and as a bulwark against the popes, who were trying to infringe on his territory. L'Áquila is one of the few cities in Italy of any importance not to have ancient precedents; instead, to populate his new town, Frederick planned to relocate the inhabitants of surrounding castles and hamlets – 99 of them in all, according to tradition, who supposedly each built their own church in the new town. The city was not actually begun until after Frederick's death, and ironically it almost immediately went over to the enemies of the Hohenstaufens; Frederick's son Manfred captured and destroyed it, and it was refounded in 1266 by Charles of Anjou.

L'Áquila's fortune was made through its loyalty to Queen Giovanna II in 1423, when the city was besieged for over a year by the Aragonese. The queen thanked the city for its steadfastness by granting it numerous privileges that helped it to become, for several centuries, the second city in the Kingdom of Naples, a chief wool and livestock market town and a producer of silk and saffron. Its success attracted Adam of Rottweil, a student of Gutenburg, who founded a printing press here in 1482, one of the first in Italy. L'Áquila's good fortune made it cocky, and in 1529 it rose up against its rulers in Naples. The Spanish viceroy quickly put an end to its pretensions and punished the Aquilani by forcing them to pay for a huge new citadel to discourage any further revolts. Much of what the Spaniards didn't destroy in their reprisal fell in the earthquake of 1703.

And yet, despite its vicissitudes, L'Áquila has managed to keep a considerable portion of its distinctive old quarters, its walls and even some of its exceptional 13th-century monuments. Grey and dignified, perhaps a little aloof and austere, with the gleaming peaks of the Gran Sasso for a backdrop, there is no city in Italy quite like it. Of all the new towns founded on the peninsula in the Middle Ages, L'Áquila is the largest and most successful; it comes as a surprise to walk its broad, straight streets and ample piazzas, and consider that this is the Middle Ages' idea of what a city should be like.

A 99-headed Fountain

L'Áquila's most famous monument, the venerable **Fontana delle 99 Cannelle**, built in 1272, stands in a corner of the city walls near the Porta Rivera, not far from the railway station on the western side of the old city. The fountain's water flows through the mouths of 93 mouldering grotesque heads and six unadorned spouts, each said to symbolize one of the 99 hamlets that were brought together to populate the city . The fountain has three sides (the one to the left is a more recent addition, built in the 16th century), and the whole is sheltered in a pretty pink-and-white chequered

Getting There and Around

Trains connect L'Áquila (with no great hurry or frequency) to Rieti in Lazio and Terni in Umbria, with connections to Rome, as well as to Pescara by way of Sulmona, the main junction for rail routes in the central Abruzzo.

L'Áquila is less than 2 hours from Rome on ARPA **buses** (Rome, **t** 06 442 33928, L'Áquila, **t** 0862 22146), with 18 departures a day (11 on Sun) from outside Stazione Tiburtina (underground line B); in Rome tickets need to be purchased before boarding from ARPA, Via Teodorico 28 (*open daily 6.30am–9.30pm*).

Tourist Information

L'Áquila: Piazza S. Maria de Paganica 5, **t** 0862 410808, **f** 0862 65442.

Centro Turistico del Gran Sasso: Corso Vittorio Emanuele 49, L'Áquila, **t** 0862 22147 (*open Mon–Fri 9–1 and 4–7, Sat 9–1*), has information on sights, hiking, winter sports and other outdoor activities in the region's mountains, as does the local office of the **Club Alpino Italiano** (*see* p.308).

Where to Stay and Eat

L'Áquila ✉ 67100

★★★★**Grand Hotel e Del Parco**, Corso Federico II 73, **t** 0862 413248, **f** 0862 65938 (*expensive*). The swish, business traveller's choice, a modern hotel overlooking a small park close to the centre with a good restaurant (*moderate*) and extras like a sauna and gym.

★★★**San Michele**, Via dei Giardini, **t** 0862 412899, **f** 0862 27060, *info@stmichelehotel.it* (*moderate*). Also modern, with large soundproofed rooms to ensure a good night's sleep and an underground car park.

★★★**Duomo**, Via Dragonetti 6, **t** 0862 410893 (*moderate*). Off Piazza Duomo, housed in a 17th-century palace; 28 slightly cramped rooms, some with views of the square.

★★★**Duca degli Abruzzi**, Viale Papa Giovanni XXIII 10, **t** 0862 28341, **f** 0862 61588 (*moderate*). A striking, somewhat eccentric bit of Modernist architecture – a rarity in Italy; inside are exceedingly comfortable and ample rooms. It's quiet and well-run, too.

★★★**Castello**, across from the castle in Piazza Battaglione Alpini, **t** 0862 419147 (*moderate*). An attractive, quite classy 44-room hotel.

★**Orazi**, Via Roma 175, **t** 0862 412889 (*cheap*). The cheapest, if not most central, option. Only two of its 10 rooms are en suite.

Ernesto, Pza Palazzo, **t** 0862 21094 (*moderate*). Traditional Abruzzese cuisine is a speciality here: home-made pasta dishes featuring truffles or saffron, *stracotto* (beef stewed in Montepulciano wine) and lamb. Book. *Closed Sun, Mon, 2 weeks in Aug and Christmas.*

Aquila da Remo, Via San Flaviano 9, **t** 0862 22010 (*moderate*). Good solid cooking in a simple setting, providing you don't mind the sometimes less than charming service of the family owners. *Closed Fri, 2 weeks in July and over Christmas.*

Trattoria del Giaguaro, Pza S. Maria Paganica 4, **t** 0862 28249 (*cheap*). Conveniently placed and slightly cheaper. *Closed Mon eves, Tues, 2 weeks in July and Aug, and Christmas.*

Dei Gemelli, near the Duomo, Via Guelfaglione 27, **t** 0862 27574 (*cheap*). Worth a detour for its great homemade pasta. *Closed Sun.*

Osteria Nudo e Crudo, Via F Cannella 9, **t** 0862 404990 (*cheap*). Cavernous, relaxed and friendly, with charming service, tasty daily specials and an excellent house wine.

courtyard. While you're there, you can try to figure out how the two sundials work on the façade of the little church opposite.

From the fountain, Via San Jacopo ascends to join Via XX Settembre, the main entry-point into the city if you're approaching from Rome. Follow Via XX Settembre straight into the shady **Villa Comunale**, turn right on Viale Francesco Crispi and then left on to the Viale di Collemaggio to reach L'Áquila's greatest Romanesque church, **Santa Maria di Collemaggio**, in open country just outside the city wall. 'St Mary of May Hill' was founded in 1270 by Pope Celestine V (*see* pp.53–4), and was freshly refurbished for the 2000 Jubilee. The church has the most sumptuous façade of any in Abruzzo, a great

rectangular Abruzzan false-front, covered in a lovely pattern of pink and white stone. Its three rounded portals are decorated with spiral mouldings and niches for saints, who have mostly vanished. Above the portals runs a pretty ribbon-like frieze, and above that are three rose windows of different patterns, the large centre one in particular a masterpiece of the stonecarver's art. The elegant interior has been stripped of its centuries' accumulation of art and debris, leaving the fancy Renaissance tomb of Celestine V as its chief decoration, though the church also contains some 15th-century frescoes, on the left-hand side of the nave, and some later ones by a pupil of Perugino on the right. Celestine granted the church the unusual privilege of a Holy Door, like that of St Peter's in Rome; they open it every year on 28 August, and anyone passing through receives an indulgence.

Around Piazza Duomo

From Via XX Settembre and the park, Corso Federico II leads into Piazza Duomo. L'Áquila is one town where the **cathedral** is the least interesting building, frequently shattered by earthquakes and now dressed in a dull neoclassical façade. On the south side of the square, next to the post office, is the much more original and nicely perverse 18th-century rococo façade of the **Santuario del Suffragio**, with opulent curves and an inscription from St John Chrysostom held by a leering skeleton, inviting us to celebrate death, not cry over it. The large, lively piazza itself has been L'Áquila's main market square ever since 1304, when Charles of Anjou granted the town the right to hold one here – you'll find produce and a variety of handicrafts on sale daily (except Sunday) from dawn to 1pm.

The neighbourhood around Piazza del Duomo is one of L'Áquila's most attractive. Walk behind the Suffragio to Via Indipendenza to see the **Cancelle**, a block of shops from the 1400s, and the ripe Baroque church of **Sant'Agostino**, with a lofty cupola and trees growing out of the cornice in the best south Italian style. Three streets east, on Via Santa Giusta, the portal and rose window of the 13th-century church of **Santa Giusta** are worth a look, the rose window embellished with 12 droll figures; all around it the streets are full of Baroque palaces. On the other side of Piazza del Duomo, on Via Sassa, the church of **San Giuseppe** contains a 15th-century equestrian tomb by Ludovico d'Alemagna, while **Palazzo Franchi**, at No.56, has a lovely Renaissance court-yard with a double loggia.

From Piazza Duomo, elegant arcaded Corso Vittorio Emanuele leads to the **Quattro Cantoni**, the 'Four Corners', the city's main crossroads. To the left, on Corso Umberto, lies Piazza del Palazzo, the palazzo in question being the **Palazzo di Giustizia**, from where Margherita of Austria, a daughter of Charles V born on the wrong side of the blanket, ruled as Governess of Abruzzo when she wasn't holding court in Penne. The bell in the palace's tower sounds 99 strokes every day at dusk, in memory, once again, of the city's origins. To the north on Via Paganica, **Santa Maria Paganica** has an unusual carved Gothic façade, at the centre of a distinguished neighbourhood with a number of palaces dating from the Middle Ages to the 1800s.

San Bernardino

On the other side of the Quattro Cantoni, Via San Bernardino leads to the master-piece of Abruzzese Renaissance art, the church of **San Bernardino**, which shines out magnificently among the more modern buildings that surround it. The great Franciscan revivalist preacher San Bernardino da Siena spent several years in the Franciscan convent in L'Áquila before he died (Bernardino's motto, 'make it sharp, make it brief and stick to the point' won him the dubious 20th-century distinction of being declared patron saint of advertising). One of his chief disciples in Abruzzo, St John of Capestrano, founded this church as his memorial. Work began in 1452, but the perfectly balanced, elegant façade was only finished by Cola d'Amatrice in 1542. It is best seen from the bottom of the stair in front of the church; we are in Abruzzo, so the roof is gable-less. The 1703 earthquake smashed the vast interior, which was rebuilt *à la* grand Baroque. San Bernardino's mausoleum and the *Tomb of Maria Periera* are both works by Silvestro d'Áquila, the master of Abruzzo sculpture and pupil of Donatello. The second chapel on the right contains a *pala* by Andrea della Robbia, grandson of the more famous Luca.

The Castello

To the north, Corso Vittorio Emanuele runs out to the shady Parco del Castello and, above it, the grand, moated **Castello**. Built in 1535 by Pier Luigi Sacrivà, it is a showpiece of Renaissance military architecture unwillingly financed by the citizens of L'Áquila, with a grand doorway, crowned by Charles V's screaming two-headed eagle (Charles, the big winner in the early 16th-century Wars of Italy, built castles like this in scores of towns to keep an eye on their inhabitants). From outside the main entrance there are fine views over L'Áquila and the surrounding mountains. The castle contains the **Museo Nazionale d'Abruzzo** (*open Tues–Sun 9–8; adm*), the region's finest, with a well-arranged collection of archaeological treasures and artworks salvaged from abandoned local churches. The biggest exhibit is on the ground floor, to the right of the entrance: the *Elephas Meridionalis*, a mighty reconstructed prehistoric pachyderm, discovered by accident near L'Áquila in 1954. The ground floor also contains an archaeological section; on the first floor the medieval section has a collection of religious art, among the highlights of which are its polychrome wooden statues, including a *St Sebastian* and a *Madonna and Child* by Silvestro d'Áquila and a fine 15th-century panel painting of *St John of Capestrano*. There are many other fine triptychs, several showing Sienese–Umbrian influence, and a detached fresco with a sweet *Madonna* by Andrea di Litio. On the next floor up there are later works by Neapolitan painters such as Mattia Preti and Andrea Vaccaro, as well as Abruzzese artists like Pompeo Cesari. The third and final floor contains 20th-century works, mainly by local artists. Concerts are held regularly in the auditorium.

South of the Gran Sasso

The SS17, the closest thing you'll find to a straight road in these mountains, runs southeast from L'Áquila along the southern flanks of the Gran Sasso, with a fair helping of distractions in the hills on both sides. North of the road the scenic SS17bis passes several rarely visited villages like **Calascio**, with its impressive ruined citadel 4,500ft up. **Castel del Monte**, further up still, has an interesting medieval core, and a good medieval church just outside town, **San Giovanni**, with a carved portal and fragments of frescoes inside; from here you can drive up to the Campo Imperatore. South of the SS17, **Fossa** has 12th-century frescoes of the *Day of Judgment* in its church of **Santa Maria ad Cryptas** that are said to have inspired Dante (*if closed, call Don Giuseppe,* ***t*** *0862 751226*). There is good skiing as well as bobsledding at **Campo Felice**, above the picturesque village of **Rocca di Cambio**, the highest in Abruzzo at 4,657ft.

Tiny **Bominaco** (near Caporciano) is the site of the most celebrated monuments in this corner of Abruzzo, two churches that formerly belonged to a fortified Benedictine abbey. The monastery dates from some shadowy three-digit year; **San Pellegrino** church is said to have been founded by Charlemagne, though it was rebuilt in 1263. The interior, rectangular in shape, with an ogival vault, is covered with an excellent example of the colourful, stylized frescoes of the period; the upper pictures include a calendar of the months and the major feast days, while others represent scenes from the New Testament, saints and geometrical patterns. The sanctuary is set apart from the nave by a marble transenna carved with a griffon with a cup, and another with a fearsome dragon – not ordinary subject matter for a Christian temple. The saint is buried under the sanctuary and it is said that you can hear his heart beating through a hole next to the altar. **Santa Maria Assunta** has none of the ancient strangeness of San Pellegrino, but is a 12th-century gem, beautifully endowed with carved doors, windows, capitals and a pulpit. Just to the west of Bominaco are the caves of the **Grotte di Stiffe** (*50min guided tours June–Sept daily 10–1 and 3–6; adm exp; call well in advance,* **t** *0862 861000 to arrange a tour in English; info@grottestiffe.it*), where about half a mile of illuminated walkway takes you along an underground river beneath an eerie assortment of stalactites and waterfalls. East of the caves, on the SS261, the little hamlet of **Fontécchio** has a little jewel of a medieval fountain.

From **Navelli**, centre of the Abruzzo's tiny saffron-growing region (they say they make the world's best), the road makes a dramatic writhing descent to Pópoli, on the Via Valeria and the Rome–Pescara *autostrada*, or you can turn eastwards to **Capestrano,** birthplace of San Bernardino's saintly follower, St John of Capestrano (1386–1456). You may see some swallows swooping about, but it's Capestrano's namesake in California where they come back every year at the same date. Here they come back when they feel like it.

Southern Abruzzo and the National Parks

For many people the highlight of the Abruzzo is its clutch of national parks, four of them including the one around the Gran Sasso, with the other three (Maiella, the Abruzzo National Park and Sirente Velino west of Pópoli) on the spine of the Apennines south of L'Áquila. All are of special interest for their rare fauna and flora, but for mountain-lovers the best might be the Montagna della Maiella, a range nearly as impressive as the Gran Sasso and considerably less touristy. Man-made sights include *Alba Fucens*, Abruzzo's most interesting archaeological site, and intriguing old towns like Sulmona, Scanno, Pescocostanzo and Tagliacozzo.

The Marsica

The region north of the Monti Simbruini (on the Lazio border) and the Monti Sirenti is known as **Marsica**, after its ancient inhabitants, the *Marsi*, who lived on the shores of Lake Fucino. The 'People of Mars' were among the most determined foes of the Romans in ancient times, and they took a prominent part in the fighting during the Social War in 90 BC. They also had a talent for medicine, using the local herbs, which gave the Romans occasion to accuse them of witchcraft.

Avezzano and *Alba Fucens*

The modern capital of the Marsica, **Avezzano**, has little to commend it, having been toppled by an earthquake in 1915 and bombed to pieces during the Second World War; the town had the misfortune of being the headquarters of the German army corps

manning the Gustav Line. Its one surviving monument, the **Castello Orsini**, has a portal with a relief celebrating the Victory of Lépanto, and contains a small modern art museum, the **Pinoteca d'Arte Moderna** (***t*** *0836 5011; open daily 8–8*). In the Palazzo Comunale there's a small museum of inscriptions and architectural fragments from the cities of the Marsica, the **Museo Lapidario Marsicano** (*open when the Comunale is, or ring* ***t*** *0863 5011*). There's a third museum in the squat fortified former arsenal at the entrance to the town: the **Museo della Civiltà Contadina e Pastorale** (*open on request,* ***t*** *0863 5021*) with earnest exhibits relating the history of the Fucino plain. Avezzano is a main departure point for the Abruzzo National Park (*see* below).

Of all the ancient cities of the Marsica, the only one to leave behind considerable traces is ***Alba Fucens***, which wasn't Marsican at all but an outpost of another people, the Fucensi, or Aequi – and as anyone in the modern village of Albe will tell you, the two didn't get along at all. After the Romans conquered it, they rebuilt the city and installed a colony of veterans to keep an eye on them both. They also used it as a prison for captured princes and generals from around the Mediterranean; even today, a more out-of-the-way spot would be hard to find. Records of later times are scarce, but it seems the city was wiped off the map by the Saracens in the 10th century.

The ruins of the **city centre**, including foundations of the forum, a basilica, baths, temples, a market and a theatre, lie in open country just outside **Albe**, a village completely rebuilt after the 1915 earthquake, 8km northwest of Avezzano. More ruins, of an amphitheatre, a long section of the original Via Valeria, and the impressive 4km

Getting Around

As a major **rail** junction, and with **bus** services to most of the area, Sulmona, near Abruzzo's main east–west and north–south arteries, is the best base for exploring. You should be aware, however, that although there are bus or train connections to most destinations in the region they are often very infrequent, so you have to be very well organized if you are depending on public transport. Buses run fairly frequently from L'Áquila to Avezzano, and from there to Pescasséroli, the administrative centre of the Abruzzo National Park. From mid-June to mid-Sept there's a direct early morning ARPA bus to Pescasséroli from Rome, returning to Rome in the evening.

There are several spectacular **roads** in the region: the SS5bis from L'Áquila to Celano, the SS84 from Lanciano to Roccaraso and the SS83 from Pescina, near Celano, through the National Park.

Tourist Information

Tagliacozzo: Via Vittorio Veneto 6, **t** 0863 610318.

Where to Stay and Eat

This area is reasonably well-served with hotels, but many are only open in the summer and winter. Although not very attractive, Avezzano has the largest choice of hotels and fairly nondescript restaurants.

Avezzano ✉ 67051

******Olimpia**, Via Tiburina Valeria km111, **t** 0863 4521, **f** 0863 452400 (*moderate*). Good for motorists (outside town, near the *autostrada* exit); a cosy place with a pool.

*****Nuova Italia**, Piazza Matteotti 1, **t** 0863 413456 (*moderate*). A cheaper option near the rail station.

Vecchi Sapori, Via Montello 3, **t** 0863 416626 (*moderate–cheap*). A good, fairly priced restaurant, with local specialities, including particularly fine pasta and lamb dishes, and fish on Friday.

Tagliacozzo ✉ 67069

*****Miramonti**, Variante Tiburtina 87, **t** 0863 6581, **f** 0863 6582 (*cheap*). Has 21 comfortable rooms and a garden. *Open all year.*

*****Albergo Bocconcino**, Via Vittorio Veneto, 25, **t** 0863 66866, **f** 0863 66867, *bocconcino@ermes.it* (*cheap*). A good central option with bright modern en-suite rooms at a reasonable price.

Carsoli ✉ 67061

Angolo d'Abruzzo, next to the station in Piazza Aldo Moro 8, **t** 0863 997429 (*expensive*). The main reason for visiting this far western corner of the Abruzzo is the call of the fork and knife at this restaurant, rated by the pros as one of the truest and most authentic taste experiences in Italy's midriff region – the home-made breads (rare in Italy), herbs of the mountains, meadow-grazed lamb and kid, and hand-made cheeses are just right. *Closed Mon, exc in Aug, and first week in July.*

circuit of walls, lie a little further afield (***t** 0863 23561; always open*). Alba was a big town, built on three hills surrounding the centre. One hill held a temple of Jupiter (now it has remains of the medieval **Castello Orsini** and the settlement around it, ruined by another earthquake); the second had a **temple of Diana**, of which the platform remains. Apollo's temple crowned the third hill, and this was recycled as the church of **San Pietro** (*ask at the bar near the entrance for the key, though it might take some time to find it*). The church as it exists today was rebuilt by the Benedictines in the 12th century, and lovingly rebuilt again after yet another earthquake levelled it in 1957; Albe is not a lucky town. There is a Cosmatesque pulpit and *pluteo*; the walls are those of the *cella* from the ancient temple, and you can still see the graffiti and scrawled drawings left by Roman prisoners of the 3rd century BC.

There's an even better church just west of Albe, in the hills above Rosciolo dei Marsi: **Santa Maria in Valle Porclaneta**, a treasurehouse of 12th- and 13th-century sculpture from the Benedictine masters of Montecassino. Outside there are fanciful modillons on the apse; inside, an intricately carved pulpit, ciborium, capitals and best of all an unusual *pluteo* where above the stone rail four slender columns support a carved wooden cornice. One of the artists, Maestro Nicolo, chose to be buried here, and he carved his own tomb in the right aisle.

West of Avezzano: Tagliacozzo and Carsóli

Named after Thalia, the Muse of Theatre, **Tagliacozzo** is an ancient, pretty town on the slopes of Monte Bove, only an hour from Tívoli and Rome. Historically it is known for the battle that took place nearby on 12 August 1268, which ended the reign of the Hohenstaufen heirs of Emperor Frederick II. As Dante described it, the Imperial forces under Conradin were caught unawares and disarmed by the clever plans and intrigues of the Angevins, led by William di Villehardouin. The site of the battle is marked by the ruined church of **Santa Maria della Vittoria**, at Scúrcola Marsicana, east of Tagliacozzo. In the town itself, the simple church of **San Francesco** has a fine rose window and portal. Tagliacozzo's secular architecture is, however, more interesting than its churches, beginning with the 14th-century **Palazzo Ducale**, a grand building on a grand piazza; the loggia on the first floor shelters fine though damaged frescoes by Lorenzo da Viterbo. The quarter around the genteel old **Piazza dell' Obelisco**, with its Renaissance obelisk, has many picturesque houses and peeling palaces from the 14th and 15th centuries. The town's theatrical connections do not lie only in its name: near the Palazzo Ducale it has a small theatre, the Teatro Thalia, where an open-air festival of theatre, music and dance is held every summer. Just east of town, the Santuario di Santa Maria d'Oriente was founded to hold a Byzantine icon from the 7th century; it also has a small but unique **Museo Orientale** (*open Mon–Sat 9–12, in summer also 3–5*), with art and archaeological finds from the East.

Carsóli, west of Tagliacozzo near the border of Lazio, was the ancient Marsi town of Carseolis, destroyed by the Romans for failing to help them against Hannibal, and rebuilt as a colony in the 3rd century BC. Carsoli's largest surviving monument is an Angevin castle, and just ouside the village, the **Santuario di Maria Santissima dei Bisognosi**, founded in 608 to house an icon of the Virgin brought on a mule back from Spain, which made it all this way before it collapsed on this spot – a heavenly sign. Inside by the altar are frescoes of Dante's *Paradiso* and *Inferno* and a crucifix donated by Pope Boniface IV as an ex-voto.

East of Avezzano: the Lake that Isn't There

If the ancient Marsi were to return to their homeland today, they would be amazed to find their lake – once the largest in central Italy – replaced by the fertile basin called the **Piana del Fucino**. But they would be the first to tell you that their *Lacus Fucinus* had an inadequate outlet and was mostly swamp, punctuated by the occasional disastrous flood. To drain it, Emperor Claudius ordered what became the greatest underground engineering work of antiquity in the year AD 54 – the 6km-long tunnel intended to spill the lake's waters into the River Liri. However, for all the skill that went into the work, the tunnel didn't work very well and eventually got blocked up. In 1240 Frederick II tried to have it unblocked, but the project was not brought to a successful conclusion until 1875, when British, Italian, French and Swiss engineers finally drained the lake, reclaiming thousands of hectares.

It's particularly hard to imagine what the Marsi would make of the huge satellite dishes of Italy's biggest telecommunications centre, the **Centro Telespaziale**, looming out of the east end of the basin. Italy has more than its share of surreal landscapes, but this one takes the cake. You can't get away from it; everywhere in the surrounding hills you look back and it is obvious that a lake belongs there, but someone stole it. The strangeness intensifies from close up, on a 50-square-mile plain of geometrically straight canals and roads, numbered like the streets in an American town. The presence of the Centro Telespaziale has brought some high-tech businesses to the area, and sightings of lost North European computer geeks, wandering aimlessly about the hills wondering what they are doing in the loneliest corner of central Italy, have become almost as common as sightings of the region's totem eagle, the *aquila reale*.

Besides witchcraft, the ancient Marsi were also noted for some strange business involving serpents. On the southern edge of the Piana del Fucino, just north of Luco dei Marsi, you can visit the Benedictine church of **Santa Maria delle Grazie**, which occupies the site of the sacred grove where the Marsi once worshipped their snake-goddess Angizia (snakes are still popular in these parts; *see* below, Cocullo).

To break the spell of the vanished lake there's the unexpectedly delightful hill town of **Celano**, just to the north, spread out beneath the skirts of its four-square **Piccolomini Castle**, which now houses the excellent **Museo Nazionale d'Arte Sacra della Marsica** (*open Tues–Sun 9–8; adm*). The Piccolomini of Siena were no mean family; at the time they built this elegant castle in their distant Abruzzo holding, one of them was installed in St Peter's: Pius II, the most refined and learned of all the Renaissance popes. Largely rebuilt after the 1915 earthquake, the castle now contains some wonders: remarkable 12th-century carvings of a jolly whale and a 'siren attacked by a griffin' (but it looks more like a caress). From San Pietro at Alba Fucens come fine and stoutly simple Abruzzese detached frescoes, 13th-century wood-carved Madonnas, and a wonderful Byzantine triptych in gold and enamel, inlaid with jewels and hundreds of minute pearls. Also from San Pietro are the original wooden 12th-century church doors, with hints of a particular Abruzzese strain of medieval mysticism. The seven levels of carved reliefs are meant to be read from the bottom up, from the Old Testament to the New, with various lions, centaurs, bulls and knights in between; the whole is thought to represent the 'triumph of the spirit over the material'. A similar door on display comes from Carsoli.

Celano is best known as the birthplace of the Blessed Tommaso da Celano, a disciple of St Francis and his first biographer; he also composed the '*Dies Irae*', the eerie medieval hymn of the dead most often heard these days in the finale of Berlioz' *Symphonie fantastique*. Nearby you can visit the stunningly steep and narrow gorge, the **Gole di Celano** (though you can only get through it when the water level is low) or head north on the scenic SS5bis towards L'Áquila, by way of the mountain resort town of **Ovindoli** and Rocca di Cambio. Ovindoli is the centre of the newest of the Abruzzo's big parks, the **Parco Regionale Sirente Velino**, created one suspects as an afterthought in a rugged and unpopulated part of the mountains, with a thriving population of boar, deer and even wolves, between 8,083ft Monte Velino and 7,634ft Monte Sirente. Most of the area is rather bare, though there are extensive beech and oak woods, and skiing and hiking at Ovindoli and a mountain plain to the north called Piano di Pezza.

East of the Piana del Fucino, on the way to Sulmona, lies **Cocullo**, famous for its bizarre 'Procession of Serpents', held on the first Thursday of every May. Live snakes are draped over a statue of Cocullo's patron, San Domenico, as well as over the more inspired locals and especially the children, who thus form a procession through the streets, uncannily coiling and writhing to the music of bagpipers come down from the Molise. There is a story that St Dominic rid the area of poisonous snakes, but scholars have a sneaking suspicion that the festival is a living folk memory of the cult of the Marsican goddess Angizia.

Sulmona

South of the Via Valeria, beautifully located in a green basin surrounded by mountains, Sulmona was a city founded by another obscure Italic tribe, the Paeligni. It is best remembered, though, as the birthplace of Ovid (43 BC–AD 17), who is now commemorated with a large 20th-century statue in the Piazza XX Settembre. Much later Sulmona became a capital of its own province, created by Frederick II. As such it grew to be a minor centre of learning and religion, home of the main abbey of the Celestine Order, and of Pietro Angeleri, who lived in the hermitage of Monte Morrone before being brought down to L'Áquila to be crowned Pope Celestine V. In the early Renaissance its craftsmen were celebrated for their gold-work, although since then they have learned a sweeter skill – what the Italians call *confetti* (*see* box below).

Sulmona lies just on the southern side of some invisible Italian Mason–Dixon line; road signs point the way to NAPOLI, while the faces and speech of the people, the aromas in the streets and the crumbling sun-bleached palazzi all conspire to create a definite air of the *Mezzogiorno*. The town centre runs along a ridge between two small rivers, the Vella and the Gízio. The main street, Corso Ovidio, cuts down the

Confetti Nuts

To Italians, *confetti* means the sweets covered in sugar of all kinds of colours that are given out to guests at a wedding. They have been a speciality of the Abruzzo since the Middle Ages, and though the original *confetti* were sugared almonds, today you can buy them with a variety of fillings that include chocolate or hazelnuts. The acknowledged capital of *confetti*-making is Sulmona, where there are any number of shops in the historic centre that sell ornate confectionery concoctions made up to look like flowers or gold and silver ornaments, and have lavish window displays to match. William di Carlo, which has its factory and showroom near the station, reckons that they are the oldest *confetti* manufacturer in the town, while another old firm, Mario Pelino, invites visitors to its Confetti Museum (*it's on Via Stazione Introdacqua 55, open Mon–Sat 9–12 and 3.30–6.30*).

Getting There and Around

Sulmona is a stop along the FS **rail** line from Rome (via Tivoli, Tagliacozzo, Avezzano and Celano) to Pescara; **buses** leave from the rail station: several each day for L'Áquila, Roccaraso, Scanno and Rivisondoli, four for Chieti and Pescara and two for Naples. There is also a twice-weekly SATAM bus over the mountains to Fiuggi in Lazio, via Avezzano; it stops on the A25 exit outside town.

Tourist Information

Sulmona: Corso Ovidio 208, **t** 0864 53276, *iat.sulmona@abruzzoturismo.it*. However you get to Sulmona, this is a town you can leave in style. In summer, they run excursions on old steam trains with equally antique cars for day trips to various points in the Abruzzo and beyond: trips run from Sulmona's station to L'Áquila and Rieti, and over the mountains to Roccaraso and Castel di Sangro; for information and schedules ring **Treni d'Epoca, t** 085 428 2097.

Scanno: Piazza Santa Maria della Valle 12, **t** 0864 74317, *iat.scanno@abruzzoturismo.it*.

Where to Stay and Eat

Sulmona ✉ 67039

*****Europa Park**, on the SS17 (off Bivio Badia) just north of town, **t** 0864 251260, **f** 0864 251317 (*moderate*). Sulmona's largest and most comfortable hotel is modern and business-orientated. Some rooms have disabled facilities, and there's also a tennis court, bar and a good restaurant.

*****Armando's**, Via Montenero 15, **t/f** 0864 210783 (*low moderate, breakfast included*). Peaceful, family-run, with a tiny garden.

***Italia**, Piazza San Tommaso 3, **t** 0864 52308 (*cheap*). For a trip back to the Italy of 40 years ago, the Italia is atmospheric and comfortable, with pleasant antique-filled rooms, run by a very charming family.

Italia, Piazza XX Settembre 22, **t** 0864 33070 (*expensive–moderate*). Another Italia offers interesting and fine variations on local cuisine: home-made pasta, and lamb with rosemary. *Closed Mon.*

Ristorante Frangio, Via Ercole Ciofano 51, **t** 0864 212773 (*moderate*). One of Sulmona's – and Abruzzo's – best restaurants, serving exquisite regional specialities accompanied

middle towards Sulmona's loveliest monument, the church and palace of **Santa Maria Annunziata**, a Gothic and Renaissance ensemble begun in 1320. Although the three portals on the palace's façade were done at different periods, the result is as harmonically sweet as *confetti*: here is a finely carved, floridly Gothic left portal, crowned by a statue of St Michael, while the middle portal is pure symmetrical Renaissance in form; the comparatively plain portal on the right was the last built, in 1522. Remarkably vivid figures of Doctors of the Church and saints stand sentry along the façade, looking down on the affairs of the Sulmonesi, while above them runs an intricate ribbon frieze; above that are three lacy Gothic windows. There are two small museums inside: the **Museo Civico** (*weekdays exc Mon 9–12.30 and 4–7, Sat and Sun 10–12.30 and 4–7; adm*) contains some of the work of the goldsmiths of Renaissance Sulmona, and local sculpture and paintings from the 16th to 18th centuries. The other is the **Pinacoteca Civica d'Arte Moderna** (*open by request, **t** 0864 210216*). The adjacent **church**'s sombre Baroque façade was rebuilt after a 1703 earthquake, yet it still complements the palace; inside is a tabernacle by the local artist Giovanni da Sulmona. Concerts are held in the palace courtyard each summer.

South of the Annunziata, Corso Ovidio passes Via Mazara on the left, with the lovely carved Romanesque portal of **San Francesco delle Scarpe** ('with shoes', because here the Franciscans wore shoes instead of sandals), but behind the portal is a Baroque rebuilding, the rest having tumbled in one of Sulmona's earthquakes – like Avezzano by a fine wine list (try the fabulous Fonte Cupa 1998). Bright, sunny yellow decor, a huge shady terrace in summer, and impeccable service. Highly recommended.

Clemente, Vico del Vecchio 16, **t** 0864 52284 (*moderate*). Offers home-made sausages and delicious local dishes, including fresh pasta with lamb sauce, saffron or mushrooms, roast kid. The desserts are good, too. *Closed Thurs.*

Mafalda, Via Solimo 20, **t** 0864 34538 (*moderate*). Just off the Corso, similar dishes are on offer in an outdoor garden. *Closed Sun in winter.*

Rigoletto, Via Stazione Introdacqua 46, **t** 0864 55529 (*moderate*). An old favourite outside Porta Napoli, offering a mix of local and rather old-fashioned dishes. *Closed Sun eve, Mon, last two weeks of July.*

Pacentro ✉ 67030

Li Caldora, Piazza Umberto I 13, **t** 0864 41139 (*moderate*). This village on the edge of the Maiella National Park has a genuine surprise: one of those perfect restaurants where the flavours – local ricotta, white truffles, mountain-grown lamb – come through like a culinary melody. *Closed Sun eve, Tues, and two weeks in Jan and Feb.*

Roccaraso ✉ 67037

*****Excelsior**, Via Roma 28, **t** 0864 602351 (*moderate*). One of the classier choices in the resort area, with well-equipped rooms. *Open mid-Dec–mid-Jan and April–Aug.*

Galleria, Viale Roma 45, **t** 0864 62278 (*moderate*). The best place to eat is hidden away in an arcade; tasty *chittara* pasta and grilled meats, including boar. *Closed Tues, exc in summer, and the last two weeks in June.*

Scanno ✉ 67038

*****Del Lago, t/f** 0864 74343 (*moderate*). A small, tranquil hotel with a garden in a lovely setting on the lake. *Open mid-Dec–mid-Jan and Mar–Oct.*

****Margherita**, Via D Tanturri 100, **t** 0864 74353 (*cheap*). A good-value hotel with simple rooms.

Agli Archetti, Via Silla 8, **t** 0864 74645 (*moderate*). A top restaurant, serving dishes made from home-grown ingredients; try the grilled lamb with pears. The ambience is all refined old elegance. *Closed Tues Oct–May.*

they do get more than their share, with big ones in 1456, 1706, 1933 and 1984. Next the Corso meets the huge Piazza Garibaldi, site of the market and the 1474 **Fontana del Vecchio**, so called because of the bust of a jovial old man on top. Running along the edge of the piazza is an unusual Gothic **aqueduct** (1256), which still supplies water to the fountain and to the rest of the town.

The next piazza opening off the Corso, Piazza del Plebiscito, is home to **Santa Maria della Tomba**, a cheerful name for a church once attached to a hospital. Inside are a number of Renaissance paintings and bits of frescoes. At the end of the Corso, the **Porta Napoli**, covered in stone flowers, was the 14th-century main gate of the town walls. North of the Annunziata, the Corso turns into Viale Roosevelt, passing the Villa Comunale and, at the northern end of town, the **cathedral**. Plain medieval outside and Baroque within, its attractions are a fine set of wood-carved choir stalls, and in the crypt a 12th-century polychrome Madonna.

Around Sulmona

Just north of Sulmona, the enormous **Badia Morronese** is the mother house of the Celestine Order, built on the spot where the hermit Pietro da Morrone, later Pope Celestine V (*see* pp.53–4) first started attracting crowds of followers; inside, the Cappella Caldora has excellent 15th-century frescoes by Giovanni da Sulmona. From here, up the slopes of Monte Morrone, you can reach the impressive stone platform that once supported a 1st century AD **Temple of Hercules**; for centuries the locals referred to the ruins as 'Ovid's villa'. And even further up the mountain is the hermitage of **Sant'Onofrio**. When Pietro da Morrone found his old cave down below too crowded with disciples and admirers, he moved up to a nearly inaccessible perch on the side of the cliffs; after his death followers built this church full of haunting, primitive frescoes over the hermit's cave (*both the temple and the hermitage open summer 9–7, winter 9–dusk; times change regularly so call in advance,* ***t*** *0864 251255*).

The Maiella National Park

There are several picturesque hill towns in the vicinity of Sulmona, especially **Pacentro**, 9km to the east, its lanes winding around the tall, white battlemented towers of the **Cantelmo Castle**. Beyond Pacentro the SS487 heads up in a serious way into the rugged Maiella Mountains, and a few winding kilometres further east, near Passo San Leonardo, reaches a T-junction where you can turn north towards **Caramanico Terme** (a pretty hill town and sulphur-water spa) and the Via Valeria, or south past the **Campo di Giove**, a winter sports centre with a cable car up the slopes of a mountain called the **Tavola Rotonda**, the 'Round Table' (7,813ft), towards the dramatic SS84 and the Sangro Valley (the Arthurian name probably isn't a coincidence; the Normans brought the stories down to southern Italy, and the Italians began to tell their own tales of *Re Artú*, who lies eternally sleeping under Mount Etna). There's a **Maiella National Park information office** in a 17th-century palace, the Casa Nanni, in Campo de Giove's main square (***t*** *0864 408102, primajella@arc.it*) which has maps and information on walking trails and the park's flora and fauna.

Pescocostanzo, **Rivisondoli** and especially **Roccaraso** (all of them stops on the Sulmona–Isérnia railway) are endowed with winter and mountain sports facilities. Pescocostanzo, which once owed allegiance to Vittorio Colonna, poet and friend of Michelangelo, is a charming little town, formerly more famous for its lace than as a ski resort, and ornamented with the lovely **Collegiata di Santa Maria del Colle** (*usually open daily for services only*), its interior adorned with excellent wood carvings, the oldest ones dating back to the 11th century.

On the SS84 between Roccaraso and Lanciano (and accessible by bus from either end), is **Taranta Peligna**, which has a cable car that rises up to the most spectacular cave in central Italy, the **Grotta del Cavallone** (4,675ft) (*open April–Sept; guided visits depart hourly and last 1½ hrs; to make sure it's open, call the Lama dei Peligni tourist office,* ***t*** *0872 916120, or call freephone (in Italy)* ***t*** *800 161088; open Mon–Sat 9–1 and 4.30–6.30; adm exp*), used as a setting in D'Annunzio's play *La Figlia di Jorio*. The cave's name, the 'Big Horse', comes from the profile carved by nature on the wall at the grandiose entrance of the grotto: other rooms are adorned with stone flowers or lace, alabaster streaks that remind Italians of ham (in the 'Sala del Prosciutto') and fairies, while the 'Sala del Pantheon' is full of curious stalagmite monsters and deities.

South of Roccaraso, near the western entrance into the Park, is **Castel di Sangro**, badly damaged in the Second World War though still preserving its ruined citadel, reached by a steep mule path. A small collection of ancient statues and bronzes found in the vicinity has been given a home inside the **Convento della Maddalena** (*open Wed–Sun 10–1 and 5–7; adm*). In the upper part of the town stands the fine Baroque church of **Santa Maria Assunta**, which retains its Renaissance plan and paintings by De Matteis and Vaccaro.

Scanno

From Cocullo or Anversa degli Abruzzi, west of Sulmona, the SS479 ascends the lovely **Valle del Sagittario**, passing through the steep Gorge of the Sagittario and alongside the pretty trout-filled Lago di Scanno. Perched high above the lake, the village of **Scanno** is one of the most popular destinations in the Abruzzo, a picturesque place that fascinated 18th-century travellers who wondered at its customs and costumes, more reminiscent of Asia Minor than Italy. Even today the women of Scanno still sometimes wear their traditional dress, with their turban-like headdresses – as much an attraction as the beautiful old village itself. All the women of the town put on traditional dress during Scanno's main festival in mid-August, which celebrates the very unusual traditional local marriage customs. On a different note, a classical music festival is also held during the same month, with concerts in the town's squares. For magnificent views of the sunset over the lake and mountains, drive up the zigzagging road from here to **Frattura**, or take the chair lift up to **Monte Rotondo**, Scanno's small winter resort.

The Abruzzo National Park

Founded in 1923 and enlarged in 1976, the park is one of Italy's oldest, covering 400 square kilometres of some of the loveliest scenery in the Apennine range, a little paradise of flowery meadows and forests of beech, pine, oak, ash, maple and yew, the last home of *Ursus arctos marsicanus*, the brown Abruzzo bear, and the Abruzzo chamois; here too are Apennine lynxes, boars, wolves, badgers, red squirrels, eagles, falcons, woodpeckers, owls and many unusual species of songbirds, all protected by law from the enthusiastic Italian hunter.

West of Cocullo lies **Pescina**, the birthplace of Cardinal Mazarin, and the SS83 that leads into the park. After passing through the **Passo del Diavolo**, the road reaches **Pescasséroli**, the largest village in the park. The main **visitors' centre**, on Viale Colli dell'Oro, has trail maps and information on where to find flora and fauna (***t** 0863 91955; open daily 9–12 and 3–7*); also visit the small **museum** (*open daily 10–1 and 3–7; adm exp*). If you want to camp, apply to the Ufficio di Zona del Parco, inside the visitors' centre, or stay in one of the nearby campsites. Bear in mind that at Easter and in July and August it's hard to find vacancies without a reservation. A pleasant excursion from Pescasséroli even for non-committed hikers is the not very difficult 2-hour walk up to the **Valico di Monte Tranquillo** (route C3 on the map). In the height of summer and in winter you can also ride Pescasséroli's cable car up to the summit of Monte Vitelle. Further south, **Opi**, **Barrea** and **Villetta Barrea** are other pretty villages in the

Tourist Information

Pescasséroli: Via Piave, **t** 0863 910461, *www.pescasséroli.net* (*open Mon–Sat 9–1 and 4.30–6.30*). The tourist office can provide information on hotels, restaurants and getting around the area, but you will need to visit one of the Abruzzo National Park information offices for maps and information about the park itself.

Park Information Offices and Visitors' Centre: the main information centre for the Abruzzo National Park is on Viale Colli dell'Oro, **t** 0863 910715. You can pick up a hiking map, information about the trails and book accommodation in the Park's refuges and campsites. Guided walks can also be arranged. Most of the towns in the region – including Opi, **t** 0863 910622; Villavallelonga, **t** 0863 949261; and Civitella Alfedena, **t** 0864 890141 – also have park information offices.

Where to Stay and Eat

Pescasséroli ✉ 67032

★★★★Grand Hotel del Parco, **t** 0863 912745, **f** 0863 912749 (*expensive*). The grandest hotel in the area, with a beautiful setting, a garden and a pool. *Open Christmas–Mar and 15 June–Sept.*

★★★Il Pinguino, Via Collacchi 2, **t** 0863 912580, **f** 0863 910449 (*cheap*). 'The Penguin' is a good choice in the park, with rooms that are far too snug for a real Antarctican.

Plistia, Viale Principe di Napoli 28, **t** 0863 910 732. Has a few simple rooms (*cheap*) and *abruzzese* cooking (*moderate*). *Closed Mon.*

park, near the Lago di Barrea and the Camosciara, where most of the park's graceful chamois live. Just outside the park the fine scenery continues around the village of **Alfedena**, built on the site of the ancient Samnite town of *Aufidena* – across the river from the modern village you can see the ancient walls and necropolis. A 3km dirt track also leads up from here to the lake of Montagna Spaccata.

Molise

Isolated, mountainous and even more sparsely populated than Abruzzo, Molise is one of the smallest and least-known regions of Italy. It belonged to the tenacious Samnites of old, and Italians still sometimes call it *Sanno*. At some point in the murky early Middle Ages it became the county of Molise and then, like the other Abruzzi, it was joined to the Kingdom of Naples. In the 14th and 15th centuries Slav and Albanian refugees from the Turkish invasion found new homes; their languages contributed to the great variety of regional dialects, and there are still cases today of neighbouring villages unable to understand one another. Recently UNESCO set up research centres in the isolated mountain communities of Montedimezzo near Vastogirardi and in Collemeluccio near Pescolanciano to study the relationship of 'man and the environment' before the old way of life is gone for good. The age-old transhumance trails – there's a very pretty one leading down from Roccamandolfi – have been declared historic monuments and are still used, not only by flocks but now for riding holidays.

Isérnia

Heading down the SS17 from Sulmona and Castel di Sangro you enter Italy's newest province, created in 1970. The dismal little capital **Isérnia** was the Samnite town of *Aesernium*, where the Italic tribes either first united against Rome, or fled after the Romans captured their capital of Corfinium in the Social Wars – at any rate Isérnia modestly puts forth a claim of being 'the first capital of Italy', although even that boast pales before the fame of its onions (fêted every 28–29 June) and its lace. Over the centuries Isérnia has been severely damaged by earthquakes – the last of them only in 1984 – and was badly bombed in 1943 so there is little to see of its old town other than the 14th-century **Fontana Fraterna**, which has somehow managed to survive. It was built using bits of Roman masonry and bears an inscription that reads AE PONT – which led to a popular belief that Aesernium gave the world Pontius Pilate.

Today, though, the town's main attraction is a Palaeolithic village that was accidentally uncovered in 1979, during the building of a new main road. At one million years old this is the most ancient evidence of human life yet discovered in Europe. There are no human remains on the site, but there are a variety of other relics such as weapons, fireplaces, face paint and so on, and plenty of remains of the huge ancestors of the elephant, deer, rhinoceros, bison, bear and hippopotamus. They are well presented, accompanied by reconstructions of life in the prehistoric villages and, unusually, multi-lingual explanations and computerized displays, in the **Museo Nazionale Santa Maria delle Monache** (*open 9–1 and 3–7; adm*), on Piazza Santa Maria.

North of Isérnia

The *comuni* in the high altitudes north of Isérnia have been compared to the isolated villages of Tibet, each perched on its lonely hilltop. Highest in all the Apennines at 4,662ft is **Capracotta**, a village immersed in woods and mountain pastures, often buried under banks of snow in the winter, so much so that there are tales of the residents having to use their upper-floor windows as doors – a fitting place for the first Italian ski club, founded in 1914. Nearby **Agnone**, the 'Athens of the Samnites', has been known for the past thousand years for its bells. One factory, the **Marinelli Pontifical Foundry**, still survives – the oldest in Italy, supplier to the Vatican and nearly every country in the world. Bells in the foundry are still made according to the ancient formula; while the molten bronze is being poured into the mould a priest is on hand to chant the medieval litanies that have always guaranteed a successful, clear-toned bell. You can see the foundry at work and visit its small **museum** (*Via d'Onofrio 14, **t** 0865 78235; open weekdays for guided tours 11–4, until 6 in July and Aug, or by request*), though with admirable reserve the company does not allow the taking of any photos. Besides bells, Agnone is known for its coppersmiths, whose workshops line the main streets of town, selling every imaginable utensil; also be sure to note the fine Romanesque portal on the cathedral of **Sant'Emidio**.

South of Agnone, **Pietrabbondante** has some of the most extensive Samnite ruins yet discovered. The site, excavated in the 19th century, was a religious sanctuary and includes a well-preserved Teatro Italico where the senate once met, complete with three rows of armchair seats and a couple of temples, all built in the 2nd century BC. The ruins are located in a green field filled with flowers, making them especially attractive (*open Mar–Oct Tues–Sun 9–dusk*). **Pescolanciano**, on the way back towards Isérnia, is dominated by its picturesque **Castello d'Alessandro**, founded in the 13th century and topped in later years by a pretty gallery. Even closer to Isérnia (8km) is the old village and 14th-century castle of **Carpinone**.

Getting There and Around

Isérnia is linked by **train** with Naples, Rome, Sulmona, Pescara and Campobasso; other trains from Naples to Campobasso pass through Benevento, then continue on to the coast at Térmoli, via Larino. **Buses** – from Naples, Rome, Cassino and Vasto to Campobasso and Isérnia – are on the whole much quicker, and less aggravating. The bus service for outlying villages is fair, and invariably departs from Isérnia or Campobasso.

Tourist Information

Isérnia: Via Farinacci 9, **t** 0865 3992, *eptisernia @moldat.molisedati.it* (*open Mon–Sat 8–2*).

Where to Stay and Eat

The few hotels that grace Molise tend to be either recently built and sterile, or old and worn at the heels – but the prices are low.

Isérnia ✉ 86170

★★★★**Europa**, on the SS 17, **t** 0865 411450, **f** 0865 235287 (*expensive*). Convenient for motorists, just off the *autostrada*. All rooms have air conditioning, satellite TV, and there's a fancy breakfast buffet. The adjacent resturant, **Pantagruel**, specializes in Molisana dishes.

★★★**La Tequila**, Via G Tedeschi 85, **t/f** 0865 412 345 (*moderate*). Just outside the centre in the new San Lazzaro area; with a pool.

★★★**Santa Maria del Bagno**, Viale Santa Maria del Bagno 1, **t** 0865 460136, **f** 0865 460129 (*cheap*). 8km northeast of Isérnia, in the little hill town of Pesche, this recently refurbished hotel is set in a garden just off the main road, with a good restaurant.

Taverna Maresca, Corso Marcelli 186, **t** 0865 3976 (*moderate–cheap*). A fine old restaurant in the old quarter, founded in 1900; memorable ravioli filled with ricotta and spinach. *Closed Sun, Aug, Christmas and Easter.*

Osteria del Paradiso, Via Occidentale 2, **t** 0865 414847 (*cheap*). A simple restaurant next to the cathedral; save room for the home-made desserts. *Closed Sun.*

Capracotta ✉ 86082

★**Montecampo**, Contrada Santa Lucia, **t** 0865 949128 (*cheap*). In the mountains and out of the way; a basic but pleasant 13-room hotel.

Agnone ✉ 86061

★★★**Sammartino**, Largo P Micca 44, **t** 0865 78239, **f** 0865 77577 (*cheap*). A comfortable hotel with an excellent restaurant, where you can dine on *sagne* (home-made pasta rhomboids) and succulent baby Molise lamb.

★★★**San Salvador**, Via Marconi 28, **t** 0865 78591 (*cheap*). Another solid choice.

Da Casciano, Viale Marconi 29, **t** 0865 77511. Here you can taste a rare dish, the lamb *sotto la coppa* (cooked under the ashes) and finish your meal with the unforgettable *ostie*, local pastry made with walnuts, chocolate, honey and wine. *Closed Tues, exc in summer, and Nov.*

Venafro ✉ 86097

Dimore del Prete di Belmonte, Via Cristo 49, **t/f** 0865 900159, *www.dimoradel.prete.it* (*expensive*). A former priest's palace, beautifully converted into a luxurious B&B with just four antique-furnished rooms. Dinner is served in the Pompeian dining room.

★★★★**Venafro Palace**, just out of town on the SS85, **t** 0865 902263, **f** 0865 903709 (*moderate*). A modern hotel which has seen better days but still has extras like a pool.

Quadrifoglio, **t** 0865 909886 (*moderate*). Near the Venafro Palace; serves the freshest of seafood (Venafro is a stop for the seafood trucks from the Adriatic to Rome), as well as other Molise dishes.

West of Isérnia

Spaghetti Western fans in Molise in the middle of August can whoop it up at an Italian 'rodeo' at **Montenero Val Cocchiara**, northwest of Isérnia; as usual in Italy, food is as much of an attraction as the events, and in this case it's barbecues. In the pre-cowboy days of the Lombards, the Benedictines built the abbey of **San Vincenzo al Volturno** to the south near **Castel San Vincenzo**, close to a small lake of the same name. Often altered, damaged and rebuilt, the abbey was last restored in the 1950s; the nearby **Crypt of San Lorenzo** managed to escape the assorted disasters that befell the abbey and preserves some interesting 11th-century frescoes. (*The complex is usually closed, but try ringing the convent's bell.*)

The most impressive castle in Molise, **Cerro al Volturno** (*privately owned but occasionally open to the public; call the town hall on* **t** *0865 953104*) was originally built by the Benedictines in the 10th century, but was rebuilt at the end of the 15th century. Appearing to grow organically out of a massive rock over the town, the castle is inaccessible except by a narrow path; in the 1920s the supporting cement bulwarks on the hill were added, all impressive enough to star on a former L200 stamp. There aren't many souvenirs to buy in Cerro, but further south, in **Scapoli**, you can visit the bagpipe (*zampogna*) display-market in the last week of July. The bagpipe has a long (and still living) tradition among the shepherds of the Molise; they still take them down to play in the streets of Rome and Naples for Christmas. The market also features pipes from Scotland, Sardinia, Hungary and other regions and countries. Alternatively, you can explore the world of bagpipes inside the **Museo della Zampogna**, in the Municipio (*open on request,* **t** *0865 954143*).

Venafro

On the road south towards Campania, **Venafro** was made famous by Horace for its olive oil. Although now more than a little run down, it is also one of the most interesting towns in Molise. Cyclopean walls run along the road leading into town, and in the Middle Ages the Roman **amphitheatre** was turned into an oval piazza, in which the arcades have been incorporated into the fronts of the houses. Portable remains of Roman *Venafrum* are now in the **Museo Archeologico** (*open Tues–Sun 9–1; adm*) in the former convent of Santa Chiara on Via Garibaldi. Of the churches the most interesting are the 15th-century **cathedral** and the **Annunziata**, a church that has preserved its Romanesque interior if not exterior, and contains in one of its chapels a series of 15th-century English alabasters. Venafro's **castle**, decorated with frescoes (14th–16th centuries), and the 15th-century fortified ducal **Palazzo Caracciolo** are still waiting for funds to be restored and opened to the public. Venafro has a couple of curiosities, too: between Via della Vergine and Via Silvano is **La Portella**, the world's smallest street at just five metres long, which was probably once a secret passage. The romantic ruins of the turret on a crag above the town are said to guard the devil's treasure.

The Matese

South of Isérnia and Campobasso is a lovely curve of snow-swept peaks and forests called the Matese, of which the southern half lies in Campania. Few Italians, much less foreigners, penetrate its quiet villages where women in traditional dress sit out in the streets over their round *tomboli* making delicate lace. The lakes of the Matese are full of waterfowl, its streams brim with fish, and its forests are home to squirrels, wildcats, wolves and other creatures seldom seen in the rest of Italy; its glens produce porcini mushrooms by the ton. The scenery is spectacular, especially around the largest of the district's several lakes, the **Lago del Matese**, with its resort of

Piedimonte Matese, both in Campania. The road back to Molise (the SS158dir) runs through the Passo del Prete Morto ('Dead Priest Pass'); the northern slopes of the Matese are equally lovely, with a wonderful quality of light that gives **Campochiaro** its name. This medieval village still retains its walls and tower; recently a huge Samnite temple complex was unearthed in the vicinity. Just to the west is the lofty little town of **Boiano** (or Bojano), the former Samnite stronghold of *Bovianum*. The upper part of town, Cívita Superiore, retains the megalithic walls and the ruins of a Lombard castle, repaired by the Normans; here the Count of Molise, Tommaso da Celano, dared to defy Frederick II. The views are great, and become fabulous if you're up to a rather stiff two-hour climb to the summit of **Monte la Gallinola** (6,309ft) – on a clear day you can see as far as the Bay of Naples. In winter there's skiing nearby at **Campitello Matese**, southwest of Boiano in the very centre of the Matese mountains.

Twin-tailed mermaids are an enigmatic symbol often encountered in the south (and elsewhere), connected to some lost strain of medieval mysticism, and particularly to the weird shrine of St Michael at Monte Sant'Angelo nearby in Puglia; you can see one on the Norman–medieval castle in **Spinete**, north of Boiano. Another hilltown further north, **Castropignano**, has an impressive, nearly impregnable castle up on a high rock, another built by the Lombards and enlarged in the 11th century by the Normans – now a picturesque ruin. In its day it apparently had 365 bedrooms, but the Duke was haunted by a fairy, who teased and harassed him no matter how often he changed his sleeping quarters until, driven to distraction, he leapt off the crag to his death. In nearby **Oratino**, the medieval tower that controlled the valley is said to guard a secret buried treasure – a nanny goat and seven kids made entirely of gold.

Saepinum

In 295 BC, the Samnite city of *Saipins* was laid waste by the Romans. The few inhabitants who were neither killed nor taken into slavery went on to found a new town for themselves, a Roman colony called *Saepinum*. As a quiet provincial town it managed to avoid most of history until the 9th century, when the Saracens destroyed it. Later in the Middle Ages, when times were surer, the site was resettled, only higher up (now modern **Sepino**), and old Saepinum was slowly covered by the dust of the ages and quarried here and there for its stone. Dilettantes began excavating the ancient town in the 18th century; nowadays groups of archaeologists come every summer. To get there by public transport take a bus from Campobasso to Sepino (*about every 2hrs, call* **t** *0874 412125 for details*), which is 2 miles uphill from the ruins, or, better still, Altilia, next to the site itself – though the latter service is very infrequent.

The charm of *Saepinum* comes partly from its remote and lovely setting in the Matese; its isolation has preserved it well, making it one of the most evocative Roman sites in all Italy – the best example there is of a small provincial city. In *Saepinum* there is very little marble, no plush villas as in Pompeii and Herculaneum, but neither are there any modern intrusions beyond a few farmhouses, making use of a column here, an architrave there; it is an ancient Anytown in the empire.

The defensive **walls** encompassing *Saepinum*, built in the diamond patterns of *opus reticulatum*, are over 1km long and defended by 27 bastions – the best preserved of which, over 35ft high, stands near the theatre. Four gates lead into the central axis of the city; from the car park at Porta di Terravecchia you pass through the walls on the *cardus maximus*. This street retains its original paving stones along the stretch closest to the heart of the town, as you approach the central crossroads with the *decumanus*, the main street of every Roman town. Here, as usual, you'll find the **Forum** and civic buildings. The slender Ionic columns on one corner belonged to the **Basilica**, the main meeting place and courts of a Roman city, with its podium for orators and lawyers. Just off it is an octagonal atrium, surrounded by the foundations of shop counters – *Saepinum*'s central market. Across from the forum itself on the decumanus are, first, on the corner, the elections office (*Comitium*), the *Curia* (town hall), a temple, believed to have been dedicated to the cult of an emperor, and then the *Terme* (baths) and the well-preserved Griffon fountain.

The decumanus continues past a house called the **Casa dell'Impluvio Sannitico**, its atrium containing a fountain and Samnite-style *impluvium* (container to collect rain water) with an inscription in Oscan, the pre-Roman language of the region; it ends at the Porta di Benevento, marked by a figure of Mars. Beyond the gate stands the funeral monument, with its inscriptions lauding the virtues of the deceased Caius Ennius Marso, one of the town's leading citizens. The **museum** adjoining the gate relates the story of the settlement (*call* **t** *0874 790207 for opening hours*).

In the opposite direction, the *decumanus* passes through *Saepinum*'s main commercial district, lined with shops, taverns and private residences. It ends at the most complete surviving gate, the impressive **Porta Boiano**, with steps to the top which you can ascend for an excellent view of the excavations. Figures of prisoners (or slaves?) stand on plinths on either side, and its inscription informs us that Tiberius and his brother Drusas paid for the fortifications. Beyond this gate is a monumental **mausoleum** of Numisio Ligure. Along the walls there are the remains of a private bath complex; beyond is the well-preserved **theatre**, with a crescent of medieval farmhouses that were built into the upper *cavea*; in its heyday the theatre seated 3,000 spectators. The stage is now occupied by another farmhouse, which contains another interesting **museum** of items such as funerary sculpture found during the digs, as well as plans and maps (*open summer 8–8; at other times call* **t** *0874 790207*).

Campobasso

The regional capital from the days of the county of Molise, Campobasso and the surrounding region hit the news in late 2002 when earthquakes rocked the area. Worst hit was the little village of San Giuliano de Puglia (near Larino, *see* below), where 29 people, including 26 six-year-olds at a school Hallowe'en party, were tragically killed. Around 3,000 people in towns and villages across the region were made homeless as buildings collapsed or began to crack, and many of the older houses are still being propped up by elaborate scaffolding.

Campobasso was once best known for its engraved cutlery – its knives, scissors and razors are still highly regarded in Italy today – and wolfmen, but is now better known as the site of the National School for Carabinieri (which has managed to keep the wolfmen under control) and its June procession, the *Sagra dei Misteri di Corpus*

Tourist Information

Campobasso: Piazza della Vittoria 14, **t** 0874 415662, **f** 0874 15370, *www.campobassonline.it* (*open Mon–Sat 8–2*).

Where to Stay and Eat

Campobasso ✉ 86100

★★★★**Hotel Roxy**, Piazza Savoia 7, **t/f** 0874 411 541 (*moderate*). A plush, modern place, with a discotheque for wild Campobasso nights.

★★★**Skanderbeg**, Via Novelli 3, **t** 0874 413341, **f** 0871 416340 (*moderate*). Another good choice, offering modern comforts with touches of Molise tradition.

★★**Tricolore**, Via San Giovanni in Golfo 110, **t** 0874 63190 (*cheap*). A little family-run hotel in one of the prettier parts of town.

Be careful about ordering 'milk' in Campobasso – it's a sweet liqueur here. There are several good restaurants, including:

Aciniello, Via Torino 4, **t** 0874 94001 (*moderate –cheap*). Simple but genuine in its atmosphere and cuisine; offers dishes like *pizza rustica* and rabbit. *Closed Sun, 2 weeks in Aug.*

Vecchia Trattoria da Tonino, Corso Vittorio Emanuele II 8, **t** 0874 415200 (*expensive–moderate*). For something more refined and less strictly local, head for one of the best restaurants in the whole Molise: specialities include zucchini flowers stuffed with ricotta, linguine with a sauce of *baccalà*, and Molise lamb. Fine local Molise wines. *Closed Sun, also on Sat in July and Aug.*

Cerchio dei Golosi (the 'gluttons' club'), Viale del Catello 16–18, **t** 0874 91135 (*moderate*). This friendly place features excellent pasta dishes, including gnocchi with walnuts and gorgonzola, unusual second courses and heavenly desserts and grappas. *Closed Sun and half of Dec.*

AF Fornaro Pizzeria, Via Conte Verde 1, **t** 0874 98513 (*cheap*). Campobasso's best pizzas come hot and crusty out of the oven of this popular pizzeria. *Closed Tues.*

Da Emilio, Piazza Spenzieri 18, **t** 0874 416576 (*moderate*). One of the best restaurants in the region, in the village of Ferrazzano. Dine out on the terrace on meals with a delightful Emilia-Romagna touch. Delicious homemade pasta; save room for the cheese. *Closed Tues, last 2 weeks in Jan and first 2 weeks in July.*

Larino ✉ 86035

★★★★**Park Hotel Campitelli 2**, Via S. Benedetto, 1, **t** 0874 823541, **f** 0874 822339 (*expensive–moderate*). This is the smartest choice here, a very modern, glassy hotel with pool, sauna and gym as well as a good restaurant serving regional specialities (*expensive*).

Domini. In the 17th century Campobasso's old *Corpus Domini* processions were banned by the bishop for making spectators laugh instead of increasing their faith; and they stayed banned until 1740, when a local sculptor named Di Zinno came up with the idea of building metal contraptions to support real people in the soaring Baroque postures of the angels and saints he carved for churches. The bishop accepted these as faith-augmenters, and indeed they are, for it seems as if faith alone is holding up the bevy of six-year-old angels and saints suspended on the 13 floats or 'Mysteries' solemnly carried on strong shoulders through the streets to the accompaniment of the local bands.

Two Museums, Two Churches and a Castle

Campobasso's attractions include the long-planned museum of Samnite antiquities, the **Museo Provinciale Sannitico**, finally open at Via Chiarizia 12 (*open 9–1 and 3–7; closed Sun*) and well worth a look to learn more about the people who held the Romans back for 50 years. The town's second museum is devoted to Christmas cribs: the **Museo Internazionale del Presepio**, Piazza della Vittoria 4 (*open weekdays 10–8*). The older, upper part of town has a couple of Romanesque churches, **San Giorgio** and

San Leonardo, and isolated on top, the **Castello Monforte** built by the Normans (now a weather station); from its upper floor you can see a large percentage of the Molise. Apparently a secret tunnel runs from the castle to a church on the periphery of town. There are scenic villages nearby, like **Ferrazzano**, with the handsome medieval/15th-century Castello Carafa and belvedere, and **Baranello**, an ancient town, the heir of the Samnite *Vairanum*. Baranello has a little **Museo Civico** at Via Santa Maria 13 (*open by request*, **t** *0874 460406*), containing Samnite artefacts, 17th- and 18th-century Neapolitan kitsch paintings, Chinese porcelains and other *objets d'art*. Nearby, on the River Biferno, you can watch a still-functioning waterwheel grind some of the grains that go into Molise's folksy cuisine. The most striking church in the area is the hilltop Romanesque **Santa Maria della Strada**, just off the SS87 north to Larino.

Larino

Between Campobasso and Térmoli on the coast (for which, *see* p.304) the main attraction is the small town of **Larino**, the Samnite *Larinum*, prettily located amid hills of olive groves. It also suffered during the 2002 earthquakes, and became the centre of operations for the relief workers during and after the disaster. The most important monument here is the **cathedral**, built in 1319 and embellished with an ornate portal in its Puglian-style façade; the nearby church of **San Francesco** has some good 18th-century frescoes. Near the cathedral take a look inside the museum of the **Palazzo Comunale**, housed in the old ducal palace (*open Tues–Fri 9–1*), three rooms which house beautiful Roman polychrome mosaics from the 2nd and 3rd centuries AD. A more substantial collection of art and artefacts from the region is waiting to be put on display in the Liberty-style Villa Zappone. Meanwhile the *Ara Frentana*, a cylindrical Roman altar, is visible by the road leading to the train station in the area that was once the centre of the ancient Samnite town. Near the station there are also the remains of a large **amphitheatre** (*open Tues–Sun 9–1*) – which in summer hosts concerts, plays and other events – and some fragments of the ancient town walls. Between 25 and 27 May, Larino holds a religious festival, the *Festa di San Pardo*, with a procession of 150 finely decorated ox carts. On the evening of the 25th the carts go from the cathedral to the original site of a Palaeochristian basilica dedicated to the three local martyrs – Primiano, Siriano and Cassio – to bring the statue of Primiano back to the cathedral for a late-night Mass. The spectacle is at its best during the return trip (2km), as the carts are escorted by thousands of people holding torches.

Albanian and Slavic Villages

In the district around Larino there are several communities of Albanians and Slavs, who still maintain their language, traditions and festivals. **Ururi**, west of Larino, is an Albanian town, as is **Portocannone**, which conserves in its Romanesque parish church an icon of the *Madonna of Constantinople*, brought over by settlers, as well as a baronial palace. The most interesting of the Slavic villages is **Acquaviva Collecroce**, where a dialect called 'Stokavo' is spoken. In the campanile of the church of **Santa Maria Esther** there is a medieval curiosity: a stone carved with the magic square of the words SATOR TENET AREPO, an ancient charm.

Language

The fathers of modern Italian were Dante, Manzoni and television. Each played its part in creating a national language from an infinity of regional and local dialects; the Florentine Dante, the first to write in the vernacular, did much to put the Tuscan dialect into the foreground of Italian literature. Manzoni's revolutionary novel, *I Promessi Sposi*, heightened national consciousness by using an everyday language all could understand in the 19th century. Television in the last few decades has performed an even more spectacular linguistic unification; although many Italians still speak a dialect at home, school and work, their TV idols insist on proper Italian.

Italians are not especially apt at learning other languages. English lessons, however, have been the rage for years, and at most hotels and restaurants there will be someone who speaks some English. In small towns and out-of-the-way places, finding an Anglophone may prove more difficult. The words and phrases below should help you out in most situations, but the ideal way to come to Italy is with some Italian under your belt; your visit will be richer, and you're much more likely to make some Italian friends.

Pronunciation

Italian words are pronounced phonetically. Every vowel and consonant is sounded. Most consonants are the same as in English, exceptions are the c which, when followed by an 'e' or 'i', is pronounced like the English 'ch' (*cinque* thus becomes cheenqway). Italian g is also soft before 'i' or 'e' as in *giro*, or jee-roh. H is never sounded; r is trilled, like the Scottish r; z is pronounced like 'ts' or 'ds'. The consonants sc before the vowels 'i' or 'e' become like the English 'sh'; ch is pronounced like a 'k' as in Chianti; gn as 'nya' (thus *bagno* is pronounced ban-yo); while gli is pronounced like the middle of the word million (Castiglione, pronounced Ca-stil-yohn-ay).

Vowel pronunciation is as follows: a is as in English father; e when unstressed is pronounced like 'a' in fate as in *padre*, when stressed it can be the same or like the 'e' in pet (*bello*); i is like the 'i' in machine; o, like 'e', has two sounds, 'o' as in hope when unstressed (*tacchino*), and usually 'o' as in rock when stressed (*morte*); u is pronounced like the 'u' in June. But beware of the Venetian accent where vowels and consonants are often slurred into a porridge of 'u's, 'v's, 'x's (pronounced 'sh') and 'z's.

The stress usually (but not always!) falls on the penultimate syllable.

Useful Words and Phrases

General

yes/no/maybe *sì/no/forse*
I don't know *Non lo so*
I don't understand (Italian) *Non capisco (italiano)*
Does someone here speak English? *C'è qualcuno qui che parla inglese?*
Speak slowly *Parla lentamente*
Could you assist me? *Potrebbe aiutarmi?*
Help! *Aiuto!*
Please *Per favore*
Thanks (very much) *(Molto) grazie*
You're welcome *Prego*
It doesn't matter *Non importa*
All right *Va bene*
Excuse me *Mi scusi*
Be careful! *Attenzione!*
Nothing *Niente*
It is urgent! *È urgente!*
How are you? *Come stai?* (informal), *come sta?* (formal)
Well, and you? *Bene, e tù/Lei?*
What is your name? *Come si chiama, Lei?*
Hello *Salve* or *ciao* (both informal)
Good morning *Buon giorno* (formal hello)
Good afternoon/evening *Buona sera* (also formal hello)

Good night *Buona notte*
Goodbye *ArrivederLa* (formal)
Arrivederci (informal)
What do you call this in Italian? *Come si chiama questo in italiano?*
What? *Che cosa?*
Who? *Chi?*
Where? *Dove?*
When? *Quando?*
Why? *Perché?*
How? *Come?*
How much? *Quanto?*
I am lost *Mi sono smarrito*
I am hungry *Ho fame*
I am thirsty *Ho sete*
I am sorry *Mi dispiace*
I am tired *Sono stanco*
I am sleepy *Ho sonno*
I am ill *Mi sento male*
Leave me alone *Lasciami in pace*
good *buono/bravo*
bad *male/cattivo*
It's all the same *Fa lo stesso*
slow *lento/piano*
fast *rapido*
big *grande*
small *piccolo*
hot *caldo*
cold *freddo*
up *su*
down *giù*
here *qui*
there *lì*

Shopping, Services, Sightseeing

I would like ... *Vorrei ...*
Where is/are?... *Dov'è/Dove sono?...*
How much is it? *Quanto costa questo?*
open *aperto*
closed *chiuso*
cheap *a buon mercato*
expensive *caro*
bank *banca*
beach *spiaggia*
bed *letto*
church *chiesa*
entrance *entrata*
exit *uscita*
hospital *ospedale*
money *soldi*
museum *museo*
newspaper (foreign) *giornale (straniero)*
chemist *farmacia*
police station *commissariato*
policeman *poliziotto*
post office *ufficio postale*
sea *mare*
shop *negozio*
telephone *telefono*
tobacconist *tabacchaio*
WC *toilette/bagno*
men *Signori/Uomini*
women *Signore/Donne*

Time

What time is it? *Che ore sono?*
It's 1 o'clock *È l'una*
It's 3 o'clock *Sono le tre*
month *mese*
week *settimana*
day *giorno*
morning *mattina*
afternoon *pomeriggio*
evening *sera*
today *oggi*
yesterday *ieri*
tomorrow *domani*
soon *fra poco*
later *più tardi*
It is too early *È troppo presto*
It is too late *È troppo tardi*

Days

Monday *lunedì*
Tuesday *martedì*
Wednesday *mercoledì*
Thursday *giovedì*
Friday *venerdì*
Saturday *sabato*
Sunday *domenica*

Numbers

one *uno/una*
two *due*
three *tre*
four *quattro*
five *cinque*
six *sei*
seven *sette*
eight *otto*
nine *nove*
ten *dieci*
eleven *undici*
twelve *dodici*
thirteen *tredici*
fourteen *quattordici*

fifteen *quindici*
sixteen *sedici*
seventeen *diciassette*
eighteen *diciotto*
nineteen *diciannove*
twenty *venti*
twenty-one *ventuno*
twenty-two *ventidue*
thirty *trenta*
thirty-one *trentuno*
forty *quaranta*
fifty *cinquanta*
sixty *sessanta*
seventy *settanta*
eighty *ottanta*
ninety *novanta*
hundred *cento*
one hundred and one *cent'uno*
two hundred *due cento*
thousand *mille*
two thousand *due mila*
million *milione*
billion *miliardo*

Transport

airport *aeroporto*
bus stop *fermata*
bus/coach *autobus/pulmino*
railway station *stazione (ferroviaria)*
train *treno*
(train) platform *binario*
port *porto*
ferry station *stazione maritimma*
ship *nave*
car *macchina*
taxi *tassi*
ticket *biglietto*
customs *dogana*
seat (reserved) *posto (prenotato)*

Travel Directions

I want to go to ... *Voglio andare a ...*
How can I get to...? *Come posso arrivare a ...?*
The next stop, please *La prossima fermata, per favore*
Where is ... /where is it? *Dove ... /Dov'è?*
How far is it to ...? *Quanto siamo lontani da ...?*
What is the name of this station? *Come si chiama questa stazione?*
When does the next train leave? *Quando parte il prossimo treno?*
From where does it leave? *Da dove parte?*
How long does the trip take? *Quanto tempo dura il viaggio?*
How much is the fare? *Quant'è il biglietto?*
Have a good trip! *Buon viaggio!*
near *vicino*
far *lontano*
left *sinistra*
right *destra*
straight ahead *sempre diritto*
forward *avanti*
back *indietro*
north *nord/settentrionale* (the North of Italy)
south *sud/mezzogiorno* (the South of Italy)
east *est/oriente*
west *ovest/occidentale*
around the corner *dietro l'angolo*
crossroads *incrosio*
fork/junction *bivio*
street/road *strada*
square *piazza*

Driving

car hire *noleggio macchina*
motorbike/scooter *motocicletta/Vespa*
bicycle *bicicletta*
petrol/diesel *benzina/gasolio*
garage (at house) *garage*
garage (for repairs) *autorimessa/garage*
service station *stazione di servizio*
This doesn't work *Questo non funziona*
mechanic *meccanico*
map/town plan *carta/pianta*
Where is the road to ...? *Dov'è la strada per...?*
breakdown *panna*
driver's licence *patente di guida*
driver *guidatore/autista*
speed *velocità*
fine *multa*
danger *pericolo*
parking *parcheggio*
no parking *divieto di sosta*
narrow *stretto*
bridge *ponte*
toll *pedaggio*
to slow down *rallentare*

Index

Main page references are in **bold**. Page references to maps are in *italics*.

Central Italy touring atlas

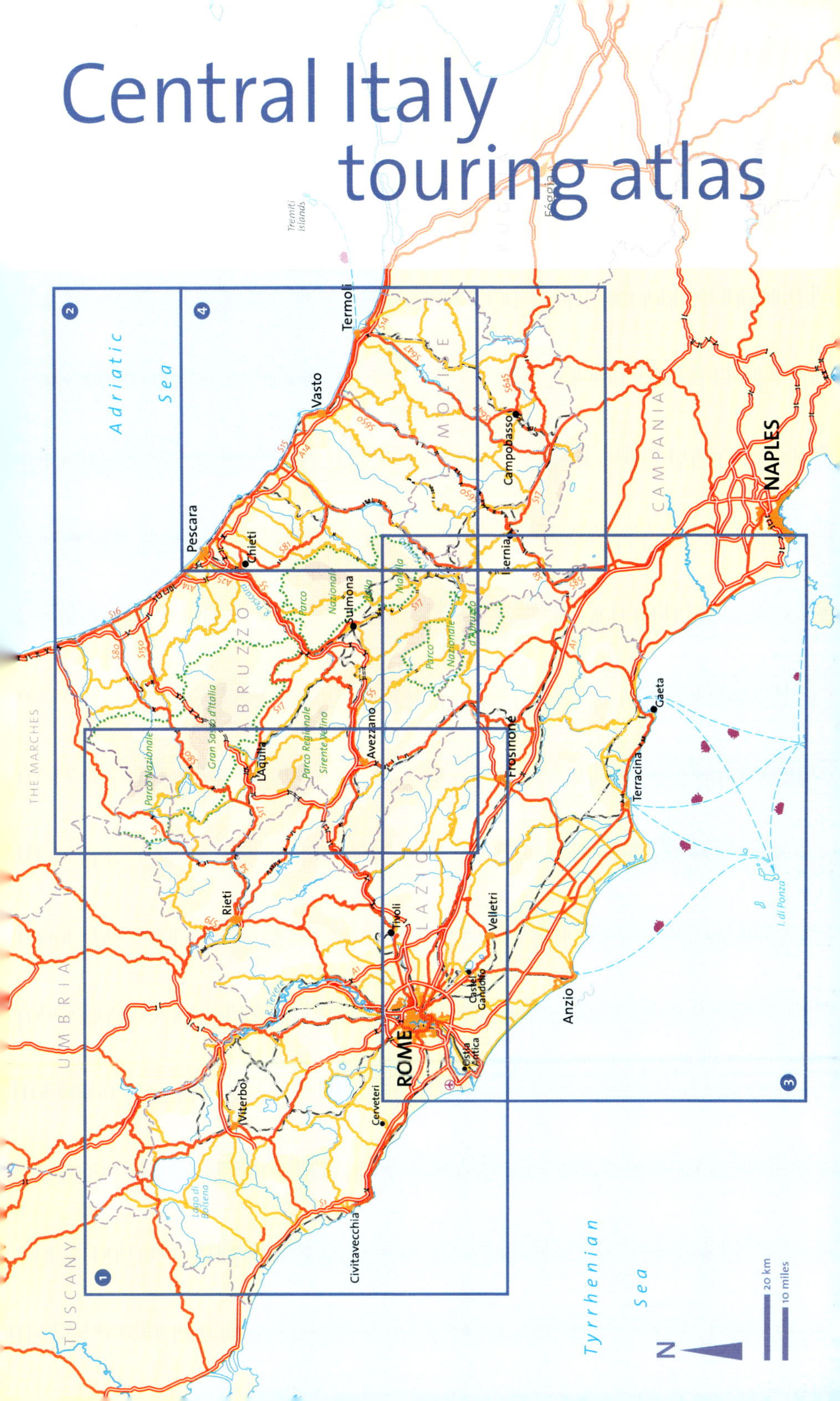

Parrano
Ficulle
Piancastagnaio
M. Labbro
Sta. Fiora
Allerona
Montecastello di Vibio
Roccalbegna
M. Rufeno
Sala
S317
Sta. Maria d. Consolazione
Todi
Castell'Azzara
Monte Rubiaglio
Titignano
Prodo
S323
Castel Viscardo
S79 bis
Collevalenza
Acquapendente
R. Tevere
S448
Semproniano
L. di Corbara
Collelungo
Montenero
M. Elmo
Castel Giorgio
Orvieto
Civitella del Lago
Camerata
S. Severo
S74
S71
Porano
Dunarob
Sorano
Cast. Rubello
Baschi
Avigliano Umbro
R. Albegna
Saturnia
Sovana
Monti Volsini
Montecchio
Toscolano
Montecastrilli
Castello del Poggio
Castel dell'Aquila
Pitigliano
Gradoli
Bolsena
Bagnoregio
Guardea
Montemerano
Lago di Bolsena
L. di Alviano
Manciano
Poggio Buco
Isola Bisentina
Lugnano in Teverina
Sambucetole
Valentano
Alviano
Olpeta
Isola Martana
Amelia
Capodimonte
Farnese
Montefiascone
Attigliano
Castro
Marta
Giove
Parco dei Mostri
Penna in Teverina
Bomarzo
Ferento
Capalbio
Orte
Castello dell'Abbadia
Canino
Santa Maria della Quercia
A1
Viterbo
Bagnaia
Soriano nel Cimino
Vulci
Tuscania
Bagni di Viterbo
Villa Lante
Monte Cimino
Necropoli dell'Olivo
Vignanello
S. Martino al Cimino
Magliano
Montalto di Castro
Monti Cimini
Monte Venere
Norchia
Caprarola
VIA AURELIA
Vetralla
L. di Vico
Villa Farnese
Villa San Giovanni in Tuscia
Ronciglione
Civita Castellana
Blera
Tarquinia
Barbarano Romano
Capranica
Castel S. Elia
Sutri
Nepi
Parco Regionale Marturanum
Bassano Romano
Calcata
Valle d. Treja
VIA CASSIA S2
S1
Monti Sabatini
Trevignano Romano
Allumiere
Golfo Aranci/ Arbatax Olbia/ Cagliari
Tolfa
Lago di Bracciano
Monti della Tolfa
Lago di Martignano
Bracciano
Civitavecchia
Vigna di Valle
Anguillara Sabazia
VIA CLAUDIA
Veio
Cerveteri
LAZIO
VIA AURELIA S1 A12
Tyrrhenian Sea
Fregene
N
Ostia
Ostia Antica
VIA CRISTOFORO COLOMBO
Fiumicino
Lido di Ostia
10 km
5 miles
Lido di Castel Fusano
VIA SEVERIANA

Spoleto
Terni
Rieti
L'Aquila
Avezzano
Tivoli
ROME
Frosinone
Velletri
Norcia
Cascia
Leonessa
Amatrice
Sibillini
Forca Canapine
Forca d'Ancarano
Sella di Leonessa
Gole di Antrodoco
Monti Reatini
Monti Sabini
Monti Simbruini
Monti Ernici
Ciociaria
Colli Albani
LAZIO
Val Nerina
Parco Naturale del Nera
Parco Nazionale
Gran Sasso d'Italia
Parco Regionale
Sirente Velino
Valle del Vomano
Lago di Campotosto
Lago di Salto
Lago di Turano
Piana del Fucino
Subiaco
Palestrina
Frascati
Fiuggi
Anagni
Alatri
Ferentino
Castel Gandolfo
Albano Laziale
Villa Adriana
Villa d'Este
Abbazia di Farfa
Abbazia di Casamari
Campo Felice
Celano
Tagliacozzo
Carsoli
Arsoli
Orvinio
Licenza
Horace's Sabine Farm
Vicovaro
Monterotondo
Mentana
Cittaducale
Antrodoco
Borgo Velino
Convento la Foresta
Convento di Fonte Colombo
Cascata d. Marmore
Piediluco
Narni
Acquasanta Terme
Arquata del Tronto
Fonte Cerreto
Assergi
Amiternum
San Vittorino
Bazzano
Valmontone
Velletri
Segni
Cori
Lanuvio
Genzano di Roma
Ariccia
Nemi
Marino
Grottaferrata
Rocca di Papa
Rocca Priora
Ciampino
Pomezia
1
2
2
3

M. Bove
Monti Sibillini
M. Sibilla
Montemonaco
Foce
Nazionale
Castelluccio
Forca d'Ancarano
M. Vettore
dei Monti
Sibillini
Arquata del Tronto
Acquasanta Terme
Forca Canapine
Ascoli Piceno
S4
S78
R. Tronto
Alba Adriatica
Civitella del Tronto
Giulianova
Campovalano
S81
Campli
S80
S16
Teramo
Morro d'Oro
Roseto degli Abruzzi
S150
Canzano
Santa Maria di Propezzano
San Clemente al Vomano
Guardia Vomano
Pineto
R. Vomano
Amatrice
Parco Nazionale
Montorio al Vomano
Atri
Silvi Alta
Silvi M
S4
Fano Adriano
S80
S491
Santa Maria di Ronzano
Tossicia
Castel Castagna
Lago di Campotosto
Prato Selva
Pietracamela
Città S. Angelo
Valle del Vomano
Isola del Gran Sasso d'Italia
S471
Gran Sasso d'Italia
Prati di Tivo
Castelli
Riserva Naturale Lago di Penne
A14
Corno Piccolo
Corno Grande
Penne
M. Camicia
Loreto Aprutino
Moscufo
Rifugio Duca degli Abruzzi
Campo Imperatore
Santa Maria in Piano
Santa Maria del Lago
Gole di Antrodoco
Fonte Cerreto
Amiternum
Assergi
Pianella
A25
San Vittorino
Gran Sasso
Castel del Monte
Chieti Scalo
Via Sabina
S17
S17bis
Bazzano
L'Aquila
Calascio
Cugnoli
R. Pescara
S5
Manoppello Scalo
Fossa
S17
Capestrano
Manoppello
Bominaco
Caporciano
Torre de' Passeri
Scafa
Serramonacesca
Navelli
San Clemente in Casauria
S. Liberatore in Maiella
Lago di Salto
Rocca di Cambio
R. Aterno
Via Tiburtina Valeria
Campo Felice
Pescorocchiano
Rocca di Mezzo
Popoli
Borgorose
Caramanico Terme
S5 bis
Parco Regionale
Parco Nazionale
S487
Rosciolo d. Marsi
Ovindoli
Corfinio
M. Morrone
Sirente Velino
Passo Leonardo
Badia Morronese
Alba Fucens
Celano
Albe
Gole di Celano
Via Tiburtina Valeria
Forca Caruso
Montagna della M
Tagliacozzo
Cocullo
Sulmona
Pacentro
Avezzano
Piana del Fucino
Pescina
S487
Campo di Giove
Anversa d'Abruzzi
Santa Maria delle Grazie
Gole di Sagittario
della Maiella
Luco dei Marsi
Marsica
Frattura
Monte Rotella
Monti Simbruini
Subiaco
M. Livata
S. Benedetto
S. Scolastica
Lago di Scanno
Scanno
Pescocostanzo
Filettino
Passo del Diavolo
Monte Rontondo
S17
Rivisondoli
Roccaraso
Campocatino
Monti Ernici
Piglio
Parco Nazionale
Pescasseroli
Fiuggi
Guarcino
Castel di Sangro
Lago di Barrea
Opi
Certosa di Trisulti
Acuto
Villetta Barrea
Monte Tranquillo
Barrea
d'Abruzzo
Aufidena
Ciociaria
Collepardo
Alfedena
Anagni
Grotta
Fumone
Sora
Lago Fibreno
Alatri
San Donato Val di Comino
Montenero Val Cocchia
1
1
3

N
10 km
5 miles
Adriatic Sea
To Split
Pescara
Francavilla al Mare
Ortona
R. Moro
San Giovanni in Venere
Fossacesia Marina
Torino di Sangro Marina
Lanciano
Orsogna
S81
S84
Rapino
Guardiagrele
A14
S15
Casalbordino
Vasto
to Tremiti Islands
Casoli
Atessa
Grotta del Cavallone
Torricella Peligna
Taranta Peligna
Termoli
Lido di Campomarino
S. Buono
S650
Villa S. Maria
Guglionesi
Portocannone
S14
Palata
Biferno
S647
Montefalcone nel Sannio
Acquaviva Collecroce
Castiglione
R. Sangro
Capracotta
Serracapriola
Ururi
Larino
Agnone
Trivento
MOLISE
Casacalenda
Pietrabbondante
Bonefro
Santa Croce di Magliano
Bagnoli del Trigno
Pescolanciano

4

LAZIO
1
ROME
GRANDE RACCORDO ANULARE
VIA TIBURTINA VALERIA
Tivoli
Villa d'Este
Villa Adriana
R. Aniene
VIA AURELIA SS1 A12
VIA PRENESTINA
VIA CASILINA
Subiaco
M. Livata
S. Benedetto
S. Scolastica
Rocca S. Stefano
S. Vito Romano
Zagarolo
Palestrina
Piglio
Paliano
Acuto
Fregene
Ciampino
Frascati
Tusculum
Grottaferrata
Rocca Priora
Valmontone
Ciociaria
Anagni
Ostia Antica
Ostia
Fiumicino
Marino
Rocca di Papa
Colli Albani
Monte Cavo
Lago di Albano
Castel Gandolfo
Albano Laziale
Nemi
Lago di Nemi
Ariccia
Genzano di Roma
VIA CRISTOFORO COLOMBO
Lido di Ostia
Lido di Castel Fusano
VIA SEVERIANA
Segni
Velletri
Rocca Massima
Lanuvio
Pomezia
Cori
Monti Lepini
Cisterna di Latina
Norba
Norma
Abbazia di Valvisciolo
Ninfa
M. Semprevisa
Sermoneta
Bassiano
Roccagorga
Aprilia
VIA APPIA
Privernum
Sezze
Latina
Priverno
Anzio
Abbazia di Fossanova
Nettuno
Parco Nazionale del Circeo
Sabaudia
San Felice Circeo
Capo Circeo
N
10 km
5 miles
I. Zannone
I. Palmarola
I. di Ponza

2
3
4
Santa Maria delle Grazie
Luco dei Marsi
Marsica
Gole di Sagittario
Frattura
Lago di Scanno
Scanno
Monte Rotella
Pescocostanzo
Rivisondoli
Roccaraso
Capracotta
Monte Rontondo
Passo del Diavolo
Parco Nazionale d'Abruzzo
Pescasseroli
Opi
Villetta Barrea
Lago di Barrea
Barrea
Aufidena
Alfedena
Castel di Sangro
Montenero Val Cocchiara
Monte Tranquillo
Filettino
Monti Simbruini
Campocatino
Monti Ernici
Guarcino
Certosa di Trisulti
Collepardo
Grotta
Fumone
Alatri
Ferentino
Veroli
Sora
Lago Fibreno
Posta Fibreno
Vicalvi
San Donato Val di Comino
Isola di Liri
Abbazia di Casamari
Arpino
Frosinone
Castel San Vincenzo
San Vincenzo al Volturno
Cerro al Volturno
Scapoli
Isernia
Atina
San Biagio Saracinesco
Ceprano
Abbazia di Montecassino
Cassino
Aquino
Cervaro
Venafro
Sacco
Grotte di Pastena
Pontecorvo
Pico
Vallecorsa
Sonnino
Monti Ausoni
Campodimele
Esperia
Ausonia
Monti Aurunci
Fondi
Tempio di Giove Anxu
L. di Fondi
Terracina
Itri
Grotta di Tiberio
Sperlonga
Formia
Minturno
Scauri
Marina di Minturno
Minturnae
Sessa Aurunca
Samnium
Pignataro Magg.
Gaeta
Serapo
Capua
Volturno
NAPLES
Lago d'Averno
Cumae
Monte Nuovo
Lago de Fusaro
Pozzuoli
Solfatara
Agnano
Baia
Bacoli
Capo Miseno
Porto Vecchio
Palau
I. Ventotene
A1
S17
S652
S85
S7
S372
S7b.d.
R. Sangro

3
2
To Split
N
10 km
5 miles
Capraia
San Domino
San Nicola
Tremiti Islands
Isole Tremiti
Francavilla al Mare
Ortona
R. Moro
San Giovanni in Venere
Fossacesia Marina
Torino di Sangro Marina
Lanciano
Orsogna
S84
S15
A14
Casalbordino
Vasto
Casoli
Atessa
Torricella Peligna
to Tremiti Islands
Termoli
Lido di Campomarino
S. Buono
S650
Villa S. Maria
Guglionesi
Portocannone
S14
Palata
Biferno
S647
Montefalcone nel Sannio
Acquaviva Collecroce
Castiglione
Capracotta
Agnone
Larino
Ururi
Serracapriola
Trivento
MOLISE
Fortore
Casacalenda
Pietrabbondante
Bonefro
Santa Croce di Magliano
Bagnoli del Trigno
Pescolanciano
S17
Santa Maria della Strada
S. Elia a Pianisi
Castropignano
Isernia
Carpinone
Frosolone
Oratino
S645
Castelnuovo d. Daunia
Campobasso
Spinete
Ferrazzano
Baranello
Cantalupo nel Sannio
Monti del Sannio
Boiano
Monti del Matese
Campitello Matese
Campochiaro
M. La Gallinola
Saepinium
Lago del Matese
SS158dir
Sepino
Passo del Prete Morto
Piedimonte Matese
Volturno
Morcone
S88